SECOND INTERNATIONAL HANDBOOK OF EDUCATIONAL CHANGE

Springer International Handbooks of Education

VOLUME 23

For further volumes:
http://www.springer.com/series/6189

Second International Handbook of Educational Change

PART 1

Editors:

Andy Hargreaves
Lynch School of Education, Boston College, Chestnut Hill, MA, USA

Ann Lieberman
Carnegie Foundation for the Advancement of Teaching, Stanford, CA, USA

Michael Fullan
OISE/University of Toronto, ON, Canada

David Hopkins
University of London, UK

Managing Editor:

Corrie Stone-Johnson

 Springer

Editors
Andy Hargreaves
Boston College
Lynch School of Education
Campion Hall
Chestnut Hill MA 02467-3813
USA
hargrean@bc.edu

Michael Fullan
University of Toronto
Ontario Institute for Studies
  in Education (OISE)
252 Bloor Street W.
Toronto ON M5S 1V6
Canada
mfullan@oise.utoronto.ca

Ann Lieberman
Carnegie Foundation for the
  Advancement of Teaching
51 Vista Lane
Stanford CA 94305
USA
annl1@stanford.edu

David Hopkins
University of London
Inst. Education
HSBC Chair iNet in
  London
United Kingdom WC1H 0AL
profdavidhopkins@hotmail.com

ISBN 978-90-481-2659-0   e-ISBN 978-90-481-2660-6
DOI 10.1007/978-90-481-2660-6
Springer Dordrecht Heidelberg London New York

Library of Congress Control Number: 2010927490

Printed on acid-free paper

Springer is part of Springer Science+Business Media (www.springer.com)

Contents

Part IV   Teaching, Learning and Change

Introduction: Ten Years of Change

Ten years ago, generational researchers Strauss and Howe (1997) anticipated a great disruption when our world would take a great turning. After three earlier turnings that defined a time of prosperity, optimism, security, pragmatism, and social conservatism in the 1950s; a period of cultural and spiritual awakening in the 1960s and 1970s; and an era of individualism, self-centeredness, and general unraveling in the 1980s and 1990s, Strauss and Howe predicted a Fourth Turning which, they claimed, will be as dramatic as the last Fourth Turning in the Great Depression of the 1930s. This turning, they argue, brings economic collapse and financial ruin, insecurity and conflict, and a shaking of society to its very foundations, with the emergence of structures, cultures, and politics, as well as value and belief systems that are profoundly different on the other side. At the Fourth Turning, people start to turn outward again, beyond themselves, in search of the spirituality, sustenance, and support that can connect them once more to their fellow women and men.

Although the Fourth Turning is borne of crisis, it beckons with the prospect of great transformations and opportunities. Yet it does not show what these are. This is a defining moment for all of us. In the midst of a great global disruption when economies are collapsing, insecurity is everywhere and some are even saying that globalization is going into reverse, it is a time in economic and educational life either to pare down our budgets, reduce our ambitions, turn in on ourselves, and keep outsiders at bay or to embark on a new course that can lead us toward a better place, a new high point of inclusiveness, security, and prosperity. Education is an essential part of the second path.

It is time, now more than ever, for a New Way of educational change that is suited to the dramatically new problems and challenges we are encountering. This New Way should build on the best of what we have learned from the Old Ways of the past, including those of the past decade, without retreating to or reinventing the worst of them. It should look abroad for intelligent alternatives and be especially alert to those educational and economic successes that also express and advance democratic and humanitarian values. It should attend to the advancement of the economy and the restoration of prosperity but not at the price of other educational elements that contribute to the development of personal integrity, social democracy, and human decency. It has to be concerned with the furtherance of economic profit yet also with the advancement of the human spirit.

Ten Years After

This second edition of the *Handbook* contains chapters that show us the possibilities for positive change. The chapters within it come from leading researchers on educational change from around the world. What has happened to the field of educational change across this 10-year period that has brought us well into the twenty-first century? Have we seen great breakthroughs and synergies of strategy and impact along with impressive new results? Or, have educational reform strategies been just as much a part of the great unraveling of overconfidence and overreach as have the bursting bubbles of speculative investment and uncontrolled indebtedness?

As the editors, and as researchers of educational change in several countries over three decades, we believe that educational change and reform strategies and their accompanying research directions have become bigger, tighter, harder, and flatter.

These trends are evident in the grand designs of political reform strategies and also in the ways that professional communities in schools have developed and done their work. These very directions that have brought us to this defining moment of educational change, however, are not the ones that will get us productively beyond it, and so the second part of this introduction sets out some anticipated and alternative directions for the future.

Bigger

Following years of frustration developing promising innovations that existed only as outliers and failed to spread, of watching pilot projects be replicated only poorly when their designs were then mandated across a system, and of seeing that early implementation of changes rarely turned into full-blown, widespread and effortless institutionalization, educational reformers began to look at more coordinated system-wide designs for reform – and research money increasingly followed them. School-based and classroom-based change was out; large-scale reform was in.

The earliest efforts were most evident in England and to some extent in Australia and New Zealand in the early 1990s. This was partly a response to the incoherence and inconsistency of preceding decades, but also an ideological onslaught on the educational establishment, as they were called, of teachers and university education professors who were deemed to be responsible for the unfocussed approaches to educational progressivism that politicians and the business community along with an increasingly irritated public associated with the economic decline of the 1980s. The mechanisms of change to bring about this ideological shift were the introduction of market competition and league tables of performance between schools, a return to traditional models of curriculum and teaching through closely prescribed curriculum contents and standards sometimes accompanied by scripted and paced models of literacy and mathematics instruction, pervasive systems of educational testing that were tied to the curriculum basics and to the criteria for market competition, and intrusive systems of surveillance by external inspection. All these were linked with high-stakes consequences of public exposure, administrative intervention, and even enforced closure for schools that performed badly.

Some years later, these basic principles and practices were largely replicated in the US federal reform strategy of No Child Left Behind with its similar emphasis on test scores, competition between schools and other education providers, and severe consequences for schools that failed to meet the legislation's compressed time lines for improvement.

Research findings reflected mounting professional and also public dissatisfaction with the limitations of this large-scale model, in terms of overemphasis on basics, teaching to the test, concentrating only on those borderline students who could offer hope of quick test-score gains, problems of recruitment and retention among teachers and leaders, and a tendency for initial test-score gains to reach an early plateau. In response, while other reformers and their research-driven supporters stayed with the large-scale reform agenda, they also looked for other sources of inspiration to improve it.

The trailblazing work of New York District 2 under the inspirational leadership of Anthony Alvarado was a key influence here. Approvingly advocated by Elmore and Burney (1997), this model of district-wide change developed a clearer, stronger, and more pedagogically constructive focus on instruction backed up by high-quality materials, a network of high-quality instructional literacy coaches, a concentration on turning principals into instructional leaders who were also required to discuss their learning and difficulties together, a system of monitoring and inspection using administrative "walk-throughs," and a clear link to transparent test-score results.

Efforts to undertake direct transplantations of this model – like all attempts to clone educational changes exactly – proved disappointing as Mary Kay Stein, Lee Hubbard, and Bud Mehan have demonstrated on the attempt to implement the District 2 model in San Diego under conditions of lesser resources, greater scope, a different political climate, and shorter time lines (Stein, Hubbard, & Mehan, 2004). But principles and practices derived from District 2 started to surface among other large-scale reform advocates who wanted better and more lasting results, a closer connection to pedagogy and instruction and better ways to engage and support teachers and leaders in the change effort.

In England, there was a similar trend during the second term of the Blair government, when there was a concerted policy effort to personalize learning, build a stronger focus on enhancing teacher professionalism, make assessment and accountability more formative, and build stronger forms of collaboration between schools (Hopkins, 2007). So although Sir Michael Barber's (2007) delivery strategy tightened the national focus around literacy and numeracy, it also increased levels of support for teachers in terms of materials, finance, and technical coaching and paid increasing attention to leadership development, especially through the establishment of a National College for School Leadership.

In Ontario, continuing commitment to test-based educational accountability was supplemented by a range of system-wide initiatives that built capacity for improvement and provided professional support. Alongside the idea borrowed from England of making tested literacy and numeracy linked to political targets for improved performance the centrepiece of its reform strategy, the province added thousands of new teaching positions to reduce class sizes in the primary grades and "student success teachers" were designated in every high school to assure that each student would be well known and supported by at least one school staff member.

At its core, the Ontario strategy focused capacity-building at the school and district levels through the support of a Literacy Numeracy Secretariat and used achievement results as a nonpunitive but specific stimulant for further reform. Like New York District 2 and England, large teams of consultants and coaches worked alongside teachers with the support of quality materials. Teacher unions were allocated $5 million to spend on professional development, successful practices were networked across schools, and underperforming schools were encouraged but not compelled to seek assistance from government support teams and higher achieving peers.

Tighter

Proponents of large-scale reform models that also offer increased support, capacity-building, and professional involvement claim that in general, bigger has been better. Authoritative independent evaluations of the Ontario experience are just starting to emerge, but the evidence from England is uneven although the trends remain positive.

In any walk of life, the more that control and intervention are orchestrated from the top, the tighter the focus must become in terms of what has to be controlled. The wider the scope of action, the more that trust, decision-making, and responsibility must be devolved downwards – what is known as the principle of subsidiarity. There are simply never enough resources to permit close control of everything from above.

The answer to this conundrum among large-scale reformers has been to establish a tight focus for control and intervention. Hence, the growing consensus has been to concentrate policy efforts, curriculum development, instructional training, intervention strategies, and improvement plans on raising test scores and narrowing achievement gaps in the tested basics of literacy and numeracy (mathematics) along with secondary school examination results.

For a while, these strategies have increased consistency across the system, heightened the sense of urgency about rectifying underachievement and mobilized support to do so, and sometimes secured public reassurance as well as political credibility in relation to the standards agenda. Early improvements are rarely sustained, though, and their validity is often contested on the grounds that results are achieved by teaching to the test and by initially low test baselines through deliberately poor preparation and hasty implementation which is only then followed by training and support – so that what appears to be an improvement is actually a recovery.

The greatest problem of the tight focus on tested and standardized basics, though, is that the efforts and activity of teachers and schools concentrate overwhelmingly on these high-stakes areas and neglect developing a curriculum or a pedagogy that will prepare students with the twenty-first century skills and capacities that are essential if we are to transform our economies and communities into creative, competitive, and inclusive knowledge societies. At the very beginning of the century, the Organization for Economic Cooperation and Development (OECD, 2001) advocated a shift in educational reform strategy toward developing these new competences and capacities. Hargreaves (2003) built on its argument and set out the case for knowledge society schools that emphasized the skills of creativity, innovation, flexibility, problem-solving, and teamwork that would fuel entrepreneurial initiative and that also promoted the skills and dispositions of inclusiveness, emotional development, community-building, and cosmopolitan awareness that are integral to social democracy. Wagner's (2009) book on *The Global Achievement Gap* also echoes the advocacy for twenty-first century corporate skills. A high-profile US Commission convened by the National Center for Education and the Economy (New Commission on the Skills of the American Workforce, 2007) that includes leading superintendents, CEOs, and two former Secretaries of Education also complains that America's obsession with tested, standardized basics is destroying its capacity to be economically creative and competitive.

The most assessment-obsessed Anglo-American nations, the United Kingdom and the United States, actually rank last and next to last on UNICEF's (2007) 21-country list of child well-being. A formidably funded and influential review of UK primary education at Cambridge University (BBC, 2009) concludes that England's reform directions have stripped innovation, creativity, and the most basic needs of child exploration and development out of young children's curriculum as all teachers' energy has been targeted toward government tests. Even the UK government's own review body points to some of the same conclusions (BBC, 2009).

In the face of global economic collapse, the dubious path of narrow standardization is now one that only educational and economic ostriches and lemmings will follow as they blindly race over the edge of an economic precipice. The ironic effect of international interest in large-scale reform is that it has exposed how the countries and systems that have actually been most successful educationally and economically are ones that provide greater flexibility and innovation in teaching and learning, that invest greater trust in their highly qualified teachers, that value curriculum breadth, and that do not try to orchestrate everything tightly from the top (Darling-Hammond, 2008; McKinsey, 2007).

High performing Singapore emphasizes "Teach Less, Learn More" and mandates 10% "white space" for teachers to bring individual initiative and creativity into their teaching. Finland – the world leader on results in the Program for International Student Assessment (PISA) tests of sophisticated, applied knowledge in mathematics, science, and literacy, as well as on international ratings of economic competitiveness – avoids national standardized tests altogether and reaches high levels of achievement by attracting highly qualified teachers with supportive working conditions, strong degrees of professional trust, and an inspiring mission of inclusion and creativity (Hargreaves, Halasz, & Pont, 2008). The Canadian province of Alberta, which tucks in just behind Finland in international PISA rankings, has secured its success, in part, by partnering with the teacher's union to develop a

9-year initiative in school-developed innovation (the Alberta Initiative for School Improvement) that involves 90% of the province's schools.

Even in the Anglo-Saxon nations, the tide of narrow standardization appears to be in retreat. Many parents and teachers in England object to young children being the most tested in the world, that country's government has put an end to all standardized testing in secondary schools, and Wales has abolished national testing altogether up to age 14 (Hargreaves & Shirley, 2009). We are at the end of a decade of large-scale limitations. The question is, What might come next?

Harder

The decade of large-scale reform has also been a decade in which evidence has replaced experience; hard data have pushed aside soft intuition and judgment. Data-driven instruction and improvement have become de rigeur elements of Anglo-American approaches to educational reform.

At first, data on student performance in examinations and standardized tests were used as crude ways to rank schools publicly and competitively, inform parent choice, pit the strong against the weak, and shame the poorest and weakest performers into pulling their socks up. Later, many countries worked at making the database more sophisticated. Progress measures were developed so schools could compare present performance to past achievement, and achievement results were contextualized in relation to the kinds of communities in which they were located. Schools could compare themselves against similarly placed peers and contact ones that were performing more strongly to access help and assistance. Many schools then started to use data to drive improvement internally. Departments were compared with departments, boys with girls, majority with minority students, second language learners with others, and so on – so that teachers could identify where they needed to concentrate their efforts and make timely interventions. Achievement data were also shared with individual students in regular one-to-one meetings to manage and monitor their progress and set goals with them for the future.

Data-driven improvement has become an integral part of the movement to develop schools into being professional learning communities (PLCs), where teachers use data and other evidence to inquire into their practice and its effects on students and make needed improvements together to address the shortcomings that they find. In the best or most advanced PLCs, a wide range of quantitative and qualitative data are used as a regular and effortless part of collective practice to inquire continuously into practice in the classroom, department, or entire school so as to keep improving in order to raise standards of achievement (Datnow, Park, & Wohlstetter, 2007).

While these developments have undoubtedly concentrated teachers' energy and efforts on identifying and responding to struggling students and groups of students who need their help the most, the enthusiastic adoption of data-driven instruction and improvement has also introduced some risks and drawbacks.

First, instead of merely respecting the value of data and objective evidence as opposed to subjective intuition, schools and systems have sometimes come to revere it above all else. In sport, Lewis (2004) has demonstrated how the Oakland A's base-ball team made the playoffs each year on a low budget simply by taking the statistic that most predicted season-long success – how often a batter reaches first base – as a basis for recruiting new players, even when those players did not intuitively strike coaches as being the most athletically likely prospects. By comparison, work on how organizations, including sports teams, achieve performance above expectations has pointed to inadvisable and ineffective ways that clubs push players to improve performance by setting targets for how many digitally tracked steps they take during a game, for example (the players simply cheat by taking more steps on the sidelines) (Hargreaves & Shirley, 2009). And Lewis (2009) again has put the other side of the evidence-based argument by highlighting one of the United States most successful pro-basketball players who consistently lifts team performance when he comes on court but whose highly complex and subtle contribution cannot be measured by any existing statistics. Sometimes the objective evidence is a good counter against intuitive judgment, but sometimes it is also insufficient, unhelpful, or just plain wrong. Experience and evidence need to be discussed in dialogue together without privileging one over the other.

Second, the quest for more and more detailed data to guide every action and decision can become obsessive and excessive. The origin of this approach is in the business practice of World Class Manufacturing which is actually a methodology of improving quality by disaggregating every part of the production process into miniscule, granular data and detail so that attention is paid relentlessly to improving every tiny aspect of that process. Numerous targets set yearly, monthly, and even weekly have red, green, or amber lights attached to them as indicators of whether or not they need real-time attention. Increasingly, frequent management of student progress and school improvement by constantly disaggregating data and targeting interventions in real time to underperforming groups or subjects represents the application of this philosophy to education. This data-driven intervention strategy can nip performance problems in the bud, but it can also divert teachers' attention and energy on to short-term tasks in easily measurable indicators of achievement and away from longer-term engagement with teaching, learning, and students within more complex sets of lasting relationships.

Third, while the best, most mature PLCs integrate and embed evidence-informed inquiry into the daily work of teaching across the curriculum, the imposition of top–down high-stakes assessments in narrowly defined basic areas such as literacy and numeracy drive many PLCs into taking a much narrower and more artificial focus. In practice, although the scope for PLCs is wide, most studies show that a majority of their activity concentrates on teachers looking at spreadsheets of student test scores together after busy days at work, then devising swift solutions to bring about the rapid improvements that will keep the forces of accountability at bay (Datnow et al., 2007; McLaughlin & Talbert, 2006).

While business and sporting organizations take metrics and indicators of improvement very seriously, there is little dispute among staff about the validity of those metrics in relation to what the organizations are trying to achieve – customer satisfaction, or the degree of stickiness that customers show in staying with a company's Web site, for example. In an age that needs to embrace innovation and creativity, the test-score metrics by which educational performance is measured are not appropriate to knowledge society goals or to many valuable educational goals more widely. So the practice ends up being distorted to fit the cheap and available metrics of test scores, rather than metrics being designed which are widely agreed as being valid in reflecting the deeper and broader goals of high-quality practice.

Flatter

In education, the work is increasingly flat. The aim is to narrow achievement gaps – to intervene so that girls catch up to boys, for example, and then so that boys can catch up to girls. These are worthy goals, but not when they are pursued relentlessly so that when any gap opens up, the immediate response is to close it. This creates a myth of the gapless school where all and any gaps, like orthodontically perfect and characterless smiles, are the target for immediate attention and elimination

In the 1960s, Young (1958) wrote a fable on *The Rise of the Meritocracy*. It depicted a society in which the goals of meritocracy had been perfectly realized – one in which everyone reached their potential and was rewarded accordingly. The result was that in a society which continued to value and reward occupations unevenly, everyone came to the often-depressing conclusion that what they got or didn't get was entirely what they deserved – a pure and incontrovertible reflection of the talents and abilities they had been allocated at birth.

Ten Years More

In most of the Anglo-American group of nations, the last 10 years have been marked by high-stakes and large-scale attention to tested basics and secondary school exam-inations, in which objective test-score data drive increasingly detailed and granular efforts at improvement in an attempt to close all gaps wherever they appear. It is increasingly clear that these emphases cannot develop or deliver the essential learn-ings that are integral to the creative and innovative knowledge societies that are our best bet for extricating ourselves from the collapse of the existing global economy.

So what directions and developments might educational change policy, practice, and research take instead? We offer the following suggestions:

First, the collapse of the global economy will grab people's attention into adopt-ing educationally driven strategies like those of Finland in turning round to become successful and competitive knowledge economies. Standardization will go into decline and innovation will emerge in its place. At first, this will appear as supple-ments to the existing diet of standardization – in after-school curriculum activities, or sheltered time for creativity or interdisciplinary studies within an otherwise standardized environment. But eventually, policymakers will have to concede that innovation and creativity require different, more flexible conditions of teaching, learning, and leadership than those that have prevailed in the managerial era of test-driven and data-obsessed educational reform. At the same time, as part and parcel of the pursuit of innovation, evidence-informed decision making will result in the consolidation of high-yield instructional strategies. The development of the teaching profession will entail incorporating a growing body of sound practice and knowledge. Around these ideas we will need to learn once more how to spread innovation through networks, relationships, and interaction and to do this more effectively than in the 1960s and 1970s.

Second, at the end of the age of materialism and of "selfish" forms of capitalism (James, 2008), we will ask bigger questions about the goals of education – about how we are preparing the next generations. Technical preoccupations with narrowing achievement gaps in the tested basics and vague allusions to developing "world class schools" that are actually importations of the technically driven principles of World Class Manufacturing, will give way to goals that embrace the forms of innovation and creativity, and the identification of effective practices that are essential for advanced knowledge economies, and the virtues of empathy and community service that are integral to more "selfless" forms of capitalism.

Third, we will or should witness the decline of the district and of district-driven reform. This will be replaced by districts fostering the creation and spread of promising practices. Teachers can only really learn once they get outside their own classrooms and connect with other teachers. This is one of the essential principles behind PLCs. Likewise, schools can only really learn when they connect with other schools – including ones outside their own immediate district. Many districts are too small to enable that learning. Others are hierarchical, bureaucratic, excessively politicized and controlling – with connections to other cities and districts being orchestrated and patrolled only by the most senior district staff who then filter what their own staff should be permitted to learn. A learning society requires schools that can connect with and learn from other schools beyond the confines and bureaucratic controls of their own districts. Without these developments, schools will become increasingly isolated and anachronistic – ill-equipped to prepare their students and themselves with the flexible learning and adaptation to change that are vital to twenty-first century economies. For this reason, face-to-face and virtual school networks that stretch across and between districts can and should become a key research and reform priority in the coming decade.

Fourth, the greater proportion of effects on student achievement comes from outside the school. Yet, being afraid to challenge parent electors about their practices and responsibilities with their children at home, policymakers have concentrated almost all their improvement efforts on the school alone – trying to improve performance within what is actually the lesser variable of influence on student achievement. The end of materialism, however, is now bringing community spirit and community responsibility back in. The highest performing nations like Finland, Singapore, the Netherlands, and Russia maintain high achievement by supporting their children in families and communities as well as in schools. Policy developments that combine district leadership with responsibility for other children's services in England are an attempt to move in the same direction. So are extended day schools, full-service schools, and community schools in other countries. In the coming decade, we will learn and commit to the idea that the strongest and most effective schools are the schools that work with and affect the communities that affect them – schools where educational leaders are also effective community leaders. This will signal an end to the misdirected assumption that all responsibility for improvement falls exclusively on the shoulders of teachers and their schools.

Fifth, management that assists the delivery and implementation of policies will give way to leadership that can build innovative professional communities. Especially challenging here will not be the task of preparing new leaders but of converting existing ones who had been appointed and had learned to survive in conditions of competition and managerialism. How to change managers responsible for faithful delivery into leaders capable of inspiring self-initiated innovation and creativity will be one of the major strategic and research tasks in the era of post-materialism and post-standardization.

Sixth, as the boomer generation retires and moves on from teaching and leading, it will be replaced by the more direct and demanding generational successors of Generation X and even more of Generation Y – sometimes called the Millennial generation (Howe & Strauss, 2000). This generation, now in its 1920s, is already introducing ideas and incorporating technologies that are closer to the cultures of today's children and youth. But it is when this generation move into leadership in great numbers toward the end of this next decade that Millennial leadership styles – more swift, assertive, direct, team-based, task-centered, and technologically savvy – will finally bring about the classroom and organizational transformations that are necessary for twenty-first century schools. A key research priority in the coming years should be on the nature and needs of the Millennial generation in teaching and leadership within our schools.

Last, global conditions of economic collapse call for greater prudence in educational spending. With financial support for learning and teaching in jeopardy, it is demonstrably no longer prudent or sustainable to finance pervasive systems of standardized testing of all students across many curriculum areas, at multiple age points by a census. Effective corporations only test samples of their products in order to ensure quality control. It is bad business and a waste of profit to test more than this. We will need to grasp that this principle also applies to education as many countries like high-performing Finland and New Zealand already accept. The excuse that industrial products don't have parents but students do as a justification for testing everyone is already on the wane with parent opposition to testing in Britain already leading to its abandonment in Wales and reductions in its scope and impact in England. Standardizing testing by census is a financial and political indulgence we can no longer afford and one that electors are increasingly opposed to. It is time to research, develop, and implement strategies of assessment that are equally accountable but economically less expensive.

The coming era of educational change needs to be an era of reduced commitments to grandiose designs and granular micromanagement of top–down reform in favor of an age of innovation and inspiration in a post-materialist world where people are increasingly prepared to look to each other in building a more hopeful and innovative society together, rather than acquisitively and self-indulgently looking only to their own families and themselves. As the Millennial generation moves into leadership, it will eventually bring about these transformations almost naturally – it is the responsibility of the rest of us in the coming years to reflect on our past policy excesses of top–down control and prepare the ground in a post-materialist and post-standardized system and society for those who will follow.

References

Barber, M. (2007). *Instruction to deliver: Fighting to transform Britain's public services*. London: Methuen.

BBC. (2009). *Primary education "too narrow"*: Retrieved February 20, 2009, from http://www.bbc.co.uk/2/hi/uk_news/education/7896751.stm.

Darling-Hammond, L. (2008). Teaching and the change wars: The professionalism hypothesis. In A. Hargreaves & M. Fullan (Eds.), *Change wars* (pp. 45–68). Bloomington: Solution Tree.

Datnow, A., Park, V., & Wohlstetter, P. (2007). *Achieving with data: How high performing schools use data to improve instruction for students*. California: Center on Educational Governance.

Elmore, R., & Burney, D. (1997). *Investing in teacher learning: Staff development and instructional improvement in Community School District #2, New York*. Washington, DC: National Commission on Teaching & America's Future & the Consortium for Policy Research in Education.

Hargreaves, A. (2003). *Teaching in the knowledge society: Education in the age of insecurity*. New York: Teachers College Press.

Hargreaves, A., Halász, G., & Pont, B. (2008). The Finnish approach to system leadership. In: Pont, B., Nusche, D., & Hopkins, D. (Eds.) *Improving school leadership* (Vol. 2, pp. 69–109). Case studies on system leadership. Paris: OECD.

Hargreaves, A., & Shirley, D. (2009). *The fourth way*. Thousand Oaks, CA: Corwin Press.

Hopkins, D. (2007) *Every school a great school*. Maidenhead, Berkshire: McGraw-Hill/Open University Press.

Howe, N., & Strauss, W. (2000). *Millenials rising: The next generation*. New York: Vintage.

James, O. (2008). *The selfish capitalist*. New York: Random House .

Lewis, M. (2004). *Moneyball: The art of winning an unfair game*. New York: W. W. Norton & Company.

Lewis, M. (2009). The no-stats all-star. *The New York Times Magazine*, February 15, 26–33, 56, 63–64.

McKinsey & Company. (2007, September). *How the world's best-performing school systems come out on top*. Retrieved November 25, 2008, from http://www.mckinsey.com/clientservice/socialsector/resources/pdf/Worlds_School_Systems_Final.pdf.

McLaughlin, M.W., & Talbert, J.E. (2006). *Building school-based teacher learning communities*. New York: Teachers College Press.

New Commission on the Skills of the American Workforce. (2007). *Tough choices or tough times – The Report of the New Commission on the Skills of the American Workforce*. Washington, DC: National Center on Education and the Economy.

OECD. (2001). *What schools for the future? Schooling for tomorrow*. Paris: OECD

Stein, M., Hubbard, L., & Mehan, H. (2004). Reform ideas that travel far afield: The two cultures of reform in New York City's District #2 and San Diego. *Journal of Educational Change, 5*(2), 161–197.

Strauss, W., & Howe, N. (1997) *The fourth turning*. New York: Broadway.

UNICEF. (2007). *Child poverty in perspective: An overview of child well-being in rich countries, Innocenti Report Card 7*. Florence: UNICEF Innocenti Research Centre.

Wagner, T. (2008) *The global achievement gap*. New York: Basic.

Young, M. (1958). *The rise of the meritocracy*. Harmondsworth: Penguin Books.

Part I
Theories of Change

Better Schools Through Better Knowledge?
New Understanding, New Uncertainty

Karen Seashore Louis

As I pointed out in the first edition of this handbook, theories of knowledge utilization and educational improvement have been closely linked since Havelock's (1969) classic literature review. This connection is also apparent in practice. On the one hand, school improvement depends on the implementation of new ideas – in the form of both programs and policies – about school organization and instruction; on the other, the refinement of theories about knowledge use depends on having schools that serve as natural loci of experimentation and change. Over the past several decades, explicit attention to dissemination and knowledge utilization have dropped from the agenda of most scholars interested in school reform and have been replaced with related but new concerns, ranging from the spread of comprehensive models to organizational learning. The purpose of this chapter is to review theories that may help to connect research on knowledge utilization with research on educational improvement. The analysis presented here assumes that the reader is familiar with the broad outlines of both school improvement and school effectiveness research (Hopkins, 2001; Sammons, 1999; Schmoker, 1999; Teddlie & Reynolds, 2000), but less familiar with research traditions related to knowledge utilization.

In the first section of this chapter, I briefly review the "state of the art" in knowledge utilization theory, and discuss how it is connected to both school effectiveness and improvement research streams. I will briefly discuss why the dominant and the challenging paradigms for knowledge utilization are not adequate to explain observed phenomena relating to knowledge flow and use in education. In the second section, I examine emerging perspectives that have the potential for altering the way in which we analyze and interpret the observed phenomena discussed in the first section. Most of the examples used in this chapter are based on research carried out in the United States, but as I note throughout, they appear to be applicable in European Union and OECD countries.

In reviewing new ideas that contribute to our understanding of knowledge utilization, it is critical that we maintain the thoroughly interdisciplinary base of this field.

K.S. Louis (✉)
University of Minnesota, Minneapolis, MN, USA
e-mail: klouis@umn.edu

A. Hargreaves et al. (eds.), *Second International Handbook of Educational Change*,
Springer International Handbooks of Education 23, DOI 10.1007/978-90-481-2660-6_1,
© Springer Science+Business Media B.V. 2010

While various writers may approach the problem of putting knowledge to work for the betterment of individuals – and/or societies – with different lenses, major reviews of the field, such as Rogers (1983) or Glaser, Abelson & Garrison (1983), demonstrate that high quality research and ideas come from disciplines ranging from agriculture to political science. The most recent review focuses on the use of behavioral and social science and draws on a wide range of experts from the media, public interest groups, and others whose focus is on dissemination (Welch-Ross & Fasig, 2007). This chapter cannot, of course, range as broadly as these synthetic reviews, and since my objective is primarily to stimulate thinking about theory, I will confine myself to a few viewpoints from political, historical, organizational, and cognitive learning theory. In each case, I will briefly illustrate how the knowledge utilization perspective is reflected in current school improvement or school reform issues.

I then turn to some elements of an intersection between knowledge utilization theories and school improvement theories that may drive us forward to a synthetic model of dissemination and utilization (D&U) that represents a paradigm shift rather than a paradigm revolution (Kuhn, 1970). Some suggestions about practical implications will also be made.

State of the Art

In 1997, when the first edition of this handbook went to press, it was the beginning of an era that posed serious challenges to the way in which educational researchers thought about change. The era of research-dissemination-diffusion-utilization (RDDU), which assumed a linear relationship between the production of new knowledge and its appearance in practice, was sharply challenged by more constructivist ideas about the relationship between knowledge production and knowledge use. Although this body of research was never as simplistic as latter-day critics contend, many studies led to the conclusion that there was no simple, direct line between knowledge production and utilization, the assumption of unidirectionality in influence dominated both policy and practice (Havelock, 1969).

Renewed D&U Theory: Bringing the "User" Back in

Huberman's review of the "state of the art" in the mid-1990s began with the accepted assumption that there is a "gap" between research knowledge and practitioner knowledge that can be bridged with calculated interventions. (See Huberman, 1994, whose work was carried out in the United States and Switzerland) Early efforts to do so have long been viewed as hyper-rational due to their assumptions that (1) the flow of knowledge should be largely one-way, from the research community to the practice community; and (2) that more sophisticated forms of knowledge packaging and communication strategies would reduce, if not eliminate, the "gap" between what was known and what people did. Huberman noted the many challenges to a rational model of knowledge use but chose to review the subtleties of the existing paradigm, arguing that five factors explained why some knowledge becomes common practice in schools, while other new ideas are rejected. These include:

- *the context of research*, including characteristics of the knowledge base and the motivation of the researcher to disseminate to practitioners;
- *the user's context*, including factors ranging from perceived needs to the perception of the value of the research information;
- *"linkage mechanisms"* between researchers and practitioners during the production and utilization phases;
- *the impacts of context and linkages on resources*, including attention, time, and acceptability of the research; and
- *the amount of effort* expended creating an appropriate environment for use, which includes both the amount and quality of dissemination effort, the "usability" of the knowledge, and the quality of planning and execution in the school or district.

Huberman focused on the role of reciprocally influential relationships in the process of knowledge utilization (Huberman, 1999), but his perspective is consistent with the main lines of dissemination research during the 1980s and 1990s, which emphasizes the dispersion of knowledge to multiple sites of practice. This perspective was reflected in programs and initiatives in a number of contexts, particularly those that emerged from the school effectiveness research tradition. For example, beginning in the late 1970s in the United States, there were a number of efforts by regional educational laboratories and individual entrepreneurs to develop research-to-practice models that translated the results of the effective schools and effective teacher research into training and support programs for local schools. Similar experiments involving collaboration between schools, trainers, and researchers were conducted in other countries (e.g., the middle schools reform efforts in the Netherlands). Thus, Huberman's review makes a bridge to alternative perspectives by emphasizing the importance of mutual influence. Huberman notes that researchers and practitioners may have a reciprocal influence on each other and suggests that the need for sustained interactivity to promote research/knowledge utilization is consistent with some elements of the contemporary constructivist approach to teaching. The latter asserts that practitioner knowledge is constructed, largely by individuals, both through reflective practice (Schön, 1983) and through more disciplined inquiry, such as action research (Carr & Kemmis, 1986; Cochran-Smith & Lytle, 1999b).[1]

Even with the modest adjustments posited by the need for mutual interaction, policymakers in most countries continue to believe that, with proper sticks and carrots, schools can be encouraged (or required) to become better consumers of

---

[1]Huberman also notes that the constructivist teaching models emphasize the need for knowledge from "outside sources," whether generated by research or through teacher inquiry, to be filtered through an interpretive individual lens.

"good research results" and programs or policies that they believe are research-based. In the United States and other countries, efforts to develop "comprehensive" school reforms that combine a research base and technical assistance for change have consumed considerable resources and energy on the part of governments, private agencies, universities, and schools. The literacy and numeracy initiatives in England stand out as clear examples of efforts to create systems change through knowledge use (Brown, Askew, Millett, & Rhodes, 2003). Still, evidence continues to mount that the "packaging" of ideas into user-friendly modules continues to reveal that there is never enough knowledge in the package to eliminate problems in use (Hatch & White, 2002) and that "co-construction" of knowledge, combined with shifting policies and resources outside the school, creates further complications and erosion of effort (Datnow, 2002). This seems to be characteristic of not only schools, but other public agencies (Landry, Lamar, & Amara, 2003).

Postmodernist Challenges to Traditional Thinking[2]

In 1997, the greatest challenge on the horizon seemed to be from "postmodernist theory" that provided a sharp critique of the renewed conceptual framework presented in Huberman's review (Watkins, 1994). Watkins begins with the observation that teachers construct knowledge as they go about their work, particularly when they engage in professional discussions around their own practice. Like many constructivists, he then goes on to equate daily efforts to solve classroom problems with research – research that is highly contextualized because it is grounded in experience. The school's process may appear nonlinear and random to outsiders, but constructivists accept that all knowledge is "local" (Geertz, 1983), contested, and partial and political (influenced by the interests of those who develop or use it).

The extreme assumption – that research knowledge is not useful to teachers – has been largely abandoned. However, given the weak results of formal R,D,D and U efforts, many researchers on both sides of the Atlantic agree that it is simply good practice to have educational practitioners involved in debating, selecting, and co-constructing practice implications (Ainscow, 2005; Cochran-Smith & Lytle, 1999a), or a modified form of postmodernism. One clear example is in policy initiatives in Europe, Canada, England, and New Zealand and Australia that attempt to foster learning communities among principals and teachers under the assumption that the right combination of reflective discussions, research-based knowledge, and motivation will lead to school improvements (ETF, N.D; Jackson, Cordingley, & Hannon, 2006; Stoll & Louis, 2007).

---

[2] Andy Hargreaves notes that one may whole-heartedly agree that we live in a postmodern era, defined by a radical shift in the nature of economies, employment, and social relations, and disagree with many of the propositions put forward by self-style postmodern thinkers (personal communication).

The notion that local invention in response to local conditions is also part of the persistent policy thrust in several countries toward deconcentration and decentralization. The "charter schools movement" in the United States, for example, is promoted as an antidote to centrally managed effectiveness programs that don't work. Proponents of charter schools, which are typically new schools founded by groups of teachers and parents, assume that improving educational performance requires invention at the lowest level, not the diffusion of centrally developed and approved ideas. This assumption has driven public-policy options in many countries, ranging from Sweden to New Zealand, based on the belief that the role of central governments is to set standards, and the role of local agencies is to figure out how to meet them.

Organizational Learning

Another wrinkle added to the knowledge utilization puzzle in the 1990s emerged from the influence of Peter Senge's work on organizational learning (Senge, 1994). The idea of organizational learning drew on a deeper knowledge base in the management literature, which pointed out, for example, that there were real differences between change that was induced by nondeliberate and random adaptation and change as a result of collective learning (Fiol & Lyles, 1985), and that learning implied both a set of conceptual frameworks through which information was processed and required the ability to learn from multiple sources (Levitt & March, 1988). Senge's contribution was to look at how organizational conditions shaped deliberate consideration of new ideas. In addition, there was immediate interest, based on his and others' work, in applying the idea that organizations can learn – from experiences and knowledge produced outside their boundaries to public agencies, including schools (Busenberg, 2001; Mahler, 1997; Senge, McCabe, Lucas, & Kleiner, 2000).

The importance of organizational learning as a challenge to the traditional D&U model is threefold.

Outside vs. inside knowledge. Like the postmodernist perspective, the organizational learning perspective presents a challenge to the notion of knowledge as something created outside of the school and then "implemented." Knowledge comes from multiple sources, includes experience as well as research. Thus, research (expert knowledge) becomes one competing resource and needs to be factored in with other sources such as (Huber, 1991, p. 88):

- drawing on knowledge available at the organization's birth (what other similar organizations have done),
- learning from experience,
- learning by observing other organizations,
- grafting on to itself the components that possess knowledge needed but not possessed by the organization, and

- noticing or searching for information about the organization's environment and performance.

Only the last two of these categories have the potential for including formal research-based knowledge.

Ambiguous quality standards. Unlike the first two perspectives, no source of knowledge is inherently privileged over other sources, whether change occurs as a result of considering new information is dependent on the particular circumstances in which the organization finds itself (Morris & Moore, 2000; van de Ven & Polley, 1992). For example, organizations that are experiencing a strong threat may be more inclined to "learn" rather than to "adapt" – if they change at all. In addition, organizations that are in an early phase of a major change process may be more likely to engage in intuitive experimentation, leading later to more purposive search and analysis that might be more clearly indicative of collective learning.

The centrality of process. The organizational learning framework, unlike the renewed D&U model or postmodernism, raises important questions around the culture of the organization along multiple dimensions, including the presence of multiple processes for dealing with new information. Experience matters, but organizations can't learn if they don't have a "learning culture" that includes features such as a willingness to experiment or improvise, cooperative rather than competitive teams or subunits, and processes for reflection and turning consensus into action (Edmondson, 2002; Huber, 1991; Miner, Bassoff, & Moorman, 2001; Pisano, Bohmer, & Edmondson, 2001).

A Critique of Postmodernism

The debates between "objectivist modernists" and "constructivist postmodernists" are based in competing assumptions about science and the nature of knowledge, in which both groups fail to reflect on the conditions of inquiry or practice that are related to the knowledge use in schools. There are also some similarities between the two: both focus on the nature of knowledge and assume, for the most part, that formal knowledge is currently produced by researchers, and knowledge utilization, whether formal or informal, takes place in the work of practice.[3] In other words, as Huberman posits, there is "a gap." In fact, both also acknowledge that the picture is more complex but have not built a theoretical base that incorporates the complexity that they acknowledge.

Postmodernism appears, on the surface, to be more flawed than the revisionist versions of traditional theory. Most basic scientists have long ago given up the straw man of radical empiricism, while it is hard to imagine most practitioners accepting the contention that their classroom practice is guided only by their

---

[3]See Dunn and Holzner (1988) for a postmodernist perspective on dissemination that is explicit about this assumption.

own interpreted experience. Furthermore, some observational empirical evidence suggests that, although there *is* a gap between what researchers think they know and how users and practitioners of various sorts behave, there is also considerable activity around knowledge utilization that does not obviously involve dark efforts to impose ideas on a passive audience.

The organizational learning perspective is appealing for a variety of reasons. It focuses clearly on the "research consumer" as a collective body, and thus fits neatly with our assumption that "the school is the unit of change" (Cuban, 1990; Fullan, 1985; Spillane & Louis, 2002). In addition, it is flexible, and allows us to think about what constitutes knowledge and knowing using our now well-embedded constructivist lenses. All in all, it feels more contemporary. It is not, however, without limitations. First, it provides us with weak guidelines for assessing what constitutes "good" knowledge for improvement. In a school setting this is a particular drawback, because judgments are always being made about the quality of what is "known" in education, whether the topic concerns the best way of teaching mathematics or the best way of assessing student learning. Thus, the organizational learning perspective has an abstract quality that bears in only a limited way on the complex, high pressure world of practicing educators. A second drawback is the limited research base: We don't know how different kinds of knowledge actually fit into the change decisions that are made by schools, nor what the implications are of the variations in knowledge for the improvement of outcomes.

An Increasing Emphasis on "Scientific Knowledge" for Policy Decisions

One thing is clear: None of the controversies surrounding theories of knowledge use have damaged "science" at all. Around the world, governments are placing more rather than less emphasis on the importance of rigorous research and "evidence-based" innovation in education, and scholars are also calling for more high quality designs, both quantitative and qualitative (Feuer, Towne, & Shavelson, 2002; Maxwell, 2004; Wolter, Keiner, Palomba, & Lindblad, 2004). In many disciplines other than education, scholars are eagerly sought out for the potential commercial value of their ideas (Blumenthal, Causino, Campbell, & Louis, 1996). The value of a scholar's "sticky knowledge" – Hippel's (1994) term for the insights from research that is not published, but can be communicated – is also apparent in education, where some researchers are in high demand among the practitioner community. This knowledge is not always purveyed by social scientists and educational developers, but the fact that some of our knowledge is not viewed as useable does not obviate observations that research finds its way into educational practice.

If we see many examples of educators looking for or using externally generated knowledge as if it had real meaning, then postmodernism's argument that all knowledge is local must be flawed. Similarly, if we see that most knowledge from the outside is viewed as suspect – or at least imperfect – until other additions have been made to it, then modernist/positivist views are also problematic. Although the revisions to traditional theory suggested by Huberman attempt to address the problematic and contingent nature of knowledge, and to suggest ways in which dissemination activities may take account of this, his discussion does not address the other issues raised by postmodernists, namely that all knowledge is local, contested, and political. Organizational learning theory has not, to date, given us much evidence about how practitioners or policymakers grapple with the wide variety of "evidence-based" innovations that are promoted by hucksters as well as scholars. And none of the perspectives help us much as we try to understand the deepening politicization of knowledge in education, in which governments privilege some research while ignoring other "rigorous" approaches, and where parents and community members (at least in the United States) want to weigh in so that their opinions about what constitutes a high quality idea will also be heard.

New Perspectives

The new perspectives on dissemination and knowledge utilization that will be described briefly below can be viewed like layers on an onion of the problem of knowledge and practice. While it is clear that philosophers – and most Western individuals – accept Descartes' dictum of "I think, therefore I am," which encapsulates the individual and psychological perspective on knowledge use, there has been a long recognition that thinking and subsequent knowing is constrained by context. Scholars have recently begun to examine these layers at a number of different levels: political, social networks, organizational fields, and cognitive responses. Each of these will be briefly examined below, and the relationship of theoretical ideas to the problem of school improvement will be suggested.

Political Agenda-Setting

Characterizing applied educational research as an underutilized treasure trove or as a vast swamp of mediocre studies of limited utility is a matter of opinion rather than objective assessment. There is, however, little question that policymakers hope for quick answers that they rarely get, and researchers want to produce definitive studies that will change the direction of education. If this is the case, why don't we see more use of rigorous research? The answer lies, in large measure, in the nature of the policy process, whether it occurs at a national, state/provincial, or local level.

The notion that knowledge use is constrained by political contexts is not new. In the late 1980s, when evaluation research was well established on the policy scene, observers began to notice that publicly funded research was often used primarily because it "fit" a set of partisan purposes that were formed prior to the availability of the results. Legislative or parliamentary staff members did not read research to find out how their elected bosses *should* vote; instead they often combed research to find results that would fit the official's or party's preferred stance. Thus, for example, even the most rigorous multimillion-dollar educational evaluations relating to supplementary educational services for less advantaged children in the United States were ignored or embraced depending on personal perspectives.

Weiss and Bucuvalas (1980) were among the first to propose that knowledge produced through more-or-less rigorous inquiry needs to pass two types of tests before it is used: a *truth test*, which helps the individual or group looking at the information to decide whether it is a reasonable approximation of "reality," and a *utility test*, by which the same groups determine whether or not it can be applied given a set of constraints, which could range from financial to potential negative consequences not considered in the research. Thus, for example, educational researchers wonder why policymakers continue to advocate for large schools and large districts when cumulative research evidence suggests strongly that size is negatively related to students' achievement (Lee & Smith, 1997; Fowler & Walberg, 1991). Yet, local school boards and their administrators can present compelling evidence to support bigger institutions that range from obvious (cost savings) to symbolic (large schools are more likely to have comprehensive programs, which increases public support for education). The research may be true, but does not yet pass the utility test.

In addition to Weiss's cogent observations, the robust line of research on the policy-making process has been driven by the observation that much of the action in policymaking occurs before any votes are taken, during the period when new ideas are introduced and become policy issues for the legislature body and the public. The most frequently cited models of policy development emphasize, like Weiss's, the chaotic and pluralistic aspects of the process in most Western countries.

Until the 1970s, research on agenda-setting tended to look for (and find) elite influence (Putnam, 1976). An alternative, while acknowledging elite bias and resistance to change in the formal system of influence, makes a key additional assumption: that "pre-political, or at least pre-decisional, processes are often of the most critical importance in determining which issues and alternatives are to be considered. . .and which choices will be made" (Cobb & Elder, 1971). This may include "nondecisions," one process by which ideas are eliminated from formal consideration. While elites may determine which issues come up, it is at this juncture that nonelite groups joust to get their knowledge and ideas into the discussion. The pre-decision process is often biased and politicized (Wolter et al., 2004, p. 521), but in other cases there are multiple points of entry, and "outsiders" who have ideas can market them freely (Edmondson, 2005; van Velzen & Louis, 2009).

The Role of Knowledge in Agenda-Setting

Explaining the complexity of the social problems to be addressed by policy is usually left to social scientists and practitioners. However, in education, researchers are ill equipped to participate in the policy-making process because they don't understand it. While educational researchers occasionally become active policy analysts, they are more likely to play an entrepreneurial role, "selling" their own findings or acting as a behind-the-scenes advisor. Researchers complain that their firm results are often ignored, while policymakers argue that the research is not useful. At the same time, professional associations representing educators are regarded as weak sources of knowledge for policy (Louis, Febey, Gordon, & Thomas, 2008). Whoever is complaining, the outcomes are the same: limited attention paid to the value of rigorous research or practice-based knowledge (Rosenbaum, 1996; Ryan, 1999).

The point is not that policy deliberately ignores research and rigorous examination of effective practice (although it sometimes does), but that the policy-making process always takes into account that "what we know," at least in the social sectors, is swamped by what we don't know. Focusing on these uncertainties often stimulates debates that further undermine the credibility of knowledge, sometimes resulting in policy statements that research was not important in determining policy when it is apparent that there is a strong research base (Brown et al., 2003).

Alternative Modes of Agenda-Setting

A recent example in the United States illustrates the problem of incorporating research and practice perspectives into agenda-setting. The federal Reading Excellence Act was based on the goal of ensuring that every child in the United States would read by the 3rd grade *and* on the assumption that we know how to teach reading. However, competing views among various actors – individuals, professional associations, and well-placed policy advisors – undermined these reasonable assumptions (Edmondson, 2005). Schisms concerned the best way to teach reading, whether reading should be taught in pre-school or earlier, and other issues. Rather than rallying the expected coalition of stakeholders, the legislation precipitated lingering divisions between agencies and researchers committed to understanding and promoting reading. If promoting reading in the early grades can be politically volatile and create vituperative debate, we cannot expect that managing change in more complex parts of the system will be less so.

Policy initiatives can also become resistant to empirical or rational analysis. For example, Technical and Further Education (TAFE) policies in Australia were influenced primarily by corporate opinions and a neoliberal rhetoric linking further education to economic expansion and work, in spite of limited empirical evidence supporting the payoff of such a shift (Ryan, 1999; Symes, Boud, McIntyre, Solomon, & Tennant, 2000). This policy process apparently lacked the pluralistic and chaotic discourse that characterized the development of the Reading Excellence Act in the United States, but did so at the cost of discouraging the inclusion of alternative ideas that might have led to a more comprehensive education policy. There is little evidence that the policy change made much of a difference in the routines and practices of universities, except on the margins (Symes et al., 2000).

What can we conclude? First, the use of knowledge in the agenda-setting process is contested and poorly understood. Second, using rigorous practice or research-based knowledge to sway opinions once the agenda is set has little impact (sad news to all of the social scientists who prepare for legislative or parliamentary testimony). Finally, in education, research on agenda-setting is very limited; we know more about how legislative agendas are set in the small, progressive state of Minnesota

(Mazzoni, 1993) than we do about larger and perhaps more typical states and much less about other countries.

The contrasting agenda-setting histories of the US reading initiative and Australia's TAFE policies reflect the problems of school improvement today. On the one hand, we observe devolution or decentralization policies that place the responsibility for knowledge utilization and change more clearly in the hands of schools. The assumption that localized processes of knowledge utilization can contribute to educational improvement is a distinct paradigm shift that has occurred on an international basis, propounded by an increasing consensus among teacher associations, politicians, and parents in countries as diverse in educational tradition as Sweden, New Zealand, the Netherlands, England, and the United States. On the other hand, political actors continue to make decisions that involve centralized, hegemonic decisions that are intended to shock the system into change – for example, efforts to introduce new standards-based reforms in previously decentralized systems.

Social Networks

Many scholars focus on the characteristics of knowledge *and* context as a predictor of use. According to many writers, educational research is likely to influence policy development when it (1) is compatible with existing belief structures, (2) diffuses rapidly throughout the organizational field so that it becomes legitimized, (3) *has prima facie* utility in local sites, and (4) is "processed" or discussed within the potential user group in ways that make it fit with local preferences (Wejnart, 2002).

Weak Ties and Diffusion

The "strength of weak ties" is a concept that explains the unexpected finding that new ideas transfer most rapidly between groups that share only a few members (Granovetter, 1973). The underlying explanation is that *very strong ties* foster "groupthink": little disagreement about preferred policy solutions occurs among groups that share common ideologies, and therefore genuinely challenging information is unlikely to be exchanged. The *absence of ties* between groups means that innovative policy ideas will not be shared at all because of limited opportunity to meet. *Weak ties*, in contrast, permit both the development of diverse ideas in independent groups and also the occasional ad hoc communication that is associated with more the rapid spread of new ideas. Weaker ties between units within the same social system can be important in generating a broader range of solutions to identified problems, or help in identifying new problems (Hansen, 1999). The implicit understanding of the importance of weak ties underlies much of the enthusiasm in several countries for developing networks among administrators and teachers in different settings (Stoll & Louis, 2007).

Recent research on policy formation and agenda-setting incorporates network studies of networks that examine weak and strong ties. In particular, research on policy networks has turned from an emphasis on bargaining to one that also includes information transfer (John, 2001) and the diffusion of innovations in the public sector (Louis, Rosenblum, Bingham-Catri, & Jones, 2003; Wejnart, 2002). This shift expands the framework to account for the emergence of competitive "issue networks" and also moves beyond examining privileged or "elite" communication relationships to more inclusive and loosely regulated forms of information exchange. A network approach argues that most connections are fluid and bound together by the trading of valuable ideas and joint work and not just the exchange of favors. The fact that these are international trends, often involving the borrowing of language and ideas between countries, suggests a strong currency for a flow of political perspective about educational reform among elites. Ideas about effective schools and effective teaching have also been widely diffused through international research networks, and later, within countries, have been influential in affecting policy discourse.

The implications for conceptualizing complex educational changes are stunning. If policymakers at all levels in the educational system are held in a large but diffuse network in which crudely defined ideas circulate, but in which some ideas come up against unpredictable exclusionary boundaries, the problem of managing change becomes enormously complex. In large systems, managing complex change requires managing the flow of knowledge – something that has become increasingly difficult in the information age. Rather than managing change, we are driven to a worldview in which embracing the apparent chaos and disorder of an evolutionary process provides the only logic for making the world better (Wheatley, 1999; Wheatley & Crinean, 2004). It is the nature of the idea and whether it "sticks" that creates structures – not the command and control apparatus.

Strong Ties: The Influence of Elite Networks on Knowledge Use and Change

The weak ties concept is compelling, but may be less applicable when complex knowledge needs to be transferred. The weak ties approach suggests that countries or states will look for solutions to educational problems quasi-independently. One government's choices will not dictate an approach to the other. "Successes" are, however, communicated in a variety of venues ranging from invitational expert conferences to OECD meetings, and governments compete to be the first to adopt solutions that look good (Berry & Berry, 1999). The problem with this pattern is that the information communicated can be weak and poorly researched, and that spread may be based more on the immediate needs of officials to "look good" than on careful analysis. Furthermore, the more complex the information, the more likely it is to be distorted during transfer.

To compensate, officials develop stronger ties with information providers, turning to trusted groups for information on complex issues. In general, when faced with complex problems, most policymakers look for acknowledged expertise that has proven helpful in the past (Salisbury, Johnson, Heinz, Laumann, & Nelson, 1989). Experts may become members of the policy elite as part of their role in regularly providing information, a trend that accelerates when legislators are faced with ever more complex research results and policy options. In countries with a professionalized civil service, inner circle policy advisors, often with ties to academia or think tanks, may come to be seen as displacing more neutral and experienced advisors.

Sustained interactions are a key to the effective transfer of complex knowledge. This is the strong ties–weak ties dilemma: Trust creates networks that not only facilitate the flow of complex knowledge, but may also serve to crowd out divergent voices and ideas. Sustained interaction facilitates consistency in "mental models" or the worldviews of parties (Huberman, 1999), and emerging research suggests that people simply do not remember factual information that challenges their mental model (Mishra & Brewer, 2003). Perhaps fortunately, networks connecting researchers and policymakers rarely generate stable or formalized strong ties. Reliance on experts does not make decision makers powerless recipients, because they pick and choose who to listen to (Lupia & McCubbins, 1994; Mishra & Brewer, 2003).

Organizational Frames: Institutional and Cognitive

In addition to the infusion of ideas related to organizational learning into educational lexicon, other recent developments in organizational studies seem to have profound implications for knowledge use and school reform. Each also contributes to the debate between the modernists and postmodernists. The first builds on the work of institutional sociologists of the 1950s and early 1960s, but takes a more radical stance in terms of the degree to which external influences condition internal stabilities in organizations, and thus affect the knowledge that will or will not be used. This school of thought, which emerged in the early 1980s, is referred to as the "new institutionalism" (Powell & DiMaggio, 1991). A second line of work, which is more recent, examines sensemaking in organizations. This perspective is consistent with the organizational learning ideas discussed above, but pays more attention to the "how" of organizational learning.

The New Institutionalism

The new institutionalism in organizational theory begins with the assumption that the patterned regularity of organizational behavior, which is particularly noticeable within sectors or industries, is a major social phenomenon that requires explanation. The assumption that repetitive social relations are facts that cannot be reduced to individual explanations is as old as the field of sociology itself. What is new about the current perspectives, however, is the emphasis placed on explaining lack of variation in organizational patterns – for example, why do all modernized countries have a higher education system that is increasingly similar in terms of types of institutions, length of study, and the names of courses of study? Why are school classrooms remarkably similar whether one is in San Francisco, Rockford, Illinois, or London?

Organizational Fields

The answer, according to institutional theory, is that the emergence of an organizational field, or a collection of organizations in the same line of business, creates both collective opportunities to influence the environment and group norms that may generate resistance to change.

> ... in the long run, organization's actors making rational decisions construct around themselves an environment that constrains their ability to change in later years. *Early adopters of organizational innovations are commonly driven by a desire to improve performance. But ... as an innovation spreads (within the field) a threshold is reached beyond which adoption provides legitimacy rather than improves performance ....* Thus organizations may try to change constantly; but after a certain point in the structuration of an organizational field, the aggregate effective of individual change is to lessen the extent of diversity within the field. (DiMaggio & Powell, 1991, p. 65) (italics added)

The spread of the community college system throughout the United States after its initial "invention" in California is an example of this – a diffusion that has now been completed virtually worldwide in developed countries. Particularly striking is its institutionalization as a system that contains both "academic" and "vocational" programs and the similarity of programs between units that avowedly respond to local labor market needs (Brint & Karabel, 1989).

Norms and Epistemic Communities

The similar nature of individual organizations within an institutionalized field is maintained not by rational choices, but by the dominance of the norms and symbols that come to exemplify "the best of what we do." Through their participation in symbolic rituals, organizational action reinforces the order of the institution and its relationship to society (Detert, Louis, & Schroeder, 2001; McLaren, 1999). To give just a small example, the use of bells in US high schools to signify the end of classes had little practical significance. Yet, in the 1960s, efforts to eliminate bells were resisted: Bells stood for the orderliness of schooling, as contrasted with the chaos of adolescence. Resistance was not a consequence of individual concerns, but of environmental pressures from the organizational field, and other constituencies who reinforce the norms and symbols. These may range from the general public (who expected bells) to the government and accrediting associations/inspectorates.

In spite of the large and small rigidities introduced into an institutionalized organizational field, change and knowledge utilization do, of course, occur. However, reforms often spread in a mimetic fashion among governments and become quickly institutionalized (DiMaggio & Powell, 1991). A clear example is the recurring waves of curriculum standards reforms in developed countries – a response to public concerns about the rigor and breadth of this highly institutionalized aspect of the education system. Because math is an area in which major comparative tests have been conducted, the similarity in curricula between provinces/states (and countries) is increasing rapidly, while other curriculum areas (art, social studies, etc.) are highly variable between schools (e.g., are not institutionalized). Why should this be the case? In making these changes, policymakers and educators rely on information from others in their field: rates of knowledge dissemination and utilization are high, and research about math curricula and its effects are widely circulated. In the case of math reforms, the institutional interests of the organizational field in preserving public confidence in their programs often stimulated very modest changes in classroom behavior (Spillane, 2000).

The "middle school movement," intended to reform schools for younger adolescents (usually 11–14-year-olds) in the United States, is another example of dissemination based on a mixture of scholarly research, information about practices in other schools, and "local knowledge." The initial period of reform was more localized and chaotic, with many efforts to invent new solutions to the problem of creating more academic engagement among early adolescents. More recently, key structural elements, such as teacher teams, interdisciplinary curriculum, and cooperative pedagogical styles, have become widely shared and legitimated, *although research supporting their value is still rather slim.* What the institutional perspective points to is the increasing similarity in features of schools that are deemed necessary in order to qualify as "a real middle school."

Institutionalism and Postmodernism

To summarize, the institutional perspective picks up the postmodernist themes of hegemony of particular ideas and forms of knowledge, but argues that these are largely created *within* the organizational field (often in response to external pressure) and are *self-sustaining*. Rather than emphasizing the "localness" of knowledge construction and use, they point to the mimetic nature of organizations within an institutionalized field as a determinant of what knowledge will be used. Educational reform within the broad organizational field is not dependent on the availability of specific externally developed models complete with training and support, although these may support change in individual schools: The intersection between pressures for change from outside, local development activities, and the rapid spread of workable ideas between adopting units determines knowledge use.

Making Sense and Giving Sense

The determinism of new institutionalism is challenged by an offshoot of the organizational learning perspective, which argues that the superficial resemblance of schools may be misleading. Effective schools research suggests that the organizational factors that matter for student achievement are not easily visible to an outsider. If the new institutionalism examines the environment for dissemination and knowledge utilization activities that affect whether information will spread within an organizational field, new ideas about sensemaking move into the interior of the school, looking at features that affect the adaptability of individual units.

There are a variety of theoretical perspectives on sensemaking and change in the educational literature, but one finding is clear: When teachers or administrators are confronted with a new set of practices (such as those emerging from research), their interpretations of it will determine whether they engage in change, resistance, or simply ignore it (Gold, 2002; Louis & Dentler, 1988). Some studies focus on individual responses to disruptions or demands for change, which examine cognitive processes used by individual teachers to understand new information that is inconsistent with what they already know (Broadway, 1999; Zembylas, 2003), while others look at the role of context and culture as conditions mediating individual change (Angelides & Ainscow, 2000; Blase & Blase, 1997; Gioia & Thomas, 1996; Harris, 1994).

What Is Sensemaking?

Sensemaking is not an event, but is ongoing, focused on extracted cues, driven by plausibility, and tied to identity construction (Weick, 1993). *Individuals* pay attention when something in their surroundings does not fit with their usual routines, and use their experience to find patterns that help to explain new situations. Similarly, *collective* sensemaking occasionally occurs as part of a deliberate activity (like strategic planning), but more often emerges from informal communication that leads to common actions or agreed-upon activities (Coburn, 2001; Donnellon, Gray, & Bougon, 1986). In education, the nature of professional communities and dialogue has emerged as a powerful factor, determining collective understanding of new ideas introduced from outside (Coburn, 2001; Honig & Hatch, 2004), as well as organizational learning, or the creation of coherent and shared explanations for "how we do things around here."

Sensemaking and Knowledge Use

Sensemaking occurs when teachers work together and learn from each other, which leads them to interpret changes in their setting and practice in a consistent and collective manner (Coburn, 2001; Craig, 1995; Louis, Febey, & Schroeder, 2005). The role of school leaders in helping to interpret new information or demands from the school's environment and their implications for collective work is increasingly important (Coburn, 2005). Recent work has focused on the role of administrator's story-telling as part of the collective interpretation (Dunford & Jones, 2000), while other research has emphasized the role of the school leader in helping to determine what information is considered worth talking about in the first place (Wahlstrom & Louis, 1993). The paradox of distributing knowledge more broadly is that it may require a significant "push" from the top of the organization (the principal or other local leader) in order for more initiative to be taken up as a more fundamental element of sensemaking. It is this paradox that has led some people to talk about "sensegiving" as typically the job of a formal leader at the beginning of a change process (Fiss & Zajac, 2006).

Sensemaking requires not only cognitive engagement with the implications of a new research-based idea, but also opportunities to learn and practice (Coburn, 2001; Marks, Louis, & Printy, 2002). In peer groups with a high rate of interaction among members, values and attitudes are redefined through frequent contact. For example, time to meet and talk allows teachers and administrators to construct interpretations of new ideas and information, and to draw implications for their own work. Thus, organizational learning is a critical outcome of sensemaking because it prevents current beliefs and experiences from interfering with teachers' and administrators' ability to implement and interpret the new expectations that come along with expectations that the shape and practice of leadership in schools will change (Kezar & Eckel, 2002; Spillane, Diamond, & Burch, 2002). Making sense of any new initiative or idea, whether research-based requires alignment with existing conditions in the school, and the manner in which a new initiative or idea is framed also affects the role of policy actors outside the school (Firestone, Meyrowetz, & Fairman, 1998; Spillane, 1998). In particular, educational professionals need to see a connection to their main task, which is supporting student learning.

Sensemaking is a form of social processing but not necessarily deep processing. Studies of sensemaking often explore micro-interactions and cultural narratives. However, casual conversations and narratives can reflect superficial behavior expectations rather than addressing core assumptions about how the school should function (Craig, 1995). In order to create a more fundamental change, both time and deeper challenges to embedded assumptions are needed (Huy, 1999; Kezar & Eckel, 2002). This focus on "sustained interactivity" meshes well with Huberman's analysis, reviewed earlier, as well as with most descriptions of the conditions that foster organizational learning.

Paradigm Shift or Paradigm Revolution?

The purpose of the above review of recent research in a number of disciplines is to point to two issues: First, there is a proliferation of research and theory bearing on the intersection of knowledge dissemination and utilization and school improvement (although many authors quoted in this chapter do not explicitly consider this issue), and second, much of this research already incorporates elements of a postmodernist position, although none of the empirical studies discussed is consciously postmodernist. The convergence taking place around the key elements of emerging views of knowledge will be considered first, and then the implications for school improvement practice:

- *All knowledge is local.* The above discussions assume that local knowledge is a key feature of the landscape of change, but most would agree that there is important knowledge that is not local. Knowledge created elsewhere must, according to all theories, be compatible with existing belief structures, diffuse rapidly through-out the organization field so that it becomes legitimized, have utility in local sites, and be "processed" in ways that make it fit with local preferences. The "new institutionalism" adds another wrinkle to this: knowledge that is widely diffused is itself institutionalized so that it can be easily legitimated and shared within the "field" of organizations, sites, or other members of the culture. Although a great deal of important knowledge may come from outside the organization, the above theories also suggest that this information is always combined with local knowledge.

- *All knowledge is contested and partial.* This is supported by most of the new theoretical advances. Sensemaking, for example, assumes that the contesting of knowledge is central to the learning process. The "new institutionalism" (at a very different level) argues that it is the incontestability of many features of an organizational field that makes it difficult to change: only where there are chaotic events that cause either insiders or outsiders to question the existing knowledge base will change/knowledge utilization occur. The contested nature of knowledge is a key element of political theory and the primary element that leads most contemporary writers to conclude that there are many ways of using knowledge, depending on the degree to which it is "solid" – for example, meets truth and utility tests – and enters the agenda-setting arena at the right time and from the right source. In the organizational learning model, it is the debate and discussion around contested or partial knowledge that leads to a new *modus operandi*, a perspective that is consistent with the sensemaking perspective.

- *All knowledge is political.* Insofar as the newer theories address power, there is a tendency to follow Macaulay's assumption that "knowledge is power" and that the creation of knowledge creates powerful settings (including constraints). None of the perspectives reviewed here adopt, however, the critical postmodernist view that power-plus-knowledge inevitably becomes an instrument of oppression. Nevertheless, political contexts are critical to understanding knowledge use, as is demonstrated by the analysis of knowledge utilization among policymakers, the "new institutionalists" observations that knowledge use is constrained as the organizational field becomes defined by both internal norms/patterns and external expectations/regulation, and the sensemaking focus on the role of designated leaders as "sensegivers."

While all of the perspectives reviewed are consistent with some of the basic tenets of postmodernist views of knowledge, they also assume that knowledge has some realist qualities, and that it can be used by individuals who have not created it. The use process is complex and difficult to predict: there will be no production function D&U models emerging from this set of scholars. But messy cannot be equated with impossible. In fact, we may draw some lessons from Bordieu and Wacquant (1992) in this regard:

> Awareness of the limits of objectivist objectivation made me discover that there exists, within the social world, and particularly within the academic world, a whole nexus of institutions whose effect is to render acceptable the gap between the objective truth of the world

and the lived truth of what we are and what we do in it. . ... It is this *double truth*, objective and subjective, which constitutes the whole truth of the social world. (Bordieu & Wacquant, 1992, pp. 254–255)

Some Implications for Practice

There are many implications of the layered approach to D&U theory proposed in this chapter. In particular, I argue that there is a self-conscious need to reintegrate our understanding of the nature of three arenas of knowledge: research results related to educational goal achievement (school effectiveness, broadly conceived), educational change processes (school improvement, broadly conceived), and the knowledge use strategies that can be pursued both inside and outside schools to improve student learning and development. None of these are inconsistent with Huberman's reformulation of traditional dissemination theory, but suggest an expanded context for thinking about D&U. In particular, we need to draw upon the research about political, historical, and organizational contexts affecting knowledge use to enrich the micro-level perspectives that are emphasized by Huberman and the sensemaking research. While it is beyond the scope of this chapter to suggest a model for D&U and school development that fully incorporates these theories, a few examples can demonstrate the practical connections:

- *Research knowledge is only one source of knowing, and its use must be negotiated during a dissemination process.* This fluid relationship – and even co-dependence – between research and practice must be acknowledged, and researchers must be prepared to be open to involvement in the development process at the user level. Much of the best practice in education is not generated by scholars in laboratories, but by teachers and school leaders in actual settings. Research enters the field at a later point, synthesizing, developing, and assessing practice-generated ideas. In case you think that this is evidence of the weakness of the field of education, the same is also true in science and engineering, where connections between universities and firms are increasingly close (Owen-Smith, 2003). On the other hand, the spread of new ideas in education, as in science and engineering, is frequently aided by research, which may codify and extend practice-based knowledge as well as making independent contributions to it. In many cases, researchers may not be as well equipped to engage in field-based development over long periods of time (they have students and new research projects to carry out), but the others may fulfill this function if they have a deep understanding of the emerging nature of the negotiated knowledge.
- *Involving potential users in research will not necessarily make research more useable – except at a particular site or among those who have been directly involved.* There has been a trend in many countries to involve practitioners in setting some research agendas (e.g., serving on peer review panels), and even as co-participants in carrying out research. This is thought to make research more grounded and, hence, useable. While it may be good for researchers to become

more connected to practice settings and vice versa, the power of site or place when it comes to change is infinite. Thus, extensive involvement of practitioners as researchers should occur for its own direct benefits, and not because it improves the possibility of dissemination and utilization.

- *The main barriers to knowledge use in the public sector accrue as a result of rigidities induced in institutionalized organizational fields, organizational designs that do not foster learning, and political agendas that are not consistent with the information.* Changing these interorganizational rigidities in the short run may be extremely difficult. The motto under these circumstances is not to engage in Sisyphysian efforts, but to "try again another day" because contextual circumstances change for reasons that have nothing to do with research or educational policy.

- *The barriers to knowledge utilization are often to be found in organizational design. This suggests that redesigning the organization should be part of any effort to engage in "sustained interactivity" around research utilization.* The emphasis on developing school self-management that is emerging in many countries should be shaped around those capacities that augment not only the ability to manage budgets and personnel policies, but also attends to the creating of schools that can learn from knowledge that is generated inside and outside the school. This objective will require policies, as well as direct training and support to schools that have previously not engaged in these efforts.

- *Some forms of useful knowledge will spread with little dissemination effort – due to organizational field compatibility or because the field develops an infrastructure to assess and legitimate the type of knowledge.* We do not always need elaborate infrastructures or sustained interactivity to ensure the incorporation of new ideas in practice – nor can we ensure that the knowledge that spreads most rapidly is "good knowledge."

- *Utilization and impact can only be assessed over the long haul.* Short-run efforts to foster major utilization are likely to appear shallow and hegemonic to practitioners, and fail to disrupt the interorganizational rigidities of the field. Policymakers and disappointed researchers are likely to view these efforts as failures and to pronounce schools as impossible to change. Thus, research-based efforts to create school reform must be based on an extended time line.

- *Creating sustained interactivity is not a solution to the D&U problem, but if it becomes a norm, it may well increase the scholarly impact because it enlarges the organizational field.* We should not limit the idea of sustained interactivity to the relationship between a "knowledge producer/researcher" and "knowledge consumers/practitioners" but focus also on formal and informal networks for transmitting knowledge between units. These networks, to be successful, must involve practice templates that combine research knowledge and practice knowledge.

References

Ainscow, M. (2005). Developing inclusive education systems: What are the levers for change? *Journal of Educational Change, 6* (2) 109–124.

Anderson, G. L. (1990). Toward a critical constructivist approach to school administration: Invisibility, legitimation, and the study of non-events. *Educational Administration Quarterly, 26*(1), 38–59.

Angelides, P., & Ainscow, M. (2000). Making sense of the role of culture in school improvement. *School Effectiveness and School Improvement, 11* (2) 145–163.

Berry, F. S., & Berry, W. D. (1999). Innovation and diffusion models in policy research. In P. A. Sabatier (Ed.), *Theories of the policy process* (pp. 169–200). Boulder, CO: Westview.

Blase, J., & Blase, J. (1997). The micropolitical orientation of facilitative school principals and its effects on teachers' sense of empowerment. *Journal of Educational Administration, 35* (2) 138–164.

Blumenthal, D., Causino, N., Campbell, E., & Louis, K. S. (1996). Relationships between academic institutions and industry in the life sciences: An industry survey. *New England Journal of Medicine, 334*(6), 368–373.

Bordieu, P., & Wacquant, L. (1992). *An invitation to reflexive sociology.* Chicago: University of Chicago Press.

Brint, S., & Karabel, J. (1989). *The diverted dream: Community colleges and the promise of educational opportunity in America: 1900–1985.* New York: Oxford University Press.

Broadway, F. S. (1999). Student teachers' sense-making of an instructional ecology. *Journal of Research and Development in Education, 32* (4) 234–245.

Brown, M., Askew, M., Millett, A., & Rhodes, V. (2003). The key role of educational research in the development and evaluation of the national numeracy strategy. *British Journal of Educational Research, 29* (5) 655–667.

Busenberg, G. J. (2001). Learning in organizations and public policy. *Journal of Public Policy, 21* (2) 173–189.

Carr, W., & Kemmis, S. (1986). *Becoming critical: Education, knowledge and action research.* London: Falmer.

Cobb, R., & Elder, C. D. (1971). The politics of agenda-building: An alternative perspective for modern democratic theory. *The Journal of Politics, 33* (4) 892–915.

Coburn, C. E. (2001). Collective sensemaking about reading: How teachers mediate reading policy in their professional communities. *Educational Evaluation and Policy Analysis, 23* (2) 145–170.

Coburn, C. E. (2005). Shaping teacher sensemaking: School leaders and the enactment of reading policy. *Educational Policy, 19* (3) 476–509.

Cochran-Smith, M., & Lytle, S. L. (1999a). Relationships of knowledge and practice: Teacher learning in communities. *Review of Research in Education, 24,* 249–305.

Cochran-Smith, M., & Lytle, S. L. (1999b). The teacher research movement: A decade later. *Educational Researcher, 28* (7) 15–25.

Craig, C. J. (1995). Knowledge communities: A way of making sense of how beginning teachers come to know in their professional knowledge contexts. *Curriculum Inquiry, 25* (2) 151–175.

Cuban, L. (1990). Reforming again, again, and again. *Educational Researcher, 19* (1) 3–13.

Datnow, A. (2002). Can we transplant educational reform, and does it last? *Journal of Educational Change, 3*(3–4), 215–239.

Detert, J., Louis, K. S., & Schroeder, R. (2001). A culture framework for education: Defining quality values for US high schools. *Journal of School Effectiveness and School Improvement, 12*(2), 183.

DiMaggio, P., & Powell, W. (1991). The iron cage revisited: Institutional isomorphism and collective rationality in organizational fields. In P. DiMaggio & Powell, W. (Eds.), *The new institutionalism in organizational analysis.* Chicago: University of Chicago Press.

Donnellon, A., Gray, B., & Bougon, M. G. (1986). Communication, meaning, and organized action. *Administrative Science Quarterly, 31* (1) 43–55.

Dunford, R., & Jones, D. (2000). Narrative in strategic change. *Human Relations, 53* (9) 1207–1226.

Edmondson, A. C. (2002). The Local and variegated nature of learning in organizations: A group-level perspective. *Organization Science, 13* (2) 128–146.

Edmondson, J. (2005). Policymaking in education: Understanding influences on the Reading Excellence Act. *Education Policy Analysis Archives, 13*(11).

ETF. (N.D). *Learning and teaching community of practice for South Eastern Europe.* Retrieved December 2007, from http://www.etf.europa.eu/web.nsf/pages/Project_area:_ SEE_VET_TT_network_EN?Opendocument

Feuer, M., Towne, L., & Shavelson, R. (2002). Scientific culture and educational research. *Educational Researcher, 31* (8) 4–14.

Fiol, C. M., & Lyles, M. A. (1985). Organizational learning. *The Academy of Management Review, 10* (4) 803–813.

Firestone, W., Meyrowetz, D., & Fairman, J. (1998). Performance-based assessment and instructional change: The effects of testing in Maine and Maryland. *Educational Evaluation and Policy Analysis, 20* (2) 95–113.

Fiss, P. C., & Zajac, E. J. (2006). The symbolic management of strategic change: Sensegiving via framing and decoupling. *Academy of Management Review, 49* (6) 1173–1193.

Fowler, W. J., Jr., & Walberg, H. J. (1991). School size, characteristics, and outcomes. *Educational Evaluation and Policy Analysis, 13*(2), 189–202.

Fullan, M. (1985). Change processes and strategies at the local level. *The Elementary School Journal, 85* (3) 390–421.

Geertz, C. (1983). *Local knowledge: Further essays in interpretive anthropology.* New York: Basic Books.

Gioia, D. A., & Thomas, J. B. (1996). Identity, image, and issue interpretation: Sensemaking during strategic change in academia. *Administrative Science Quarterly, 41* (3) 370–403.

Glaser, E. M., Abelson, H. H., & Garrison, K. N. (1983). *Putting knowledge to use: Facilitating the diffusion of knowledge and the implementation of planned change.* San Francisco: Jossey - Bass Publishers.

Gold, B. (2002). *Social construction of urban education: New Jersey whole school reform and teachers' understanding of social class and race.* New York: Pace University.

Granovetter, M. (1973). The strength of weak ties. *American Journal of Sociology, 6* (6) 1360–1380.

Hansen, M. T. (1999). The search-transfer problem: The role of weak ties in sharing knowledge across organizational subunits. *Administrative Science Quarterly, 44* (1) 82–111.

Harris, S. G. (1994). Organizational culture and individual sensemaking: A schema-based perspective. *Organization Science, 5* (3) 309–321.

Hatch, T., & White, N. (2002). The raw materials of reform: Rethinking the knowledge of school improvement. *Journal of Educational Change, 3* (2) 117–134.

Havelock, R. (1969). *Planning for innovation through the dissemination and utilization of knowledge.* Ann Arbor: Institute for Social Research, University of Michigan.

Hippel, E. V. (1994). "Sticky Information" and the locus of problem solving: Implications for innovation. *Management Science, 40* (4) 429–437.

Honig, M., & Hatch, T. (2004). Crafting coherence: How schools strategically manage multiple, conflicting demands. *Educational Researcher, 33* (8) 16–30.

Hopkins, D. (2001). *School improvement for real.* New York: Routledge.

Huber, G. P. (1991). Organizational learning: The contributing processes and the literatures. *Organization Science, 2* (1, Special Issue: Organizational Learning: Papers in Honor of (and by) James G. March), 88–115.

Huberman, M. (1994). Research utilization: The state of the art. *Knowledge and Policy, 7* (4) 13–33.

Huberman, M. (1999). The mind is its own place: The influence of sustained interactivity with practitioners on educational researchers. *Harvard Educational Review, 69* (3) 289–319.

Huy, Q. N. (1999). Emotional capability, emotional intelligence, and radical change *Academy of Management Review, 24* (2) 25–345.

Jackson, D., Cordingley, P., & Hannon, V. (2006). *Networked learning communities: Programme, policy environment and the potential of participatory evaluation.* Retrieved December 17, 2007, from http://networkedlearning.ncsl.org.uk/knowledge-base/conference-papers/networked-learning-communities-programme-policy-environment.doc

John, P. (2001). Policy networks. In K. Nash (Ed.), *The Blackwell companion to political sociology*. Oxford: Oxford University Press.

Kezar, A., & Eckel, P. (2002). Examining the institutional transformation process: The importance of sensemaking, interrelated strategies, and balance. *Research in Higher Education, 43* (3) 295–328.

Kuhn, T. (1970). *The structure of scientific revolutions* (2nd ed.). Chicago: University of Chicago Press.

Landry, R., Lamar, M., & Amara, N. (2003). The extent and determinants of the utilization of University Research in Government Agencies. *Public Administration Review, 63*(2), 192–205.

Lee, V., & Smith, J. (1997). High school size: Which works best and for whom? *Educational Evaluation and Policy Analysis, 19*(3), 205–227.

Levitt, B., & March, J. G. (1988). Organizational learning. *Annual Review of Sociology, 14*, 319–340.

Louis, K. S., & Dentler, R. (1988). Knowledge use and school improvement. *Curriculum Inquiry, 18* (1) 32–62.

Louis, K. S., Febey, K., Gordon, M., & Thomas, E. (2008). State leadership for school improvement: An analysis of three states. *Educational Administration Quarterly, 44* (4) 562–592.

Louis, K. S., Febey, K., & Schroeder, R. (2005). State-mandated accountability in high schools: Teachers' interpretations of a new era. *Educational Evaluation and Policy Analysis, 27* (2) 177–204.

Louis, K. S., Rosenblum, S., Bingham-Catri, D., & Jones, L. (2003). *Dissemination systems in vocational education: Observations across three cases*. Minneapolis: National Center for Career and Vocational Education, University of Minnesota.

Lupia, A., & McCubbins, M. D. (1994). Who controls? Information and the structure of legislative decision making. *Legislative Studies Quarterly, 19* (3) 361–384.

Mahler, J. (1997). Influences of organizational culture on learning in public agencies. *Journal of Public Administration Research and Theory: J-PART, 7* (4) 519–540.

Marks, H., Louis, K. S., & Printy, S. (2002). The capacity for organizational learning: Implications for pedagogy and student achievement. In K. Leithwood (Ed.), *Organizational learning and school improvement*. Greenwich, CT: JAI.

Maxwell, J. (2004). Causal explanation, qualitative research, and scientific inquiry in education. *Educational Researcher, 33* (2) 3–11.

Mazzoni, T. (1993). The changing politics of state eduation policy making: A 20 year Minnesota perspective. *Educational Evaluation and Policy Analysis, 15*(4), 357–379.

McLaren, P. (1999). *Schooling as a ritual performance: Toward a political economy of educational symbols and gestures* (2nd ed.). Lanham, MD: Rowan and Littlefield.

Miner, A. S., Bassoff, P., & Moorman, C. (2001). Organizational improvisation and learning: A field study. *Administrative Science Quarterly, 46* (2) 304–337.

Mishra, P., & Brewer, W. F. (2003). Theories as a form of mental representation and their role in the recall of text information. *Contemporary Educational Psychology, 28* (3) 277–303.

Morris, M. W., & Moore, P. C. (2000). The lessons we (don't) learn: Counterfactual thinking and organizational accountability after a close call. *Administrative Science Quarterly, 45* (4) 737–765.

Owen-Smith, J. (2003). From separate systems to a hybrid order: Accumulative advantage across public and private science at research one universities. *Research Policy, 32* (6) 1081–1104.

Pisano, G. P., Bohmer, R. M. J., & Edmondson, A. C. (2001). Organizational differences in rates of learning: Evidence from the adoption of minimally invasive cardiac surgery. *Management Science, 47* (6) 752–768.

Powell, W. W., & DiMaggio, P. J. (1991). *The new institutionalism in organizational analysis.* Chicago: University of Chicago Press.

Putnam, R. (1976). *The comparative study of policy elites.* Englewood Cliffs, NJ: Prentice Hall.

Rogers, E. (1983). *Diffusion of Innovations* (3rd ed.). New York: Free Press.

Rosenbaum, J. (1996). Policy uses of research on the high school-to-work transition. *Sociology of Education* (extra issue), 102–122.

Ryan, R. (1999). How TAFE became "Unresponsive": A study of rhetoric as a tool of educational policy. *Australian and New Zealand Journal of Vocational Education Research, 7* (2) 105–126.

Salisbury, R. H., Johnson, P., Heinz, J. P., Laumann, E. O., & Nelson, R. L. (1989). Who you know versus what you know: The uses of government experience for Washington lobbyists. *American Journal of Political Science, 33* (1) 175–195.

Sammons, P. (1999). *School effectiveness: Coming of age in the 21st century.* New York: Taylor and Francis.

Schmoker, M. (1999). *Results: The key to continuous school improvement.* Alexandria: Association for Supervision and Curriculum Development.

Schön, D. (1983). *The reflective practitioner: How professionals think in action.* New York: Basic Books.

Senge, P. (1994). *The fifth discipline: The art and practice of the learning organization.* New York: Currency Doubleday.

Senge, P., McCabe, N. C., Lucas, T., & Kleiner, A. (2000). *Schools that learn: A fifth discipline fieldbook for educators, parents, and everyone who cares about education.* New York: Doubleday.

Spillane, J. (2000). Cognition and policy implementation: District policymakers and the reform of mathematics education. *Cognition and Instruction, 18* (2) 141–179.

Spillane, J., Diamond, J. B., & Burch, P. (2002). Managing in the middle: School leaders and the enactment of accountability policy. *Educational Policy, 16* (5) 731–762.

Spillane, J., & Louis, K. S. (2002). School improvement processes and practices: Professional learning for building instructional capacity. In J. Murphy (Ed.), *Challenges of leadership* (pp. 83–104). Chicago: National Society for the Study of Education.

Spillane, J., Reiser, B. J., & Reimer, T. (2002). Policy implementation and cognition: Reframing and refocusing implementation research. *Review of Educational Research, 72* (3) 387–431.

Spillane, J. P. (1998). State policy and the non-monolithic nature of the local school district: Organizational and professional considerations. *American Educational Research Journal, 35* (1) 33–63.

Stoll, L., & Louis, K. S. (Eds.). (2007). *Professional learning communities.* Milton Keynes: Open University Press/New York, McGraw-Hill.

Symes, C., Boud, D., McIntyre, J., Solomon, N., & Tennant, M. (2000). Working knowledge: Australian Universities and "Real World" education. *International Review of Education, 46* (6) 565–579.

Teddlie, C., & Reynolds, D. (2000). *The international handbook of school effectiveness research.* New York: Falmer.

Van de Ven, A. H., & Polley, D. (1992). Learning while innovating. *Organization Science, 3* (1) 92–116.

Van Velzen, B., & Louis, K. S. (2009, January 4–7) *The Netherlands: An individualistic policy culture.* Paper presented at the annual meeting of the International Congress of School Effectiveness and School Improvement, Vancouver, BC.

Wahlstrom, K., & Louis, K. S. (1993). Adoption revisited: Decision-making and school district policy. In S. Bachrach & R. Ogawa (Eds.), *Advances in research and theories of school management and educational policy* (Vol. 1, pp. 61–119). Greenwich, CT: JAI.

Warren, D. I. (1970). Variations on the themes of primary groups: Forms of social control within school staffs. *Sociology of Education, 43*(3), 288–310.

Watkins, J. (1994). A postmodern critical theory of research use. *Knowledge and Policy, 7* (4) 55–77.

Weick, K. E. (1993). The collapse of sensemaking in organizations: The Mann Gulch Disaster. *Administrative Science Quarterly, 38* (4) 628–652.

Weiss, C., & Buculvalas, M. (1980). *Social science research and decision making.* New York: Columbia University Press.

Wejnart, B. (2002). Integrating models of diffusion and innovation: A conceptual framework. *Annual Review of Sociology,* 23, 297–326. Palo Alto, CA: Annual Reviews.

Welch-Ross, M. K., & Fasig., L. G. (Eds.). (2007). *Handbook on communicating and disseminating behavioral science/[edited by].* Los Angeles: Sage Publications.

Wheatley, M., & Crinean, G. (2004). *Solving, not attacking, complex problems a five-state approach based on an ancient practice.* Retrieved from 2/11/05 http://www.margaretwheatley. com/articles/solvingnotattacking.html

Wheatley, M. J. (1999). *Leadership and the new science: Discovering order in a chaotic world.* San Francisco: Berrett-Koehler.

Wolter, S., Keiner, E., Paloma, D., & Lindblad, S. (2004). OECD examinaters' report on educational research and development in England. *European Educational Research Journal, 3* (2) 510–546.

Zembylas, M. (2003). Interrogating "Teacher identity": Emotion, resistance, and self-formation. *Educational Theory, 53* (1) 107–127.

Innovation and Diffusion as a Theory of Change

Tom Bentley

In 1991, a Finnish computer science student named Linus Torvalds announced, in an email to an Internet news group:

> I'm doing a (free) operating system (just a hobby, won't be big and professional) . . . this has been brewing since April, and is starting to get ready (Steinberg, Mulgan, & Salem, 2005).

By 2002, the system that Torvalds had developed, Linux, had claimed 25% of the world market for server operating systems, drawing on an estimated 8,000 person hours of developer time. It now supports a burgeoning range of software applications and services, shaped and spread by enthusiastic user communities and used by some of the world's largest public and private organisations.

The key to its rapid evolution and spread was its open, free nature. Torvalds deliberately shared the program, encouraged its replication and use and invited modifications and improvements which he vetted and adopted and as such the core operating system continued to evolve.

Open-source programmes are perhaps best known for the challenge they present to the dominant incumbent in the world of proprietary computer software, Microsoft. The challenge is not just to the quality and cost of products, but the operating philosophy behind them: Open source appeals to many who somehow feel that the tools to create and manipulate knowledge and information are best shaped by an ethic of openness, creativity and collaboration (Leadbeater, 2008).

Open-source methods have led to many other powerful ways of creating, refining and sharing knowledge. One of the best known is Wikipedia, the online encyclopaedia that now holds more than 1 million articles in over 100 languages. Wikipedia is created by its users and edited by volunteers according to open editorial standards.

The Internet is making possible mass-scale applications of knowledge and knowledge-sharing, which could be powerful, if not revolutionary, when applied the task of improving the quality and of reach public education.

T. Bentley (✉)
Policy Director for Julia Gillard, Deputy Prime Minister and Education Minister,
Melbourne, Australia (writing in a personal capacity)
e-mail: tombentley@fastmail.fm

A. Hargreaves et al. (eds.), *Second International Handbook of Educational Change*,
Springer International Handbooks of Education 23, DOI 10.1007/978-90-481-2660-6_2,
© Springer Science+Business Media B.V. 2010

There is no shortage of visionaries who can see the potential. For example, Jimmy Wales, Wikipedia's founder, recently coauthored an article with Richard Baraniuk calling for an "open education revolution":

> We want to infect you with the dream that anyone can become part of a new movement with the potential to change the world of education. (Wales & Baraniuk, 2008)

Baruniuk, a professor of engineering at Rice University in Texas, is the founder of Connexions, an "open-source media platform" designed to encourage the sharing and adaptation of educational materials. Connexions provides an online environment in which learners and educators can freely access, share and adapt learning materials on any subject.

In November 2008, Connexions announced a collaboration with the South Africa–based Shuttleworth Foundation to "jointly develop one of the world's largest, most comprehensive sets of free online teaching materials for primary and secondary school children."

For Wales and Baruniuk, changing the nature of educational textbooks and teaching resources is just the start. They see these methods as part of a mission to transform the nature of education itself, just as new collaborative technologies and methods are having radical, disruptive effects on the organisation of science, commerce, and cultural production.

In the same year, Paul Miller, a young researcher and entrepreneur in London, launched the School of Everything with a group of friends (School of Everything, 2008). The School of Everything describes its mission as "Everyone has something to teach, everyone has something to learn." It offers a simple, Web-based system, through which members can find people offering to teach in any area of knowledge and register to offer their own expertise.

School of Everything is setting out to reinvent adult education. Early signs are promising: Following 2 years of development, its public launch in September 2008 was followed by thousands of members signing up every month. Though its founders do not see themselves as business entrepreneurs, it has been deliberately established as a for-profit entity, in part to bypass the difficulties of operating in the world of public education, with its bureaucratic management structures, closed accreditation systems and incremental timescales.

A Shifting Landscape

These examples point to a profound shift in the organisation of work and learning that has been gathering force for a generation. Information has become pervasive through the networking of information and communications technologies (ICTs). Value is increasingly added through the creation and embedding of knowledge into products, services and organisations, and the most successful ways to innovate and undertake large-scale adaptation have become significantly more interactive and open.

The shift applies to every sector – in the corporate world, investment in research and development is increasingly undertaken through open, collaborative processes which seek to attract and motivate contributors from far-flung networks spanning countries, sectors, and firms rather than seeking to direct innovation through dedicated research labs, proprietary pipelines, or closed policy silos (Chesbrough, 2003).

In the public realm, civil society is using the same methods to mobilise campaigns, activism, and journalism through open, user-driven networks. Ohmynews.com, the Korean-based citizen journalism project, produces news and commentary generated by its network of more than fifty thousand user-contributors in more than one hundred countries. Avaaz.org – motto: "the world in action" – has built a global Web-based community to campaign on issues from human rights to climate change and poverty. It has attracted more than three million members and regularly mobilises hundreds of thousands to lobby meetings like the 2008 EU leaders' summit on climate change.

These examples share common features:

- They are *open*, making transparent their own structures, operating processes and content to an unprecedented degree, and allowing access to users and participants with few restrictions.
- They are highly *networked*, operating through structures which enable rapid lateral transfer of new material across networks of users who cut across institutional, sectoral or geographical boundaries.
- They are *user driven*, affording a new level of empowerment and contribution to participants who might previously have been thought of as passive consumers or inexpert students.

The combination of these three features means that the activities they create can be highly *self-organising*, relying on emergent structures and distributed decision making to allocate resources and coordinate projects, and highly *differentiated*, responding to the varying needs of their users instantly through the terms on which they choose to participate and in the process generating personalised services and experiences.

These features have led some to declare a new era of participatory democratic innovation which shakes the foundations of our professionally dominated and proprietary systems of institutional and economic life (Benkler, 2006).

Such changes have obvious importance for the way we understand and approach change in education. They point to the potential of emergent, networked innovation as a means to achieving rapid and widespread change.

But dynamic new movements and transformative ideas have been with us for much longer than the last generation. Some wither on the margins, while many turn out not to fulfil their radical promise. Others are absorbed into the wider pattern of economic and social life without revolution.

New educational eras have been boldly predicted many times before, premised on "scientific" measurements of intelligence, the professionalization of teachers, the role of the state in making schooling universal, the introduction of computers into classrooms, and more recent advances in neuroscience.

This chapter examines the importance of the new innovation movement for the organisation of K-12 education and the potential for its methods and tools to extend the repertoire of educational change.

Beyond its potential, we should ask whether the growing emphasis on innovation and diffusion amounts to a model of systemic change relevant to the governance, leadership, and reform of mass schooling systems. There are many barriers to such change, including sunk investment in old models, producer capture and the cost of making disruptive transitions.

But there is also no question regarding the fact that education is already part of the global shift: Linus Torvalds was a student when he posted his program (as was Mark Zuckerberg, the founder of Facebook, the social networking tool). Many of the most influential innovations, such as the World Wide Web itself, have emerged from public education and research institutions.

This is not surprising: Any approach to enquiry and innovation which treats knowledge as a common good, pursues collaboration as a means to deeper under-standing, and encourages open exchange and dialogue owes much to long-standing educational traditions.

But in the last century the dominant methods for governing and improving pub-lic education systems have taken quite different forms. While there have been many innovations, successful reform strategies and fiercely competing intellectual and ide-ological currents in education policy, deep systemic change has remained elusive, despite the central political status that education policy now enjoys in most countries and the intense focus on improving outcomes that accompanies this status.

This chapter examines whether the growing emphasis on innovation and diffu-sion amounts to a model of systemic change relevant to the governance, leadership, and reform of mass schooling systems.

It argues that the conditions for systemic adoption of this approach to learning and adaptation are not in place in most school systems despite the welter of inno-vative activity and the growing emphasis on spreading it. Accurate understanding of the real causes of rigidity and "adaptive flexibility" in school systems is a pre-condition of understanding how innovation can lead to deep, beneficial, educational change.

The Need for Systemic Change

The current pressure on schooling arises from twin drivers. The first is to ensure and demonstrate better attainment across *all* students and schools, and narrow the gap between the highest- and lowest-achieving students. The second pressure is to respond to the ever-growing range of need and demand, expressed as social and cultural diversity; greater student mobility; changing student, family and employer expectations; growing economic inequality; and geographical polarisation.

Public recognition of education as a central determinant of social and economic success – both for individuals and for whole societies – continues to grow. But educational performance is both cause and consequence – mirror and mould – of a society's success. So the practice of education is entangled, inevitably, in wider processes of change including urbanisation and industrialisation, family formation and the renegotiation of gender roles, mass migration and the emergence of new knowledge economies from India and Brazil to Finland and Malaysia.

As a result, of course, education systems are under constant pressure to improve fast enough to meet this heightened demand, while simultaneously adapting to the effects of wider social, economic and technological change, in real time, on the systems themselves. Any strategy for adaptation and improvement through innovation must therefore address these complex, ongoing interactions – between the impact of schools' performance on the capabilities of the communities they serve and on schools of changes to the economic, social, demographic and technological context in which they operate.

The challenge under those circumstances is to build systems which can improve their own core performance by focusing on priority outcomes like literacy and numeracy and essential standards of equity or fairness, while also actively reflecting the heterogeneity and diversity of the societies they serve.

Under these conditions – where education is expected to deliver often dramatic improvements in performance with often only modest injections of extra funding and simultaneously expected to respond and adapt to an increasingly diverse and vociferous range of demands – it is no surprise that innovation is also in demand.

Nor is it in short supply. New tools and practices are continuously being generated from both within and beyond formal education. They range from breakthrough pedagogies to concentration-enhancing drugs, digital learning assistants and communities of practice to corporate engagement strategies and models of system reform.

But despite the success of some strategies, few would claim that education systems are improving or adapting at the rate or depth that is really needed, or of the examples with which we began this chapter. The questions which are continuously raised in educational debate are how to find more powerful ways to select and run with the right innovations and how to spread them effectively across whole systems of organisation (Dede, Honan, & Peters, 2005). In the case of public education, those systems are often very geographically dispersed and organisationally fragmented.

The Dominance of the Bureaucratic Paradigm

In the second half of the twentieth century, education policies focused on achieving universal coverage for the core years of schooling. In its last 2 decades, the focus shifted towards pushing up quality through standards-based reform. Most countries have national education policies clustered around the following themes:

- standards-based measures to improve attainment in essential outcomes, especially numeracy and literacy;
- reporting, assessment and accountability based on key performance indicators;
- new infrastructure, including the overhaul and modernisation of school buildings and the introduction of ICT hardware and networks;
- reduction of class sizes and training of new teachers;
- finding, training and rewarding high-performing educational leaders;
- funding and growing childcare and early years centres;
- increasing post-compulsory participation by expanding higher education and creating new schoolwork pathways and higher vocational qualifications;
- reshaping the educational workforce to emphasise flexibility, professional development, specialisation of professional and paraprofessional roles and performance management;
- civic engagement and citizenship among young people;
- targeted strategies to tackle underperformance among specific, deprived social groups and in marginalised urban or rural areas.

This list masks many important variations in the ways that each reform can be approached. Among others these variations reflect policy choices about the measurement of attainment, funding, curriculum prescription, the role of government and non-government schooling providers and the structure of the teaching workforce. But with few exceptions, the reform agenda across OECD nations revolves around the same governance paradigm and the ongoing dominance of public bureaucracies in managing schooling and school reform.

In this model, responsibility for educational management and improvement is coordinated through a *tri-level* structure of central agencies, local authorities or school districts and individual schools. The centre makes policy, sets rules of accountability and allocates funding; a layer of local or regional authorities conducts planning and coordination and individual schools operate according to their own mix of leadership, community expectation and organisational capability within the prevailing environment.

This model is almost universal, though the relative power of each layer varies. Its ubiquity means that no reform strategy will be successful without explicitly addressing and aligning actions at each of the three levels (e.g., see Michael Fullan's theory of tri-level reform) (Fullan, 2005).

But while active alignment of the three levels is clearly essential, it is equally striking that the tri-level schema applies equally to the internal organisation of the typical school as well as to the wider system, indeed, to many different kinds of organisation.

In fact, other educational innovations tend to be channelled through and absorbed into this institutional paradigm as part of the enduring operating framework for schooling. As such, the tri-level framework provides the setting for the standards-based reform strategies of the last generation and helps to explain both their successes and shortcomings.

Standards-based reform uses a simple, powerful set of tools to pursue better outcomes. They are as follows:

- Creating formal performance objectives and standardising measures of performance;
- Targeting resources and prioritising key outcome measures;
- Strengthening and simplifying accountability structures;
- Building professional development and continuous improvement strategies;
- Centralising control over investment budgets, performance measures, curriculum specification, accountability structures and inspection systems;
- (Often) decentralising and deregulating other aspects of school resourcing and organisation, including school budgets, support services and professional development, creating new managerial flexibilities for school leaders.

The major policy trend, over a generation, has been the creation of a single framework through which to pursue continuous improvement in school performance by identifying standards, resourcing schools to meet them and making schools, students and professionals accountable for their attainment. This trend has occurred, of course, at the same time as the shift in public administration towards decentralisation and devolution in the organisation of public services through reforms broadly associated with the "new public management". These reforms, which have applied to education as much as to anything else, have encouraged contracting out of key services, entry of new service providers into areas of state monopoly and devolution of management control towards the local level, for example, through school-level autonomy over budgets, teacher recruitment and procurement of support services. If differentiation and responsiveness have been achieved through administrative devolution and operational flexibility, they have been accompanied by the standardisation and hardening of measurement and accountability structures.

The aim of the reform strategies using this approach has been to ensure that each school has appropriately focused capacity and incentives to improve its own performance through participation in a common system of governance and accountability. Schools are then supported or rewarded to the extent that they are deemed to have under- or over-performed.

Some of these strategies have been highly effective (Levin, 2008). But this strategic focus has never, as far as I know, led to the replacement of the traditional model of bureaucratic governance.

Why is the Bureaucratic Model So Resilient?

One explanation, I believe, for the persistence of this model is that it fits hand in glove with a model of schooling itself which is deeply rooted in public imagination and in our wider systems of social and economic organisation. Centuries-old habits are hard to break and lead to the formation of powerful vested interests. Traditional forms of schooling are especially susceptible to producer capture given the relatively weak voices of users (students and parents). The costs sunk over generations into schooling infrastructure and industrial organisational models mean that moving to alternative patterns of organisation and delivery can be expensive, although some more networked and open models could eventually reduce overheads and encourage more innovation.

But even where vested interests are weak or have been swept away by reform or market competition, the model does not seem to have changed radically. Successful private schools rarely stray from the organisational form or the regulatory methods found in state sectors and often generate their own intermediate bureaucracies to coordinate, regulate and manage support services in the absence of public school boards or local government. Across countries and cultures, the received definition of an "effective school" has also become remarkably similar, influenced by both the international research movement on school improvement and the internationalisation of performance indicators and measurement. The effective school is characterised by strong, purposeful leadership; an ordered, stable setting that sustains a consistent focus on learning, held in place by a clearly defined hierarchy of professional roles and organisational systems and cultures which support continuous review and improvement within the organisational framework.

Of course there are many variations and inflections, from specialist curricula to religious or community ethos. But the organisational core remains recognisable across sectors and cultures – and it aligns seamlessly with the wider governance framework.

This might prompt many discussions, but our focus is on what shapes the flow of innovation and adaptation. Traditional models of bureaucracy are usually characterised as rigid, rule based, and internally focused. Many reformers and reform strategies have worked to inject openness, contestability and explicit goal-setting into the workings of these systems. But perhaps the explanation for their resilience lies in their peculiar flexibility rather than their closed nature.

Much recent thinking about the shaping of social and economic behaviour has focused on the evolution, through open and self-organising processes, of *complex adaptive systems*. Rather than the formal, rational goals and accountabilities of the institutional framework, which is the focus of so much school reform, this thinking focuses on the patterns and dynamics of behaviour in systems which hold together without explicit systems of command.

Human behaviour is adaptive in the sense that it continuously adjusts to changing environments and new experience, even without conscious decision making. A burgeoning literature on game theory and behavioural and institutional economics provides a rich new source of insight into these patterns and the fact that social and organisational behaviour forms complex, durable patterns which often subvert or contradict both chains of command and the "common sense" of market incentives (Homer-Dixon, 2006; North, 2005).

The evolution of these adaptive systems can lead to increasingly complex patterns of specialisation, interdependence and self-organisation which hold together different needs, functions and interests in a wider community (Wright, 2001).

Such systems contain many diverse parts but still operate as coherent wholes which generate more than their sum (Chapman, 2003). Ecosystems function in this way, with clear hierarchies, specialised division and sharing of labour between species and within groups, a constant, evolving mix of competition and collaboration and physical boundaries set and shaped by the interaction between landscape, population and capability. A school system could be characterised in the same way, except that its evolution is directed by human intentions and norms and not simply by competition and natural selection.

My argument here is that the bureaucratic model is adaptive, but that it is not necessarily designed to optimise learning outcomes for all of its participants. Instead, it enables its members – schools, administrators, teachers and so on – to coordinate the process of continuous adaptation to changing student identities, changing socio-economic conditions and changing policy requirements, through an ordered, incremental process of adjustment, refinement, and organisational learning. The bureaucratic model is not impervious to change: It offers a particular kind of flexibility which makes adaptation manageable, as long as the changes can be accommodated within its own organisational parameters. The system is implicitly geared towards maintaining the integrity of *its own* design.

This layering allows reliable organisation of teaching and learning and progression of cohorts of students, simultaneously with the day-to-day adjustment and improvisation needed to accommodate changing needs and behaviours – each box in the diagram in Fig. 1 simultaneously represents a unit of formal accountability and a domain of local knowledge and authority with its own leadership, power structure, informal social relationships, shared culture and so on.

Fig. 1 The tri-level adaptive structure of schools and school systems

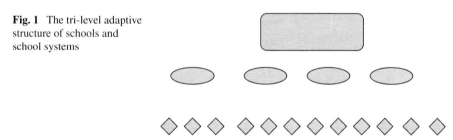

The remarkable durability of these routines in the face of change may be explained partly by the mutual dependence of policy makers, administrators and practitioners on its orderly structure for the implementation of their own central objectives. They make ordered learning possible by creating the predictability and responsibilities needed to organise at large scale.

As Christensen, Horn and Johnson put it:

> In every organisation there are forces that shape and morph every new innovative proposal so that it fits the existing organisation's own business model, rather than fitting the market it was intended to serve. (Christensen, Horn, & Johnson, 2008)

All durable systems set parameters on the scope of what they can accommodate. If an innovation has to pass through these processes and routines – what Christensen et al. describe as a "legislative process" – in order to win legitimacy and be taken up across the operating system, it is inevitable that it will be shaped and implemented by the perspectives, interests and dominant methods in that existing system.

Stemming the Flow of Learning

But if the system as a whole increasingly requires rapid, powerful flows of innovation, these underlying sources of order also present a major constraint.

The same structures which make ordered learning possible also set boundaries which limit its possibilities by limiting the scope of inquiry, interaction and information flow in teaching and learning.

At the level of practice, many teachers seek ways around these limitations, but most remain within the boundaries of classrooms, year groups and a preset curriculum. Some of the most powerful educational innovations are disruptive: They require radically different patterns of organisation, using time, space, information and people differently in the learning process, in order to achieve their potential impact. But as Richard Elmore has persuasively argued, the multiple layering of organisational systems and authority, and the strong separation of the core technical and practical knowledge of teachers from the organisational knowledge and authority of educational administration, creates a potent "buffering" effect.

Thus policy makers and experts are insulated from the classroom, and individual teachers are insulated from the expertise and exposure to new practice that might make them directly accountable for generating the best possible outcomes (Elmore, 2000).

These properties have not escaped the notice of educational leaders. The need for "adaptive work" as part of any change strategy is increasingly accepted as part of the lexicon of educational reform. (Heifetz & Linsky, 2002) In this context, adaptive work means mobilising people to solve problems or meet challenges which go *beyond* the existing capabilities or technical solutions at their disposal (Bentley & Wilsdon, 2003).

Adaptive strategies therefore seek explicitly to *build a new capacity* which can be used to support higher student achievement and to build a culture of "high expectations" which seeks permanently to overcome an institutionalised status quo of student underachievement.

Two elements in particular stand out as features of these reform strategies: the focus on developing *leaders* who can successfully raise expectations and the focus on starting (or restarting) *new organisations* – academies, charter schools and so on – as a way to disrupt these patterns.

But while the introduction of fresh external stimulus may be recognised as essential to the prospects of systemic change, how best to combine them with the resources of the existing system remains a challenge unmet. In short, educational reform has become more adept at creating new directions and new models in the last generation, but still struggles to gain leverage for these innovations across whole systems.

In the context of the tri-level governance framework, this creates a deep *systemic tension:* Focusing on performance regimes in pursuit of higher standards from the centre requires strengthening of vertical chains of command and reinforcement of the structures which create functional standardisation and fragmentation.

At the same time, meeting the needs of an increasingly diverse student body by utilising a burgeoning range of expert knowledge and evidence about effective learning practices requires much greater levels of flexibility and direct collaboration with the wider world.

This combination of stability and incremental change allows the traditional model of schooling, and of bureaucratic school systems, to adapt continuously to all kinds of external change, and therefore to deflect the disruptive potential of almost any innovation, whether it comes from above, below or around the corner.

While reform strategies continue to rely on the ongoing consistency at the core of the system – such as those required by standardised reporting processes, outcome measures and benchmarked features of effective schools – they will inevitably help to reinforce and embed the core institutional design. Meanwhile, the adaptive resilience of the wider system is just as likely to be filtering and interpreting the signals being sent from the policy centre, and in the process reducing their impact.

Making Innovation Systemic

Yet if this were the whole story, it would be hard to account for the many different ways in which innovation *is* generated and spread across existing education systems.

Of course, much of the current wave of open, networked innovation has its roots in long-standing educational thinking and practice. The School of Everything is a self-conscious twenty-first century manifestation of Ivan Illich's "de-schooling" ideas, while the principles of systems thinking and reflective practice flow directly from thinkers like John Dewey and Donald Schön to contemporary scholars like Lawrence Lessig and Etienne Wenger.

Most school systems make significant investments in infrastructure for knowledge transfer, whether through professional development programs or technology networks, research laboratories or leadership institutes. Most schools participate in partnerships, exchange programs and self-generated improvement projects of some sort. The question is not whether resources for innovation exist, but whether the wider whole of the system manages to create more than the sum of its individual parts.

Some of the more breathless theories of networked innovation would suggest that its spread depends almost entirely on the kind of spontaneous, organic and self-organising growth shown by the viral spread of Web-based phenomena.

But a longer view would acknowledge that the most influential innovations are often the result of deliberately crafted strategies and that innovation has its greatest impact precisely when it is integrated with, or replaces, existing systems.

Christensen's analysis of the growth of disruptive innovation helps here: Genuinely disruptive innovations, in order to achieve their full impact, must initially be developed to "compete against non-consumption", that is, for use by those for whom the current industry standard is not accessible, affordable or sufficiently valuable. If new innovations are tested immediately against the industry standard, they will come up short because they are more expensive, lower in quality or do not benefit from an existing infrastructure.

But if innovations can grow in a space where previously a group of users was unserved – teenagers listening to transistor radios who could not have afforded the expensive table-top version, for example – then they may, over time, develop to the point where they can genuinely compete with and supplant existing industry standards.

Take a political example: the 2008 US Presidential election broke all records for campaign fund-raising and produced an unprecedented surge in voter turnout for the Obama campaign by successfully integrating long-established methods of political communication and campaign coordination with forms of Internet-based mobilisation pioneered *as an alternative* to the dominant approach since 2000. The Obama campaign produced a winning synthesis of traditional political organisation and open, networked activism which has helped to break the mould of US politics. It could not have done so without building on the growth of alternative spaces and user groups of pro-Democratic activists, but it could not have changed the national political landscape without integrating these methods into an adapted (and highly adaptive) national campaign infrastructure which built on long-standing party and fund-raising structures.

The lesson is that, rather than seeking only to subvert or bypass the adaptive capacity of existing systems, change strategies based on innovation and diffusion must harness them. Too often innovation is assumed to flow from one of three sources:

- from competition between schools, or from "quasi market" policy measures which replicate the effects of open competition, such as publishing performance league tables.
- from new knowledge, primarily created upstream from teaching and learning in the fields of basic research. For example, advances in neuroscience or ICT create insights about the nature of learning which can be fed scientifically into the design of curriculum, teaching and assessment programmes.
- from the interaction between teachers and learners; it is context specific and organic and cannot be generalised in ways that go beyond professional judgement and discretion; it therefore emerges from the bottom up, and should be recognised by policy makers through respect for professional autonomy and creativity.

While each of these has some truth, it fails to capture the systemic properties – we need a larger, more robust schema which shows how multiple sources of innovation can form part of a more robust *innovation system*.

According to the leading Australian researchers Jonathan West and Keith Smith, innovation systems embody five essential functions.

- Identifying opportunities;
- Creating and spreading knowledge and skills;
- Developing new organisations and production capacity;
- Managing risk and uncertainty;
- Building and maintaining essential infrastructure (West & Smith, 2005).

Different sectors, argue Smith and West, may adopt radically different ways of fulfilling these functions – but they are all present in systems which successfully adapt over time to changing conditions through the flow of innovation. Most importantly, innovation systems that succeed over time are grounded in the repeated, practical effort by participants to solve problems and challenges they encounter in the course of trying to improve what they currently do.

Crucially, Smith and West remind us that successful innovation systems are not driven exclusively by a single external factor, such as the rate of technical invention or the pressure of market competition. Instead, successful innovation systems are ones in which a plurality of competing approaches, collaborative problem-solving and a constant interchange between specialist expertise and practical experience become embedded in the organisation, culture and market structure of a given field.

Looking at the five together it is striking that some, like creating new knowledge and skills or developing new organisations, tend to receive disproportionate attention in education policy. For example, many school reform strategies now seek to create new organisations, such as the British Government's Academy program or Chicago's Renaissance 2010. Others, such as New York City or England's National College for School Leadership, have created academies and institutes to instil high impact practices among emerging leaders.

But while each of these elements may be highly desirable, depending on the specific need or opportunity it is addressing, it clearly will not bring systemic change unless it is combined in the right way with a wider set of activities.

Taking Diffusion Seriously

The flow, or diffusion, of innovation through these wider systems of activity is mediated by all the same influences which shape and characterise systems of human organisation. So strategies for diffusion must be based on our understanding of the ways in which people actually come to learn and adjust their own behaviour in social groups and organisations (Bentley, 2007).

They include the following:

- *Imitation:* people take up new practices when they observe them in situ, that is, see them being modelled successfully by others;

- *Iteration:* new practices are developed, accepted, improved and embedded through repetition and routine, not through one-off interventions;
- *Improvisation:* necessity is the mother of invention, as the old saying goes. When we are confronted by the need to act in changed or unfamiliar circumstances, we are more likely to try things we have not done before;
- *Inspiration:* stories narrated in compelling ways are far more likely to elicit positive responses than instructions, injunctions or more abstract descriptions of why change is needed;
- *Immigration:* moving people into new settings is often highly effective in bringing new practices to bear, rather than trying to move ideas separately from the people who enact them;
- *Interpretation:* the ability to recognise patterns and draw conclusions from complex sets of information about activities is crucial to whether or not innovations are successfully evaluated and adopted over time. As Lester and Piore argue, innovation requires the capacity to draw meaningful conclusions under conditions of sustained uncertainty, as well as to respond to unambiguous evidence of effectiveness. (Lester & Piore, 2004)

These forms of learning, of course, feature in the repertoires of great teachers. Ironically enough, they rarely appear explicitly in innovation strategies designed for the larger systems that teachers inhabit.

Can Open Innovation Work in Real Communities?

Hume, a local government area in the metropolitan area north of Melbourne, Australia, is characterised by ethnic and cultural diversity and economic struggle. It includes Broadmeadows, site of a Ford motor manufacturing plant, which is an important source of jobs and investment, but cannot sustain the whole local economy. Hume also includes Melbourne international airport, a crucial economic asset and source of thousands of jobs.

Hume exemplifies many features of the new global economy – diversity, inequality and dynamism – which do not neatly fit into an idealised, traditionally planned definition of place or community. Thirty-five different languages are spoken by its people. But their achievement is limited by Hume's location, which makes many job and learning opportunities difficult to access, and by the impact of economic disadvantage and social fragmentation. School reform to drive up standards is an obvious way to tackle this challenge and improved schooling outcomes is high on the agenda of the state, local and federal governments. But Hume has also chosen a different kind of response: the Hume Global Learning Village™.

Hume's Global Learning Centre, a sleek steel and glass building in the town centre, is designed as a hybrid: It houses the Council Chamber, a welcoming café and a public library. It provides conference and seminar facilities and Internet services for local learners: teenagers using them after school, mothers learning English, or workers looking to improve their ICT skills. As Vanessa Little, the Learning Community's General Manager, explains, there are so many kinds of community resource in the building that there is very little space for her own team.

But there are good reasons for the close proximity of so many different functions. The centre is part of a much more ambitious strategy to link together the traditional elements of Hume's educational infrastructure – schools and colleges – with many other activities and sites of learning that can impact positively on learning outcomes. In *Learning Together*, the centre outlines a vision of "a learning community where people embrace learning as a way of life, for all their life, thereby creating a community that values learning as the key to strengthening individual and community wellbeing." Hume's strategy is to transform and enhance what is achieved within its education institutions by linking them directly to its wider communities.

This means myriad projects, organised around themes like inspiring lifelong learning; learning in community settings; language, literacy and numeracy; ICT uptake and village networking. Threaded through them is a hard, practical focus on developing skills and learning with tangible benefits. But the activities reach into places where the traditional bureaucratic model rarely gets: recruiting women from new migrant communities to create digital records of songs, stories and oral history; attracting teenagers to download, create and exchange their own learning materials; holding an annual State of Learning research conference; mentoring and "inspiring learners" programmes that put high-profile individuals who grew up in the area in touch with Hume's current youngsters.

Many of these activities are familiar to educators. But there are few places where they are systematically connected to the development of formal education services. Hume's model for doing so is a wide-ranging partnership of institutions, a network capable of combining to raise money, offer shared services and jointly plan new infrastructure. As part of the same regeneration process, many of Hume's government schools are being rebuilt and reconfigured into a smaller number of learning centres designed to offer a new range of learning pathways to all their students.

The Global Learning Village does not act as a traditional corporate or bureaucratic centre; when it needs a legal entity to form a partnership or bid for funding, one of its network members steps forward. It is not a direct replacement for the existing governance institutions or service providers, but by designing itself to further the whole population's learning interests, it can bring these other institutions together to create entirely new options.

The Hume Global Learning Village is one illustration of how open systems of governance and learning can support more ambitious educational strategies. It uses practice-based innovation to generate collective action to change the *context* in which individual experience and service delivery occur. In doing so, it seeks to adjust the broad institutional parameters which frame the ongoing, incremental processes of educational participation. Crucially, it connects the workings of formal education providers with the many other dimensions of learning and sources of innovation that exist beyond their formal boundaries. It seeks to create community, as well as to serve it.

Innovation comes from multiple sources; but it may be best understood as the product of dissonance or incongruity, the clash between expectation and reality or the gap between the ideal standard and the particular form.

Hume's innovation is perhaps a response to the gap between the diversity and inequality of its community. In successful learning systems, dissonance is not screened out or neutralised, but used as the stimulus for a continuous pattern of experimentation, evaluation, collaboration and exchange; that is the theory of change which educational innovators should seek to enact.

Conclusion: An Architecture for Systemic Innovation

Whether or not Hume offers a powerful innovation that can be successfully adopted across whole systems of education is impossible to tell for now.

But there may be one overall conclusion to draw from its approach, from the "open-source learning" innovations featured at the beginning of this chapter and from the overall analysis of systemic change that I have presented.

The new theories of innovation and adaptive systems offer an opportunity for a new synthesis between schools of educational thought which have traditionally emphasised either the authority of expertise transmitted through vertical chains of authority or the necessity of understanding grounded in the experience of learners and the emergence of communities of practice.

As I argued, successful open systems are not governed by free-for-alls. An essential feature of open-source programming is that it maintains a clear editorial hierarchy and quality standards against which any adjustment can be judged. The crucial feature is that access to these standards, and the opportunity to test out new ways of meeting them, is openly shared.

Twenty-first century education cannot succeed without becoming more explicit or authoritative about the meaning of understanding and excellence. But the ways in which these definitions of excellence are applied: in school selection criteria, professional standards for educators, methodologies for student assessment and the expectations of the wider community could all be radically improved if they were subject to the rigours of open, user-driven testing and codevelopment of new methods.

Whether these methods become mainstays of our next education system depends on whether the institutional architecture underpinning mass education can be designed to make these standards and processes transparent to the people who use and depend on them rather than to the current closed communities of administrators and experts.

For example, such an architecture might include systems for the following:

- individual digital record keeping and portfolios;
- formative assessment and peer-to-peer exchange;
- open access curriculum standards and specifications, and open archives of curriculum content and learning resources;

- network-based user communities, both of educational practitioners and of students, clustered around specific shared interests;
- area-based information about social and economic outcomes, services and community structure, integrated across different public agencies and openly available for community use;
- funding and regulation of education providers which did not discriminate by sector or function, for example, between private schools or public technical colleges, but which explicitly sought accountability for public outcomes for any kind of organisation receiving public subsidy or protection;
- opening of educational infrastructure and facilities to wider, plural forms of community use, as many jurisdictions are now doing;
- harmonisation of regulatory regimes designed across different countries and jurisdictions to encourage diversity of practice and model, but make possible higher levels of mobility and "interoperability" between systems;
- development and research programmes based on open, collaborative platforms and specialised clusters of innovators;
- home-school-community services designed to support the educational "coproduction" of families and informal community networks.

There are certain to be many more applications. The crucial point is not that we should continue searching for the most powerful innovations, but that education needs an architecture which is capable of harnessing the flow of innovations far more effectively.

We are far more likely to be successful in building this "supporting infrastructure" for systemic, adaptive learning if it is built in ways which make the standards, content and terms of participation for public education radically more open than they have been over the last century. The tools with which to build such an open architecture are currently emerging around us.

References

Benkler, Y. (2006). *The wealth of networks: How social production transforms markets and freedom.* New Haven: Yale University Press.

Bentley, T. (2007). 7 kinds of learning. In S. Parker & S. Parker (Eds.), *Unlocking innovation: Why citizens hold the key to public service reform.* London: Demos.

Bentley, T., & Wilsdon, J. (2003). *The adaptive state.* London: Demos.

Chapman, J. (2003). *System failure: Why governments must learn to think differently.* London: Demos.

Chesbrough, H. (2003). *Open innovation: The new imperative for creating and profiting from technology.* Cambridge, MA: Harvard Business School Press.

Christensen, M., Horn, B., & Johnson, C. (2008). *Disrupting class: How disruptive innovation will change the way the world learns* (p. 74). New York: McGraw Hill.

Connexions: Sharing Knowledge and Building Communities. (2009). http://cnx.org/, accessed February 28, 2009

Dede, C., Honan, J., & Peters, L. (2005). *Scaling up success: Lessons learned from technology-based educational improvement.* San Francisco: Jossey-Bass.

Elmore, R. (2000). *Building a new structure for school leadership*. Washington, DC: Albert Shanker Institute.

Fullan, M. (2005). *Leadership and sustainability*. Thousand Oaks, CA: Corwin.

Heifetz, R., & Linsky, M. (2002). *Leadership on the line*. Cambridge, MA: Harvard Business School Press.

Homer Dixon, T. (2006). *The upside of down: Catastrophe, creativity and the renewal of civilisation*. London: Souvenir Press.

Leadbeater, C. (2008). *We think: Mass innovation, not mass production*. London: Profile Books.

Lester, R., & Piore, M. (2004). *Innovation: The missing dimension*. Cambridge, MA: Harvard University Press.

Levin, B. (2008). *How to change 5000 schools*. Cambridge, MA: Harvard Education Press.

North, D. C. (2005). *Understanding the process of economic change*. Princeton, NJ: Princeton University Press.

School of Everything. (2008). http://schoolofeverything.com/, accessed February 28, 2009.

Steinberg, T., Mulgan, G., & Salem, O. (2005). *Wide open: Open source methods and their future potential*. London: Demos.

Wales, J., & Baraniuk, R. (2008). An open education revolution, Project Syndicate, http://www.project-syndicate.org/commentary/wales1, accessed February 28, 2009.

West, J., & Smith, K. (2005). Australia's innovation challenges: Building an effective national innovation system. *Melbourne Business Review*, www.utas.edu.au/business/AIRC, accessed 17 May, 2008.

Wright, R. (2001). *Nonzero: The logic of human destiny*. New York: Vintage.

The Psychodynamics of Educational Change

Chris James

Educational change can take many forms. It may be equivalent to or an extension of something familiar, may restore expertise in an aspect of practice long forgotten, and may add skills and experience without a sense of loss. Radical educational change may be fundamental, requiring a substantial reorientation of practice or the way practice is organised. However, such a change may not be particularly disruptive to any sense of well-being because it is appropriate, required and timely. So, although the change may break important attachments to ways of working and expose relatively trivial habits and expectations, it may at the same time launch a new and exciting enterprise or endeavour. Moreover, whilst the change may generate great anxiety and apprehension, there is no powerful sense of loss; the change may even be experienced as revitalising and energising. Even if the hoped-for expectations do not materialise and the venture does not succeed, the accustomed sense of self-limitation has been broken. Not all educational change is experienced so positively. When the change is unwelcome, involves the loss of important attachments that cannot be restored and does not have an acceptable purpose, there may be considerable mental disturbance resulting from internal conflicts and the loss of meaning (Marris, 1974). The experience of educational change may therefore be complicated, and making sense of it can be extremely problematic. This chapter makes sense of some of these complexities in the sometimes disturbing experience of educational change.

The chapter draws upon a set of interlinked concepts known as system psychodynamics (see James & Connolly, 2000; James, Connolly, Dunning, & Elliott, 2006, 2008; Obholzer & Roberts, 1994), which use concepts from analytical psychology (Gabriel, 1999; Hirschhorn, 1988; Kets de Vries, 1991; Papadopoulos, 2006) and systems theory (Hanna, 1997; Miller & Rice, 1967; von Bertalanffy, 1968) to interpret individual and group behaviours in social settings. In system psychodynamics theory, a number of concepts are central:

C. James (✉)
University of Bath, Bath, England
e-mail: c.james@bath.ac.uk

A. Hargreaves et al. (eds.), *Second International Handbook of Educational Change*,
Springer International Handbooks of Education 23, DOI 10.1007/978-90-481-2660-6_3,
© Springer Science+Business Media B.V. 2010

- *social defences*, which are the behaviours that individuals and groups adopt to protect themselves against unacceptable feelings that may imperil their senses of identity, legitimacy and value;
- *unconscious mental activity* and its influence on individual and group behaviours;
- *boundaries*, which are places of discontinuity in an individual's external social world, within an individual's inner psychic structure, and between an individual's internal and external worlds and which can be powerfully influenced by affective experience;
- *the primary task of work groups*, which is what work groups feel they should be doing, along with work group mentalities;
- *basic assumption tendencies* in group behaviour where groups in work settings put their efforts into meeting their unconscious needs instead of working on the primary task; and
- *affective containment* by individuals and in organisations.

The foundational axiom of system psychodynamics is that feelings powerfully influence individual and collective organisational practice and changes to those practices. So, regardless of any intentions to retain a cognitive rationale for practice and a cognitive perspective on educational change, feelings dominate. Systems psychodynamics enable that affective influence to be understood.

This chapter explores the reasons for the high level of affective intensity in educational institutions. It then sets out what may lie behind responses to educational change and, using concepts from systems psychodynamic theory, explores those responses in greater depth. In shedding light on change processes from this affective standpoint, the chapter also seeks to offer pointers for those leading and managing change in schools and colleges.

Feelings and Educational Institutions

For a variety of reasons, schools and colleges are places with high levels of affective intensity (James, 1999, 2008a; James & Connolly, 2000; James et al., 2006). For teachers, the work of teaching and organising in schools can call up a whole range of feelings (Beatty, 2000; Hargreaves, 1998a, 1998b). Learning requires motivation, which has an affective component. If the pupils are not motivated to learn, the teacher has to engender it and provoke the feelings that are part of it. Teaching is an uncertain and unpredictable practice, which can bring feelings of both excitement and anxiety. Teachers' and educational leaders' relationships with pupils, parents and close working colleagues can have a powerful affective aspect as typically do most social relationships that add to the affective intensity. Schools and colleges are institutions, which means they have important and significant social purposes. The responsibility carried by those who work in them arguably increases the affective intensity of their work. Importantly, many teachers have a very powerful attachment (Fonagy, 2001) to their work. It has meaning for them. For the pupils, learning is associated with risk and uncertainty, so they may well feel excited and energised *and* apprehensive and fearful as they learn. In their lives in and out of school, pupils may experience a whole range of unfamiliar and unmanageable feelings, which may be brought into the classroom in ways that can be difficult to control.

The Affective Experience of Educational Change

While some educational change is easily accepted and can even be energising, invigorating and uplifting, unwelcome change can be profoundly disturbing and disorientating. There are two main reasons for the effect of unwelcome change: the disruption of defensive behaviours and the complex feelings that result from loss of meaning.

Much organisational practice in work settings involves defensive behaviours (social defences) that are intended to protect against the experience of unacceptable feelings or the prospect of that experience (Argyris, 1985; Menzies, 1960; Obholzer & Roberts, 1994). The same is true in schools and colleges – perhaps more so because of the affective intensity of educational work (Dunning, James, & Jones, 2005; James & Connolly, 2000). So, a good deal of educational practice, although it may have an explicit cognitive rationale, is actually intended to defend against the prospect of experiencing difficult feelings and to optimise the probability of experiencing positive ones. The requirement to change practice, especially if the change is not welcome, may cut across the "conservative impulse" to preserve and safeguard the predictability of life of those concerned (Marris, 1974). It may therefore be accompanied by feelings of loss, insecurity and inadequacy, which may all bring other distressing feelings such as anxiety. Thus, educational change may require a change in practice, which in itself can be associated with difficult feelings and anxieties, which are explicitly intended to protect against other difficult feelings and anxieties. So, change can bring an extra burden of difficult feelings and anxieties (James & Connolly, 2000; James et al., 2006). It is no surprise therefore that the conservative impulse in educational practice can be strong and can overwhelm adaptive capacity, which is the readiness and capability to learn and change. Unwelcome change that disrupts the familiar practice pattern can as a result generate high levels of anxiety. It can also call up powerful internal conflicts, which can influence responses to change that need to be resolved.

Educational change can also result in the loss of meaning. Throughout our lives we attach meaning to significant practices, physical objects and the people around us (Fonagy, 2001). In educational change, significant objects and aspects of educational work – teaching and organising – may be discarded, deemed redundant and lost and the attachment to them threatened or broken. Realisation that the meaningful object no longer exists requires that our mental energies "are withdrawn from its attachment to this meaningful object" (Freud, 1925, p. 15x). This requirement to withdraw from an attachment and to reattach to other objects demands a fundamental restructuring of meaning. This restructuring can provoke high levels of anxiety and generate conflicting feelings, which can influence behaviour. Those concerned may experience two powerful impulses: firstly, to return to the time before the loss, and secondly, to reach a state of mind where the past is forgotten, both of which are practically impossible. The struggle to resolve this conflict and to begin to restore a sense of equilibrium can take time and energy and can drain people's vitality. Recovery from the feelings generated by loss depends on restoring a sense that the lost attachment can still give meaning to the present. However, when the sense of loss is extreme, it can impair the ability to attach meaning to subsequent events and lessen the ability to learn from them and to begin to understand how to resolve the conflicting feelings. Individuals may also seek to withdraw from the kinds of social experiences that may help them. So, a teacher whose work is profoundly affected and radically changed in an unwelcome way by an educational change may find it impossible to become motivated to work in the new way and in the new setting, may withdraw from contact with colleagues, and may feel unable to "move on" from the sense of loss (Marris, 1974).

Social Defences in Educational Institutions

Social defences are patterns of behaviour that are often routinised and taken for granted and that have the purpose of reducing the prospect of unacceptable feelings – typically anxiety – or eliminating influences that are experienced as potentially threatening a person's mental survival (Gabriel, 1999). They may be present in existing individual and organisational practice, and individuals and groups may resort to them in the face of unwelcome educational change. Typically, they are not deliberately or consciously engaged in unconscious processes but are largely the result of them. Understanding social defences can therefore give important insights into the experience of educational change and how to manage change appropriately.

Social defences can become so deeply embedded in organisational practices that their defensive purpose may not be immediately apparent or understood by those who engage in them. Indeed, for a variety of reasons individuals and groups are likely to cover over the affective rationale with an apparently valid and sensible cognitive explanation of their behaviour. Whilst social defences offer protection from affective pain and danger, they can also distance the individual and the group from their experience of the external world (Obholzer & Roberts, 1994). In that regard, they support and protect the ego.

From a Freudian perspective, the ego is the part of the psyche that links with the external reality of the environment. The ego also has the task of mediating between the id, which in Freudian terms is the location of unconscious excitations and desires and what he called "a cauldron full of seething excitations" (Freud, 1933, p. 106), and the superego, which is the part of the psyche that is responsible for self-criticism and self-monitoring. The ego ideal, though a contested concept, is generally considered to be an amalgam of the desired yet often conflicting features and representations that the ego attempts to emulate (Gabriel, 1999). The ego's tasks of arbitrating between these three "harsh masters" (Gabriel, 1999, p. 308) and mediating between the individual's internal world and their environment are substantial. They involve keeping the boundary between the individual's internal and external worlds, self-preservation, and maintaining the mental integrity between the psyche's different components. It is no surprise that in the face of such challenging work as teaching or changing teaching or organisational practice in schools and colleges that individuals and groups resort to defensive behaviours to support the ego in its work.

Basically, social defences take five different forms, which are linked and can occur in combination: rituals and routines, projection and introjection, regressions, repressions and resistance and splitting.

Rituals and Routines

Organisational rituals and routines are the practices that one is repeatedly engaged in and that then become taken-for-granted ways of working. Such behaviours may have little apparent connection to any rational understanding of experience or may have a cognitive rationale that overlays and belies their deeper affective purpose. They can be engaged in individually or collectively (Menzies, 1960). Importantly, rituals and routines satisfy both the conservative impulse (they provide a consistent secure pattern) and the protective purpose (they afford a defence against difficult feelings). So, for example, having regular seating arrangements in the school staffroom avoids any conflicts that might ensue and associated difficult feelings that might be generated if there was a free-for-all for seats at lunchtime. The arrangement might also provide a secure place that contrasts with the relative chaos outside the staffroom. The long-established tradition in the UK of pupils addressing their teachers as "Sir" and "Miss" arguably has the purpose of reducing the affective content of pupil–teacher relationships. Perhaps school uniform is simply a way of protecting against the difficult feelings that may result from pupils being allowed to wear what they want to. Educational change may well alter defensive routines and the order they give and may also involve the loss of an attachment to a "much loved" way of working. Taken to extremes rituals and routines can develop into obsessions and compulsions. They can be very damaging to organisational effectiveness if the routine takes up resources that can be used on the organisation's primary task (see below). When engaged in collectively, rituals and routines and the set of shared assumptions and beliefs on which they are based provide a frame of reference for establishing meaning and significance. This frame of reference and the associated routinised and ritualised practices can become an important dimension of the organisational culture (Alvesson, 2002; Schein, 1992). The protective purpose of rituals and routines and attachments to them can help explain why culture change in schools and colleges can be so difficult.

Projection and Introjection

Although many writers from a range of fields use the terms "feeling" and "emotion" as synonyms (Goleman, 1995; Hochschild, 1983; Niedenthal, Krauth-Gruber, &

Ric, 2006; Oatley & Jenkins, 1996), others, such as Forgas (2000) and Fineman (2003), distinguish between the two on the basis that feelings are what is experienced, whilst emotions are feelings that are displayed. Such a distinction is helpful because it gives an additional analytical dimension, and on that basis emotions become particular kinds of actions, which have an affective rationale. However, feelings are also important rationales for actions that might not be described, as emotions and many actions can have a powerful affective component. There is thus a good case for arguing that all actions, including emotions, are feelings that are shown to others. When the feeling associated with an action is very apparent, for example, a teacher very heatedly arguing against a proposed educational change at a staff meeting, that feeling is very easily and consciously experienced by all those witnessing the event. The impression is that the feeling has "moved" from the teacher to those listening, who may then feel similarly angry. If feelings are expressed less overtly or less straightforwardly, the feelings may only be experienced unconsciously. Nonetheless, they are still experienced by others, and again, the feelings still seem to have moved, albeit unconsciously. The apparent movement of feelings in this way is known as projection (Diamond, 1993; James et al., 2006; Obholzer & Roberts, 1994).

Projected feelings may be "taken in" by others, which is a process known as introjection (Diamond, 1993; James et al., 2006; Obholzer & Roberts, 1994). The essence of the feelings and what the feeling represents become part of the recipient and turn into a so-called internal object (Diamond, 1993). During early development, children introject "parents" and "important others" who give security and reassurance. Later, the child may introject the parental ego ideal and superego to assemble a set of principles, a sense of conscience, an internal arbiter and censor. If the child introjects a parental superego that is punishing and harshly judgmental, he/she may as an adult become a severe judge of others and highly critical of what they do (Diamond, 1993). As a social defence, introjection can work in various ways. For example, in the process of implementing unwanted educational change, individuals may introject the feelings of security and assuredness projected by a wise and thoughtful head teacher so that the head teacher becomes internalised as a good object, in this instance a protector from the difficult feelings generated by the undesirable change. The introjection of the projections of a critical and judgemental manager can paradoxically be protective if the projections feel "right" and resonate with internal feelings of inadequacy and incompetence in the recipient. The introjection gives a sense of consistency between the recipient's internal and external worlds. It is important for those managing educational change to learn to accept and respond to the projections of others without introjecting them. The introjection of others' projections is likely to be unhelpful regardless of whether the projections are positive or negative (James & Vince, 2001).

When feelings have been introjected, the recipients may be unable to distinguish between their own feelings (those that have originated within them) and those that have been projected by others that they have introjected (James & Vince, 2001). In those circumstances, it is quite possible for the projected feelings to be used by the recipient as rationales for their own actions. This process forms the basis of a social defence known as projective identification, which was first identified by Melanie Klein (Likierman, 2001; Segal, 1979). Projective identification is an attempt to control the other by means of projections. The subject (the person doing the projecting) imagines he/she is "inside" the other. The recipient of the projections may not be aware that their behaviour is being controlled in part at least by the other. An example would be a situation where the deputy principal does not want to implement a required curriculum change because of the unbearable anxiety it would provoke. The anxiety may be projected toward the principal ("I don't think it would be a good idea to bring in the change until at least next year, I don't think the staff would like it"). The principal may well introject the projection and delay the implementation. The deputy principal has created a proxy character to act on his behalf and he can then distance himself from the decision.

Regression

Regression is when people return to a childlike state of dependency, helplessness and immaturity when faced with difficult situations that generate threatening feelings. Put simply, "Adults take on childlike roles" (Diamond, 1993, p. 6). This defence is generally not particularly effective or successful. Even in the regressed state, the individual or group still experiences anxiety, and the more primitive level of ego functioning resulting from the regressed state means that the threat is less easily coped with. Despite its ineffectiveness, regression is a familiar response to the uncertainties and threats that can come with organisational change such as leadership transitions, changes in organisational objectives or radical changes in practice. As a consequence, groups may regress in their relationships with the leader, perhaps forming subcultures that may become more like that of a group of children with a parent, or the group members might fantasise about the possibility of remaining in a secure place ("We don't have to change do we? Why can't the school stay as it is?") or returning to a former "safer" time, perhaps referring to it as "The good old days". The recipient of the projections that result from regression may experience them consciously or unconsciously, a process that is known as transference. He/she may start behaving on the basis of the projections that he/she has introjected (see above), which is known as counter-transference in this context. So, in the example above, the leader of the group may begin to feel like a parent to the "regressed children" and start acting in that way.

Covert coalitions are social defences that are linked with regression and projection, which provide protection from painful feelings by establishing "a more durable set of relationships" (Hirschhorn, 1988, p. 63). These relationships typically reflect family relationships such as parent–child or sibling relationships. So, for example, a young newly qualified teacher may form a covert coalition with the more experienced head teacher, treating him as a father figure in order to gain protection from the anxieties associated with starting teaching. The head teacher's response may be to become a kindly father-figure, thus colluding in the coalition. In educational change, problems may arise in this example when the young teacher's expertise develops and she seeks to break out of the relationship against the head teacher's perhaps unconscious wishes, or if the young teacher is unable to respond to a change that the head teacher is advocating and is keen to implement.

Repression

Repression is a social defence that consigns threatening or painful desires, thoughts and feelings to the unconscious, thus preventing them from being experienced consciously (Diamond, 1993; Gabriel, 1999). The repressing process begins in early life and continues throughout adulthood. It contributes to the formation of the personal unconscious (see below). If the repression is incomplete, the contents of the unconscious may emerge. A repressed thought or feeling may emerge relatively harmlessly, although perhaps embarrassingly as a parapraxis or Freudian slips, as such occurrences are more colloquially known. Serious repression failures may threaten an individual's deeply seated senses of lack of self-worth and vulnerability and may therefore provoke intense anxiety. Periods of stress, exceptional tiredness and the introjections of others' projections, all of which are probably more likely to happen during times of educational change, can undermine the repressing process and allow unconscious content to reach consciousness resulting in increased levels of anxiety. In organisations, individuals and groups may adopt rituals and routines and other defensive behaviours to support the repression process. Changes in these individual and organisational practices may therefore be highly threatening.

Denial is a defence that involves painful or unacceptable aspects of the internal or external world being denied but without their "being excluded from consciousness" (Gabriel, 1999, p. 293) in the way that occurs in repression. The presence of denial may be confirmed by the process of negation, which is when an idea is repeatedly and firmly ruled out when such an overt rejection is not really called for. So for example, a colleague who is anxious about the implications of a change to a teaching programme (but is in denial about it) may persistently say how happy he is about the change and how unconcerned he is about it (the process of negation).

Resistance

Resistance is a direct refusal to accept information or to defy or oppose a proposal, request or order of some kind (Fineman, 2003; Gabriel, 1999). It usually has an unconscious origin and may not appear reasonable or rational, and those resisting may not be able to articulate any rationale. Resistance results from a powerful and deeply seated sense of anxiety, which, in turn, may result from a perceived threat to an individual's sense of their identity, esteem and worth. Imposed educational change may be experienced as just that kind of threat, which is why opposition to it can be so strong. As with all social defences, but particularly so with resistance because of its direct oppositional nature, it may not be possible to overcome resistance by authority, regardless of its legitimacy. In the face of direct compulsion, the mode of resistance may simply take on a different form.

Splitting

In the social defence of splitting, contradictory feelings about objects and experiences that generate painful or threatening internal conflicts are separated and perceived as either ideal (all good) or persecutory (all bad) (Halton, 1994). It is a very common defence in organisations – especially those under stress – and the consequences may be very damaging. Splitting may result in reaction formation when the threatening impulse is repressed, leaving in its place the diametrically opposite feeling. For example, the quite natural anxiety about change in familiar practices may be so firmly repressed that the change is only seen as good with no negative anxiety-provoking aspect to it at all. In response to unwelcome educational change and the resulting organisational stress, individuals and groups such as school leaders, the local authority, the school board or the government may be viewed as either "on our side" or "the enemy". Experiences during the change process such as meetings may be described as either "excellent" and or "rubbish". The way a department in a school has responded to change may be seen by the principal as "absolutely marvellous", whereas the response to another department may be viewed as "dreadful, as usual". In both examples, the reality may be more complex.

The split and separated feelings may be projected to other individuals, groups or institutions by means of actions that are driven by the separated feelings (Diamond, 1993; Dunning et al., 2005; Obholzer & Roberts, 1994). So, in response to unwanted change, a head teacher may be heard blaming "the stupid politicians for interfering in education". His unacceptable feelings about the imposed change are separated and projected towards the government. A group of disillusioned teachers discussing the implementation of a new teaching programme may be heard saying the "teaching in this new way would be fine if it wasn't for that group of trouble makers in year 10". The anxieties associated with the implementation are separated from other feelings and projected towards the group of pupils. If splitting and projection are persistent and widespread, they can result in a blame culture, where anything unacceptable or mistakes are always another's fault. Taken to extremes, it can lead to bullying where an individual or group is *always* the recipient of blame. Ultimately, it can result in scapegoating where the recipient of the difficult projected feelings eventually leaves the group or organisation taking the difficult feelings with them, much to the pleasure – and relief – of those left behind (Dunning et al., 2005). In bullying and scapegoating, there is usually a fit between those projecting and those introjecting, so often organisational scapegoat will themselves feel a sense of release and liberation if they leave. It is as if their departure feels right to them. So, for example, a head teacher seeking to bring much-needed change in the face of continual conscious and unconscious hostile projections from the staff, governors and parents may come to the view that "it would be better for all concerned if I left and allowed someone else to take up the challenge" with a sense of relief all round.

The Unconscious at Work in Schools

It is now widely accepted that we are not fully conscious of all our mental functioning and that there are unconscious processes at work in our minds. However, what the unconscious part of the mind is and what it does remain open for debate, as indeed does the whole notion of where it is. In the modern era, two main perspectives on the unconscious, those of Freud and Jung, have dominated.

From a Freudian perspective, the content of the unconscious is the outcome of repression (see above) and thus contains hidden and potentially threatening urges, ideas and feelings (Gabriel, 1999). Jung, who was for a time a student of Freud, generally agreed with this conception but argued that this personal unconscious also contained "semi-impressions, which had never sufficient intensity to reach consciousness but have somehow entered the psyche" (Jung, 1927, para. 321).

Jung argued that what Freud had described was the personal unconscious, which was unique to each individual. Compared to this, Jung contended that there was also a substantial collective unconscious (Hauke, 2006). It was on this idea (as well as Freud's deterministic position and his narrow linking of libido with sexuality) that Freud and Jung disagreed, a disagreement that in effect ended their working relationship. The central feature of Jung's conceptualisation of the collective unconscious was the notion of the archetype (Lawson, 2008).

From the Jungian standpoint, human consciousness grew out of the unconscious mental processes of the primitive ancestors of human beings who lived largely in a state of preconsciousness. In this primitive form, instinctual behaviour would have dominated and the individuals would be unable to distinguish between their internal mental world and the external world. Both would have been as one. The residues of those instincts have remained in the human psyche as archetypes, which are archaic structures within the psyche that have become embedded over generations. Archetypes predispose us to particular behaviours. Metaphorically, an archetype can be viewed as the bed of a river that has long since dried up, but should the rains come, the water may begin to flow and may then become a raging torrent. So, typically, we may not be consciously aware of archetypes much as we may not notice a dried up watercourse when we view a landscape or walk through it. However, in appropriate circumstances, the archetypes may become actualised – the rivers flow – and may condition our behaviour sometimes very powerfully. Importantly, archetypal structures are widely shared amongst all humans. This notion gives rise to the idea of the collective unconscious, from which it can be asserted that, despite substantial cultural differences, the dominant underpinnings of human functioning are in fact broadly similar. Jung used the term "archetype" in a very broad and perhaps even confusing way, referring to the following: archetypal events, such as birth, death, separation from parents, initiation and marriage; archetypal figures, for example, mother, hero, swindler and wise man; archetypal symbols such as the sun, water, the cross and the snake; and archetypal motifs, such as the Apocalypse, the Deluge, the Creation, and the Night Journey (Samuels, 2006). The notion of the collective unconscious and archetypal structures has important implications. For example, behaviour resulting from an actualised archetype can be very powerful, a notion that "gains its way against all reason and will, or else produces conflict of pathological dimensions, that is to say neurosis" (Jung, 1936, para. 99). The existence of archetypal structures may have a role in establishing the notion of a "vocation" such as teaching and the desire to respond to such a calling. Changing behaviours that are strongly conditioned by the actualisation of an archetype may be difficult and may be resisted by those being asked to change. So when asked to fill in forms detailing the attainment of tightly defined competences by her pupils (as required by a new policy), the devoted, charismatic, passionate teacher may well respond with some feeling: "I didn't come into teaching to do this!" or "Please tell me exactly how my precious pupils will benefit from this pointless exercise!" An interpretation of this event would be that the teacher's commitment to her pupils, which is underpinned by the forceful activation of archetypal structures, is being blocked by a requirement to undertake work that she considers to be of little value in fulfilling her commitment, hence she seeks to resist and reject the requirement.

Henderson (1962) has proposed the notion of a cultural unconscious that "lies between" and mediates the influences of the personal unconscious and the more archaic and primordial collective unconscious with its archetypal structures. It "is built up through many exposures to cultural canons of taste, of moral principles, of social custom, and of religious symbolism" (p. 8). Such an idea is attractive and its potential mediating role immediately apparent. The cultural unconscious is linked to and influenced by the collective unconscious. Over time, the cultural unconscious has influenced the archetypal tendencies and predilections of the collective unconscious. At the same time, there would be a similar linkage and interplay between the cultural unconscious and conscious mental processes. The cultural unconscious could also have a role in influencing what is repressed into the individual unconscious. Thus, although teaching or being the head teacher of a school may have archetypal foundations, the actualisation of the archetypes may be conditioned culturally. So, for example, the work of the teachers in a science department in a school may be powerfully underpinned by the actuation of archetypal structures in the collective unconscious, which drives a desire to "educate the next generation." That desire is conditioned by perhaps unwritten cultural assumptions on which the practice of teaching in the department, the school and the profession more generally is based. Those taken for granted assumptions may in part both influence and be influenced by repressed desires in connection with teacher–pupil relationships.

Boundaries and Educational Change

The work of schools shapes organisational and intrapersonal boundaries and at the same time is shaped by those boundaries. There are physical boundaries, for example, around classes, the school grounds and particular parts of the school, such as the staff room. There are boundaries between different groups – between pupils and staff, the leadership team and the teaching staff, the administrative staff and the teachers, and the cleaners and the ground staff. There are also task boundaries that distinguish what is legitimate work in the school and what is not. As with any work organisation, schools function because of boundaries of a whole range of different kinds. Intrapersonal boundaries of the kind discussed in the previous section between the collective unconscious, the cultural unconscious and the personal unconscious also configure what goes on in schools.

In system psychodynamics, the boundary represents structural inconsistency and discontinuity (Heracleous, 2004; Lamont & Molnar, 2002), and boundaries can be internal as well as external (Hirschhorn, 1988; Roberts, 1994; Schneider, 1991). Gabriel (1999) asserts that "The first boundary we discover is that which separates us from an external world" (p. 98). This boundary is the ego. From an organisational standpoint, Hernes (2004) argues that boundary formation in organisations is not incidental but is inherent to the process of organising and to the organisation itself. Boundaries are not therefore by-products of organising; rather, organisations evolve through the process of setting boundaries. As such, organisational boundaries are not fixed and static but may be variable, unclear and, to varying degrees, permeable (Paulsen & Hernes, 2003; Perrow, 1986; Scott, 1998; Weick, 1979, 1995).

Organisational boundaries can be experienced and analysed from a number of perspectives (Hernes, 2004). Various kinds of boundary have been identified: authority, political, task and identity boundaries (Hirschhorn & Gilmore, 1992); functional, hierarchical and inclusionary boundaries (van Maanen & Schein, 1979); and behavioural and normative boundaries (Scott, 1998). Leach (1976) defines boundaries as spatial, temporal and psychological, a view supported by others (Stapley, 1996) and Diamond, Allcorn and Stein (2004). Hanna (1997) considers that physical boundaries are also important.

Czander (1993) argues that all organisational conflicts are related to boundaries in some way. As points of where difference is distinguished and experienced (Heracleous, 2004; Lamont & Molnar, 2002), boundaries will be places of tension and affective intensity (Douglas, 1966; Hernes, 2004). Boundary violations are articulated and experienced as conflicts and may well escalate into major incidents in individual and organisational life. For this reason, people may be reluctant to protect boundaries, or may protect them more vigorously than might be expected (Czander, 1993).

The maintenance of boundaries is critical to organisational success (Czander, 1993; Diamond et al., 2004) despite the sense that in current ways of working in education and other settings boundaries may be disappearing (Hirschhorn & Gilmore, 1992). The management and maintenance of organisational boundaries is therefore an important organising practice. Similarly, securing and sustaining the boundary between individuals' internal and external worlds and between the different parts of the psyche, for example, between the conscious and non-conscious elements, is crucial to survival in work settings.

It is difficult to think of an educational change that does not involve a reconfiguration of individual and organisational boundaries. A change to the teaching task means a reworking of the task boundaries. A change in practice demands a change in the role boundaries – which capabilities are now within the role boundary and which are not? A change in organisational responsibilities will require a similar redrawing of role boundaries. Altering the school timetable shifts time boundaries. Changing pastoral care responsibilities will almost certainly require a reworking of psychological boundaries. Varying a teacher's regular teaching room requires a change in physical boundaries. Given that boundaries have a conservation function and given that existing boundaries are frequently points of conflict, it is no surprise that unwelcome educational change (and therefore boundary change) can be so problematic.

The Primary Task in Educational Change and the Work Group Mentality

The primary task is what an individual, group or organisation feels it must do to survive and to continue and to carry on (Rice, 1963). If the task that the work group is engaged upon is widely sanctioned within the organisation and by key external stakeholders, organisational success can result (James et al., 2006). Clarifying the primary task of a work organisation may be difficult but is arguably crucial in improving organisational effectiveness, especially in schools (James & Connolly, 2000). An organisation that focuses its resources on the primary task is said to have a work group mentality (Bion, 1961). Typically however, work on the primary task carries a high level of anxiety, and this is especially the case in work in schools and is part of the reason why schools are places of high affective intensity. This task-related anxiety may be exacerbated in times of educational change, when the task may be redefined, when the definitions of successful task completion are altered or when a change is required in established ways of successfully completing or performing the task. In these circumstances, and indeed under normal circumstances, because of the primary task–anxiety link, work-group members may seek to avoid working on the primary task and turn instead to basic assumption tendencies.

Basic Assumption Tendencies and Change Processes in Groups

A basic assumption tendency is when the group avoids primary task-related work and concentrates instead on meeting its unconscious needs (Bion, 1961). There are different forms of basic assumption mentality, and they are not fixed. Moreover, a group may move between a work group mentality and a basic assumption mentality.
  There are several kinds of basic assumption tendency (Bion, 1961).

- Fight and flight (baF) occurs when the group behaves as if it has met to flee from or fight something.
- Basic assumption dependency (baD) arises when the group acts as if it has met to be sustained by a leader on whom it depends.
- Basic assumption pairing (baP) is when the group functions as if the members have met together in order that two people can pair off and create a new and as yet unborn leader.
- Basic assumption oneness (baO) is where members join and surrender themselves to the group, thereby experiencing well-being and wholeness (Turquet, 1974).
- Basic assumption me-ness (baM) is when the members of a group behave as is they are not a group but are separate and distinct individuals for whom "groupness" is an anathema (Lawrence, Bain, & Gould, 1996).

Following a study of successful schools in disadvantaged settings, I have examined the associations between the different basic assumption tendencies and the different facets of joint working or collaborative practice in school staff work groups (James, 2008b). I found that fight or flight, dependency and pairing are associated with the group's relationship with the primary task. In the successful schools, while the work group tendency was evident, this was due in part at least to the highly meaningful nature of the given, normative primary task. Thus, the staff group's work on this task satisfied a deeply rooted and perhaps unconscious need.

By contrast, oneness and me-ness are associated with the deeply seated ambivalence that individuals feel about group membership. These simultaneous and conflicting feelings result from desire to join the work group along with anxieties that joining the group will result in some form of psychic annihilation. In collaborative practice, both collective and individual endeavours are valued. The "collective" pre-dispositions of oneness and me-ness and the behaviours they underpin must therefore be held together in dynamic tension in a staff work group for successful joint working.

Two new basic assumption tendencies concerning the learning and change that are inherent in reflective practice emerged from this work. In basic assumption change (baC), the group behaves as if current practice is not – and will never be – good enough. This basic assumption drives a powerful desire in the group to change its practice. By contrast, in basic assumption stasis (baS), the group behaves as if it must stay as it is in order to survive. Both baC and baS are driven by anxiety. In the change mode, the anxiety may be founded on a lack of self-worth and a desire to counter a sense of personal and organisational. With the stasis tendency, the anxiety may be that change will bring chaos and insecurity. Both change and stasis must be held together in a dynamic tension and their concomitant anxieties contained (see below) if collaborative practice is to be successful.

In educational change, alterations to the task may heighten the anxieties associated with it, and as a result, the staff may begin engaging in fight/flight, dependency and pairing ways of working. If there are disruptions to the composition of the working group, the group may move to either individual atomised functioning (me-ness) or may give up their individual autonomy, sacrificing it for the good of the group oneness – neither of which is ideal. In the face of educational change, the group may start working in a change mode and may rush wholeheartedly into the proposed change and indeed any other change that comes along. On the other hand, the group may adopt a stasis mode of working, refusing to adapt in any way and resisting the change.

The Importance of Affective Containment by Individuals and Organisations During Educational Change

When there are difficult feelings in an organisation, for example, during a time of educational change, people are more likely to seek to protect themselves from them

(Dunning et al., 2005). Schools are places where feelings are always concentrated and where there are often difficult feelings present. During times of change, affective intensity and the likelihood of difficult feelings being present will increase. One response might be exerting affective control to minimise or even eradicate the difficult feelings from teaching, organising and change in educational institutions. However, even though feelings are very difficult to deal with, they are essential in helping to motivate actions and are a prerequisite for practice. The same applies to changing educational practice; feelings support the will to change and are dominant in the experience of change.

An alternative to affective control is affective containment. Affective containment is the process of providing an environment that brings about effective and authentic receptiveness and reflection. The idea was first developed by Bion (1961) to describe the creation of the conditions during psychoanalysis under which the experience of feelings, especially anxiety, can be accommodated securely, articulated and reflected upon. A containing environment for emotions (feelings that are shown) contrasts with a controlling environment where feelings are restrained, hidden and not allowed to become apparent as emotions. In controlling environments, difficult feelings have to be managed in other ways. If those feelings are hard to bear, individuals and groups may attempt to protect themselves by adopting defensive behaviours. In addition, the sense of "being controlled" may itself be experienced as a threat, which may in turn generate unacceptable feelings. Environments that seek to bring about affective control may therefore create more problems than they solve.

During educational change, affective containment can be very important. It can allow feelings to come to the surface, to be talked about and reflected upon. The difficult feelings can be accepted by others (as opposed to being introjected) and, in an important leadership act, can be reconfigured and returned to the others in an acceptable form (James & Jones, 2007). The containment processes can prevent the development of defensive routines in the face of change, enable the meaningful objects that may be lost during the change to be appropriately valued, and can facilitate re-attachment to the new.

Concluding Comments

This chapter has addressed the sometimes destabilising experience of educational change. By drawing on system psychodynamic theory, it has sought to explain and interpret individual and group responses to educational change. A number of systems psychodynamics theory concepts have been employed in this endeavour. They are social defences, the influence of unconscious mental activity, organisational and individual boundaries, the primary task of work groups and work group mentalities; basic assumption tendencies in group behaviour particularly in relation to collaborative practice; and affective containment by individuals and in organisations. Although the reasons for initiating change may be varied and the responses to change may be very wide ranging and unpredictable, systems psychodynamic theory can offer some very powerful insights into understanding the educational change process and how it might be better managed and led.

References

Alvesson, M. (2002). *Understanding organizational culture*. London: SAGE.

Argyris, C. (1985). *Strategy, change and defensive routines*. Boston: Pitman.

Beatty, B. R. (2000). The emotions of educational leadership: Breaking the silence. *International Journal of Leadership in Education, 3*, 331–357.

Bion, W. R. (1961). *Experiences in groups and other papers*. London: Tavistock.

Czander, W. (1993). *The psychodynamics of work and organisations*. New York: Guilford Press.

Diamond, M. A. (1993). *The unconscious life of organisations: Interpreting organisational identity*. London: Quorum Books.

Diamond, M. A., Allcorn, S., & Stein, H. (2004). The surface of organisational boundaries: A view from psychoanalytic object relations theory. *Human Relations, 57*, 31–53.

Douglas, M. (1966). *Purity and danger*. London: Routledge.

Dunning, G., James, C. R., & Jones, N. (2005). Splitting and projection at work in schools. *Journal of Educational Administration, 43*, 244–259.

Fineman, S. (2003). *Understanding emotion at work*. London: SAGE.

Fonagy, P. (2001). *Attachment theory and psychoanalysis*. London: Other Press.

Forgas, J. P. (2000). Introduction: The role of affect in social cognition. In J. P. Forgas (Ed.), *Thinking and feeling: The role of affect in social cognition*. Cambridge: Cambridge University Press.

Freud, S. (1925). *Mourning and melancholia* (Vol. IV, 1925 ed.). London: Vintage.

Freud, S. (1933). *New introductory lectures on psychoanalysis* (Vol. 2). Harmondsworth: Penguin.

Gabriel, Y. (1999). *Organizations in depth*. London: SAGE.

Goleman, D. (1995). *Emotional intelligence: Why it can matter more than IQ*. New York: Bantam.

Halton, W. (1994). Some unconscious aspects of organisational life. In A. Obholzer & V. Z. Roberts (Eds.), *The unconscious at work* (pp. 11–18). London: Routledge.

Hanna, D. (1997). The organisation as an open system. In A. Harris, N. Bennett, & M. Preedy (Eds.), *Organisational effectiveness and improvement in education*. Buckingham: Open University Press.

Hargreaves, A. (1998a). The emotional practice of teaching. *Teaching and Teacher Education, 14*(8), 835–854.

Hargreaves, A. (1998b). The emotions of teaching and educational change. In A. Hargreaves, A. Lieberman, M. Fullan, & D. Hopkins (Eds.), *The international handbook of educational change* (pp. 558–575). London: Kluwer Academic Publishers.

Hauke, C. (2006). The unconscious: Personal and collective. In R. K. Papadopoulos (Ed.), *The handbook of Jungian psychology* (pp. 54–73). London: Routledge.

Henderson, J. (1962). The archetype and culture. *The archetype: Proceedings of the second international congress of psychology*. Zurich, New York: S. Karger.

Heracleous, L. (2004). Boundaries in the study of organisations. *Human Relations, 57*(1), 95–103.

Hernes, T. (2004). Studying composite boundaries: A framework of analysis. *Human Relations, 57*, 9–29.

Hirschhorn, L. (1988). *The workplace within: Psychodynamics of organisational life*. Cambridge, MA: MIT Press.

Hirschhorn, L., & Gilmore, T. (1992, May/June). The new boundaries of the 'boundaryless' company. *Harvard Business Review, 70*, 104–115.

Hochschild, A. R. (1983). *The managed heart: Commercialisation of human feeling*. Berkeley: University of California Press.

James C. R. (1999). Institutional transformation and educational management. In T. Bush, L. Bell, R. Bolam, R. Glatter, & P. Ribbins (Eds.), *Educational management: Redefining theory, policy and practice* (pp. 142–154). London: Paul Chapman Publishing/SAGE.

James, C. R. (2008a). Teaching as affective practice. In H. Daniels, J. Porter, & H. Lauder (Eds.), *Companion in education*. London: Routledge.

James, C. R. (2008b). *Collaborative practice in schools: Developing understandings of educational organising using systems psychodynamics theory*. Annual Conference of the American Educational Research Association, New York, 24th–28th March, 2008.

James C. R., & Connolly, U. (2000). *Effective change in schools*. London: Routledge Falmer.

James, C. R., & Jones, N. (2007). A case study of the mis-management of educational change: An interpretation from an affective standpoint. *Journal of Educational Change, 9*, 1–16.

James, C. R., & Vince, R. (2001). Developing the leadership capability of headteachers. *Educational Management and Administration, 29*, 307–317.

James, C. R., Connolly, M., Dunning, G., & Elliott, T. (2006). *How very effective primary schools work*. London: SAGE.

James, C. R., Connolly, M., Dunning, G., & Elliott, T. (2008). High attainment schools in disadvantaged settings: An interpretation of significant characteristics from a system psychodynamics perspective. *International Studies in Educational Administration, 36*(2), 66–79.

Jung, C. G. (1927). The structure of the psyche. In H. Read, M. Fordham, & G. Adler (Eds.), *The collected works of C. G. Jung* (Vol. 9i, paras. 112–147). London: Routledge and Kegan Paul.

Jung, C. G. (1936). The concept of the collective unconscious. In H. Read, M. Fordham, & G. Adler (Eds.), *The collected works of C. G. Jung* (Vol. 9i, paras. 1112–1147). London: Routledge and Kegan Paul.

Kets de Vries, M. F. R. (1991). *Organisations of the couch*. San Francisco: Josey Bass.

Lamont, M., & Molnar, V. (2002). The study of boundaries in the social sciences. *Annual Review of Sociology, 28*, 167–195

Lawrence, W. G., Bain, A., & Gould, L. J. (1996). The fifth basic assumption. *Free Associations, 6*, 28–55.

Lawson, T. L. (2008). *Carl Jung: Darwin of the mind*. London: Karnac.

Leach, E. (1976). *Culture and communication*. Cambridge: Cambridge University Press.

Likierman, M. (2001). *Melanie Klein: Her work in context*. London: Continuum.

Marris, P. (1974). *Loss and change*. London: Routledge Kegan Paul.

Menzies, I. (1960). A case study in functioning of social systems as a defence against anxiety. *Human Relations, 13*, 95–121.

Miller, E., & Rice, A. K. (1967). Systems of organisation. In A. D. Coleman & W. H. Bexton (Eds.), *Group Relations Reader 1* (pp. 43–68). Jupiter, FL: A. K. Rice Institute.

Niedenthal, P. M., Krauth-Gruber, S., & Ric, F. (2006). *Psychology of emotion: Interpersonal, experiential and cognitive approaches*. London: Psychology Press.

Oatley, K., & Jenkins, J. M. (1996). *Understanding emotions*. Oxford: Blackwell.

Obholzer, A., & Roberts, V. Z. (1994). *The unconscious at work*. London: Routledge.

Papadopoulos, R. K. (Ed.). (2006). *The handbook of Jungian psychology*. London: Routledge.

Paulsen, N., & Hernes, T. (2003). *Managing boundaries in organisations: Multiple perspectives*. Basingstoke: Palgrave Macmillan.

Perrow, C. (1986). *Complex organisations – A critical essay* (3rd ed.). New York: McGraw-Hill.

Rice A. K. (1963). *The enterprise and its environment*. London: Tavistock.

Roberts, V. Z. (1994). The organisation of work: Contributions from open systems theory. In A. Obholzer & V. Z. Roberts (Eds.), *The unconscious at work*. London: Routledge.

Samuels, A. (2006). The archetypes. In R. K. Papadopoulos (Ed.), *The handbook of Jungian psychology* (pp. 177–195). London: Routledge.

Schein, E. H. (1992). *Organisational culture and leadership*. San Francisco: Jossey Bass.

Schneider, S. C. (1991). Managing boundaries in organisations. In M. F. R. Kets de Vries (Ed.), *Organisations of the couch*. San Francisco: Josey Bass.

Scott, W. R. (1998). *Organisations – rational, natural and open systems*. Englewood Cliffs, NJ: Prentice-Hall.

Segal, H. (1979). *Klein*. London: Fontana.

Stapley, L. (1996). *The personality of organisation*. London: Free Association Books.

Turquet, P. M. (1974). Leadership – the individual and the group. In G. S. Gibbard, J. J. Hartman, & R. D. Mann (Eds.), *Analysis of groups*. San Francisco, CA: Jossey Bass.

van Maanen, J., & Schein, E. H. (1979). Towards a theory of organisational socialisation. In B. Staw (Ed.), *Research in organisational behaviour* (Vol. 1). Greenwich, CA: JAI Press.

von Bertalanffy, I. (1968). *General systems theory*. New York: George Brazillier.

Weick, K. E. (1979). *The social psychology of organising* (2nd ed.). New York: Random House.

Weick K. E. (1995). *Sensemaking in organisations*. Thousand Oaks, CA: SAGE.

Moving Change: Evolutionary Perspectives on Educational Change

Stephen E. Anderson

The recognition that the implementation of changes in the professional beliefs and knowledge, behaviors, organizational conditions, and outcomes of people working in schools and school systems takes place over time is a fundamental precept in educational change theory, research, and practice. The aim of this chapter is to provide a concise overview of significant conceptual tools developed by education change theorists for describing, studying, and explaining that process as it plays out over time at different levels – e.g., individual, program, school, and school system. Given the volume of published research on educational change over the past 50 years, it is perhaps surprising that our understanding of the process dimensions of educational change remains limited to a few core concepts that once articulated have assumed a taken-for-granted status. This chapter revisits these concepts, highlights key areas of debate or lack of conceptual clarity, and suggests areas for further research regarding the processual nature of education change, particularly in terms of stage or phase theories of change over time. For each level of change considered, reference is made to key sources in the literature for the prevailing conceptual models of the temporal dimensions of the change process. While other publications might have been selected, these have been chosen because they are widely cited and applied in the literature on educational change, and because they draw attention to many of the key ideas and issues in considering change as a process that evolves through identifiable personal and organizational stages or phases over time.

Change as a Developmental Personal Process

Credit the developers of the Concerns-Based Adoption Model (CBAM) for their seminal conceptualization of change as a developmental process in attitudes and behaviors for individuals attempting to put new ideas and practices into use (Hall & Loucks, 1977, 1978; Hall, Loucks, Rutherford, & Newlove, 1975; Loucks &

S.E. Anderson (✉)
Ontario Institute for Studies in Educational Change, University of Toronto, Toronto, ON, Canada M5S 1V6
e-mail: sanderson@oise.utoronto.ca

A. Hargreaves et al. (eds.), *Second International Handbook of Educational Change*, Springer International Handbooks of Education 23, DOI 10.1007/978-90-481-2660-6_4, © Springer Science+Business Media B.V. 2010

Hall, 1977; see Hall & Hord, 2006, for a recent comprehensive overview of CBAM and supporting research). The basic ideas are straightforward. One dimension of change is represented as a developmental sequence of "Stages of Concern" that reflect a person's (e.g., a teacher) disposition or attitudes toward a change that he or she is attempting to put into practice (voluntarily or as an organizational mandate). A second dimension focuses on a developmental progression in a person's behaviors as he or she prepares for, begins, masters, and refines the use of new professional practices, referred to as "Levels of Use."

Through studies of experienced teachers implementing changes in curriculum and teaching (referred to as innovations), the CBAM developers identified and defined seven Stages of Concern. At Stage 0, Awareness, a teacher has little knowledge about or interest in the change. At Stage 1, Informational, the teacher is interested in learning more about the change and the implications of its implementation. Teacher concerns at Stage 2, Personal, reflect anxieties about the teacher's ability to implement the change, the need for change, and the personal costs of getting involved. Stage 3, Management, concerns intensify as the teacher first begins to cope with the logistics and new behaviors associated with putting the change into practice. At Stage 4, Consequence, teacher concerns focus on the impact of the change on students in their classrooms and on ways of modifying the innovation or its use to improve its effects. Teacher interest in working with other teachers to jointly improve the benefits of implementing the change for students is manifested in Stage 5, Collaboration, concerns. At some point in the change process, teachers may develop Stage 6, Refocusing, concerns. These teachers think about making major modifications in the use of the innovation, or perhaps replacing it with something else. The intent of the developers of the CBAM framework was not simply to create a research-based framework for understanding teacher change, but also to create ways to assess teachers' feelings and experience with innovative practices, and to use this information to provide interventions that would address their concerns.

The image of affective "stages" that a teacher (or anyone implementing a change in practice) progresses through over time is somewhat misleading. It is grounded in the notion (supported by research) that as teachers (both novice and experienced) become aware of, learn about, try out, and master the use of new teaching methods and programs their feelings about the change often evolve from a predominant focus on self (high Personal concerns), to task (high Informational and Management concerns), to impact (high Consequence and Collaboration concerns). Where things can get confusing, however, is if education researchers or practitioners misinterpret the CBAM framework as a necessary and lockstep evolution in the concerns of innovation users, rather than a possible progression dependent upon the influence of other factors at play in the implementation context. CBAM theory posits that the nature and intensity of individual concerns about the implementation of new ideas and practices across and within each stage will be higher or lower, depending not only on the person's progress in mastering the change, but also on the organizational conditions (e.g., administrative and collegial support, fit with prior beliefs and practices) associated with the change, and the perceived impact or results of the change for those affected (teachers, students). Without effective professional development inputs during the time in which teachers are learning to use new teaching strategies and programs, for example, teachers may experience unresolved Personal and Management concerns that can lead to frustration, resistance, or even abandonment of the change. Furthermore, interventions that do effectively resolve early stage concerns do not necessarily stimulate more intense concerns at subsequent stages in the model. Researchers applying the CBAM have discovered, for example, that even with repeated use of a new practice and adequate professional assistance, teachers may incorporate new teaching methods and programs into routine patterns of use without necessarily shifting their concerns toward refinement of the innovation based on observed evidence of student impact. Research on teacher collegiality and professional community suggests that the shift into more intense Consequence or Collaboration stage concerns may be less a function of teachers' individual mastery in the use of new programs and practices than of whether the organizational culture of the school in which they work emphasizes improvement in student learning through shared goals, teacher collaboration, and ongoing teacher learning activities (e.g., Anderson, 1997; Dufour, Eaker, & Dufour, 2005; Little, 1982; Rosenholtz, 1989).

A second element of potential confusion in applying this stage theory of teacher feelings about implementing new practices is that teachers are likely to experience and express concerns that link simultaneously to multiple "stages" in the model. It is the relative intensity of their concerns related to one or more stages that distinguish teacher attitudes toward a particular change they are involved with, not the mere presence or absence of concerns. For example, a teacher who is preparing or just starting to use some new teaching method might be genuinely wondering about the potential benefits of the innovation for student learning compared to current practices (Consequence concerns), while being predominantly concerned with figuring out how to integrate the use of that method into his/her daily lesson plans, and with attaining a basic level of comfort and competence in how he or she applies it in the classroom with students (Management concerns). In other words, at this point in their mastery of the use of the new method teachers are more preoccupied with the logistics and skill of doing it than with assessing and judging its effects on students and modifying it accordingly. It is not the case, however, that they do not care about student impact. In a metaphorical if not a real sense, it may be more appropriate to think of the different categories of concerns less as distinct stages than as notes in a musical chord that can be played in ways that give emphasis to different feelings depending on the teachers' progress in context. The CBAM developers refer to change users' concerns profile across the stages. A profile may reflect multiple peak concerns, not a single dominant focus on one stage. The theoretical and practical meaning of "stage" in this well-known model of the evolution of teachers' dispositions toward the implementation of changes in practice would benefit from further research.

The second dimension of the CBAM framework for understanding, assessing, and facilitating teacher change refers to a behavioral progression in knowledge and skills associated with mastering the use of new programs and practices, described as Levels of Use. Progression from one level to the next is marked by key decision points and corresponding behaviors in several domains associated with the change: acquiring information, assessing, sharing, planning, status reporting, performance, and knowledge. Levels 0 (Nonuse), I (Orientation), and II (Preparation) describe the behaviors of teachers vis-a-vis an innovation before they actually begin using it in the classroom. Teachers at Level I, Orientation, are seeking or receiving information about the change, but have not yet committed (or been committed) to implementation, whereas at Level II, Preparation, a teacher is actively planning to begin implementing the program or practice at a later date. Once teachers actually begin to operationalize their use of the innovation in the classroom, they enter Level III, Mechanical Use. Teachers at this level are struggling with the logistics of implementation (e.g., lesson and resource planning, classroom management, record keeping) and with attaining basic mastery of the new teaching skills. Any changes they make in their use of the innovation are likely to be teacher-centered, that is, aimed at making use of the innovation more manageable and easier to practice. A teacher who establishes a pattern of regular use and who makes few adaptations in his/her use of the new program and practices is said to have attained Level IVA, Routine Use. Many teachers will settle in at a Routine Level of Use once the new program or practice gets integrated into their ongoing repertoire of teaching strategies, materials, and so on. Some teachers, however, may begin making adjustments in their use of the program or practice based on evaluations of its impact on students. This is characterized as Level IVB, Refinement Use. If they actively seek out and interact with other teachers to collectively and collaboratively modify their use of the innovation to improve student results, they are engaged in Level V, Integration, behaviors. Eventually, some teachers may exhibit Level VI, Renewal, behaviors. Teachers at this level are actively exploring alternative programs and practices or major changes in the innovation.

Similar to the Stages of Concern, the CBAM Levels of Use concepts and framework describe a possible – not an inevitable – progression of individual innovation user behaviors associated with mastering the implementation of new programs and practices in teachers' work. As a developmental model of innovation user behaviors over time, however, the Levels of Use concepts and framework are more inclusive of alternative outcomes of use than the Stages of Concern. The behavioral model recognizes the practical reality that many educators engage in all sorts of professional learning experiences (Orientation) that lead to greater awareness and knowledge about programs, ideas, and practices that they may never end up implementing. It distinguishes people who are planning and otherwise getting ready to try out something new (Preparation) from those who are actually applying it in their work (Mechanical Users and beyond). Most importantly, the model accommodates the fact that some innovation users (perhaps most), after an initial period of mastering the logistics and basic skills required to implement the program or practice (Mechanical), will settle into a personally comfortable Routine Level of Use. The factors that lead some educators to engage individually or collectively in deliberate impact assessment and modification of their use of new programs and practices (Refinement, Integration) are not well understood. As noted for the arousal of impact-focused concerns, this may be less generally a function of individual pro-fessional orientations and skills than of workplace-specific norms and arrangements that give more or less emphasis to results. The original CBAM research and theory were developed prior to the contemporary curriculum content and student perfor-mance standards and accountability policy era. The incidence of impact-focused levels of user behaviors (Refinement, Integration, Renewal) linked to the imple-mentation of new programs and practices may be more prevalent nowadays given the changes in the policy context. Again, the theory that supports this developmental model of change would benefit from further research.

The common sense appeal of the Levels of Use (and Stages of Concern) concepts and frameworks relates to their generic applicability to any new policy, program, and professional practices that require expected implementers to alter current pro-fessional beliefs and behaviors. Just because it resonates well with people's practical experience, however, does not mean that it makes perfect sense as a developmen-tal model of change. One source of persistent confusion has to do with the nature and definition of professional expertise as it relates to the implementation of new programs and practices. Implicitly we can infer that someone (e.g., a teacher) who has sufficiently mastered his/her use of a new program or practice to move from an assessment of Mechanical Use to Routine or Refined Use has attained a higher skill level. Some CBAM researchers, however, note that implementers may routinize the use of new programs and practices at sub-optimal levels of expertise (Anderson, 2006). In other words, they are implementing the practices on an ongoing basis, and are comfortable with the way they are doing it, but demonstrate low levels of understanding and skill in their use (and are probably not aware of that discrepancy).

Our understanding of teacher and principal growth from novice to expert gen-erally and with regard to the use of specific teaching and leadership strategies remains poorly developed. When it comes to teachers, in particular, our notions of developing expertise are confounded with notions of fidelity and with compliance. Fidelity refers to the degree to which someone, such as a teacher, is implement-ing a program or practice in accordance with the way that program or practice is designed to be used (Fullan, 1982). Compliance adds the prescriptive expectation that particular forms or patterns of practice are not merely professionally desir-able, but are formally required by some external authority (e.g., school system policy and/or administrators). Some change researchers and theorists have argued that it is appropriate to view and assess changes in teacher practices as a process of behavioral change that progresses incrementally toward conformance with ideal images of implementation, when supported by effective leadership, resources, and technical assistance (e.g., Leithwood & Montgomery, 1982). From this perspec-tive, variability in the ways that teachers implement new programs and practices reflects variations in teacher understanding and skill in the use of those particu-lar programs and practices. To the extent that these variations are conceived as a linear progression of behaviors that approximate a desired pattern of use, this rep-resents a normative developmental model of teacher change over time. Others have similarly distinguished variations in teacher use of specific programs and practices as ideal, acceptable, or unacceptable relative to prescriptive definitions of what the innovation would look like in practice if implemented well, but without arguing that the variations represent developmental steps in mastering its use (e.g., Hall & Hord, 2006).

Our conceptions and understanding of variability and growth in teacher implementation of educational innovations are further complicated by the recognition that innovations are typically multi-dimensional (Fullan, 1982; Hall & Loucks, 1981; Leithwood, 1981). In broad terms, educational innovations for teachers may involve changes in materials (curriculum content, textbooks), practices (e.g., teaching or assessment strategies, grouping practices, classroom management), and beliefs (ibid). The exact nature and extent of change within each of these dimensions, however, is innovation and context specific. The adoption of a new textbook, for example, is a change in materials that may or may not fit with teachers' prior beliefs and practices. Furthermore, for a group of teachers simultaneously learning to implement the same new teaching strategy (e.g., guided reading), the gap between their prior beliefs, understanding, and practices and those associated with use of the new strategy may vary in magnitude and complexity for different individuals. Leithwood (1981) proposed a generic framework of ten dimensions that might be implicated in the implementation of any change in teaching and learning (not all changes would necessarily affect all dimensions), and that could be used as a tool for comprehensively describing and assessing use of different components of a change. For our discussion here, the basic point to highlight is that for a given set of innovation users, implementation progress relative to expected and ideal patterns of implementation may vary for different dimensions. Considered from this perspective, the idea that teachers or anybody implementing changes in their professional practice may move through holistically defined but empirically identifiable stages or levels of concern and skill in their use of that change gets murky indeed. Intuitively, no one disputes that implementing changes in current practices is not a single event, but rather an evolution in attitudes, understanding, and behaviors for those involved over time. The theoretical concepts that we use to describe and explain this process, however, are not resolved.

Program and School Change as an Organizational Process over Time

The preceding section examines developmental theories of change in educational settings from the vantage point of the individuals attempting to implement changes in programs and practices. This section focuses on process theories concerning the implementation of new educational policies, programs, and practices over time more from an organizational perspective. Key sources for the original ideas date from the 1970s and 1980s in the research and writing of Berman and McLaughlin (1976; Berman, 1978, 1980, 1981), Fullan (1982, 2007), Fullan and Pomfret (1977), Miles and Huberman (Miles, 1983; Huberman & Miles, 1984), and a few others (e.g., Corbett, Dawson, & Firestone, 1984). There are four core ideas that have become ingrained in the discourse on educational change – (1) that change is an organizational process over time; (2) that the process can be described and explained in terms of three broad phases; (3) that activities associated with different phases are interactive, not necessarily sequential in time; and (4) that change over time is less a process of direct replication than one of mutual adaptation. This conceptualization of change as an organizational process over time has been applied to the investigation of educational changes that take the form of new programs (e.g., a new curriculum, a new textbook, a set of packaged set of activities and materials for a specific curriculum area) and new instructional strategies (e.g., cooperative group learning, particular assessment techniques, specific classroom management strategies), as well as to the study of the adoption and implementation of models for whole school reform.

First is the idea that change is a process and not an event (Fullan, 1982; Hall & Loucks, 1977). This idea emerged as a rebuttal to the misguided expectation by policy makers and external program developers that putting new programs and policies into practice was equivalent to the simple replacement of one technology with another, an event commonly referred to as innovation adoption. This concept worked well when applied to the diffusion and adoption of technological innovations (e.g., new types of seeds by farmers) (Rogers, 2003). Education change researchers discovered early on that public announcements declaring the adoption of new policies or changes in educational products (e.g., curriculum content, textbooks, program kits) and practices (e.g., team teaching, teaching methods) at the classroom, school, school district, or school system levels did not guarantee that practitioners at the local level would change what they were doing (Charters & Jones, 1973). As characterized by Berman (Berman, 1981; cf. Fullan, 1982, 2007), change is an implementation-dominant process not a technology-dominant process, and the progress and outcomes of the implementation process are highly contingent upon interaction of the innovation with local context factors (e.g., perceived need and motives for change, innovation quality and complexity, fit with prior practices and beliefs, funding, resources and working conditions to enable change, quantity and quality of technical assistance, leadership stability and skill, participation in decision making by key stakeholder groups, competing priorities and expectations).

In their early research and writing, Berman and McLaughlin (1976) employed the concept of "stages of innovation" to characterize the overall organizational process through which school district and school personnel engage in efforts to replace, modify, or supplement current professional practices with new ones over time. They defined three stages: initiation, implementation, and incorporation. Each stage is associated with different activities and decisions concerning the selection, use, support, and progress in putting the change into practice on the part of local actors in their respective roles. Initiation encompasses decision-making activities about the reasons for change, selecting solutions (new programs and practices), implementation planning, and seeking resources. Implementation refers to the stage during which local educators are actually attempting to put the selected change into practice. Typically, this involves activities that lead to adaptations in the innovation as well as changes and modifications in the organizational setting and behaviors. Incorporation refers to activities associated with the continuation of what was originally a change into ongoing organizational routines and work practices. Berman and McLaughlin noted that decisions and actions at earlier stages affect what happens at later stages. From their research on the implementation of some 280 federally funded educational change projects in the United States, they concluded that while the focus of change was generally predictable from the content of the change initiative, the actual progress and outcomes of change were highly dependent upon local decisions and actions vis-à-vis its adoption, use, and continuation and upon the degree of specificity or uncertainty about the image of what the change should look like once put into practice.

Fullan (1982) nudged the conceptualization of the change process in organizations away from the linear notion of stages. He referred instead to three broad "phases" of change: initiation (also referred to as adoption or mobilization), implementation (or initial use), and continuation (cognate terms include incorporation, routinization, institutionalization). While he did not explain his decision to employ the concept phase instead of stage, his explanation of this model of the change process clearly indicates that he was striving to develop a way of thinking and talking about change in organizational practices that could account for the fact that it is "not a linear process," even though it occurs over time. Like Berman and McLaughlin, Fullan asserted that what happens at one phase strongly affects events and outcomes at later phases. But he added the nuance that events associated with a particular phase can feed back into and alter decisions and actions taken previously, and employed two-way arrows in a conceptual diagram to try to capture the interactive relationships between actions within each phase, as opposed to portraying change as a deterministic causal chain of events. Nonetheless, the metaphorically sequential image of a change progressing through the phases over time remained powerfully embedded in this conceptualization of change. In a later work, citing the research and thinking of Matthew Miles, Fullan further elaborated on what he then characterized as the "Triple III" model of change: initiation, implementation, and institutionalization (Video Journal of Education, 1992). Implementation success (defined as putting the change into practice and sustaining that practice) depended upon the quality of attention and action given to distinct conditions and activities associated with each phase: Initiation (high-profile need, clear model of change process, strong advocate, active initiation); Implementation (orchestration, shared control, pressure and support, technical assistance, rewards); and Institutionalization (embedding, links to instruction, widespread use, removal of competing priorities, continuing assistance).

Berman (1981) reconceptualized his original stage constructs of the change process as "sub-processes" related to specific functions and activities within an organizational system. According to this organizational systems view, a change can be said to occur when existing organizational routines are replaced or modified such that the system enters a different state of organizational behaviors and attendant relationships, materials, and so on, depending on the content and scope of the change. While this occurs over time, Berman deliberately avoided the language and images of linearity in the activities associated with the three sub-processes: mobilization, implementation, and institutionalization. The sub-processes co-exist as change-related functions in the organization, and the activities linked to those sub-processes can overlap in time and interact in mutually influential ways. The activities associated with certain sub-processes, however, may be more prominent in the actions of local actors at different times in the history of a change initiative, and the roles that those actors play in the change process can vary for different sub-processes. Mobilization activities include developing an image of the desired change (e.g., needs assessment, goal setting, product adoption), planning for implementation, and lobbying internally and externally for support (commitment, political support, resources, etc.). Implementation encompasses two broad functions that local educators engage in as they attempt to put new programs and practices into action – clarification and adaptation. Clarification is linked to activities such as professional development that help implementers figure out exactly what and how to do the change and how it differs from what they were doing before. Adaptation refers to local activities that lead to modifications in the content or design of the change as originally presented, as well as to the changes in behaviors and knowledge that they experience as a result of the process. Institutionalization happens when a system stabilizes into a changed state of routine behaviors, and is manifested through activities that demonstrate the assimilation of new practices into the ongoing behaviors of organizational members affected by the change, and by incorporation of these new routines into associated organizational decision-making processes (e.g., budget, staffing, support services). For purposes of this discussion, the key idea advanced by Berman is that organizational change is more appropriately conceived of as a change of state in an organizational system of behaviors, arrangements, and processes that occurs as a result of actions taken within different sub-processes of the system, but not as a predictable progression through developmental stages or phases over time. Berman's ideas foreshadowed much of the contemporary thinking about schools and school systems as complex adaptive systems, but these ideas did not catch on at the time.

What did capture the attention of educational change scholars and practitioners was the idea that various implementation outcomes were possible (where outcomes refer to the use of new programs and practices, not to the effects of their use on students or organizational effectiveness and efficiency). Berman and McLaughlin (1977; cf. Berman, 1978) distinguished four possible outcomes, differentiated in terms of the changes that result through the implementation process in implementer behaviors and in the new program or practices, i.e., the innovation. Non-implementation (or symbolic implementation) describes a state in which no change occurs either in implementer behaviors or in the innovation. Co-optation describes a situation in which the implementers modify the new program or practice to conform to what they were already doing, resulting, as well, in no substantive change in organizational work practices (though sometimes the users adopt new ways of talking about what they do that promotes an illusion of change in beliefs and behaviors). Berman and McLaughlin (op cit) reported that *mutual adaptation* was the most common implementation outcome associated with successful change. Under these circumstances, the implementation process results in changes in implementer behaviors in the direction of those envisioned by the innovation developers and promoters, as well as in adaptations in the innovative program or practice in response to local circumstances. The fourth implementation outcome, technical implementation, refers to the rational planning image that implementers of an innovation will alter their existing behaviors in compliance with the ideal forms of practice as specified in new policies, programs, or practices, with minimal changes in the design, content, and procedures of the innovation. Berman and McLaughlin reported that they did not actually find examples of this outcome in their investigation of the implementation of federally funded educational innovation projects in the United States (ibid). Other education change researchers, however, argued that the change projects that Berman and McLaughlin studied simply did not include procedurally specific programs and practices that were known to yield demonstrably positive effects if faithfully implemented as designed (Crandall, 1983) when conditions conducive to successful implementation were in place (e.g., leadership, good training, resources). While it is debatable whether any new program or practice is ever exactly replicated by users in different settings, the idea that the quality of education could be substantially improved if only teachers and principals would carefully replicate "best practices" that have worked well for desired educational goals in schools serving similar students with similar resources remains deeply ingrained in the discourse on educational change.

Fullan drew a distinction between two organizational approaches to implementation – a fidelity approach and an adaptive approach (Fullan, 1982, 2007; Fullan & Pomfret, 1977; cf. Berman, 1980). The fidelity approach is most appropriate when procedurally clear new programs and practices are introduced in settings where there is a good match between local needs and goals and the selected change, where local resources and conditions are adequate to support the implementation of that change as designed, and when the likely effects of innovation use have been previously demonstrated in similar settings. Under these circumstances, organizational expectations and support for change may aim for the ideal of technical implementation of the change, whether that outcome is achieved or not. The adaptive approach is more appropriate when the technology of innovation use is not well specified, the claimed benefits of implementation are not well supported by evidence, and the local needs and resources conditions are not well matched to the change. Under these circumstances, the expected outcome would be mutual adaptation.

Whether by design or by default, mutual adaptation remains the most realistic conceptualization of what happens when educators genuinely attempt to implement new ideas, programs, and practices, i.e., changes occur both in implementer behaviors and in the innovation as initially conceived and designed by those promoting the change. Has our understanding of the process of mutual adaptation evolved since the original formulation of these ideas in the 1970s? The simple answer is not much. Analysis and discussion of mutual adaptation as a phenomenon has tended to focus less on the "mutual" dimensions of adaptation, than on whether and how implementers alter the change as originally introduced. The most common strand of inquiry and discussion reaffirms the idea already noted that under certain conditions (e.g., an uncertain technology, poor fit between the innovation and the "problem" it is supposed to address, inadequate resources, ineffective leadership and assistance) the degree of adaptation to the innovation will be greater than under the opposite conditions. From this perspective, mutual adaptation is commonly characterized in quantitative terms as a matter of degree. Berman and McLaughlin (1977) also used the term *mutation* to describe what happens when implementers modify the design and content of a change as they put it into practice. Hall and his colleagues introduced the idea that for innovations that are procedurally well specified, there can be a point of "drastic mutation" beyond which so much modification has occurred in the program or practice as initially presented that it is no longer appropriate to claim that the original innovation has been implemented (Hall & Hord, 1987, p. 137). No one, however, has presented empirical evidence to suggest any uniform or alternative stages or developmental patterns in the process of mutual adaptation over time.

Datnow, Hubbard, and Mehan (2002) present a more elaborated conception of mutual adaptation in which context constitutes the critical explanatory dimension, rather than characteristics of the innovation, the implementation support system, and time. Their research and analysis focused on the fate of changes (e.g., comprehensive school reforms) originating externally to schools and school districts attempting to put them into practice. While employing the familiar language of reform adoption, implementation, and sustainability (i.e., continuation or institutionalization) to organize their account and analysis of change over time, they reject technical rational linear conceptions of the change process. They define implementation simply as "doing the reform," and building upon the earlier work of Berman and McLaughlin, Fullan, and others, they argue that implementer adaptation of new policies, programs, and practices in relation to varied components or dimensions of local context is the normal process of change, even in situations involving highly prescriptive innovations. Their theoretical and research-based conceptualization of context and the adaptation process, however, adds complexity and depth to our understanding of this phenomenon. First, they propose that mutual adaptation might be more appropriately conceived of as a process of "co-construction" between those who design, advocate, or facilitate the implementation of a change and those expected to participate in enacting the change. Second, they argue that this co-construction process is subject to the varied interests, actions, and influence of all stakeholders implicated in implementation decisions and actions acting from the situational position of their particular roles and social contexts Third, they argue that context is often misconceived as a system of lower levels (e.g., classroom, school) embedded within higher or broader levels (e.g., district, community, state). This metaphor tends to promote hierarchical and unidirectional perspectives on implementation in which local actors are portrayed as simply reacting to changes and pressures originating from external sources. Datnow, Hubbard, and Mehan argue instead for what they call a relational sense of context. From this perspective, people implicated in different functions of the overall enterprise of public education – e.g., state policy making, state education agency activities, district office work, school administration, classroom teaching, parental and community involvement, being students – each enact their role in particular social contexts. These social contexts co-exist in interconnected sets of relationships. Actions taken in one context create outcomes and conditions which can permeate through these interlocking relationships to influence subsequent actions in other contexts in unpredictable ways. The unpre-dictability arises in part from the unique histories, socio-cultural characteristics and relationships, and social structural conditions of the different interacting con-texts. In order to understand mutual adaption in the implementation of educational change, one has to examine the interconnections among these contexts and how people involved in implementation respond in terms of the specific characteristics of the contexts within which they play out their roles in the process. The overall process (inter-contextual connections, communication between contexts, and pre-vailing responses within contexts) is strongly influenced by those actors whose organizational, political, or social positions allow them to exert the most power over how reform efforts and responses to them are defined and the corresponding courses of action that are taken. This relational and dynamic view of actions taken within and between interlocking contexts does not privilege a priori the influence of actions taken in one context over another. Change is multi-directional, not uni-directional. Datnow, Hubbard, and Mehan provide examples of local adaptations of school reform initiatives to a variety of structural and cultural contextual condi-tions – school organizational constraints, overlapping reform initiatives, state and district policies, linguistic diversity, and educator beliefs about student abilities, teaching and learning.

Datnow, Hubbard, and Mehan's account of the mutual adaptation process is consistent with complexity theory perspectives on social organizations as complex adaptive systems in which change occurs as a non-linear dynamic process over time (Kauffman, 1995; Waldrop, 1992; cf. Fullan, 2003). Actions taken in any spe-cific socio-organizational contexts that are interlinked and implicated in adopting, implementing, and sustaining the change have unpredictable effects (including no effects) on organizational conditions and actions in other contexts. To posit pre-dictable stages and outcomes of implementation is meaningless in this view. The overall model of the implementation of school reforms and programmatic changes in educational settings, however, preserves the basic distinction in chronological time between deciding to change (adoption), doing the change (implementation), and sustaining (or abandoning) the changes over time.

All analysts of the process of planned changes in education talk in both a chrono-logical time and an organizational sense about the continuation or sustainability of changes in programs and practices beyond early experiences with implemen-tation. While there is no fixed timeline, the basic idea is that some innovations lead to enduring changes in the way educators go about doing their work; that is, they become routine features of ongoing practice. Others only lead to temporary modifications in behaviors that are abandoned after some recognizable period of initial use. Changes may be abandoned for any number of reasons – e.g., loss of funding or other resources required to sustain the program or practice, evidence or perceptions of ineffectiveness, low leadership pressure and support, the presence of other priorities competing for people's time and energy, and staff turnover. As previously reviewed, change researchers and theorists have identified a number of organizational conditions and management practices and innovation characteristics that affect the likelihood that a given change in a particular setting will be sustained or not (Anderson & Stiegelbauer, 1994; Berman, 1981; Fullan, 1982; Miles, 1983). The key point is the idea that some efforts to change do result in what systems and complexity theorists refer to as a state change for the people and organizations involved. That is, the changes become more than passing perturbations in the way people conduct their work.

The idea of a change in state (as opposed to a stage or phase in change) makes sense, but is not without its own conceptual and empirical conundrums. One has to do with the multi-dimensionality of change. Thus, some components of a change may get institutionalized and sustained as a feature of ongoing practice while others do not. Second has to do with the loosely coupled nature of schools and school systems as organizations. Thus, a change that affects multiple settings (classrooms, schools, district offices), or multiple contexts as conceptualized by Datnow and her colleagues, might get sustained in some contexts but not in others. Even in those where it does carry on, it is likely to take different forms as a result of the contextually sensitive adaptation process.

Third has to do with the magnitude of the change in terms of the actual difference it makes in prior patterns of work for the educators involved. Numerous analysts of planned educational change draw a distinction between changes which may result in people refining existing practices, replacing existing practices, or adding new practices to existing patterns of work, but which do not alter the fundamental nature of that work. Elmore (1995) describes this as the difference between first-order and second-order change. The idea of changes and improvements that are more profound and far reaching in their consequences for how schools and school systems are organized, the professional work of educators, and the nature and outcomes of student learning, than simply changing materials, learning a new teaching strategy, enabling people to work together (rather than individually) to try to improve what they do, and so on, is intellectually and politically appealing, but challenging to define and identify empirically. Perhaps we will know it when we finally experience it? Suffice it to say that most educational change initiatives are more about modifying the existing state of school organization and educational practice than about fundamentally changing that state. Conceptually and instrumentally, the idea of a state change in education runs into difficulties when we try to define the parameters and boundaries of the phenomenon or system that is potentially undergoing a non-trivial change in "state." These concepts are hard to apply at the organizational levels of schools, districts, or state/national educational systems.

Regardless of the organizational level or magnitude of change at hand and in mind, the long-standing notion of institutionalization as a final stage or phase of planned change is challenged by the contemporary ideology of continuous improvement in the context of standards-based and results-oriented education accountability systems. The idea that even new programs and practices that are successfully put into practice may eventually be subject to major modifications or replacement was noted long ago by the developers of the Concerns-Based Adoption Model, in the form of the Refocusing Stage of Concerns and Renewal Level of Use behaviors (Hall & Hord, 2006; Hall & Loucks, 1977, 1978). Crandall, Eiseman, and Louis (1986) posed the question of whether institutionalization or renewal was the more appropriate organizational goal for the introduction of school improvement–oriented policies, programs, and practices. Over the past 20 years, the entrenchment of national and state accountability systems linked to curriculum content standards, student performance standards, student performance targets, large-scale testing of student performance, and mandatory consequences (rewards, assistance, sanctions) at the school and district levels based on evidence of performance is fueling and sustaining the idea of continuous improvement in the quality of teaching and learning in schools.

Drawing upon studies of sustained (5–10 years) improvement efforts at the school and district levels, Anderson & Kumari (2008) distinguishes the organizational practice of continuous improvement from the evidence of impact over time on student learning and the quality of teaching. They report that schools and school districts that engage in sustained improvement efforts may evolve through successive phases of improvement marked not only by the introduction of new or revised instructional programs and practices, but also by changes in the organizational structures and processes to support ongoing change, when there is compelling evidence that further improvement requires rethinking the existing support system for improvement. The latter point is key. It arises from the recognition that sustained improvement in student learning can stall in two significant ways. First, the support system as currently organized may reach a limit in terms of its capacity to effectively reach and provide ongoing support for improvement to all teachers, principals, and schools that it is intended to serve. Second, after a period of change, student learning levels can reach a point where evidence of improvement plateaus (cf. Fullan, 2003; Hopkins, 2007). Further improvement will not be accomplished simply by doing more of the same. These findings are discussed further in the succeeding section on educational change at the system level (district, state, nation).

System-Wide Change and Improvement in Student Learning

The idea of continuous improvement as applied to educational change has brought student learning outcomes more explicitly into theories and models of change. But what does it mean for student learning to continuously improve in a school, a school district, a school system? Is it incremental growth on set indicators of academic achievement for all students? Is it mainly about bringing low-performing students up to the level of their higher performing peers? Does it involve changing the standards and expectations as student performance rises? Does it happen in ways that can be characterized as phases, stages, or changes in state? Empirical and conceptual accounts of student learning *over time* in the context of educational change are recent and associated mainly with studies of large-scale reform at the state/national and school district levels (Fullan, 2000). Some well-known and researched examples at the district level include the decentralization reform in the Chicago School Systems (Bryk, Sebring, Kerbow, Rollow, & Easton, 1998; Simmons, 2006) and the case of Community School District #2 New York City (Elmore & Burney, 1997). Longitudinal investigations of improvement at the state/national level are more difficult to come by. Two prime examples are an evaluation of the National Literacy and Numeracy Strategies in the United Kingdom (Earl et al., 2003; cf. Fullan, 2003; Hopkins, 2007) and the controversial accounts of and debates about state-wide improvement and equity in student achievement across Texas in the 1990s (e.g., Scheurich & Skrla, 2001; Skrla, Scheurich, Johnson, & Koschoreck, 2001a; Valencia, Valenzuela, Sloan, & Foley, 2001).

The breadth and depth of longitudinal research on large-scale reform at this level is insufficient to generalize with much certainty about patterns of change over time. We can, however, highlight some key findings and ideas emerging from this research. One is the phenomenon of plateaus in the trajectory of aggregate improvement in student learning over time. While this has been noted in long-term studies of school-level improvement (e.g., Anderson & Kumari, 2008; Anderson & Stiegelbauer, 1997), it is more profoundly evident in evaluations of system-wide reforms involving large numbers of schools and districts. Analysts of the British government's Literacy and Numeracy Strategies reform, for example, chart significant improvements in the percentages of elementary school students performing at or above government-prescribed standards on standardized tests of reading and mathematics during the first 3 years (1997–2000), a reduction in the gap between higher and lower performing students, and a phenomenal scaling-up of the number of schools and local education authorities reporting these positive results (the story and data are reviewed in Hopkins, 2007; also Fullan, 2003). Student performance across the system, however, leveled off for about 3 years and only began to rise again around 2004 and 2005. Hopkins attributes the early gains to the government's success in designing and intensively supporting a rigorous standards-based national curriculum development and implementation reform. In short, a national infrastructure of policies, resources, training, technical assistance, and monitoring to support implementation of the literacy and numeracy initiatives was effectively put into place. Citing the reform's director, Michael Barber, Hopkins refers to this period of the reform as a time and strategy of informed prescription. Informed prescription worked to get the curriculum reform into place with significant gains in student learning, but did not result in the ideal of continuous improvement once the initial gains settled in. Hopkins attributes the revitalization of improvements in student performance after a 3- or 4-year plateau to a deliberate shift in the government's strategy for improvement to what Barber conceptualized as informed professionalism. The impetus and support for ongoing improvement was redirected from a dependency on external direction and expertise to developing local leadership for improvement, and to encouraging and supporting lateral networking among schools and school personnel about promising practices and solutions to locally contextualized needs and challenges for improvement. The government reorganized its support for improvement less around technical implementation of the literacy and numeracy reforms, and more around developing and sustaining the capacity of school personnel to lead and make improvements together. For purposes of this discussion of phases, stages, or state changes in the process of educational change, the exact details of this shift in government strategy are less relevant than the evidence of the plateau effect in improvement student learning over time, and the

British government's strategic decision that further improvement meant rethinking and reorganizing the support system for change within the parameters of national goals.

The student achievement plateau phenomenon, followed by a restructuring of the system support system and then by renewed evidence of student performance gains, is also reported for the Ontario government's literacy initiative (Campbell & Fullan, 2006) and in longitudinal analyses of decentralization reforms, district organization and support, and student outcomes in the Chicago school system (Bryk et al., 1998; Simmons, 2006). The Chicago case adds some additional complexity to this pattern. As recounted by Simmons (2006), the Chicago reform has moved through three phases of improvement relative to student performance and to the district role and relationships with schools. Each phase of reorganization was preceded by a period of system-wide improvement in standardized test scores leading to a 2- to 3-year plateau in student performance gains. The complexity in this picture arises from the fact that the improvement gains varied for different sets of schools. Focusing on the low-performing elementary schools in 1990 (82% of the city's 429 regular elementary schools), Simmons shows how test scores declined initially in all these schools, began to rise in 1992, and plateaued 1993 and 1995. Among these schools, however, Simmons identifies half as "high-gain" schools that showed evidence of significant improvements in student performance, while the other half were "low-gain" schools that showed minimal overall improvement in this phase. The scores leveled off for both sets of schools, but at different performance thresholds. Following a partial recentralization of the district authority and reorganization of district direction, support, and intervention for school improvement, student achievement scores improved significantly among all these schools from 1995 and 1999, but stalled again between 1999 and 2001, leading to another reorientation and reorganization of district-level involvement in supporting ongoing improvement efforts in the schools. This change was followed by renewed evidence of improvement in the high-gain schools, but did not have an effect on the stalled achievement test results in the low-gain schools. Again, our purpose here is not to explore the details of the district improvement strategies and their evolution over time, but rather to highlight some patterns of change associated with a long-term system-wide improvement effort. The Chicago case reinforces the expectation that a system-wide improvement strategy is likely to result in short-term improvement in student performance followed by a leveling off or plateau in student learning gains, and that further improvement may require strategic rethinking and reorganization of system-level leadership and support for change at the school level. The difference in the Chicago case is the recognition that the pattern of gains and plateaus may vary for schools in varying circumstances across the system. Thus, the support system for improvement has to become increasingly differentiated in response to the performance trends and circumstances of individual schools and sets of similar schools. Elmore and Burney (1997) also talk about the development of a district approach to improvement in NYC District #2 that became increasingly responsive to differential progress in achieving school improvement targets in the context of district-wide goals.

A different scenario of wide-scale improvements in student performance over a sustained period of time occurred in Texas during the 1990s and into the current century. The history of this process and controversies surrounding the social and educational implications of the results are widely documented, e.g., Haney, 2001; Klein, 2001; Scheurich & Skrla, 2001; Skrla et al., 2001a, 2001b; Valencia et al., 2001. Texas was one of the first states in the United States to introduce a standards-based curriculum aligned with a state accountability system that included annual criterion-based testing of student performance on the curriculum, state-mandated performance indicators and reports, and public ratings of schools and school districts on the basis of student performance (aggregated and disaggregated by student characteristics, such as race and family income). Over a 10-year period, schools and districts across the state charted remarkable gains in student achievement on the state tests, and a significant narrowing of gaps in performance between racially and socio-economically different sub-groups of students. Controversy surrounding the results centered on claims that the state curriculum standards and tests were set at a low level of expectations for student learning, that Texas students did not perform nearly as well on nationally normed tests, that the state education agency inflated performance ratings by manipulating minimum pass standards, that the accountability pressures led teachers to concentrate classroom instruction more on preparing students for the tests than on learning per se, and that the claimed improvements in student learning, particularly for minority and poor students, were more illusory than real. By 2001, as seen elsewhere, student results had plateaued, but had plateaued at relatively high levels, with many schools and districts reporting 80% or more of their students performing at or above the state's minimum standards for acceptable performance in reading, writing, and mathematics. The state's response at this point was not to rethink and reorganize its support system for ongoing improvement under the existing curriculum regime. Instead, the state introduced a more challenging curriculum and testing system. In essence, the state raised the bar of standards and acceptable performance. The immediate effect was a decline in student, school and district performance levels. This created a new context and stimulus for improvement (and an impression that some schools and districts that were high performing under the old system were not so effective after all). Here is not the place to engage in the debate on the educational and social significance of the Texas miracle from 1991 to 2001 (see the works cited). The Texas case is, however, important to this discussion of the conceptual, methodological, and political complexities of measuring and judging continuous improvement in student learning over time. It reminds us of the implications of stability and change in how we assess and judge the quality and change in student learning over time. It also illustrates that when confronted with what may be an inevitable leveling off of gains in student learning across a system, system authorities can respond in different ways. In England and in Chicago, they reoriented and reorganized the external support systems to achieve better quality implementation within the existing curriculum and accountability system. In Texas they changed the curriculum and performance standards, with no major shift in state support for implementation of altered expectations and accountability requirements. It remains to be seen whether Texas schools will,

on a wide scale, register renewed gains with a more challenging curriculum and performance standards, but low investment at the state level in whether and how this
might require change in the infrastructure of system support for improvement at the
school and district levels.

Concluding Remarks

The aim of this chapter was to review and discuss different ways in which education change researchers and analysts have conceptualized, studied, and explained
the process of change over time, particularly in terms of successive stages, phases,
or states. Popular concepts used to make sense of change over time were discussed as an individual phenomenon and as an organizational phenomenon at the
level of schools and school systems (district, state, nation). These included the
developmental schema of affective Stages of Concern and behavioral Levels of
Use applied to individuals implementing innovations associated with the Concerns-
Based Adoption Model (Hall & Hord, 2006); the three-stage/three-phase mobilization, implementation, and institutionalization model of planned changes in program
and practices in organizations (Berman, 1981; Berman & McLaughlin, 1977; Fullan,
1981, 2007); continuing developments in understanding the phenomena of mutual
adaptation (Datnow et al., 2002) and the sustainability of change; and recent
attempts to conceptualize and describe what continuous improvement looks like at
the school and school system levels in terms of both student outcomes and system-
level organization (e.g., Anderson & Kumari, 2008; Fullan, 2003; Hopkins, 2007).
While many of the concepts reviewed are well known and often applied, this review
draws attention to some of the knotty conceptual problems associated with their
application to empirical findings from research on educational change. On the basis
of this review, I argue that the fit of these theoretical concepts to practice should
not be taken for granted by education researchers and practitioners. More research
effort is needed to deepen theoretical development along these lines in our ongoing
efforts to construct a discourse that accurately describes and explains educational
change. In sum, as knowledge workers in the field of educational change, we need
to continually challenge and refine our conceptions and explanations of the change
process over time.

References

Anderson, S. E. (1997). Understanding teacher change: Revisiting the concerns based adoption
    model. *Curriculum Inquiry, 27*(3), 331–367.
Anderson, S. E., & Kumari, R. (2008). Understanding the practice of continuous improvement in
    schools. *International Journal of Educational Development, 29*(3), 281–292.
Anderson, S. E., & Stiegelbauer, S. (1994). Institutionalization and renewal in a restructured
    secondary school. *School Organisation, 14*(3), 279–293.
Berman, P. (1978). The study of macro- and micro-implementation. *Public Policy, 26*(2), 157–184.

Berman, P. (1980). Thinking about programmed and adaptive implementation strategies and situations. In H. Ingram & D. Mann (Eds.), *Why policies succeed or fail*. Beverly Hills, CA: Sage.

Berman, P. (1981). Educational change: An implementation paradigm. In R. Lehming & M. Kane (Eds.), *Improving schools: Using what we know* (pp. 253–286). Beverly Hills, CA: Sage Publications.

Berman, P., & McLaughlin, M. (1976). Implementation of educational innovation. *Educational Forum, 40*(3), 345–370.

Bryk, A., Sebring, P., Kerbow, D., Rollow, S., & Easton, J. (1998). *Charting Chicago school reform*. Boulder, CO: Westview Press.

Campbell, C., & Fullan, M. (2006). *Unlocking the potential for learning: Effective district-wide strategies to raise student achievement in literacy and numeracy*. Toronto, ON: Ontario Literacy and Numeracy Secretariat, Project Report.

Charters, W. W., & Jones, J. (1973). On the risk of appraising non-events in program evaluation. *Educational Research, 2*(11), 5–7.

Corbett, H. D., Dawson, J., & Firestone, W. (1984). *School context and school change: Implications for effective planning*. New York: Teachers College Press.

Crandall, D., Eiseman, J., & Louis, K. S. (1986). Strategic planning issues that bear on the success of school improvement efforts. *Educational Administration Quarterly, 22*(3), 21–53.

Datnow, A., Hubbard, L., & Mehan, H. (2002). *Extending educational reform: From one school to many*. London, NY: RoutledgeFalmer.

Dufour, R., &, Eaker, R. (Eds.). (2005). *On common ground: The power of learning communities*. Bloomington, IN: National Educational Service.

Earl, L., et al. (2003). *Watching and learning 3. Final report of the external evaluation of England's national literacy and numeracy strategies*. Nottingham: Department for Education and Skills.

Elmore, R. (1995). Getting to scale with good educational practice. *Harvard Educational Review, 66*(1), 1–26.

Elmore, R., & Burney, D. (1997). *Investing in teacher learning: Staff development and instructional improvement in Community School District #2, New York City*. New York: Consortium for Policy Research in Education and National Commission on Teaching and America's Future.

Fullan, M. (1982). *The meaning of educational change*. New York: Teachers College Press.

Fullan, M. (2000). The return of large scale reform. *Journal of Educational Change, 1*(1), 5–28.

Fullan, M. (2003). *Change forces with a vengeance*. London, NY: RoutledgeFalmer.

Fullan, M. (2007). *The new meaning of educational change* (4th ed.). New York: Teachers College Press.

Fullan, M., & Pomfret, A. (1977). Research on curriculum and instruction implementation. *Review of Educational Research, 47*(1), 335–397.

Hall, G., & Hord, S. (1987). Change in Schools: Facilitating the Process. Alhang, NY: State University of New York Press.

Hall, G., & Hord, S. (2006). *Implementing change: Patterns, principles, and potholes* (2nd ed.). Boston: Pearson Education, Inc.

Hall, G., & Loucks, S. (1977). A developmental model for determining whether the treatment is actually implemented. *American Educational Research Journal, 14*(3), 273–276.

Hall, G., & Loucks, S. (1978). Teacher concerns as a basis for facilitating and personalizing staff development. *Teachers College Record, 80*(1), 36–53.

Hall, G., & Loucks, S. (1981). Program definition and adaptation: Implications for inservice. *Journal of Research and Development in Education, 14*(2), 46–58.

Hall, G., Loucks, S., Rutherford, W., & Newlove, B. (1975). Levels of use of the innovation: A framework for analyzing innovation adoption. *Journal of Teacher Education, 26*(1), 52–56.

Haney, W. (2001). The illusion of educational equity in Texas: A commentary on 'accountability for equity'. *International Journal of Leadership in Education, 4*(3), 267–275.

Hopkins, D. (2007). *Every school a great school*. Berkshire, England: Open University Press, McGraw-Hill.

Huberman, M., & Miles, M. (1984). *Innovation up close: How school improvement works.* New York: Plenum.

Kauffman, S. (1995). *At home in the universe: The search for the laws of self-organization and complexity.* New York: Oxford University Press.

Klein, S. (2001). Is there a connection between educational equity and accountability. *International Journal of Leadership in Education, 4*(3), 261–266.

Leithwood, K. (1981). Dimensions of program innovation. *Journal of Curriculum Studies, 13*(1), 25–36.

Leithwood, K., & Montgomery, D. (1982). Evaluating program implementation. *Evaluation Review, 4*(2), 193–214.

Little, J. W. (1982). Norms of collegiality and experimentation: Workplace conditions of school success. *American Educational Research Journal, 19*(3), 325–340.

Loucks, S., & Hall, G. (1977, February). Assessing and facilitating the implementation of innovations: A new approach. *Educational Technology, 17*(2), 18–21.

Miles, M. (1983). Unraveling the mystery of institutionalization. *Educational Leadership, 41*(3), 14–19.

Rogers, E. M. (2003). *Diffusion of innovations*(5th ed.). New York: The Free Press.

Rosenholtz, S. (1989). *Teachers' workplace: The social organization of schools.*White Plains, NY: Longman.

Scheurich, J., & Skrla, L. (2001). Continuing the conversation on equity and accountability: Listening appreciatively, responding responsibly. *Phi Delta Kappan, 83*(4), 322–326.

Simmons, J. (2006). School reform in Chicago, 1988–2005. In *Breaking through: Transforming urban school districts*(chap. 1, pp. 11–23). New York: Teachers College Press.

Skrla, L., Scheurich, J. J., Johnson, J., & Koschoreck, J. (2001a). Accountability for equity: Can state policy leverage social justice? *International Journal of Leadership in Education 4*(3), 237–260.

Skrla, L., Scheurich, J. J., Johnson, J., & Koschoreck, J. (2001b). Rejoinder: Complex and contested constructions of accountability and educational equity. *International Journal of Leadership in Education, 4*(3), 277–283.

Valencia, R., Valenzuela, A., Sloan, K., & Foley, D. (2001). Let's treat the cause, not the symptoms: Equity and accountability in Texas revisited. *Phi Delta Kappan, 83*(4), 318–321, 326.

Video Journal of Education. (1992). Managing change: The dynamics of change. *Video Journal of Education, 2*(4).

Waldrop, M. (1992). *Complexity: The emerging science at the edge of order and chaos.* New York: Simon and Schuster.

A Temporary, Intermediary Organization at the Helm of Regional Education Reform: Lessons from the Bay Area School Reform Collaborative

Ann Jaquith and Milbrey McLaughlin

The Bay Area School Reform Collaborative (BASRC) was invented in 1995 as an ad hoc intermediary organization. It was created in response to a national challenge from philanthropist Walter Annenberg and his half-billion-dollar gift to American public education. The William and Flora Hewlett Foundation responded with $25 million to support the creation of a San Francisco Bay Area regional education reform initiative. BASRC was charged with the goal of stimulating and supporting education reform in the Bay Area and working to close the achievement gap among students of different race and language backgrounds. During its 10-year history, BASRC pursued its mission by making grants to support schools' reform work and establishing a regional collaborative of member schools, districts, support organizations, and funders. BASRC's reform efforts proceeded in two phases. During Phase I of its work (1996–2001), BASRC funded 86 "Leadership Schools" in 6 Bay Area counties. By the fall of 1999 the initial $50 million had been matched by $62 million more in public and private funds.[1] During Phase II (2001–2006), BASRC invested in reform efforts in four *focal* districts and featured coaching as a reform strategy. The Hewlett and Annenberg Foundations provided $40 million in funds and other sources contributed a total of about the same amount. Throughout, the Collaborative's signature reform tool was the school-based Cycle of Inquiry, in which teachers used student data to assess and plan for instruction.[2]

BASRC's Organizational Form

BASRC was an organization of a particular stripe. As an *intermediary*, BASRC operated between districts and schools and funders. The Collaborative vetted

M. McLaughlin (✉)
Stanford University, Stanford, CA, USA
e-mail: milbrey@stanford.edu

[1]BASRC's regional membership also included an additional 146 Membership Schools, 40 districts, and several regional school reform support organizations and foundations which participated without funding.

[2]See McLaughlin and Mitra (2004).

A. Hargreaves et al. (eds.), *Second International Handbook of Educational Change*,
Springer International Handbooks of Education 23, DOI 10.1007/978-90-481-2660-6_5,
© Springer Science+Business Media B.V. 2010

participation in the reform effort, carried out an oversight role, and enacted a vision of whole school/whole district reform. As a *temporary* organization, funding periods defined its lifespan. According to a founding board member, there was never any intent to make BASRC a permanent addition to the Bay Area's education landscape.

Intermediary organizations have evolved as a response to a number of policy problems – how to make effective use of scarce resources, how to foster the spread of ideas and technologies, and how to coordinate missions across organizational and political lines. Likewise, temporary structures spring up in both public and private sectors to carry out special missions. Though both organizational forms are valued as promising policy responses, empirical research about the function and contribution of temporary intermediaries is limited. This chapter draws on 10 years of site-based and survey research in BASRC schools and districts to consider BASRC as a temporary intermediary charged with regional education reform. As background for the analysis, we first discuss the general opportunities and challenges associated with intermediary organizations and temporary structures. To identify and illustrate lessons for policy and practice, we then turn to BASRC's experience as a temporary intermediary charged with bringing about education reform in the San Francisco Bay Area.

Intermediary Organizations

The appearance of intermediaries in both public and private sectors reflects the contemporary appeal of interactive, boundary-spanning organizations dispatched to connect organizations and individuals. Intermediaries of various descriptions generally are capacity-building organizations, operating to increase the capability of individuals, organizations, or systems.[3] Several features of intermediary organizations make them uniquely suited to play the roles of connector and broker. Many intermediaries are non-system actors and so have flexibility not available to public agencies. They enjoy multiple connections and complex relationships that permit them to act across institutional domains. Intermediaries such as BASRC live "at the boundaries...neither 'of' the system nor wholly outside it" (McDonald, McLaughlin, & Corcoran, 2002, p. 6). A positional aspect that adds value is their "betweenness" (Botes & Mitchell, 1995; Scott, 2003). Intermediaries can move between public and private agencies, individual and organizational concerns, and institutions with a nimbleness typically unavailable to bureaucracies or public agencies. Intermediaries "add value to the world mostly through what they enable *other* players to do (or do better)" (Briggs, 2003, p. 3).

---

[3] Initial conceptions of intermediaries featured them as mediating structures linking "the individual in his private life and vast institutions of the public order" (Berger, 1976; Kerrine & Neuhaus, 1979, p. 10). Subsequently, intermediaries' roles extended to include inter-institutional and inter-organizational transactions of various sorts.

However, intermediaries wrestle with their own set of positional challenges. Intermediaries such as BASRC must determine the appropriate balance between delivering their own vision and building the capacity of the organization they are trying to help (Sherman, 2002). To what extent does an intermediary see itself as transforming the field by imposing knowledge and skills, versus supporting a change that is coming from within the organization with which it works (Wynn, 2000)? Similarly, staff experience and background influence relationships intermediaries can establish with focal organizations and the organization's credibility (Honig, 2004). Do actors associated with an intermediary have credibility in the array of institutions with which they interact?

A related challenge involves establishing channels to enable a two-way communication between the intermediary and its target – channels that provide ongoing information about what client organizations need and enable intermediaries to be responsive in a dynamic environment. Briggs (2003) describes the environment in which intermediaries exist as "fluid, where demand for what they do can shift or erode, where the functions of intermediaries and other players may overlap, where the rules are ambiguous" (p. 2). Responding strategically to clients' shifting and evolving needs requires that intermediaries know what is needed when and are able to scan the environment and adapt well (Briggs, 2003, pp. 9–15). Funder relationships also test many intermediaries when they seek to attend to funders' interests while remaining faithful to their own goals as an organization, a problem of serving "many masters" (Briggs, 2003).

Temporary Organizations

Temporary organizations such as BASRC are created with a specific purpose and duration in mind. They are "defined as a set of diversely skilled people working together on a complex task over a limited time period" (Goodman & Goodman, 1976, p. 494). Temporary organizations assume varied forms and missions – such as presidential commissions, task forces, negotiating teams, research and development projects, and structures charged with providing a particular service. Their charter confines their mission and the organization's termination is tied to a specified time or event – when the commission or task force completes its work, and when an experiment, pilot project, or reform initiative ends. "These new structures are *themselves* innovations in the larger system – innovations designed to further installation of other, more specific innovations in target systems" (Miles, 1964, p. 19n).

Temporary organizations are created to do something that existing, permanent organizations cannot do, or accomplish easily. Typically they are invented to bypass "anti-change" elements in permanent organizations, to focus on a problem outside the purview of existing systems, or take on a problem for which permanent organizations have no regularly specified procedures or capacity. "They are formed with a sense of making a difference" (Goodman & Goodman, 1976, p. 496). Temporary organizations are distinctive in their ability to focus on a discrete task, and operate on a narrowed, finite time table. To accomplish their charge, they need to keep a steady pace and cannot put off decisions in the way permanent organizations often can.

Time presents perhaps the greatest problem to both the temporary system and the organizations or systems it seeks to influence. Many temporary organizations operate under unrealistic timelines – constraints imposed at their creation that often reflect insufficient initial understanding of the scope and complexity of the task assigned. Further, temporary organizations' schedules as developed by funders or commissioners often overlook or minimize the start-up requirements of getting a new structure staffed and up and running. Implicit in the plans for temporary organizations frequently is the assumption that they will be "good to go" once the doors are opened and the first check is cut. Yet, staffs responsible for carrying out the organization's work need clear specification of rules, expectations, and procedures. These organizational processes and procedures take time to establish, yet funding and activity schedules often neglect this important management task for the new, temporary organization (Miles, 1964). Temporary organizations also commonly experience difficulty establishing effective, credible channels of communication with clients in permanent systems. Building the relationships essential to an effective communication strategy takes staff-intensive effort – a resource in short supply in a temporary organization on a fast pace to meet ambitious goals.

The "extra-system" character of temporary organizations provides flexibility and protection from the daily pressures felt by actors in permanent systems. This feature permits single-mindedness but it also can isolate temporary organizations and their staff from real-world dynamics. Being cut off in this manner can generate "them/us" divisions and "boutique" products impractical in the everyday context of permanent organizations. The education reform arena is replete with examples of initiatives nurtured in a special project setting but unsustainable once special funding and attention end – pilot projects that led nowhere.

Miles (1964) and others who study temporary systems comment on a tendency toward "grandiose, unattainable goals" (p. 481). Unrealistic goals may reflect the relative freedom from the constraints of permanent organizations and the warrant to think broadly. But they can also be "excessively noble in sentiment and impossibly difficult" (op. cit.). Temporary organizations walk a fine line between imagining the innovative "out of the box" plan for action, and simultaneously considering the doable.

And, temporary organizations often confront resistance *because* they are temporary. Perhaps nowhere more than in the field of education are actors cynical about the "flavor of the month" or the next good idea brought into a district by a well-intentioned group or task force. Educators often dismiss projects associated with temporary organizations as efforts to be endured but ultimately dismissed as "here today, gone tomorrow" resources. Temporary organizations such as BASRC, then, face special obstacles when it comes to handing off their efforts to permanent systems. Have they fostered change in attention, systems, and resources that will be continued, or will the target organization return to the *status quo* once the temporary structure is dismantled?

BASRC in Action

BASRC's founding was big news; the size of its purse and its ambitious, innova-tive mission created significant buzz in the Bay Area public education community.[4] BASRC brought a vision of regional educational reform, tools and strategies for achieving this vision, and resources in the form of dollars and technical sup-ports. BASRC's theory of change featured elements of school and district culture it assumed essential to improved student outcomes – a professional learning com-munity focused on inquiry and evidence-based decisions about practices. In many respects, BASRC functioned as planners and funders intended, moving between schools, districts, support providers,[5] funders, and others to advance its mission of regional reform. In other respects, the Collaborative fell short of its goals; many schools and districts struggled to carry out BASRC's mission and among those that did, the end of the initiative saw serious questions of sustainability.

Many of these shortfalls can be understood in terms of BASRC's organizational form. Here we explore the strengths and weaknesses of BASRC as a temporary intermediary. First, we look at the roles BASRC assumed and the ways in which it added value and promoted reform. Then we turn to the challenges that frustrated BASRC's efforts. What factors in the sites and the Collaborative itself account for the significant variation seen in the implementation and outcomes of BASRC's efforts? Finally, we consider the lessons BASRC's experience teaches about the role and function of a temporary intermediary at the helm of regional education reform.

BASRC as Reform Agent

The Collaborative constructed three broad roles to implement its reform goals: *grant maker, broker, and educator.*

Grant maker. BASRC acted as a scout for funders, establishing application and vetting procedures for the schools or districts. Funders expected that BASRC would develop a reform with coherence at the initiative level, capable of generat-ing regional reform capacity. Through its support of Leadership Schools and focal districts, BASRC re-granted over $100 million to support locally proposed reform efforts. Not surprisingly, educators were positive about BASRC's funding for their reform efforts and appreciative of the Collaborative's flexibility compared to that of public agencies. They also were positive about BASRC's accountability strategy, the Review of Progress – a strategy designed to establish and enforce standards for self-regulation and mutual accountability among its members. The R.O.P. process asked schools to document their reform progress and state their plans for the fol-lowing year. This document underwent a peer review process by colleagues and

---

[4]Wildermuth (1995).

[5]BASRC termed individuals and organizations providing technical assistance to BASRC schools "support providers."

BASRC coaches through the local collaborative network. Ultimately, the R.O.P. was intended as a way for BASRC to hold schools accountable for making reform progress and to provide guidance to schools as they refined their reform goals.

Broker. BASRC played different brokering roles at different times and for different constituencies. Sometimes the Collaborative connected individuals and groups both inside and outside the system. For instance, BASRC brokered relationships with other support providers such as content-focused professional development on reading. At other times, BASRC brokered knowledge, by helping to translate, coordinate, and align perspectives on reform practices within and across the regional participants.

BASRC defined its broker role in two complementary ways: as a builder of ties and as a convener of stakeholders. BASRC brought educators together from a wide variety of school contexts through its Summer Institutes, role-alike networks, and Best Practices Institutes. Participants generally viewed these activities positively. A number of district administrators and principals commented that they had few opportunities to engage with educators outside their district and that they found these cross-school and -district conversations stimulating and valuable.

Despite the value experienced by those who participated in these opportunities to connect with other educators and experts, these brokering efforts experienced limited success. Attendance was spotty; competing demands for time and attention figured prominently as obstacles. Though a temporary organization operates in time and space apart from the permanent organizations it seeks to inform or change, the individuals who are the focus of such efforts rarely have the luxury to suspend their daily responsibilities. And the sprawling geography of the Bay Area region meant that participation in BASRC events required significant commute time, extending time away from schools and offices. The BASRC-supported professional exchanges educators reported valuing most involved opportunities without demands of travel and daylong meetings. For instance, though almost half of the principals reported that they had not attended a BASRC regional convention, nearly half said that they found opportunities to work with other schools in their district's local collaborative very or extremely useful. Similarly, a district administrator said that BASRC's local collaborative strategy "opened up an opportunity for us to join in partnership within our own district that we might not have thought of." BASRC's most effective brokering supports ultimately may have existed in the relationships and structures it built on the ground, up-close rather than regional exchanges.

Educator. Central to BASRC's educator role were strategies, tools, and technical assistance for teachers and administrators to learn about the Cycle of Inquiry, its foundational process for using data to investigate practice and plan for change that promised to increase student achievement. During Phase I, that support featured workshops and Summer Institutes as well as on-site assistance from BASRC staff. During Phase II, BASRC supported coaches at both school and district levels to provide hands-on assistance with the Cycle of Inquiry and other elements of its reform vision. Many teachers and administrators said that they would not have made progress in the areas of evidence-based decision making and comfort with data without BASRC. A teacher commented:

BASRC's biggest contribution—they made you do these Cycles of Inquiry. Initially like "oh my God." But in retrospect, in addition to all of the staff development and materials, were the concepts and structures and systems that would never have been established had it not been for their guidance and requirements.

Some administrators described BASRC's concentration on inquiry in terms of culture change. "This has been a major shift—really looking at what we do, what we need based on data, based on how well we know the district. [The BASRC coach] was really able to pull it together and drive it home." In particular, they commented about how a major part of the "culture change" BASRC enabled was to get beyond the "culture of nice," to analyze their own work critically and ask tough questions ". . .and say if that's not working well, then let's throw it out."

To expose BASRC members to new ideas, the Collaborative offered various 1-day or multi-day sessions focused on promising practices. Presentations by experts provided teachers, administrators, and local collaborative coaches with concrete examples of practices. BASRC's various professional development offerings received generally high marks from participants and positive recognition of BASRC's educator role throughout the Collaborative's duration. A teacher stressed how important it was for a district team to be off-site, hearing about promising strategies, and "talk about some issues that are vital to the district." Another district superintendent thought "BASRC provides the type of professional development that can grow capacity in a district."

However, response to BASRC's education efforts was not uniformly positive, and varied in both reception and consequence depending on site or individual readiness to learn. Schools and districts primed to begin, or just embarking on, the use of evidence-based practices were quicker to credit BASRC with building their local capacity. In particular, districts *ready* to engage BASRC's vision reported that the Collaborative's tools, procedures, and coaching enabled them to go to the next stage and, by their report, change culture. BASRC staff's feedback in this context often was deemed "excellent" because "working from the outside, they look at us through a different lens." Teachers and administrators talked about BASRC as "providing needed focus," "a facilitator," "a vehicle for change," "a kick in the butt," "an external force to keep you moving," and "preventing [the district] from staying stuck in management-type things."

Not all BASRC staff experienced a smooth course working with schools or districts, however. Some coaches described difficulties in using some BASRC tools to help teachers learn. These differences turned less on the nature of the feedback BASRC coaches and others provided than on administrator and teacher willingness to hear critical feedback about the progress of their reform efforts. Across all of the focal districts and schools, BASRC tools, supports, and coaches added greatest value in schools and districts already committed to reform and eager for support. Districts and schools with less concrete engagement with education reform often experienced BASRC's efforts as "all process and no product," and "providing too little direction." These different assessments of BASRC's work highlight the significance of "readiness" as an important aspect of BASRC's ability to achieve, given its status as a temporary organization.

Its status as an intermediary provided BASRC a high degree of independence and agency in pursuing regional reform. Participating Bay Area schools and districts valued the Collaborative's flexible organizational structure and resources. However, though BASRC can count some important accomplishments in its decade of regional reform work, it also struggled with many of the obstacles associated with temporary systems and intermediary organizations – challenges that ultimately limited the Collaborative's impact in the region. BASRC's experience provides instructive perspective on the limits of this organizational form as a reform agent.

Ambitious Scale and Scope: Struggles with Regional Diversity

In theory, an intermediary organization ought to be able to educate and build capacity at the same time. In practice, educating and building capacity within a complex, interdependent, and loosely coupled system such as the San Francisco Bay Area proved to be an overly ambitious undertaking. The bold scale and scope of BASRC's work meant that the organization faced the difficult task of providing services and resources across the broad and differentiated population of Bay Area schools and districts. BASRC's reform vision – culture change in schools and districts that supported evidence-based decision making and attention to equity – made the outsider's role an especially challenging one. BASRC was not attempting to "deliver" a well-specified reform package; rather, the Collaborative sought to introduce the tools and habits that would enable participating sites to make fundamental change in the business of schooling and conceptions of practice. BASRC's executive director described it "not as a program but a vision – a vision of what schools should look and feel like."

The Collaborative's initial 86 Leadership Schools varied significantly in student demographics, faculty background, community contexts, and grade levels. And most important to the outcome of BASRC's work, Leadership Schools joined the Collaborative with substantively different reform histories. Some Leadership Schools had extensive experience with the evidence-based, whole-school reform efforts BASRC promoted. Others, especially schools with a poor track record of student achievement, had little to no experience with the strategies BASRC advanced.

Many schools felt BASRC's tools and strategies did not meet their needs. Schools advanced in evidence-based practices found various BASRC technical assistance and support efforts too elementary, while many schools new to inquiry found sessions too abstract to be useful to them (McLaughlin & Mitra, 2004). BASRC recognized these problems but had insufficient capacity to provide Leadership Schools with tailored supports. BASRC sought to meet requests for site-specific technical assistance by underwriting support providers for each Leadership School. In some instances, these matches were effective; in many others, however, successful matches were not made. Schools discovered that the "pool" of support providers in the region was thin and that available support providers either did not fit their needs or were ineffective. Staffing constraints, an insufficient number of qualified support providers, and the Collaborative's own relative newness to the enterprise often constrained BASRC to a "transmission" role and, as a teacher put it, "produced lots of big fat binders."

In its Phase II work, to move away from standardized tools and strategies, BASRC hired school- and district-level coaches, as well as local collaborative coaches, to work with teachers and administrators. In practice, however, the work of transforming the culture of even a single district consisting of multiple schools, each with its own different context and needs, proved a complex and demanding task. One way BASRC responded to this challenge was to keep its tools and technical assistance relatively non-specific in terms of content. This strategy reflected a philosophical commitment on BASRC's part to site-based input and local development of specific reform plans and strategies. But this approach left many responsible for carrying out reform efforts in schools and districts frustrated and unclear about how to proceed. As a reform coordinator in a focal district put it, "BASRC staff contributed with implementing change without a recipe but with the ingredients." It soon became apparent that in schools and districts lacking substantial experience with inquiry, more concrete guidance was needed – especially in light of the relatively limited timeframe under which reformers were operating.

Many protocols ran into problems because of the significant variation among settings in which they were used. In some schools, protocols did not connect with teachers' day-to-day realities; in others, protocols were ineffective because, as a coach put it, "the protocol didn't teach them anything new." The Literacy Learning Communities or the Equity Learning Communities BASRC introduced as a way to support teachers' implementation of reform strategies never came together for similar reasons. The diversity of teachers' experiences, expertise, and commitments to various literacy programs meant that a single "curriculum" or focused discussion was difficult to stage.

Ambitious Goals: Too Much, Too Soon

BASRC's goals were broad and ambitious – in retrospect, too much so given the organization's capacity and timeline. The Collaborative was commissioned to "close the achievement gap," to build appetite and capacity for regional change – a breathtaking charge resonant with worries about temporary systems, that in the presence of high-flying, unattainable goals, "failure and disenchantment are practically guaranteed" (Miles, 1964, p. 481). BASRC's status as a regional intermediary stretched its capacity to respond effectively to the diverse needs and experience of participants. Its temporary status compounded the problem. Since the Collaborative was not in it for the long haul, many schools and districts poised to take advantage of BASRC's resources were unable to reach "take off" point during their participation in the Collaborative. This outcome might have been different had BASRC been able to target intensive, site-specific resources. The Collaborative had insufficient organizational capacity to scan the region for these resources. But even if its plan of action had allowed such focusing, its temporary status made BASRC relatively inflexible in terms of pace of change, and so unable to make the adjustments in timelines and expectations a permanent intermediary could.

Staffing Issues and a Tight Timeline

BASRC introduced its two-tier coaching strategy – executive coaches to work with the superintendent and school coaches to work at the school level – as a way to honor the organization's belief in the importance of ground-level development while also providing material, specific implementation assistance. Though BASRC expended much effort and many resources to do a better job of supporting the reform progress of its diverse membership, the Collaborative's coaches struggled with their task.

BASRC's coaching staff, though they were educators with substantial reform experience, generally did not bring the background needed on the ground. Coaches shared no common experience with each other and in some instances even with their "coachee." For example, only one of the BASRC school-level coaches had been a principal. And though all executive coaches were former superintendents, only one of the executive coaches engaged to "teach" BASRC had previous district experience with BASRC. Further, one executive coach questioned "the assumption that if you hire people who have been successful superintendents, that was going to be good for coaching. . ."

In addition, the Collaborative's coaching staff was new to the challenges before them. Their own lack of clarity about their roles and the expectations hampered their ability to promote BASRC's vision or bring coherence to the initiative. The coaches had little opportunity to develop a shared understanding about ways to respond to members' different styles, needs, and expectations. As a consequence, both executive and school coaches were uncertain about how much latitude they had to create site-specific plans. The local collaborative coaches (LoCoCos), who were district employees hired to support BASRC's work in the district, also wished for more role clarity. But perhaps more important, they wished for more time. LoCoCos often felt overwhelmed. They described their coaching role as "like a second full-time job."

These staffing issues with BASRC coaches responsible for carrying out Phase II reform work in focal districts and schools meant that, in practice, BASRC's coaching model was unevenly implemented and the pace of the reform left little opportunity for mid-course correction at any level.

Sustaining Reform: Managing the Handoff

Temporary organizations such as BASRC must, at some point, hand off their work to permanent organizations. Creators of temporary organizations expect that these provisional resources will engender change in systems, organizations, and individuals – new practices that are incorporated into permanent organizations' routines and norms. On sustainability grounds, BASRC's impact on Bay Area education has been disappointing. The Collaborative did accomplish some changes in district systems, but they were few. In one focal district, the local collaborative structure is in place, which "would not have happened" without BASRC. In other districts and schools, some BASRC practices remain, such as "selecting and tracking target students" and convening school leadership teams.

Signs are that the reforms BASRC championed will fade in many schools and districts. For example, though several BASRC Phase I schools that were in Phase II focal districts continued and deepened their inquiry-based reform work, by 2005, schools new to BASRC had caught up, with teacher survey data showing the same inquiry levels. However, both groups showed decline during the final year when BASRC funding support had been reduced, suggesting that inquiry practices had not been embedded in school culture in ways that were sustainable in the longer term, even in schools with almost a decade of BASRC experience. One district administrator says that in order to sustain the district's conversations about evidence-based learning it needs "to continue its relationship with BASRC" because the "personnel resources and ...the opportunity to talk about education ...at different levels" is even more helpful than the financial resources. The district has not created its own internal structures and knowledge resources to continue these sorts of cross-level educational conversations when this temporary system disappears. According to their BASRC executive coach, BASRC's failure with this district is "sobering, given how many resources and how much time has gone into that district."

The lack of adequate resources comprises a significant obstacle to sustainability. BASRC's flagship reform, the Cycle of Inquiry, requires dedicated staff and attention. It is not a reform to be "learned" and then considered self-winding. Change of the sort BASRC promulgated and tools such as the Cycle of Inquiry require ongoing learning and support if they are to deepen, spread, and retain vitality. The Cycle of Inquiry requires time for individual practitioners to collect and analyze data as well as reflect on practice. These activities must in turn be supported by data collection and analysis capacity at both the school and district levels. When BASRC funding ended, so did dedicated attention to a Cycle of Inquiry in most all schools and focal districts. As a temporary intermediary, BASRC introduced reforms that generally could not be sustained by existing district budgets and staff – especially in a context of high stakes accountability and state mandated curriculum – even when administrators were supportive.

Significant turnover in district and school staff also compromised the sustainability of BASRC tools and vision. The reform BASRC brought to participating schools and districts was not one of simple activity structures, but one that assumed change in organizational culture, norms, and expectations. So as staff left, so did the vision. Further, BASRC's executive coaches worked only with the superintendent – other central office administrators were not included in coaching or, in some instances, in feedback sessions. BASRC elected this strategy on the assumption that Superintendents would be most comfortable and candid in a one-on-one coaching format. However, this tactic meant that other central office administrators were not brought into the district reform effort in a meaningful way, and so were unable to provide substantive support. Yet, experience teaches that middle management backing is key both to implementing and sustaining district-wide reforms (Spillane & Burch, 2004).

All of these factors contributed to a survey-based conclusion of little "BASRC district effect." Responses from district administrators in districts participating in Phase I *and* Phase II show no significant differences over time (1998–2004) in their assessments of "district reform leadership" or "central office reform culture" – two scales measuring key aspects of BASRC's focal district strategy such as support for schools' focus on teaching and learning and use of data as a basis for decision making (reform leadership), and district's active involvement in school reform and district administrators' learning (reform culture).[6] However, a modest "BASRC effect" is evident in the 4 Phase II focal districts. Compared to 11 non-focal districts, they started with lower district indicators of reform culture and caught up to or surpassed the non-focal districts on measures of distributed leadership; district central office reform culture at the end of Phase II. Survey and interview data suggest that some BASRC-related change in district office culture was beginning to occur as the initiative drew to an end.

As a temporary organization, BASRC could not continue supports for participating districts once its funding came to an end. Because the Collaborative did not achieve the degree of system and organizational change it sought, it was unable in most cases to hand off its reform strategies and programs. The overall demand on participating schools and districts made by BASRC strategies and vision was greater than could be sustained on a permanent basis, all things equal. Despite funders' intent and the Collaborative's innovative work, BASRC in the end functioned more as a "special project" than the transformative force for education reform its supporters imagined.

Lessons for the Field: Temporary Systems, Intermediaries, and Culture Change

Can a temporary intermediary organization stimulate and sustain learning and growth on the ground? The response, drawing on BASRC's experience, is "it depends." The success of an ad hoc reform intermediary hinges critically on the readiness and capability of target organizations to take advantage of the tools and resources it provides, connections to additional resources it facilitates, and the school and district subscription to the overall operating vision. In BASRC's case, its status as a temporary intermediary compromised its ability to be an effective outside reform resource. In hindsight, this shortfall reflects to a significant extent the mismatch between BASRC's timeline and the pace of reform progress in many participating districts. Many schools and districts simply were not ready or able to engage the reform process BASRC assumed, and BASRC had neither

---

[6]BASRC District Administrator Survey – 1998, 2002, 2004.

the time nor the resources to respond effectively to these different paces of reform. BASRC's own management strategies are equally important to understanding the Collaborative's relatively disappointing impact on education reform in the Bay Area. In this case we consider lessons for the field based on BASRC's experience.

Address Sustainability Issues at the Start

Temporary organizations assuming a change agent's role must continually attend to sustainability issues once the funding clock starts ticking. Given a limited timeline to meet goals and the challenges inherent in creating sustainable solutions, temporary organizations need to focus on the attitudes and structures necessary to support and sustain the new practices from the beginning of their relationship.

Commitment. One important aspect of sustainability resides in the initial commitment of participants. In retrospect, many BASRC staff wonder how committed Collaborative participants really were to making the fundamental changes BASRC advocated – or whether primary motivation for some participants lay in the possibility of new funds.

BASRC conceived of its reforms in terms of learning, and an implicit assumption was made that, once learned and value demonstrated, tools and routines such as the Cycle of Inquiry would be incorporated into school and district practices. Sustainability issues associated with allocation of needed resources – such as funds, personnel, and time – were not addressed directly at the outset. Furthermore, key players in focal districts often did not recognize the kinds of supports that were needed to sustain the work. Even districts inclined to sustain and even extend BASRC reforms found themselves scrambling to do so as funding drew to an end. We saw that while commitment may be an essential element of a successful handoff, more is needed to embed reform goals and practices.

Organizational "hooks". A deficiency of organizational "hooks" to which individual participants could attach their new perspectives and learning diminished the spread and sustainability of BASRC tools and vision. A number of teachers commented on the lack of expectations for them to share what they learned at BASRC gatherings, such as the network meetings. Others felt unable to act on BASRC's tools and reform strategies once they returned to their "regular jobs" because they lacked the warrant or support to do so. Explicit understandings and expectations about how the information, tools, and resources BASRC provided would be brought back to districts and schools – and explicit hooks for them – might have broadened their impact on practice or system routines.

Likewise, by expressly defining an "emissary" role for BASRC participants, the Collaborative might have lessened the "them/us" feelings sometimes expressed by non-participants – feelings that BASRC activities and mission had nothing to do with them or that participants received special resources and treatment. In some instances, educators participating in the Collaborative were relatively isolated. In one district, for example, an effective local collaborative structure added sustained value and connections to participants, but created resentment feelings elsewhere in the district "that some of the schools were the 'special schools' that went up and did BASRC stuff, and some of them weren't." The whole-school, whole-district message was not uniformly received or understood and BASRC strategies did not address effectively issues of "spread" beyond BASRC participants.

Temporary Organizations Require Strategic Site Selection

BASRC's decade at the helm of regional education reform provides clear instruction about the importance of a "match" between the capacities and mission of a temporary intermediary and its reform target. BASRC was most successful in supporting sustainable reform in schools and districts that were ready to take up its vision of reform and experienced in the evidence-based strategies used to advance it. Schools and districts less far along this reform path generally found BASRC's tools and resources less valuable (funding excepted), and struggled to apply the loosely defined BASRC protocol and strategies to their settings. These sites, just getting started, had scant experience with inquiry and were unfamiliar with a culture of evidence-based reflection and focused critique.

Culture change takes time. But as a temporary organization, BASRC lacked a timeline compatible with this goal. Schools and districts "ready" for BASRC had histories with similar reform strategies; their growth and change with BASRC support reflected much more than their years with the Collaborative. In hindsight, it seems that a temporary organization of BASRC's tenure is ill-suited to promote a significant normative and skill-based reform in settings lacking foundational experience and readiness. Almost all of the sites were moving toward BASRC's vision of reform, but more time was needed for them to get there than was available under BASRC's grant-supported tenure. In these instances, a permanent organization able to partner over an extended period of time and provide "just in time" resources would seem a more effective reform agent. An important lesson from BASRC's experience is that readiness to pursue a particular reform vision is essential when the reform time frame is delimited and goals are ambitious.

Measurable Goals

BASRC was "accountability lite." The Leadership School application of Phase I as well as the needs assessments and related requirements associated with Phase II membership asked educators to set out clear goals and strategies for meeting them. However, little clarity existed throughout the Collaborative's life about what participating schools and districts were accountable for and on what timeline. Looking back, several BASRC leaders regret the absence of a memorandum of understanding to anchor expectations for both the Collaborative and participants.

BASRC's single-minded reform focus was not matched in participating districts, especially as state and federal high-stake accountability requirements turned up pressure for improved student achievement. Even without considerations such as those brought by No Child Left Behind, participating schools and districts by and large did not share BASRC's sense of urgency about either a pace of change or expected outcomes. Thus, as grant periods neared their end, both local educators and BASRC staff were unclear about what was expected of participating schools and districts, and when and how it would be measured. Reflecting on the Phase II experience and its variable outcomes, BASRC's head school coach said "I think we would all agree that from the very beginning we formed partnerships with districts that were rather vague agreements and we didn't really investigate the district's capacity to do the work, certainly at the district level."

BASRC's experience highlights the need for measurable goals and agreed-upon indicators, especially when the relationship is a temporary one aiming at sustainable outcomes. BASRC's executive coach, who initially resisted setting targets because they conflicted with what he called his "constructivist approach to learning," reflected on this lesson: "I want to be clear that the next time we go out with something we want to accomplish, that we're clear about it. . .even if they [participating districts] don't approve the goals, at least we'll have clear, measurable goals [to hold them accountable]."

Balancing the Tension Between Prescribing and Co-constructing

BASRC's process-heavy approach proved difficult for a temporary organization to execute effectively, especially when its "clients" were a diverse lot. In theory, BASRC's coaching approach might have been a way to create a balance between prescribed practices and local adaptations. However, given the bumpy start of the coaching strategy and the relatively short time it was in place, the Collaborative's experience supplies a cautionary tale about implementation but little solid evidence of the value of coaching as a way to achieve this balance.

Another way to address the diversity in BASRC's clients might involve a differentiated portfolio of tools, resources, and approaches. BASRC had limited success dealing with member diversity across the region. To this point, the head executive coach advised: "Even though lots of money has been poured into these districts over the years, they were not all on the starting block. So their level of readiness to accomplish what we wanted to accomplish was very different. And so we need differential models. We need [models for] places where we start at ground zero, and we need [models] for places where we can enter and really accelerate their movement forward."

In addition to the intrinsic initial value of a diversified portfolio, this capacity in a permanent or semi-permanent intermediary would allow response to any falloff in effort that might occur due to factors such as turnover in leadership or teaching positions. Intermediaries can act as relatively stable actors in the unstable environment in which schools are located. The instability of the political context in which schools reside makes it extremely difficult for schools and districts to adopt a long-term vision for success and then sustain the organizational capacity to achieve this vision over time. An intermediary organization can become the keeper of the vision and can respond flexibly to fill the different needs that emerge as districts move to implement their reform strategies. However, as a temporary organization BASRC could not assume that role.

Managing Temporary Organizations

BASRC was "building the plane while flying it." Plans were developed as the initiative went along; tools and strategies were tweaked or modified along the way. Leadership Schools – especially those new to evidence-based reform – found the Collaborative's ongoing adjustment of protocols and strategies somewhat problematic during Phase I. The significant sea changes of focus on the district during Phase II were even more unsettling to participants. Changes in priorities, direction, or routines that occurred during the first years of the focal district strategy further complicated basic issues such as a lack of clear role definition for coaches and the introduction of insufficiently specific reform tools.

Role Clarity

BASRC's experience suggests that in order to interpret successfully the Collaborative's vision – and stay true to that vision – coaches and other staff required a greater degree of clarity than they achieved about both the vision and the practices intended to support it. An executive coach remarked on the absence of a well-developed conception when work began with the superintendents. "When I took this job I knew some parts of it would be under construction, but I thought there would be a more well-thought out model, and there wasn't. But it has been pretty much 'stumble your way through'...."

School-level coaches worried from the start about expectations, what they were supposed to do, and how to assess their work. One said: "We're still trying to figure it out, what our theory of action is..." And another pointed to the organization's own structure as an issue: "We're independent contractors. There is no loop for us to enter into. We're sort of out of the loop."

If time and resources had been dedicated at the outset to allow them to work together to define their roles and establish explicit expectations, the coaches might have achieved the clarity and common language they sought. Role ambiguity created stress within the organization as well. As a temporary organization, the amount of "start up time" that BASRC could afford to spend building its own foundation of resources was limited. The BASRC staff responsible for the school coaching strategy recognized the problems stemming from this initial lack of role clarity:

> ... real live bodies are out in the field every day and they're doing something. And I have more questions about, (a) what are you doing? Are you clear about the outcomes that you're hoping to achieve when you're out there? (b) how does the school work and the district work inform itself?

School and district participants similarly were unclear about their roles and responsibilities to the Collaborative. For example, many Summer Institute attendees were surprised by the expressed expectation that they would take what they learned back to their respective schools and districts, to help others understand BASRC's vision and goals, and to gain support for BASRC-related activities. Additionally, Summer Institute participants repeatedly pointed out that it took them 3 entire days to grasp BASRC's vision and tools, but they would have very limited time in the context of their day-to-day activities to present their knowledge to others.

Conclusions

Where BASRC's vision of inquiry and evidence-based reform was realized, even if incompletely, the power of its conception of what was needed to bring about education reform (i.e., changes in organizational culture and the integration of evidence-based practices at both the school and district level), as well as the value of the resources it brought to the task were evident. This conclusion from BASRC's 10-year experience confirms funders' and founders' vision about the focus and character of significant education reform, especially reform addressing equity of educational outcomes.

However, other lessons offer a cautionary tale: BASRC's organizational form was ill-suited to its mission and charge. As a regional intermediary with limited capability to differentiate its tools and resources, the Collaborative was unable to provide an effective response to the significant diversity in experience, district contexts, and student demographics existing in its broad membership. Even though BASRC employed application procedures designed to reduce member variability in such important dimensions as reform appetite, buy-in, and capacity, local differences in these elements nonetheless thwarted BASRC in its role as educator. As a consequence, the scope of BASRC's change agent responsibilities overreached the organization's ability to respond in both phases of its work. Over time, BASRC might have been able to evolve a way of working with schools and districts that provided both consistency of vision and opportunities for local adaptation. The Phase II coaching strategy held promise to this effect. But the Collaborative's status as a temporary organization meant that, except for schools and districts experienced in inquiry and ready to take up the reform BASRC envisioned, reformers sought too much, too soon. The organization had insufficient time to work with participants to make adaptations or even to develop the internal community of practice BASRC staff needed to carry a confident, consistent message to schools and districts.

BASRC's experience counsels that a temporary organization generally is a poor choice to bring about change in norms and values, or to teach complex skills of the sort required by the Collaborative's evidence-based reform. For many of participating schools and districts, BASRC's strategies could not be fully mastered and its tools could not be deeply embedded in everyday work in the period of time available. BASRC's experience affirms and illustrates the vulnerabilities associated with both temporary and intermediary organizations (see Table 1). It advises that,

Table 1 Distinguishing features of temporary and intermediary organizations

	Temporary organization	Temporary intermediary	Intermediary organization
Strengths	• Created to solve a particular problem • Diversely skilled staff • Decisive actor • Aims for quick results	• Flexible actor • Broker • Designed to develop innovative solutions	• Capacity builder • Grant maker • Non-system actors • Connector of disconnected agencies and institutions
Challenges	• Limited timeline to: (1) Build shared understanding of task among diverse, "temporary" staff (2) Develop relationships w/"target" organization (3) Establish effective communication channels (4) Meet own ambitious goals • Isolated from "real world" • Create sustainable solutions	• Acquiring inside knowledge and legitimacy • Assembling necessary organizational capacity	• Manage own vision with specific needs of target organization • Have needed organizational capacity to: (1) Scan the environment for needs (2) Respond flexibly to shifting needs in a dynamic environment (3) Manage scale and scope of work • Manage relationships with funders; serve "two" masters

to be successful, a temporary, intermediary organization promoting regional education reform needs either to provide specific, discrete assistance, or to be extremely strategic in its choice of reform sites, assuring both readiness for and explicit commitment to reform. BASRC's mission called for a stable presence in the region, one that was capable of working over time with schools and districts as they developed their reform goals and achieved the degree of readiness necessary to use the rich array of resources the Collaborative provided. Its organizational form frustrated that mission.

References

Botes, J., & Mitchell, C. (1995, November). Constraints on third party flexibility. *Annals of the American Academy of Political and Social Science, 542*, 168–184.

Briggs, X. (2003). *Working the middle: Roles and challenges of intermediaries*. The Art and Science of Community Solving Project, Harvard University.

Goodman, R. A., & Goodman, L. P. (1976, September). Some management issues on temporary systems: A study of professional development and manpower—the theatre case. *Administrative Science Quarterly, 21*, 494–501.

Honig, M. I. (2004, January 1). The new middle management: Intermediary organizations in education policy implementation. *Educational Evaluation and Policy Analysis, 26*(1), 65–87.

Kerrine, T. M., & Neuhaus, R. J. (1979). Mediating structures: A paradigm for democratic pluralism. *The Annals of the American Academy of Political and Social Science, 446*(1), 10–18.

McDonald, J. P., McLaughlin, M. W., & Corcoran, T. (2002). *Agents of reform: The role and function of intermediary organizations in the Annenberg Challenge.* Paper presented at the AERA.

McLaughlin, M., & Mitra, D. (2004). *The cycle of inquiry as the engine of school reform: Lessons from the Bay Area School Collaborative San Francisco, CA: Bay Area School Collaborative.* San Francisco: Center for Research on the Context of Teaching.

Miles, M. B. (1964). *Innovation in education.* New York: Teachers College Press.

Scott, W. R. (2003). Institutional carriers: Reviewing modes of transporting ideas over time and space and considering their consequences. *Industrial and Corporate Change, 12*(4), 879–894.

Sherman, A. L. (2002). *Empowering compassion: The strategic role of intermediary organizations in building capacity among and enhancing the impact of community transformers.* Charlottesville, VA: Hudson Institute.

Spillane, J., & Burch, P. (2004). *Leading from the middle: Mid-level district staff and instructional improvement.* Chicago: Cross City Campaign for Urban School Reform.

Vargo, M. (2004). Choices and consequences in the Bay Area School Reform Collaborative: Building the capacity to scale up whole-school improvement. In T. K. Glennan, S. J. Bodily, J. R. Galegher & K. A. Kerr (Eds.), *Expanding the reach of education reforms: Perspectives from leaders in the scale-up of educational interventions.* Santa Monica: RAND Corporation

Wildermuth, J. (1995, May 18). $50 million to improve Bay Schools. *San Francisco Chronicle* (p. 1).

Wynn, J. (2000). *The role of local intermediary organizations in the youth development field.* Chicago, IL: The Chapin Hall Center for Children at the University of Chicago.

Change from Without: Lessons from Other Countries, Systems, and Sectors

Andy Hargreaves

Change Alternatives

When Galileo first constructed a telescope and saw that Venus transited around the Sun and not vice versa, and it was concluded that this must also be true of the third planet from the Sun – the Earth – Europeans had to confront the idea that everything did not revolve around them.

Teachers can also only really learn once they get outside their own classrooms and connect with other teachers: when they can see beyond the immediate world that surrounds them. This is one of the essential principles behind professional learning communities. Likewise, schools can only really learn when they connect with other schools – including ones outside their own immediate districts. And the same is true of countries.

In the early twentieth century, educational ideas used to spread around the world freely and in many directions. This is when learning theory was inspired and influenced by European psychologists and philosophers like Piaget, Froebel, Montessori, Pestalozzi, and Vygotsky. Now, ideas circulate more among the globally dominant Anglo-American group of nations and then outwards to other countries through international lending and donor organizations such as the World Bank. Whereas the ideas that circulated almost a century ago were largely pedagogical and psychological ones that involved professional educators, today's globally circulating ideas in education are institutional and systemic and are more confined to politicians, bureaucrats, and their advisors – they are ideas about how to change education on a large scale across entire systems and countries in relation to particular visions of economic reform.

A. Hargreaves (✉)
Boston College, Boston, MA, USA
e-mail: hargrean@bc.edu

A. Hargreaves et al. (eds.), *Second International Handbook of Educational Change*,
Springer International Handbooks of Education 23, DOI 10.1007/978-90-481-2660-6_6,
© Springer Science+Business Media B.V. 2010

The Anglo-Saxon Obsession

In one sense, these developments are a good thing. Especially in America, for too long, educational reform strategies had been circulated incestuously within districts, states, and the country at large. The source of inspiration might shift – from New York City to Cincinnati and Chicago and then to Boston or Denver – but ideas moved around mainly internally – recycling ideological obsessions with tested achievement targets, accountability requirements, greater independence for charters and pilots, and performance-related pay for teachers. All these have been locked within an economic ideology of market competition, measurement-driven performance, granular analysis of data on quality, and the exercise of accountability in relation to standards, targets and outcomes.

The ironic effect of contemporary international interest in large-scale reform, though, is that it has exposed how the countries and systems that have actually been most successful educationally and economically are the ones that provide greater flexibility and innovation in teaching and learning, that invest greater trust in their highly qualified teachers, that value curriculum breadth, and that do not try to orchestrate everything tightly from the top (Wei et al., 2009; McKinsey, 2007).

Most market-driven and individualistically oriented countries in the Anglo-American group of nations suffer from wide achievement gaps between children from poor and rich families respectively, rank poorly in early child-care provisions (except for New Zealand), score particularly badly in child well-being (the UK and U.S. ranking last or next to last out of 21 developed countries) (UNICEF, 2007), and register much higher rates of stress and mental illness, especially among the young, compared to more mainland European-style systems and economies (James, 2008)

By comparison, high-performing Singapore emphasizes "Teach Less, Learn More" and mandates 10% "white space" for teachers to bring individual initiative and creativity into their teaching. Finland – the world leader on results in the Program for International Student Assessment (PISA) tests of sophisticated, applied knowledge in mathematics, science, and literacy, as well as on international ratings of economic competitiveness – avoids national standardized tests altogether and reaches high levels of achievement by attracting highly qualified teachers with supportive working conditions, strong degrees of professional trust, and an inspiring mission of inclusion and creativity (Hargreaves, Halasz, & Pont, 2008). The Canadian province of Alberta, which tucks in just behind Finland in international PISA rankings, has secured its success, in part, by partnering with the teachers' union to develop a 9-year initiative in school-developed innovation (the Alberta Initiative for School Improvement) that involves 90% of the province's schools.

Among a number of emerging reviews of international practice (e.g. McKinsey, 2007), a state-of-the-art review for the U.S. National Staff Development Council of teacher education and professional development practices in the highest-performing countries reveals that high performance is associated with highly qualified teachers being accorded wide professional flexibility for curriculum and pedagogical decisions within broad boundaries (rather than prescribed and standardized requirements) in countries and systems where teachers are well supported in their schools and accorded considerable public and political respect (Darling-Hammond et al., 2009).

What can be learned from international comparative examples such as these, and just as importantly, how can this learning be organized most effectively? What can we take from other effective systems, and how can we learn from the best of them?

Change Travel

Reform is like ripe fruit. It does not usually travel well. In a classic set of studies, Mary K. Stein and her colleagues (Stein, Hubbard, & Mehan, 2004) have examined the destinations and destinies of successful reforms originally designed for New York District 2 in the 1990s. With a tight and detailed design focused on specified literacy instruction, learner-centered leadership, intensive coaching, and a relentless preoccupation with results, a successful reform in New York District 2 was transposed, along with some of its architects and implementers, to the city of San Diego. After some initial increase in measured attainment, the attempt to impose an instant solution on San Diego that had been developed over many years in New York was then declared a failure. The researchers identified many reasons for this, including:

- Military-based and larger San Diego was more conservative yet had less local capacity than smaller District 2 within high-capacity, chutzpah-like New York.
- San Diego's reforms were imposed in 2 years, whereas New York's had been developed over a decade.
- Large and complex secondary schools were included in the San Diego reform, unlike District 2.
- As San Diego's reform mill became increasingly grueling, resentment grew against the interlopers responsible for its implementation.
- Understandings of literacy and instruction that had taken a decade to develop in District 2 were interpreted more superficially in the fast-track reform environment of San Diego.

Stein and colleagues go on to document that a little less was lost in translation with a further attempt at implementation in Philadelphia as implementers tried to be more sensitive to differences of context.

Attempts to transplant reform designs from one country to another in wholesale fashion suffer from the same historic fallacies as the efforts to copy or replicate innovative, lighthouse, or model schools. Attempts to transplant the innovative designs that are evident in many model schools often stumble because implementation timelines are shorter, leaders are less charismatic or exceptional, staff are "captives" of a preceding culture rather than drawn to the school by its mission or being handpicked by the principal, resources are scarcer, and – in consequence – understanding of and

capacity to enact the complex principles and practices that make up the model school
are weak (Fink, 1999).

A second fallacy in trying to spread school-level reform is that if whole systems
cannot be copied, at least particular elements can. This leads to a search for silver
bullets of educational change – easily separated practices or elements that appear to
work well in a group of pilot or outlier schools and that seem to be worth mandating
for or spreading to the rest. Technology is a common temptation. Small schools are
another – ignoring the fact that a badly led or dysfunctional small community, or one
that perpetuates poor teaching and learning practices, can be more claustrophobic
and stressful for staff and students alike than a larger, more anonymous institution
that at least has some variety within it (McQuillan & Englert, 2001).

This fallacy and failing also occurs at the international level of policy borrowing
and policy transfer. For example, from the complexity of high-performing Finland,
policy-makers might be and have been drawn to the fact that all Finnish teachers have masters' degrees and then embark on certifying all their own teachers to
Masters level (McKinsey, 2007). But just as when college-educated teachers were
upgraded in many countries in the 1970s to acquire bachelor of education degrees
on often indifferent, part-time courses, the acquisition of an additional masters-level
qualification in other countries can lose the rigor that first defined it and connected
it to its already highly qualified applicants in the case of Finland. It can become
a merely symbolic process of certification, rather a substantive process of quality
improvement.

In educational reform, Sarason (1990) pointed out everything is connected to
everything else. You cannot change one thing without changing the rest. Cherry-
picking particular policies like small schools or masters' degrees fails to grasp how
they are interconnected with a whole array of other elements. But as we have seen,
trying to transpose an entire system can be culturally inflexible and ineffective too.
Despite these documented difficulties, whole reform designs or isolated elements
of them are often exported impulsively from one country to others. The reasons are
usually ones of ideological compatibility with favored agendas of market competition and political control over the education agenda, and cultural affinity among
the English-speaking nations, along with the physical travel of a very small number
of international consultants or policy pollinators among and beyond them. One key
instance concerns the transposition of national policy strategies from England to
other English-speaking countries. These policy strategies center on setting imposed
targets in tested literacy and numeracy at different age points along with curricular
and training emphases in these core subjects. Strangely, England ranks relatively
poorly on international tests in literacy. The record of its literacy strategy has been
labeled as unsuccessful, contrived, or stuck even by its proponents (e.g. Barber,
2007); parents are increasingly opposed to the testing of younger children (Honore,
2008); and the scope of standardized testing is already being severely scaled back
(Hargreaves & Shirley, 2009). Yet, the country's emphasis on standardized testing
and governmentally imposed system-wide targets has been eagerly adopted by both
Ontario and Australia, even though they already rank among the world's leaders in
literacy attainment (Levin, 2008). These ready-made solutions seem to be going in

search of problems that do not exist or making up ones that aren't there, rather than local problems giving rise to their own solutions.

Change Lessons

This does not mean that we cannot or should not learn from other contexts. But we should do so intelligently in relation to clear principles and multiple examples, sensitively in relation to differences in context, and interactively through dialogue among educators at all levels within and across the respective systems rather than confining discussions and decisions to only the most senior leaders in the system. Let's look at three examples by way of illustration.

Finland

Finland receives a lot of international policy attention. It ranks number one on most PISA assessments, has the narrowest achievement gaps in the developed world, and is a world leader in corporate transparency and economic competitiveness. In 2007, I took a team there for the Organization for Economic Cooperation and Development (OECD)to examine the relationship between leadership and school improvement (Hargreaves et al., 2008). Drawing on our evidence and on the growing body of other literature on the Finnish experience (Aho et al., 2006; Castells & Himanen, 2004; Grubb, 2007; Sahlberg, 2006), this is what we concluded.

After being one of the most backward economies in Europe in the 1950s and after an international banking crisis, the loss of its Russian market, and the escalation of unemployment rates to almost 19% in the early 1990s, Finland consciously connected economic transformation toward being a creative and flexible knowledge economy to the development of a significantly more decentralized education system. This effort has been coordinated at the highest political level where chief executive officers (CEOs) from leading companies like Nokia meet regularly with university presidents in a science and technological development committee chaired by the prime minister.

The coherence is not merely bureaucratic and governmental, but visionary and inspirational. Finns have a common vision that connects their creative high-tech future to their past as creative craftspeople. There are more composers and orchestral conductors per capita in Finland than in any other developed country, and all young people engage in creative and performing arts until the end of their secondary education.

This vision is shared at every level among Finns since teachers create their country's future as a creative and inclusive nation. Though teachers are paid only at the OECD average, teaching in Finland is highly competitive with only a one-in-ten chance of acceptance to teacher education programs in primary education. Retention is high among Finnish teachers because conditions are good and trust is high. All

Finnish teachers are awarded masters' degrees. Finns control quality at the most important point – the point of entry.

Within broad guidelines and with minimal steering by the state, highly qualified teachers create curricula together in each municipality for the children they know best. Curricula and pedagogy are not separate – they are in a common tradition of what continental Europeans call "didactics". The sense of delivering a curriculum devised by others from afar is utterly alien to Finnish educators. Finnish educators are grateful that they are not constantly bombarded by government initiatives, like the Anglo-Saxon nations.

In small classes rarely larger than 24 students, and with generous definitions of special educational needs, the push for quality is driven largely by quietly lifting all children up from the bottom, one at time, through knowing them well in small classes, having specialist support as needed, and not having to deal with excessive paperwork and endless external initiatives.

Principals work across schools, sharing resources where they are needed, and feeling responsible together for all the children and young people in their town and city, not acting competitively only for the children in their own school.

Assessment strategies are largely diagnostic forms of assessment-for-learning and internal to the school. External accountability is confidential and undertaken on a sample basis for monitoring purposes only, not as a census of everyone.

Principals are seen as being part of a "society of equals" in their schools, not as line-managers. They are often recruited from within their schools and they engage in considerable informally distributed leadership with their colleagues. Principals may not be recruited from outside education, and many principals teach for at least 2 h per week. Leaders teach and teachers lead. Teachers say that if the principal is indisposed or ineffective, they take over the school as it belongs to all of them.

Finland has a strong system of social support and investment funded by high taxes that characterizes much of continental Europe so that people have security of housing, of support for parental leave so families can care for young children, of early childhood education, and of care and livelihood in old age.

Some market-oriented advocates dismiss the high-performing Finnish example as simply too different (New Commission on the Skills of the American Workforce, 2007). Or they highlight weaknesses such as Finland's impending generational crisis of leadership succession, as a way of occluding the strengths. Or they choose single items such as awarding teachers masters' degrees, that are applied and imposed in isolation and disembodied from the democratic and inclusive context of the rest of the system and society (Barber & Mourshed, 2007). Or they overly celebrate how the system succeeds without Anglo-Saxon systems of standardized testing (Sahlberg, 2006).

And yet, the broad principles of developing an inspiring and inclusive mission that attracts into the profession high-caliber people capable of creating curriculum together for children they know well in smaller classes is much more readily transferable. So too is the importance of active trust among and for the teaching profession, and the synergy of educational and economic improvement with social and public investment more widely.

Without an inspiring and inclusive mission, high trust for professionals and strong social support throughout the society, other less successful measures such as market incentives have to be used to attract and retain highly qualified professionals. Without highly qualified professionals, teaching cannot be trusted so much, which increases the argument for external accountability, standardized curriculum, and government intervention. But these measures then destroy nations' capacities to be competitive and creative knowledge economies. Last, without small classes in which teachers know their children well, individual knowledge of children's needs has to be developed in other ways, through batteries of data on standardized tests.

Tower Hamlets

If Finland seems too culturally homogeneous for other countries to be able to copy, let's turn to an interesting and more diverse outlier in England instead. After the collapse of London's docking industry in the 1970s, when supertankers and container ships could no longer navigate the tight bends of the River Thames, new waves of immigrants moved into the newly impoverished area of Tower Hamlets – many from rural areas of Bangladesh, one of the world's poorest countries. Despite the reconstruction of part of the Docklands into a fashionable global finance and media center of Canary Wharf, the white-collar workers who came and went on the new high-tech transit line were barely aware of the immigrant community in their midst whose people found little skilled employment in the office towers of glass and steel.

Tower Hamlets' Bengali community suffered from high unemployment rates and some of the greatest incidences of poverty in the country with more children on free school meals than almost anywhere else. Educators' aspirations for student achievement were startlingly low and in 1997, Tower Hamlets was proclaimed the country's worst-performing Local Education Authority, with the lowest-performing primary school in the nation.

Ten years later, the transformation of the schools in Tower Hamlets is dramatic. The schools perform around and above the national average. On standardized achievement tests, General Certificate of Secondary Education (GCSE) examination results, and rates of students going on to university, the borough ranks as the most improved local authority in Britain. It has significantly reduced achievement gaps in relation to children with special educational needs, those from cultural minorities, and those on free school meals. These gains have been achieved with largely the same population and are reflected in Figs. 1 and 2 in relationship to the more modest national gains posted in the same time period.

Figure 1 refers to the percentage of students gaining five or more passing scores at grade C and above in their crucial GCSE secondary school examinations. Grade C is typically the minimum required to move on to university-bound programs.

Figure 2 displays the percentage of students at key Stage 2 (age 11/the last year of primary school) who attain Level 4 proficiency in English literacy.

What explains this system wide turnaround? In a large-scale research project co-directed with Alma Harris called *Performing Beyond Expectations*, I have studied

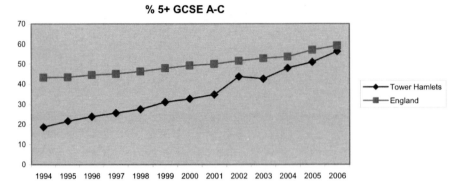

Fig. 1 Secondary school examination results in Tower Hamlets

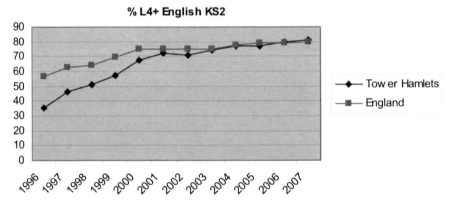

Fig. 2 Primary school literacy achievement in Tower Hamlets

the secrets of Tower Hamlet's success in association with my research colleague Alan Boyle (Hargreaves & Shirley, 2009). At the center of the story are the following components:

- The *visionary leadership* of a new director (superintendent) who was a self-confessed workaholic and who believed that "poverty is not an excuse for poor outcomes," that aspirations should be extremely high, that efforts to meet these aspirations should be relentless, and that everyone should work on this together;
- The *successful succession* of this first driving leader by a more developmentally inclined, yet equally persistent one, with just a short period of instability in between where the results took a slight dip;
- The ability to attract *high-quality teachers who stay* with the borough, after a period of weeding out overseas teachers who were drawn more to enjoying a brief life excursion in London than a long-term professional commitment to the schools;

- A commitment developed with the schools' leaders to set and reach ambitious *shared targets* for improvement in "a culture of target setting" so that "everybody owns them";
- A shared philosophy that *it is better to have ambitious targets and just miss them than have more modest targets and meet them*;
- *Mutual trust and strong respect* where "lots of our schools work very closely together and with the local authority" and where inspectors' reports refer to the "enthusiasm and high level of morale among the workforce";
- *Knowledge of and presence in the schools* which provides support, builds trust, and grounds intervention in consistent and direct personal knowledge and communication more than in the numerical data that eventually appear on spreadsheets;
- A commitment to *cross-school collaboration,* so that when one secondary school went into "Special Measures" (similar to "corrective action" in the United States) after taking in Somali students from refugee families in a neighboring authority, all the other secondary schools rallied round to help;
- A *resilient but not reckless* approach to external government pressure and policy – accepting the importance of testing and targets, but deciding to set their own targets and resisting the politically motivated pressure to build new (and partly privately funded) high-school academies since the authority already had high-trust relationships with its schools that now performed very well;
- *Positive business partnerships* with corporations in Canary Wharf that model a new form of "corporate educational responsibility" with schools; and
- *Strengthening of community relations and engagement.* Tower Hamlets schools affect the communities that affect them. They have done this by working with faith-based organizations and forming agreements with imams from this largely Muslim community to counter the effects of children taking extended absence from schools to attend and then stay on after family events such as funerals in Bangladesh. This includes announcements at school and at prayer in the mosque that extended absences will be treated as truancy because the educational achievement of the young people and the development of the community's future capacity matter that much. Tower Hamlets has also developed some of its schools into community centers that keep a school open from 8:00 am until 10:00 pm – providing resources and recreation for both students and the community's adults. Last, the employment of large numbers of classroom assistants and other staff from the community to support teachers builds strong relationships and trust between professionals and community members and enables and encourages some of these community members to go on to become professionally trained teachers themselves.

Educators in Tower Hamlets possess a robust and resilient sense of purpose; enjoy successful and sustainable system leadership that stays close to and is undertaken with schools; commit to professionally shared targets rather than politically arbitrary ones; establish an ethic of schools helping schools and the strong supporting the weak; and commit to a kind of community development that penetrates all aspects of a cohesive and coherent change process, while still respecting and even enhancing the special expertise of educators in boosting achievement. One of Tower Hamlet's visionary leaders sums it up well: It's "not just about the data. It's actually knowing the school, knowing the community, knowing about history, knowing about the staff—all of that."

Performing Beyond Expectations

The study of Tower Hamlets is part of a larger investigation into unexpectedly high performance in other sectors and its implications for educational improvement. One of these sectors is sport.

Sport has started to undergo a revolution in evidence-based improvement. In *Moneyball*, Lewis (2004) describes how the Oakland Athletics baseball team of the 1990s managed to outperform most competitors, even after its financial backers had pulled out, by paying relentless attention to the statistic that best predicts season-long high performance: on-base percentage (the percentage of times a player can reach first base from the plate where he bats). "The most important, isolated offensive statistic is the on-base percentage," Lewis notes (p. 58). So the Oakland Athletics set about recruiting players who had a high on-base percentage and batters were urged to attend to it – to do anything it took to get on base, even drawing a "walk" or being hit by a pitch.

Systematically attending to this single statistic throughout the club's selection, organization, and playing strategies got it into the play-offs season after season, despite falling levels of investment. Before, coaches had recruited players who reminded them of themselves – big guys who could hit a ball hard. Now, the Oakland Athletics had some of the most peculiarly built players in baseball, but what they could all do was get on base consistently!

The parallel in football is Prozone: a computer program that can track players' performance throughout a game – monitoring and measuring energy levels, areas of the pitch covered, and number of successful and unsuccessful passes made – backwards, forwards, and sideways.

An English Premiership football club we have been studying employs a single Prozone analyst. Many Premiership clubs have entire Prozone analysis teams while at the other end of the scale, one low-ranking second division team's Prozone analyst fell off the floodlights in a rainstorm while recording the game with his camera! The Premiership Prozone analyst we interviewed, who made the program the subject of his master's degree, described how multiple cameras are typically positioned around the ground to track players during each game. Individual player patterns and profiles are subsequently compiled from the accumulated data. The key question, though, is how are the data used to improve performance?

In the extreme case, our interviewee described how some managers had tried installing electronic chips in their players' boots to measure the number of steps they took per game as an indicator of energy expenditure. Some managers then set "step" targets to increase the energy that players used. However, players got around this by taking extra little steps off-field when they were retrieving the ball and the camera couldn't follow them. The same kind of cheating occurs in education when targets for increased test scores are imposed on teachers who take their own extra little steps such as teaching to the test in order to produce the necessary numbers.

By comparison, the Premiership Club Prozone director invites players in to discuss their data. At first, only a trickle of players come to see him, but as players' subsequent performance improves, their peers take notice and are very soon following their team-members' footsteps to join this intelligent community of soccer learners who analyze data to improve performance together. Whether they concern individual student achievement, or comparative international performance, the most productive uses of data in education similarly occur not by imposing unwanted targets that lead to unnecessary expenditures of energy on superfluous extra steps, but by building intelligent communities of professionals and policy-makers who look at data together in shared commitments to improvement.

Conclusion

All policies start somewhere but most of them travel poorly. The past is a foreign country and too much nostalgia or amnesia about it impairs the intelligent immigration of its policy strategies into the present. This is the danger when presidents, prime ministers, and premiers try to replicate what worked for them as students in the past across entire policy systems in the present. Other countries and other sectors that seem to show exemplary success can equally be sources of disappointment if their strategies are adopted inflexibly and simplistically because of cultural familiarity or political plausibility.

Policy principles are much more transposable and transportable if they are interpreted intelligently within communities of practice among and between those who are their bearers and recipients. Indeed, it is these communities of practice and the ways they engage with past policies and comparative policies elsewhere in order to make committed and sincere efforts to improve together that will prove to be the ultimate test bed of effective as well as sustainable policy development and implementation. Seeds travel better than ripened fruit and so does the germination and cross-pollination of policy change.

In a high-performing country, a remarkably successful district, and a sports club that performs far beyond expectations, we have begun to discern what some of these common principles of high performance can be, including in contexts of low resources and even outright adversity.

What they point to is not what has characterized many Anglo-American reform strategies over the past 2 decades – bureaucratic standardization that stunts creativity, cutthroat competition that widens achievement gaps and pits the strong against the weak, obsessions with the independent authority of objective data and autocratically imposed targets that make everyone expend fruitless energy on taking unnecessary extra steps to create the appearance of improvement, and the reduction of leaders who develop their community's purposes to managers who merely implement the purposes of others and who are turned over with increasing frequency or ferocity if they fail to deliver.

Instead, what we have encountered is the importance of inspiring missions that connect the future to the past and draw the best people to the organization; leaders who know their people and how to get them to work well together in interchangeable roles and positions and who are able to stay long enough to see their work through; cultures of trust, cooperation, creativity, and responsibility; intelligent use of data that serves as a conscience that checks people and not as an all-powerful force that drives them; and commitment to the cause of community development, even among competitors who are galvanized by a common cause that transcends their differences and rivalries.

As we strive to extricate ourselves from the worst economic catastrophe for 70 years, it is time to move beyond the failed solutions of the last 2 decades, to abandon the ingrained ideologies of bureaucratic prescription and market competition, to resist the temptations to inflict our own educational biographies and the opportunities they gave us on a present population whose success may require different solutions, and to avoid transplanting simple solutions from plausible models of success elsewhere. Our task instead is to work together in relation to an inspiring purpose that can lift us all and commit us to helping each other, and to learn from the common principles that underpin inspirational success, far beyond expectations, in systems and sectors beyond and beside us.

In the Renaissance, it was the telescope that got us to see beyond ourselves. In the twenty-first century, it's more of a metaphorical Global Positioning System (GPS) that will help us locate and navigate inspiring sectors and systems, and that will help us learn how to extricate ourselves from the economic calamity that has befallen us. In the end, this will be achieved by no more slick solutions for achieving success in low-tax systems, but by truly investing in the quality, creativity, and community of the only sustainable resource we can ultimately rely on – the future generations of our people and those teachers who we call and depend on to educate them.

References

Aho, E., Pitkänen, K., & Sahlberg, P. (2006). *Policy development and reform principles of basic and secondary education in Finland since 1968*. Washington, D.C: World Bank.

Barber, M. (2007). *Instruction to deliver: Fighting to transform Britain's public services*. London: Methuen.

Castells, M., & Himanen, P. (2004). *The information society and the welfare state: The Finnish model*. New York: Oxford University Press.

Fink, D. (1999). The attrition of change: A study of change and continuity. *School Effectiveness and School Improvement, 10*(3), 269–295.

Grubb, W. N. (2007, October). Dynamic inequality and intervention: Lessons from a small country. *Phi Delta Kappan, 89*(2), 105–114.

Hargreaves, A., Halász, G., & Pont, B. (2008). The Finnish approach to system leadership. In Pont, B., Nusche, D., & Hopkins, D. (Eds.), *Improving school leadership, Vol. 2: Case studies on system leadership* (pp. 69–109). Paris: OECD.

Hargreaves, A., & Shirley, D. (2009). *The fourth way*, Thousand Oaks, CA: Corwin Press.

Honore, C. (2008). *Under pressure*. New York: HarperOne.

James, O. (2008). *The selfish capitalist*. New York: Random House.

Levin, B. (2008). *How to change 5000 schools: A practical and positive approach for leading change at every level.* Cambridge: Harvard Education Press.

Lewis, M. (2004). *Moneyball: The art of winning an unfair game.* New York: W. W. Norton & Company.

McKinsey & Company. (2007, September). *How the world's best-performing school systems come out on top.* Retrieved on November 25, 2008, from http://www.mckinsey.com/clientservice/socialsector/resources/pdf/Worlds_School_Systems_Final.pdf

McQuillan, P. J., & Englert, K. S. (2001). The return to neighborhood schools, concentrated poverty, and educational opportunity: An agenda for reform. *Hastings Constitutional Law Quarterly, 28*(4), 739–770.

New Commission on the Skills of the American Workforce. (2007). *Tough choices or tough times: The report of the new commission on the skills of the American workforce.* Washington, DC: National Center on Education and the Economy.

Sahlberg, P. (2006). Education reform for raising economic competitiveness. *Journal of Educational Change, 7*(4), 259–287.

Sarason, S. B. (1990). *The predictable failure of educational reform.* San Francisco, CA: Jossey-Bass.

Stein, M., Hubbard, L., & Mehan, H. (2004). Reform ideas that travel far afield: The two cultures of reform in New York City's District #2 and San Diego. *Journal of Educational Change, 5*(2), 161–197.

UNICEF. (2007). *Child poverty in perspective: An overview of child well-being in rich countries, Innocenti Report Card 7.* Florence: UNICEF Innocenti Research Centre.

Wei, R.C., Darling-Hammond, L., Andree, A., Richardson, N., & Orphanos, S. (2009). *Professional learning in the learning profession: A Status Report on Teacher Development in the United States and Abroad.* Dallas, TX, National Staff Development Council.

Positive Pressure

Michael Fullan

Educational systems are known to be loosely coupled, fragmented, and overloaded with piecemeal initiatives. Under these conditions, there is a lot of room for inertia – things like to keep on doing what they are already doing. Yet, improvements in the performance of schools are badly needed. What forces could possibly and positively move whole systems toward substantial and continuous improvement?

When we first turned out the phrase "pressure and support" in the early 1990s, it became an instant hit. People could pick whichever concept they were predisposed to like and give lip service to the other. Politicians in particular loved the pressure part. What should have been an integrated set became two pillars.

Now that we have much more experience under our belts, it is time to take stock and clarify what forms of pressure and support in combination are effective. To do this, I (1) stipulate two advance criteria; (2) consider bad or negative forces of pressure; (3) identify a core list of integrated elements of positive pressure; and (4) furnish a case example to show that these ideas can and are being embedded in reality.

The two criteria to judge effectiveness are as follows:

1. Is a given pressure or support action *motivational*? That is, does it cause people to put in the effort to get good results?
2. Do the set of pressure and support policies and actions address improvement of the *whole system*?

By "motivational," I do not mean that an action today will motivate people tomorrow, but rather if a particular action is taken with a degree of persistence it will incrementally and perhaps dramatically gain on the motivational problem.

Whole system is an entire state, province, or country. It is what we call "tri-level reform" – the school and community, the district, and the government. All schools. All children. Our question in this chapter is, why some forms of pressure

M. Fullan (✉)
OISE/University of Toronto, Toronto, ON, Canada
e-mail: mfullan@oise.utoronto.ca

A. Hargreaves et al. (eds.), *Second International Handbook of Educational Change*,
Springer International Handbooks of Education 23, DOI 10.1007/978-90-481-2660-6_7,
© Springer Science+Business Media B.V. 2010

work, while others don't? By "work," I mean that they motivate lots of people to change the whole system. One final foundational point: Inertia works because it is organic – nobody has to do anything for it to be effective. Negative pressure doesn't work because it is ad hoc or inorganic. Positive pressure will work when it becomes organically part and parcel of system functioning.

Negative Forms of Pressure

To recall, negative pressure is ad hoc and extraneous to the system culture. To the extent that some forms of negative pressure are built-in they actually serve the forces of inertia. I take up five forms of negative pressure:

1. blind sense of urgency
2. pressure without means
3. punitive pressure
4. groupthink
5. win–lose competition

The more the system fails, the greater the blind sense of urgency. Kotter (2008) talks about this as a false sense of urgency:

> With a false sense of urgency an organization does have a great deal of energized action, but it's driven by anxiety, anger and frustration, and not a focused determination to win. . . With false urgency, the action has a frantic feeling: running from meeting to meeting, producing volumes of paper, moving rapidly in circles, all with a dysfunctional orientation that often prevents people from exploiting key opportunities and addressing gnawing problems (p. x).

This is a recipe for burnout and cynicism. It saps people's energy while they never learn what to do. People get discouraged and lose hope.

Along with a blind sense of urgency is mounting "pressure without the means" to act on it. This is pressure without a theory of action. It shows the failures and the goals but no way of getting there. It omits or gives lip service to "capacity-building" – how to build the individual and collective knowledge, skills, competencies, and motivation necessary to work on the problem.

Pressure without means can afford to have ridiculous goals. No Child Left Behind (NCLB) Act in the United States is a prime example – well-intentioned with lofty goals (such as every child will have a qualified teacher by 2014 or every child will perform at a world-class level in literacy, math, and science, and so on) and without any strategy to get there, it becomes a fantasy. Fantasies left to rot become nightmares.

The more that blind sense of urgency and lofty goals without means prevail, the more the next bad step is likely to occur: tightening the screws with punitive pressure. Accountability with teeth, proponents say, is necessary to show people that we are serious. We will leave no child left behind because we say so, and we mean it.

Punitive pressure is what most authoritarian regimes and individuals reach for when all else fails. It doesn't take a psychology graduate to know that punitive pressure doesn't work. It can work in narrow situations such as standing over a person's shoulder with a gun or its equivalent. But even this doesn't work if the person doesn't have the capacity to do what needs to be done.

Pfeffer and Sutton (2000) identify the problem as "fear prevents acting on knowledge." They found that organizations that were weak on generating and using knowledge had an atmosphere of fear and distrust. They identify two specific consequences of fear mongering. The first problem is that it causes people to focus on short-term immediate results even if they have to cheat or fudge the books to show that they met targets. The second adverse consequence is that it fosters selfishness and individualism. Look after number one, blame others—survival of the sneakiest.

Fourth, *groupthink* is interesting because it can cut both ways – to prevent action and to encourage ill-considered action. "Groupthink" is a term coined by Janis (1982) that describes "a mode of thinking that people engage in when they are deeply involved in a cohesive in-group, when the members' striving for unanimity overrides their motivation to realistically appraise alternative courses of action" (quoted in Wilson, 2007, p. 202). Many examples of negative pressure including our entire list can be attributed to the unexamined assumptions of the in-group going along with the policies and strategies promulgated by a central few.

Groupthink can serve inertia in another way. When teachers tacitly or otherwise fail to face up to poor performance of their peers by reinforcing the norms of the privatization of teaching, they are engaged in an act of groupthink. Groupthink is one of inertia's best friends.

Finally, certain forms of competition unleash negative pressure. When there is an unfair playing field, when certain groups do not have the capacity to be competitive, when some people are left out, competition actually *increases* the gap between high and low performers. Win–lose competition acts like Pfeffer and Sutton's fear mongering. Some individuals win, but at the expense of the system.

What makes the set of the five forms of negative pressure perverse is that they almost always appear together. The mind that thinks up any one of the forms is very likely to find and embrace all forms. One can almost see Douglas McGregor (1960) turn in his grave. Theory X assumptions are alive and well in the land of negative pressure:

– The average human being has an inherent dislike of work and will avoid it if he or she can.
– Because of their dislike for work, most people must be controlled and threatened before they will work hard enough.
– The average human being prefers to be directed, dislikes responsibility, and desires security above everything else. (Theory Y is the opposite where you expect people to rise to the occasion if you treat them well and enable their development.)

Positive Pressure

The opposite of negative pressure is not no pressure. No pressure is complacency. No pressure is inertia's other best friend. Fortunately, there are forms of pressure that palpably meet our two criteria: they are motivational, and they are such for hordes of people. They require a degree of sophistication and perseverance to master and to kick in, but they are practically powerful. They don't work overnight, but they are not long-term either – benefits (remember our large-scale criterion) can be obtained in 2 or 3 years, and then leveraged for greater gain thereafter.

We have identified and used five forms of positive pressure:

1. sense of focused urgency
2. partnerships and peers
3. transparency of data
4. nonpunitive accountability
5. irresistible synergy

I define these in turn and then provide a case example of them in action. Recall that Kotter did not like frenetic urgency. But he also knows about inertia. After examining about 100 large-scale change initiatives, he formed the following conclusion:

> Incredibly, we found that in over 70 percent of the situations where substantial changes were clearly needed, either they were not fully launched, or the change efforts failed, or changes were achieved but over budget, late, and with great frustration. We also found that in about 10 percent of the cases, people achieved more than thought would have been possible (p. vii–viii).

Kotter (2008) states,

> The winning strategy combines analytically sound, ambitious but logical goals with methods that help people experience new, often very ambitious goals, as exciting, meaningful, and uplifting – creating a deeply felt determination to move to make it happen, and win, now (p. 47).

This is moral purpose with a focus: a confident but humble sense of real hope that this can be done; ideas for acting on the goals; a wraparound sense that there is no time to waste; and a can-do attitude that this will be achieved by the whole team through engaged partnership.

Second, the partnership is crucial in two respects. One is vertical. Central leaders make it clear that they will provide direction and stay the course, but they also are committed to acting through two-way partnerships. Participation is made more meaningful and powerful through the use of horizontal peer learning strategies – within schools, across schools, and across districts. The idea is to learn about implementation from peers during implementation. Knowledge flows and a sense of identity grows with wider circles of peers. Yes there is lots of peer support, but one of the most powerful forms of pressure comes from engaged peers with a sense of urgency. The power of peers is that there are so many of them.

Third, transparency of data is essential and can and must be made into a powerhouse. Transparency is about two things: results and practice (i.e., the practices that caused the results). The good news is that both of these components are now recognized as crucial and are being developed in tandem. This is about assessment of learning (especially higher order skills), and the link to precise, high-yield instructional practices that produce such learning for all students.

There is still in the education field too much assessment (without adequate links to instructional practice) and too much stick wielding. Cisco, Intel, and Microsoft have just partnered with leading academics to produce new assessments linked to powerful instructional practices for the twenty-first century skills (Partners in Education Transformation, 2009). This initiative promises to develop and make available higher order assessments, and equally importantly to identify the effective instructional practices associated with the accomplishment of these new learning goals.

Transparency of data about results and practice is powerful positive pressure when used with the other four pressure elements in this section. It exposes not only results, but practices that produce the results. It generates specific, precise, visually clear images of what works. It is accessible for all as it takes all the excuses off the table.

Nonpunitive accountability must accompany transparency. Openness will do its work if people do not run away. The combination of positive pressures actually helps people to experience success, thereby motivating them to do even more. Nonpunitive accountability plays down "judgmentalism" in favor of high expectations in your face. Achievement data, effective practices, decisions about progress or not, are relentlessly pursued and portrayed. These practices act as (effective) accountability but accountability per se is not the main point. The value of relentless nonpunitive accountability is that it is a *powerful strategy for improvement* with external accountability as a natural by-product.

Finally, positive pressure is never piecemeal. The only chance to alter the course of inertia (because it is embedded culture) is to attack the cultural core itself in order to create a new replacement organic culture with positive pressure and support seamlessly built-in. Thus, coherence, alignment, and synergistic integrated forms of the first four positive pressures working in concert need to be established as "the new way we do things around here."

A Case Example

The previous section could be written off as mere theory. It is not. There is now a powerful growing presence of many countries, provinces, and states committed to what Michael Barber, Fullan, and MacKay (in press) calls "the professionalization of system reform." There is not total agreement, but a growing commitment on the part of politicians and professionals to put these ideas into practice, and yes, with a sense of urgency.

We can look for many manifestations of this in the coming year(s), and here I report on only one, namely, the case of Ontario where we have been using and studying the role of positive pressure since 2003 (see Fullan, 2010, and Levin, 2008). Here are some of the main elements expressed in reference to the five components of positive pressure presented in the previous section.

The Ontario public school system consists of 2 million students, 4,000 elementary schools, and 900 secondary schools within 72 districts. From 1995 to 2003, it was a stagnant system in terms of literacy and numeracy achievement – essentially flatlined and had actually lost ground with respect to high school graduation rates.

With a new government in 2003, and a commitment to educational improvement as measured by student learning, the province formulated a strategy based on purposeful, positive pressure. Based on the five elements of pressure outlined in the previous section, the strategy created a powerful base for improvement.

A Sense of Focused Urgency

Being elected in 2003, the new government immediately announced a small number of ambitious goals: improve literacy, numeracy, and high school graduation. The other elements of positive pressure created the essential means of getting there but let's stay with urgency for a moment. Urgency is not (although it could be) a crisis. In all cases, it is a sense of deep dissatisfaction with the status quo and a corresponding ambitious but manageable focus. The government set targets, roughly committing to going from 54% high proficiency in literacy and numeracy in grades 3–6 to 75%; and from 68% high school graduation to 85%.

These three priorities were stated and reiterated in all educational pronouncements. The priorities gained greater prominence by the establishment of an informed "guiding coalition" (GC), chaired by the premier and included the top officials (minister, deputy minister, advisers). The GC is a kind of "feet to the fire" mechanism that constantly puts pressure on the priorities, strategies, and progress. It was clear to all that literacy, numeracy, and high school graduation represented a small core set of urgent ambitious priorities.

It is interesting to observe that negative or frenetic sense of urgency always loses steam. It has no focus or momentum. Focused urgency maintains and even gains energy. When the government was re-elected in 2007, after four successful years, it was not complacency but greater urgency that characterized the mood. The premier commented just after the election in 2007 that he had changed in two ways since 2003, namely, (a) he was more confident about being on the right track and (b) more impatient. With positive pressure, urgency (partly because of initial success) actually intensifies as you go.

Partnership and Peers

A second form of powerful pressure consists of strategies that cause peers to interact and learn from each other in implementing improvements. Central leadership provides direction, a sense of urgency, a concern with monitoring results and invests in strategies whereby peers can learn from each other. I mention a few here.

One is called "schools on the move" where over 100 schools (currently) have been identified as experiencing 3 years of gains in literacy and numeracy. These schools are profiled by name, demographics, strategies used, and results obtained. Funds are made available to other schools to learn from these schools – not in a hierarchical, superior sense of accomplishment, but rather, "this is hard work let's learn from those who are making progress."

Other similarly based strategies include "networked learning communities," "districts learning from other districts" achieving success in district-wide reform, and schools facing difficult challenges being paired with other schools facing similar challenges but experiencing success.

In all these strategies, peers learn specifically from each other about what is working. Of course, there is plenty of support, but there is also a built-in form of pressure that happens organically. Nothing is more powerful than positively driven peer pressure.

Transparency of Data

Transparency or openness of data, as will be recalled, refers to two elements that must be connected. One is data on student achievement – performance data over time and disaggregated so that it is clear which groups are doing well or not. The other component is transparency of practice. We have to be able to access and learn from others who are employing more effective instructional practices in getting greater achievement results with given groups of students.

We have just seen in the previous strategy (peers learning from each other) how this works to get at effective instructional practice. Here we add the outcome data. It is crucial to note that there is a very close integration between instruction and assessment in these strategies. Schools examine and get better at identifying the *causal* relationships between particular instructional actions and specific student engagement and learning.

In Ontario, we pursue this from two perspectives, what I would call micro- and macro-viewpoints. Micro is the school; macro is the district or state. At the school level, in addition to promoting instructional practices in the classroom that closely link to diagnostic assessment (the daily two-way street between diagnosis and instruction), we foster three school assessment perspectives. First, schools begin to compare themselves with themselves – where were we last year on literacy achievement, the condition this year, and what do we aspire to for the next year. Second, schools are enabled to compare themselves with schools in similar circumstances (what we call "statistical neighbors"). This "apples to apples" comparison is valuable and stimulating especially when used in conjunction with peer learning strategies. Third, we help schools compare their performance to a larger external standard such as 95% success or the provincial target.

The macro use is from the district or province vantage point. Here, we have employed nonpunitive strategies. We have created a "statistical neighbors" database. All 4,000 elementary schools are on the database. They are organized into four bands – those schools facing the most challenging circumstances, two groups in the middle, and a fourth set situated in the least challenging contexts. Other demographic data are included: size of school, rural/urban, percent of ESL students, percent of special education students, and so on. Finally, each schools' student achievement data are included – grade 3 and grade 6 percentages of students achieving proficiency on the state tests in reading, writing, and mathematics – six scores in all for each school, year after year.

The province monitors results, has a turnaround schools strategy (see below), and invests in helping school principals learn how to use statistical neighbors to monitor their own performance, to learn from others, and to work on strategies that will beget better results.

Transparency as can be seen is a pressure point. What makes it a positive pressure is that it is used largely nonpunitively, and the information is readily and easily accessible, not just for learning outcomes, but also as a route to learning about the practices that produced the results.

All of this is reinforced by negotiating annual targets (in the six results areas) based on existing and previous performance. Every school and every district is always cognizant of how well it has been doing or not in comparison with its own previous efforts, and in terms of what its peer schools are accomplishing.

Nonpunitive Accountability

One of the most perplexing problems in large-scale reform is how to turn around large numbers of poor performing or nonperforming (coasting) schools. We have already seen that punitive accountability backfires. Absence of pressure honors inertia. The previous three forms of positive pressure already stimulate action and improvement. A focused sense of urgency gets people's attention; partnership and peer learning increase support, and also pressure from successful cases (it is being done in circumstances similar to ours); transparency of data makes it even more evident who is successful and who is not.

These three forces, however, are not powerful enough to improve the whole system. This is where nonpunitive accountability comes in because it puts the spotlight on all the schools and their performance. We have already seen that transparency of performance data and practice stimulates improvement for many schools. Nonpunitive accountability puts acceptable "teeth" in the change proposition. Here is how it works in practice.

First, in the face of poor or stagnant performance, leaders make it explicitly clear that the schools in question are not to blame. We call this nonjudgmentalism. Poor performance is recognized – transparent data tell us so – but the entire initial response focuses on capacity-building rather than criticism. Put another way, it is best to test the capacity-building hypothesis – if knowledge and skills were developed would better performance ensue – rather than dwell on whose fault it is – the latter being a classic de-motivator.

Again, this is not just theory. We have done it with success through a strategy called the Ontario Focused Intervention Partnership (OFIP). As whole system (all schools) reform unfolds, it is necessary to elevate expectations for all schools in an explicit action-oriented manner. OFIP is a natural next step to focusing energy and capacity-building because it "picks up" schools that are, so to speak, not responding. We have three categories of OFIP schools:

1. OFIP1 ($N = 36$): these are schools whose students are achieving below 35%, as measured by the percentage of students achieving the high standard provincial average of 75%;
2. OFIP2 ($N = 200$): schools whose students are achieving 35–50%;
3. OFIP3 ($N = 755$): schools whose students are scoring 50–74%, but are coasting (i.e., their student achievement is between 50 and 74% but is flatlined or declining over a 3-year period).

Three points are crucial here. First, the focus is on *all* schools not just the so-called "low performing schools." Over 1,000 (25% of all) elementary schools are involved, including those schools that seem to be doing okay but actually are "cruising" showing no improvement over a given 3-year period.

Second, OFIP schools are publicly labeled (any district could identify its nine or ten OFIP schools by name), but do not feel stigmatized. They are not treated as "failing schools,", but rather as schools in need of capacity-building. In some sense, it is all in the attitude – Theory Y not Theory X: treat people nonjudgmentally, invest in their capacity-building, and (in most cases) reap the reward. Third, these schools really do get specific capacity help – the kind of help that is being discovered and delivered from the three previous positive strategies.

All of this is increasingly specific. The name of the game is clarity, precision, and relentless implementation of effective practices. The key to success is consistent implementation of a few key strategies and time for staff to work together with a specific focus. All staff is engaged in the development of the school improvement plan and the monitoring of progress in achieving the goals in their school improvement plans. All OFIP schools are required to have in place:

- Uninterrupted blocks of time for literacy and numeracy
- A common assessment tool for primary and junior divisions
- A school improvement team that uses the school effectiveness framework as a guide to examine data, identify instructional intervention, and to plan for next steps in meeting ambitious targets for student learning
- A school improvement plan (SIP) revised based on the school's self assessment and linked to the board improvement plan (BIP)
- Resources to implement a comprehensive literacy and numeracy program across the school

- A process to regularly monitor the growth and progress of specific students to ensure equity of outcome
- Interventions for struggling students

We could be much more specific if space permitted but basically OFIP helps lower performing or stagnant schools install practices of schools that are highly effective. And it does this without "attitude." The result is that most OFIP schools improve – in 2007–2008, OFIP schools moved ahead 10 percentage points higher compared to the non-OFIP schools. No OFIP school, as I have said, feels negatively labeled. This is positive pressure at its best.

But, what if schools or certain districts (with high numbers of OFIP schools) do not improve? First, this is a much smaller number compared to systems that have a punitive accountability. Second, the pressure on nonresponsive schools and districts is mounting. The small number of schools and districts not moving forward become more and more noticeable. And yes, eventually direct intervention on the part of governments aimed at school districts, not improving despite all efforts, is necessary. But this (because of the strategy) is in a very small number of situations. When direct intervention is exercised under these (relatively last resort and small number of cases), it is applauded by the public and peer districts (as in "it is about time someone intervened").

The lesson here is first use indirect means of pressure such as the three addressed earlier in this section, add more direct, but still positive measures as in the OFIP strategy, and then take more serious interventionist action in those (few cases) failing to move forward.

Irresistible Synergy

The previous four positive pressure points when pursued in an integrated fashion create relentless synergy. Strategies are focused, aligned, comprehensive, and based on partnership. They foster concentrated practice linked to results. Through purposeful action people become more skilled, as they become more skilled they become clearer (skill produces clarity), and as skill and clarity combine they generate *shared* ownership.

The corresponding positive results themselves are further energizers. Literacy and numeracy increased by 13% (using a very high standard of proficiency) across 4,000 schools in 4 years: high school graduation rates increased from 68 to 77% over the same period; morale of teachers and principals increased; and the percentage of new teachers leaving the profession by their 4th year plummeted from 32 to 9%.

Conclusion

Ontario is not a conclusive case. It still has not yet met its ambitious targets, let alone full success. It is difficult to maintain the sense of urgency. Perhaps the pressure points are not strong enough. But the main line of argument holds. Specific, synergistic positive pressures are powerful in motivating very large numbers of system members to put in the individual and collective effort essential for getting continuous results.

I mentioned earlier the notion of culture as being organic –norms and values built-in that come to have their own momentum. Let's take accountability in terms of it being either a negative or positive culture. Strong accountability measures (our negative pressure points) occur when the system is not improving itself. This, as I have argued, produces even more negativism. By contrast, positive pressure results in a new culture in which the system is committed to and engaged in improving. I like Hargreaves and Shirley's (2009) statement that accountability is the gap that exists where responsibility stops. In other words, if (intrinsically motivated) responsibility is full bore, accountability is redundant. It is a natural and self-evident by-product of intrinsically driven individual and collective responsibility. You still need external accountability, but in synergistic positive pressure cultures internal and external accountability merge.

These advanced forms of integrated positive pressure for whole systems are fairly recent phenomenon – barely 5 years old. But they augur well for the future because they get results. This makes it politically attractive. It is still tough for politicians because the methods are indirect. They prefer "do this, get that" short-term strategies. But the strategies are still politically attractive because they do get results in relatively short time frames – 2 to 3 years, not 5–10.

Globally, attention is now beginning to shift to whole system reform because some countries are noticeably doing better through the explicit use of the strategies identified in this chapter. Barber and Mourshed's (2007) *How the world's best performing systems come out on top* is a case in point. People are now beginning to benchmark not just outcomes, but also policies and strategies.

My prediction is that this whole system reform work, undergirded by positive pressure components, will take off in the next 2–3 years. We will come to know a lot more about the nature, value, and indispensability of positive pressure in large-scale reform. It's about time, and desperately needed in the world of educational reform.

References

Barber, M., Fullan, M., & MacKay, T. (in press). *International education dialogue*. Melbourne, Victoria: Centre for Strategic Education.

Barber, M., & Mourshed, M. (2007). *How the world's best performing systems came out on top*. London: McKinsey & Co.

Cisco, Intel, & Microsoft. (2009). *Partners in education transformation*. Author.

Fullan, M. (2008). *The six secrets of change*. San Francisco: Jossey-Bass.

Fullan, M. (2010). *All systems go*. Thousand Oaks, CA: Corwin Press.

Hargreaves, A., & Shirley, D. (2009). *The fourth way*. Thousand Oaks, CA: Corwin.

Janis, I. (1982). *Groupthink*. Boston: Houghton-Mifflin.

Kotter, J. (2008). *A sense of urgency*. Boston: Harvard Business Press.

Levin, B. (2008). *How to change 5000 schools*. Cambridge, MA: Harvard Education Press.

Levin, B., Glaze, A., & Fullan, M. (2008). Results without rancor or ranking. *Phi Delta Kappan, 90*(4), 273–280.

McGregor, D. (1960). *The human side of enterprise*. New York: McGraw-Hill.

Pfeffer, J., & Sutton, R. (2000). *The knowing-doing gap*. Boston: Harvard Business School Press.

Wilson, D. (2007). *Evolution for everyone*. New York: Delacorte Press.

Education for an Interdependent World: Developing Systems Citizens

Peter M. Senge

The work described here was only possible because of the many pioneers of the systems thinking movement in public education and the founders of the more recent SoL Education Partnership – Burlington, Vermont; Murphy School District in Pheonix, Arizona; the Hewlett-Woodmere District in Long Island, New York; the E3 Initiative and the Washington Sustainability Education Association; Sustainable St. Louis; Jaimie Cloud of the Cloud Institute for Sustainability Education; and Lees Stuntz of the Creative Learning Exchange, dedicated to fostering networks of collaboration among systems thinking educators. A special thanks also to Linda Booth Sweeney, who has served as coordinator of the Partnership in its formation and now supports capacity building and research in several of the sites. See the Creative Learning Exchange www.clexchange.org, The Cloud Institute for Sustainability Education

Education for Today's World, Not Yesterday's

I believe that the Industrial-Age education system that has spread around the world in the past 150 years will change dramatically in the coming decades.

This will not happen because such a change is easy. Indeed, as most educators know only too well, few institutions are more resistant to innovation and change than primary and secondary education. It will happen because fundamental change is necessary if human society is to survive and thrive in the world in which we now live. The Industrial Age is ending, and the changes coming will not be possible

P.M. Senge (✉)
MIT and SoL (The Society for Organizational Learning), Cambridge, MA, USA
e-mail: diane@solonline.org

www.sustainabilityed.org, ISEE Systems www.iseesystems.com, and The Waters Foundation.

A. Hargreaves et al. (eds.), *Second International Handbook of Educational Change*,
Springer International Handbooks of Education 23, DOI 10.1007/978-90-481-2660-6_8,
© Springer Science+Business Media B.V. 2010

without recreating the two central institutions, business and education, which have been the primary propagators of the Industrial Age worldview and skillset.[1]

Economic globalization has brought extraordinary material benefits and unimaginable dangers. For the first time in human history, billions of people share a material standard of living previously unimaginable, just as more share reasonable expectations of long life, democratic processes, and formal education than at any previous time. Just so, human beings are destroying other species and ecosystems at unprecedented rates and altering their ecological environment locally and globally as never before. The average American causes a ton of material waste to be generated *per day*, including the gaseous waste by-products of industrial life like greenhouse gas emissions.

According to Jason Clay of the World Wildlife Fund, to support today's global economy takes 1 1/4 Earths. Soon it will be more. But we have only one Earth, and the inevitable adjustment to living within the scope of her generosity grows more severe every year we continue down the "take-make-waste" industrial path.

The challenges ahead will be social and cultural as well as economic and ecological – indeed they are inseparable. According to the World Bank, the poorest quartile of the world's people saw their income share of global income fall from 2.5 to 1.4% from 1975 to 2000. Globalization has caused a collision of cultures as well as economic systems, with many around the world fighting to preserve traditional cultural identity against the spread of western style consumerism, while massive joblessness spreads as rural economies decline and tens of millions are forced to migrate to cities. In this sense, global terrorism, fueled by millions of disaffected youth with little hope for a positive future, is as inevitable a by-product of the spread of modern industrial development as is global climate change.

While most individuals and organizations are still largely in denial regarding the profound changes required to meet these challenges, more and more business-, civil-society, and governmental leaders (mostly in local government in the US) not only see the changes needed but are busy bringing them into reality (Senge et al., 2008). Fortunately, this revolution also includes a growing number of educators and communities, some of whose examples are mentioned in the following section.

These innovators are guided by imagining a different path into the future, one that leads toward *regenerative* economic system in place of the *extractive* system that has dominated the Industrial Age. They are guided by simple but profound questions. Why could we not emulate nature in creating "circular economies" with little or no waste? Why could we not interact across cultural differences with the

---

[1]Many have argued that the industrial age ended decades ago, as the world of smokestacks and mass production was replaced by that of bits and bytes. But this confuses shifts in dominant technologies with shifts in the underlying values and processes that defined the industrial age. More steel is produced in the world today than ever before. So, too, are more automobiles produced and more coal burned. Indeed, shifts in dominant technologies are a defining feature of the industrial age, what Lewis Mumford and others called the "Age of the Machine." See "The Myth of the Machine, Vol. 1: Technics and Human Development," New York: Harcourt Brace, Jovanovich 1967.

aim of learning rather than domination, fostering a new renaissance as has happened before when established cultures were forced to face radical new ideas? Why could globalization not represent mindful stewardship of the Earth's treasures rather than mindless consumerism, awakening us to our sacred identity as *homo sapiens*, the "wise species"?

The key, to paraphrase Shakespeare, lies not in our stars but in ourselves. Below the multiple symptoms of social and ecological imbalances sits a growing gap in awareness between the nature of our reality and the nature of our thinking, symbolized in the following figure:

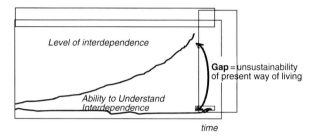

Fig. 2

Global industrial expansion has woven a web of interdependence, the likes of which has never before existed. The average pound of food travels 2,000 miles prior to its purchase by an American consumer. Many of our everyday goods travel much further.

Conversely, the by-products of our ways of living likewise travel around the world. For example, the greenhouse gasses emitted by Americans' cars and SUVs, along with our video games, flat panel TVs, and Web surfing (whose electricity is powered mostly by burning coal), 20% of worldwide emissions, contribute to shrinking glaciers, reduced spring runoffs, and hundreds of millions of chronically dehydrated people in northern India. Weather instability, flooding, and rising sea levels affect a great many more.[2] Soon, the same statement will be valid in reverse: as China's and India's surging economies eclipse that of the United States in greenhouse emissions (China's already has). Never before in human history have people's daily choices on opposite sides of the globe been so entangled.

But while this web of interdependence has been growing, our capacity to understand interdependence has not; indeed you could argue that it has steadily deteriorated over centuries. As humans have moved from tribal to agrarian societies and more recently to the modern industrial society, our sense of connection to the larger living world has progressively become more and more tenuous. For example, recent studies have shown that many American children believe that their food

---

[2]In 2007, Oxfam estimated that the costs to the world's poor of adapting to global climate change (including costs due to loss of crops, spread of tropical diseases, and migration) exceeded $50 billion. (see www.oxfam.org) This figure is expected to rise sharply in the coming years.

comes from the grocery store, and most have no concept of seasonality in food, since all foods are available at all times.

Because this decline in capacity to understand interdependence has happened over many generations, it has largely gone unnoticed. Native peoples do not need to read books to understand their dependence on and responsibilities to "Mother Earth"; it constitutes the very roots of their culture. Farmers likewise must understand the dance of sun, wind, rain, soil nutrients, and water flows or they cannot survive as farmers. We need to understand neither, and consequently do not.

As this gap grows, our way of living becomes increasingly unsustainable. Very few adults today understand the global economy, let alone where the goods they buy come from, or the social and environmental by-products of the global supply chains through which they move. Few know, for example, that the worldwide expansion of industrial agriculture, mostly to serve middle-class consumers in the north, which displaces tens of millions of rural residents per year due to falling farmer incomes, is a major source of greenhouse gases (not only CO_2 from shipping food around the world but methane from the expansion of livestock to meet growing demands for meat), and has caused the loss of over a billion hectares of topsoil in the past 50 years, more than the size of India and China combined.

While there are many facets of the malaise of global industrial society, it is hard to imagine much real change without beginning to address this gap between our growing interdependence and our ability to understand that interdependence. No technological fixes are likely to solve climate change alone. No global government is likely to suddenly appear to deal with the growing stresses of food and water. No enlightened corporate responsibility movement will miraculously change the DNA of global business so that short-term profit comes into balance with long-term contribution to people and planet.

All of these changes, and more, *will only happen as our thinking changes*. The institutions of the modern world work as they do because of how we work. How we think and interact shape their policies and practices, neither of which is likely to change on their own.

Thinking Newly, Educating for New Thinking

Time does not go backward. Our task is not to re-create yesterday's cultures of interrelatedness but tomorrow's. This will require deep change in all the primary institutions that shape modern society – none of which is more important than education because none has a larger long-term impact.

"To be a teacher is to be a prophet," said Gordon Brown, former Dean of the MIT School of Engineering and a founding inspiration to the systems thinking in education movement. "We are not preparing students for the world of today, or the world that teachers have grown up in; we are preparing students for a world that we can barely imagine." Education is the one social institution with a 50-year-plus time horizon. Business does not have this. Government does not have this. The media does not have this. But, school, by its nature, does. That is why education is always a key to the future direction of a society.

When education is driven by incessant pressures to perform on standardized tests, get good grades, and get into the right college, in order to get a good job and make lots of money, then education reinforces the consumerism and economic orthodoxy that drive the present global business system. When it is oriented around deeper questions of human and social development, it can contribute distinctly to the larger needs of a society needing desperately to reorient its priorities. In this sense, education is a natural leader in this time of "great turning," when the Industrial Age is dying and, as Vaclav Havel put it, "something new, still indistinct, is struggling to be born."

While this might sound romantic or grandiose, I believe the kids in school sense the significance of the moment. More than ever before in history, today's young people grow up with an awareness of the world. They know about climate change. They know about our addiction to fossil fuels. They know about the persisting gap between rich and poor. They are often in direct communication with friends in other countries, and they know about the struggles of the world's cultures to live respectfully with one another. As such they are disengaged when education that will shape their future does not address the imbalances, and when it does, they thrive.

Young people know that we are "living into" a new global society. What they don't know is whether their teachers know about it. What they don't know is do adults care enough and have enough courage to re-create education to match *their* world. Regardless of how they express it, they know that the only citizenship that matters today is global citizenship, how the people of the world work together to, in the words of Buckminster Fuller, "create a world that works for everyone."

The overarching aim of education must become developing "systems citizens," a generation of young people whose capacity to understand interdependence is commensurate with the interdependence that shapes our lives. This aim will take us all into new territory. No one knows how to do it. There is no set curriculum, anymore than there is agreement on the processes of learning that will be needed.

Moreover, educators won't be able to do this by themselves. The modern school is an expression of public priorities and sits within a complex web of societal accountabilities. In the Industrial Age, school became the domain of specialists who taught fragmented subjects in a way that was fragmented from the lives of the learners and the larger community (Senge, 2000). Re-creating education will be a job for communities committed to a future that has a future, not just for professional educators.

Our efforts to explore this new landscape through the SoL Education Partnership focus on four foundational changes[3]:

---

[3] SoL (the Society for Organizational Learning – www.solonline.org) is a network of individuals and organizations who work together around the world for systemic change. The SoL Education Partnership focuses primarily on communities within the US where educators, local businesspeople and government, and youth organizations are working together to create a climate for continuing innovation toward educating systems citizens.

- systems thinking,
- authentic youth engagement,
- rethinking schools as learning communities, and
- education for sustainability.

The overarching aim is not educational reform but recontextualizing the whole process of education: starting with young children learning how to be more responsible for their own school environment and gradually moving to interconnecting diverse stakeholders in tackling complex real-life community issues. In this process, students stop being passive recipients of someone else's curriculum and become active agents in developing a sense of responsibility and efficacy for an interdependent world.

Systems Thinking

The first systems thinking classes at Orange Grove Middle School started in 1988, instigated by Frank Draper, a science teacher, and encouraged by Mary Scheetz, then Orange Grove's principal. When my wife, Diane, and I first visited Frank's 8th grade science class in 1991, it was hard not to notice that something was different. First, Frank was nowhere to be seen. In fact there was no teacher in the room. A couple of students had some questions about their library research, and Frank had gone to the library with them (remember, this was much before the Internet). But, to our amazement, the classroom had not descended into chaos. Instead, the thirty or so students were glued to their new MacIntosh computers, two to a machine, deeply engrossed in their conversations with one another.

We learned that Frank and his colleague Mark Swanson had designed their semester science curriculum around a real project, the design of a new state park to be developed on the north of Tucson. After studying the sorts of conflicts that inevitably arise in park and wilderness area management, they were working with a STELLA-based simulation model that showed the impacts of different decisions.[4] They had an overall budget and prescribed mission based on environmental-quality, economic, and recreation and education targets they set for the park. At the time, there were working on designing the park's trail system. Once they would lay out a proposed trail, the simulation model calculated the environmental and economic consequences, prompting energetic debates over trade-offs among different options.

We had only been standing in the back of the room for a few minutes, and a couple of young boys came and grabbed us. "We need your opinion," Joe said. "Billy (the boy's partner) has a trail system that he thinks is great because it makes a lot of money (routing hikers past the best views), but it also does a lot of environmental

---

[4]STELLA and ITHINK are products of ISEE Systems, Hanover, New Hampshire: www.iseesystems.com

damage. Mine avoids the environmental impact areas, but he thinks it is too close to the Indian Burial Grounds and will stir up protests."

We listened for a while as the two boys explained their different trails and showed us some of the simulated consequences. There were no black and white answers, and it was clear that they understood this. This was about design and making choices. The bell rang signaling the end of the period, and they said goodbye, agreeing as they left to come back after school to see if they could agree on a proposal to share with the rest of the class at the end of the week. (Eventually, the students' proposals and analyses were presented to the actual park planning commission at the end of the term.)

Barry Richmond has identified eight constituent thinking skills that comprise a broad definition of systems thinking[5]:

- *Dynamic Thinking* – seeing patterns of change over time rather than focusing only on isolated events.
- *System as Cause Thinking* – recognizing that problems and their solutions are endogenous: They arise within a system, not from outside.
- *10 K Meters Thinking* – being able to step back and see the big picture.
- *Operational Thinking* – understanding how the structure of a system causes its behavior, and that the same basic structures apply to all systems. Understanding stocks and flows.
- *Closed-Loop Thinking* – recognizing feedback: Any action has consequences that can influence that action again.
- *Nonlinear Thinking* – knowing that feedback loops interact to produce changing responses over time.
- *Quantitative Thinking* – being able to consider and include all variables, even those that cannot be measured in standard units.
- *Scientific Thinking* – recognizing that all models are working hypotheses to be rigorously built, tested, and refined.

In that particular project at the Orange Grove, the students were learning to see change – the consequences of how the park's trail system was laid out – as differing patterns of behavior over time (Richmond's "dynamic thinking"). This was also illustrated earlier, when I argued that many of today's most pressing problems could be understood as arising from a particular pattern of behavior over time: the growing gap over time between interdependence and our understanding of interdependence.

The students were also practicing stepping back to see how one change can have many different effects as the change plays out in a larger system, and how that system has its own distinctive characteristics and generates particular forces (10 K meter thinking and system as cause thinking).

---

[5] See "Tracing Connections: Voices of Systems Thinkers," forthcoming (2010).

And, they were learning how to formulate a hypothesis: what sorts of consequences they expected from different changes and testing their expectation against a formal model of the system (scientific thinking).

The students also learned a variety of conceptual tools for mapping systems and for expressing and communicating with others about their understanding of interdependence. Again, these were applied to real-life situations the children could identify with, including ones drawn from their own lives. Today, tools like "behavior-over-time graphs," "connection circles," "causal loop diagrams," and "system archetypes" are introduced as early as third and fourth grade, and young children are invited to look at daily experiences like how trust builds or deteriorates in a friendship, or what happens in breaking a bad habit (Quaden, Ticotsky, & Lyneis, 2009). As students get older, they can naturally extend these tools to more complex subjects, including developing their own simulation models.[6] This develops not only deep content knowledge but thinking skills to see how common system dynamics can underlay very different situations.[7]

"Our approach was to invite kids to consider a worldview of complex interdependent systems. Instead of abstract learning, we use simulations to begin to confront and to penetrate this world of interdependence as it is embodied in particular real-life situations, and how these systems relate to other systems," says Frank Draper.

This work is challenging and requires dedicated teachers like Draper and Swanson willing to wrestle with some timeless questions, as well as newer ones brought to light by the systems worldview – like, What if the education process throughout primary and secondary school continually build on children's innate curiosity and capacity to construct their own understanding rather than digesting a teacher's understanding? Learning through doing is ultimately essential for retention and meaningfulness, but how can this learning be extended to more complex subjects where the consequences of our actions are no longer immediate? What really are our innate capacities to understand complexity, and how far could this intelligence develop if it were really nurtured?

Authentic Youth Engagement

What was equally evident from the outset at Orange Grove was the engagement of the students. What made the state park exercise so engaging for them?

---

[6]See, for example, Diana Fisher, "Modeling Dynamic Systems: Lessons for a First Course," available at www.iseesystems.com. In this book, Fisher shares examples of remarkable student work that includes college and post-graduate level work done by high school students versed in systems modeling tools.

[7]The idea of "generic structures" is a cornerstone of systems education and ranges from simple dynamic structures like delays that arise in virtually all social systems (and confound decision-makers expecting immediate results from their actions) to more involved structures like "aging chains" which arise in diverse settings from demographics to product life cycles.

First, they were wrestling with real-world problems rather than artificial school-room exercises. They could identify not only with the challenges of developing a new state park but also with the benefits of designing the park well.

Second, they were thinking for themselves. They knew there was no single right answer to the challenges they were facing. Ultimately, they had to understand better what would happen if different decisions were made, and they had to frame trade-offs. There was no single formula presented by the instructor to gain the right answer. Rather, they had to sort out their own thinking about a real issue and explore different proposals – ultimately coming to their own conclusions.

Third, the teachers operated as mentors, not instructors. The teacher's role was not to give a prescribed method or guide the students to a predetermined right answer. Indeed, the teachers did not know the best outcome and were colearners with the students. But the teachers' roles were no less crucial: They had to help the students make sense of the outcomes of different experiments. Having been involved in building the computer simulation gave them important knowledge for this task but no simple answers: A complex dynamic simulation model will often respond to changes in ways that its developers do not anticipate, as different feedback interactions play out over time.

So, the learning project was mutual for teacher and student. Though they had built the simulation model, it *was* a model and thus, by definition, incomplete. Indeed, one of the teachers' roles was to help the students appreciate the assumptions upon which the model was based, and to invite the students to critique those assumptions and consider the implications of alternative assumptions, a critical aspect of scientific reasoning.[8]

Lastly, working with partners drew the students into a joint inquiry. This not only enabled them to get to know one another but forced them to continually confront alternative views and assumptions. This drew students into a natural process of seeing how each of us reasons from past experiences and assumptions to draw conclusions that guide our actions, and to becoming more open to testing their reasoning.

Of course, human beings follow such processes of inferential reasoning all the time, but it is often easier to see how this works in another situation, since our own reasoning is often "transparent" or invisible to us. Educators understand the importance of reflection – learning how to examine our own assumptions and reasoning – but it remains an elusive educational goal, all but completely ignored by traditional schooling. Didactic instruction bypasses it entirely. Teachers' efforts to try to get students to reflect is easily undermined by teachers' authority and formal power, which intimidates students programmed to seek correct answers. As Scheetz said, reflection requires safety, which benefits from an environment of mutual inquiry. In this sense, students helping one another reflect is a powerful approach that goes well beyond teacher-centered strategies.

---

[8]For examples of students developing their own simulation models see D. Fisher, "Modeling Dynamic Systems: Lessons for a First Course", Second Edition, available from iseesystems.com

For example, consider the followed (slightly stylized) interaction between Joe and Billy working on their park trail system.

> Billy: " Your trails are a bad idea because they are too close to the Indian burial grounds. You shouldn't do that."
>
> Joe: " Who says? There are no rules that say we can't do that. They do a lot less environmental damage than yours."
>
> Billy: "Yeh, mine *are* a problem. But what is worse?"
>
> Joe: "I didn't really think about the burial grounds. Maybe there is a way to avoid the burial grounds and also do less environmental damage also?"
>
> Billy: "Yeh. Maybe, but I wonder how much less money we'll make; the park has to generate enough money to stay open. Let's try some other routes."

In this simple interaction, the two boys are practicing Richmond's "operational thinking," understanding how specific features of the structure of a system cause its behavior (such as how trail location affects visitor hiking patterns, environmental effects, and park revenues) and how changes in that structure can change system behavior.

As important, the boys are engaging in a critical collaborative learning process: probing one anothers' ways of thinking through the design problem they face and, in the process, making their own thinking more explicit. Plus, they are helping one another – neither is right or wrong, both are learning. Joe hadn't really thought about the Indian burial grounds as a constraint; this was outside the assumptions upon which he was operating. Likewise, Billy had not paid a lot of attention to the environmental damage of his trails because he was focused on maximizing hiker traffic and park revenues. Both become more aware of taken-for-granted assumptions through the other's inquiry. Both conclude that there may still be better overall designs if they expand their assumption sets. In short, the boys are mastering the basics of reflective learning based on collaborative inquiry, becoming more aware of their own taken-for-granted assumptions through thinking together.

Of course, such interactions only work if there is mutual respect. It is easy to imagine two young boys simply arguing about who is right, and never challenging their own reasoning.

This is why educators like Scheetz understand that realizing the benefit of systems thinking tools depends on the overall school environment. "An environment where learning is likely to occur," said Principal Mary Scheetz, "is one that is safe and secure, and where taking risks is OK."

What if we saw learning how to see systems as inseparable from learning how to see one another? What if we saw the foundation for systems citizenship as a seamless blend of cognitive and interpersonal skills in learning about complexity, anchored in learners' ongoing discovery about what it means to grow as a human being in relationship with one another? What if teachers, as well as other adults working with kids, saw themselves as mutual learners along with the students?

Rethinking Schools as Learning Communities

Early on in Orange Grove's movement toward adopting systems thinking and "learner-centered learning," the staff realized that their success depended on the overall learning culture at the school, starting with how they interacted with one another.

For example, teachers often espouse an ideal of collaboration but lack practical experience at truly creating a collaborative work environment. Of all professions, teaching is among the most individualistic. Whereas most people in business or architecture or law have an acute sense that their accomplishments are the result of a team effort (even though some individuals may have more visibility to a customer or a client), teachers typically operate in a highly fragmented world of *their* courses and *their* students. Working as teams does not come easily to teachers who have spent most of their lives in an educational system that emphasizes individual performance and competition, reinforced by a professional work environment that forces them to practice their craft alone much of the time.

It takes time and commitment to go beyond platitudes about collaboration. "Of all the changes I tried to lead as principal, helping teachers learn how to team was probably the most difficult," says Scheetz. She personally led several-day retreats, where teachers began to reflect and listen to one another more deeply and to build different capacities for dealing with the inevitable conflicts that arise between different teachers' lesson plans or strategies with particular kids. "There is so much more potential for collaborative solutions than normally gets realized given the professional isolation common to most schools," says Scheetz.

Scheetz and assistant principal Tracy Benson (who later succeeded Scheetz) made sure collaboration became part of teachers' daily lives by redesigning the school schedule so that all teachers had 45–60 min free to clinic with one another, each day. "Collaboration only starts to make a difference when teachers have time to practice coordinating in real time," says Benson. "They need to know what Billy's teacher found out in his first period class or how a new systems idea that is suppose to integrate across civics and science is actually playing out for the kids. This is what actually helps them feel like a team."

Gradually, Orange Grove's teachers began to build a larger vision of the type of school culture they wanted to create. "We have to lead by example," said Martha Jones (check name), a history teacher. "If we show respect to the kids and to one another, the kids see that." Over time, the Orange Grove teachers found that their hard work in developing themselves as a learning community started to reshape how they interacted. "Any topic we talk about is a process of building a community," said Tom Keys, a math teacher. "Dealing with all our differences is the key to building our shared vision."

As the teachers developed as a team, so did their understanding of how specifically to move toward the overall school environment they envisioned. In the end, this came down to one idea: respect. "Teachers are always trying to improve discipline. We took a radical approach: we abandoned all the rules," said Jones. "We eventually came up with one rule: show respect. We don't put one another down. We have to continually learn to listen to one another, not just superficially but actually."

Building learning communities does not stop at the four walls of the school. School cultures based on genuine respect and student engagement affect how people think and act and naturally start to bridge to encompass the larger community. Ironically, building this larger community is often more common in poorer settings, where resources are scarce and people must work together.

The Murphy School District in Pheonix, one of the founders of the SoL Education Partnership, is one of the poorest in America. Yet, the members of the community have succeeded in creating networks of mutual support that have led to delivery of food and clothing to those in need, a decrease in youth violence, domestic abuse and substance abuse, and an increase in student achievement over the past 3 years. A recent study by SoL researcher Dennis Sandow found that the "Students and their families, as well as the neighborhoods within Murphy School District, all benefit from a large, collaborative social system whose members include but are not limited to not-for-profit, government, faith-based and business organizations, teachers, councilors, parents, and Murphy School District graduates. There is a single (although unstated) purpose to this social system: to generate health and well being for Murphy School District students, families and neighbors" (Sandow, 2006).

Traditionally, the professional isolation of teachers is mirrored by the way schools see themselves as isolated institutional entities sitting apart from the larger communities in which they are embedded. This tragically often becomes a self-fulfilling prophesy: Isolated schools contribute little to their communities and in turn fail to tap the potential engagement and support from those communities. As this happens, the reciprocal benefits from acknowledging and cultivating the interdependence between school and community are lost.

"Maybe it is the harsh circumstances of Murphy, but it has always been obvious that if school here is to succeed it must become a hub for community building," says superintendent Paul Mohr, a founding member of the SoL Education Partnership. "When that happens, the benefits for students as well as adults can go well beyond what educators can do on their own." Over the past 5 years, student achievement at Murphy has increased significantly because of, according to Sandow, the larger "social system supporting the Murphy School District student's academic achievements."

What if "school" was defined not by institutional geography but by the geography of students' lives? What if the "teachers" were not just the professional educators but all the adults (and the older youth) with whom a student interacts? What if we assumed that sustaining innovation in education will only occur to the extent we develop collaborative networks linking local business, local social services and government organizations, and families who share a common vision of supporting kids in their development? What if we realized that whatever shortage we perceive in teachers is but an artifact of the fragmentation of school from the larger community – that, in fact, there are vast numbers of potential teachers waiting to be asked to help?

What would this mean for how education works in general and for nurturing systems citizens in particular – through reconnecting school and the larger communities to create a rich laboratory for students learning how to build healthy interdependence here and now?

Education for Sustainability: Making Systems Citizenship Real

The Monte del Sol charter school in Santa Fe, New Mexico, came up with a simple way to start reconnecting school to the larger community, the school's innovative "community learning project" requirement. Here's how it works.

Every tenth grader at Monte del Sol can identify something she or he wants to learn that someone in the community can teach her or him. The resulting project then constitutes one of his or her five required courses for the year. I have met students at Monte del Sol who have learned carpentry, consulting, and community organizing. As important as what they learn is how they learn it. Freed from the classroom, they re-create the oldest form of education, apprenticeship. Not only does this lead toward learning that has real meaning to them, it connects many adults with students and gives them a sense of being meaningful contributors in the school, paving the way for both to work together for building healthier and more sustainable communities.

Jaimie Cloud of the Cloud Institute, a national leader in education for sustainability for over a decade, identifies seven primary "habits of mind" to be cultivated in education for sustainability (Federico, Cloud, Byrne, & Wheeler, 2009):

- *Understanding of Systems as the Context for Decision Making*. The extent to which one sees both the whole system and its parts as well as the extent to which an individual can place one's self within the system
- *Intergenerational Responsibility*. The extent to which one takes responsibility for the effect(s) of her/his actions on future generations
- *Mindful of and Skillful with Implications and Consequences*. The extent to which one consciously makes choices and plans actions to achieve positive systemic impact
- *Protecting and Enhancing the Commons*. The extent to which one works to reconcile the conflicts between individual rights and the responsibilities of citizenship to tend to the commons
- *Awareness of Driving Forces and their Impacts*. The extent to which one recognizes and can act strategically and responsibly in the context of the driving forces that influence our lives
- *Assumption of Strategic Responsibility*. The extent to which one assumes responsibility for one's self and others by designing, planning, and acting with whole systems in mind
- *Paradigm Shifting*. The extent to which one recognizes mental models and paradigms as guiding constructs that change over time with new knowledge and applied insight

Cloud sees education for sustainability as integrating ideas and approaches from many different content areas, like "ecological literacy" (science principles and natural laws that help understand the interconnectedness of humans and all of the Earth's systems), system dynamics and systems thinking, "multiple perspectives" (truly valuing and learning from the life experiences and cultures of others), "sense of place" (connecting to and valuing the places in which we live), "sustainable economics" (study of the connections between economic, social, and natural systems), citizenship, participation and leadership (the rights, responsibilities, and actions associated with participatory democracy toward sustainable communities), and creativity and visioning (the ability to envision and invent a rich, hopeful future).

Obviously, education for sustainability is more than just new curriculum. It is about how the content and process of education can be interwoven with *real-life contexts* to create opportunities for young people to lead in building sustainable communities and societies. In short, real education for sustainability is only possible in concert with systems thinking, authentic youth engagement, and rethinking schools as learning communities to catalyze a radical shift. No longer is education something that adults do to kids. Education becomes a joint learning process for communities learning to become more sustainable.

For example, before I knew of the Monte del Sol charter school in Santa Fe, local businesspeople had given me an impressive local magazine, "Sustainable Santa Fe." In addition to high-quality articles focused on community sustainability challenges and innovative responses by local organizations, I noticed the editorial byline: In order to advertise in the magazine, companies had to first meet certain criteria of waste management and energy efficiency. So, not only did the magazine feature sustainability-oriented stories, it fostered healthy competition among local businesses for positive brand image. It was only later that I discovered that the magazine was in fact a product of a group of Monte del SoL students teaming up with local community mentors in desktop publishing. Indeed, it was the students who had the idea of the advertising criteria.

In such projects, students become catalysts for engaging their communities, as they have at Brewster, New York High School, where science teacher Scott Beall created a novel way to teach 10th and 11th grade science, "Do Right Enterprises." Beall told his largely conservative school board he was connecting meaningful science education with developing entrepreneurial skills. In fact, he had a bigger aim. For example, Brady teaches students how to conduct energy audits and then engages local businesspeople as clients. Not only do the students learn how to apply science to practical analysis, even local businesses start to reduce their energy (and carbon) footprint. Along the way, the students discover the difference they can make to their community.

"We thought we were doing the students a favor by letting them come in and gather some data from our restaurant," said one local businessperson. "We had no idea how much waste they would find, and how much money we could save."

The difference for student learning, even as defined more traditionally, is dramatic. "There is no doubt that the kids in the "Do Right" course learn as much science content as counterparts in more traditional science classes," says Beall. In fact, their New York Regents' science exam results tend to be as high or higher than counterparts in more traditional classrooms. "There are many ways you can design meaningful service learning sustainability projects with particular curricular content in mind," says Beall. "The big payoff is student motivation and a completely different understanding of what it means to *do science* rather than do schoolroom exercises."

When education for sustainability is connected to authentic youth engagement, learning naturally becomes intertwined with youth leadership development. "I think we tend to greatly underestimate young people's capacities as leaders," says Les Omotani, superintendent of the Hewlett-Woodmere district and another SoL Education Partnership founder. Starting several years ago, Omotani invited high school students to learn the disciplines of learning organizations and how to become systems thinkers and to serve as facilitators for community dialogues that the school hosts. "The young people learned that they could help adults have meaningful conversations about how to make the community, including the schools, more healthy," says Omotani. "The adults at Hewlett-Woodmere have learned to listen to and support the students' voice and come to see the students as important leaders, a view that many of the young people have accepted as well." The whole process is anchored in the yearlong Youth Leadership Forum, which invites students to focus on their own development as servant-leaders and systems thinkers, including change projects they shape themselves. Projects in recent years have included replacing disposable cups with reusable cups in the school and a "bag the bag" project that produced and promotes the use of reusable bags, rather than plastic bags, in the community.

"It's hard for me to imagine achieving the changes ahead without empowering the voice of young people to take responsibility for their own future," says Omotani, "rather than graduating disempowered and disengaged high school students angry at the irresponsibility they see all around them. We believe that a twenty-first century high school education must not only prepare our graduates for higher education and how to make a living but perhaps more importantly to prepare them to live (create) a sustainable and high quality of life!"

Stories like these also implicitly raise basic questions about how education for sustainability might address fundamental developmental needs for teenagers long neglected by traditional secondary education.

For most of human history, by the age of thirteen to fifteen, children had gone through some sort of rite of passage that signaled their joining the adult community. It was well understood that it was important that they discover how they could contribute to that larger community. Confining students in their mid-teens to classroom instruction and traditional academic exercises not only fails to tap their creativity, it also ignores fundamental developmental needs to deepen their sense of personal purpose and to learn how they can make a difference. It is impossible to know how much of the anomie and developmental anxiety young people encounter later in life, in their twenties and thirties, has its roots in neglecting these developmental requirements in their teens.

Noted anthropologist Edward Hall, who had spent his life studying child-rearing in diverse cultures, felt that confining young adults to schoolroom learning "(ignores) the primate base we are built upon. . . Until a generation ago, males were warriors at the age of 18. . . with all that energy, those glands going like mad, they shouldn't be in school. They're tearing things apart! We should educate them before and after" (Hall, 1980, 1988).

What if we learned once more how to create meaningful rites of passage for entering young adulthood, and this were integrated into the educational process? How much of the frustration for students and teachers alike would be alleviated if we stopped seeing traditional classroom education as the anchor in secondary education and school became more a sort of base camp for young people exploring how to deepen their own sense of responsibility and efficacy – and the content of the curriculum were organized around this core developmental need? What if we stop seeing them as school children and, as Omotani says, saw them as important leaders in building more sustainable communities? How much would this contribute to the shifts desperately needed in awareness, understanding, and values needed to build a more sustainable world?

Learning that Lasts

These schools afford a rare opportunity to glimpse the longer-term consequences of education for systems citizenship. Orange Grove was one of the first public schools in the US to adopt systems thinking, authentic youth engagement (what they called "learner-centered learning"), and building schools as learning communities, starting in the late 1980s. (Education for sustainability was not a term used explicitly then, but many of the school's projects focused on these priorities.) Now, thanks to a recently released video documentary, we can see some of the longer-term effects.

Filmmaker James Morrison and former Orange Grove teacher Joan Yates recently brought together seven former Orange Grove students, including several who had been part of an earlier PBS satellite video program when they were students, 14 years earlier. The former students' reflections indicate powerful life lessons tracing to their experiences as middle schoolers.

"My overwhelming positive recollection was one of being involved in what I was doing; there not being a set outcome; of learning on the go, of presenting at the end of the day a result that was *totally mine*, that didn't conform to a typical school-sheet form," says James, now an attorney. "I remember that as a very powerful thing. I really felt like I was seeing real world results."

The systems perspective was very real for the kids when they were students, as evident in these quotes from the original video: "I like the flexibility." "You use it almost automatically: just like that, you analyze a problem as a system." "We are so much more motivated than kids in other schools." "You learn so much more than you would if it was just paperwork."

And, it clearly had stuck with them 14 years later. Dave (a high school teacher today) talked of seeing a classroom as a system: "From the minute they walk in from home, managing thirty kids in a room five times a day is all about the systems."

Nat (now a medical resident) commented: "(I notice) how often people use the word "system" and why the levers people try fail. In a recent documentary on New Orleans (after Hurricane Katrina), I was struck by how often people said that we need to use a systems approach so that this does not happen again: the failure in the levies happened because multiple parts of the system that should have been considered were not, whether it was wetlands or the height of the levies or whatever – people just didn't consider how all of this would interact."

"It (systems thinking) really made us think out of the box, rather than just follow the easiest answer or the first answer that comes to you," according to Athena, a dentist today.

Interestingly, one of the lasting effects of their systems thinking work as teenagers was a sense of humility that had carried into their careers as adults: "Systems thinking teaches you to not take the straight line path between point A and point B," said James. "That's such an important lesson, not just for children, but for everyone. The ultimate lesson of systems thinking is that it's always more complicated than you think. As a parent, I cannot think of anything more important I could teach my children, because it goes to addressing so much in our society – not just what we do as professionals, but for who we are as people and how we interact with our community and how we interact with the world at large. I think systems thinking is an imperative for how we educate our children, both now and in the future."

In the original video, Scheetz talked about the importance of creating "simulations where students learn how to make decisions to improve a system." Interestingly, when the adult students go together, several reflected on what they had learned from the systems simulations they had done years earlier.

"In an ideal world, patient care would work like a good simulation," said Nat. "You come with your set of knowledge but you have access to people you consult with. A cohesive approach is especially important with complicated patient illnesses."

Others talked about a city planning simulation they had done as students and the lessons it had left, like understanding trade-offs in making decisions. "I had located the school next to a shopping mall," said Kelly, now a nurse, "because I thought getting kids to shop would be good for the economy. But, it also promoted truancy. I hadn't thought about that."

The adult former students also talked about the importance of collaboration and learning from one another as a defining feature of their Orange Grove experience. In the original video, many of the students' comments had focused on the importance of working together: "Working together we get to know one another... You learn more trust." Another commented: "You had a partner and you could converse a lot... there was so much freedom but you also had a goal."

Fourteen years later, Andy (now a trade negotiator at the Department of Commerce) commented, "(In order to get things done) you are completely dependent on your ability to understand other people's thinking... (for example in negotiations with the Chinese) to understand their positions, what sorts of pressures people feel domestically from their constituents. It's really hard to shift from a 'push' type of argument, trying to convince someone, to 'pulling' them towards you. Making that sort of mental transition was really beneficial in my work." Interestingly, in the original video, 13-year old Andy had commented, "You really have to start to learn to listen to other people... because you may actually be wrong." Seeing this, Andy commented, "I had not realized how much of this insight came from the 8th grade."

Appreciating collaboration is rooted in understanding the limits of each person's mental models, starting with your own. "You have your perspective and you have to seek others' views," said Nat. "You learn pretty quickly that the docs are pretty knowledgeable but so too are the nurses and the support staff, and many have been in the trenches a lot longer than you have. You need to pay attention to one another and actively seek their advice."

Clearly, for these young adults, systems thinking and learning collaboratively had shaped their worldviews in profound ways. In Andy's words: "The real question is, are you, when you are the person in a position of power, willing to let it go? Are you willing to ask, 'I don't know – what do you think?'" For Athena, "Yes, we learned to look for more complexity, but also to look to our peers." For Nat, "I think we learned how to actively seek out knowledge together." For Dave, "When you look at other middle schools and you talk with other people, this really was a different place."

Conclusions

"Education is the most powerful weapon, which you can use to change the world," said Nelson Mandela. As concerns grow around the world around "sustainability" and the overall path of global industrial development, businesses, NGOs, and governments are stepping forward to confront increasingly critical issues around food, water, climate change, destruction of ecosystems, waste and toxicity, and growing gaps between rich and poor. But, if you believe that the shifts ahead will be cultural, not just technical, the potential role of education looms large.

Hoping to direct attention to this role, the United Nations declared the decade from 2005 to 2014 the decade of "Education for Sustainable Development."[9] This is encouraging, but the response in schools to date far less than what is needed. Today, what passes for sustainability education mostly is reworked environmental science curricula, even though the UNESCO emphasizes that it is about more than ecology but affects an "integrated approach to education, learning and life." Still, few school systems have reprioritized their goals. Most teachers remain focused on "teaching to the test," seeking to improve student achievement in traditional subjects. Few business and public-sector leaders have stepped forward to "connect the dots" between essential long-term societal changes and a fundamental rethinking

---

[9]See portal.unesco.org/education/en/ev.php-URL_ID=27234&URL_DO=DO_TOPIC&URL_SECTION=201.html

of the aims of primary and secondary education. Lofty sentiments do not make a revolution – yet that is exactly what we need.

In my view, two things are missing.

First, we must build a meaningful consensus as to the scope and substance of education for the twenty-first century and how it differs from education in the past. Perhaps, the vision of systems citizenship can help focus this budding consensus. Whether we are ready or not, young people will inherit a world in which they are first and foremost global citizens, not national citizens. Unlike any time in human history, young people today grow up with an awareness of the world, and with increasing connections to other young people around the world. It is irresponsible that they should leave secondary school without understanding how the global economy works, or understanding the basic interconnections between healthy economies, healthy societies, and healthy ecosystems. It is tragic that they should leave without genuine curiosity about and engagement with other cultures, for which, often, they need but to travel across their city.

I believe that *systems thinking provides the missing intellectual and cognitive underpinning for education for global citizenship*. This is starting to be understood among business and civil society leaders. "If I reflect on what many organizations have been going through, the whole awareness of sustainability has been growing because systems thinking, in different forms, is enabling us to see much more interdependencies than we have seen in the past," says Andre van Heemstra of Unilever Management Board. He adds: "It is those interdependencies which make you conclude that it is more than stupid, it is reckless to think of commercial sustainability in isolation of either social or environmental sustainability" (Senge et al., 2008, p. 217).

Barry Richmond's eight "systems thinking skills" offer a starting point in translating the need for systems thinking into the curricula and pedagogy needed to achieve it. By building upon the foundations of critical thinking and scientific reasoning, Richmond offers a bridge to mainstream ideas that are widely accepted. He extends these to incorporate thinking and learning skills almost completely missing in education today: namely, "the endogenous viewpoint" and learning how to identify feedback dynamics and understand the nonlinear ways complex systems can respond to simple changes. Long regarded as the stuff of graduate education, 20 years of evidence now exists to show that, done well, these skills can be nurtured in primary education and developed to remarkably advanced levels in secondary education, not just for an elite but for the majority of students.

Today many educators embrace goals like students "should know how to think systemically." But little will change without rigorous programs of study, teacher training, and curriculum development. When combined with developments in education for sustainability and reflection and youth engagement, I believe there is much to build upon to create such programs.

Second, we must face the fact that it is unlikely that basic innovation in education will be accomplished by educators working alone. The failures of endless "educational reform" movements to produce large-scale lasting changes offer mute testimony to forces that work to conserve the status quo in public education. The problem is not that educators do not have new ideas. The problem is that we, as a society, demand that education continue to operate in the main as it did when we were children. This immense cognitive anchor becomes the source of the political movements that inevitably rise up to squelch meaningful experimentation, the sine quo non of innovation. This inherent conservatism will continue to thwart innovation until communities of leaders from *education, business, civil society, and local government start working together* to support ongoing basic innovation, not remediation in public education.

We do not need to have all the answers worked out in advance in order to build these coalitions. We do need to have the capacity as communities to prioritize and persist in supporting new thinking and new practice. We don't just need teachers who are "prophets," as Gordon Brown called for. We need diverse leaders from all sectors willing to travel together into a future we can only begin to imagine. Education for life after the Industrial Age requires realizing that humans will actually be living together differently in the coming decades or they will not be living much at all – and that young people often have deeper intuitions than do adults regarding the changes coming.

Through the SoL Education Partnership, we are working together to embody and explore in several communities around the country what these new partnerships can look like. In particular, we are working to connect innovators from business and civil society with their counterparts in education. Many businesspeople live in a world where either you innovate or die. They understand how to manage the risks that come with experimentation, how to focus on testing new ideas in local ways before they are extended prematurely to broad application, how to finance and assess innovation. But to date, the businesspeople drawn into working on education have mostly been reacting to perceived shortcomings in schools, rather than focusing on the real needs of creating sustained innovation.

A natural alignment exists between innovators in the private sector and innovators in education, but this alignment has not yet developed sufficiently to have large-scale impact. Leaders in the private sector know that they need people who can think for themselves; solve complex problems in creative teams; work effectively with people from different cultures; and maintain a global, longer term perspective while dealing with immediate problems at hand. Yet, relatively few of our schools are focusing on these requirements in educating students, and most school systems and state departments of education are still sadly out of touch with these very real needs.

Lastly, pursuing both this new consensus and building these new cross-sector partnerships will, I believe, bring us as a society to confront a core unasked question: *In a world of growing interdependence, what is the purpose of education?*

There is a timeless aspect of the purpose of education, enabling young people to grow as healthy and contributing human beings. Most people drawn to teaching as a life work are drawn because of this calling, to be part of how children and young people grow and develop as human beings. This is the love of learning for its own sake.

But there is also a timely and contextual aspect of education, which starts with recognizing the specific challenges society faces and how education must be part of solving these problems. This is the aspect of education that Nelson Mandela reminds us of, and it is to this aspect that education for systems citizenship points.

No one works consciously to destroy ecosystems, or to widen the gap between rich and poor, or to use water and topsoil more rapidly than they are replenished, or to increase concentrations of greenhouse gases to the point of destabilizing global climate. All these changes occur as unintended by-products of business-as-usual. The problem is that, whether as businesspeople, consumers, or voters, we tend to operate with blinders. Individuals make decisions, like the products we buy, with virtually no awareness of the consequences of their choices for others. Companies maximize profits with little attention to the larger social costs, like the costs of climate change. Governments pursue national interests with little regard to the fact that all nations' interests are now increasingly bound together.

We have the sustainability issues that we have because, as individuals, organizations, and societies, we are unable to see the larger systems we have created that shape modern society, and we are unable to work together across institutional and national boundaries to create alternative systems.

Our core task is simple – to create a truly *regenerative economy and society,* one that operates based on the defining principle of all interdependent living systems: Life creates conditions for life. It is time to recognize that young people have the largest stake in the unsustainable future we are now shaping, and they are more than ready to share in creating an alternative. Are we?

References

Federico, C., Cloud, J., Byrne, J., & Wheeler, K. (2009). *Kindergarten through twelfth-grade education for sustainability*. Accessed 23 July, 2009, from http://www.sustainabilityed.org/what/education_for_sustainability/documents/K12Chapter.PDF

Hall, E. (1980). *Beyond culture*. New York: Doubleday.

Hall, E. (1988, Spring 12–14). The drive to learn. *Santa Fe Lifestyle*.

Quaden, R. A., Ticotsky, A., & Lyneis, D. (2009). *The shape of change*. Accessed 23 July, 2009, from www.clexchange.org

Sandow, D. (2006). *Murphy School District's learning communities*. Piper Foundation research paper. Phoenix, Arizona: Virginia Piper Charitable Trust.

Senge, P. (2000). The industrial age system of education. In P. Senge, N. Cambron-McCabe, A. Kleiner, T. Lucas, & B. Smith (Eds.), *Schools that learn* (pp. 27–58). New York: Doubleday.

Senge, P., et al. (2008). *The necessary revolution: How individuals and organizations are working together to create a sustainable world*. New York: Doubleday.

Social Movement Organizing and Equity-Focused Educational Change: Shifting the Zone of Mediation

Michelle Renée, Kevin Welner, and Jeannie Oakes

In the first edition of this handbook, we recommended significant shifts in the way education change is understood and pursued. Specifically, we argued that reforms seeking to disrupt historic connections among race, social class, educational opportunities, and schooling outcomes are likely distorted or abandoned altogether during the implementation process. To succeed, such "equity-focused" change must move beyond conventional change to address a series of unique political and normative challenges (Oakes, Welner, Yonezawa, & Allen, 1998). A related recommendation from that earlier chapter was that the processes of formulating, adopting, and implementing include the active participation of members of less powerful communities as well as the professionals and elites who typically lead reforms. Finally, we joined many others in recommending that education leaders be held accountable for providing all students with a high-quality education and, in particular, for ensuring that the least well-off students are provided with the learning resources they need. Here too, however, we argued that the form of accountability most likely to support the implementation of equity-focused change is the accountability of policy makers and school officials to the public and, most notably, to members of marginalized groups whose educational chances depend on such reforms.

An emerging body of research documents how social movement organizations around the nation have, over the past decade, furthered all three of these recommendations. This updated chapter use Welner's "zone of mediation" (Oakes et al., 1998; Welner, 2001) to illuminate how social movement organizations are beginning to shift the boundaries, structure, and substance of local- and state-level education reform. The zone of mediation describes the potential of these organizations to bring greater balance to policy deliberations, increasing the probability of the initiation and sound implementation of equity-focused change.

The chapter begins with an explanation of the zone of mediation – describing the nature and use of the concept. We identify the types of forces that shape the zone and describe the potential role of social movement organizations as one of those

J. Oakes (✉)
Presidential Professor of Educational Equity, UCLA; Director, Educational Opportunity and Scholarship, The Ford Foundation, New York
e-mail: j.oakes@fordfound.org

A. Hargreaves et al. (eds.), *Second International Handbook of Educational Change*,   153
Springer International Handbooks of Education 23, DOI 10.1007/978-90-481-2660-6_9,
© Springer Science+Business Media B.V. 2010

forces. We then review recent studies that document how social movement organizations are building on the legacy of the civil rights movement to advocate for more equitable school policies and practices. Next, we apply the theoretical construct of the zone of mediation to two examples from our work in California – a statewide "opportunity-to-learn" campaign led by a coalition of community-based and legal-advocacy organizations and a grassroots movement in Los Angeles to make college preparatory courses the default curriculum for all students. We conclude with an analysis of three elements that we think are key to the future success of social movement organizations in shifting the zone of mediation to make schools more equitable: (a) the practice of participatory inquiry, (b) the need to address the political and normative aspects of education reform, and (c) the importance of efforts being grounded in the theory that schools are a key component of the larger political economy.

Reintroducing the Zone of Mediation

The equity-focused reform process is unique. These reforms tend to face daunting normative and political obstacles at both the initiation and implementation stages. Quite often, the environment for potential equity-focused reforms is simply not hospitable toward forward movement. In our studies of detracking reforms, for example, we repeatedly observed this inhospitability; teachers and school leaders have explained to us that the politics of schools and neighborhoods would never allow for meaningful changes to elite, high-track classes (Oakes, 1992, 2005; Welner, 2001).

A decade ago, when we wrote our chapter for the first edition of this handbook, we criticized the dominant educational change literature for failing to adequately account for the normative and political barriers standing in the way of such equity-focused reform. That literature, we contended, assumes well-meaning actors who, if given the technical tools and shown the way, will move forward with school improvement efforts. While this dynamic might exist for purely technical reforms, it is rarely recognizable for reforms that strongly implicate issues of race, class, and language-minority status.

To help illustrate the forces – particularly technical, normative, political, and inertial forces – that create the environment surrounding a potential reform, we described a zone of mediation:

> [Schools are] situated within particular local enactments of larger cultural norms, rules, incentives, power relations and values. These forces promote either stability or change, and they accordingly set the parameters of beliefs, behavior, and policy in schools. The intersection of forces around a particular issue shapes the zone of mediation for that issue. Such forces may include such far-reaching items as legislation, judicial decisions, foundation support, demographics, housing and nutritional needs, economic and market forces, social/state political climates, educational influence groups (such as teacher unions), district history, individual players within districts, their political ambitions, and the media. (Welner, 2001, p. 95)

> Each reform proceeds within a unique context. This context, . . . the zone of mediation, is shaped by a myriad of forces. When forces are added, subtracted, strengthened or weakened, the zone shifts. With each shift, the zone becomes more receptive or more hostile to the reform. From this perspective, the reform process is a battle over contextual turf. (Welner, 2001, p. 223)

The zone framework calls our attention to the forces that continually shape and reshape the context for reform. Each new reform rests atop multiple layers of social and political history, as well as past experiences with education reforms.

The zone framework also highlights why a reformer attentive to just technical interventions will likely fail to advance equity-focused change. Such change requires a fundamentally different understanding than do changes in the overwhelmingly technical realm – for example, changing approaches to teaching mathematics, acquiring and using new instructional technologies, or even most reforms designed to foster healthier school cultures. These technical changes are not simple, particularly when they deviate from the culturally established "grammar of schooling" (Tyack & Cuban, 1995), but compared to equity-focused change, they do not implicate substantial normative and political issues. That is, they tend to require only relatively small changes in core normative beliefs about who can learn and in the need to overcome political opposition related to issues of race and social class. If reformers create an environment where technical needs are met (i.e., where school structures changes and resources are put in place), but they neglect the political and normative environment, an equity-focused change is unlikely to be successfully initiated or implemented (Welner, 2001; see also Oakes & Rogers, 2006).

We've also criticized mainstream school change literature for "emphasiz[ing] concerns that are normatively and politically neutral, such as the need for schools to become 'learning organizations' where teachers and administrators act as 'change agents' skilled at dealing with change as a normal part of their work" (Welner, 2001, p. 12; see also Oakes & Rogers, 2006). This same approach can be seen in recent attempts at so-called "whole school reform," which is similarly focused on carefully planned organizational change (see Berends, Bodilly, & Kirby, 2002). In the service of implementing the school improvement plan, whole-school reformers address such items as getting the pieces in place, creating buy-in, instituting staff development, acquiring resources, and developing and empowering leadership. While careful planning, resources, buy-in and leadership certainly do help to create a more hospitable environment for reform, this is what we call a "neutral" reform approach. When it comes to equity-focused reform, these neutral elements are insufficient to create a healthy change context.

In this regard, we think it important to draw a distinction between *school improvement*, which depends overwhelming on a healthy within-school culture, and *third-order change* (Welner, 2001), which depends not only on within-school culture but also greatly depends on the context surrounding the school. Third-order changes are "fundamental changes which seek to reform core normative beliefs about race, class, intelligence and educability held by educators and others involved with our schools" (Oakes et al., 1998, p. 968).[1] While school improvement is intended to better accomplish current school goals, third-order reform is intended to shift those goals to become more equity-focused.

Third-order changes tend to directly oppose and confront prevailing external forces and, therefore, are most likely to fall outside the zone of mediation. Moreover, the process of implementation often results in a watering down of reforms' equity-focused aspects. We call this process "downward mutual adaptation:"

> [T]he changes [to an equity-focused reform] that arise as a result of interaction with pre-existing school context will almost always be in the direction of less equity. That is, the pressures from the school and the community will likely favor the dominant societal actors (the local elites) at the expense of the reform's intended beneficiaries. (Welner, 2001, p. 228)

As explained throughout this chapter, these concepts of the zone and of downward mutual adaptation illustrate why political mobilization is crucial for the success of third-order, equity-focused reform. Community organizing and other forms of political mobilization can help shape a zone of mediation in the direction of more equity. The principal at a school with a recently initiated detracking reform, for example, is more likely to push forward with the reform if any voices of discontent are balanced by voices praising the effort.

This chapter fleshes out these ideas, again considering the equity-focused reform dynamic and again applying the zone framework to help explain the importance of addressing norms and politics. Our specific emphasis in this chapter concerns social movements. In our chapter a decade ago, we illustrated the zone concept while describing the role of court orders. Like such mandates, social movements and community organizing can play an important reform role, and we contend here that this role has generally been misunderstood and underestimated and has too often been ignored.

Our current emphasis on social movements should not, however, detract from our broad contention about the zone of mediation: many scholars and policy makers have fallen into the trap of looking to just one type of "force" – whether technical, legislative, judicial, or social movement – as having the sole potential to bring about change. By pushing social movements to the forefront, we are in no way minimizing the importance of other forces shaping the zone; rather, this chapter serves to introduce social movement organizations as one critical and increasingly active force.

---

[1] Larry Cuban (1992) set forth a framework with a two-part typology for educational change, distinguishing between changes of different magnitude. He categorized changes that simply improve the efficiency and effectiveness of current practices as "first-order" or "incremental" changes, and he categorized those changes that seek to alter the basic ways that organizations function as "second-order" or "fundamental" changes. Our "third order changes" are fundamental (second-order) changes that also seek to reform educators' and community members' core normative beliefs about such matters as race, class, intelligence, and educability.

Reshaping the Zone Through Social Movements

The role of social movement organizations in equity-focused education change is perhaps best understood in the context of recent social movement theories, which focus on both political processes and identity formation. Pursuant to this approach, social movements are first and foremost identified by the presence of protest, or "contentious actions" (Tarrow, 1998). By definition, social movements challenge the technical, political, and normative aspects of the existing political system. Social movement organizations are also defined as organizations that engage in forming new collective identities (Whittier, 2002). That is, at the same time that social movement organizations aim to transform the external political system through protest, they also aim to transform the role of individuals and groups in that system (generally by increasing the power of traditionally marginalized groups). And social movement organizations share common features of all organizations: internal structures, regular participants, defined goals, and technical skills and resources (Della Porta & Diani, 1999). Social movement organizations vary significantly – some are multinational, are well funded and engage in multiple issues; others are small and focus on just a single local issue. Most exist somewhere in between.

Current social movement organizing for school equity builds on the long history of activism in African American, Latino, Asian American, and Native American communities. The Civil Rights Movement is perhaps the most well-known social movement in American history. Though the Civil Rights Movement was focused on achieving equity for African Americans across all sectors of society, educational equity was clearly at its center. Similarly, prior to *Brown*, Latino communities in California and elsewhere organized and litigated to fight segregation and inadequate educational opportunities (Donato, 1997). Beginning at the time of the Treaty of Guadalupe Hidalgo, which annexed the American Southwest, and continuing to the present day, organizing in Latino communities has included student protest, leadership development, and the creation of Latino community organizations (Delgado Bernal, 2003; San Miguel & Valencia, 1998). Some of the established organizations that currently work on education reform around the nation, such as the NAACP and MALDEF, have direct roots in the Civil Rights Movement.

A small but growing body of literature is beginning to document the recent wave of social movement organizing focused on education reform. The Industrial Areas Foundation (IAF) is perhaps the best-studied example of modern education organizing. The IAF began with Saul Alinsky's work in Chicago's poor neighborhoods in the 1930s, helping ordinary people organize to solve local community problems. Self-interest, collective power, and relationships were central to Alinsky's organizing approach. Drawing from labor organizing movements, he taught neighborhood residents to identify problems in their communities and use confrontational tactics such as sit-ins and boycotts to improve their lives. In Alinsky's view, collective power was the only tool available to poor people for wresting concessions from the rich and powerful and for countering their use of wealth and political position to maintain their advantages (Alinsky, 1971). These ideas remain at the core of contemporary organizing, although today's grassroots efforts also reflect the legacy of the Civil Rights Movement, which infused organizing with an emphasis on learning and leadership development (Oakes & Rogers, 2006; Payne, 1995; Ransby, 2003).

Shirley (1997, 2002) and Warren (2001) provide extensive case studies of the development and impact of the Alliance school network built by the Texas IAF. Ernesto Cortes and the group's organizers built on local movements to form the Alliance Schools Project in Texas. Local parents and community members learned to use contentious action to develop what they called "fear and loathing relationships" with elected officials, which held those officials accountable for improving schools in some of the state's most impoverished neighborhoods of color (Shaw, 2001). At the same time, however, the Alliance Schools Project augmented their repertoire of strategies beyond direct confrontation to include mutually supportive, if sometimes confrontational, relationships between communities and local schools.

Over time, this productive combination of "relational" strategies – powerful community engagement and strong accountability – was recognized and supported by the state legislature and department of education. The network of Alliance schools has been granted financial resources supporting teacher professional development and student academic assistance. Teachers, principals, and parents within the network of schools meet to collaborate, learn, and campaign for additional resources, helping to enhance and sustain the reform. Notably, throughout the evolution of the project, the work has maintained its organizing edge – with community members judging educators and officials by actions and results (rather than promises), giving them credit when they have advanced the group's agenda and criticizing them loudly when they have not.

Setting aside for a moment the normative and political context, one can identify within this reform elements that are often advocated by mainstream school reformers: collaborative school environments, professional development, resources to help students succeed, and even waivers from restrictive top–down rules. These can be thought of as the "technical" elements of the Texas IAF reform. But describing the reform only in terms of those technical elements neglects the reality that in most jurisdictions normative and political forces, as well as inertial forces, would likely keep this reform from going forward; what differed in Texas was the social movement (Oakes, 1992; Oakes & Rogers, 2006; Welner, 2001).

The Texas IAF challenged the forces that created the preexisting zone of mediation as well as the inequitable education system in Texas. The participation of community members, parents, teachers, and others who developed the Alliance schools brought about the technical changes, but they did so by also bringing about political changes (community members gained an authentic role in school decision making) and normative changes (IAF members countered stereotypes, increased the social capital of their community, and helped to shift fundamental ideas about the cause of inequity in Texas schools). That is, these political and normative changes made possible by organizing strategies shifted the zone to make it more hospitable to the technical changes. While the technical knowledge likely existed prior to the social movement, the reform could not feasibly have been initiated or implemented without that movement.

The impact of social movement organizing on the zone of meditation is also illustrated by the normative changes resulting from the activities of Comité de Padres Latinos (COPLA), a community organization of Latino parents in Carpentaria, California. Delgado-Gaitan (2001) describes how engaging in school reform "changed [the parents'] perception about their lives from one of deficit to empowerment [which] led to the cultural changes in the family, the community and in their personal lives" (p. 175). These are not isolated, insignificant examples. A national study by Gold, Simon, Mundell, and Brown (2004) located over 140 education organizations with an active membership base, working on equity, building cross-community alliances, developing democratic leadership, and aiming to improve the civic participation and power of low-to-moderate communities. After synthesizing information about these organizations, they concluded that organizing "creates the political will to address problems that would otherwise go unattended for lack of an organized constituency demanding attention to them" (p. 705). Most recently, Mediratta and her colleagues (2008) found that by creating political contexts (zones of mediation) hospitable to equitable education change, community organizing in eight communities around the country produced tangible effects on policy and resource decisions, school-level improvements, and student outcomes.

This emerging body of literature documents the increasing engagement of social movement organizations in education reform, as well as the ways in which social movement organizations intentionally and explicitly address the political and normative aspects of reform and thereby reshape the zone. Yet, as we explained above, no single force is responsible for shaping the zone; in each of the case studies we encountered, social movement organizations interacted with other forces (many hostile to the reform efforts) to reshape the zone and redefine their schools.

To further illustrate the role of social movement organizations, we present two case studies of social movement organizing from our research in California (Oakes & Rogers, 2006; Renee, 2006). These examples demonstrate how the organizations act as a force and how they interact with other forces (economy, history, courts, politicians, school administrators, etc.) to shape the zone. The first focuses on a statewide campaign to ensure all California students have an equal opportunity to learn. The second is an example of education reform at the local level – a coalition of grassroots organizations formed to advocate for the implementation of a curriculum policy extending college preparation to all students in the Los Angeles Unified School District (LAUSD). Both cases involve the joining together of grassroots, advocacy, legal, and research organizations to form coalitions capable of generating enough power to alter technical policies, political relationships, and normative beliefs.

Case Study #1: Education Adequacy and Opportunities to Learn in California

By the turn of this century, California's once first-rate education system had crumbled. The state ranked below almost every other state in the number of counselors and teachers per student; hundreds of schools and thousands of classrooms were overcrowded; only 69 students of every 100 who were in 9th grade 4 years earlier actually graduated from high school, and only 27 of those 69 graduates had passed the courses required for entry into any of the state's 4-year public colleges (Rogers, Oakes, Terriquez, & Valladares, 2007). Layered on top of this inadequacy was significant inequality; the state's growing Latino and African American student populations were far more likely to bear the brunt of resource shortages and lack of educational opportunity. Subsequently their rates of graduation and college preparation lagged far behind those of Whites and Asians.

Little meaningful reform had been forthcoming to counter these problems. Students ill-served by the schools 20 years earlier found their own children to be equally ill-served, or worse. And, as easy as it was for some policy makers to recognize and decry inequalities and other weaknesses in the school system, it had been extraordinarily difficult to initiate and implement policies that substantially reform the system. To some extent, this is because change must overcome inertial forces, such as educators and others who want to continue doing things the way they've always been done. To some extent, too, it is because of normative and political forces.

Challenging these forces in California were forty-eight students and their parents, supported by a team of advocates, who filed a lawsuit (*Williams v. State of California*) in the spring of 2000. These families argued, on behalf of a class of over a million students, that California's governor, State Board of Education, and State Superintendent of Public Instruction failed to provide them with qualified teachers, basic educational supplies, and safe classrooms and school facilities. Their case alleged that the state violated the students' constitutional right to an education. The plaintiffs, who were nearly all African American, Latino, and Asian Pacific Islander students attending predominately non-White schools, also argued that students of color and low-income students disproportionately experienced the lack of basic educational resources. Their bottom line was that all students must receive certain basic resources in order to learn and that the state had a legal responsibility to ensure that schools are adequately resourced.

As is generally the case with major education rights litigation, a cadre of public interest law firms represented the interests of the *Williams* plaintiffs.[2] Unique to *Williams*, however, was the extent of engagement from the very outset between the lawyers and a group of grassroots community advocates and educational researchers. Aware of past long-term failures of much equity-focused litigation, this coalition determined that sustained community engagement was critical to maintaining public pressure on policy makers and in particular for ensuring that the equity intent of any new laws or regulations survived through implementation. In this regard, it is noteworthy that the legal team set aside staff time and organizational resources to support the learning and mobilization of community organizations engaged with the *Williams* litigation. The result was that the inertial, normative,

---

[2]In this case, the firms included the ACLU of Northern and Southern California, Public Advocates, and MALDEF, as well as pro bono counsel from the San Francisco firm, Morrison & Foerster.

and political forces shaping the zone of mediation were all challenged – by the litigation itself, but also by grassroots organizing that targeted political and normative resistance to change.

For a group of California social justice organizations, *Williams* was an opportunity to collaborate with each other, building their own base of members concerned about education, and helping to address the inequalities in California's education system. A newly formed collection of local community organizations, state chapters of national grassroots organizations, research institutes, and advocacy groups approached philanthropic organizations with a proposal for a collaborative campaign to further the education justice goals of the *Williams* litigation. Two statewide collaboratives were formed – the Campaign for Quality Education (CQE) and the Educational Justice Collaborative (EJC). The CQE is a loose coalition of California education justice organizations that meet to build alliances and coordinate statewide campaigns. Its structure and development were facilitated by Californians for Justice, a statewide student organization. The EJC is a collaborative effort between UCLA's Institute for Democracy, Education, and Access (IDEA) and over 30 activist and advocacy organizations, with the express goal of improving the equity of California schools. The EJC does not run campaigns. Rather, it provides the time and space for different organizations to study issues, form relationships, exchange ideas and strategies, and build organizational capacity to engage with policy makers and the media. These two statewide collaboratives overlap in membership as well as in their focus issues (Oakes & Rogers, 2006).

As the *Williams* litigation made its way through the courts and the eventual negotiated settlement, California's educators, students, and policy makers were debating a related policy: the impending implementation of a new high school exit exam. Organizers participating in the CQE and EJC began to look for ways to address this combination of issues. At a grassroots level, students, parents, and advocates pointed to the unfairness of denying high school diplomas to students denied opportunities – those who attended poorly maintained and under-resourced schools. From their perspective, the exit exam seemed to be punishing students for politicians' failure to adequately fund schools. As these community groups began to develop campaigns, they collectively turned for assistance to the researchers at UCLA's IDEA (including authors Renee and Oakes) affiliated with the EJC.

During these meetings, we heard them articulate their concerns and recognized the match between their theories and the "opportunity to learn" theories discussed in the education literature. Specifically, we heard in these ideas the call for resource and practice standards needed to ensure that all students have the opportunity to perform at a high level (Guiton & Oakes, 1995; O'Day et al., 1993). In daylong retreats with these community activists and advocates, researchers shared studies on opportunities to learn, and the community activists applied the research concepts to their campaigns around *Williams* and the high school exit exam policy. The research was helpful to them, but it was not received without critique; many lamented that the published research had missed key components of equal educational opportunity, such as the need for standards to address access to culturally relevant curriculum, respectful teachers, and dignity. The process of learning about research and,

more importantly, of engaging and exchanging ideas with researchers allowed organizers and advocates to grapple with key concepts and apply empirically derived
knowledge to their campaigns.

Armed with the "opportunity to learn" framing, several EJC organizations
embarked on multiple education equity campaigns across the state. As one example, professional legal advocates at the organization *Public Advocates* used the
opportunity-to-learn framing to develop legislation to create opportunity-to-learn
standards.[3] At the same time, the CQE focused its opportunity-to-learn campaign on
delaying the high stakes consequences of the high school exit exam. The mobilization against what they termed "the diploma penalty" began in 2002 and continues as
we write this. It has included many forms of protest: rallies, petition drives, policy
advocacy, public testimony, publication of reports, and litigation.

The impact of this work is neither straightforward nor easy to measure. The campaign to derail California's high school exit exam had an important "win," in the
form of a 2-year delay in the requirement that high school students pass the exam
in order to graduate. Nevertheless, the diploma penalty was implemented for the
Class of 2006 – a result at direct odds with a key goal of the organizations. Yet the
implementation did include exceptions for English Learners and special education
students, something the organizations and others fought hard to bring about. The
campaigning also resulted in new state funding and education programs to assist
students not initially able to pass the exam. But the impact of this social movement
organizing can only partially be measured by dollars spent, legislation passed, or
test scores raised.

We have, in the past, described how the success of equity-focused reform efforts
is found, in part, simply in the struggle to improve schools (Oakes & Rogers, 2006;
Renee, 2006; Welner, 2001). During that struggle, educators and others learn about
their own values and beliefs, challenge accepted norms and politics, and develop
technical skills, as they pave the way for future efforts. Similarly, a large part of the
success of the organizing against the California High School Exit Exam is found
in the broader, ongoing political and normative arenas. Students and parents from
low-income communities of color forced their concerns and ideas directly into this
state-level policy debate. Their steady and determined protest and demand to be
included provoked a very public debate around the implementation of the exam and
the inadequacy of California's public schools. Young people testified at the State
Board of Education, community organizers lobbied the legislature, and the media
covered much of the protest. The result was a shift in the zone of meditation surrounding state education policy. The parameters of a feasible exit exam policy correspondingly shifted. The resulting zone – in particular, the new political context –
became more hospitable to conversations about the adequacy and equity of the
education system.

---

[3] Though the legislation was introduced in the California Senate, it did not pass (SB 495, 2003; SB
550, 2003).

Organizing also created a normative shift. By being physically present in the debate, low-income parents and students directly challenged the deficit notion that the achievement gap is the result of their apathy or low desire for an education. Instead, the public and policy makers were confronted with the reality that parents and students were not only concerned but were also demanding that the education system change. One visible result was that policy makers began talking more about providing all students in California with basic learning resources alongside their more conventional concerns about the "achievement gap" and "failing students."

The *Williams* litigation itself resulted in a more traditional, technical change, although the plaintiffs did not secure a legal victory that established these opportunities to learn as a constitutional right. Instead, Governor Arnold Schwarzenegger settled the *Williams* lawsuit at the outset of his first term in office. The settlement included nearly a billion dollars set aside to correct the most egregious resource shortages in the state's lowest performing schools. It also included significant new accountability requirements for monitoring students' access to basic education resources that make state and county governments more accountable to students and parents. Importantly, and in contrast to much earlier litigation focused on civil rights and education rights, the settlement did not end the involvement of the plaintiffs and their supporters. Grassroots organizations around the state continue to use the new complaint process created by the *Williams* settlement as a tool for engaging parents and students in improving schools. This new process allows parents, students, and community members to file a grievance about inadequate educational resources or unsafe school conditions. School and county officials are required to respond to and, as appropriate, fix the problems.

In this way and others, *Williams* brought about ongoing political change in addition to the structural, technical changes in state policy. The relationships and alliances built during the litigation have continued, as groups work toward the equitable implementation of the settlement. Advocacy organizations have helped draft implementing legislation in the California legislature. When these organizers and advocates come across technical problems, they turn to the research and researchers they know and trust. Grassroots organizations have testified, written letters, and met with elected representatives to ensure that the legislation moves through the policy process. Acting in concert, these organizations – advocacy, grassroots, and research – are developing community-led research projects as well as student and parent campaigns to ensure that the equity intent of the legislation is maintained through implementation.

In our earlier work (Oakes et al., 1998; Welner, 2001), we warned that a zone of mediation hospitable to equity-focused reform could not be maintained unless one of two things happened. Pursuant to the first possibility, the forces that originally created the hospitable zone remain in place, although we have viewed this possibility as particularly problematic when reform was initiated with court involvement. A second possibility involves the emergence of new force or (preferably) set of forces to sustain a hospitable political and normative environment. The California case study illustrates the potential of this latter approach.

Case Study #2: College Preparation for All in the Los Angeles Unified School District

The second case study takes place during the same timeframe as the opportunity-to-learn campaign described above. Although education adequacy and the California High School Exit Exam were dominating state policy debates, grassroots organizations in Los Angeles were beginning to look for ways to engage in education equity reform at the local level. If the data about student opportunities and outcomes looked bad statewide, they paled in comparison to those in Los Angeles. The second largest school district in the nation, LAUSD, educates more than 700,000 young people, including high percentages of low-income students and English learners. In 2002, the district produced only about 48 graduates for every hundred 9th graders 4 years earlier, and only 20 of these hundred 9th graders graduated from high school qualified for a 4-year college. These low numbers of college-prepared students were not terribly surprising, given that most of the LAUSD high schools provided the college preparatory course sequence to only a fraction of their students. Moreover, many of the district's college preparatory courses were being taught by teachers without the proper subject matter certification, took place in overcrowded schools and classrooms, and often proceeded with inadequate curriculum materials. As in the state, LAUSD students of color and low-income students disproportionately experienced these resource shortfalls (UCLA IDEA, 2004).

In 2003, community organizers in Los Angeles decided to challenge these inequities. Early on, they contacted researchers at UCLA IDEA and asked for data regarding high school graduation and college preparation rates in the communities' schools. Community organizers, parents, and students were outraged when they saw, across the large district, the stark disparities in access to college preparatory coursework. The data (presented on straightforward maps and tables) showed that schools in low-income communities of color offered significantly fewer opportunities offered significantly fewer opportunities for students to graduate high school prepared to enter California colleges and universities. At the time these meetings were taking place, the United Way published a "Latino Scorecard" grading the quality of life for Latinos in Los Angeles. The education system received a "D" grade.

Moving from outrage to action, the organizers pursued approaches to change LAUSD policy to make a college preparatory curriculum the default curriculum for all students – students would have to affirmatively opt out in order to enroll in classes with a less-challenging curriculum. The organizers quickly found an ally in LAUSD School Board President Jose Huizar and his chief of staff, Monica Garcia. The region of the school district President Huizar represented had some of the lowest rates of college preparatory offerings, undoubtedly influencing his decision to take on the issue. Community organizers guiding the emerging campaign made a concerted effort to broaden the base of their coalition – reaching out to other community organizations, the teachers union, and school district insiders. They organized themselves into key teams to create a policy proposal, develop political support in the district and community, and produce a media campaign around the issue. For a year, they worked to increase the sense of urgency around the issue and to build a critical mass of supporters.

Prior to the school board vote, the organizations involved in this effort formalized their collaboration by officially creating Communities for Educational Equity (CEE). By June 2005, CEE had helped President Huizar draft and pass a districtwide resolution making the college preparatory sequence of courses the default curriculum for all students; this sequence also became a graduation requirement beginning with the high school graduating class of 2016.[4] Members of the community had built effective alliances with researchers, teachers, administrators, and elected officials, changing the nature of policy discussions and solutions. Their involvement and the alliances they formed helped policy makers to understand the academic desires and needs of their communities, building a zone of mediation – a policy making context – that was hospitable to this equity-focused reform.

Yet passing this resolution turned out to be just the beginning for the CEE. With their sweeping new reform in place, CEE organizers are ensuring that the equity intent of their resolution survives implementation. Most of the pressures and forces that preexisted their reform effort – that created a relatively inhospitable zone for the reform – were undoubtedly still in place, so if the CEE's own pressures had disappeared, the zone might have quickly shifted back. Implementation of the reform would then have looked very different from the CEE intent.

Accordingly, CEE members pushed to ensure that community organizations had an official role within the LAUSD team charged with implementing the reform. They also insisted that their concerns continue to be addressed by district officials during the reform's implementation. In addition, the CEE organizations collectively, and successfully, applied for a grant from the Bill and Melinda Gates Foundation. With significant support from this foundation, and with input from the community as well as education researchers, CEE has developed an effective community-based implementation strategy at eight core families of schools (high schools and the junior high and elementary schools that feed into them). The goals and new resources for these "collaboratives" were celebrated at a widely reported joint press conference held by the CEE groups, the LAUSD superintendent, and city officials. In each of these sites, the community groups now have both dollars and legitimacy as they use social movement strategies (relationship building, contentious action when needed, and constant monitoring) to fight for changes in schools' structures, curriculum, and teaching.

This ongoing effort – the "insider" involvement of the community groups on district implementation teams and their "outsider" monitoring of that implementation – has taken place with much less public attention compared to the initial campaign. But this long-term commitment to the issue has elevated the reform to a different level of sustainability and potential success. These community members and the ones discussed in the first case study realized that state policy debates, local outrage, and their increased capacity to collaborate change the nature of the policy discussion, shifting the zone to one now open to new equity-focused reform efforts.

---

[4]Resolution to Create Educational Equity in Los Angeles Through the Implementation of the A-G Course Sequence as Part of the High School Graduation Requirement (Board President Jose Huizar, author), passed 6-1 by the LAUSD Board of Education in June 2005.

They researched reform ideas, built collaborations across organizations, agencies, and political offices, and thus increased their ability to disrupt established norms and politics. The result on a technical level was unambiguous: the passage of a resolution that structurally changed the curriculum of the second largest school district in the nation. But this was only the most visible success. At a political level, community concern was legitimized and responded to, from policy development through passage and now into implementation. On a normative level, a policy that prepares all children to have the choice to go to college challenges deficit notions about who is capable of high academic success. Another normative and political shift arises from the long-term engagement of low-income communities and communities of color, defying common beliefs that these communities are not invested in the education system.

Conclusion

Community organizations and community involvement are really about the full participation of all voices – of all segments of that community. In our earlier discussion of top–down reform, we warned that court orders and policy mandates provide, at best, temporary disruptions of an inequitable status quo. Once the mandate disappears, the reform's survival depends on the presence of some other set of forces that will create a hospitable zone. We argued that to remain receptive to an equity-focused policy, reformers must build a normative, political, and technical foundation (Oakes & Rogers, 2006; Welner, 2001). The needs and concerns of all parts of a school's community should be considered. Although the voices of so-called "local elites" (Oakes & Lipton, 2002; Wells & Serna, 1996) have long been heard, the same is not true of voices representing students of color and those whose parents have less wealth and formal education. As described in this chapter, community organizing has the potential to create balance among all these voices and concerns and, as a result, the potential to create equitable schools.

References

Alinsky, S. D. (1971). *Rules for radicals: A practical primer for realistic radicals* (1st ed.). New York: Vintage Books.

Berends, M., Bodilly, S., & Kirby, S. N. (2002). Looking back over a decade of whole-school reform: The experience of new American schools. *Phi Delta Kappan, 84*(2), 168–175.

Cuban, L. (1992). Curriculum stability and change. In P. Jackson (Ed.), *Handbook of research on curriculum* (pp. 216–247). New York: Macmillan.

Delgado Bernal, D. (2003). Chicana/o education from the civil rights era to the present. In J. Moreno (Ed.), *The elusive quest for equality: 150 Years of Chicano/Chicana education* (pp. 77–108). Cambridge: Harvard Educational Review.

Delgado-Gaitan, C. (2001). *The power of community: Mobilizing for family and schooling.* Lanham, MD: Rowman & Littlefield Publishers.

Della Porta, D., & Diani, M. (1999). *Social movements: An introduction.* Oxford: Blackwell Publishers.

Donato, R. (1997). *The other struggle for equal schools: Mexican Americans during the civil rights era*. Albany, NY: State University of New York Press.

Gold, E., Simon, E., Mundell, L., & Brown, C. (2004). Bringing community organizing into the school reform picture. *Nonprofit and Voluntary Sector Quarterly, 33*(3), 54S–76S.

Guiton, G., & Oakes, J. (1995). Opportunity to learn and conceptions of educational equity. *Educational Evaluation and Policy Analysis, 17*(4), 323–336.

Mediratta, K., Shah, S., McAlister, S., Fruchter, N., Mokhtar, C., & Lockwood, D. (2008). *Organized communities, stronger schools*. Providence, RI: Annenberg Institute for School Reform.

Oakes, J. (1992). Can tracking research inform practice? Technical, normative, and political considerations. *Educational Researcher, 21*(4), 12–21.

Oakes, J. (2005). *Keeping track: How schools structure inequality* (2nd ed.). New Haven, CT: Yale University Press (First edition in 1985).

Oakes, J., & Lipton, M. (2002). Struggling for educational equity in diverse communities: School reform as social movement. *International Journal of Educational Change, 3*, 383–406.

Oakes, J., & Rogers, J. (2006). *Learning power: Organizing for education and justice*. New York: Teachers College Press.

Oakes, J., Welner, K. G., Yonezawa, S., & Allen, R. (1998). Norms and politics of equity-minded change: Researching the "zone of mediation." In M. Fullan (Ed.), *International handbook of educational change*. Norwell, MA: Kluwer Academic Publishers.

O'Day, J.A. & Smith, M.S. (1993). Systemic reform and educational opportunity. In S. Furham (Ed.), *Designing coherent education policy: Improving the system*. San Francisco: Jossey-Bass Publishers.

Payne, C. M. (1995). *I've got the light of freedom: The organizing tradition and the Mississippi freedom struggle*. Berkeley: University of California Press.

Ransby, B. (2003). *Ella Baker and the Black freedom movement: A radical democratic vision*. Chapel Hill: University of North Carolina Press.

Renee, M. (2006). *Knowledge, power and education justice: How social movement organizations use research to influence education policy*. Unpublished doctoral dissertation, University of California, Los Angeles.

Rogers, J, Oakes, J., Terriquez, V., & Valladares, S. (2007). Roadblocks to college. In D. Mitchell (Ed.), *California policy options 2007*. Los Angeles, CA: UCLA School of Public Policy.

San Miguel, G., Jr., & Valencia, R. (1998). From the treaty of Guadalupe Hilgado to Hopwood: The educational pight and struggle of Mexican Americans in the Southwest. *Harvard Education Review, 68*(3), 353–412.

Shaw, R. (2001). *The activist's handbook: A primer for the 1990s and beyond*. Berkeley: University of California Press.

Shirley, D. (1997). *Community organizing for urban school reform*. Austin: University of Texas Press.

Shirley, D. (2002). V*alley Interfaith and school reform: Organizing for power in South Texas* (1st ed.). Austin: University of Texas Press.

Tarrow, S. G. (1998). *Power in movement: Social movements and contentious politics* (2nd ed.). Cambridge [England], NY: Cambridge University Press.

Tyack, D., & Cuban, L. (1995). *Tinkering toward utopia: A century of public school reform*. Cambridge, MA: Harvard University Press.

UCLA IDEA, (2004). *The education gap in Los Angeles county*. Los Angeles: UCLA Institute for Democracy, Education, and Access (IDEA), available online at www.ucla-idea.org/publications/

Warren, M. R. (2001). *Dry bones rattling: Community building to revitalize American democracy*. Princeton, NJ: Princeton University Press.

Wells, A. S., & Serna, I. (1996). The politics of culture: Understanding local political resistance to detracking in racially mixed schools. *Harvard Educational Review, 66*(1), 93–118.

Welner, K. G. (2001). *Legal rights, local wrongs: When community control collides with educational equity.* Albany, NY: SUNY Press.

Whittier, N. (2002). Meaning and structure in social movements. In D. Meyer, N. Whittier, & B. Robinson (Eds.), *Social movements: Identity, culture and the state* (p. 366). New York: Oxford University Press.

Community Organizing and Educational Change

Dennis Shirley

As recently as the late 1990s, the concept of *community organizing for educational change* would scarcely have registered a blip on the proverbial screen of most change theorists. The first foray into research on this topic, documenting the origins, growth, and impacts of the "Alliance Schools" of the Industrial Areas Foundation (IAF) in Texas (Shirley, 1997), generated some interest, but many considered the Alliance Schools to be an idiosyncratic appearance on the educational landscape and expected community organizing for educational change to dissipate as had so many other change efforts before it. After all, what were the chances that a network of schools organized through community-based organizations (CBOs) founded by the flamboyant, willfully adversarial Saul Alinsky, with institutional membership made up of inner-city African American and Latino churches, could have any lasting impacts on low-achieving schools in a state as famously conservative as Texas? Furthermore, unlike the Accelerated Schools, the Comer Schools, or the Coalition of Essential Schools, the Alliance Schools lacked a powerful, well-positioned academic leader such as Hank Levin (at Stanford), James Comer (at Yale), or Ted Sizer (at Brown) heading the network, with a resultant diminished impact on education anticipated.

But contrary to expectations, community organizing for educational change – referred to here interchangeably with "education organizing" for reasons of brevity – did not disappear into the ever-expanding roster of failed change initiatives. Although Ernie Cortés, the Southwest Executive Director of the IAF, was not based in a university, his talents as a community organizer and his successes in launching the Alliance Schools led him to receive a prestigious MacArthur "genius" award as well as a Heinz award for civic leadership. Cortés skillfully recruited dozens of academic allies to leadership seminars for community leaders in Texas, and soon prominent authors as diverse as psychologist Seymour Sarason (2002), political scientist Robert Putnam (Putnam, Feldstein, & Cohen, 2003), and economist Paul Osterman (2003) were writing about the Alliance Schools. Significantly, they were

D. Shirley (✉)
Boston College, Boston, MA, USA
e-mail: shirleyd@bc.edu

A. Hargreaves et al. (eds.), *Second International Handbook of Educational Change*,   169
Springer International Handbooks of Education 23, DOI 10.1007/978-90-481-2660-6_10,
© Springer Science+Business Media B.V. 2010

not only seeking to understand, but actively promoting the Alliance Schools as a new model of educational and social change.

Texas was not the only site experiencing a renaissance of community organizing with a concomitant expansion of organizing into education in the 1990s. In 1999 a second study, Marion Orr's *Black Social Capital: The Politics of School Reform in Baltimore, 1986–1998*, appeared and documented the capacity of a predominantly African–American CBO named BUILD ("Baltimoreans United In Leadership and Development") to bring corporate and civic leaders in that city to sign a "Commonwealth Agreement" pledging unprecedented support for urban high school graduates to receive scholarships at area colleges and universities or well-paying jobs with health care benefits in the private sector. Soon, cities around the United States were imitating Baltimore's Commonwealth Agreement, thereby demonstrating the ability of a relatively small CBO in an aging industrial city to expand the educational "zone of mediation" (Welner, 2001, p. 94) to enhance the public good.

From those early efforts to today, the field of community organizing for educational change has exploded. Leading scholars at schools of education in the United States increasingly are focusing their research and graduate-level courses on this area. Mark Warren at Harvard, initially trained as a sociologist, has turned from his first masterly overview (2001) of the multifaceted political agenda of the IAF in the Southwest to focus exclusively on community organizing and educational change throughout the United States (2005; forthcoming). Milbrey McLaughlin at Stanford, dismayed by the findings of "misery research" (2008, p. 176) indicating the inability of policy reforms to impact school-site issues without considerable grassroots leadership at the local level, has come to focus her latest research (2009) on community organizing as a powerful resource for knowledge utilization and capacity enhancement. Jeannie Oakes, John Rogers, and Martin Lipton, at the University of California Los Angeles, have broken new ground (2006) by reconnecting community organizing explicitly with the democratic theorizing of John Dewey and extending it in new directions that blend on-the-ground research with equity-driven change strategies. A cohort of scholars affiliated with Brown University and the Annenberg Institute (Mediratta, Shah & McAlister, 2009) have developed a sophisticated blend of research strategies that have pushed beyond the earlier almost exclusive reliance on qualitative research to include hierarchical regression analyses that document strong correlations between high levels of intensity of community organizing in Alliance Schools in one city (Austin, Texas) and pupil achievement gains on Texas' standardized tests. In March 2008, a Community and Youth Organizing Special Interest Group (SIG) was approved by the American Educational Research Association, thereby adding an important academic imprimatur for this new scholarly field. Finally, during the US presidential campaign of 2008, the fact that Hilary Clinton had written her undergraduate senior thesis on Saul Alinsky and Barack Obama had been a community organizer in Chicago brought international attention to the continuing relevance of organizing as a change strategy.

These gains of community organizing as a field of scholarship have not been hermetically sealed off from broader research developments and policy recommendations in the area of educational change. David Cohen (1990), Linda Darling-Hammond (1990), and Seymour Sarason (1974, 1995a) have all long argued that local adaptations and leadership are indispensable if any policy reforms at the state or federal level are to have a chance of success, with Sarason (1995b) taking the lead in insisting that at some point power relations and strategic conflict are necessary to disrupt the ossified patronage machines that have corrupted too many public school systems. Michael Fullan began his *Turnaround Leadership* (2006) not with a focus on superficial gimmicks to "game the system" to raise pupil test scores but with a deep and probing examination of the impacts of rising inequality on a wide variety of indicators including education outcomes, income levels, and life expectancy. His foremost recommendation for attacking this inequality was simple and direct: "First, focus on the societal problem of income differential and employ direct community-based short-term and long-term strategies," he wrote (2006, p. 9). Likewise, Andy Hargreaves (2002) has written of the need to conceptualize educational change as part of a broad, equity-driven social movement that engages all sectors of the public, and Andy Hargreaves and Dean Fink (2006), in identifying social justice as one of seven key principles of sustainable leadership, have viewed a renewal of public engagement with public education as a central component of any durable change strategy.

On the basis of the foregoing observations, one could argue that we are now approaching an important confluence between a rising tide of community-organizing efforts and broader developments in theorizing and enacting educational change. Yet, the rapid rise of education organizing has in many ways outpaced the ability of change theorists to keep pace with developments. Furthermore, occasional fireworks such as Aaron Schutz's in-depth critique (2007) of Jeannie Oakes and John Rogers' *Learning Power*, Francesca Polleta's (2002) forthright description of a macho organizing style that is still evident in many CBOs, and the "marriage made in hell," which was described by one grantmaker who tried to build a coalition between two CBOs (MacKinnon, 2006, p. 11), indicate that community organizing for educational change is much more incomplete and contested than the more positively inflected earlier accounts (Shirley, 1997, 2002; Warren, 2001) suggested.

Three Questions

Community organizing as a new field of study in educational change is thus characterized by a rapid rise in visibility, a plurality of different forms of organizing that blend with other approaches to change, and scholarly controversies about the theories-in-action and outcomes of organizing. In light of this situation, the present chapter seeks to answer the following sets of questions:

- First, what is it that makes education organizing different from other forms of parent and community relationships with schools, as articulated by Joyce Epstein (2001) in her oft-cited six-fold model of parent involvement? How many groups currently are engaged in education organizing, and what kinds of change strategies do they typically use?

- Second, what evidence do we have that education organizing improves conditions in struggling schools and communities? Do we have evidence of improved pupil achievement, high school graduation rates, or greater civic engagement among students and parents in schools that have been the foci of organizing efforts? On the other hand, when education organizing appears to be ineffective or counterproductive, what seem to be common problems that lead to such outcomes?
- Third, how might education organizing best be understood in regard to recent reforms related to high-stakes testing and accountability? In light of these reforms, what role should organizing play in a repertoire of change strategies in the future? Furthermore, how might researchers best study education organizing in the future?

Origins of Community Organizing for Educational Change

Although some recent work (Orr, 2007; Payne, 1995; Ransby, 2003) has directed attention to Ella Baker, Fannie Lou Hammer, and other leaders of the civil rights movement in regard to community organizing, the genesis of most historical scholarship (Horwitt, 1992; Santow, 2007; Warren, 2001) on community organizing begins decades earlier, with attention focused on Saul Alinsky's work in the "Back of the Yards" immigrant neighborhood in Chicago in the 1930s. Alinsky, a biographer of Congress of Industrial Organizations (CIO) founder and leader John Lewis (Alinsky, 1949), took from Lewis key principles of union organizing and essentially transferred them with some modifications to the neighborhood or community setting. To do so, Alinsky had to shift his focus from attacks simply upon employers alone to include the complex web of governing elites and private and public social service providers that failed to improve conditions in the poorest communities. By garnering a number of unexpected victories in neighborhoods filled with immigrants who neither spoke English nor enjoyed high levels of social trust with one another, Alinsky demonstrated that the democratizing potential of the labor movement could be extended beyond the workplace into the community, thereby inspiring thousands of activists and community leaders to study the principles of community organizing and to enact them in their own settings (Alinsky, 1946; Horwitt, 1992).

Scholars have noted that Alinsky generally kept his distance from issues of educational change, preferring to deal with more familiar bread and butter issues such as job creation services, housing provision, and health care (Fish, 1973; Shirley, 1997). When Alinsky organizations in Chicago attempted to become involved in school reform in the late 1960s and early 1970s, they were outmaneuvered by the district's ability to contain and ultimately destroy their attempts to start experimental schools through a strategy of attrition (Fish, 1973). The lesson seemed to be that schools, with their complex bureaucracies, specialized knowledge and modes of operating, and vast professional apparatuses, were off limits to and impenetrable by the urban poor. While many community groups sprang up in the 1970s and 1980s to support or battle school busing, or to champion or to denounce various court orders of federal mandates to support English-language learners or children with disabilities, when it came to their understandings of power, these groups often shared more in common with single-issue organizations such as the National Council for Learning Disabilities or the National Association for Bilingual Education than they did with the Alinsky model of multi-issue and multi-class "people's organizations" that focused on fundamental political change across the social spectrum.

It was not until 1985 that the Allied Communities of Tarrant (ACT), an affiliate of Alinsky's IAF, demonstrated that community organizing could turn around a troubled school in an urban setting. Morningside Middle School, located in an African–American working-class neighborhood in Fort Worth, Texas, was in such trouble at that point in its history that even an Alinsky-affiliated group was welcome to try its hand at turning it around. The school was besieged with gangs who made a mockery of its educational aspirations; the recently retired principal had had his jaw broken when trying to break up a scuffle on a basketball court; and when the new principal, Odessa Ravin, arrived for her first day, she found that her office had been firebombed the night before and she had to set up shop in the school's library.

Ravin connected with ACT, and together they rolled out classic community organizing strategies. Drawing upon local leaders affiliated with churches and schools, ACT began making *home visits* to all of the parents of Morningside students – a task that was expedited by the concentration of parents in two large housing projects adjacent to the school. *House meetings* were convened in the homes of parents and teachers who met with organizers to air grievances and to identify *winnable victories* that they could pursue to build confidence and establish momentum. *Research actions* into school district policies, Texas state laws on education, and potential political allies unfolded. *Accountability sessions* in which public officials and business leaders promised to support ACT's agenda for educational change and community development created vivid public dramas that allowed local leaders to develop new political voices and to create long-term strategies that would improve community conditions. In the course of 2 years, the middle school went from dead last – twentieth of twenty middle schools on Texas' standardized tests in the Fort Worth Independent School District – to third.

This kind of education organizing is quite different from the traditional forms of parent–teacher involvement that have been documented by Epstein (2001). As several scholars have noted, those traditional forms really have no public-forming dimension, but in many ways exemplify the individual client, consumer, or even customer-oriented approach that has become dominant in many privatized, market-driven analyses of educational change (Schutz, 2006; Shirley, 1997; Warren, 2005). Such approaches largely restrict parents to the role of passive consumers of pre-established school curricula, with their involvement limited to volunteering at the school, tutoring the child at home, or enriching the child's learning through accessing educational resources affiliated with but not embedded in the school. Indeed, Epstein's original model did not even include community (rather than just parent) involvement, and when it was belatedly added (Epstein, 2001), it altogether failed to address asymmetrical power relationships between communities and schools – a shortcoming noted by scholars more attuned to the manner in which schools actively reproduce social inequalities (Lareau & Shumar, 1996; Schutz, 2006).

Community organizing for educational change, then, must be understood as a form of *public* engagement for *public* schools. The emphasis by community organizers is not on an individual's *human* capital, nor even on his or her *social* capital, but more on the development of *political* capital to change power relationships in a community, city, or state to empower the marginalized and disenfranchised (Alinsky, 1971; Chambers, 2003; Stone, Henig, Jones, & Pierannunzi, 2001). Nor is community organizing directed toward establishing programs – a point of view that emerged most famously when Alinsky (1965, p. 41) attacked the War on Poverty as a form of "political pornography" for providing services disconnected from community empowerment. While programs often are battled for and their acquisition can be celebrated as real advances, the ultimate goal, Alinsky contended, should be to develop power through authentic "people's organizations" that effectively articulate community concerns and impact the overall distribution of power and influence in a city or state.

Even among social justice activists, community organizing is often conflated with advocacy or social movements, although organizers themselves take great pains to avoid such confusion. Organizers do not view themselves as conducting advocacy as much as developing independent, non-partisan CBOs that will impact politics from the position of intermediary institutions that are beholden to no special interest groups. Nor do they view themselves as part of social movements, which they typically view as driven by single issues that lead to the loss of organizing capacity when goals are achieved (Chambers, 2003). Rather, the intention is to attack a broad array of community issues through multiracial, multiclass organizations that endure over time and that continually are reorganizing and expanding, by identifying and training grassroots community leaders.

Estimates suggest that there are approximately 800 community organizing groups in the United States today (Warren, 2010). Roughly 500 of those 800 groups are now working in the area of school reform. These groups span a broad spectrum, from entities like the Oakland Community Organization (OCO) affiliated with the national People's Institute for Community Organizing (PICO) to groups such as the Dudley Street Neighborhood Initiative (DSNI) in Boston and the Logan Square Neighborhood Association (LSNA) in Chicago. These latter groups are unaffiliated with larger national networks and have truly developed grassroots campaigns that have successfully improved their communities and schools (Medoff & Sklar, 1994; Warren, 2010).

What kinds of strategies and campaigns do CBOs engaged in education organizing typically develop? They usually are working in the poorest communities of color in a metropolitan region in the United States and are concentrating their efforts on those schools that have the least qualified teachers, most staff turnover, and worst records in a district in regard to pupil achievement and high school graduation rates (Mediratta et al., 2009). Conditions of concentrated poverty, higher rates of unemployment, and environmental racism make for challenging work, so organizers need to be selective in choosing organizing "handles" (in the argot of organizers themselves) that will lead to palpable victories rather than reinforce a sense of fatalism and despair.

In my early work with the IAF in Texas, many of these early organizing efforts focused on what some might consider to be insignificant, almost trivial matters, such as the circulation of petitions to install a new traffic light at a busy intersection near an urban elementary school or efforts to press city councillors to fund a community center or library close by a school. Many of the early efforts did not begin in schools themselves. Rather, they emanated from community conditions close by schools that threatened children, such as a crack house across the street from a middle school or a junkyard infested with rats behind an elementary school that outraged community residents.

By attacking those visible insults to their communities, parent leaders, educators, and community organizers have developed increasingly sophisticated campaigns in recent years that have capitalized upon the human capital of academic allies situated in universities and, in some cases, developed their own research and development projects. In New York City, for example, the Community Collaborative to Improve District 9 Schools in the South Bronx developed a teacher support program with that city's public schools that reduced teacher attrition from 28 to 6.5% in targeted schools in the space of a single year (Academy for Educational Development, 2006). In Philadelphia, high school activists with "Youth United for Change" exposed the way in which one of the only three secondary schools in the city that achieved "adequate yearly progress" (AYP) cheated by posting answers to anticipated test questions on walls where tests were administered (Shah & Mediratta, 2008). In Chicago, the LSNA and other community groups created a "Grow Your Own" teacher preparatory program linked with area universities to prepare poor and working-class parents, many with immigrant backgrounds, to become certified teachers (Warren, 2005). Beyond an immediate metropolitan area, statewide campaigns by CBOs have persuaded policymakers to pass legislation providing additional resources for schools that collaborate with CBOs in Texas (Shirley, 1997) and have led to litigation to improve funding for children in the poorest and most disenfranchised communities in California (see chapter "Social Movement Organizing and Equity-Focused Educational Change: Shifting the Zone of Mediation" by Renée, Welner, & Oakes, this book).

However, while these kinds of strategies and outcomes are encouraging, most of the CBOs engaged in education organizing have only one or two organizers focused on education, and they operate with small budgets, generally in the range of $150,000–$200,000 per year (Mediratta, Fruchter & Lewis, 2002; Warren & Wood, 2001). With such small staff and financial resources, the CBOs have to develop the unpaid leadership of community members. For groups such as the IAF and PICO that rely on congregationally based community organizing, churches, synagogues, temples, and mosques contribute annual dues to support the CBO. Other groups solicit individual memberships, such as is the case with the many affiliates of the Association of Communities Organized for Reform Now (ACORN). Still, for comparative purposes, we should note that just two direct service providers in the San Francisco Bay area have combined annual budgets of over $13 million, 179 staff members, and over 100 regular volunteers (McLaughlin et al., 2009). Hence, in spite of the growth of education organizing and a string of victories in the past 15 years, organizing remains a comparatively small phenomenon in a larger social ensemble of diverse public, nonprofit, and private entities.

Questions of Evidence

It is difficult to conduct rigorous research on education organizing because the process of organizing is so multifarious and unpredictable. In many ways, only case studies, with appropriate analysis of pupil achievement data and other school district records, enable one to get an overview of the organizing process and its impacts. My own early examination of the impact of education organizing on pupil achievement in the Alliance Schools of the IAF in Texas documented modest gains at the elementary school level and none at the middle or high school level (Shirley, 1997). My subsequent examination of three Alliance Schools in the Rio Grande Valley of Texas showed no test score gains in one elementary school with high levels of parent engagement, high gains in a second elementary school with high levels of parent engagement, and modest gains in a middle school with a faculty that was polarized with the school administration about the Alliance Schools project (Shirley, 2002). Other authors (Osterman, 2003; Putnam et al., 2003; Sarason, 2002; Warren, 2001) who studied the Alliance Schools generally relied on that earlier research or did not discuss test score results beyond brief presentations of achievement gains of individual schools.

In 2002, the Charles Stuart Mott Foundation funded the Institute for Education and Social Policy, then at New York University and now at Brown, to begin a systematic investigation into the diverse modalities of education organizing and their impacts on pupil learning. The research team identified seven urban school districts and targeted schools that were working closely with CBOs for in-depth study. Their research methods included 321 interviews, 509 teacher surveys, 124 youth member surveys, and 241 surveys of non-educators involved in community organizing for educational change (Mediratta et al., 2009). School district pupil achievement results, graduation rates, and enrollments in college preparatory courses were also studied to illuminate correlations between organizing strategies and orthodox measures of educational improvement. Among the findings were the following:

- People Acting for Community Together (PACT) in Miami used a congregationally based organizing approaching matching parents with partner schools to focus on literacy instruction in elementary schools, and those schools improved from 27% pupils at proficiency in 2001 to 49% in 2005, far outpacing a demographically similar comparison set of schools in grades 3 and 4;
- Measuring the intensity of collaboration with the local IAF affiliate, Austin Interfaith, the Alliance Schools in Austin, Texas, with higher levels of faculty engagement in education organizing showed larger percentages of students

meeting minimum standards on Texas' state test when controlled for student SES, limited English proficiency, and after controlling for the effect of baseline test scores;

- A campaign by the OCO broke up that city's largest and most dysfunctional high schools, with the new, small schools showing improved graduation rates, increased enrollment in college-preparatory coursework, and improved ratings on California's Academic Performance Index;
- On a survey distributed across seven sites, young people who affiliated with education organizing projects reported on a higher level of civic engagement than a national comparison group and organizing experience was a significant predictor of enhanced academic motivation ($p = 0.004$).

Perhaps the most interesting finding of the research team was that community organizing is correlated with higher levels of social trust within schools and between schools and community members. Previous research has found social trust in schools to be a prerequisite for raising pupil academic achievement (Bryk & Schneider, 2004). Surveys of teachers in the Alliance Schools in Austin showed that schools that had high levels of involvement with Austin Interfaith had higher levels of teacher–parent trust, sense of school community and safety, an achievement oriented culture, and parent involvement in the school than schools with less involvement. High levels of community organizing were also associated teacher–teacher trust, teachers' commitment to their school, and teachers' peer collaboration. The survey data indicate that organizing appears to be associated with a dilution of the individualism (Lortie, 1975) and privatism (Little, 1990; Zahorik, 1987; Zielinsky & Hoy, 1983) among teachers that research has found to be inimical to the creation of learning-enriched schools (Rosenholtz, 1989). Given organizers' stated rhetoric about drawing individuals out of their isolation and creating new political capacity for attacking tenacious social problems, the survey data point to significant success in achieving these goals.

Education Organizing in the Age of Accountability

It would take too long to provide a full history of the rise of the standards and accountability movements in the United States since the issuance of the Nation at Risk report by White House in 1983 (National Commission on Excellence in Education, 1983. Much scholarly ink (Center on Education Policy, 2007a, 2007b; Gamoran, 2007; Hamilton et al., 2007; Nichols & Berliner, 2007) has been spilled documenting the rise of standardized testing to increase accountability in education, and the (hotly debated) blessings and curses that have ensued. In general, most of these debates have focused on student achievement results on test scores, with special attention devoted to the impact of the No Child Left Behind (NCLB) Act on schools.

Yet from the very first plan for a system of public schools in Virginia proposed by Thomas Jefferson in 1779 through Horace Mann's advocacy of "common schools" in the 1830s through battles for equity and integration that animated the Civil Rights movement and galvanized further social justice struggles that continue up to the present day, American education has always been closely intertwined with ideals of civic engagement (Shirley, 2010). An inclusive definition of "accountability," therefore, must include themes of *community* and *public accountability* that have become marginalized from mainstream educational discourse since *A Nation at Risk* was issued. We know that many sectors of the public – especially those who do not speak English and the have least financial capital and the least formal education – are not in a position to influence the formation and implementation of policy in the United States (Rogers, 2006). Hence, new forms of community and public accountability need to be developed to create a truly inclusive public sphere, such as the following:

- Through modalities of "empowered participatory governance" (Fung & Wright, 2003) that place a premium on easily accessible deliberative forums that allow individuals and groups to engage in the political process without presuming a high level of technical and bureaucratic skill;
- Through creating new cultures of "collaborative transparency" (Fung, Graham, & Weil, 2007) that use house meetings and home visits to enable parents and community members to understand not just pupil test score results, but also educational choices that teachers make and why;
- Through school-based "accountability sessions" in which public officials and business leaders commit to community-initiated policy reforms, with ongoing evaluation and reporting embedded into accountability processes (Shirley, 1997, 2002).

Still, while all of these forms of community and public accountability are desirable, they need to be placed in relationship to recent educational changes that have radically restructured education today. How, for example, does community organizing for educational change interact with the recent drive for clearer standards, more testing, and more accountability in terms of pupil achievement?

To answer this question, Michael Evans and I (2007) studied three CBOs and their interpretations of the impact of NCLB on organizing. The three groups were ACORN Chicago, PACT in Miami, and the IAF in Texas. Drawing upon interviews of educators and organizers, CBO reports, and a wide range of school district data, the following findings emerged:

- ACORN Chicago used the "highly qualified teacher" definitions provided by NCLB as a point of departure to document a crisis of teacher quality in Chicago, with high schools in particular unable to retain certified teachers over time; this documentation then contributed to the creation of a "Grow Your Own" teacher preparatory program (www.growyourownteachers.org) that tailored teacher education coursework to community members with a commitment to teaching in their neighborhood schools;

- PACT in Miami found that public achievement data gave organizers a "handle" for working with parents and community members to understand low pupil test score results in PACT-affiliated schools; this access to information was then utilized to adopt a literacy program in PACT partnership schools that led to improved test scores;
- The IAF found that educators in Texas were becoming skilled at "gaming the system" by excluding low-achieving pupils from schools on test days, reclassifying them as special education students, and narrowing the curriculum to tested subjects; in addition, educational administrators used NCLB as a pretext to exclude parents from schools, arguing that they needed to focus all of their efforts on meeting AYP under NCLB guidelines.

These findings indicate that NCLB and the broader accountability movements have had multiple impacts on the field of education organizing. In the case of Chicago ACORN and PACT in Miami, CBOs were able to use provisions of the act to gather and interpret data and to shape policy in such a way as to improve teacher quality and to raise pupil achievement. Here, the two CBOs served as policy mediators that used provisions of the act to increase civic engagement and improve educational outcomes.

In the third case of the Texas IAF, however, community organizers experienced the more heavy-handed and ethically dubious strategies of "educational triage" (Booher-Jennings, 2005) that appear to have led a mere 15% of American educators to believe that NCLB is improving American education (Public Agenda, 2006). These findings indicate that in the Texas setting a new form of "civic triage" (Shirley, 2008) has occurred that resembles the "decline of the local" in contemporary education articulated by Foster (2004, p. 176) in one of his last papers. Rene Wizig-Barrios, an organizer with The Metropolitan Organization (TMO) affiliated with the IAF in Houston, described the conditions there as follows:

> One of our principals was told by her district to make sure that homeless kids in a shelter shouldn't show up on testing day because they would depress the scores. Other principals have abolished free time for kids in first, second, and third grade. Principals tell us that they want to meet with us and work with us but that they're so much under the gun to raise test scores that they just can't make the time. And now we have this new law in Texas which says that if kids don't pass the TAKS [Texas Assessment of Knowledge and Skills] reading test in third grade they can be held back. That kind of pressure seems to us to be way too great to put on kids who are that little, and it's a major source of fear and stress for the teachers.

Wizig-Barrios noted that it was unclear how many of these actions were caused by NCLB. "It's hard to tell what comes from the principal, the district, the state, or NCLB," she said. Nonetheless, when the larger "policy narrative" places such enormous stakes on test score results, the exact source of the pressures on schools may be less important than understanding the cumulative effect (Gerstl-Pepin, 2006, p. 146).

The Three Contradictions of Education Organizing

In this chapter, three sets of permanent tensions in the field of education organizing have become salient. These are contradictions that are inherent in the very different kinds of organizational settings community organizers and educators inhabit and are related to the compatible but also distinct goals aspired to by educators and organizers. On the one hand, each of the contradictions can appear somewhat abstract and ambiguous; however, in the daily, street-level work of education organizing, they surface repeatedly and illuminate the different ways that educators and organizers frame issues and seek to bridge, amplify, and extend them across settings (Snow & Benford, 1988). The ability of educators and organizers to adjudicate these differences successfully is crucial, I argue, to their ability to engage in cross-organizational learning and field-building processes that are needed to restructure relationships between schools and communities beyond single-shot, grant-funded programs that expire far too quickly when budgets get tight and inadequate capacity has been developed.

The first contradiction concerns the *tension between the educational and the political*. Ideally, political processes support learning, but we know of many cases in which struggles for power come to preoccupy educators and community members. In the case of one Alliance School in the Rio Grande Valley, for example, my earlier research (2002) showed that battles over educators' autonomy, administrators' exhortations to teachers to support the IAF organization, and teachers' intense identification with their academic subject areas and relative disinterest in pupil's community backgrounds led to a long, grinding stalemate. Other research describes educators who resent the intrusive interventions of special interest groups who seek to mobilize power to foist their particularistic agendas on the public schools (Binder, 2004; Bryk, Sebring, Kerbow, & Rollow, 1999; Nespor, 1997). On the other hand, researchers with social justice values (Oakes & Lipton, 2002; Welner, 2001) have found that educators' claims to specialized professional knowledge are sometimes used to undermine efforts to develop more democratic and inclusive schools. The point here is not to adjudicate the veracity of either interpretation, but simply to note the presence of a major fault line that can separate and polarize schools and communities.

The second contradiction concerns *the relationship between the community and larger macro-level contexts of change*. Leading change scholars (Elmore, 2004; Fullan, 2001; Hargreaves & Fink, 2006; Hopkins, 2007) often emphasize the national or even international contexts of educational change, but grassroots organizers generally prefer activating community actors to develop "civic capacity" (Stone et al., 2001) to solve local problems. On the one hand, this preference for the local bespeaks a long-standing Jeffersonian tradition in American political thought and, in the case of congregational community organizing, extends the notion of "subsidiarity" that is a cornerstone of Catholic social thought. However, the increasingly transnational nature of urban populations – with millions of immigrants moving regularly in well-defined circuits between their home nations and employment centers in remote corners of the globe – is requiring new elasticity of approaches and a fundamental rethinking of traditional organizing strategies. For example, the IAF increasingly frames its work in terms of "broad-based organizing" rather than community organizing, and groups such as ACORN, the Center for Community Collaborations, and the Public Education Network have developed a sophisticated repertoire of digitally-mediated campaigns and reporting that are accessible around the globe to those with a PC, an electrical outlet, and a modem. Yet, as this greater technical capacity and professional expertise of organizers expands, one may anticipate that it will be increasingly difficult to maintain credible and deep connections with local communities. It surely can be done, but only with exceptionally adroit and principled leadership.

The third contradiction concerns issues of *representation and legitimacy*. Who really represents "the community"? The term is often used as a simplistic slogan-system. City councilors, school board members, and mayors are all elected through democratic processes, but in some framings, they are seen as not only distant from but opposed to the individuals who elected them (as well as those who abstained from voting or could not vote). On the other hand, CBOs generally only represent a sliver of a population, yet are able to advance claims of universality for a given neighborhood or part of a city while avoiding normal electoral processes altogether. In many cities there are numerous CBOs, often with conflicting agendas, that contend with equal assertiveness that they are the "authentic" representatives of communities. Such claims can give way to demagoguery and de facto misrepresentation of the diversity that exists in communities. At the same time, however, it is by no means clear that elected officials do not distance themselves from their communities for a variety of complicated reasons, and hence need continual pressure from below to assure that they indeed serve their constituencies.

These contradictions are pervasive in community organizing for educational change. Educators learn that a community organization is coming to a school to attend a faculty meeting and fears of intrusiveness and manipulation are raised immediately. A second community organization seeks to develop local political capital to attack academic underachievement and dangerous neighborhood conditions, but is not able to negotiate the maze of local, state, and federal guidelines that lead educators to pay more attention to the requirement to reach AYP than to improve school safety and student learning. A third community organization develops a campaign to provide health clinics in inner-city schools but then is outmaneuvered by school committee members who mobilize religious fundamentals who raise fears that contraceptives will be distributed through the clinics.

Such is the complicated political terrain in which education organizing occurs. Such organizing involves a never-ending oscillation between the educational and the political, the local and the cosmopolitan, and the community and its representatives. In this dynamic and contested field, there are abundant opportunities to improve neighborhood safety, increase student achievement, and advance community development. There are also, however, an equally large number of opportunities for individuals to derail promising school improvement initiatives by defending professional prerogatives, failing to develop effective guiding coalitions, and simply failing to understand the complicated internal workings of schools in the first place.

Yet lest these many problems with educational organizing be misunderstand as grounds for inaction, one must hasten to add that opportunity costs of a particularly devastating kind and scope are incurred when educators marginalize community engagement, overemphasize top-down management rather than bottom-up activism, and mystify the role of power and politics in educational change (Ginwright, Noguera, & Cammarota, 2006; Sarason, 2005b). Educators often overstate technical considerations in educational change that advantage their own status and knowledge and minimize political and cultural factors that parents and community members seek to bring to their relationships with schools (House & McQuillan, 2005). On the one hand, this reliance upon technical procedures in adjudicating conflicts is understandable for educators or for any "street-level bureaucrats" who engage with a fractious and assertive public (Lipsky, 1983. But educators cannot forget the political decisions that shape the broader social context and have an enormous import for children and their schools.

In one recent study, for example, the United States ranked next to last in a roster of 30 nations ranked by child poverty rate, exceeded only by Mexico (United Nations Children's Fund, 2004, p. 28). Thirteen million children in the United States now grow up below the poverty line, and numerous indicators of child well-being reflect steady declines in the past two decades (Annie E. Casey Foundation, 2005). Who should be held "accountable" for leaving so many children behind in poverty when other nations with far less wealth and power outperform the United States on these indicators? The consequences of neglectful policies and values injurious to children spill over into schools and communities on a daily basis and suggest that educators have a civic responsibility, as part of their vocation, to remedy the most egregious forms of social injustice that afflict the most vulnerable members of their schools and communities.

Conclusion

We now have a significant and ever-growing body of literature indicating positive consequences from community organizing for educational change. The findings discussed in previous sections indicate that education organizing has an important role to play in contemporary educational change. Positive impacts were found when organizations such as Chicago ACORN and PACT in Miami studied data and used it to develop new strategies of school site and district-level change; when groups such as the OCO promoted a small school reform that improved Oakland's ratings on the multifaceted indicators of California's Academic Performance Index; and when young people affiliated with education organizing in Philadelphia rated more highly on civic engagement than a national comparison group of students.

On the whole, the research on education organizing has been positive in tenor. Nonetheless, some areas of concern must be addressed for the future of this change approach if it is to expand beyond its first innovative phase and is to become anchored in schools and districts as a visible, effective, and sustainable strategy. First, community organizers and educators need much more assistance with capacity enhancement to overcome the fault lines that can divide local political leaders from the professional autonomy and respect sought by educators. Second, the balance between the local grassroots nature of change and broader national and even transnational developments will need to be reconceptualized to link the ensemble of strategies developed by community organizers in the past to the complex new demographic and technological challenges of the present. Finally, issues of representation and legitimacy will continue to need to be adjudicated and clarified so that single individuals or small groups do not assert themselves as community representatives when they in point of fact may only be representing themselves.

In the years to come, it will be necessary for community organizers and educators to deepen their collaborations and to structure educational change in such a way that community development and school improvement are mutually supportive undertakings that are sustainable over time. To do so, at a certain level, it will be necessary for community organizations to continue their crucial contribution by revitalizing democracy and expanding the public sphere. Educators in turn will need to find new ways to network not only with one another but also to reach out to community members to confront common problems, to share expertise, and to slowly but surely transform schools from islands of bureaucracy to centers of civic engagement. The interdependent relationship between democracy and education may remain fractious and demanding, but it also remains indispensable.

References

Academy for Educational Development. (2006). *Lead teacher report: Second year report submitted to the community collaborative to improve Bronx schools*. Washington, DC: Academy for Educational Development.

Alinsky, S. (1946). *Reveille for radicals*. New York: Vintage.

Alinsky, S. (1949). *John L. Lewis: An unauthorized biography*. New York: Vintage.

Alinsky, S. (1965). The war on poverty—political pornography. *Journal of Social Issues, 11* (1), 41–47.

Alinsky, S. (1971). *Rules for radicals: A pragmatic primer for realistic radicals*. New York: Vintage.

Annie E. Casey Foundation. (2005). *KIDS COUNT data book*. Baltimore, MD: Author.

Binder, A. (2004). *Contentious curricula: Afrocentrism and creationism in American public schools*. Princeton, NJ: Princeton University Press.

Booher-Jennings, J. (2005). Below the bubble: Educational triage and the Texas accountability system. *American Educational Research Journal, 42* (2), 231–268.

Bryk, A. S., & Schneider, B. L. (2004). *Trust in schools: A core resource for improvement*. New York: Russell Sage Foundation.

Bryk, A. S., Sebring, P. B., Kerbow, D., Rollow, S., & Easton, J. Q. (1999). *Charting Chicago School reform: Democratic localism as a lever for change*. Boulder, CO: Westview.

Center on Education Policy. (2007a). *Answering the question that matters most: Has student achievement increased since No Child Left Behind?* Washington, DC: Author.

Center on Education Policy. (2007b). Choices, changes, and challenges: Curriculum and instruction in the NCLB era. Washington, DC: Author.

Chambers, E. T. (2003). *Roots for radicals: Organizing for power, action, and justice*. New York: Continuum.

Cohen, D. K. (1990). A revolution in one classroom: The case of Mrs. Oublier. *Educational evaluation and policy analysis, 12* (3), 327–345.

Darling-Hammond, L. (1990). Instructional policy into practice: "The power of the bottom over the top." *Educational Evaluation and Policy Analysis, 12* (3), 339–347.

Elmore, R. (2004). *School reform from the inside out.* Cambridge: Harvard Education Press.

Epstein, J. (2001). *School, family, and community partnership: Preparing educators and improving schools.* Boulder, CO: Westview Press.

Fish, J. H. (1973). *Black power/white control.* Princeton, NJ: Princeton University Press.

Foster, W. P. (2004). The decline of the local: A challenge to educational leadership. *Educational Administration Quarterly, 40* (176), 176–191.

Fullan, M. (2001). *The new meaning of educational change* (3rd ed.). New York: Teachers College Press.

Fullan, M. (2006). *Turnaround leadership.* San Francisco: Jossey-Bass.

Fung, A., Graham, M., & Weil, D. (2007). *Full disclosure: The perils and promise of transparency.* New York: Cambridge University Press.

Fung, A., & Wright, E. O. (2003). *Deepening democracy: Institional innovations in empowered participatory governance.* London: Verso.

Gamoran, A. (2007). *Standards-based reform and the poverty gap: Lessons for No Child Left Behind.* Washington, DC: Brookings.

Gerstl-Pepin, C. I. (2006). The paradox of poverty narratives: Educators struggling with children left behind. *Educational Policy, 20* (1), 143–162.

Ginwright, S., Noguera, P., & Cammarota, J. (2006). *Beyond resistance! Youth activism and community change.* New York: Routledge.

Hamilton, L. S., Stecher, B. M., Marsh, J. A., McCombs, J. S., Robyn, A., Russell, J. L., Naftel, S., Barney, H. (2007). *Standards-based accountability under No Child Left Behind: Experiences of teachers and administrators in three states.* Santa Monica, CA: RAND.

Hargreaves, A. (2002). Sustainability of educational change: The role of social geographies. *Journal of Educational Change, 3*, 189–214.

Hargreaves, A., & Fink, D. (2006). *Sustainable leadership.* San Francisco: Jossey-Bass.

Hopkins, D. (2007). *Every school a great school: Realizing the potential of system leadership.* Maidenhead: Open University Press.

Horwitt, S. D. (1992). *Let them call me rebel: Saul Alinsky—His life and legacy.* New York: Vintage.

House, E. R., & McQuillan, P. J. (2005). Three perspectives on school reform. In A. Lieberman (Ed.), *The roots of educational change: International handbook of educational change* (pp. 186–201). Dordrecht, Holland: Springer.

Lareau, A., & Shumar, W. (1996). The problem of individualism in family-school policies. *Sociology of Education, 69*, 24–39.

Lipsky, M. (1983). *Street-level bureaucracy: Dilemmas of the individual in public services.* New York: Russell Sage Foundation.

Little, J. W. (1990). The persistence of privacy: Autonomy and initiative in teachers' professional relations. *Teachers College Record, 91* (4), 509–536.

Lortie, D. C. (1975). *Schoolteacher: A sociological study.* Chicago: University of Chicago Press.

MacKinnon, A. (2006). *Principles for effective education grantmaking.* Portland, OR: Grantmakers for Education.

McLaughlin, M. (2008). Beyond "misery research"—New opportunities for implementation research, policy, and practice. In C. Sugrue (Ed.), *The future of educational change: International perspectives* (pp. 175–190). New York: Routledge.

McLaughlin, M. (2009). *Between movement and establishment.* Palo Alto, CA: Stanford University Press.

Mediratta, K., Fruchter, N., & Lewis, A. (2002). *Organizing for school reform: How communities are finding their voice and reclaiming their public schools.* New York: New York University, Institute for Education and Social Policy.

Mediratta, K., Shah, S., & McAlister, S. (2009). *Community organizing for stronger schools: Strategies and successes*. Cambridge, MA: Harvard Education Press.

Medoff, P., & Sklar, H. (1994). *Streets of hope: The fall and rise of an urban neighborhood*. Boston: South End Press.

Milbrey, M., Scott, R.W., Deschenes, S., Hopkins, K., & Newman, A. (2009). *Between movement and establishment: Organizations advocating for youth*. Palo Alto, CA: Stanford University Press.

National Commission on Excellence in Education (1983). *A nation at risk: The imperative for educational reform*. Washington, DC: United States Department of Education.

Nespor, J. (1997). *Tangled up in school: Politics, space, bodies, and signs in the educational process*. Mahwah, NJ: Erlbaum.

Nichols, S. L., & Berliner, D. C. (2007). *Collateral damage: How high-stakes testing corrupts America's schools*. Cambridge, MA: Harvard Education Press.

Oakes, J., & Lipton, M. (2002). Struggling for educational equity in diverse communities: School reform as a social movement. *Journal of Educational Change, 3* (3–4), 383–406.

Oakes, J., Rogers, J., & Lipton, M. (2006). *Learning power: Organizing for education and justice*. New York: Teachers College Press.

Orr, M. (2007). Community organizing and the changing ecology of civic engagement. In M. Orr (Ed.), *Transforming the city: Community organizing and the challenge of political change* (pp. 1–27). Lawrence, KS: University Press of Kansas.

Osterman, P. (2003). *Gathering power: The future of progressive politics in America*. Boston: Beacon Press.

Payne, C. (1995) *I've got the light of freedom: The organizing tradition and the Mississippi freedom struggle*. Berkeley, CA: University of California Press.

Polletta, F. (2002). *Freedom is an endless meeting: Democracy in American social movements*. Chicago: University of Chicago Press.

Public Agenda. (2006). *Reality check 2006, issue number 3: Is support for standards and testing fading?* New York: Public Agenda.

Putnam, R., Feldstein, L., & Cohen, D. (2003). *Better together: Restoring the American community*. New York: Simon & Schuster.

Rogers, J. (2006). Forces of accountability? The power of poor parents in NCLB. *Harvard Educational Review, 76*(4), 611–641.

Rosenholtz, S. (1989). *Teachers' workplace*. New York: Longman.

Santow, M. (2007). Running in place: Saul Alinsky, race, and community organizing. In M. Orr (Ed.), *Transforming the city: Community organizing and the challenge of political change* (pp. 28–55). Lawrence, KS: University Press of Kansas.

Sarason, S. B. (1974). *The psychological sense of community: Prospects for a community psychology*. San Francisco: Jossey-Bass.

Sarason, S. B. (1995a). *School change: The personal development of a point of view*. New York: Teachers College Press.

Sarason, S. B. (1995b). *Parental involvement and the political principle: Why the existing governance structure of schools should be abolished*. San Francisco: Jossey-Bass.

Sarason, S. B. (2002). *Educational reform: A self-scrutinizing memoir*. New York: Teachers College Press.

Schutz, A. (2006). Home is a prison in the global city: The tragic failure of school-based community engagement strategies. *Review of Educational Research, 76* (4), 691–743.

Schutz, A. (2007). Education scholars have much to learn about social action: An essay review. *Education Review, 10* (3). Retrieved 26 April, 2008, from http://edrev.asu.edu/essay/v10n3index.html

Shah, S., & Mediratta, K. (2008). Negotiating reform: Young people's leadership in the educational arena. *New Directions in Youth Development, 117*, 43–59.

Shirley, D. (1997). *Community organizing for urban school reform*. Austin: University of Texas Press.

Shirley, D. (2002). *Valley Interfaith and school reform: Organizing for power in South Texas.* Austin: University of Texas Press.

Shirley, D. (2010). A brief history of public engagement for public education. In M. Orr & J. Rogers (Eds.), *Public engagement for public education.* Palo Alto, CA: Stanford University Press.

Shirley, D., & Evans, M. (2007). Community organizing and No Child Left Behind. In M. Orr (Ed.), *Transforming the city: Community organizing and the challenge of political change* (pp. 109–133). Lawrence: University Press of Kansas.

Snow, D. A., & Bendford, R. D. (1988). Ideology, frame resonance, and participant mobilization. In B. Klandermans, H. Kriesi, & S. Tarrow (Eds.), *From structure to action: Social movement participation across cultures* (pp. 197–217). Greenwich, CT: JAI Press.

Stone, C. N., Henig, J. R., Jones, B. D., & Pierannunzi, C. (2001). *Building civic capacity: The politics of reforming urban schools.* Lawrence: University Press of Kansas.

United Nations Children's Fund. (2004). *The state of the world's children 2005.* New York: Author.

Warren, M. R. (2010). Community organizing for education reform. In M. Orr & J. Rogers (Eds.), *Public engagement for public education.* Palo Alto: Stanford University Press.

Warren, M. R. (2001). *Dry bones rattling: Community building to revitalize American democracy.* Princeton: Princeton University Press.

Warren, M. R. (2005). Communities and schools: A new view of urban education reform. *Harvard Educational Review, 75,* 133–173.

Welner, K. G. (2001). *Legal rights, local wrongs: When community control collides with educational equity.* Albany: State University of New York Press.

Zahorik, J. (1987). Teachers' collegial interaction: An exploratory study. *The Elementary School Journal, 87* (4), 385–396.

Zielinsky, A., & Hoy, W. K. (1983). Isolation and alienation in the elementary schools. *Educational Administration Quarterly, 19* (2), 27–45.

Recent Developments in the Field of Educational Leadership: The Challenge of Complexity

Bill Mulford

In this "golden age" of school leadership (Anderson et al., 2007; Day & Leithwood, 2007) the field is faced with the fact that "new managerialism" which embraced managerial efficiency and effectiveness through bureaucracy and accountability as key levers for reforming schools has failed. It is argued that it is time that the professionals and educational leaders strive to ensure what happens now and in the future is what they want to happen (Gronn, 2003; Hargreaves & Fink, 2006; Hyman, 2005; Leadbeater, 2004a; MacBeath, 2006; Mulford, 2003a; OECD, 2006). However, overcoming the gap between dependence on, or a feeling of the inevitability of, system or school bureaucracies as the means of achieving what they want and their preferred model of seeing schools as social centres and learning organisations remains a challenge.[1]

In order to achieve greater professional control, educational leaders need to understand and be able to act on the context, organisation and leadership of the school, as well as the interrelationship among these three elements. A single input by a leader can have multiple outcomes. Success, therefore, will depend on which elements and in what sequence the educational leader chooses to spend time and attention on (Mulford, 2007b; NCSL, 2007). Recent developments in the field suggest the elements for successful educational leadership involve being contextually "literate", organisationally "savvy" and leadership "smart". To add to the complexity, successful educational leaders are the prime vehicle for linking all three elements.

This chapter draws on mainly Western literature to examine each of these elements and then the interrelationships among them.

B. Mulford (✉)
University of Tasmania, Tasmania, Australia
e-mail: bill.mulford@utas.edu.au

[1] See, for example, the OECD (2001a) scenarios for future schools and feedback from educational leaders on the most likely and preferred scenarios in the next 5–10 years (Mulford, 2007a).

A. Hargreaves et al. (eds.), *Second International Handbook of Educational Change*, Springer International Handbooks of Education 23, DOI 10.1007/978-90-481-2660-6_11, © Springer Science+Business Media B.V. 2010

Contextually "Literate"

Context matters. School leaders need to be contextually literate. A context involving rapid advances in science and technology, increased globalisation, changes in demography, including in the nature of work, and pressures on the environment argues for educational leaders achieving balances between and/or choosing between competing forces and a broadening of what counts for good schooling (Mulford, 2008).

Choices between competing forces make the most sense when they foster stability (in the form of a school's collective capacity to learn) for change, independence rather than dependence, community rather than individualism and heterogeneity rather than homogeneity. Broadening what counts for good schooling needs to include excellence and equity as well as cognitive and non-cognitive (especially personal and social skills) (Mulford, 2002; Mulford and Edmunds, 2010). In such a context school leadership has been found to be intense, varied, accountable and rewarding (NCSL, 2007).

Achieving Balance and/or Choosing between Competing Forces

There are at least four sets of competing contextual pressures on schools. In what follows, these are examined under the following broader headings: continuity and constant change, dependence and independence, individualism and community, and homogeneity and heterogeneity.

Continuity and/or Constant Change

In contrast to past continuity, recent times have been witness to constant change, a stream of new movements, new programs and new directions. Unfortunately, some in education seem to be forever rushing to catch the next bandwagon that hits the scene – "unfortunately" because there is increasing evidence that many a school and school system and their children have been badly disillusioned by the galloping itinerant peddlers selling the new movements (sometimes the new and ever changing ministers of education and/or departmental officials).

The main challenge in such a situation, a world of massive and constant change, is how to foster enough internal stability in people and the organisation in which they work and study in order to encourage the pursuit of change. Stability for change, moving ahead without losing our roots, is the challenge (Peters, 1987).

It is quite incorrect to assume that a school is effective only if it is undergoing change. Change may be in an inappropriate direction, for example, towards a facade of orderly purposefulness (Sergiovanni, 1990). Change may also involve the use of inappropriate measures of success, especially when they are merely procedural illusions of effectiveness (Meyer & Rowan, 1978). The difficulty of providing output measures by which education's success can be measured has often led to the elevation in importance of "approved" management processes. These processes include program planning budgeting systems, school-based management, charters/partnership agreements and strategic plans. Such processes contribute an illusion of effectiveness and become desired outputs in themselves, thus deceiving outside observers and many of those in schools as well. Such deception should have no place in good education.

In a changing world it might be more helpful to remember Noah's principle: One survives not by predicting rain (change) but by building arks. Amid uncertain, continually changing conditions, many schools are constructing arks comprising their collective capacity to learn; they are striving to become intelligent, or learning, organisations (Mulford, 2003c).

Dependence and/or Independence

A second fundamental issue relates to the balance between the competing factors of dependence and independence and the current imbalance favouring dependence. This situation is most easily seen in the over-dependence many of those in schools place on "leaders" outside schools, often engendered by the overconfidence of these "leaders" in their own abilities or importance.

There seem to be a lot of people who want to tell those in schools what to do. This situation is unfortunate because many of those doing the telling do not seem to want to accept responsibility for their advice, are not around long enough to take responsibility for their directions and may even seek to prevent fair and open assessment of the changes they promulgate.

We cannot avoid change; indeed we may wish to seek, embrace and even thrive on it. Education is an integral part of our society and must anticipate change as being one of the constants it will face. Whether these changes result in Frankensteins, or gentle, functional, collaborative and sustainable butterflies, depends largely on the response of those in schools. Hyman (2005), for example, who left 10 Downing Street after many years as speech writer and advisor to the prime minister to work as an assistant to the head teacher at London's Islington Green School, concludes that:

> Perhaps the biggest eye-opener for me on my journey has been how the approach I had been part of creating, to deal with 24-hour media and to demonstrate a decisive government, was entirely the wrong one for convincing frontline professionals, or indeed for ensuring successful delivery. Our approach to political strategy has been based on three things: momentum, conflict and novelty, whereas the frontline requires empowerment, partnership and consistency. (Hyman, 2005, p. 384)

Individualism and/or Community

Religious institutions no longer attract or have an impact on the young, families are dysfunctional more often than ever before, some children are malnourished, drug addiction is a scourge and many prime-time television programs can be vacuous and educationally bankrupt. It is a time when advertisers and their clients have succeeded in not only rushing children through their developmental stages into a false sense of maturity but have also managed to link identity and status to brand names, and gang members; athletes, and narcissistic celebrities are the admired adolescent role models (Goodlad, 1994).

Although schools do have the responsibility of care for students, at the same time debate continues as to whether schools should be dealing with these broad social issues (Bernstein, 2000). It may be unreasonable to expect the schools to pick up the slack in such situations but if the home cannot and the school does not pick up the responsibility for our young then who will? Who will counter, for example, the pressure inherent in much of our "modern" society to act alone rather than with, or for, the community? We need to be reminded that change for the sake of change, including technological change, is not necessarily good; it must be tempered with wisdom, compassion and justice.

A different generation, those born from the 1980s onwards, the New Millenial Learner (NML), now populate our schools – as students and, increasingly, as staff. The NML are the first generation to grow up surrounded by digital media, and much of their activity involving peer-to-peer communication and knowledge management is mediated by these technologies (Howe & Strauss, 2000). Also called "Homo Zappiens" (Veen, 2003), this generation has made popular the less controllable "socially" oriented technologies such as blogs, wikis, tagging and instant messaging (Pedro, 2006).

In this individualistic, technology-mediated world, a skills crisis would indeed be bad enough but a values crisis would be devastating. For example, turning back the tide of a "virtual", computer-based cyberspace existence, with its stress on individualism and encouragement to dissociate oneself from an increasingly challenging world, is vital for our future survival. For, as Peck (1987) has reminded us, a community is a place where conflict can be resolved without physical or emotional bloodshed and with wisdom as well as grace. A community is a group that "fights gracefully".

A generation that is unable to feel for others is incapable of creating the social trust that is so essential to maintain culture. And, as it is in the broader culture, so it is in schools. For example, it has been demonstrated that where teachers' trust in principals is undermined by perceptions of principal co-option of top-down system change initiatives, especially when unsupported by teachers, it results in teacher alienation and feelings of disempowerment, which can then bring teacher strategies of resistance to the fore (Bishop & Mulford, 1999).

Homogeneity and/or Heterogeneity

If you look for common denominators in successful schools, you will see that a strong indicator is to find a way to get some of the staff and students to do a radical thing, to take the initiative, to take risks. If a system is too tight for this there will be no search and no development and if there is no search and no development there is no learning.

One lesson in this context is that reductionist approaches in education, to the complexity that is the world of the teacher and the student, should not go unchallenged. Uniformity for schools and education systems in aims, in standards and in methods of assessment is a complexity-reducing mechanism. It is far tidier to have a single set of aims for all, a single curriculum for all, a single set of standards for all and a single array of tests for all than to have locally developed approaches to school improvement.

Homogeneity of outcome for the future of our schools and society is not necessarily the highest pinnacle and attempts to reach it may have backfired in terms of student attitudes to school. International research (OECD, 2004) shows, for example, that more than a quarter of students agrees or strongly agrees that school is a place where they do not want to go. In countries such as Belgium, France and Hungary, where there is a high level of homogeneity in the education system, the proportion ranges from 35 to 42% while in countries such as Denmark, Mexico, Portugal and Sweden, where there is less homogeneity, the figure is less than 20%.

In fact, UK researchers are:

> beginning to encounter students expressing doubts about the genuineness of their school's interest in their progress and well-being as persons, as distinct from their contributions to their school's league table position. [The result is that] contract replaces community as the bond of human association. (Fielding, 1999, p. 286)

Broadening What Counts as Good Schooling

The forces and factors increasingly permeating our schools show that to achieve their purposes there is a pressing need to broaden what counts for "good" schooling. Measures of successful student achievement in a knowledge society are increasingly being seen as wider than the cognitive/academic; it is more personalised and involves achieving both excellence and equity (DfES, 2005; Leadbeater, 2004a; OECD, 2001b; World Bank, 2005). If we stress only scientific and technological knowledge, or only literacy and numeracy, we could languish in other respects, including physically, aesthetically, morally and spiritually.

Howard Gardner understood the need to broaden what counts for good schooling with his conceptualisation of multiple intelligences. His most recent work (Gardner, 2007) continues this understanding by defining the abilities that will be needed in times of vast change as his five "minds for the future"; that is, disciplinary, synthesising, creating, respectful and ethical minds. In linking this broadening of what counts for good schooling to school leadership, Leo (2007) points out that:

> a key question for school leadership is how to develop more imaginative approaches to educational assessment that illuminate how schools develop capabilities such as motivation and creativity and to ensure that these are among the outcomes of education for all students. (Leo, 2007, p. 10)

Consistent with this argument to broaden what counts is a range of impressive research using data from the British cohort study. This data base followed all children born in the United Kingdom in the first week of April 1970 and surveyed them again in 1975, 1980, 1986, 1991 and 1996. At age 10, in 1980, over 12,000 children were tested for mathematics and reading ability and the psychological attributes of self-esteem and locus of control. The children's teachers were questioned about their behavioural attributes of conduct disorder, peer relations, attentiveness and extraversion. In 1996, at age 26, information was collected on highest qualification attained, earnings and periods of unemployment.

The author of one of these studies, Leon Feinstein, an economist, summarises his findings as follows:

> ... attentiveness in school has been shown to be a key aspect of human capital production, also influencing female wages even conditioning on qualifications. Boys with high levels of conduct disorder are much more likely to experience unemployment but higher self-esteem will both reduce the likelihood of that unemployment lasting more than a year and, for all males, increase wages. The locus of control measure ... is an important predictor of female wages .... Good peer relations are important in the labour market, particularly for girls, reducing the probability of unemployment and increasing female wages. ... [These results] suggest strongly that more attention might be paid to the non-academic behaviour and development of children as a means of identifying future difficulties and labour market opportunities. It also suggests that schooling ought not be assessed solely on the basis of the production of reading and maths ability. (Feinstein, 2000, pp. 22, 20)

These results have been confirmed in other longitudinal research by Carneiro, Crawford, and Goodman (2006) where it was found that 7- and 11-year-old children who exhibited social maladjustment were less likely to stay on at school post-16 (after taking into account cognitive ability and other family background factors); did less well in terms of performance in higher education; were more likely to display negative adolescent outcomes, such as trouble with the police by age 16 and teenage motherhood; and even conditioning on schooling outcomes were more likely to have both lower employment probabilities and lower wages at age 33 and 42.

Carneiro and colleagues (2006) believe their findings are consistent with another research (e.g., Cunha, Heckman, Lochner, & Masterov, 2005) which shows that non-cognitive skills are more malleable than cognitive skills. This finding suggests that schools can have a greater effect on students' non-cognitive than cognitive outcomes. Cunha and colleagues (2005, p. 1) also remind us that "remediation of inadequate early investments [in such areas of social skills] is difficult and very costly".

Organisationally "Savvy"

School organisation also matters. Educational leaders need to be organisationally savvy. They need to be able to build capacity. Broadening the way schools are organised and run would see a move from the mechanistic to an organic, living system; from thin to deep democracy; from mass approaches to personalisation through participation; and from hierarchies to networks. The emphasis would very much be on social capital, learning organisations, collective teacher efficacy and communities of professional learners.

From Mechanistic to Organic, Living Systems

In her book, *Finding Our Way: Leadership for an Uncertain Time*, Wheatley (2005) employs two competing metaphors – "organisations as machines" and "organisations as living systems" – as explanation for both organisations and leadership that differ radically in their functioning and outcomes. The "machine" metaphor encourages a view of organisation as a fixed structure of some sort, a structure consisting of parts that need to be "oiled" if they are to function together smoothly. From this view, organisations require effortful monitoring, coordination and direction by someone, typically a "leader".

Wheatley (2005, p. 4) notes that "in the past few years, ever since uncertainty became our insistent twenty-first century companion, leadership strategies have taken a great leap backward to the familiar territory of command and control". Such leadership, aiming to increase employees' certainty about their work (and increase the school's level of accountability to government and the public) is mostly transactional. This means that, in the case of school organisations, teachers are assumed to be motivated by the promise of such extrinsic, positive rewards as money and status and opposing, extrinsic, negative impacts such as school reconstitution and public shaming through the publication of league tables.

Transactional, command and control forms of leadership on the part of principals further manifest themselves in the close supervision of teachers, specification of the one best model of instruction which all teachers must use, centralised decisions about how time in the classroom is to be used together with very long lists of curriculum standards or expectations which teachers are required to cover with students. Teachers are allowed little autonomy over their work in classrooms, their voices are heard weakly, at best, in school-wide decision making and yet they are held almost entirely accountable for student achievement (Day & Leithwood, 2007).

An organic, or "living systems", metaphor encourages a view of organisation as a process, one of constant adaptation, growth and becoming that occurs naturally and inevitably in response to a strong desire for learning and survival. As Wheatley describes it:

> the process of organizing involves developing relationships from a shared sense of purpose, exchanging and creating information, learning constantly, paying attention to the results of our efforts, co-adapting, co-evolving, developing wisdom as we learn, staying clear about our purpose, being alert to changes from all directions. (Wheatley, 2005, p. 27)

A description of organisation-as-living-system bears a strong resemblance to accounts of organisational learning in schools (Mulford, Silins, & Leithwood, 2004; Silins & Mulford, 2002a), professional learning communities (Stoll et al., 2006) and the OECD (2001b, 2006) scenarios for future schools as social centres and learning organisations. The ongoing eight-country research project on successful principalship (see, for example, Gurr, Drysdale, & Mulford, 2005; the edited book by Day & Leithwood, 2007) strongly suggests that successful principals thought of their organisations as living systems, not machines.

From Thin to Deep Democracy

Furman and Shields (2003) argue that there is a need to move our schools from "thin" conceptions of democracy based in the values of classical liberalism, and its concern with the right of the individual to pursue his or her self-interest and the resolution of conflict through "democratic" majority voting, to a notion of "deep" democracy. Dewey (in Furman & Shields, 2003) saw "deep" democracy as involving respect for the worth and dignity of individuals and their cultural traditions, reverence for and the proactive facilitation of free and open inquiry and critique, recognition of interdependence in working for the common good, the responsibility of individuals to participate in free and open inquiry and the importance of collective choices and actions in the interest of the common good.

Furman and Shields (2003) state that "deep" democracy needs to be practised in schools. However, as a consequence of risk of chaos and loss of control from the forces on schools, the typical pattern they perceive is that students

> are expected to conform to hierarchically imposed decisions about what they study and teach and when, what the outcomes of instruction should be, how to behave and talk, and even how they look. . . . [In fact,] learning democracy may be one of the least experiential aspects of K–12 curricula. (Furman & Shields, 2003, p. 10)

The results of a recent analysis of school principal training in the Australian State of Tasmania (Mulford, 2004) leads one to suggest that the same could be said about the adults in schools within bureaucratically designed systems. "Deep" democracy needs to be practised by them but it may be the least experienced aspect of their working world, especially when it comes to their own professional development.

Personalisation through Participation

A major debate taking place in the United Kingdom about the future shape of public services picks up on the confused organisational situation for those in schools. This debate is pitched into the chasm between the way public institutions work and how users experience them. For example, in the education sector it has been argued by Leadbeater (2004a) that efficiency measures based on new public management as reflected in:

> [t]argets, league tables and inspection regimes may have improved aspects of performance in public services. Yet the cost has been to make public services seem more machine-like, more like a production line producing standardised goods. [And, I would add, increasingly create dependence on the system.] . . . It is . . . clear that the State cannot deliver collective solutions from on high. It is too cumbersome and distant. The State can only help create public goods – such as better education – by encouraging them to emerge from within society. . . . That is, to shift from a model in which the centre controls, initiates, plans, instructs and serves, to one in which the centre governs through promoting collaborative, critical and honest self-evaluation and self-improvement. (Leadbeater, 2004a, pp. 81, 83, 90)

It is further argued (Leadbeater, 2004a, 2004b, 2005) that public services can be improved by focussing on what is called "personalisation through participation".

The "pay off" of personalisation is believed to be increased knowledge, participation, commitment, responsibility and productivity. Thus personalisation can be seen to be both a process and outcome of effective public organisations, including schools.

A personalised public service is seen as having four different meanings:

- Providing people with a more customer-friendly interface with existing services.
- Giving users more say in navigating their way through services once they have access to them.
- Giving users more direct say over how the money is spent.
- Emphasising users are not just consumers but co-designers and co-producers of a service.

As we move through these four meanings, dependent users become consumers and commissioners then co-designers, co-producers and solution assemblers. In schools, learners (students and staff) become actively and continually engaged in setting their own targets, devising their own learning plan and goals and choosing among a range of different ways to learn. As we move through these four meanings, the professional's role also changes from providing solutions for dependent users to designing environments, networks and platforms through which people can together devise their own independent and interdependent solutions. (NCSL, 2005a)

From Hierarchy to Networks

Leadbeater (2005) believes that personalised learning will only become reality when schools become much more networked, collaborating not only with other schools, but with families, community groups and other public agencies. Arguably one of the best funded and continuous school networks – The Network Learning Group (NLG) with its hub at the United Kingdom's National College for School Leadership (NCSL) – summarises its learning about the advantages of networks in comparison to traditional hierarchically designed organisations (NCSL, 2005b) as greater sharing, diversity, flexibility, creativity, risk taking, broadening of teacher expertise and learning opportunities available to pupils, and improved teaching and pupil attainment. They point out that while there is no blueprint for an effective network, it is possible to identify factors that successful networks have in common:

- Design around a compelling idea or aspirational purpose and an appropriate form and structure.
- Focus on pupil learning.
- Create new opportunities for adult learning.
- Plan and have dedicated leadership and management.

But Leadbeater (2005, p. 22) warns that the collaboration needed for effective networks "can be held back by regulation, inspection, and funding regimes that encourage schools to think of themselves as autonomous, stand-alone units". Levin (NCSL, 2005b, p. 6) agrees, pointing out that there "are inevitable tensions between the idea of learning networks, which are based on ideas of capacity building as a key to reform, and ... reform through central policy mandate". Rusch (2005), in fact, concludes that networks cannot be controlled by the formal system. She questions the role of the system in effective school networks, identifying competing institutional scripts between what is likely to be required by networks as opposed to the system as follows:

- Structures are seen as malleable in networks but fixed and hierarchical in the system.
- Conflict is open and valued in networks while it tends to be hidden and feared in the system.
- Communication is open and unbounded in networks but controlled and closed in the system.
- Leadership tends to be fluid in networks while it is hierarchical and assigned in the system.
- Relationships are egalitarian in networks but meritocratic in the system.
- And, finally, knowledge and power based on inquiry and learning is valued in networks while expertise and knowing are valued in the system.

Social Capital and Communities of Professional Learners

Arguably, the two organisational concepts that underpin schools as social centres and learning organisations, organic systems, deep democracy, personalisation through participation, and networking are social capital and communities of professional learners.

Social Capital

The idea of social capital has enjoyed a remarkable rise to prominence. By treating social relationships as a form of capital, it proposes that they are a resource, which people can then draw on to achieve their goals. It also serves alongside other forms of capital (e.g., economic, human, cultural, identity and intellectual) as one possible resource and accepted contributor to our individual, community and national wellbeing. International bodies such as UNESCO, OECD and World Bank have engaged in extensive conceptual, empirical and policy related work in the area and a number of websites are devoted entirely to the area.[2]

---

[2]For example: http://www.socialcapitalgateway.org/

What do we mean by "social capital"? The World Bank (Grootaert, Narayan, Jones, & Woolcock, 2004, p. 3) concludes that social capital "is most frequently defined in terms of the groups, networks, norms, and trust that people have available to them for productive purposes". As well as this generally accepted definition, Grootaert et al. (2004, p. 4) point out that common distinctions are made among "bonding", "bridging" and "linking" forms of social capital. "Bonding" social capital refers to "ties to people who are similar in terms of their demographic characteristics, such as family members, neighbours, close friends and work colleagues". "Bridging" social capital is also horizontal in nature but refers to "ties to people who do not share many of these characteristics". However, it continues to connect "people with more or less equal social standing". "Linking" social capital operates across power differentials and thus is seen vertical in nature. It refers to "one's ties to people in positions of authority such as representatives of public (police, political parties) and private (banks) institutions".

Knowing the definition of social capital and its different forms is helpful, but it does little to assist educational leaders with the challenges in building social capital in schools. A way through this situation is for the educational leader to see bonding social capital as that occurring among work colleagues within schools. It is the most developed area in the research literature (Goddard, Hoy, & Woolfolk Hoy, 2004; OECD, 2004; Ross, Hogaboam, & Gray, 2004; Somech, 2002; Stoll et al., 2003). Bridging social capital can be taken as that occurring between schools. This area is a recent but growing one in the research literature, especially in the area of networking (see the previous subsection) (Hopkins, NCSL, 2005b; Kanter, 1994; Leadbeater, 2005). Linking social capital can be understood as that occurring between a school and its community. While there is a long research tradition in this area it tends to be unidirectional, concentrating on what the community can do for the school, rather than the other way around (Jolly & Deloney, 1996; Kilpatrick, Johns, Mulford, Falk, & Prescott, 2001).

The research evidence is clear in its strong support for all three forms of social capital. The outcomes are impressive, not the least of which being improved student engagement, academic performance and later life chances, improved teaching and learning, reduced within school variation and retention of teachers in the profession, and increased individual and community capacity to influence their own futures.

However, the research also points to many challenges to overcome at the contextual, organisational and individual levels including the current accountability press, especially system preoccupation with a limited number of academic performance outcomes; the micro politics of schools such as contrived collegiality, groupthink and conflict avoidance; differences between policy development and its implementation; dedicated leadership; large, secondary, high-poverty schools; and professional autonomy.

Communities of Professional Learners

Where do we take this research evidence on the importance of and challenges to social capital? The way forward is to see the task as establishing communities of professional learners (CPL) and to see it as developmental *starting* with the building of social capital. A message arising from the research is that those in schools must learn how to lose time in order to gain time. Awareness of, and skill development in, group and organisational processes is a first step towards any effective change. Instead of others trying to insert something into a school's (or community's) culture, the school, and especially its leadership, should first be trying to help that culture develop an awareness of and responsiveness to itself (Scribner, Hager, & Warne, 2002).

In brief, the position taken identifies three major, sequential and embedded elements in successful school reform. It takes the two elements in the definition of social capital, "groups, networks, norms, and trust" and "for productive purposes", and extends them to include a third element, learning. The first element in the sequence relates to the community, how people are communicated with and treated. Success is more likely where people act rather than are always reacting, are empowered, involved in decision making through a transparent, facilitative and supportive structure, and are trusted, respected, encouraged and valued. It is a waste of time moving to the second element until such a community is established. The second element concerns a community of professionals. A community of professionals involves shared norms and values including valuing differences and diversity, a focus on implementation and continuous enhancement of quality learning for all students, de-privatisation of practice, collaboration, and critical reflective dialogue, especially that based on performance data. However, a community of professionals can be static, continuing to do the same or similar thing well. The final element relates to the presence of a capacity for change, learning and innovation – in other words, a community of professional learners (CPL) (Mulford, 2007d).

Each element of a CPL, and each transition between them, can be facilitated by appropriate leadership and professional development. Also, each element is a prerequisite for the other; they are embedded within each other with only the emphasis changing. For example, when learning is occurring there is still a need to revisit the social community and the professional community, especially where there has been a change of personnel and/or a new governmental direction announced.

Using this analysis of bonding, bridging and linking social capital to understand the importance of, challenges to and developmental nature of CPLs can assist the educational leader in better translating the research into policy and practice. It can help him or her to do the following:

- understand better and be able to take action on the intricacies involved in moving a school, or part of a school, from where it is now to becoming truly a place of ongoing excellence and equity without those in schools being "bowled over" by the demands for change that surround them;
- target appropriate interventions to ensure more effective progression through the stages. In targeting interventions recognition will need to be given to the fact that it is a journey and that actions at one stage may be inappropriate, or even counterproductive, at another stage; and,
- support the position that a school will need to be evaluated differently depending on the stage it has reached.

Changing the organisation of and leading schools and school systems so they become CPLs will not be for the faint of heart. It will require schools and their leaders to radically rethink how they operate. As Leadbeater (2005) points out, many of the basic building blocks of traditional education – such as the school, the year group, the class, the lesson, the blackboard and the teacher standing in front of a class of 30 children – could be seen as obstacles. All the resources available for learning – teachers, parents, assistants, peers, technology, time and buildings – will have to be deployed more flexibly than in the past. School leadership in such organisations will certainly be less lonely and more collaborative and professionally interactive than ever before (NCSL, 2007).

Leadership "Smart"

Educational leadership matters (Day & Leithwood, 2007; Fullan, 2005; Hallinger, 2007; Hargreaves & Fink, 2006; Leithwood, in press; Leithwood, Day, Sammons, Harris, & Hopkins, 2006; Marks & Printy, 2004; McREL, 2005; Silins & Mulford, 2004), is changing (Leithwood et al., 2006; NCSL, 2007) and, given the changing context and organisational response, needs to be smart. Unfortunately, in this situation the plethora of advice about "strong", adjectival, one-size-fits-all school leadership (e.g., instructional, transformational and distributed) is anachronistic. Successful educational leadership is more complex; it needs to be able to see and act on the whole, as well as on the individual elements, and the relationships among them over time (i.e., in a developmental manner). As Hargreaves and Fink (2006) point out, it is a meal not a menu, with all pieces needing to fit together in different ways at different times.

A lack of time and professional isolation are major barriers to collaborative endeavours. Donaldson (2001, p. 11) describes some major attributes of schools that contribute to what he calls a "leadership-resistant architecture" reflected in a "conspiracy of business". There is, according to Donaldson, little time for the school leader to convene people to plan, organise and follow through. Contact and the transaction of business often take place "catch-as-catch-can". Opinion setting and relationship building in schools, he argues, are mostly inaccessible and even resistant to the principal's formal attempt to guide and structure the direction of the school. Consistent with the findings from the Australian LOSO project (see the next section), it was found that the larger the school the more complex and impersonal the environment and the fewer the opportunities a principal was likely to have for individual relationship building or problem solving.

It may in fact be that "strong", visible, visionary leadership is dysfunctional. A research by Barnett, McCormick, and Conners (2001) is key in this context, showing as it does the positive effects of principals demonstrating individual concern and building relationships but the negative effects of being inspirational and visionary. While one leadership style or approach may work well for some leaders, most have a range of leadership styles.

Dinham's (2007, p. 37) research examining schools achieving outstanding educational outcomes found that "the turning-around and lifting-up processes can take around 6–7 years to accomplish". In this situation, successful leaders adapt and adopt their leadership practice to meet the changing needs of circumstances in which they find themselves (see, for example, Hallinger, 2007; Leo, 2007). As schools develop and change, different leadership approaches will inevitably be required and different sources of leadership will be needed so that the development work keeps moving. A one-size-fits-all, adjectival style or approach to leadership, or checklists of leadership attributes, may seem superficially attractive but can often limit, restrict and distort leadership behaviour in ways that are not always conducive to school development and improvement.

On this point, it is interesting to note that proponents of instructional (Hallinger, 2005), transformational (Leithwood et al., 2006) and distributed leadership (Spillane, 2006) have, over time, moved well away from the one-size-fits-all, charismatic, heroic model of school leadership and expanded their understandings to include aspects of the context, antecedent conditions (e.g., school level, size and SES) and school mission, culture and a reinforcing structure (especially developing people, collaboration and monitoring) and instructional program. For example, Hallinger (2007) calls for an integrative model of educational leadership which links leadership to the needs of the school context, Leo (2007) focuses on the role of social context and socio-cultural factors on achievement motivation and Mulford (2003b) calls for an awareness of balance and learning.

Interrelationships among Context, Organisation and Leader: Two Models Meeting the Challenge of Complexity

The final section of this chapter outlines two models based on an Australian research that take the evolving, broader and more complex approach to educational leadership. The models are fully consistent with the advice in other sections to meet the following: achieve balance and/or choose between competing contextual forces; broaden what counts as good schooling; and broaden the way schools are organised and run, especially as social centres and learning organisations, organic, living systems, deep democracies, networks, personalisation through participation, and social capital developers through communities of professional learners.

The first is a model of successful school principalship based on the evidence from qualitative in-depth case studies of five best practice Tasmanian schools that constitute part of an eight-country exploration of successful school leadership (the Successful School Principals Project – SSPP) (see, for example: Gurr et al., 2005; Mulford, 2007b, 2007c). The second is a model of leadership for organisational learning and student outcomes (LOLSO) based on quantitative survey evidence from over 95 principals, 3,700 teachers and 5,000 15-year-old high school students in South Australia and Tasmania. Details of the samples, methodologies, related literature reviews and so on can be found elsewhere (see, for example: Silins & Mulford, 2002a, 2002b; Silins, Mulford, & Zarins, 2002; Silins & Mulford, 2004), as can the application to policy (Mulford, 2003a, 2003d).

Successful School Principals Project (SSPP)

Findings from the SSPP case studies suggest that successful school principalship is an interactive, reciprocal and evolving process involving many players, which is influenced by and in turn influences the context in which it occurs (see Fig. 1). Further, the findings demonstrate that successful principalship is underpinned by the core values and beliefs of the principal. These values and beliefs influence the principal's decisions and actions regarding the provision of individual support and capacity building, and capacity building at the school level, including school culture and structure. The principal's core values and beliefs, together with the values and capacities of other members of the school community, feed directly into the development of a shared school vision, which shapes the teaching and learning – student and social capital outcomes of schooling. To complete the proposed model requires a process of evidence-based monitoring and critical reflection, which can lead to school maintenance, change and/or transformation. The context and the successful school principal's values form the "why" of the model; the individual support

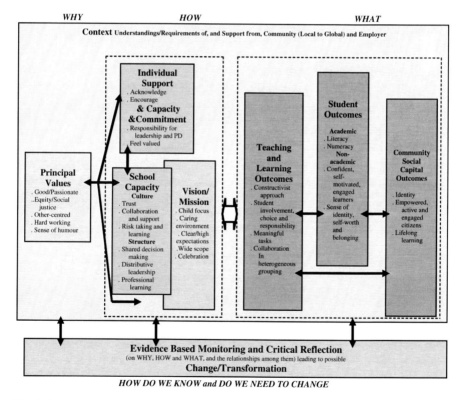

Fig. 1 SSP model

and capacity, school capacity and school vision/mission form the "how"; and the teaching and learning, student and community outcomes form the "what". The evidence-based monitoring and critical reflection on the "why", "how" and "what" and the relationship among them form the final section of the model, the "how do we know" and "do we need to change" element.

Leadership for Organisational Learning and Student Outcomes (LOLSO)

Evidence from LOLSO surveys clearly demonstrate that leadership that makes a difference is both position based (principal) and distributive (administrative team and teachers) (see Fig. 2). Further, it was found that the principal's leadership needs to be transformational – that is, providing individual, cultural and structural support to staff; capturing a vision for the school; communicating high performance expectations and offering intellectual stimulation. However, both positional and distributive leadership are only indirectly related to student outcomes. Organisational learning (OL), involving three sequential stages of trusting and collaborative climate, shared

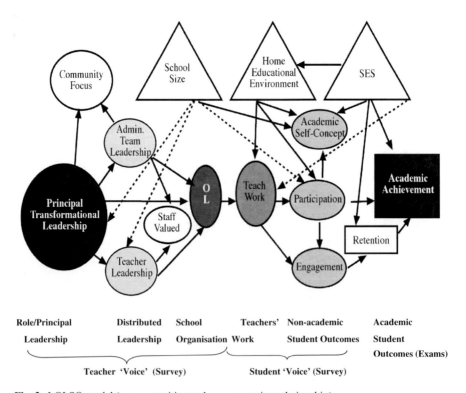

Fig. 2 LOLSO model ($\longrightarrow$ = positive and =--→ negative relationship)

and monitored mission and taking initiatives and risks supported by appropriate professional development, was found to be the important intervening variable between leadership and teacher work and then student outcomes. That is, leadership contributes to OL, which in turn influences what happens in the core business of the school: teaching and learning. It influences the way students perceive that teachers organise and conduct their instruction and their educational interactions with, and expectations of, their students.

Students' positive perceptions of teachers' work directly promote their participation in school, academic self-concept and engagement with school. Student participation is directly and student engagement indirectly (through retention) related to academic achievement. The contextual variables of school size, socioeconomic status (SES) and, especially, student home educational environment make a positive or negative difference to these relationships (as indicated in Fig. 2). However, this was not the case in terms of teacher or leader gender or age, having a community focus or student academic self-concept.

Summary

As we have seen over the course of this chapter, a great deal of a school's success depends on which areas of school life the educational leader chooses to spend time and attention on. As a single input by a leader can have multiple outcomes, a leader needs to be able to see and act on the whole, as well as on the individual elements, and the relationships among them (NCSL, 2005c).

The chapter moved through evidence on three elements: context, organisation and leaders. Context related to the forces currently pressing on schools and the implications of these forces for schools and their leaders. School organisation focused on evolving models that moved beyond the outmoded and ineffective bureaucratic model to communities of professional learners. Evidence on leaders questioned whether one type of leadership fits all contexts and organisations and subsequently what it meant to be a successful leader. A great deal of promise was found in the evidence on successful leaders building school capacity and doing this in a developmental way.

To be successful on all these fronts and how they interrelate is the biggest current leadership challenge. Within this complex challenge, school leaders must be part of ongoing conversations about context and its implications for schools. Leaders need to understand and be able to act on the evolving and preferred organisational models for schools. And, leaders need to be able to understand and act on the quality evidence that is now accumulating on being a successful school leader.

With the eminent retirement of a larger-than-normal proportion of our nation's school leaders (Anderson et al., 2007), there is no better time to act on these challenges. Will education systems and, more importantly, the profession take up the challenges? And, will they actually use quality evidence (OECD, 2007), such as that provided in this handbook, in schools and school systems to enable us to move forward? This is a plea for us to move beyond mere technical competence in school leadership. Galton (2000, p. 203) makes this point well in terms of teachers:

> By making certain techniques mandatory you run the danger of turning teachers into technicians who concentrate on the method and cease to concern themselves with ways that methods must be modified to take account of the needs of individual pupils. As we face the demands of a new century, creating a teaching profession which while technically competent was imaginatively sterile would be a recipe for disaster. (Galton, 2000, p. 203)

As it is for teachers, so it is for school leaders. (PricewaterhouseCoopers, 2007)

There is clearly a need to achieve better balances in our world, including between learning what the political and bureaucratic systems require of individual leaders and what practising professionals require of themselves and their colleagues. On the basis of the available research, I believe this balance can best be achieved by groups of educational leaders, or professional collectives and alliances, setting, negotiating and delivering their own agendas. This position is also consistent with the emerging priorities for successful educational leadership detailed in this review. After all, participation in context, organisation and leadership, including policy making, not only enhances efficiency in implementation, but also contributes to the creation of more pluralistic and democratic political systems (Lecomte & Smillie, 2004).

A Concluding Comment

Recent developments in the field of educational leadership demonstrate that it is more complex, nuanced and subtle than previously portrayed. It may be that we need to take models such as SSPP and LOLSO, as well more recent work by Heck and Hallinger (2009), Mulford and Edmunds (2009) and Sammons et al. (2009), further by having a set of models representing different groupings of variables and their relationships and sequences, for example for high-poverty, rural, inner city, primary and/or public schools. On the other hand, when lost in the complex, "swampy" ground of schools and their environments a simple "compass" (head roughly west, be "instructional", "transformational" and/or "distributive") may be felt to be much more helpful than the detailed road maps in linking leadership with improving learning in schools. However, in an age of "global positioning systems" and models based on quality evidence that are complex enough to come close to the reality faced by schools and are predictive in that they link leadership and student outcomes, such a simplistic response does education and its continued reform a deep disservice.

References

Anderson, M., Gronn, P., Ingvarson, L., Jackson, A., Kleinhenz, E., McKenzie, P., et al. (2007). *Australia: Country Background Report. OECD Improving School Leadership Activity.* A report prepared for the Australian Government Department of Education, Science and Training. Melbourne: ACER.

Barnett, K., McCormick, J., & Conners, R. (2001). Transformational leadership in schools: Panacea, placebo or problem? *Journal of Educational Administration, 39*(1), 24–46.

Bernstein, B. (2000). *Pedagogy, symbolic control and identity: Theory, research, critique.* Lanham, Maryland: Rowman & Littlefield.

Bishop, P., & Mulford, B. (1999). When will they ever learn? Another failure of centrally imposed change. *School Leadership and Management, 19*(2), 179–187.

Carneiro, P., Crawford, C., & Goodman, A. (2006). Which skills matter? London: Centre for the Economics of Education, London School of Economics. http://cee.lse.ac.uk/cee%20dps/ceedp59.pdf

Cunha, F., Heckman, J., Lochner, J., & Masterov, D. (2005). Interpreting the evidence of life cycle skill formation. London: NBER Working Paper 11331. http://papers.nber.org/papers/w11331

Day, C., & Leithwood, K. (Eds.). (2007). *Successful principal leadership in times of change: An international perspective.* London: Springer.

DfES. (2005). http://www.everychildmatters.gov.uk/aims/ (accessed on 27/3/2006).

Dinham, S. (2007). *Authoritative leadership, action learning and student accomplishment.* ACER Research Conference 2007, 'The Leadership Challenge: Improving learning in schools', Melbourne, 12–14 August.

Donaldson, G. (2001). *Cultivating leadership in school: Connecting people, purpose and practice.* New York: Teachers College Press.

Feinstein, L. (2000). *The relative economic importance of academic, psychological and behavioural attributes developed in childhood.* London: Centre for Economic Performance, London School of Economics and Political Science, University of London.

Fielding, M. (1999). Target setting, policy pathology and student perspectives: Learning to labour in new times. *Cambridge Journal of Education, 29*(2), 277–287.

Fullan, M. (2005). *Leadership and sustainability: System thinkers in action.* Thousand Oaks, CA: Corwin Press, Toronto Principals Council.

Furman, G., & Shields, C. (2003, April) *How can leaders promote and support social justice and democratic community in schools?* Paper presented to the annual meeting of the American Educational Research Association, Chicago, IL.

Galton, M. (2000). Big change questions: Should pedagogical change be mandated? Dumbing down on classroom standards: The perils of a technician's approach to pedagogy. *Journal of Educational Change, 1*(2), 199–204.

Gardner, H. (2007). *Five minds for the future.* Boston: Harvard Business School Publications.

Goddard, R., Hoy, W., & Woolfolk Hoy, A. (2004). Collective efficacy beliefs: Theoretical developments, empirical evidence, and future directions. *Educational Researcher, 33*(3), 1–13.

Goodlad, J. (1994). *Educational renewal: Better teachers, better schools.* San Francisco: Jossey-Bass.

Gronn. P. (2003). *The new work of educational leaders.* London: Paul Chapman Publishing.

Grootaert, C., Narayan, D., Jones, V., & Woolcock, M. (2004). *Measuring social capital.* Washington DC: The Word Bank, Working Paper No. 18.

Gurr, D., Drysdale, L., & Mulford, B. (2005). Successful principal leadership: Australian case studies. *Journal of Educational Administration, 43*(6), 539–551.

Hallinger, P. (2005). Instructional leadership and the school principal: A passing fancy that refuses to fade away. *Leadership and Policy in Schools, 4*(3), 1–20.

Hallinger, P. (2007). *Research on the practice of instructional and transformational leadership: Retrospect and prospect.* ACER Research Conference 2007, 'The Leadership Challenge: Improving learning in schools', Melbourne, 12–14 August.

Hargreaves, A., & Fink, D. (2006). *Sustainable leadership.* San Francisco: Jossey-Bass.

Heck, R., & Hallinger, P. (2009). Assessing the contribution of distributed leadership to school improvement and growth in math achievement. *American Educational Research Journal, 46*(3), 659–690.

Howe, N., & Strauss, W. (2000). *Millennials rising: The next great generation.* New York: Vintage Original.

Hyman, P. (2005). *1 out of 10: From downing street to classroom reality*. London: Vintage.

Jolly, D., & Deloney, P. (1996). *Integrating rural school and community development: An initial examination*. Paper presented at the Annual Conference of the National Rural Education Association, San Antonio, Texas, 11–14 October.

Kanter, R. (1994, July). Collaborative advantage: The art of alliances, *Harvard Business Review, 72*(4), 96–108.

Kilpatrick, S., Johns, S., Mulford, B., Falk, I., & Prescott, L. (2001). *More than education: Leadership for rural school-community partnerships*. Canberra: Rural Industries Research and Development Corporation. http://rirdc.gov.au/reports/HCC/02-055sum.html

Leadbeater, C. (2004a). *Learning about personalisation: How can we put the learning at the heart of the education system?* London: UK Department for Education and Skills.

Leadbeater, C. (2004b). *Personalisation through participation*. London: DEMOS.

Leadbeater, C. (2005). *The shape of things to come*. London: DfES Innovation Unit. www.standards.dfes.gov.uk/innovation-unit

Lecomte, H., & Smillie, I. (2004). *Ownership and partnership: What role for civil society in poverty reduction strategies?* Paris: OECD.

Leithwood, K. (in press). Transformational school leadership. In E. Baker, B. McGaw, & P. Peterson (Eds.), *International encyclopaedia of education*. Oxford: Elsevier.

Leithwood, K., Day, C., Sammons, P., Harris, A., & Hopkins, D. (2006). *Seven strong claims about successful school leadership*. Nottingham: National College for School Leadership.

Leo, E. (2007). *Take me to your leader: Leadership and the future*. ACER Research Conference 2007, 'The Leadership Challenge: Improving learning in schools', Melbourne, 12–14 August.

MacBeath, J. (2006). *Leadership as a subversive activity*. Melbourne: Australian Council for Educational Leaders Monograph No. 39.

Marks, H., & Printy, S. (2004). Principal leadership and school performance: An integration of transformational and instructional leadership. *Educational Administration Quarterly, 39*(3), 370–397.

McREL. (2005). *The future of schooling: Educating America in 2014*. Colorado: Mid-continent Research for Education and Learning.

Meyer, J., & Rowan, B. (1978). Notes on the structure of educational organisations: Revised Version. Paper prepared for the Annual Meeting of the American Sociological Association. Reported in J. Hannaway, Administrative structures why do they grow? *Teachers College Record, 79*(3), 416–417.

Mulford, B. (2002). The global challenge: A matter of balance. *Educational Management & Administration, 30*(2), 123–138.

Mulford, B. (2003a). *School leaders: Challenging roles and impact on teacher and school effectiveness*. Paris: Commissioned Paper by the Education and Training Policy Division, OECD, for the Activity 'Attracting, Developing and Retaining Effective Teachers'. http://www.oecd.org/dataoecd/61/61/2635399.pdf

Mulford, B. (2003b). Balance and learning: Crucial elements in leadership for democratic schools. *Leadership and Policy in Schools, 2*(2), 109–124.

Mulford, B. (2003c). Leadership in education: Losing sight of out interests? In N. Bennett, M. Crawford, & M. Cartwright (Eds.), *Effective educational leadership* (pp. 3–13). London: Open University Press & Paul Chapman Publishing.

Mulford, B. (2003d). The role of school leadership in attracting and retaining teachers and promoting innovative schools and students. Canberra: Review of Teaching and Teacher Education, Commonwealth Department of Education Science and Training. http://www.dest.gov.au/NR/rdonlyres/161EEEC9-713A-40CD-9E87-2E5ACA1E19A3/1661/leadership.pdf

Mulford, B. (2004). Congruence between the democratic purposes of schools and school principal training in Australia. *Journal of Educational Administration, 42*(6), 625–639.

Mulford, B. (2007a). *Overview of research on Australian educational leadership 2001–2005*. Melbourne: Australian Council for Educational Leaders Monograph No. 40.

Mulford, B. (2007b). Successful school principalship in Tasmania. In C. Day & K. Leithwood (Eds.), *Making a difference: Successful school leadership in eight countries*. London: Springer.

Mulford, B. (2007c). Successful school leadership: What and who decides? *Australian Journal of Education, 51*(3), 228–246.

Mulford, B. (2007d). The challenge of building social capital in professional learning communities: Importance, challenges and a way forward. In L. Stoll & K. Seashore Louis (Eds.), *Professional learning communities: Divergence, detail and difficulties* (pp. 166–180). London: Open University Press/McGraw Hill.

Mulford, B. (2008). *The leadership challenge*. Melbourne: Australian Council for Educational Research, Australian Education Review 53.

Mulford, B., & Edmunds, B. (2009). *Successful school principalship in Tasmania*. Launceston: Faculty of Education, University of Tasmania. http://fcms.its.utas.edu.au/educ/educ/

Mulford, B., & Edmunds, B. (2010). *Educational investment in Australian schooling: Serving public purposes in Tasmanian primary schools*. Launceston: Faculty of Education, University of Tasmania. http://fcms.its.utas.edu.au/educ/educ/

Mulford, W., Silins, H., & Leithwood, K. (2004). *Educational leadership for organisational learning and improved student outcomes*. Dordrecht, The Netherlands: Kluwer Academic Publishers.

NCSL. (2005a). *Learning-centred leadership: Towards personalised learning-centred leadership*. Nottingham: National College for School Leadership.

NCSL. (2005b). *Establishing a network of schools*. Cranfield: Network Learning Group, National College for School Leadership.

NCSL. (2005c). *Emerging lessons from NCSL research activity*. Nottingham: National College for School Leadership.

NCSL. (2007). *What we know about school leadership*. Nottingham: National College for School Leadership.

OECD. (2001a). *New school management approaches*. Paris: OECD.

OECD, (2001b). *What school for the future?* Paris: OECD.

OECD. (2004). *Learning for tomorrow's world: First results from PISA 2003*. Paris: OECD.

OECD. (2006). *Think scenarios, rethink education*. Paris: OECD.

OECD. (2007). Evidence in education: Linking research and policy. Paris: OECD.

Peck, S. (1987). *The different drum: Community making and peace*. New York: Simon & Schuster.

Pedro, F. (2006). *The new millennium learners: Challenging our views on ICT and learning*. Paris: Paper for the OECD-CERI New Millennium Learners activity. http://oecd.org/document/56/0,2340,en_2649_35845295_38358584_1_1_1_1,00.html

Peters, T. (1987). *Thriving on chaos*. London: Harper and Row.

PricewaterhouseCoopers. (2007). *Independent study into school leadership*. London: Department of Education and Science, Project RB818.

Ross, J., Hogaboam, A., & Gray, P. (2004). Prior student achievement, collaborative school processes and collective teacher efficacy. *Leadership and Policy in Schools, 3*(3), 163–188.

Rusch, E. (2005). Institutional barriers to organisational learning in school systems: The power of silence. *Educational Administration Quarterly, 41*(1), 83–120.

Sammons, P., Gu, Q., Day, C., & Ko, J. (2009, April). *Exploring the impact of school leadership on pupil outcomes: Results from a study of academically improved and effective schools in England*. Paper presented at AERA, San Diego.

Scribner, J., Hager, D., & Warne, T. (2002). The paradox of professional community: Tales from two high schools. *Educational Administration Quarterly, 38*(1), 45–76.

Sergiovanni, T. (1990). *Value-added leadership: How to get extraordinary performance in* schools. London: Harcourt Brace Jovanovich.

Silins, H., & Mulford, B. (2002a). Leadership and school results. In K. Leithwood & P. Hallinger (Eds.),*Second international handbook of educational leadership and administration* (pp. 561–612). Norwell, MA: Kluwer Academic Publishers.

Silins, H., & Mulford, B. (2002b). Schools as learning organisations: The case for system, teacher and student learning. *The Journal of Educational Administration, 40*(5), 425–446.

Silins, H., & Mulford, B. (2004). Schools as learning organisations: Effects on teacher leadership and student outcomes. *School Effectiveness and School Improvement, 15*(3–4), 443–466.

Silins, H., Mulford, B., & Zarins, S. (2002). Organisational learning and school change. *Educational Administration Quarterly, 38*(5), 613–642.

Somech, A. (2002). Explicating the complexity of participative management: An investigation of multiple dimensions. *Educational Administration Quarterly, 38*, 341–371.

Spillane, J. (2006). *Distributed leadership.* San Francisco: Jossey-Bass.

Stoll, L., Bolam, R., McMahon, A., Thomas, S., Wallace, M., Greenwood, A., et al. (2006). *Professional learning communities: Source materials for school leaders and other leaders of professional learning.* London: Department of Education and Skills, Innovations Unit.

Stoll, L., Fink, D., & Earl, L. (2003). *It's about learning: And it's about time.* London: Falmer Press.

Veen, W. (2003). A new force for change: Homo Zappiens. *The Learning Citizen, 7*(1), 5–7.

Wheatley, M. (2005). *Finding our way: Leadership for an uncertain time.* San Francisco: Berrett-Koehl.

World Bank. (2005). *Expanding opportunities and building competencies for young people: A new agenda for secondary education.* Washington, DC: World Bank.

Large-Scale Reform in the Era of Accountability: The System Role in Supporting Data-Driven Decision Making

Amanda Datnow and Vicki Park

The contemporary education policy marks a shift away from the idea that change happens organically, one school at a time. Instead, there is a focus on creating a systematic infrastructure to support change across a large number of schools at once. Within this decade, we have witnessed several types of large-scale reform efforts in the United States and across other Western countries, including state and federal systems of standards and accountability and system-wide implementations of literacy and numeracy programs, among others.

In the United States, the shift to large-scale reform was crystallized in the No Child Left Behind Act (NCLB) of 2001 which instituted a new accountability system based on assessments and standards. As the reauthorization of the Elementary and Secondary Education Act (ESEA), NCLB followed up on the ideas laid forth in governmental plans and policies beginning in the 1990s. However, this new policy gave the federal government unprecedented authority in several ways by "crea[ting] stern directives regarding test use and consequence; put[ting] federal bureaucrats in charge of approving state standards and accountability plans; set[ting] a single nationwide timetable for boosting achievement; and prescrib[ing] specific remedies for under-performing schools" (Finn & Hess, 2002, p. 2).

NCLB is the first federal comprehensive educational framework consisting of standards, assessments, and accountability. NCLB is particularly noteworthy because it moves past the traditional focus on schooling "inputs" and holds educators responsible for student performance results (Dembosky, Pane, Barney, & Christina, 2005; Ingram, Louis, & Schroder, 2004; Lafee, 2002). Under this system, the mechanisms for accomplishing these goals emphasize data-driven decision making (i.e., test scores, yearly progress reports), the implementation of evidence-based practices, and increased school choice for parents. NCLB requires states to have standards detailing content for student learning. Testing is also mandatory for students in most grades, and results are intended to be used to drive instruction and teaching practices. In addition, student performance data must be disaggregated

A. Datnow (✉)
University of California San Diego, San Diego, CA, USA
e-mail: adatnow@ucsd.edu

A. Hargreaves et al. (eds.), *Second International Handbook of Educational Change*,
Springer International Handbooks of Education 23, DOI 10.1007/978-90-481-2660-6_12,
© Springer Science+Business Media B.V. 2010

based on major demographic classifications such as race/ethnicity, socioeconomic status, gender, disability, and language. Systematic testing is also coupled with pre-scriptive intervention remedies for schools not meeting Adequate Yearly Progress (AYP). Schools are pushed to improve under threat of sanctions that ultimately allow parents to opt out of low-performing schools. Additionally, guidelines for enhancing teacher quality are laid out.

Thus, the current era of large-scale educational reform is marked by standards, assessments, and accountability. These policy tools are held together by assump-tions of the need for policy coherence, system alignment, and coordination among various education agencies. Standards, tests aligned to standards, and accountability systems are stronger policy instruments because they attempt to directly influence instruction and student outcomes. However, the instruments are still relatively weak because the how and why of teaching and learning remain unaddressed. Standards provide guidance on classroom content but do not assist teachers in translating stan-dards into effective instructional practices. Given the flexibility that states have in determining standards and proficiency levels, metrics of student performance can also be misleading, since some states opt for less rigorous standards and minimum competency measures of learning rather than the world-class standards touted by NCLB (NCES, 2007).

Even in the era of large-scale educational reform ushered in by NCLB, determin-ing effective instructional practices and measuring learning remain elusive goals. Moreover, capacity building for the core technology of education (Spillane, Reiser, & Reimer, 2002) – teaching and learning – has not been apparent in NCLB. Thus, the work of changing practices to meet more stringent accountability demands has been left to educators at the school and district levels, hence setting the stage for system-wide movements toward data-driven decision making (DDDM).

In this chapter, our purpose is to open up the "black box" of large-scale educa-tional change, specifically focusing on a reform movement that results from the current era of accountability: data-driven decision making. We first present the "co-construction" framework as a way to understand large-scale reform and then examine research and theories of action behind DDDM. Our focus here is on the system, or school district level, where large-scale efforts to engage educators in the use of data often are initiated. We summarize with conclusions and implications for further research.

Understanding Large-Scale Educational Reform Through the Co-construction Framework

In our earlier work (e.g., Datnow, Hubbard, & Mehan, 2002; Datnow, Lasky, Stringfield, & Teddlie, 2006), we have found the "co-construction" perspective to be a useful heuristic for examining the dynamics involved in the implementation of large-scale educational change. The co-construction perspective extends the mutual adaptation theory coined in the Rand Change Agent study (Berman & McLaughlin, 1978) and elaborates on how the interconnections between actors and the wider social and political sphere shape policy implementation (Datnow et al., 2002). Co-construction draws upon the socio-cultural tradition which identifies personal, interpersonal, and community "levels" or "planes" of interaction (Rogoff, 1995; Tharp, 1997). Furthermore, co-construction, like mutual adaptation, views organizations as embedded within successively contextualized layers (McLaughlin & Talbert, 1993), but it extends the context to include the broader social system and political economy.

The co-construction approach has a number of specific dimensions. Most important is the idea of a relational sense of context (Datnow et al., 2002). By this we mean that people's actions cannot be understood apart from the setting in which the actions are situated; reciprocally, the setting cannot be understood without understanding the actions of the people within. A relational sense of context does not privilege any one context; rather it highlights the reciprocal relations among the social contexts in the policy chain (Hall & McGinty, 1997). Because contexts are inevitably connected (Sarason, 1997), multiple layers of the social system must be considered (Datnow et al., 2002). Of course, at a given point in time, a researcher will foreground interactions among social actors in one context and locate others in the background; but in order to allow for complete analysis, the interconnections among contexts throughout the system need to be described (Hall & McGinty, 1997; McLaughlin & Talbert, 1993; Sarason, 1997).

The relational sense of context builds on but also moves beyond the embedded sense of context notion that has dominated many analyses up to now. While definitions vary, embedded context typically refers to classroom as nested in broader system layers (Fullan, 1991) or interactional "planes" (Rogoff, 1995). This conception is important because it calls attention to the fact that face-to-face interaction occurs within wider dimensions of social life. However, it often puts only one site in the center. Furthermore, the embedded sense of context can be susceptible to the conceptual traps of structural determinism and uni-directionality, implying that policy only travels in one direction, usually from the top to down (Datnow, Hubbard, & Mehan, 2002). By contrast, the relational sense of context does not automatically assign a sense of importance to any one context but rather highlights relationships among contexts as key focus for analysis. As Cohen, Moffitt, and Goldin (2007) noted, implementation of policy is a complex process; policy aims, instruments, implementers' capabilities, and the environment of practice all interact to produce policy outcomes (p. 71).

Accordingly, the co-construction perspective rests on the premise of multi-directionality: that multiple levels of educational systems may constrain or enable policy implementation and that implementation may affect those broader levels. In this view, political and cultural differences do not simply constrain reform in a top–down fashion. Rather, the causal arrow of change travels in multiple directions among active participants in all domains of the system and over time. This grammar makes the reform process "flexible" and enables people who have "different intentions/interests and interpretations [to] enter into the process at different points along the [reform] course. Thus many actors negotiate with and adjust to one another within and across contexts" (Hall & McGinty, 1997, p. 4).

Given that it takes into consideration political and cultural differences, co-construction also acknowledges the role of power (Datnow et al., 2002). The co-construction perspective recognizes that people in organizations at all levels contribute to the policy-making process and that process is characterized by continuous interaction among agents and actors within and between levels of the system. However, differential access and use of power are affected by a person's position in the system (Firestone, Fitz, & Broadfoot, 1999). For example, unlike policymakers whose main role is to help design policy, implementers (whether they are situated at the state, district, or school levels) are simultaneously the object of reform and the agents of change. Consequently, implementers tend to carry the bulk of the weight in adjusting or conforming to policy mandates.

Most studies that look across contextual levels take an embedded sense of context. If we were to take an embedded sense of context, we would assume that events at higher levels of the context occur first and are more important analytically. We might also assume that policies originating in "higher" levels of context cause or determine actions at lower levels. However, this may limit our understanding of educational reform, as we will explain. This conceptualization makes the reform process flexible, with people who have "different intentions/interests and interpretations [and who] enter into the process at different points along the [reform] course. Thus many actors negotiate with and adjust to one another within and across contexts" (Hall & McGinty, 1997, p. 4). As with Elmore's (1979–1980), "backward mapping" concept, we also do not assume that policy is the only, or even major, influence on people's behavior. Individuals at the local level do indeed make decisions that affect not only policy implementation, but sometimes also the policy itself. This emphasis upon multi-dimensionality marks the co-construction perspective of reform implementation and departs from the technically driven, uni-directional conceptions of educational change.

We believe that formulating implementation as a co-constructed process coupled with qualitative research is helpful in making sense of the complex, and often messy, process of large-scale educational reform. Even when policies are seemingly straightforward, they are implemented very differently across localities, schools, and classrooms (Elmore & Sykes, 1992). We will call up the co-construction framework as we discuss DDDM.

District Level Reform and Data-Driven Decision Making

In the current policy environment, districts have emerged as key players in educational reform. More than ever before, districts are helping schools to focus on student achievement and quality of instruction (McIver & Farley, 2003; Togneri & Anderson, 2003). They have done so by learning to strategically engage with state reform policies and resources, with DDDM being a key ingredient.

When the term data-driven decision making is raised, people often ask, exactly, "what data are you referring to?" When using the phrase data-driven decision making, we refer to the process by which individuals or groups think about and use data. Some scholars make delineations between concepts such as data, informa-tion, and knowledge (Mandinach, Honey, & LIght, 2006). In these cases, data are defined as "raw" pieces of facts while information and evidence are described as an interpretation of data. Since all data, including those collected from formal research projects, are designed and gathered based on theoretical and methodological per-spectives, this distinction narrowly defines data and ignores the importance of data collection methods. In contrast to these narrow definitions, Earl and Katz (2002) adopt a broader view on what constitutes data. They argue that data are "summaries that result from collection of information through systematic measurement or obser-vation or analysis about some phenomenon of interest, using quantitative and/or qualitative methods" (p. 4). Data are not characterized based on their visual repre-sentation (e.g., whether they are numbers or words or "raw facts") but by the quality of their collection and synthesis. Furthermore, evidence refers to the interpretation arising out of data synthesis and analysis that is then used as a justification for spe-cific purposes such as supporting a course of action or confirming or disconfirming assumptions (Lincoln, 2002).

When referring to data use by individuals in schools and districts, we specifically refer to broad categories of information including (Bernhardt, 1998):

1. Demographic data, including attendance and discipline records;
2. Student achievement data, which encompasses not only standardized data but also formative assessments, teacher developed assessments, writing portfolios, and running records;
3. Instructional data, which focuses on activities such as teachers' use of time, the pattern of course enrollment, and the quality of the curriculum; and
4. Perception data, which provides insights regarding values, beliefs, and views of individuals or groups (e.g., surveys, focus groups).

As noted above, with the advent of No Child Left Behind, many districts are relying on these kinds of data (though often primarily those listed in number two, student achievement data) to inform decisions. A recent national study of the impact of NCLB reveals that most districts are allocating resources to increase the use of student achievement data to inform instruction in schools identified as needing improvement (Center on Education Policy, 2004). Similarly, summarizing findings across several major recent studies of high-performing school districts, Anderson (2003) writes:

> Successful districts in the current era of standards, standardized testing, and demands for evidence of the quality of performance invest considerable human, financial and technical resources in developing their capacity to assess the performance of students, teachers and schools, and to utilize these assessments to inform decision-making about needs and strate-gies for improvement, and progress towards goals at the classroom, school, and district levels (p. 9).

Supporters of data-driven decision making practices argue that effective data use enables school systems to learn more about their school, pinpoint successes and challenges, identify areas of improvement, and help evaluate the effectiveness of programs and practices (Mason, 2002).

Previous research, though largely without comparison groups, suggests that DDDM has the potential to increase student performance (Alwin, 2002; Doyle, 2003; Johnson, 1999, 2000; Lafee, 2002; McIntire, 2002). Student achievement data can be used for various purposes including evaluating progress toward state and district standards, monitoring student progress, evaluating where assessments converge and diverge, and judging the efficacy of local curriculum and instructional practices (Cromey, 2000). When school-level educators become knowledgeable about data use, they can more effectively review their existing capacities, identify weaknesses, and better chart plans for improvement (Earl & Katz, 2006).

Data-driven decision making is also critical to identifying and finding ways to close achievement gaps between white and minority students (Bay Area School Reform Collaborative, 2003; Olsen, 1997). One of the expected outcomes of using evidence to base decisions is the questioning of long-held assumptions about students and student achievement. In some instances when educators are confronted with evidence that challenges their views about students' abilities, data can act as a potential catalyst for changing perceptions (Datnow & Castellano, 2000; Skrla & Scheurich, 2002). Armstrong and Anthes (2001) indicated that comparisons to high-performing schools with similar student demographics helped teachers in lower-achieving schools to stop blaming students' background for low academic results. Skrla and Scheurich (2002) suggested that the Texas accountability system's emphasis on disaggregating student data by subgroups helped to displace, but not eliminate, deficit views of students. Similarly, Woody's (2004) survey of educators' views on California's accountability system found that larger data patterns increased teachers' awareness of inequities in student outcomes.

Prior research on DDDM indicates several key strategies, or areas of work, particularly when the reform is initiated by a system as part of a large-scale educational reform effort. First of all, studies indicate that using data must be a key feature in reform plans rather than a supplemental or sporadic activity (Datnow, Park, & Wohlstetter, 2007; Supovitz & Taylor, 2003; Togneri & Anderson, 2003). Becoming a learning organization necessitates a collaborative environment in which teachers and administrators have multiple opportunities and resources to examine and interpret data, followed by time to develop an action plan to change behavior. Furthermore, the effective use of data must occur at the district, school, and classroom levels (Armstrong & Anthes, 2001; Datnow et al., 2007; Kerr, Marsh, Ikemoto, Darilek, & Barney, 2006; Supovitz & Taylor, 2003; Togneri & Anderson, 2003; Wayman & Stringfield, 2006). Because DDDM is a system-wide activity, the co-construction framework is a helpful way for thinking about the activities and interrelationships of the individuals involved, up, down, and around the system.

Also, in districts where DDDM is prevalent, there is often a culture of inquiry (Earl & Katz, 2006) that supports data use at all levels. Districts are actively transforming their professional development practices from ones that focus on compliance to support in order to build the capacity of their staff to participate in decision-making processes and create an organizational culture of inquiry

(Petrides & Nodine, 2005). A culture of continuous improvement accompanies this culture of inquiry. Also, inclusiveness in the DDDM process is often prevalent. Not only are principals privy to repositories of assessment data, but teachers are as well. Teachers are often encouraged to take a close look at grade-level and class-room data and share and discuss the data with each other (Armstrong & Anthes, 2001).

As part of engaging in DDDM, districts often create a closer alignment between the curriculum and state standards. This typically involves creating benchmarks and standards for each grade level. Increasingly, districts are also implementing regular assessments throughout the school year in order to make sure that student progress toward standards is regularly monitored and that instructional adjustments are made accordingly (Armstrong & Anthes, 2001; Petrides & Nodine, 2005). Scorecards are also utilized as a management tool to monitor and measure the progress of schools as well as to assist districts and school in aligning their goals (Petrides & Nodine, 2005).

However, data need to be actively used to improve instruction in schools, and individual schools often lack the capacity to implement what research suggests (Wohlstetter, Van Kirk, Robertson, & Mohrman, 1997). The implementation of NCLB has set the stage for schools to become "data-rich" but not necessarily for teachers to be effective data users; in other words, the presence of data alone does not lead to substantive and informed decision making. Thus, districts play a key role in developing capacity and structures to enable effective data use. Previous studies on the implementation of DDDM confirm that structural enablers, effec-tive leadership, and positive socialization toward data use impact its effectiveness (Armstrong & Anthes, 2001; Datnow et al., 2007; Ingram et al., 2004).

In districts that support DDDM, the superintendent and school board members often know how to lead and support data use. Districts often have staff that work as liaisons with principals and individual schools (Armstrong & Anthes, 2001). Some districts are hiring instructional guides for each school to help faculty interpret stu-dent achievement data and to develop plans for improving outcomes. Overall, strong leaders, committed to utilizing data for decision making and knowledgeable about the process, are essential to ensuring that a positive culture for data use is imple-mented at the school level (Dembosky et al., 2005; Marsh et al., 2005; Petrides & Nodine, 2005). They lead by creating an atmosphere where data use practices are relevant for instructional decision making.

School systems that are more successful in data use also tend to balance both standardization and flexibility (Datnow et al., 2007; Marsh et al., 2005). A degree of autonomy and flexibility for teachers is necessary in order to maintain the per-spective that decisions are based on data rather than predetermined conclusions. In schools where DDDM practices became a core element for improvement processes, central office administrators, principals, and lead teachers expected data to be used to inform and justify decisions. Whether teachers have the flexibility to reorganize their student groups based on benchmark assessments, re-teach previous topics out-side the scope and sequence of the curriculum, or alter the pace of the curriculum impacts the degree to which data will be used to guide decisions.

Teachers need time to review and make sense of data if it is going to affect their instruction. In districts and schools that use data effectively, time is reallocated in the school day for reflection and professional development (Datnow et al., 2007; Feldman & Tung, 2001; Halverson, Grigg, Prichett, & Thomas, 2005; Marsh et al., 2005). Group-based inquiry or "collaborative data teams" have been found to be successful in implementing DDDM across a system due to the broad participation from a diverse array of staff including teachers and administrators (Mason, 2002). School systems are also starting to data reflection protocols in order to guide these data meetings (Datnow et al., 2007). These structured data discussions provide teachers with continuous and intensive opportunities to share, discuss, and apply what they are learning with their peers (Garet, Porter, Desimone, Birman, & Yoon, 2001; Wilson & Berne, 1999). Once teachers identify instructional and learning gaps, improvement efforts may be blocked if teachers are unaware of intervention or instructional strategies. Leaders can address these needs by developing external partnerships to help build system-wide capacity (Anthes & Armstrong, 2001; Datnow et al., 2007).

Studies consistently suggest that as part of their capacity-building efforts, districts often provide professional development for principals and teachers so that they can learn to use data effectively (Petrides & Nodine, 2005; Togneri & Anderson, 2003). This is very important, as a perpetual problem that many schools face in making data-driven decisions is the lack of training regarding how to incorporate data into the school improvement process (Cromey, 2000). The onslaught of "drive-by" training sessions (Elmore, 2002) that do little to address the specific needs of schools and teachers cannot support the ongoing learning that is required for capacity building (Darling-Hammond & McLaughlin, 1995). Instead, effective professional development provides teachers with continuous and intensive opportunities to share, discuss, and apply what they are learning with other practitioners (Garet et al., 2001; Wilson & Berne, 1999). In order for this to occur, system-level support needs to be in place. In addition to consistent structured time for collaboration and professional learning, schools need strategies for planning, sharing, and evaluating their efforts.

Thus, developing teachers' capacity to become effective at using data to inform their instruction requires actions at multiple levels. Studies have suggested that school systems empower teachers to use data to inform their instruction and learning by: (1) investing in user-friendly data management systems that are accessible to teachers; (2) offering professional development for staff in how to use data and how to make instructional decisions on the basis of data; (3) providing time for teacher collaboration; and (4) connecting educators within and across schools to share data and improvement strategies (see Datnow et al., 2007). However, it is important to note that teachers need not only the capacity but also the *empowerment* to make instructional decisions based on data. School and system leaders need to provide scaffolds of support, but at the same time allow teachers enough flexibility to act on the basis of an informed analysis of multiple sources of data about their students' progress.

Overall, school systems play an increasingly pivotal role in leading and partnering with school sites to make data-driven practices an engine of reform. However, it is at the school level where everything comes together – and where DDDM is co-constructed by local educators (Datnow et al., 2007). School leaders provide time for meeting to discuss data, flexibility for re-teaching, and curriculum and material resources in order to facilitate data-driven instruction. Schools also develop their own assessments and tools for acting on data, which were often created by teachers working together. Like the systems, schools also function as places to build human and social capital in the form of building the knowledge and skills of teachers, a process which happened through professional development, instructional leadership, and networking among teachers. Schools also play a critical role in providing the expectations for data-driven instruction among teachers, as well as creating a climate of trust and collaboration so that teachers can work in professional learning communities to improve their practice (Datnow et al., 2007).

Thus, in DDDM, we see that reform success is a joint accomplishment of individuals and policies at multiple levels of the system. Broader federal and state accountability policies provide an important frame for the work that happens at the system and school levels. Although the crux of the work around data use takes place at the school and district levels, NCLB has helped to provide the political leverage needed in order for districts to stimulate improvement at the school level. The federal government holds states, districts, and schools accountable for student performance. States set curriculum standards and also hold schools and districts accountable. However, DDDM is in the work of teachers and administrators. As Dowd (2005) explains, "data don't drive," and therefore local educators co-construct the outcomes of this reform in their daily work with each other and with students.

Conclusion

When we examine events and actions across various contextual levels in the policy chain, we find that conditions at the federal, state, district, school, and design-team levels all co-construct the implementation of large-scale educational reform. Whereas a technical-rational view of educational change might suggest that implementation is an activity restricted to a group of people in schools at the bottom of the policy chain, we see here that implementation is a system-wide activity, even when the desired change is mainly at the school level. However, the various policy levels have varying degree of influence, and varying levels of connection with each other in the schools and districts. These findings point to the need for viewing events in broader contextual levels not just as "background" or "context" but as important, dynamic shaping forces in the large-scale educational reform process.

In order to fully understand the co-construction of a multi-level reform like the ones discussed here, researchers would ideally gather detailed, longitudinal case-study data on the district, state, community, and other systemic linkages that might influence large-scale educational change efforts. Multiple schools and school systems would be involved. The study might employ a mixed-methods design that supplements the qualitative data with valid and reliable measures of student achievement over at least a 3-year period. Survey data gathered from teachers and principals would also be very useful in assessing the extent to which educators at the school level have been engaged in reform efforts. For example, teachers and principals could be asked about the presence of systemic structural supports (e.g., collaboration time, networks), professional development, and resources devoted to assist in the reform effort.

Examining the co-construction of reform and the linkages across the educational system would likely provide insights that can inform the fields of educational research, policy development, and evaluation. However, there is a dearth of empirical research with the primary goal of identifying or describing such linkages. This gap in the reform literature reflects a systemic weakness in understanding why reform efforts have not been more successfully sustained. Clearly, educational reform involves formal structures, such as district offices, state policies, and so on. It also involves both formal and informal linkages among those structures. Yet, reform involves a dynamic relationship, not just among structures but also among cultures and people's actions in many interlocking settings. It is this intersection of culture, structure, and individual agency across contexts that helps us better understand how to build positive instances of large-scale educational change.

References

Alwin, L. (2002). The will and the way of data use. *School Administrator, 59*(11), 11.

Anderson, S. (2003). *The school district role in educational change: A review of the literature.* Ontario: International Centre for Educational Change, Ontario Institute of Studies in Education.

Armstrong, J., & Anthes, K. (2001). *Identifying the factors, conditions, and policies that support schools' use of data for decision making and school improvement: Summary of findings.* Denver, CO: Education Commission of the States.

Bay Area School Reform Collaborative. (2003). *After the test: Using data to close the achievement gap.* San Francisco: Author.

Berman, P., & McLaughlin, M. W. (1978). *Federal programs supporting educational change, Vol. VIII.* Santa Monica, CA: Rand.

Bernhardt, V. L. (1998). *Multiple measures.* Invited Monograph No. 4. CA: California Association for Supervision and Curriculum Development (CASCD).

Center on Education Policy. (2004). *From the capital to the classroom: Year 2 of the No Child Left Behind Act.* Washington, DC: Author.

Cohen, D. K., Moffitt, S. L., & Goldin, S. (2007). Policy and practice. In S. Furhman, D. Cohen, & F. Mosher (Eds.), *The state of education policy research* (pp. 63–85). Mahwah, NJ: Lawrence Erlbaum Associates, Inc.

Cromey, A. (2000). *Using student assessment data: What can we learn from schools?* Oak Brook, IL: North Central Regional Educational Laboratory.

Darling-Hammond, L., & McLaughlin, M. W. (1995). Policies that support professional development in an era of reform. *Phi Delta Kappan, 76*(8), 597–604.

Datnow, A., & Castellano, M. (2000). Teachers' responses to success for All: How beliefs, experiences, and adaptations shape implementation. *American Educational Research Journal, 37*(3), 775–799.

Datnow, A., Hubbard, L., & Mehan, H. (2002). *Extending educational reform: From one school to many.* London: RoutledgeFalmer Press.

Datnow, A., Park, V., & Wohlstetter, P. (2007). *Achieving with data: How high-performing school systems use data to improve instruction for elementary students.* A report commissioned by the NewSchools Venture Fund. Los Angeles, CA: Center on Educational Governance.

Datnow, A., Stringfield, S., Lasky, S., & Teddlie, C. (2006). *Integrating educational systems for successful reform in diverse contexts.* New York: Cambridge University Press.

Dembosky, J. W., Pane, J. F., Barney, H., & Christina, R. (2005). *Data driven decisionmaking in Southwestern Pennsylvania School Districts.* Working paper. Santa Monica, CA: RAND

Dowd, A. C., (2005). *Data don't drive: Building a practitioner-driven culture of inquiry to assess community college performance.* Boston: University of Massachusetts, Lumina Foundation for Education.

Doyle, D. P. (2003). Data-driven decision-making: Is it the mantra of the month or does it have staying power? *THE (Technological Horizons in Education) Journal, 30*(10), 19–21.

Earl, L., & Katz, S. (2002). Leading schools in a data rich world. In K. Leithwood, P. Hallinger, G. Furman, P. Gronn, J. MacBeath, B. Mulford, & K. Riley (Eds.), *The second international handbook of educational leadership and administration.* Dordrecht, Netherlands: Kluwer.

Earl, L., & Katz, S. (2006). *Leading schools in a data rich world.* Thousand Oaks, CA: Corwin Press.

Elmore, R. F. (1979–1980). Backward mapping: Implementation research and policy decisions. *Political Science Quarterly, 94*(4), 601–616.

Elmore, R. F. (2002). *Bridging the gap between standards and achievement: The imperative for professional development in education.* Washington, DC: Albert Shanker Institute.

Elmore, R., & Sykes, G. (1992). Curriculum policy. In P. W. Jackson (Ed.), *Handbook of research on curriculum.* New York: Macmillan.

Feldman, J., & Tung, R. (2001). *Whole school reform: How schools use the data-based inquiry and decision making process.* Paper presented at the 82nd annual meeting of the American Educational Research Association in Seattle, WA.

Finn, C. E., & Hess, F. M. (2004). On leaving no child left behind. *Public Interest, 157,* 35–57.

Firestone, W. A., Fitz, J., & Broadfoot, P. (1999). Power, learning, and legitimation: Assessment implementation across levels in the United States and the United Kingdom. *American Educational Research Journal, 36*(4), 759–793.

Fullan, M. (1991). *The new meaning of educational change.* London: Cassell.

Garet, M., Porter, A. C., Desimone, L., Birman, B. F., & Yoon, K. S. (2001). What makes professional development effective? Results from a national sample of teachers. *American Educational Research Journal, 38*(4), 915–945.

Hall, P. M., & McGinty, P. J. W. (1997). Policy as the transformation of intentions: Producing program from statutes. *The Sociological Quarterly, 38,* 439–467.

Halverson, R., Grigg, J., Prichett, R., & Thomas, C. (2005). *The new instructional leadership: Creating data-driven instructional systems in schools* (Wisconsin Center for Education Research Working Paper No. 2005-9). Madison, WI: Authors.

Ingram, D. Louis, K. S., Schroeder, R. G. (2004). Accountability policies and teacher decisionmaking: Barriers to the use of data to improve practice. *Teachers College Record, 106*(6), 1258–1287.

Johnson, J. H. (1999). Educators as researchers. *Schools in the Middle, 9*(1), 38–41.

Johnson, J. H. (2000). Data-driven school improvement. *Journal of School Improvement, 1*(1), XX.

Kerr, K. A., Marsh, J. A., Ikemoto, G. S., Darilek, H., & Barney, H. (2006). Strategies to promote data use for instructional improvement: Actions, outcomes, and lessons from three urban districts. *American Journal of Education, 112*(3), 496–520.

Lafee, S. (2002). Data-driven districts. *School Administrator, 59*(11), 6–7, 9–10, 12, 14–15.

Lincoln, Y. S. (2002). *On the nature of qualitative evidence.* A paper presented for the Annual Meeting of the Association for the Study of Higher Education. Sacramento, CA.

Mandinach, E. B. Honey, M., & Light, D. (2006). *A theoretical framework for data-driven decision making.* Paper presented at the annual meeting of AERA, San Francisco.

Marsh, J. A., Kerr, K. A., Ikemoto, G. S., Darilek, H. Suttorp, M., Zimmer R. W., et al. (2005). *The role of districts in fostering instructional improvement: Lessons from three urban districts partnered with the Institute for Learning*. Santa Monica, CA: Rand Corporation.

Mason, S. (2002, April). *Turning data into knowledge: Lessons from six Milwaukee Public Schools*. A paper presented at the annual conference of AERA, New Orleans.

McIntire, T. (2002). The administrator's guide to data-driven decision making. *Technology and Learning, 22*(11), 18–33.

McIver, M., & Farley, L. (2003). *Bringing the district back in: The role of the central office in improving instruction and student achievement* (Report No. 65). Baltimore: Center for Research on the Education of Students Placed at Risk, John Hopkins University.

McLaughlin, M. & Talbert, J. E. (1993). *Contexts that matter for teaching and learning: Strategic opportunities for meeting the nation's standards educational goals*. Stanford, CA: Stanford University Center for Research on the Context of Secondary School Teaching.

National Center for Educational Statistics. (2007). *Mapping 2005 proficiency standards onto the NAEP scales* (NCES-2007-482). US Department of Education. Washington, DC: Author.

No Child Left Behind. (2002). Public Law 107–110.

Olsen, L. (1997). The data dialogue for moving school equity. *California Tomorrow Perspectives, 5*, 48–61.

Petrides, L., & Nodine, T. (2005). *Anatomy of school system improvement: Performance-driven practices in urban school district*. San Francisco, CA: NewSchools Venture Fund.

Rogoff, B. (1995). Observing sociocultural activity on three planes: Participatory appropriation, guided participation, and apprenticeship. In J. V. Wertsch, P. Del Rio and A. Alvarez (Eds.), *Sociocultural studies of mind* (pp. 139–164). Cambridge: Cambridge University Press.

Sarason, S. (1997). Revisiting the creation of settings. *Mind, culture, and activity, 4*(3), 175–182.

Skrla, L., & Scheurich, J. (2001). Displacing deficit thinking. *Education and Urban Society, 33*(3), 235–259.

Spillane, J. P., Reiser, B. J., & Reimer, T. (2002). Policy implementation and cognition: Reframing and refocusing implementation research. *Review of Educational Research, 72*(3), 387–431.

Supovitz, J., & Taylor B. S. (2003). *The Impacts of standards-based reform in Duval County, Florida, 1999–2002*. Philadelphia, PA: Consortium for Policy Research in Education.

Tharp, R. G. (1997). *From at risk to excellence: Research, theory, and principles for practice, research report #1*. Santa Cruz, CA: Center for Research on Education, Diversity and Excellence.

Togneri, W., & Anderson, S. (2003). *Beyond islands of excellence: What districts can do to improve instruction and achievement in all schools*. Washington, DC: Learning First Alliance.

Wilson, S., & Berne, J. (1999). Teacher learning and the acquisition of professional knowledge: An examination of research on contemporary professional development. *Review of Research in Education, 24*, 173–209.

Wohlstetter, P., Van Kirk, A. N., Robertson, P. J., & Mohrman, S. A. (1997). *Organizing for successful school-based management*. Alexandria, VA: Association for Supervision and Curriculum Development.

Woody, E. L. (2004). *Voices from the field: Educators respond to accountability*. Berkeley, CA: Public Analysis of California Education.

Teacher Emotions in the Context of Educational Reforms

Michalinos Zembylas

The ever-expanding field of teacher change informs us that reform in schools is about conflict, unpredictability, resistance, and some loss in self-image. Teachers are considered by most policymakers, curriculum developers, and school change experts to be instrumental in the process of educational change (Datnow, 2000; Fullan, 1998; Hargreaves & Fullan, 1998; Hargreaves, Earl, & Ryan, 1996; McLaughlin, 1998). Yet teachers respond to school reforms in a variety of ways: Some teachers are happy to support and sustain reform efforts, whereas others feel fear, frustration, or loss and resist such efforts (Datnow, 1998; Datnow & Castellano, 2000; Hargreaves, 1994, 1997, 1998a, 1998b, 2004, 2005; Lasky, 2005; Van Veen & Sleegers, 2006; Van Veen, Sleegers, & van de Ven, 2005; Zembylas & Barker, 2007). However, reform efforts rarely address the emotions of change for teachers and the implications of educational reforms on teachers' emotional well-being (Hargreaves, 2004; Van Veen & Lasky, 2005).

Over the last few years, two reviews of research on teachers' meanings regarding educational practice (van den Berg, 2002) and policy implementation and cognition (Spillane, Reiser, & Reimer, 2002), and a special issue on emotions, identity, and change of *Teaching and Teacher Education* (Van Veen & Lasky, 2005), have brought attention to the emotional impact of reform efforts on teachers. Both of these reviews, as well as the articles published in the special issue of *Teaching and Teacher Education*, emphasize the need for research that pays attention to the emotional aspects of teacher practice and reform initiatives and moves beyond a "dispassionate cognitive perspective" (Spillane et al., 2002, p. 401) of teacher sense-making. Spillane and his colleagues state specifically that emotions are an "overlooked and understudied aspect of the social sense-making with respect to reform" (p. 411); similarly, Van Veen and Lasky (2005) assert that the ways teachers experience reform is fundamentally emotionally laden, and thus research on these issues can inform change theory and professional development.

M. Zembylas (✉)
Open University of Cyprus, Nicosia, Cyprus
e-mail: m.zembylas@ouc.ac.cy

A. Hargreaves et al. (eds.), *Second International Handbook of Educational Change*, 221
Springer International Handbooks of Education 23, DOI 10.1007/978-90-481-2660-6_13,
© Springer Science+Business Media B.V. 2010

In this chapter, I offer a critical synthesis and analysis of contemporary work on the importance of teacher emotions in relation to educational change. My purpose is not to provide a comprehensive review of current literature on teacher emotions and educational reforms but rather to engage in a discussion of contemporary work, focusing on what seem to me two major issues that run through recent research on teacher emotions and educational change. These issues are: (1) space and time as sources of social and emotional support for teachers in reform contexts; (2) the interplay among teacher emotions, identity, and politics. My discussion is informed by and contextualized in my own research in the area for the last 10 years, and my goal is to make a contribution to the ongoing conceptual analysis of investigations on teacher emotions in the context of educational reform. This chapter also explores the implications for practice and policy from the development of spaces for teachers to process their feelings about change. While more work is being done in the area of teacher emotions and the impact of high-stakes accountability and stress-inducing reforms (e.g. Troman & Woods, 2000; Vandenberghe & Huberman, 1999), research on teachers' emotional efforts in the context of reforms has not been the subject of extensive research and thus requires more in-depth analysis (Day, 2002). In a world of unrelenting and even repetitive change (Abrahamson, 2004), understanding the emotional aspects of educational change is essential, if reform efforts are to be more meaningful and successful.

Emotionality and Educational Reform: An Overview

Emotion and change are closely linked (Hargreaves, 2004). Teachers' emotional responses toward change are the result of the ways teachers perceive, interpret, and evaluate their relationship with the changing environment (Blase, 1986; Troman & Woods, 2001). When teachers resist reform efforts, it is often because it threatens their self-image, their sense of identity, and their emotional bonds with students and colleagues by overloading the curriculum and intensifying teachers' work and control from the outside (Hargreaves, 1994, 2005; Nias, 1999a, 1999b; van den Berg, 2002; Zembylas, 2005b). Teachers' resistance to change has often been attributed to stubbornness, lack of imagination, and laziness. However, teachers grasp the negative consequences the reform agenda – often imposed from the outside – will have on them and their students; therefore, teachers resist reforms when the rhetoric of change does not match with the reality of their everyday classroom practices (Bailey, 2000; Schmidt & Datnow, 2005). Emotional disappointment with reform arises not only because of the unwanted imposition of reform demands, but also because of the cumulative effects of the repetitive and contradictory nature of such demands (Little, 1996, 2000). Van Veen et al. (2005) and Van Veen and Sleegers (2006) extend the work of Little and further show that even when teachers subscribe to the reform agenda, the working conditions under which the reform has to be implemented elicit more negative emotions than one would expect on the basis of the teachers' (cognitive) assent. It is not surprising, then, that attempts for educational change may be unsuccessful not only because they may exclude rather than include teachers, but also because these attempts may have predominantly negative emotional implications for teachers (Hargreaves, 2004).

There are many models of school reform that are based on the idea that change is a problem to be solved through appropriate needs assessment, followed by the implementation of appropriate strategies. Such perspectives on school reform are based on the idea that change is primarily a "rational" and "technical" process. The difficulty with such models of reform is that they overemphasize the rational and consequently do not take into account the complexity, ambiguity, and uncertainty acknowledged to be part of change in schools (Hargreaves, 1994, 2000, 2005; Nias, 1999a, 1999b). Rationality is often the driving force behind reform initiatives. In such circumstances, teachers' emotional responses to change are often seen less important.

However, change does not only occur as a result of outlining a set of problems to diagnose and solve (Vince & Broussine, 1996). It can also be approached through identifying the emotions (e.g., anxiety and loss) and relations of collegiality and trust that challenge the ways in which teachers think and feel about themselves and others. In the last two decades, educational reformers have emphasized the importance of collegial relations, collaborative networks, and trust among teachers in enriching the school organizational climate while also providing teachers powerful opportunities for self-renewal (Alfonso & Goldsberry, 1982; Hargreaves & Dawe, 1990; Little, 1990; Marlow & Nass-Fukai, 2000; Sergiovanni, 1992; Wallace, 1998). True collegiality, according to Marlow and Nass-Fukai (2000), involves ongoing professional interaction and trust; in these interactions there is validation of colleagues as equals. Despite the conceptual vagueness of the terms "collegiality" and "trust," professional collegial relationships are suggested as one way to reduce isolation and develop greater coherence and integration to the work of teaching (Little, 1990).

Several authors acknowledge the advantages of social and emotional support in teachers' efforts to cope with change (Hargreaves, 1994, 2001a, 2001b, 2004; Nias, 1998, 1999a, 1999b; Van Veen & Lasky, 2005). For example, Nias (1999a) argues that collegial relations appear to strengthen the moral perspectives and values of teachers. "Collegial" or "collaborative" teacher cultures (Nias, 1989) are characterized by mutual support and caring, in which

> individuals feel able to express their emotions, negative and positive, to admit to failure and weakness, to voice resentment and frustration, to demonstrate affection. By contrast, a culture of individualism tends to increase emotional stress for its members by fostering an illusion that others are coping and that one's own fears are born of a unique incompetence; by requiring individuals to pretend to feelings they do not own; by failing to promote the habit of day-to-day communication so that small interpersonal or professional differences build up into major problems. (Nias, 1999a, p. 235)

Nias (1998) also emphasizes that teachers who have the time or subject matter relatedness value talking and listening as a means of sharing emotional experiences – especially, in times of frustration or despair such as during stressful reform efforts. The benefits of this kind of teacher talk are important: First, teachers get to know one another much better, both personally and professionally; second, teacher talk builds trusting relationships and mutual openness; and third, teachers develop a shared language that contributes to the success of what they do (Nias, 1998). Interpersonal relationships among teachers contribute to the emotional health of the staff group; these relationships have added benefits such as improved cooperation, communication, and emotional commitment (Ashforth & Humphrey, 1995; Leithwood, Menzies, Jantzi, & Leithwood, 1999). Hence, trust and emotional support among teachers seems to facilitate effective and meaningful collaborative working relationships.

Increasingly, change theorists acknowledge that resistance to change is part of the process – in fact, it has a modifying influence – and that the ambivalence and confusion teachers have toward change can be understood on the basis of how individuals respond to change and why they change. To accept reform costs teachers some loss in self-image and vulnerability (Hargreaves, 1998a, 1998b, 2000; Nias, 1999a, 1999b). This threat to self-esteem and the resulting vulnerability can work against reform efforts (Lasky, 2005; Kelchtermans, 2005). There needs to be acknowledged, of course, that sometimes reform is needed, even conceding that it will be emotionally destructive for some teachers who are involved. Nevertheless, as Blackmore (1996, 1998a, 1998b) argues, the issue is not so much about the rational vs. emotional views of reform, but it is about issues of commitment to certain values and certain types of social relationships. That is, Blackmore asserts, change theorists still fail to consider how individuals' emotions intersect with the politics of change. Thus, any attempt to understand school reform needs to take into consideration both the individual and the collective coping practices of teachers. Evans (1996) suggests that change has emotional investment which cannot be altered by rational explanation or technical approach alone; change is part of the context of specific relationships with friends, colleagues, family and how change impacts on such relationships. Thus social, emotional, and material support for teachers during times of reform is necessary for the emotional well-being of teachers, as well as for the successful implementation of reform efforts (Hargreaves, Earl, Moore, & Manning, 2001; Van Veen et al., 2005).

Finally, in my own work, I have used the metaphorical term *spaces for coping* with change (Zembylas, 2005a; Zembylas & Barker, 2007) to identify the spatiality and politics of emotional relations and understandings of teachers' responses to educational reform. Space may sound like a vague metaphor until we realize that it describes experiences of everyday life (Palmer, 1993). We know what it means to experience a sunrise; we know what it means to be on a crowded rush-hour bus. In teaching, teachers know best what it is to be pressed, their space diminished by the urgency of demands, especially in the context of reform efforts that may exclude them. Needless to say, there is ample evidence of the chances of innovations when teachers feel some ownership of the change process (Fink & Stoll, 1996; Fullan, 1993; Sarason, 1990). But regardless of whether teachers feel ownership of the change process or not, they somehow have to make an affective meaning of change and move on. The term "spaces for coping" is used precisely to describe this notion: the literal and metaphorical spaces that teachers create to cope with change and make sense of their feelings about the change processes; thus teacher emotions are unavoidably social and political.

The notion of "space" and its political implications are important because their relevance is seen as central to school reform efforts (Baker & Foote, 2006; Hargreaves, 2001b, 2004, 2005). The idea of "spaces for coping" may be utilized as an overarching concept, because it helps us identify the intersection between individual experiences and social power relations (Beatty & Brew, 2004; hooks, 1991) or structural and cultural working conditions (Kelchtermans, 2005). In other words, spaces for coping are places where it is possible to explore how teachers' emotional responses are socially and politically contextualized (Zembylas, 2005a). Thus, spaces for coping imply defenses or resistances that may have to be breached for change to occur. But the creation of spaces of coping may also imply resisting those tendencies to clutter up a renewed consciousness about teaching; it is then that possibilities are opened up for real change.

Space and Time as Sources of Social and Emotional Support for Teachers in Reform Contexts

A key idea of spatial theorists is that space is fundamental to social life; social spaces are produced and transformed by our practices (Harvey, 1989; Rose, 1993). There is a co-constructive relationship among individuals, groups, and their environments; in other words, our social space is producing and is produced by us. Space is conceptualized as an arena of social, historical, and political relations that imply certain assertions about social interaction, race, class, gender, identity formation, and power (Soja, 1989, 1996). According to this conception, our being-in-the-world is simultaneously historical, social, political, and spatial; social acting, then, has to be understood within spatial contexts. The field of geography has contributed significantly to our understanding of the role of spatiality in human relations, although more often than not space has been theorized in ways that have been complicit to the exploitation of individuals (Rose, 1993).

What seems to be an important contribution of spatial theories to the discussion here is the notion that spatial aspects create emotional experiences in teaching. Spatial aspects such as physical closeness, social relations, moral values, professional ideas, and power relations are characteristics of schools. Hargreaves (2001a, 2001b) has utilized the term *emotional geographies* to emphasize the spatial and experiential patterns of closeness and/or distance in human interactions or relationships within schools. He identifies five key emotional geographies of teaching: sociocultural, moral, professional, political, and physical distance. It is important to reiterate the three caveats that Hargreaves (2001a) suggests regarding emotional geographies of teaching. The first one is that there are no "universal" rules of emotional geography in teaching, meaning that there is no ideal closeness or distance between teachers and others that is culture free. The second caveat is that emotions have imaginary geographies of psychological closeness as well as physical ones.

And the third caveat is that distance and closeness are not just structural or cultural conditions that shape teachers' interactions but active accomplishments by teachers who make or remake the emotional geographies of their interactions.

In addition to the social and political understanding of space, time also constitutes human experience and thus change over time has to be examined in relation to the spaces in which it acquires meaning (Louis, 2006). Again, Hargreaves' contribution is important here because as it is shown through his work, the issue of time is significant in understanding the emotions of change. For example, the sustainability of change is part of the social and emotional geography of a school (Goodson, Moore, & Hargreaves, 2006) and teachers' age and career stages are inextricable aspects of spaces of change (Hargreaves, 2005). Teachers' emotional responses to educational change, then, are as much a matter of spatial politics of reform as it is a historical matter of teachers' concerns. Time and space are inevitably interpreted through teachers' emotions and identities and thus the historical organization of spaces of reform is a constitutive element in teachers' professional development (Baker & Foote, 2006).

A similar term by Spillane (1999), *teachers' zones of enactment*, refers to the social and political spaces in which reform initiatives are encountered within the worlds of practitioners; it is within these zones that "teachers notice, construe, construct, and operationalize the instructional ideas advocated by reformers" (p. 144). Both Hargreaves' "emotional geographies" and Spillane's "zones of enactment" offer important contributions to discourses on educational reform: they emphasize the (positive or negative) "emotional labor" (Hochschild, 1983) involved in teachers' efforts to cope with change as well as the need that teachers' emotional responses must be considered when reform efforts are undertaken. More recently, Beatty and Brew (2004) have also examined how *emotional epistemologies* address the power of connecting with self and others in emotional meaning-making, which may very well underlie "emotional geographies" and "zones of enactment."

In my own work, I have built on these ideas and conceptualized a term that captures more specifically the collection of teachers' efforts and practices to deal with the emotional aspects of educational reform. For this purpose, I suggested the term *spaces for coping* to theorize space by bringing together the various kinds of modalities – emotional, political, cultural, and social – that produce an active (not a passive) locus of interactions and relationships among teachers (Zembylas & Barker, 2007). This term articulates a conceptualization of space as a *product* (Lefebvre, 1991) that contains (1) the social relations among teachers, students, and parents, along with the specific organization of the school; and (2) the emotional labor – positive and negative – of teachers as a result of their involvement in reform efforts. Spaces for coping are products of physical, social, moral, professional, and political processes enacted by teachers in the context of educational reform.

By spaces for coping, I mean those spaces emergent through the enactment of practices that attempt to deal with educational reform in terms of awareness, thinking, feeling, and relating. This term does not merely represent a metaphorical conceptualization of space but an understanding of coping in terms of signifying practices and processes. In other words, the term "spaces for coping" captures the inseparable components of the dynamics of spatial production. The concept of spaces for coping explores how efforts to attend to and through processes and practices can work to extend rather than diminish the emotional field in which teachers move. This extension is facilitated by a deepening of the analysis of teachers' emotional entanglements with change. Therefore, the emphasis is on how spaces for coping with change provide contexts through which to apprehend issues of emotionality and educational reform.

For example, in many of the studies cited so far investigating teacher emotions and educational reform as well as in my own research, it is shown how teachers strive to balance their personal goals for reform, their emotional responses, and the external pressures. Opportunities like time and space set aside for conversations with their colleagues or for planning or practicing ideas provide teachers with sources of social and emotional support in their efforts to deal with change. Each teacher's understanding of the reform effort is clearly very different from that of other teachers within the same school. In a sense, then, teachers' struggles with the reform efforts constitute highly individual tales. Teachers embrace or reject reform for quite different reasons; they bring to the reform efforts certain commitments and have particular emotional responses that effectively undermine or support the proposed changes (Schmidt & Datnow, 2005). On the one hand, teachers, who are against the reform effort, may find ways to "adjust" the reform to their own needs and beliefs; on the other hand, others who embrace the reform efforts, value time and space opportunities so that they can be more successful in implementing the reform (see Zembylas & Barker, 2007). As it is shown through existing research, teachers who are in an environment of uncertainty use time and space in their own ways to create practices of coping with the reform efforts.

What I want to suggest here, then, is that sensitivity to teachers' needs for emotional and social support is essential to reform efforts. Creating networks of support that strengthen collegiality and trust can gradually make space for the feelings that help weave community and cultivate relationships. There are always the mixed feelings of excitement and anxiety teachers have at the outset of a new reform effort. Opportunities for time and space as sources of emotional and social support may work well for teachers, especially for those who resist change. On the one hand, having such opportunities might create opportunities for the future transformations of those teachers who initially resist change. On the other hand, it should not be ignored that such opportunities may in fact subvert reform efforts, despite the fact that "oppositional" teachers find their much-needed support to cope with change (see Zembylas & Barker, 2007).

Teacher collegiality and trust are based not only on contextual factors (e.g., time, subject matter relatedness), but also on personal moral values (Hargreaves, 1994; Van Veen & Sleegers, 2006). Teachers' moral values contribute to the school emotional culture and subcultures and affect teachers' emotional practices in school reform efforts. Often, some teachers' coping practices with reform efforts have damaging consequences for their effectiveness in the classroom and for their capacity to connect with students (Hargreaves, 2000; Woods, Jeffrey, Troman, & Boyle, 1997), because external reform efforts can work against the moral values and beliefs held by these teachers. In addition to the fact that the personal self-image and identity of teachers is usually at stake, teachers' efforts result in the adoption of often insufficient coping practices such as retreatism or downshifting (Troman & Woods, 2000). Thus, change for some teachers can invoke a sense of powerlessness (Smylie, 1999) and vulnerability (Kelchtermans, 1996, 2005; Lasky, 2005), when teachers evaluate their capacities, values, and will to respond to change as incompatible. Inevitably, then, teacher emotions are interwoven with issues of power, identity, and resistance in the context of educational reform (Zembylas, 2005a, 2005b).

The Interplay Among Teacher Emotions, Identity, and Politics

Recent research on teacher emotions and educational change also shows the multiple links among teacher emotions, identity, and politics (e.g. see Hargreaves, 2005; Kelchtermans, 2005; Van Veen & Lasky, 2005; Zembylas, 2003, 2005a, 2005b). This line of work provides evidence about the ways in which teacher emotions and identity formation play a central role in the circuits of power that constitute teacher-selves. The critical understanding of this process in contexts of educational reform is crucial, if we are also to explore the possibility of creating new forms of teacher-selves that escape normative responses to change. For example, it is shown that teacher identity is not fixed but is constantly becoming in spaces that are embedded in the interplay between emotions and actions, on the one hand, and the political conditions within a school, on the other; this interplay mediates the emotionally laden interpretation of reform policies (Zembylas, 2005b). This line of thinking – which is grounded on a poststructuralist theorization of emotions, identity, and power in education (Boler, 1999; Zembylas, 2005a) – provides a different lens than the usual sociocultural framework that has been used to understand teacher emotions and identity in school reform efforts (e.g., see Hargreaves, 1998a, 2000, 2005; Lasky, 2005; Van Veen & Sleegers, 2005). Most sociological studies on this subject emphasize how teacher emotions are socially constructed but often assume a givenness to teacher-self and identity – the processes of social construction pertain only to how social situations shape the *expression* and *experience* of teachers' emotional states (Zembylas, 2005a). On the other hand, the approaches that are based on feminist and poststructuralist perspectives examine the transaction among larger social forces and the inner psychic aspects and highlight how teachers participate in emotional practices by adopting or resisting – *in action* – particular emotion discourses. The advantage of feminist and poststructuralist approaches compared to other approaches is that feminist and poststructuralist approaches focus on the role of emotional and social practices of teachers and avoid privileging self-consciousness, that is, they reject the assumption that one's awareness of being is separate from the socially constructed world (Boler, 1999).

In particular, feminist and poststructuralist approaches draw attention to a deeper and more complex understanding of the role of power relations in the context of educational change. As Abu-Lughod and Lutz argue, power is an integral part of emotions, identity politics, and change, because "power relations determine what can, cannot, or must be said about self and emotion, what is taken to be true or false about them, and what only some individuals can say about them. [. . .] . . . [This idea] show[s] how emotion discourses establish, assert, challenge, or reinforce power or status differences" (p. 14). By recognizing the role power relations play in constructing emotions of change, a better understanding of the personal, cultural, political, and historical aspects of teacher identity formation might be gained. For this reason, I have termed this work *genealogies of emotions in teaching* (Zembylas, 2005a, 2005b). Following Foucault's genealogical method (1983a, 1983b, 1984), I have argued that constructing genealogies of emotions in teaching casts light on how emotions are located and represented in teachers' pedagogies and on teachers' personal and professional development. In particular, genealogies of teacher emotions in contexts of educational reforms describe events, objects, persons, and their relationships that are present or absent in the realization of the emotions related to change, and the ways that these emotions are experienced in relation to teacher-self (individual reality), others (social interactions), and school politics and culture (sociopolitical context). For example, it has been shown that analysis of identity politics and power relations in the context of school reform enriches our understanding of the *fear* and *suspicion* that teachers often feel when they are faced with change (Zembylas & Barker, 2007).

The existing research on teacher emotions, identity, and politics in the context of reform highlights two important issues. First, it is valuable to gain an understanding of the constitution of teacher subjectivities within a historical and spatial framework of how meaning intersects with emotional experiences of change. Only by interrogating the temporal and spatial contexts from which questions of identity are posed can we trace how teacher identity is subjected to the social and emotional practices of change. As Bauman (1991, 2004) argues, identities in contemporary world are undergoing a process of continual transformation and emotional ambivalence is a compelling notion of understanding the changing nature of social life and personal experience. This kind of analysis problematizes the "emotional regulation" that is often demanded from teachers and highlights the process with which *emotional rules* are constructed in relation to change, that is, how power relations and identity politics shape the expression of emotions by permitting teachers to feel some emotions and by prohibiting them to feel others. This lesson turns our attention to the view that emotions are essentially embedded in identity politics and power relations; thus, emotional regulation is not only an individual process (which is how it is usually presented by psychologically grounded literature; see, e.g., Sutton & Wheatley, 2003) but also a political one. By understanding how emotional rules and expectations are historically contingent, teachers and teacher educators may begin to deconstruct the power relations and identity politics that seek to "regulate" teachers' lives.

The second issue has to do with the importance of the emotional aspects of the negotiation of change in the context of school reforms and the role of self-discipline, self-esteem, and professional norms in teaching. Professional values and norms, as Kelchtermans (2005) points out, ought to be conceptualized as inextricable aspects of teacher identity and the cultural and structural working conditions; these norms are continually (re)constructed and/or reproduced through interactions of domination and resistance. For example, it is shown in various studies that a teacher's relation to oneself is marked by self-policing of emotional conduct according to the demands of a particular educational reform (Hargreaves, 2005; Lasky, 2005). Thus, there is a lot to be gained from developing accounts that are suspicious of appeals to emotional well-being tied to rationalizations and instrumental goals of educational reforms. Such appeals to emotional well-being tied to rationalizations need to be examined in terms of how they shape the meaning and drive the direction, goals, emotional conduct, and motivation of teachers involved in reform efforts. New theoretical frameworks, such as those of feminist theories and poststructuralism, can be helpful in identifying how problematic are some of the underlying assumptions of reform and show that power and resistance can be productive in efforts to subvert normalizing practices (see Zembylas, 2005a).

Clearly, then, emotions in the context of educational reforms are not only a private matter but also a political space, in which students and teachers interact with implications in larger political and cultural struggles (Albrecht-Crane & Slack, 2003; Zembylas, 2005a, 2005b). The notion of "politics" here refers to "a process of determining who must repress as illegitimate, who must foreground as valuable, the feelings and desires that come up for them in given contexts and relationships" (Reddy, 1997, p. 335). That is to say, power is located in emotional expression (Campbell, 1997) – in who gets to express and who must repress various emotions. The *politics of emotions*, therefore, is the analysis that challenges the cultural and historical emotion norms with respect to what emotions are, how they are expressed, who gets to express them, and under what circumstances. It is in this sense that it may be argued that there is always something political in which teachers and students are caught up as they relate emotionally to one another in contexts of reform, because power relations are essentially unavoidable; there are always some norms influencing emotion discourses and emotional expressions during reform efforts. A careful analysis of the interplay among teacher emotions, identity, and politics provides openings for a critical intervention in a much larger debate about professional subjectivities in schools. The need for a deeper conceptualization of this interplay among teacher emotions, identity, and politics can guide future efforts to understand the power and the limitations of the political merits or demerits of any emotional regime within the space of educational reform efforts.

Implications

Overall, the findings from research on teacher emotions in the context of educational reforms highlight two issues: First, how schools structure teacher interactions in ways that hinder or promote the processing of teacher emotions; and, second, how teachers respond emotionally to professional expectations and norms (Ball & Cohen, 1996; Hargreaves, 2000; Kelchtermans, 2005; Spillane, 1999). My analysis in this chapter has emphasized that a teacher's emotional development in the context of educational reform efforts is profoundly influenced by his or her participation in particular forms of discursive and emotional practices at school. By analyzing this idea in such terms, I wish to avoid a suggestion that subordinates the individual to the social and loses sight of the reciprocal relation between the two. As I have indicated, existing research shows that there is a great deal at stake in the emotional regimes of schools under reform. However, teacher communities are able to constitute spaces that have the potential to subvert disciplinary mechanisms and practices.

My analysis here also identifies an idea that is found in previous studies about teachers' responses to educational change. That is, it is shown how teachers differ in fundamental emotional ways with regard to how they create spaces for coping with reform efforts. Yet, more recent studies indicate that these differences are not idiosyncratic ones but are related to the sociopolitical culture of school. These findings suggest that working conditions, social relations, and moral/personal values and concerns engage teachers emotionally with the reform effort and signify what is at stake for them, regardless of whether teachers support or object the reform initiatives (see also Hargreaves, 2004, 2005). Educational change, then, is inevitably a deeply emotional sense-making experience for teachers. Consequently, allowing emerging feelings to be dealt with is not about helping teachers to feel "better" about reform pressures, but is a valuable contribution to teachers because it helps them practically to find ways of integrating and/or reconciling opposing or conflicting feelings about reform. On the one hand, teachers must understand that in the process of educational change, conflict, tensions, and disturbance to long-held beliefs are not to be feared; on the other hand, teachers also need the emotional and social support to take reasonable risks to cope with reform (Schmidt & Datnow, 2005).

However, it is often assumed that all or most teachers will produce a uniform set of responses to reform – that is, they will want to teach and behave in the manner expected of them (Hargreaves, 1994). Such demand for uniformity highlights the power relations involved in reform efforts and seeks to limit teachers' role to that of a technician. Therefore, an implication of this finding is that reformers have to acknowledge the significance of emotional diversity and provide opportunities for teachers to create their own spaces of coping with change. Change is not about forcing all teachers to subscribe enthusiastically to new ideas; a reform process needs to allow teachers to carve out spaces for themselves in order to work individually and collaboratively and find ways to reflect on their practices. Teachers need space and time to make sense of change and to make reform efforts part of their own teaching. In their own classroom, teachers hold the power for the success or failure of school reform efforts (Sarason, 1996).

The findings of existing studies in this area add support to the research which suggests that teacher emotions, identity politics, and power relations have substantial effects on classroom practice and reform efforts (Beatty & Brew, 2004; Hargreaves, 2001a, 2001b; Little, 1996, 2000; Nias, 1999a, 1999b). These findings are not so unusual; however, it seems that these issues need to be directly addressed in schools undergoing reform, because stressed and unhappy teachers can subvert reform efforts in unexpected ways (Datnow, 1998; Datnow & Castellano, 2000). In some respects, the success of reform efforts that are based on collaborations among teachers is directly related to the relationships that these teachers develop. Not surprisingly, then, teacher collegiality and trust create distinctive emotional geographies that influence reform efforts in two ways. First, teacher collegiality that is also based on friendship and trust may intensely compete with interests for a successful reform effort; and second, teacher collegiality that is based on politeness and avoidance of conflict may end up subverting the reform effort because the real issues are not addressed (Zembylas & Barker, 2007). The contribution of existing studies lies in the finding that while social sharing and collegial relationships create important spaces for teachers to cope with change in a nonthreatening environment, it is also possible that these spaces may simultaneously undermine the reform effort.

In an increasingly changing educational environment, it has never been more necessary to develop an in-depth understanding of teacher emotions in the context of reform. Building a better emotional understanding of educational reform expectations, teachers, administrators, and reformers will become able to form more productive alliances (Hargreaves & Fullan, 1998), and redefine the emotional geographies of their relationships to make them more effective in dealing with the emotional risks of change. Better emotional understanding, as Hargreaves (2001b) argues, implies a reversal in many educational policies and policy processes. Such policies must seriously consider the emotional implications of reforms that demand teachers to implement content and learning standards, to limit teachers' time out of class to interact with others, and to standardize teachers' interactions with those around them. Future research in this area needs to further clarify how different policies may enable productive spaces of dealing with change, while exposing the constraints of any taken-for-granted assumptions about educational reforms.

References

Abrahamson, E. J. (2004). *Change without pain: How managers can overcome initiative overload, organizational chaos, and employee burnout*. Boston: Harvard Business School.

Abu-Lughod, L., & Lutz, C. A. (1990). Introduction: Emotion, discourse, and the politics of everyday life. In C. Lutz & L. Abu-Lughod (Eds.), *Language and the politics of emotion* (pp. 1–23). Cambridge: Cambridge University Press.

Albrecht-Crane, C., & Slack, J. (2003). Toward a pedagogy of affect. In J. D. Slack (Ed.), *Animations (of Deleuze and Guattari)* (pp. 191–216). New York: Peter Lang.

Alfonso, R. J., & Goldsberry, L. (1982). Colleagueship in supervision. In T. Sergiovanni (Ed.), *Supervision of teaching* (pp. 90–107). Alexandria, VA: Association for Supervision and Curriculum Development.

Ashforth, B. E., & Humphrey, R. H. (1995). Emotion in the workplace: A reappraisal. *Human Relations, 48*(2), 97–125.

Bailey, B. (2000). The impact of mandated change on teachers. In N. Bascia & A. Hargreaves (Eds.), *The sharp edge of educational change* (pp. 112–128). London: Falmer Press.

Baker, M., & Foote, M. (2006). Changing spaces: Urban school interrelationships and the impact of standards-based reform. *Educational Administration Quarterly, 42*, 90–125.

Ball, D. L., & Cohen, D. K. (1996). Reform by the book: What is—or might be—the role of curriculum materials in teacher learning and instructional reform? *Educational Researcher, 25*(9), 6–8.

Bauman, Z. (1991). *Modernity and ambivalence.* Cambridge, UK: Polity Press.

Bauman, Z. (2004). *Identity.* Cambridge, UK: Polity Press.

Beatty, B., & Brew, C. (2004). Trusting relationships and emotional epistemologies: A foundational leadership issue. *School Leadership and Management, 24,* 329–356.

Blackmore, J. (1996). Doing emotional labor in the educational market place: Stories from the field of women in management. *Discourse, 17*(3), 337–352.

Blackmore, J. (1998a). The politics of gender and educational change: Managing gender or changing gender relations? In A. Hargreaves, A. Lieberman, M. Fullan, & D. Hopkins (Eds.), *International handbook of educational change* (pp. 460–481). London: Kluwer.

Blackmore, J. (1998b). *Troubling women: Feminism, leadership and educational change.* London: Open University Press.

Blase, J. J. (1986). A qualitative analysis of sources of teacher stress: Consequences for performance. *American Educational Research Journal, 23,* 13–40.

Boler, M. (1999). *Feeling power: Emotions and education.* New York: Routledge.

Campbell, S. (1997). *Interpreting the personal: Expression and the formation of feelings.* Ithaca, NY: Cornell University Press.

Datnow, A. (2000). Implementing an externally developed school restructuring design: Enablers, constraints and tensions. *Teaching and Change, 7,* 147–171.

Datnow, A. (1998). *The gender politics of educational change.* London: Falmer.

Datnow, A., & Castellano, M. (2000). Teachers' responses to success for all: How beliefs, experiences, and adaptations shape implementation. *American Educational Research Journal, 37,* 775–799.

Day, C. (2002). School reform and transitions in teacher professionalism and identity. *International Journal of Educational Research, 37,* 677–692.

Evans, R. (1996). *The human side of school change: Reform, resistance, and the eal-life problems of innovation.* San Francisco: Jossey-Bass Publishers.

Fink, D., & Stoll, L. (1996). *Changing our schools: Linking school effectiveness and school improvement.* Bristol, PA: Open University Press.

Fullan, M. (1993). *Change forces: Probing the depth of educational reform.* New York: Falmer Press.

Fullan, M. (1998). The meaning of educational change: A quarter of a century of learning. In A. Hargreaves, A. Lieberman, M. Fullan, & D. Hopkins (Eds.), *International handbook of educational change* (pp. 214–231). London: Kluwer.

Goodson, I., Moore, S., & Hargreaves, A. (2006). Teacher nostalgia and the sustainability of reform: The generation and degeneration of teachers' missions, memory, and meaning. *Educational Administration Quarterly, 42,* 42–61.

Hargreaves, A. (1994). *Changing teachers, changing times: Teachers' work and culture in the postmodern age.* New York: Teachers College Press.

Hargreaves, A. (1997). *Rethinking educational change with heart and mind.* Alexandria, VA: Association for Curriculum and Development.

Hargreaves, A. (1998a). The emotional practice of teaching. *Teaching and Teacher Education, 14,* 835–854.

Hargreaves, A. (1998b). The emotional politics of teaching and teacher development: With implications for educational leadership. *International Journal of Leadership in Education, 1,* 315–336.

Hargreaves, A. (2000). Mixed emotions: Teachers' perceptions of their interactions with students. *Teaching and Teacher Education, 16,* 811–826.

Hargreaves, A. (2001a). Emotional geographies of teaching. *Teachers College Record, 103,* 1056–1080.

Hargreaves, A. (2001b). The emotional geographies of teachers' relations with colleagues. *International Journal of Educational Research, 35*, 503–527.

Hargreaves, A. (2004). Inclusive and exclusive educational change: Emotional responses of teachers and implications for leadership. *School Leadership & Management, 24*, 287–309.

Hargreaves, A. (2005). Educational change takes ages: Life, career and generational factors in teachers' emotional responses to educational change. *Teaching and Teacher Education, 21*, 967–983.

Hargreaves, A., & Dawe, R. (1990). Paths of professional development: Contrived collegiality, collaborative culture, and the case of peer coaching. *Teaching and Teacher Education, 6*, 227–241.

Hargreaves, A., Earl, L., & Ryan, J. (1996). *Schooling for change*. London and New York: Falmer Press.

Hargreaves, A., Earl, L., Moore, S., & Manning, S. (2001). *Learning to Change Teaching Beyond Subjects and Standards*. San Francisco: Jossey-Bass.

Hargreaves, A., & Fullan, M. (1998). *What's worth fighting for out there*. New York: Teachers College Press.

Harvey, D. (1989). *The condition of postmodernity*. Cambridge, MA, Oxford, UK: Blackwell.

Hochschild, A. R. (1983). *The managed heart: Commercialization of human feeling*. Berkeley: University of California Press.

hooks, B. (1991). *Yearning: Race, gender and cultural politics*. London: Turnaround books.

Kelchtermans, G. (1996). Teacher vulnerability: Understanding its moral and political roots. *Cambridge Journal of Education, 26*, 307–324.

Kelchtermans, G. (2005). Teachers' emotions in educational reforms: Self-understanding, vulnerable commitment and micropolitical literacy. *Teaching and Teacher Education, 21*, 995–1006.

Lasky, S. (2005). A sociocultural approach to understanding teacher identity, agency and professional vulnerability in a context of secondary school reform. *Teaching and Teacher Education, 21*, 899–916.

Lefebvre, H. (1991). *The production of space*. London: Basil Blackwell.

Leithwood, K. A., Menzies, T., Jantzi, D., & Leithwood, J. (1999). Teacher burnout: A critical challenge for leaders of restructuring schools. In R. Vandenberghe & A. M. Huberman (Eds.), *Understanding and preventing teacher burnout: A sourcebook of international research and practice* (pp. 85–115). Cambridge: Cambridge University Press.

Little, J. W. (1990). The persistence of privacy: Autonomy and initiative in teachers' private relations. *Teachers College Record, 91*, 509–536.

Little, J. W. (1996). The emotional contours and career trajectories of (disappointed) reform enthusiasts. *Cambridge Journal of Education, 26*, 345–359.

Little, J. W. (2000). *Emotionality and career commitment in the context of rational reforms*. Paper presented at the annual meeting of the American Educational Research Association, New Orleans, LA.

Louis, K. (2006). Change over time? An introduction? A reflection? *Educational Administration Quarterly, 42*, 165–173.

Marlow, M. P., & Nass-Fukai, J. (2000). Collegiality, collaboration, and kuleana: Three crucial components for sustaining effective school-university partnerships. *Education, 121*, 188–194.

McLaughlin, M. (1998). Listening and learning from the field: Tales of policy implementation and situated practice. In A. Hargreaves, A. Lieberman, M. Fullan, & D. Hopkins (Eds.), *International handbook of educational change* (pp. 70–85). London: Kluwer.

Nias, J. (1989). *Primary teachers talking: A study of teaching and work*. London: Routledge.

Nias, J. (1998). Why teachers need their colleagues: A developmental perspective. In A. Hargreaves, A. Lieberman, M. Fullan, & D. Hopkins (Eds.), *International handbook of educational change* (pp. 1257–1271). Dordrecht: Kluwer Academic Publishers.

Nias, J. (1999a). Teachers' moral purposes: Stress, vulnerability, and strength. In R. Vandenberghe & M. Huberman (Eds.), *Understanding and preventing teacher burnout:*

A sourcebook of international research and practice (pp. 223–237). Cambridge, UK: Cambridge University Press.

Nias, J. (1999b). Teaching as a culture of care. In J. Prosser (Ed.), *School culture* (pp. 66–81). London: Paul Chapman Pub.

Palmer, P. (1993). *To know as we are known: Education as a spiritual journey*. San Francisco: Harper & Row.

Reddy, W. M. (1997). Against constructionist: The historical ethnography of emotions. *Current Anthropology, 38*, 327–340.

Rose, G. (1993). *Feminism and geography: The limits of geographical knowledge*. Minneapolis: University of Minnesota Press.

Sarason, S. B. (1990). *The predictable failure of educational reform: Can we change course before it's too late?* San Francisco: Jossey-Bass Publishers.

Sarason, S. (1996). *Revisiting "The culture of the school and the problem of change."* New York: Teachers College Press.

Schmidt. M., & Datnow, A. (2005). Teachers' sense-making about comprehensive school reform: The influence of emotions. *Teaching and Teacher Education, 21*, 949–965.

Sergiovanni, T. J. (1992). *Moral leadership: Getting to the heart of school improvement*. San Francisco: Jossey-Bass.

Smylie, M. A. (1999). Teacher stress in a time of reform. In R. Vandenberghe & A. M. Huberman (Eds.), *Understanding and preventing teacher burnout: A sourcebook of international research and practice* (pp. 59–84). Cambridge: Cambridge University Press.

Soja, E. (1989). *Postmodern geographies: The reassertion of space in critical social theory*. New York: Verso.

Soja, E. (1996). *Thirdspace: Journeys to Los Angeles and other real and imagined places*. Cambridge: Blackwell Publishers.

Spillane, J. P. (1999). External reform initiatives and teachers' efforts to reconstruct their practice: The mediating role of teachers' zones of enactment. *Journal of Curriculum Studies, 31*, 143–175.

Spillane, J. P., Reiser, B. J., & Reimer, T. (2002). Policy implementation and cognition: Reframing and refocusing implementation research. *Review of Educational Research, 72*, 387–431.

Sutton, R., & Wheatley, K. (2003). Teachers' emotions and teaching: A review of the literature and directions for future research. *Educational Psychology Review, 15*, 327–358.

Troman, G., & Woods, P. (2000). Careers under stress: Teacher adaptations at a time of intensive reform. *Journal of Educational Change, 1*, 253–275.

Troman, G., & Woods, P. (2001). *Primary teachers' stress*. New York: Routledge/Falmer.

Van den Berg, R. (2002). Teachers' meanings regarding educational practice. *Review of Educational Research, 72*, 577–625.

Van Veen, K., & Lasky, S. (2005). Emotions as a lens to explore teacher identity and change: Different theoretical approaches. *Teaching and Teacher Education, 21*, 895–898.

Van Veen, K., & Sleegers, P. (2006). How does it feel? Teachers' emotions in a context of change. *Journal of Curriculum Studies, 38*, 85–111.

Van Veen, K., Sleegers, P., & Van de Ven, P-H. (2005). One teacher's identity, emotions, and commitment to change: A case study into the cognitive–affective processes of a secondary school teacher in the context of reforms. *Teaching and Teacher Education, 21*, 917–934.

Vandenberghe, R., & Huberman, A. M. (1999). *Understanding and preventing teacher burnout*. Cambridge, UK: Cambridge University Press.

Vince, R., & Broussine, M. (1996). Paradox, defense and attachment: Accessing and working with emotions and relations underlying organizational change. *Organization Studies, 17*, 1–21.

Wallace, J. (1998). Collegiality and teachers' work in the context of peer supervision. *The Elementary School Journal, 99*, 82–98.

Woods, P., Jeffrey, B., Troman, G., & Boyle, M. (1997). *Restructuring schools, reconstructing teachers*. Buckingham: Open University Press.

Zembylas, M. (2003). Interrogating "teacher identity": Emotion, resistance, and self-formation. *Educational Theory, 53*, 107–127.

Zembylas, M. (2005a). *Teaching with emotion: A postmodern enactment.* Greenwich, CT: Information Age Publishing.

Zembylas, M. (2005b). Discursive practices, genealogies and emotional rules: A poststructuralist view on emotion and identity in teaching. *Teaching and Teacher Education, 21*, 935–948.

Zembylas, M., & Barker, H. (2007). Teachers' spaces for coping with change in the context of a reform effort. *Journal of Educational Change, 8*, 235–256.

The Micropolitics of Educational Change and Reform: Cracking Open the Black Box

Joseph Blase and Lars Björk

The first studies of micropolitics of education were published during the mid-1980s (Ball, 1987; Blase, 1987). Two decades later, a small but significant number of studies have been completed, some of which have centered on the micropolitics of educational change and reform. In 1998, Blasé conducted a comprehensive review of the micropolitics of educational change; this chapter highlights primary studies from that review but emphasizes more recent relevant work.

Micropolitics remains a fact of life in educational settings, and during times of change, such politics tend to increase and intensify. This chapter presents a review of studies that have generated findings on the micropolitics of educational change and reform. The chapter opens with an overview of macro– and micro–educational politics. Following this, a section focusing on the micropolitics of life in schools illustrates the ubiquitous nature of this important phenomenon in schools. Subsequent sections form the heart of this chapter and highlight findings about teachers, school principals, middle-level administrators (i.e., central office staffs), district superintendents, and school boards. Each section describes micropolitical factors that facilitate and impede school reform. The chapter closes with a brief discussion of directions for future research and a conclusion.

The Macropolitics and Micropolitics of Education

Generally speaking, the term "politics" refers to decisions about the allocation of valued goods for a particular society or organization – for example, who gets what, how, and when. Macropolitics and micropolitics (i.e., organizational politics), two broad aspects of the politics of education, refer to similar conflictual and cooperative processes and similar concepts including individual and group interests, power and influence, strategic interaction, values, and ideologies (Ball, 1987; Barott & Galvin, 1998; Blase, 1991; Blase & Blase, 2000; Marshall & Scribner, 1991; Spring, 1997,

J. Blase (✉)
University of Georgia, Athens, GA, USA
e-mail: blase@uga.edu

A. Hargreaves et al. (eds.), *Second International Handbook of Educational Change*, 237
Springer International Handbooks of Education 23, DOI 10.1007/978-90-481-2660-6_14,
© Springer Science+Business Media B.V. 2010

1998; Wirt & Kirst, 1992). In the United States, macropolitics of education may describe the school's external environment and its relationships at the local, state, and federal levels (Willower, 1991) as well as the interaction of private and public organizations within, between, and among levels (Cibulka, 2001; Marshall & Scribner, 1991; Spring, 1997; Wirt & Kirst, 1992).

In recent decades, several waves of school reform have dominated the macropolitics of education in the United States. Firestone (1990) notes that although efforts to improve public schools began in the late 1970s, the release of a Nation at Risk in 1983 launched an era of educational reform "that is arguably the most intense, comprehensive and sustained effort to improve education in America's history" (Bjork, 2001a, p. 19). Media coverage of the report heightened concern for the condition of public education, shaped the perception that the nation's schools had failed the nation's children and economy, and stimulated calls for reform.

Other reports over long periods have reflected separate yet related reform themes (Bacharach, 1990; Firestone, Fuhrman, & Kirst, 1990; Lane & Epps, 1992; Murphy, 1990). The first wave (1983-1986), which began with the release of the Nation at Risk Report (1983), was followed in rapid succession by similar commission and task force reports that called for using student test scores to hold schools accountable, increasing graduation requirements, lengthening the school day and year, and increasing the rigor of teacher licensure requirements (Björk, Kowalski, & Young, 2005). Legislative accountability measures lessened district policy-making prerogatives by shifting decision making to states.

An analysis of second-wave reports (1986–1989) suggests a continuation of accountability themes as well as greater emphasis on higher-order thinking skills, problem solving, computer competency, and cooperative learning. Importantly, many reports made a compelling case that schools should be responsible for ensuring that all children learn, particularly "at risk" children living in poverty (Murphy, 1990). In addition, efforts to establish teacher empowerment and strengthen teaching professionalism contributed to the devolution of decision making and governance from the district level to school councils. These shifts coupled with high stakes accountability attempted to alter both conventional practices and power configurations at the district and school levels (Björk, 1996; Murphy, 1990).

Third-wave (1989–2003) reform reports criticized previous commission reports for their focus on organizational and professional issues rather than on student well-being and student learning. These reports offered two canons to guide reform including recentering the profession to focus on student learning and realigning schools to support families as a way to enhance children's capacity to learn. In 2002, the enactment of the No Child Left Behind Act (NCLB) reiterated previous school accountability themes and underscored the importance of ensuring that all children learn. NCLB shifted accountability from the building level to the individual child and introduced the notion of holding school superintendents, principals, and teachers responsible for bridging the learning gaps for different groups of children. The NCLB coupled hardnosed accountability measures, performance timetables, and remedies with parsimonious federal support; consequently, many critics have characterized it as the largest underfunded federal education mandate in US history (Björk et al., 2005). Although it is generally agreed that NCLB has heightened attention to glaring inequities in student academic performance, many speculate that raising the bar to successively higher levels of performance until 2014 may result in a declaration that schools have failed and thus justify the offering of vouchers as an alternative way to fund public education (Björk et al., 2005).

Indeed, nationally initiated legislation in the United States and the external collection of private and public organizations with interest in such legislation have had significant effects on politics at the district and school levels (Barott & Galvin, 1998; Blase, 1991, 1998; Cibulka, 2001; Datnow, 2000; Fuhrman & Elmore, 2004; Mawhinney, 1999; Oakes, Quartz, Ryan, & Lipton, 2000; Sarason, 1990, 2004; Smith, Miller-Kahn, Heineke, & Jarvis, 2004).

> The building or site level is the immediate organizational unit within which the principal and classroom teacher work, children are instructed and direct supervision occurs. At the same time, it is important to recognize that the school is nested in multilevel governmental structures. The organizational politics of the building site is the micropolitics of a subunit of a larger complex organization: the school district. In turn, the school district is a local government unit, variously connected to other local governments, as well as to the state and national governments (Barott & Galvin, 1998, p. 312).

In fact, in recent years macropolitical influences have strengthened in many parts of the world, and this has resulted in increased political conflict at the local and school levels, notably in the context of reform adoption and implementation processes (Ball, 1994; Blase, 1998; Cibulka, 2001; Hoyle, 1999; Lindle, 1999; Mawhinney, 1999). Consequently, beginning in the early 1990s, policy studies in education have increasingly investigated implementation processes associated with school reform at the local level.

> Those actually implementing policy in schools turned out to be the final policy makers, as evidence mounted that they could reshape or resist the intentions of policies adopted at higher levels. From these not entirely surprising revelations, it was only a short jump to the beginning of the systematic study of the dynamics of the "micropolitics" within the schools (Boyd, 1991, p. vii).

Not surprisingly, theoretical and empirical work has underscored stark differences between policy rhetoric and the reality of policy implementation, referred to as the "implementation gap" or "black box" of educational reform (e.g., Datnow, 2000; Mawhinney, 1999; Scribner, Aleman, & Maxcy, 2003).

Micropolitical Perspectives and Educational Change and Reform

Studies of the micropolitics of educational change and reform have relied heavily on Ball's (1987) and Blase's (1991) perspectives. Ball's approach emphasizes the politics of conflict:

I take schools, in common with virtually all other social organizations, to be arenas of struggle; to be riven with actual or potential conflict between members; to be poorly co-ordinated; to be ideologically diverse. I take it to be essential that if we are to understand the nature of schools as organizations, we must achieve some understanding of these conflicts (Ball, 1987, p. 19).

Blase (1991) constructed a more inclusive definition of micropolitics from an exhaustive review of the literature that includes conflictive and cooperative processes:

Micropolitics refers to the use of formal and informal power by individuals and groups to achieve their goals in organizations. In large part political action results from perceived differences between individuals and groups, coupled with the motivation to use power to influence and/or protect. Although such actions are consciously motivated, any action, con-sciously motivated, may have "political significance" in a given situation. Both cooperative and conflictive actions and processes are part of the realm of micropolitics. Moreover, macro and micropolitical factors frequently interact (Blase, 1991, p. 11).

More recently, Blase and Blase (2002) have argued that micropolitics is a critical aspect of many organizational structures and processes, and often constitutes the *central mechanism* through which major organizational outcomes related to school change and reform are produced:

An organization's political processes, for example, a school's formal and informal (e.g., organizational stakeholders and their power sources, interests, ideologies, and interchanges) as well as its political culture (e.g., patterns of interests, ideologies, decision making, power distribution) dramatically influence most school outcomes, including teaching and learning. The degree to which political processes and political culture account for a given out-come (e.g., decision, policy, program, practice, event) varies, of course, from one school to another and, over time, within the same school. (p. 10).

In essence, micropolitics processes and structures make up the "political culture" of a school and account for both stability and change in school settings; certain political forces work to sustain (maintain) the status quo, while other political forces serve the interests of change and reform (Ball, 1987; Blase, 1991, 1998; Blase & Blase, 2002; Burlingame, 1988; Burns, 1961; Malen, 1994; Townsend, 1990). "The strong advocacy of some and the strong opposition of others...will be called into service to bring about or successfully oppose the innovation under consideration" (Mangham, 1979, p. 133).

Typically, externally imposed initiatives to change and reform schools must con-tend with existing internal political cultures that promote and protect the school's status quo (Ball, 1994; Blase, 1991, 1998; Cusick, 1992; Elmore, 2004; Gronn, 1986; Gtazek & Sarason, 2007; Lukes, 1974; Sarason, 1990, 2004). With refer-ence to the micropolitics of change, Mangham (1979) stated, "[S]o significant is the collection of forces which underpin behavior in organizations that it is surprising that any changes ever manage to be promulgated let alone implemented" (p. 122). Sarason (1990) wrote,

Schools will accommodate (change) in ways that require little or no change...the strength of the status quo—its underlying axioms, its pattern of power relationships, its sense of tradition and, therefore, what seems right, natural, and proper—almost automatically rules out options for change in that status quo (p. 35).

During periods of externally imposed change and reform, school-based political interaction tends to intensify, and new micropolitical processes and structures emerge and become more visible in formal and informal areas of school life. Specifically, change dynamics – uncertainty, diversity, ambiguity, and goal disparity and complexity tend to exacerbate political interaction within the school (Blase, 1998).

The Micropolitics of Life in Schools

In the past two decades, empirical political studies have revealed strong findings about the ubiquitous and natural occurrence of micropolitics in the everyday life of schools. Topics studied include personnel evaluation (Bridges & Groves, 1999), superintendents and interest groups (Björk & Lindle, 2001), teacher induction (Kelchtermans & Ballet, 2002a), beginning teacher development and micropolitical literacy (Kelchtermans & Ballet, 2002b), teacher supervision and evaluation (Cooper, Ehrensal, & Bromme, 2005; Stronge & Tucker, 1999), school-level management teams (Cranston & Ehrich, 2005), educational interest groups (Johnson, 2001), and court-ordered desegregation (Goldring & Crowson, 2001).

A number of studies of teacher–student interactions and instructional and social issues in the classroom have demonstrated the degree to which micropolitics pervades life in schools (Anton, 1999; Bloome, Carter, Christian, Otto, & Huart-Faris, 2005; Cazden, 2001; Connell, 1985; Gilbert & Yerrick, 2001; Gutierrez & Rogoff, 2003; Lee, 2006; Lightfoot, 1983; McDevitt, 2004; McNeil, 1983; Morgan, 2001; Nias, 1989; Pauly, 1992; Pollard, 1985; Powell, Farrar, & Cohen, 1985; Sedlak, Wheeler, Pullin, & Cusick, 1986; Waller, 1932; Winograd, 2002; Woods, 1990). Powell et al. (1985) and Sedlak et al. (1986) found that interaction between classroom teachers and students was essentially political; interactions were based primarily on power dynamics; "negotiation" between teachers and students produced "understandings," "bargains," and "treaties" that defined and controlled all aspects of classroom life. These findings have been confirmed by Winograd (2002), who reported that students' resistance to teachers' authority resulted in negotiated political agreements in the classroom. Anton (1999) found that interactive exchanges between students and teachers in learner-centered, second language classrooms were characterized by negotiation of form, content, and classroom rules of behavior, and such political processes created environments conducive to learning.

McDevitt (2004) specifically studied issues of pedagogical and cultural appropriateness that arose between teachers and students from two disparate cultures of learning; she found that conflicts were resolved by negotiating course content and classroom procedures. Lee (2006) and Bloome et al. (2005) found that language, patterns of interaction, and activities used in classrooms were negotiated, a finding consistent with Pauly's (1992) conclusion that "education is the result of working agreements that are hammered out by the people in each classroom, who determine the rules, the power relationships, and the kinds of teaching and learning that will take place there" (pp. 13–14). Such findings are also consistent with how informal language used in classrooms to promote learning (e.g., African American English paralinguistic practices) resulted from cultural negotiations and power relations linked to race, class, and ethnicity (Cazden, 2001; Gutierrez & Rogoff, 2003; Morgan, 2001). In contrast, Gilbert and Yerrick (2001) found that the quality of science instruction was subverted by negotiation between students and teachers in the context of low academic expectations in rural, underrepresented school contexts.

The Micropolitics of Educational Change and Reform

A growing number of micropolitical studies address relationships at various levels of school organization that range from the nature of teacher engagement in school reform processes to superintendent–board interaction in district governance processes. General studies of school reform can also be interpreted from a micropolitical standpoint. *Taken together, these studies demonstrate the critical role of micropolitics, a role that appears to facilitate and support as well as impede and inhibit educational change and reform.*

Teachers and Educational Change and Reform

A number of studies have demonstrated that teachers' political participation in school-wide decision making, classroom autonomy, empowerment, and reflective critique of curriculum and instruction have *facilitated* successful school reform efforts (Allen, 1993; Blase & Blase, 2001; Bredeson, 1989; Brimhall, 1993; Corbett & Rossman, 1988; Melenyzer, 1990). Smylie and Brownlee-Conyers (1990) described teachers' use of specific political strategies to develop innovative collaborative relationships with principals. Scribner, Sawyer, Watson, and Myers (2007) found that teacher problem-finding teams employed autonomy and relational leadership skills to facilitate collaboration and to avoid marginalization by principals. In a micropolitical study of a school's implementation of site-based management, Somich (2005) found that when teachers' political involvement in school increased, teachers' classroom instruction benefited significantly. Reed (1992) reported that teachers who defined efficacy as greater formal authority in school-wide decision making were seen as more politically important than colleagues who participated primarily to facilitate classroom instruction and implement site-based initiatives. The work of Chrispeels and Martin (2002), Goldring and Simms (2005), Firestone and Fisler (2002), Feuerstein and Dietrich (2003), and Goodman (2006) affirmed the significance of teachers' political involvement in school-wide and interorganizational relationships: when teachers participated in negotiating a redefinition of roles, building trust, setting agendas and standards, and confronting sources of conflict, they frequently facilitated reform. Heck, Brandon, and Wang (2001) found that decentralized (school-based) decision making was successful when teacher participation focused on improving student learning and selection of issues addressed in Site-based Decision Making (SBDM) meetings. Achinstein (2002) demonstrated that collaborative reform efforts in schools with strong professional learning communities generated constructive political conflict crucial to organizational learning. Johnson (2004) reported that leadership teams in several Australian schools enacted school reform through primarily positive political approaches; they conceptualized, negotiated, and implemented reforms via consensually and morally based approaches sensitive to teacher professionalism.

There is also evidence that teacher-related micropolitical factors – classroom territoriality norms, protectionist orientations to outside intrusions, resistance to internal threats of work intensification, and relationships of power and negative forms of politics within classrooms *impede* school change and reform (Altrichter & Soukup-Altrichter, 2000; Cusick, 1992; Gitlin, 2001; Pauly, 1992; Powell et al., 1985; Sedlak et al., 1986). Moreover, confusion about roles and authority in school-level decision making, and structural factors (e.g., inadequate planning time and administrative control of planning topics and outcomes) interfere with collegial dialogue (Gitlin, et al., 1992). Other teacher-related micropolitical factors that interfere with reform include adversarial factions with competing interests that fail to share resources (Robertson & Briggs, 1994), domination of governance processes by particular teacher groups and the types of strategies teachers used to pursue their interests (Peterson & Solsrud, 1993), compliant orientations toward principals (Allen, 1993; Blase & Blase, 2001), resistance to decentralization by veteran teachers (Heck et al., 2001), and conflict arising from partial faculty involvement in school planning (Mintrop, Gamson, McLaughlin, Wong, & Oberman, 2001).

Micropolitical factions do not only facilitate or impede reforms, but also alter and adapt them. For instance, in a 5-year case study of inquiry-based school reform, Stokes (2000) reported that responses of teachers and other stakeholders, largely defined by political forces (e.g., emotional and ideological differences), transformed a "literacy" project into one that emphasized "equity."

Principals and Educational Change and Reform

The importance of the principal's role in *facilitating* school reform has been widely discussed in the restructuring literature. Studies of several models of school reform – Coalition of Essential Schools (Hall & Placier, 2003); the New American Schools project (Berends, Bodily, & Kirby, 2003), and the Bay Area School Reform Collaborative (BASRC) (Copeland, 2002) – have identified that principals are central to successful implementation. Maxey and Ngyuyen (2006) assume that distributing, sharing, and facilitating leadership are inherently political, and principals who engage in facilitative leadership and work with and through others are engaged in the politics of power sharing. Principals' political role in facilitating reconfiguration of school structures and governance processes to ensure higher levels of collaboration and teamwork has been examined by a number of scholars (Berends, et al., 2003; Blase & Blase, 2001; Blase, Blase, Anderson, & Dungan, 1995; Etheridge & Hall, 1995; Firestone & Fisler, 2002; Freeman, Brimhall, & Neufeld, 1994; Hall & Placier, 2003; Murphy & Louis, 1994; Smylie, Wenzel, & Fendt, 2003; Somich, 2005; Reitzug, 1994; Rollow & Bryk, 1995; Rulfs, Crocker, Wright, & Petrie, 2001).

Successful school reform has been strongly associated with principals' facilitative leadership and specific political practices including empowering teachers (Berends et al., 2003; Blase & Blase, 2001; Hall & Placier, 2003; Smylie et al., 2003; Rulfs et al., 2001; Somich, 2005), team building (Farrell, 2003; Somich, 2005), enhancing parent and community participation in democratic governance processes (Berends et al., 2003; Copeland, 2002; Farrell, 2003; Flinspach, Easton, Ryan, O'Connor, & Storey, 1994; Goldberg & Morrison, 2003; Lopez, Scribner, & Mahitvanichcha, 2001; Rollow & Bryk, 1995), managing internal conflict (Beck, 1993; Goldberg & Morrison, 2003; Hall & Placier, 2003; Peterson & Warren, 1994), developing teachers' capacity for critique (Reitzug, 1994), maintaining balance between district-level initiates and school-based initiatives (Conley & Goldman, 1994; Goldberg & Morrison, 2003), challenging teachers to transform schools (Prestine, 1994), maintaining accountability of organizational stakeholders (Bondy, Ross, & Webb, 1994; Feuerstein & Dietrich, 2003; Lopez, et al., 2001), and using high stakes accountability to garner support for school reform (Spillane et al., 2002). Moreover, these studies demonstrate that principals' facilitative leadership is correlated with the development of democracy in schools and substantial increases in teachers' sense of political efficacy.

In contrast, studies have demonstrated that a control-oriented political approach to school reform on the part of principals (i.e., unwillingness or inability to let go of power to enact democratic facilitative leadership approaches) has been a major *impediment* to successful school reform (Blase, 1991; Cooper et al., 2005; Datnow & Costellano, 2003; Kilgore & Jones, 2003; Finnan & Meza, 2003; Maxey & Nguyen, 2006; Robertson & Briggs, 1994; Rollow & Bryk, 1995; Scribner et al., 2007; Smith, 1995). Malen and Ogawa (1988) were among the first to report that even properly conceived structural approaches to educational innovation and reform (e.g., wherein school-based councils had broad jurisdiction and decision-making authority) were easily sabotaged by principals' predisposition to "control" interactions with teachers and parents. Implementation studies of school reform, including the *Success for All Project* (Datnow & Costellano, 2003), the *Comer School Development Process (CSDP)* (Payne & Diamond, 2003), *The Modern Red Schoolhouse* (Kilgore & Jones, 2003), *Accelerated Schools Project* (Finnan & Meza, 2003), and earlier studies of Chicago school reform initiatives (Rollow & Bryk, 1995) have also affirmed that principals who worked to control or mediate school reform impeded its success.

More specifically, studies have found that principals have impeded school reform initiatives by controlling discourse, maintaining power, and preventing power sharing with teachers via a wide array of political tactics such as an unwillingness to facilitate shared leadership, failing to empower teachers, opposing collaborative work, dismissing agendas, marginalizing dissenters, intimidating teachers, postponing meetings with teachers, limiting access to information, providing misinformation, holding traditional expectations of self and teachers, undermining trust, and practicing favoritism and exclusion (Blase & Blase, 2003; Bredeson, 1993; Brown, 1994; Datnow & Costellano, 2003; Cooper et al., 2005; Etheridge & Hall, 1995; Finnan & Meza, 2003; Gitlin, et al., 1992; Kilgore & Jones, 2003; Lonnquist & King, 1993; Murphy & Louis, 1994; Reitzug & Cross, 1994; Scribner, et al., 2007; Smylie & Crowson, 1993).

Middle-Level Administrators and Educational Change and Reform

Central office efforts to *facilitate* processes and protect schools engaged in restructuring from interference have been important to achieving successful implementation of school reform. Although central office administrators are often viewed as technocrats responsible for carrying out bureaucratic operations such as program planning, budgeting, compliance, accountability, and reporting, politically, they are not benign functionaries. As professional staff, their expert knowledge enables them to influence strategic policy decisions at the district and school levels. Björk (2001b) found that a district financial officer institutionalized a building-centered financial system that was essential to implementing decentralized decision making in schools. Spillane et al. (2002) found that central office staff functioned as sense makers, mediated district accountability policies, and used accountability policies as levers to support educational reforms. Studies have also revealed that central office support for training principals and teachers in collaborative processes facilitated implementation of decentralized decision making (Slavin, Madden, Shaw, Mainzer, & Donnelly, 1993; Smylie & Crowson, 1993). A study of collaboration within an external coalition of partners (university, district, and computer manufacturer) highlighted the importance of both central office strategy and resource control for school-level innovation (Baker, 1994). Morgan and Peterson (2002) found that multilevel collaboration among central office staffs enhanced superintendents' work as instructional leaders in their districts.

In contrast, studies also indicate that central office administrators *impede* school reform. Skrla, Reyes, and Scheurich (2000) reported that male-dominated societal and district office professional norms, and the use of coercive political pressure, effectively prevented female superintendents from publicly acknowledging gender-based discrimination. Rusch (2005) described a similar pattern of influence—in particular, how organizational cultures at the district office level created institutional scripts that sanctioned talk about school reform and inhibited learning among professionals. Björk (2001b) found that central office staffs leveraged internal and external influence among community interest groups and school board members to resist school decentralization initiatives that reduced their influence and threatened their positions. Honig (2003) reported that central office staffs defended conventional administrative roles until they were effectively threatened by school reform progress or marginalized by school reform initiatives. Glassman and Fuller (2002) found that superintendent evaluation practices illuminated the politics of local decision making and highlighted the role played by multiple and diverse constituency groups within central office professional staff, who required the inclusion of student achievement data in the evaluation protocol.

Superintendents and Educational Change and Reform

Superintendents who maintain high levels of involvement in instructional matters play a crucial role in launching and sustaining district-level-initiated educational reforms (Björk, 1996, 2000). Recognition of their contribution to the improvement of learning and teaching has advanced efforts to redefine their roles as instructional leaders (Björk et al., 2005: Peterson & Barnett, 2005); this has also heightened interest in the politics of the superintendency. Superintendents' capacity to work effectively within community and school board political dynamics and build community-based business coalitions has been directly related to the success of district reform initiatives. Such political capacities have provided the continuity necessary for long-term change initiatives (Björk, 2000, 2005; Glassman & Fuller, 2002).

The importance of district-and-school-level leadership in launching and sustaining educational reforms specifically in high-poverty schools has been described by Berends et al. (2003). These researchers found that superintendents were instrumental in building organizational political support needed to establish a professional climate to advance teaching and learning as well as effectively communicating with the public about the purpose and status of change initiatives. Goldring and Sims (2005) reported that superintendents' efforts to build collaborative partnerships in the community based on trust and power sharing were key factors in initiating and sustaining educational reforms.

A growing academic literature on the role of female superintendents in educational reform shows that relational ways of working have enabled them to survive in office and successfully engage in district-level educational reform efforts. Ortiz (2001, 2002) found that female superintendents' knowledge of community power structures and cultural practices in Hispanic communities contributed to their longevity and success in reforming educational programs. Owen and Ovando (2000) reported that superintendents who were knowledgeable about community cultural and political contexts were particularly adept at coalescing interest groups, building coalitions, negotiating agreements, forcing concessions when required, and empowering others, all of which were associated with effective educational change. In addition, Grogan and Blackmon (2001) and Skrla, Scott, and Benestante (2001) found that understanding constituent group interests, school board power structures, and competing community values enabled superintendents to protect their positions and unify board members, build coalitions, counter adverse interest group politics, and achieve district educational reform goals.

Although the role of superintendents is pivotal to facilitating educational reform, the ways in which their political behavior *impedes* progress cover a wide spectrum of organizational issues (Björk, 2001b, 2005; Björk & Lindle, 2001; Bloom & Erlandson, 2003; Brunner, 2000; Hoffman & Burrello, 2004; Keedy & Björk, 2002; Kelsey & Lupini, 2001). Along these lines, Björk (2001c) found that a superintendent stalled district-initiated decentralization efforts when he acquiesced to pressure from the school board to retain a politically connected central office staff member who opposed the change. In addition, superintendents' failure to support school site policy decisions, provide adequate time for decision making, clarify the role of principals, and develop assessment criteria relevant to principals' new leadership roles has inhibited educational reform efforts. Hoffman and Burrello (2004) reported that superintendents' needs for power and control and their reluctance to release test scores to reduce unfavorable political exposure undermined attempts to improve teaching and learning in low-achieving schools. Superintendents have also hindered reform by failing to clarify ambiguous governance procedures (Bondy et al., 1994), trust the professional judgments of teachers, provide adequate funding and resources (Murphy & Louis, 1994), and support principals in conflicts with others (Crowson & Boyd, 1991). The use of top-down mandates to create school-based collegiality among teachers (i.e., "contrived collegiality Hargreaves, 1991)" and extending inordinate power to school principals involved in site-based management have also been linked to adverse effects on school reform (Smylie & Crowson, 1993).

School Boards and Educational Change and Reform

Throughout the history of American education, schools have been viewed as extensions of local communities bound by shared social, economic, and political circumstances. Alsbury (2003) and Björk (2000) found that political configurations of school boards were influenced by changes in community values and power structures, which, in turn, can *facilitate* or *impede* school reform. Shipps (2003) contends that school board policy making is influenced by multiple coalitions, the composition of which affects reform agendas. The dynamic relationship between communities and schools provides a framework for understanding school board responses to calls for school reform in the context of declining financial resources and politicization of educational policy making (Björk, 2005; Björk & Keedy, 2002; Johnson, 1996). Clearly, some view school boards as unworkable and detrimental; others see them as viable political forums in which individuals and groups openly express real needs and interests and reconcile differences through consultation and negotiation (Björk, 2005; Björk & Gurley, 2005).

Unfortunately, there is very little empirical research on school boards in general. Björk (2000) discovered that some boards were remarkably consistent and resilient in their efforts to engage community interest groups, factions, and citizens to successfully advance school district reform. On the other hand, Glass, Björk, and Brunner (2000) found that many school boards' primary expectations for superintendents have emphasized effective management of district affairs rather than instructional leadership or school change and reform. Louis and King (1993) discovered that educational reform efforts were *impeded* because the school board required teachers to share negative feedback about reform that potentially threatened the board's willingness to continue its support. Feuerstein and Dietrich (2003) found that local political turbulence and interest group conflict frequently impeded the ability of schools to implement state-initiated academic standards and testing.

Future Research

Although research on the micropolitics of educational change and reform has increased significantly during the past decade, much more work will be required on all aspects of this incredibly complex, dynamic, and unpredictable phenomenon, particularly research on central office administrators and school boards. We suggest that future research employ a broad theoretical perspective of micropolitics that requires, among other things, investigation of cooperative and conflictive processes, overt and covert forms of political activity, the activities of relevant stakeholders, and the impact of school context, including macro-level factors. Methodologically, it will be important to employ both quantitative and qualitative research approaches at this early stage of inquiry. We especially need long-term, retrospective studies (Hargreaves & Goodson, 2006), and also real-time observational studies at the school level to capture the dynamic interplay of micropolitical factors that evolve in situ and that transform change and reform efforts and outcomes in unpredictable ways (Stokes, 2000).

Studies of both successful and unsuccessful school change and reform initiatives would provide invaluable insights about related micropolitical configurations. Recently, the effects of NCLB and high stakes testing legislation in the United States have begun to emerge (Jennings & Rentner, 2006). It will be important to examine whether such heavy-handed, top-down, control-oriented approaches to school reform spawn the type of positive, facilitating school-based micropolitical processes and structures that appear to be essential to authentic school reform. The evidence from a range of other countries that have previously adopted similar measures and from states that had already adopted more centralized curriculum along with high stakes testing suggests that they will not (Hargreaves, 2003).

In addition, future micropolitical studies must devote greater attention to the historical and cultural context of schools (Blase, 1998; Chrispeels & Martin, 2002; Pillay, 2004), including gender, race, and ethnicity (Datnow, 1998). Unfortunately, individuals and groups often experience intense stress and strain stemming from educational change and reform; however, very little research has addressed this crucial aspect of micropolitics (see Troman & Boyle-White, Durham, Leithwood, etc). Furthermore, few studies have attempted to uncover subtle and covert types of micropolitics such as the politics of powerlessness by stakeholders who practice "silence" in the face of school change (Pillay, 2004). Both of these areas provide fertile ground for political research. Datnow (1998) found that micropolitics was the centerpiece to adoption processes preceding implementation (i.e., how schools decide whether to implement a change project or approach); this suggests that greater attention to such factors would be worthwhile.

Smith, et al. (2004) have argued that educational reform at all levels of the educational hierarchy and in varying degrees is, in large part, a "political spectacle"; that is, more symbolic than substantive. Using Edelman's (1985, 1988) theory of political spectacle (which includes elements such as symbolic language, dramaturgy, illusions of rationality, democratic processes, and front-and-back stages), Smith et al. contend that political spectacle currently dominates American politics, and NCLB is but one conspicuous example of political spectacle. Needless to say, under such circumstances, authentic reform cannot be expected. Relatedly, Ball (2003) has discussed the relationship between educational change and reform as "spectacle" and performativity whose performances of organizations and individuals represent their respective value. Study of these fascinating phenomena would open new and exciting aspects of the micropolitics of educational change and reform.

Conclusion

This chapter has focused on micropolitical studies of change and reform at the school and district levels. In each case, micropolitics *impedes* or *facilitates* school change and reform. Our examination of the extant research underscores the dramatic transformative effects of micropolitical processes and structures on internally and externally initiated school change. To be sure, cracking open the black box of educational change and reform reveals stunning differences between the intent of educational reform policies and the reality of school-based implementation efforts. Our review also reveals that, generally speaking, uses of positive forms of micropolitics (e.g., empowering, collaborative, problem centered) by political stakeholders, such as teachers, school principals, and central office administrators, are associated with facilitating school change and reform. Conversely, uses of negative forms of micropolitics (i.e., controlling and self-serving) is associated with impeding school change and reform. There is little question on the fact that school-based micropolitics pervade all aspects of educational change and reform and have the potential to promote successful and/or unsuccessful change. Despite this conclusion, educational policy makers and school district and building-level school administrators frequently fail to adequately acknowledge or address micropolitical features of their work. Further, university-based administrator and teacher education programs typically do little or nothing to equip students with relevant micropolitical knowledge and skill.

For these and other reasons, decades of research indicate that successive iterations of reform have failed to produce significant, enduring changes in school improvement. Oakes et al. (2000) are not alone in contending that the educational "reform mill" (p. 264) rarely delivers improvements in student achievement. "[It] grinds out reworked versions of the status quo that do little to address whatever initially motivated the reform. . ..[D]isappointed policy makers, the public, and educators judge the reform to be misguided, poorly implemented, or both; and the next reform, waiting in the wings with new funding or new leadership, takes center stage" (p. 264). Long ago, in commenting on educational change and reform, Sarason (1971) observed, "The more things change the more they remain the same" (p. 297). Recently, he declared, "the one thing that history of educational reform indisputably proves is that the more things change the more they do not remain the same but rather do or will get worse" (2004, p. 25).

> Schools and school systems are political organizations in which power is an organizing feature. Ignore [power] relationships, leave unexamined their rationale, and the existing system will defeat efforts at reform. This will happen not because there is a grand conspiracy or because of mulish stubbornness in resisting change or because educators are uniquely unimaginative or uncreative (which they are not) but rather because recognizing and trying to change power relationships, especially in complicated, traditional institutions, is among the most complex tasks human beings can undertake (Sarason, 1990. p. 7.)

The implications are clear. As scholars we must substantially increase our efforts to understand micropolitics and educational change and reform. As policy makers, educational administrators and teachers we must learn to create the positive, robust type of political processes and structures in schools that lead to school improvement.

References

Achinstein, B. (2002). Conflict amid community: The micropolitics of teacher collaboration. *Teachers College Record, 104*(3), 421–455.

Allen, L. R. (1993). *The role of voice in shared governance: A case study of a primary school.* Unpublished Doctoral Dissertation, University of Georgia.

Alsbury, T. (2003). Superintendent and school board member turnover: Political versus apolitical turnover as a critical variable in the application of dissatisfaction theory. *Educational Administration Quarterly, 39*(5), 667–698.

Altrichter, H., & Soukup-Altrichter, K. (2000, April). *The micropolitics of quality assurance in schools.* Paper presented at the Annual Conference of the American Educational Research Association, New Orleans.

Anton, M. (1999). The discourse of a learner-centered classroom: Sociocultural perspectives on teacher-learner interaction in the second-language classroom. *The Modern Language Journal, 83*(3), 303–318.

Bacharach, S. (Ed.). (1990). *Educational reform: Making sense of it all.* Boston: Allyn & Bacon.

Baker, L. M. (1994, April). *The politics of collaboration: How an educational partnership works.* Paper presented at the Annual Meeting of the American Educational Research Association, New Orleans.

Ball, S. J. (1987). *The micro-politics of the school: Towards a theory of school organization.* New York: Methuen.

Ball, S. J. (2003). The teacher's soul and the terrors of performativity. *Journal of Education Policy, 18*(2), 215–228.

Barott, J. E., & Galvin, P. F. (1998). The politics of supervision. In G. R. Firth & E. F. Pajak (Eds.), *Handbook of research on school supervision* (pp. 310–336). New York: Simon and Schuster Macmillan.

Beck, L. G. (1993). Cultivating a caring school community: One principal's story. In J. Murphy & K. S. Louis (Eds.), *Reshaping the principalship: Insights from transformational reform efforts.* Thousand Oaks, CA: Corwin Press.

Berends, M., Bodilly, S., & Kirby, S. (2003). New American schools: District and school leadership for whole school reform. In J. Murphy & A. Datnow (Eds.), *Leadership lessons form school reforms* (pp. 109–134). Thousand Oakes, CA: Corwin.

Björk, L. (1996). The revisionists' critique of the education reform reports. *Journal of School Leadership, 7*(1), 290–315.

Björk, L. (2000). The transformative role of superintendents: Creating a community of learners. In P. Short & J. Scribner (Eds.), *Case studies on the superintendency* (pp. 41–60). Lancaster, PA: Technomic Publishing.

Björk, L. (2001a). Preparing the next generation of superintendents: Integrating professional and experiential knowledge. In C. C. Brunner & L. Björk (Eds.), *The new superintendency* (pp. 19–54). Amsterdam: JAI Elsevier Science Ltd.

Björk, L. (2001b). Institutional barriers to educational reform: A superintendent's role in district decentralization. In C. C. Brunner & L. Björk (Eds.), *The new superintendency* (pp. 205–228). Amsterdam: JAI Elsevier Science Ltd.

Björk, L. (2001c). The role of the central office in decentralization. In T. Kowalski & G. Perreault (Eds.), *21st century challenges for school administrators* (pp. 286–309). Lanham, MD: Scarecrow.

Björk, L. (2005). Superintendent-board relations: An historical overview of the dynamics of change and the sources of conflict and collaboration. In G. Peterson & L. Fusarelli (Eds.), *The district superintendent and school board relations: Trends in policy development and implementation* (pp. 1–22). Charlotte, NC: Information Age Publishers Inc.

Björk, L., & Gurley, K. (2005). Superintendent as educational statesman and political strategist. In L. Björk & T. Kowalski (Eds.), *The contemporary superintendent: Preparation, practice and development* (pp. 163–186). Thousand Oakes, CA: Corwin.

Björk, L., & Keedy, J. (2001). Politics and the superintendency in the USA: Restructuring in-service education. *Journal of In-Service Education, 27*(2), 275–302.

Björk, L., Kowalski, T., & Young, M. (2005). National reports and implications for professional preparation and development. In L. Björk & T. Kowalski (Eds.), *The contemporary superintendent: Preparation, practice and development* (pp. 45–70). Thousand Oakes, CA: Corwin.

Björk, L., & Lindle, J. (2001). Superintendents and interest groups. *Educational Policy, 15*(1), 76–91.

Blase, J. (1987). Political interactions among teachers: Sociocultural context in the schools. *Urban Education, 22*(3), 286–309.

Blase, J. (Ed.). (1991). *The politics of life in schools: Power, conflict, and cooperation.* Newbury Park, CA: Sage.

Blase, J. (1998). The micropolitics of educational change. In A. Hargreaves, A. Lieberman, M. Fullan, & D. Hopkins (Eds.), *International handbook of educational change* (pp. 544–557). Great Britain: Kluwer.

Blase, J., & Blase, J. (2000). The micropolitics of instructional supervision: A call for research. *Educational Administration Quarterly, 38*(1), 6–44.

Blase, J., & Blase, J. (2001). *Empowering teachers: What successful principals do.* Thousand Oaks, CA: Corwin.

Blase, J., & Blase, J. (2002). The micropolitics of instructional supervision: A call for research. *Educational Administration Quarterly, 38*(1), 6–44.

Blase, J., & Blase, J. (2003). *Breaking the silence: Overcoming the problem of principal mistreatment of teachers.* Thousand Oakes, CA: Corwin.

Blase, J., Blase, J. R., Anderson, G., & Dungan, S. (1995). *Democratic principals in action: Eight pioneers.* Thousand Oaks, CA: Corwin Press.

Bloom, C., & Erlandson, D (2003). African American women principals in urban schools: Realities, (re) constructions, and resolutions. *Educational Administration Quarterly, 39*(3), 339–369.

Bloome, D., Carter, S., Christian, B., Otto, S., & Huart-Faris, N. (2005). *Discourse analysis and the study of classroom language and literacy events: A microethnographic perspective.* Mahway, NJ: Lawrence Erlbaum.

Bondy, E., Ross, D., & Webb, R. (1994, April). *The dilemmas of school restructuring and improvement.* Paper presented at the Annual Meeting of the American Educational Research Association, New Orleans.

Boyd, W. L. (1991). Foreword. In J. Blase (Ed.), *The politics of life in schools: Power, conflict, and cooperation* (pp. vii–ix). Newbury Park, CA: Sage.

Bredeson, P. V. (1989). Redefining leadership and the roles of school principals: Responses to changes in the professional work-life of teachers. *The High School Journal, 23*(1), 9–20.

Bredeson, P. V. (1993). Letting go of outlived professional identities: A study of role transition and role strain for principals in restructured schools. *Educational Administration Quarterly, 29*(1), 34–68.

Bridges, E. M., & Groves, B. R. (1999). The macropolitics and micropolitics of personnel evaluation: A framework. *Journal of Personnel Evaluation in Education, 13*(4), 321–337.

Brimhall, P. A. (1993, April). *Restructuring and teacher empowerment.* Paper presented at the Annual meeting of the American Educational Research Association, Atlanta.

Brown, D. F. (1994, April). *Experiencing shared leadership: Teachers' reflections.* Paper presented at the Annual meeting of the American Educational Research Association. New Orleans, LA.

Brunner, C. C. (2000). Unsettled moments in settled discourse: Women superintendents' experiences with inequity. *Educational Administration Quarterly, 36*(1), 76–116.

Burlingame, M. (1988). Review of the micro-politics of the school: Towards a theory of school organization. *Journal of Curriculum Studies, 20*(3), 281–283.

Burns, T. (1961). Micropolitics: Mechanisms of institutional change. *Administration Science Quarterly, 6,* 257–281.

Cazden, C. B. (2001). *Classroom discourse: The language of teaching and learning.* Portsmouth, NH: Heineman.

Chrispeels, J. H., & Martin, K. J. (2002). Four school leadership teams define their roles within organizational and political structures to improve student learning. *School Effectiveness and School Improvement, 13*(3), 327–365.

Cibulka, J. G. (2001). The changing role of interest groups in education: Nationalization and the new politics of education productivity. *Educational Policy, 15*(1), 12–40.

Conley, D. T., & Goldman, P. (1994). Ten propositions for facilitative leadership. In J. Murphy & K. S. Louis (Eds.), *Reshaping the principalship: Insights from transformational reform efforts* (pp. 237–262). Thousand Oaks, CA: Corwin Press.

Connell, R. W. (1985). *Teachers' work.* Sydney: George Allen & Unwin.

Cooper, B., Ehrensal, P., & Bromme, M. (2005). School level politics and professional development: Traps in evaluating the quality of practicing teachers. *Educational Policy, 19*(1), 112–125.

Copeland, M. (2002). The bay area school reform collaborative. In J. Murphy & A. Datnow (Eds.), *Leadership lessons from comprehensive school reforms* (pp. 159–183). Thousand Oakes, CA: Corwin.

Corbett, H. D., & Rossman, G. B. (1988, April). *How teachers empower subordinates: Running good schools.* Paper presented at the annual meeting of the American Educational Research Association, New Orleans.

Cranston, N., & Ehrich, L. (2005). Enhancing the effectiveness of senior management teams in schools. *Leadership and Management, 33*(1), 79–91.

Crowson, R. L., & Boyd, W. L. (1991). Urban schools as organizations: Political perspectives. *Politics of education yearbook* (pp. 87–103). London: Taylor & Francis.

Cusick, P. A. (1992). *The educational system: Its nature and logic.* New York: McGraw-Hill.

Datnow, A. (1998). *The gender politics of educational change.* London: Falmer Press.

Datnow, A. (2000). Power and politics in the adoption of school reform models. *Educational Evaluation and Policy Analysis, 22*(4), 357–374.

Datnow, A., & Costellano, M. (2003). Success for All. In J. Murphy & A. Datnow (Eds.), *Leadership lessons from school reforms* (pp. 184–208). Thousand Oakes, CA: Corwin.

Edelman, M. (1985). *The symbolic uses of politics*. Urbana, IL: University of Illinois.

Edelman, M. (1988). *Constructing the political spectical*. Chicago, IL: University of Chicago Press.

Elmore, R. (2004). Change and improvement in educational reform. In D. T. Gordon & P. A. Graham (Eds.), *A nation reformed? American education 20 years after a nation at risk* (pp. 23–28). Cambridge, MA: Harvard Education Press.

Etheridge, C. P., & Hall, M. L. (1995, April). *Challenge to change: The Memphis experience with school-based decision making revisited*. Paper presented at the annual meeting of the American Educational Research Association, San Francisco.

Farrell, G. (2003). Expeditionary learning schools: Tenacity, leadership and school reform. In J. Murphy & A. Datnow (Eds.), *Leadership lessons from school reforms* (pp. 21–36). Thousand Oakes, CA: Corwin.

Feuerstein, A., & Dietrich, J. (2003). State standards in the local context: A survey of school board members and superintendents. *Educational Policy, 17*(2), 237–256.

Finnan, C., & Meza, J. Jr. (2003). The Accelerated Schools Project: Can a leader change the culture and embed reform? In J. Murphy & A. Datnow (Eds.), *Leadership lessons form school reforms* (pp. 83–107). Thousand Oakes, CA: Corwin.

Firestone, W. A. (1990). Continuity and incrementalism after all: State responses to the excellence movement. In J. Murphy (Ed.), *Educational reform movement of the 1980s: Perspectives and cases* (pp. 143–166). Berkeley: McCutchan.

Firestone, W., & Fisler, J. (2002). Politics, community, and leadership in a school-university partnership. *Educational Administration Quarterly, 38*(4), 449–493.

Firestone, W. A., Fuhrman, S., & Kirst, M. W. (1990). An overview of educational reform since 1983. In J. Murphy (Ed.), *Educational reform movement of the 1980s: Perspectives and cases* (pp. 349–364). Berkeley: McCutchan.

Flinspach, S. L., Easton, J. Q., Ryan, S. P., O'Conner, C., & Storey, S. L. (1994, April). *Local school councils during four years of school reform*. Paper presented at the annual meeting of the American Educational Research Association, New Orleans.

Freeman, D. J., Brimhall, P. A., & Neufeld, J. (1994, April). *Who's in charge now? A principal's endeavors to empower teachers*. Paper presented at the annual meeting of the American Educational Research Association, New Orleans, LA.

Fuhrman, S. H., & Elmore, R. F. (Eds.). (2004). *Redesigning accountability systems for education*. New York: Teachers College Press.

Gilbert, A., & Yerrick, R. (2001). Same School, separate words: A sociocultural study of identity, resistance and negotiation in a rural, lower track science classroom. *Journal of Research in Science Teaching, 38*(5), 574–598.

Gitlin, A. (2001). Bounding teacher decision making: The threat of intensification.*Educational Policy, 15*(2), 227–257.

Gitlin, A., Bringhurst, K., Burns, M., Cooley, V., Myers, B., Price, K., et al. (1992). *Teachers voices for school change: An introduction to educative research*. New York: Teachers College Press.

Glass, T., Björk, L., & Brunner, C. C. (2000). *The study of the American superintendency2000: A look at the superintendent in the new millennium*. Arlington, VA: American Association of School Administrators. Lanham, MD: Scarecrow.

Glassman, N., & Fuller, J. (2002). Superintendent evaluation: Concepts, practices, an outcome-related case. In B. Cooper & L. Fusarelli (Eds.), *The promises and perils facing today's school superintendents* (pp. 133–152). Lanham, MD: Scarecrow Press.

Goldberg, B., & Morrison, D. (2003). Co-Nect: Purpose, accountability and school leadership. In J. Murphy & A. Datnow (Eds.), *Leadership lessons form school reforms* (pp. 57–82). Thousand Oakes, CA: Corwin Press.

Goldring, E., & Crowson, R. (2001, April). *School leadership and the micropolitics of disman-tling court-ordered desegregation.* Paper presented at the annual meeting of the American Educational Research Association. Seattle, Washington.

Goldring, E., & Simms, P. (2005). Modeling creative and courageous school leadership through district-university partnerships.*Educational Policy, 19*(1), 223–249.

Goodman, J. (2006). *Reforming schools: Working within a progressive tradition.* Albany, NY: State University of New York Press.

Grogan, M., & Blackmon, M. (2001). A superintendent's approach to coalition building: Working with diversity to garner support for educational initiatives. In C. C. Brunner & L. Björk (Eds.), *The new superintendency* (pp. 95–114). Amsterdam: JAI Elsevier Science Ltd.

Gronn, P. (1986). Politics, power and the management of schools. In E. Hoyle (Ed.), *The world yearbook of education 1986: The management of schools* (pp. 45–54). London: Kogan Page.

Gtazek, S. D., & Sarason, S. (2007). *Productive learning: Science, art, and Einstein's relativity in educational reform.* Thousand Oaks, CA: Corwin.

Gutierrez, K., & Rogoff, B. (2003). Cultural ways of learning: Individual traits or repertoires of practice. *Educational Researcher, 32*(5), 19–25.

Hall, P. M., & Placier, P. L. (2003). The coalition of essential schools. In J. Murphy & A. Datnow (Eds.), *Leadership lessons form school reforms* (pp. 209–238). Thousand Oakes, CA: Corwin Press.

Hargreaves, A. (1991). Contrived collegiality: The micropolitics of teacher collaboration. In J. Blase (Ed.), *The politics of life in schools: Power, conflict, and cooperation* (pp. 46–72). Newbury Park, CA: Sage.

Hargreaves, A. (2003). *Teaching in the knowledge society: Education in the age of insecurity.* New York: Teachers' College Press.

Hargreaves, A., & Goodson, I. (2006). Educational change over time? The sustainability and non-sustainability of three decades of secondary school change and continuity. *Educational Administration Quarterly, 42*(1), 3–41.

Heck, R., Brandon, P., & Wang, J. (2001). Implementing site-based managed education changes: Examining levels of implementation and effort. *Educational Policy, 15*(2), 302–322.

Hoffman, L., & Burrello, L. (2004). A case study illustration of how a critical theorist and a con-summate practitioner meet on common ground. *Educational Administration Quarterly, 40*(2), 28–289.

Honig, M. (2003). Building policy from practice: District central office administrators' roles and capacity for implementing collaborative educational policy. *Educational Administration Quarterly, 39*(3), 292–338.

Hoyle, E. (1999). The two faces of micropolitics. *School Leadership and Management, 19*(2), 213–222.

Jennings, J., & Rentner, D. S. (2006). Ten big effects of the No Child Left Behind Act on public schools. *Phi Delta Kappan, 88*(2), 110–113.

Johnson, B. (2004). Local school micropolitical agency: An antidote to new managerialism. *School Leadership & Management, 24*(3), 266–286.

Johnson, B. L. (2001). Micropolitical dynamics of education interests: A view from within. *Educational Policy, 15*(1), 115–134.

Johnson, S. M. (1996). *Leading to change: The challenge of the new supeintendency.* San Francisco, Jossey-Bass.

Keedy, J., & Björk, L. (2002). Superintendents and local boards and the potential for commu-nity polarization: The call for political strategy skills. In B. Cooper & L. Fusarelli (Eds.), *The promises and perils facing today's school superintendents* (pp. 103–128). Lanham, MD: Scarecrow Press.

Kelchtermans, G., & Ballet, K. (2002a). The micropolitics of teacher induction: A narrative-biographical study on teacher socialization. *Teaching and Teacher Education, 18*, 105–120.

Kelchtermans, G., & Ballet, K. (2002b). Micropolitical literacy: Reconstructing a neglected dimen-sion in teacher development. *International Journal of Educational Research, 37*, 755–767.

Kelsey, G., & Lupini, D. (2001). Legislative change and the superintendency in British Columbia. In C. C. Brunner & L. Björk (Eds.), *The new superintendency* (pp. 229–246). Amsterdam: JAI Elsevier Science Ltd.

Kilgore, S., & Jones, J. (2003). The modern red schoolhouse: Leadership in comprehensive school reform initiatives. In J. Murphy & A. Datnow (Eds.), *Leadership lessons from school reforms* (pp. 37–56). Thousand Oakes, CA: Corwin.

Lane, J., & Epps, E. (Eds.). (1992). *Restructuring schools: Problems and prospects*. Berkeley: McCutchan.

Lee, C. (2006). "Every good-by ain't gone": Analyzing the cultural underpinnings of classroom talk. *International Journal of Qualitative Studies in Education, 19*(3), 305–327.

Lightfoot, S. L. (1983). *The good high school: Portraits of character and culture*. New York: Basic Books.

Lindle, J. C. (1999). What can the study of micropolitics contribute to the practice of leadership in reforming schools? *School Leadership & Management, 19*(2), 159–170.

Lopez, G., Scribner, J., & Mahitivanichcha, K. (2001). Redefining parental involvement: Lessons from high performing migrant-impacted schools. *American Educational Research Journal, 38*(2), 253–288.

Louis, K. S., & King, J. A. (1993). Professional cultures and reforming schools: Does the myth of Sisyphus apply? In J. Murphy & P. Hallinger (Eds.), *Restructuring schooling: Learning from ongoing efforts* (pp. 216–250). Newbury Park, CA: Corwin.

Lukes, S. (1974). *Power: A radical view*. London: MacMillan Press.

Malen, B. (1994). The micropolitics of education: Mapping the multiple dimensions of power relations in school politics. *Journal of Education Policy, 9*(5 & 6), 147–167.

Malen, B., & Ogawa, R. (1988). Professional-patron influence on site-based governance councils: A confounding case study. *Educational Evaluation and Policy Analysis, 10*(4), 251–270.

Mangham, I. L. (1979). *The politics of organizational change*. Westport, CT: Greenwood Press.

Marshall, C., & Scribner, J. D. (1991). "It's all political": Inquiry into the micropolitics of education. *Education and Urban Society, 23*(4), 347–355.

Mawhinney, H. B. (1999). Reappraisal: The problems and prospects of studying the micropolitics of leadership in reforming schools. *School leadership & Management, 19*(2), 159–170.

Maxey, B., & Nguyen, S. (2006). The politics of distributed leadership: Reconsidering leadership distribution in two Texas elementary schools. *Educational Policy, 20*(1), 163–196.

McDevitt, B. (2004). Negotiating the syllabus: A win-win situation? *ETL Journal, 58*(1), 3–9.

McNeil, L. (1983). Defensive teaching and classroom control. In M. Apple & L. Weis (Eds.), *Ideology and practice in schooling* (pp. 114–142). Philadelphia: Temple University Press.

Melenyzer, B. J. (1990, November). *Teacher empowerment: The discourse, meanings and social actions of teachers*. Paper presented at the National Council of States on Inservice Education. Orlando, FL.

Mintrop, H., Gamson, D., McLaughlin, M., Wong, P., & Oberman, I. (2001). Design cooperation: Strengthening the link between organizational and institutional change in schools. *Educational Policy, 15*(4), 520–546.

Morgan, C., & Peterson, G. (2002). The role of the district superintendent in leading academically successful districts. In B. Cooper & L. Fusarelli (Eds.), *The promises and perils facing today's school superintendents* (pp. 175–196). Lanham, MD: Scarecrow.

Morgan, M. (2001). The African-American speech community: Reality and sociolinguistics. In A. Duranti (Ed.), Linguistic anthropology: A reader. Malden, MA: Blackwell.

Murphy, J. (1990). The reform of school administration: Pressures and calls for change. In J. Murphy (Ed.), *Educational reform movement of the 1980s: Perspectives and cases* (pp. 277–304). Berkeley: McCuthan.

Murphy, J., & Louis, K. S. (1994). (Eds.). *Reshaping the principalship: Insights from transformational reform efforts*. Thousand Oaks, CA: Corwin.

Nias, J. (1989). *Primary teachers talking: A study of teaching as work*. London: Routledge.

Oakes, J., Quartz, K. H., Ryan, S., & Lipton, M. (2000). *Becoming good American schools: The struggle for civic virtue in education reform.* San Francisco: Jossey-Bass.

Ortiz, F. (2001). Using social capital in interpreting the careers of three Latina superintendents. *Educational Administration Quarterly, 37*(1), 58–85.

Ortiz, F. (2002). Executive succession processes and management success for Latina superintendents. In B. Cooper & L. Fusarelli (Eds.), *The promises and perils facing today's school superintendents* (pp. 21–40). Lanham, MD: Scarecrow.

Owen, J., & Ovando, M. (2000). The superintendent as political leader. In J. Owen & M. Ovando (Eds.), *Superintendents' guide to creating community* (pp. 32–44). Lanham, MD: Scarecrow.

Pauly, E. (1992). *The classroom crucible: What really works, what doesn't, and why.* New York: Basic Books.

Payne, C., & Diamond, J. (2003). The comer school development process. In J. Murphy & A. Datnow (Eds.), *Leadership lessons form school reforms* (pp. 239–260). Thousand Oakes, CA: Corwin.

Peterson, G., & Barnett, B. (2005). The superintendent as instructional leader: Current practice, future conceptualizations, and implications for preparation. In L. Björk & T. Kowalski (Eds.), *The contemporary superintendent: Preparation, practice and development* (pp. 107–136). Thousand Oakes, CA: Corwin.

Peterson, K., & Solsrud, C. (1993, April). *Leadership in restructuring schools: Six themes on the worklines of principals and teachers.* Paper presented at the annual meeting of the American Educational Research Association, Atlanta.

Peterson, K. D., & Warren, V. D. (1994). Changes in school governance and principals' roles: Changing jurisdictions, new power dynamics, and conflict in restructured schools. In J. Murphy & K. S. Louis (Eds.), *Reshaping the principalship: Insights from transformational reform efforts* (pp 219–236). Thousand Oaks, CA: Corwin.

Pillay, V. (2004). Towards a broader of the micropolitics of educational change. *Perspectives in Education, 22*(1), 129–138.

Pollard, A. (1985). *The social world of the primary school.* London: Holt, Rinehart & Winston.

Powell, G., Farrar, E., & Cohen, D. K. (1985). *The shopping mall high school: Winners and losers in the educational marketplace.* Boston: Houghton Mifflin.

Prestine, N. A. (1994). Ninety degrees from everywhere: New understandings of a principal's role in a restructuring essential school. In J. Murphy & K. S. Louis (Eds.), *Reshaping the principalship: Insights from transformational reform efforts* (pp. 123–143). Thousand Oaks, CA: Corwin Press.

Reed, C. J. (1992, April). *Political basis of teacher response to opportunities for involvement in school site policy curriculum decisions.* Paper presented at the annual meeting of the American Educational Research Association, San Francisco.

Reitzug, U. C. (1994). A case study of empowering principal behavior. *American Educational Research Journal, 31*(2), 283–307.

Reitzug, U. C., & Cross, B. E. (1994, April). *A multi-site case study of site-based management in urban schools.* Paper presented at the annual conference of the American Educational Research Association, New Orleans.

Robertson, P. J., & Briggs, K. L. (1994, April). *Managing change through school-based management.* Paper presented at the annual meeting of the American Educational Research Conference, New Orleans, LA.

Rollow, S. G., & Bryk, A. S. (1995). *Politics as a lever for organizational change.* Washington, DC: Office of Educational Research and Improvement.

Rulfs, S., Crocker, C., Wright, P., & Petrie, G. (2001). Principal leadership skills needed to transform the culture of a struggling school. In T. Kowalski & G. Perreault (Eds.), *21st century challenges for school administrators* (pp. 320–334). Lanham, MD: Scarecrow.

Rusch, E. (2005). Institutional barriers to organizational learning in schools systems: The power of silence.*Educational Administration Quarterly, 41*(1), 83–120.

Sarason, S. B. (1971). *The culture of the school and the problem of change* (2nd ed.). Boston: Allyn & Bacon.

Sarason, S. (1990). *The predictable failure of educational reform.* San Francisco: Jossey-Bass.

Sarason, S. (2004). *And what do you mean by learning?* Portsmouth, NH: Heinemann.

Scribner, J., Sawyer, R., Watson, S., & Meyers, V. (2007). Teacher teams and distributed leadership: A study of group discourses and collaboration. *Educational Administration Quarterly, 43*(1), 67–100.

Scribner, J. D., Aleman, E., & Maxcy, B. (2003). Emergence of the politics of education field: Making sense of the messy center. *Education Administration Quarterly, 39*(1), 10–40.

Sedlak, M. W., Wheller, C. W., Pullin, D. C., & Cusick, P. A. (1986). *Selling students short: Classroom bargains and academic reform in the American High School.* New York: Teachers College Press.

Shipps, D. (2003). Pulling together: Civic capacity and urban school reform. *American Educational Research Journal, 40*(4), 841–878.

Skrla, L., Reyes, P., & Scheurich, J. (2000). Sexism, silence, and solutions. Gaining access to the superintendency: Head hunting, gender, and color. *Educational Administration Quarterly, 36*(1), 44–75.

Skrla, L., Scott, J., & Benestante, J. (2001). Dangerous intersection: A meta-ethnographic study of gender, power, and politics in the public superintendency. In C. C. Brunner & L. Björk (Eds.), *The new superintendency* (pp. 115–131). Amsterdam: JAI Elsevier Science Ltd.

Slavin, R. E., Madden, N. A., Shaw, A. H., Mainzer, K. L., & Donnelly, M. C. (1993). In J. Murphy & P. Hallinger (Eds.), *Restructuring schooling: Learning from on-going efforts* (pp. 84–113). Newbury Park, CA: Corwin.

Smith, M. L., Miller-Kahn, L., Heinecke, W., & Jarvis, P. F. (2004). *Political spectacle and the fate of American schools.* New York: Routledge-Falmer.

Smith, W. E. (1995, April). *A case study of principal leadership: Dilemmas in implementing shared decision making.* Paper presented at the annual meeting of the American Educational Research Association, San Francisco.

Smylie, M. A., & Crowson, R. L. (1993, April). *Principal assessment under restructured governance.* Paper presented at the annual meeting of the American Educational Research Association, New Orleans, LA.

Smylie, M., Wenzel, S., & Fendt, C. (2003). The Chicago Annenberg Challenge: Lessons on leadership for school development. In J. Murphy & A. Datnow (Eds.), *Leadership lessons form school reforms* (pp. 135–158). Thousand Oakes, CA: Corwin.

Smylie, M. A., & Brownlee-Conyers, J. (1990). *Teacher leaders and their principals: Exploring new working relationships from a micropolitical perspective.* Paper presented at the annual meeting of the American Educational Research Association, Boston.

Somich, A. (2005). Teachers' personal and team empowerment and their relations to organizational outcomes: Contradictory or compatible construction. *American Educational Research Journal, 41*(2), 237–266.

Spillane, J. P., Diamond, J. B., Burch, P., Hallett, T., Jita, L., & Zutners, J. (2002). Managing in the middle: School leaders and enactment of accountability policy. *Educational Policy, 16*(5), 731–762.

Spring, J. (1997). *Political agendas for education: From the Christian Coalition to the Green Party.* Mahwah, NJ: Lawrence Erlbaum.

Spring, J. (1998). *Conflict of interests: The politics of American education* (3rd ed.). Boston: McGraw Hill.

Stokes, L. (2000, April). *Micropolitical realities as context for inquiry-based school reform.* Paper presented at the annual meeting of the American Educational Research Association, New Orleans.

Stronge, J. H., & Tucker, P. D. (1999). The politics of teacher evaluation: A case study of new system design and implementation. *Journal of Personnel Evaluation in Education, 13*(4), 339–359.

Townsend, R. G. (1990). Toward a broader micropolitics of schools. *Curriculum Inquiry, 20*(2), 205–224.

Waller, W. (1932). *The sociology of teaching*. New York: John Wiley.

Willower, D. J. (1991). Micropolitics and the sociology of school organizations. *Education and Urban Society, 23*, 442–454.

Winograd, K. (2002). The negotiative dimension of teaching: Teachers sharing power with the less powerful. *Teaching and Teacher Education, 18*(3), 343–362.

Wirt, F. M., & Kirst, M. W. (1992). *Schools in conflict: The politics of education* (3rd ed.). Berkeley, CA: McCutchan Publishing.

Woods, P. (1990). *Teacher skills and strategies*. London: Falmer Press.

Part II
Systemic Change

How Government, Professions and Citizens Combine to Drive Successful Educational Change

Michael Barber

For much of the twentieth century, the story of education systems in developed countries was one of expansion – universal elementary education, then universal secondary education, and finally major growth in post-secondary and higher education. Details of how this occured varied from country to country, but no one doubted its importance. Underlying economic and social imperatives drove it forward. Even unskilled work in developed industrial economies benefitted from universal education. As the century unfolded, the nature of work became more technically demanding and more specialised, resulting in a demand for higher standards of basic education and a capacity for individuals to specialise and keep on learning.

From the late 1970s onwards, the technological revolution and globalisation accelerated the demand for an educated workforce, and from the early 1990s, with the end of the Cold War, these forces intensified. The premium for an individual of a good education and for a country of a good education system became ever more apparent. Governments, from the 1980s onwards, began to demand more of public education. They were no longer interested just in quantity; they wanted quality. Where once they had asked about numbers of places, now they asked about results.

Furthermore, changes in the economy also limited the extent to which governments could go on raising taxes to provide public education systems. Increasingly governments wanted improved results without necessarily a commensurate increase in investment. In any case, these economic pressures coincided with social pressures. The growing evidence that achievement was strongly correlated with social class (in England, for example) or with race (in the US, for example) led to demands from many quarters for improved performance. Thus, by the end of the twentieth century, in ways that had not been true 50 years earlier, the social and economic drivers of educational change reinforced each other.

Public education systems struggled to respond to these pressures. They had, after all, not been established with change in mind; still less with any sharp focus on

M. Barber (✉)
Head of McKinsey & Company's Global Education Practice, SW1Y 4UH, London, UK
e-mail: michael_barber@mckinsey.com

A. Hargreaves et al. (eds.), *Second International Handbook of Educational Change,*
Springer International Handbooks of Education 23, DOI 10.1007/978-90-481-2660-6_15,
© Springer Science+Business Media B.V. 2010

results. When the then British prime minister James Callaghan made a speech about education in 1976, he felt obliged to explain himself because at the time it was an unusual thing to do. "There is nothing wrong," he said, "with non-educationalists, even a prime minister, talking about education now and again." His main point was clear:

> In today's world higher standards are demanded than were required yesterday and ....therefore we demand more from our schools than did our grandparents. (quoted in *The Learning Game*, pp. 33–34, Indigo, 1997)

In England, the need to understand educational change can be dated from that moment. In most of the developed world, it can be dated from around that time. Since then we have become much better informed than we were about the ingredients of successful educational change. The development of this knowledge began at the level of school.

In the 1980s, a series of major reports from outstanding academics, such as Rutter et al. (1979) and Mortimore (1988), gave us for the first time a clear definition of school effectiveness. The picture they painted then has been refined somewhat in the decades since but has not been substantially altered. Then, in the mid-1990s, the focus shifted from school effectiveness (what an effective school looks like) to school improvement (how to achieve effectiveness). Since then we have moved on again. Now research about whole education systems, not just individual schools, is reaching a similar point not least as a result of the development of well-founded international comparison. We are becoming much clearer about what effective systems look like. The current picture will surely be clarified and refined in decades to come, but the central question of educational change is this: What kind of reforms and what approaches to implementation will be most successful in enabling systems to *achieve* effectiveness? This debate is only just beginning, and there is much more to learn.

In this chapter, I will set out some admittedly early thinking on the question of system improvement based in part on the research, in part on debates of education reform in more than 20 countries around the world, and in part on my direct experience in England with both managing reform of the school system (from 1997 to 2001) and leading the prime minister's Delivery Unit (from 2001 to 2005) for Tony Blair, which provided the opportunity to learn about reform of other large public systems such as health and policing. The value here is that while some of the knowledge about improving education systems will, of course, come from within education research, much, I believe, will also come from examination of the reform of large public systems in general. What they have in common may well be more important than their differences. In this chapter, I will do the following:

- Describe the three paradigms of public service reform – "twenty-first-century solutions" – which I have put forward in previous and recent publications, relating them throughout to education reform and giving examples from around the world.

- Extend the argument by analyzing the relationship between government and professions, a central issue in all education reform and one that the three paradigms on their own do not sufficiently explain.
- Draw some conclusions both for government and for leaders of education systems.

The first two sections draw heavily on my pamphlet *Three Paradigms of Public Sector Reform* (Barber, 2007), while the third and fourth parts draw similarly on the postscript in my book *Instruction to Deliver* (Barber, 2008a). This essay is also a refinement of my chapter in *Change Wars* (Barber, 2008b). The aim is to arrive at a first sketch of a complete theory of educational change.

Twenty-First-Century Solutions

How do we go about ensuring that the public services, especially education, are good enough that increasing numbers of wealthy people still choose them, thus binding them to the system and thereby securing the support to generate enough revenue to ensure both steadily improving performance and increasing equity? Successful efforts to create effective education, health, policing, and social security systems suggest that there are three paradigms for reform in large-scale systems, that each is suitable in different circumstances, and that, regardless of which approach is selected, the government at the centre of the system has a crucial role to play. I should say at the outset, therefore, that full-scale privatization has not been included as an option. While it is theoretically feasible, no government of a developed country has applied it to education for the good reason that while it might in theory deliver efficiencies, it would be entirely inconsistent with equity.

Three Paradigms for Large-Scale Public Service

There are three paradigms for the reform of any large-scale public service: command and control, devolution and transparency, and quasi-markets. Figure 1 shows these three paradigms.

Command and Control

Command and control is often the first choice of governments that want urgently to enact change – and to be seen to be enacting it. As the phrase implies, it involves top–down management approaches and conveys at least an impression of government taking charge. If executed well, it can be highly effective. Good examples of this paradigm include the UK government's National Literacy Strategy from 1997 to 2001 and its approach to reducing health service waiting times from 2000 to 2005. It should be noted, however, that there is nothing worse than command and control incompetently implemented.

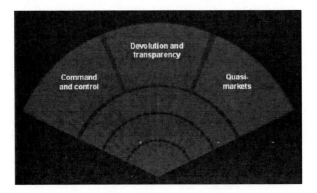

Fig. 1 Three choices for large-scale system reform

A refinement of this paradigm is also top–down, but it is built and designed much more explicitly in consultation and potentially in collaboration with other key stakeholders, such as teachers and local authorities. Perhaps, rather than top–down, it should be described as "government-led." A good example of this is the education reform in Ontario since 2003, where educators have been successfully led by the government to pursue the moral purpose of higher standards of literacy and numeracy.

The danger of this variation is that it becomes a soft, pragmatic compromise and can therefore be ineffective. In Ontario, the existence of clear targets, strong emphasis on capacity building, and the fact that the strategy was a reaction to a period of bitterness and conflict have all contributed to avoiding such an outcome. The question faced there is whether in the next phase the government can build effectively on the strong foundations already laid, because as performance improves, further improvements may depend on greater specification of teaching approaches – always a sensitive issue in relations between the teaching profession and the government.

Quasi-Markets

The second paradigm is quasi-markets. Given the stunning gains in productivity and customer services brought about in recent decades by the global market economy and the difficulty governments have had in delivering improved public services, the idea of applying market forces to public systems without full-scale privatization has obvious attractions. Quasi-markets make the introduction of elements of the private sector feasible by introducing options such as retaining public control of the commissioning of services but having private or voluntary-sector providers deliver them. Examples include many IT systems in governments around the world and the use of independent-sector providers of routine operations in the UK health-care system, and private providers of public schools in Philadelphia, which, recent evidence suggests, have been modestly successful.

However, applying marketlike pressures within a public service is not always straight forward. One must be able to define a clear customer, offer customer choice, bring in new providers, and ensure that the use of money reflects the choices made by the customer. Charter school programs in New York State and California and voucher programs in Milwaukee, Wisconsin, and Florida are examples of quasi-markets in action. Evidence of impact is so far mixed, however, and success seems to depend on the precise design of the program. For example, Swedish education reform, which has brought in new providers and offered much greater choice, appears to have had modest positive effects, while the radical restructuring of England's National Health Service along quasi-market lines is bringing increasing evidence of positive impact. Meanwhile, evidence from the Organisation for Economic Co-operation and Development (OECD) – Programme for International Student Assessment (PISA) international comparisons of education systems in the developed world are neutral on the benefits or otherwise of quasi-market reforms.

What of situations in which a government wishes to reform a service without resorting to command and control, but where the conditions for the success of quasi-markets are not present? For example, in the provision of prisons, courts, or policing, it is either not possible or not desirable to define a customer and offer choice from a range of providers. In relation to education, a government may seek a means of improvement, but for political, ideological, or indeed pragmatic reasons, it may reject market thinking.

Devolution and Transparency

In the third paradigm, devolution and transparency, the government can devolve responsibility to the frontline units delivering the relevant service and then use transparency – making public the results in a way that allows comparisons to be made – to drive performance. Units that succeed can be rewarded and potentially expanded; failing units can be made subject to interventions and ultimately shut down. To work, this model depends on genuine devolution of operational control along with accountability. The benefits have been limited at best in some US school districts where accountability has been devolved to principals without offering them commensurate operational flexibility. The New Zealand school reforms of the early 1990s, those in Victoria, Australia, under the Kennett government of the late 1990s, and those in England from 1988 onwards are examples of this philosophy being applied to public education systems.

The model can operate in a fully public system – the most famous example being the New York City Police Department, where the Compstat process generated competition between precinct commanders – or within a service in which a mix of public and private providers compete on equal terms. "Compstat" became the term used for generating weekly data on each crime type for each precinct and then using that data to hold precinct commanders to account for their performance. This can also be done by separating payer and provider and encouraging competition for contracts offered by the government or its agencies. This approach has been widely adopted with significant success in a variety of public services. Examples include the use of private prisons and the contracting out of local education services in the UK. It seems clear that this approach can only work if, in those cases where performance is very poor in specific schools or local systems in education, the government has both the will and means to intervene effectively. This is by no means straightforward, and many American states are struggling with this challenge as the impact of the No Child Left Behind legislation is increasingly felt.

Where fully applied, the devolution and transparency model has proved sufficiently beneficial that some informed commentators have suggested applying it fully to all government services (see Osborne & Hutchinson, 2004). Moreover, it has the advantage that it can be applied in combination with the quasi-market approach. For example, while the quasi-market approach has been put in place in some public school systems, it is important to acknowledge that it has limitations in this sector. In a true market, the customer may change providers regularly. But parents are naturally reluctant, for good reason, to change their child's school often. For this reason, market pressures on schools tend to be weak. If, however, as is the case in England, New Zealand, and Holland, devolution and transparency are also introduced, pressure for school improvement tends to be significantly strengthened. The evidence from OECD–PISA international comparisons, particularly its most recent report published in November 2007 (OECD, 2007), suggests that moves in favour of both devolution and transparency are generally associated with better performance – though of course much depends on the precise detail.

To some degree, these paradigms will be familiar to any government, and there is intense ideological and political debate about the merits of each. The truth is that each model is appropriate in different circumstances, and all may be deployed within a system, with the balance between them changing over time.

Changing Approaches for Changing Performance

In *Good to Great* (2001), Jim Collins explains the characteristics that distinguish great companies from good ones. More recently, in *Good to Great in the Social Sector* (2005), he explains that similar characteristics apply to all good organizations, regardless of whether they are in the business or social sector. Unfortunately, some organizations, including many of those that have historically been insulated from the pressures of the market, cannot yet call themselves "good." In the UK prime minister's Delivery Unit, we developed an extended, four-point scale designed to encompass the full range of performance for the various public services whose improvement was sought (Fig. 2). The scale also suggests what the consumer reaction is likely to be at each point on the scale.

This categorization is crude but useful. Generally speaking, when services are "awful" and users are exiting the system, command and control solutions are appropriate. This is certainly true in a crisis, but it also applies in circumstances of endemic underperformance. In such cases, the public, and even the workforce

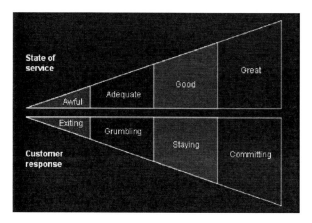

Fig. 2 A four-point scale for public services

within the service, will usually accept (albeit perhaps reluctantly) strong government intervention as long as it is effective. This is, after all, how the market handles bankrupt companies and how CEOs deal with underperforming companies. England's National Literacy and Numeracy Strategies, for example, were justified by the fact that elementary school literacy had barely improved in the 50 years leading up to the mid-1990s and the country's math standards lagged behind those in comparable countries.

Once adequate performance is established – which in itself is a huge task – the benefits of command and control are less clear. Governments find it hard to sustain the focus and drive on which command and control depends. Frontline leaders find themselves constrained by government regulation. Moreover, while shifting performance from "awful" to "adequate" is a substantial achievement, it does not satisfy the consumer, who continues to grumble until performance improves substantially. In the end, achieving "great" performance in the public sector requires unlocking the initiative, creativity, and motivation of leaders throughout the system, rather than just those at the top. This cannot be done without substantial devolution and/or providing the freedoms of a quasi-market. In short, as Joel Klein, Chancellor of the New York City School system, says, "You can mandate 'awful' to 'adequate,' but you cannot mandate 'greatness'; it must be unleashed" (Barber, 2008a, p. 337).

The Role of Government

Reforming a large public service is a sophisticated challenge. Whichever paradigm is chosen, it will work only if three underlying roles are performed by government (Fig. 3): capability, capacity, and culture; performance management; and strategic direction.

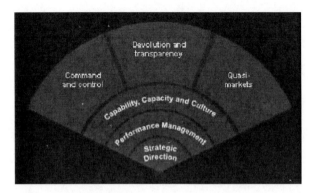

Fig. 3 Three necessary underpinnings for reform

The first requirement relates to the capability, capacity, and culture of the service in question. This means that the people who provide the service must have or must acquire the right skills, sufficient resources must be allocated to get the job done, and an appropriate performance mindset must be established among those providing the service. The precise nature of the required mindset will differ depending on the stage of reform. The final section of this chapter debates this issue in depth.

The second requirement is that the government secures rigorous performance management. None of the three paradigms can work without it. Performance management starts with information: data on performance are essential so that service providers can see how they are doing and can benchmark their performance against others. The public, the ultimate funder of the service, also needs to see the return it is getting on its investment. Neither parents nor patients can exercise choice without good information. And as governments move away from command and control, the capacity to intervene when part of a service is underperforming, remains crucial. Again, this cannot be done without reliable, up-to-date information on performance. This explains why currently the development of refined and high-quality data systems is high on the list of priorities for many education systems.

Third, because public-service reform is complex and only possible over several years, strategic direction is necessary. Developing a good strategy is a sophisticated challenge for a large business. In a political environment, with all its attendant pressures, this challenge is even more daunting. A small, well-qualified, courageous group – a kind of "guiding coalition" (Kotter, 1996) must oversee the sequencing and implementation of reform. The group that oversees the education reform in Ontario is a fine example. Given the controversy such reform often generates, only a sustained, well-thought-out strategy will work. Moreover, those responsible need to learn as they go because not all outcomes can be anticipated. This means designing by learning rapidly what is working, what is not working, and how the environment is changing. In short, what the literature calls adaptive leadership (see Heifetz, 1994) needs to be exercised by this group. The support for the strategy should build over time, both within the public service itself and among the public.

Building on this kind of thinking, the UK prime minister's Strategy Unit in its recent document on the next stage of public service reform (Cabinet Office, 2008) suggests there are four essential roles for government.

1. Leading change
2. Guaranteeing standards and fairness
3. Investing for the long term
4. Capacity building and connecting

Leading change, the document explains, is similar to the description above of setting strategic direction. Guaranteeing standards and fairness describes a role for government in which, even in a largely good or great system, it would be willing to intervene to secure a minimum acceptable standard of performance or to guarantee fairness among different interest groups or sectors of the population.

Investing for the long term is an argument for ensuring the funding is in place not just for the current year but also for the strategic period ahead. There is no doubt that an investment perspective is critical to enabling long-term strategic change and funding systems that depend on sources of income liable to wild fluctuations (e.g., property taxes) are likely to be less successful. Similarly, the process for the allocation of funding is also critical – transparency and steadiness help.

Finally, capability building and connecting builds on the points made above about capacity, capability, and culture and emphasises in addition the important role government can play in connecting across service boundaries or between education and business, for example. In a democracy, government has a legitimacy in making these connections that no other actor has. The more it is able to develop trust-based relationships with key stakeholders, the more likely it is to succeed. Its store of political capital at any given moment will also be a factor influencing its ability to succeed.

Government and the Teaching Profession

The most critical relationship of all for successful educational change is that between government and the teaching professions. For example, there was some frustration among many teachers in England in the 1990s and early 2000s as the education reform unfolded, though it has now diminished. Even now, much more could be achieved if the relationship between the teaching profession and government was one that – in the word of the 2008 Ontario Education White Paper – "energized" all those involved.

The state of affairs in England's education system in the late 1980s and early 1990s was unacceptable; performance fell short of both public expectations and the demands of the economy, so reform was necessary. There is no doubt government made mistakes along the way – governments always will. But despite mistakes, the education service significantly improved in England, not just for pupils but also for teachers and other staff because of, not in spite of, the government's efforts. Test scores are higher at primary level. Secondary school performance are also much improved. There are also far fewer pupils failing schools. Moreover, teachers are better supported, better trained, and better paid than ever before. No one faced with the facts can dispute this, but it does not solve the problem of the strained relationship between the teaching profession and government over that 20-year period; the question is whether we can learn from that experience – and parallel reform efforts elsewhere – to develop a conceptual framework for thinking about this relationship, which is at the heart of education reform.

Unless the relationship between teachers and government is soundly based, it is a problem for everyone. Such a strained relationship is a problem for government because the credibility with the public of a teacher will always be much higher than that of a minister or a civil servant and, more importantly, because well-motivated teachers will do a better job. It is a problem for the professionals themselves because if they are dissatisfied, their careers will be less rewarding than they might have been, and by suggesting to people that reform is not working, they undermine the long-term prospects of fully tax-funded services. Above all, it is a problem for citizens because even if it does not affect the quality of their services – which in some cases it might – they will often feel a sense of confusion about what is happening and where the services for which they pay their taxes are headed.

Part of the answer to this problem lies with globalisation and technology, which are transforming services of all kinds everywhere. Those who work in media and communications or financial services, for example, have seen their working lives and organizations transformed since the 1980s. This is true for many professions in the private sector – architects, accountants, and lawyers, for example – whose working methods have been changed utterly. Globalisation and technology influence services such as health, policing, and education, which are in the public sector, just as much as they shape those in the private sector. The difference is that in the public services, the changes that result are inevitably – precisely because the services are public – mediated through government. When governments urge educators to be "world class," they are giving voice to what the global market demands in other services. When doctors struggle with the impact of technology on medicine, they are facing what the market drives in other sectors. When police try to keep pace with organized crime, they are competing directly with an endlessly innovating – albeit in this case illegal and immoral – global business.

Charles Clarke, former education secretary of England, makes this case in his chapter in *Public Matters: The Renewal of the Public Realm* (2007). He argues that technological and scientific innovation, empowered and assertive consumers, and growing concern about professional standards have dramatically changed the rules of the game and contributed to a mutual lack of confidence between government and the professions.

So when public service professionals complain that government has driven too much change, often the drivers (hidden though they might be) are these wider forces. This does not excuse a government from coming up with too many initiatives or making mistakes, but it does help to explain why governments around the world generally want more change while simultaneously public service professionals complain about overload. Moreover, while it is true that there has been immense change in many education systems since the 1980s, it is not true that it is more than in many other sectors; indeed, it may overall have been less.

For example, one of the most glaring gaps between the public and business sectors is in the attitude to customers. Public service professionals still too often take customers for granted and expect them to be grateful; very few professionals in the business sector can afford to take this attitude. In another example, in relation to the widespread availability of information, many people are now able to be their own lawyer or doctor or teacher up to a point, thanks to the Internet. It is easy for the professional, once revered specifically for his or her expertise, to feel threatened or defensive in these circumstances – but in fact the existence of many better-informed citizens or customers is potentially a major gain. The challenge for teachers is to build unshakeable partnerships for performance with those they serve – that is, pupils and parents.

Consider performance data: Most teachers and head teachers I know hate published performance data, but this is the era of global media and freedom of information. University vice-chancellors do not like published data either, but *The Times* does, student websites do, and so do several outlets on a global basis. In Berlin recently, I saw that the front-page headline on the city's main paper related to a website which enabled schoolchildren to rank their teachers across the city. Comparative data will out. Moreover, citizens and customers demand data and will not give it up. The only question, therefore, for teachers is whether they would prefer government to organize and provide reliable, published comparative performance information – in which case there can be an ongoing dialogue with them about what is included and how it is presented – or a major media organization to do it instead – in which case there will be no such dialogue.

I emphasize this point because I believe that the two main drivers of teachers' frustration in England, as in theUS, since the 1980s have been the pressures of accountability and the pace of change, yet both of these are ultimately spurred on not just by government but also by globalisation and technology. When government makes mistakes or suffers "initiative-itis," it compounds the problem. Government hugely influences how these forces play out, so of course it bears huge responsibility. But unless this bigger picture is understood, we will never unravel the complexities of the relationship between government and professions.

The central issue, therefore, beyond the competence of government, is how to construct a more effective relationship between government and teachers – one in which they develop a deeper understanding not just of each other's views of the world but also of the profound forces that are reshaping everyone's world and the implications of these forces for education.

In the first broadly successful phase of Blair's education reform between 1997 and 2000, one of the government's mistakes in relation to the teaching profession was, in the words of John Kotter, "undercommunicating the vision by a factor of 10 (or 100 or even 1,000)" (Kotter, 1996, p. 4) To be sure, the government wrote what was widely recognized to be an ambitious white paper and promoted it. It consulted widely in its formation, too. It sent out pages of regulations and guidance on everything from the far-flung corners of school governance (unimportant) to the sequence of teaching phonics (vital). In what was widely seen as an innovation (remarkably), ministers and officials visited schools all the time. Alongside these efforts to communicate directly with the school workforce, government also ran a largely successful media strategy aimed, of course, at parents and taxpayers rather than teachers. The message here was that performance in the education system was not good enough, failure would be tackled vigorously, and poor schools would be closed. Parents and taxpayers heard and generally warmed to the message. The error was a simple and obvious one: Teachers read the newspapers like everyone else and heard the government's message to parents loud and clear; understandably they did not pay as much attention to the guidance and white papers so they did not necessarily understand the strategy or its moral purpose.

The government understood this challenge soon enough and began to respond. It reduced the paper going into schools dramatically, but obviously this did not convey the vision in the way Kotter suggests. It realized that in order to do this, it needed intermediaries. Government could not communicate directly with more than 400,000 teachers, so it focused on head teachers. For example, in September 2000, it took a road show around the country: five cities in 5 days, five hundred heads in each venue – like a band on tour. Ministers, leading officials, and successful head teachers explained the vision and the strategy and debated them vigorously with the very engaged participants. These events were a great step forward and valued greatly by those who attended, but what about Kotter's point? This was the boldest direct communication exercise ever attempted by the Department for Education in England up to that time, yet that week just 10% of head teachers in the country participated in the events.

The government needed the following: briefer, clearer, more memorable messages that resonated; to spend even more time than it did on the road; to integrate the media and direct communications approaches; to sustain the same messages for longer period; fewer distractions; constant, genuine interaction; and more intermediaries. The purpose, after all, was a better society – not, as many teachers understandably thought, hitting government targets. Others in addition to head teachers should have been effectively mobilized, such as local authority chief executives, chief education officers (now called Directors of Children's Services), and heads of university schools of education. Not all of these people would have agreed with the government by any means, but it would have greatly helped if they had understood.

I have spent some time discussing these communication efforts to make a more general point about the need to invest in much greater, deeper communication between professions and the government. Moreover, communication needs to be two way, interactive, and sustained. Much of policy in England from 1997 to 2000 was of the "shock therapy" variety. The government had set out to jolt a system from its comfort zone and deliver some results. It was largely successful, but could it have achieved what it did with a different approach, investing more deeply (and inevitably more slowly) in two-way communication early on? Or would it have lost momentum and found the cutting edges bevelled off its policies? There is no easy answer to these uncomfortable questions.

This takes us back to the idea of a guiding coalition. It is necessary to have a small group at the centre of a change who know what they want to do and how they plan to go about it, but over time this group must widen. This is why Michael Fullan and I talk about "ever-widening circles of leadership;" the guiding coalition can stay at the centre, but it needs consciously and constantly to build leadership capacity throughout the service for which it is responsible. In Ontario's education reform, this has been done well.

In the second Blair term, Estelle Morris began and then Charles Clarke and David Miliband completed a process of building a social partnership with teacher leaders. In return for active involvement in the policy process, the unions (all but one of them) agreed to greater flexibility in working practices. This inspired the foundation of something that could be much more radical; imagine a joint declaration that, for example, the teaching profession and government would strive to achieve world-class performance – defined and specified – with both accepting their share of responsibility for achieving it. This points the way to the next phase of my argument: What is needed is not just better communication, but a shared understanding of what is required to achieve world-class public services and a shared commitment, given the huge investment over the past decade in England (and still flowing, albeit more slowly, in the next decade), that this is what this country needs to see delivered. Making this happen will require courageous leadership – not just in government but also in the professions. Whether it will emerge remains to be seen, but given that the alternative, over a generation, could be frustration, conflict, disappointing performance, the flight from the public realm of those who can afford the private alternative, and thus a residual set of poor public services for poor people, it must be worth a try.

Moving Towards World-Class Education

In this final section, I want to set out a conceptual framework that might provide an underpinning for this long-term shared understanding between government and the professions. The basis of the framework is that the nature of reform and therefore the nature of the relationship between professions and government needs to change and adapt as services improve.

The starting point is the scale presented in Fig. 2. As discussed previously, this crude scale establishes four states: awful, adequate, good, and great. In terms of reform, it establishes three phases or transitions: (1) awful to adequate, (2) adequate to good, and (3) good to great.

My argument is that as systems pass through these three transitions, the nature of the relationship between government and the professions needs to adapt and the dialogue between them needs to develop accordingly.

To take a large education system through these three transitions is a major task by any standards. To take them all the way from "awful" to "great" is surely at least a decade's work. Any government, along with its allies in the professions, needs to be committed for the long haul. Indeed, given the vagaries of democracy, it is always possible that governments of differing parties will be involved, as in the 1990s in education reforms in England, Texas, and North Carolina. Given the long timelines, the key is for those leading the reforms to have two timetables in mind: one leading to short-term results, and the other leading ultimately to world-class performance. Both are essential; the former because without short-term results, neither those within the system nor those using it will have any confidence that progress is being made, and the latter because world class is the ultimate goal. Thus, in the awful-to-adequate phase, it is right to emphasize reducing outright failure and achieving a jump in the next year's test results, just as the management of a failing company must first stop leaking cash and then build some confidence among investors. The key, though, is to take these sometimes drastic actions in a way that does not undermine progress towards the long-term goal. For example, Michael Fullan and I emphasize in our conversations the importance of building the underlying capability and capacity of a workforce and a system through *every* policy (Barber, 2008a, p. 375).

Since 2003, the Government of Ontario has consciously modelled its strategy for improving literacy and numeracy in schools on our experience in England between 1997 and 2001, but it has also consciously varied the strategy, with greater emphasis on partnership, less prescription, fewer "distracters" (as they call them), and a language about capacity building and sustainability. They still have targets, but the government does not publish league tables (it leaves that to the newspapers), which means it can deflect this criticism. Interestingly, the results so far in Ontario are very similar to that in England – really substantial progress beginning to plateau, but so far not enough to hit an ambitious target. The test will be whether in the next phase they can avoid the long plateau seen in England. I believe they have a strong chance, partly because performance in Ontario was already better than in England when they began, so shock therapy was not judged necessary, and partly because leaders there have been careful to bear the long term in mind throughout the first phase. It will depend whether it can sustain partnership as the strategy becomes more precise and specific. Certainly, the dialogue throughout with the teacher unions, principals, and school boards has been focused on building partnership and appears to have developed and sustained a shared sense of moral purpose.

This is just one interesting contrast. On the basis of education reforms such as these in other countries and my own experience in England in health and policing as well as education, it is possible to set out a framework for the changing nature of the dialogue that moves the conversation on as the system goes through the transitions towards world class. The basic premise is that awful-to-adequate phase may involve shock therapy and therefore a top–down approach, but the further you move towards world class, the less a government's role is prescriptive, and the more it becomes enabling. Meanwhile, the professions need to move in the other direction to, at the world-class end, leading or driving the reform.

Table 1 How the relationship between government and professions could transform public service

Phase of development	Awful to Adequate	Adequate to Good	Good to Great
Chief focus of system	Tackling under-performance	Improvement	World-class performance
Role of Government	Prescribing	Regulating	Enabling
Role of profession	Implementing	Accommodating	Leading
Nature of relationship	Top-down and antagonistic	Negotiated and pragmatic	Principled and strategic
Time horizon	Immediate	Medium-term	Continuous
Chief outcomes	Reduced failure	Uneven improvement	Consistent quality
What citizens think	Reduced anxiety	Growing satisfaction	Active engagement

At the outset, though, we need some understanding of what it takes to be world class. In education, we have this knowledge from a series of international benchmarking studies. What marks out the best systems in the world is that they recruit great people into teaching and invest in their skills effectively both at the start of their careers and throughout them so that they teach lessons of consistently high quality.

This consistency is crucial, and it begins and ends in teachers' classrooms. In other words, it can only be brought about by frontline professionals who share the mission, benefit from excellent management, and are given the tools and incentives to deliver consistent high quality by an enabling government. With this background, then, the framework described in Table 1 can be developed as the starting point for dialogue.

At the very least, a framework such as this could provide a common language for the dialogue between government and the professions. That alone would be a major improvement on talking past each other, which has seemed so common in many countries. Two factors should enable it. The first is that even when a system is awful, there are plenty of head teachers and teachers who are doing an outstanding job. Right from the outset, government needs to foster a strong relationship with those in any service who are out in front. If these school leaders can express impatience with the slow pace of change, it helps to counterbalance the drag effect of those who want to slow things down. Indeed, this alliance with successful leaders is a key part of that process of building ever-widening circles of leadership, as previously mentioned. The second enabling factor is the vastly improved information

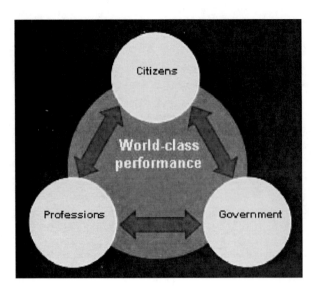

Fig. 4 World class performance

available about the performance of public services. These data – everything from the published performance data to the growing range of international benchmarks – provide (and in the future will provide even better) the evidence base on which to have this conversation. Charles Clarke, former secretary of state for education in England, argues that part of the new relationship would need to be long-term pay settlements, which are both more flexible and more explicit about professionals' responsibilities to develop their skills continuously, with government accepting responsibility for making this possible. The 3-year pay settlement for teachers in England announced in January 2008 may point the way. In Ontario, similarly, a long-term (4 year) pay deal was agreed upon in 2005 as a conscious step towards removing a "distracter."

New insights into this set of questions appear in a recent publication (Cabinet Office, 2008) from the prime minister's Strategy Unit in the UK, which establishes a conceptual framework for the next stage of reform of the public services in the UK, as illustrated in Fig. 4.

The document argues powerfully that whereas in the last decade the relationship between government and professions has been the chief focus of reform, in the next decade the relationship between citizens and professionals will become central.

To quote, *Excellence and Fairness* argues:

"We know that services need clear standards but that, following our first phase of reform, persisting with too may top-down targets can be counterproductive; we know services must value professionals if we are to foster innovation and excellence; we know that while central government must be a key player in driving better public services there are limits to what it can achieve and if it seeks to do too much it will stifle local initiative; and we know that vital though user choice is, it needs to be complemented with other approaches if we are really to empower citizens. So our established strategies now need to be accompanied by a new phase of reform:

- Developing new approaches to *empowering citizens* who use public services: both extending choice and complementing it with more direct forms of individual control, such as personal budgets in areas like care; opportunities for people to do more themselves, such as manage their own health; stronger local accountability, such as directly-elected police representatives; and providing greater transparency of performance.
- Fostering a *new professionalism* across the whole public service workforce, from the dinner lady to the head teacher, from the hospital porter to the consultant. This combines increased responsiveness to users, consistent quality in day-to-day practices and higher levels of autonomy from central government wherever those at the front line show the ambition and capacity to excel and greater investment in workforce skills.
- Providing strong *strategic leadership* from central government to ensure that direct intervention is more sharply concentrated on underperforming organisations, while the conditions are created for the majority to thrive more autonomously."

Whether this precise mix is appropriate for every country, the direction is likely to be similar across the developed world and will increase the need to establish a principled relationship between government and public service professionals. The demand for public services of real quality that are available to all is overwhelming; those who work in the public services would surely prefer to be more motivated and more successful (rather than less), while governments in the next decade will find they need to sign up to this vision too if they are to succeed in meeting bold aspirations. Without something along these lines, we are likely to see public education systems collectively – government and the school workforce – fail to implement reform successfully or to communicate to the users and to those who pay for the services where they are heading and how they are doing. As a consequence, a spiral of decline would set in. If government and the teaching profession aim their messages only at each other and appear to be at loggerheads, then the public will inevitably be both sceptical and confused.

If instead they combine in implementation and communication, they could be unstoppable. Easy to say, but very hard to do in practice, since this will require major culture change all round. It will require professions that embrace transparency, recognize the value of consistently high-quality and reliable processes, as well as personalization, and instead of saying "slow down," they would promote greater urgency. It will require governments to engage in constant, informed dialogue, stick to priorities, avoid gimmicks, and admit mistakes. Delivering sustained system improvement and consistent world-class performance will be an exacting challenge for whole systems. System leaders around the world are just beginning to understand what it will take.

References

Barber, M. (2007). *Three paradigms of public-sector reform*. London: McKinsey & Company.

Barber, M. (2008a). *Instruction to deliver: Tony Blair, the public services and the challenge of achieving target*. London: Politico.

Barber, M. (2008b). From system effectiveness to system improvements: Reform paradigms and relationships. In A. Hargreaves & M. Fullan (Eds.), *Change Wars* (pp. 71–96). Bloomington, IN: Solution Tree.

Clarke, C. (2007). Competition for social justice: Markets and contestability in public services. In P. Diamond (Ed.), *Public matters: The renewal of the public realm* (pp. XX–XX). London: Politico.

Collins, J. (2001). *Good to great and the social sectors: Why business thinking is not the answer.* New York: Collins.

Collins, J. (2005). *Good to great.* New York: Harper Business.

Heifetz, R. A. (1994). *Leadership without easy answers.* Cambridge, MA: Belknap.

Kotter, J. (1996). *Leading change.* Boston: Harvard Business School.

Mortimore, P., Sammons, P., Stoll, L., Lewis, D., & Ecoh, R. (1988). *School matters: The junior years.* London: Open Books.

OECD. (2007, December). PISA report. Paris: OECD.

Osborne, D., & Hutchinson, P. (2004). *The price of government: Getting the results we need in an age of permanent crisis.* New York: Basic Books.

PMSU/Cabinet Office. (2008). *Excellence and fairness.* London: Crown copyright.

Rutter M., Maughan, B., Mortimore, P., & Ouston, J. (1979). *Fifteen thousand hours.* London: Paul Chapman Publishing Ltd.

Educational Change and Demographic Change: Immigration and the Role of Educational Leadership

Pedro A. Noguera

Although the United States is a nation of immigrants, having been populated largely through waves of migration by people from nations and territories throughout the world (people of African and indigenous descent being the most notable exceptions to this pattern), immigration has historically been a source of controversy and conflict. Throughout American history, each wave of immigration has been greeted by hostility, discrimination, and, in some cases, fierce opposition from groups who arrived not long before. In each case, the right of new migrants to settle and reside in the United States has been challenged both on the basis of the perceived threat they posed to the economic security and well-being of those who came before and on the basis of their presumed cultural incompatibility with American social norms (Roediger, 1991). Ironically, even groups that today seem to be completely accepted and integrated within the social fabric of American society – Germans, Italians, Irish, and Jews – were once subjected to attacks and concerted opposition to their entry and settlement by others that charged they were unwanted and "unassimilable" (Brodkin, 1992; Takaki, 1989).

This chapter examines the factors influencing how schools are responding to the demographic changes that are being brought about as a result of immigration. It focuses upon what educational leaders can do to address some of the educational controversies that often accompany demographic change. It will show that while many of the controversies that schools find themselves confronting are framed around questions related to language acquisition (English immersion vs. bilingual education) and to a lesser degree tracking (due to the tendency to place English-language learners (ELLs) in non-college prep classes) and student achievement, concerns and unease related to the changing nature of the American population are often at the root of these conflicts. Current trends suggest that as immigrants settle in communities throughout the United States and begin to transform the social landscape of American society, controversies over what role schools should play

P.A. Noguera (✉)
New York University, New York, NY, USA
e-mail: pan6@nyu.edu

A. Hargreaves et al. (eds.), *Second International Handbook of Educational Change*, Springer International Handbooks of Education 23, DOI 10.1007/978-90-481-2660-6_16, © Springer Science+Business Media B.V. 2010

in integrating the children of immigrants and shaping the future of American society will become increasingly intense. Educational leaders who understand how to address the educational needs of immigrant students will be in a better position to respond to these controversies, and their leadership may prove to be extremely important to communities that are grappling with the changes that result from the arrival of new immigrants.

Many of the approaches described in this chapter for addressing the needs of immigrant students are entirely unaddressed by the predominant theories of educational change that are promulgated by mainstream educational researchers. In a departure from these technical approaches to leadership, the ideas presented here are part of a growing body of the theories-in-action literature which advocate an approach to narrowing of achievement gaps, examining achievement data, structuring literacy strategies, and employing various combinations of pressure and support to immigrant students in a manner that takes account of the dynamic nature of change in the social context that impacts schools and student learning (Bryk & Schnieder, 2003; Lipman, 2002; Noguera, 2004). Unlike educational theories that ignore ethnic, socio-economic, and linguistic differences among students, this chapter was written with the explicit purpose of providing concrete recommendations to educational leaders regarding what they can do to play a positive and supportive role in helping their schools and the larger society adjust to and capitalize on inevitable demographic change.

Understanding the New Immigration

Most demographers and economists predict that no matter how many guards are deployed at the southern border or how high the fences are erected, immigrants, both legal and undocumented, will continue to find ways to enter the United States.[1] As my colleague Marcelo Suarez-Orozco has put it, "[I]mmigration is not only our past, it is our destiny".[2] Since 1990, the United States has experienced the greatest influx of immigrants in its history (Suarez-Orozco & Suarez-Orozco, 2001), and once again, it finds itself embroiled in a bitter conflict over whether or not the new arrivals, particularly the undocumented, have a right to remain. Public schools find themselves at the center of the nation's controversy over the rights of immigrant children because unlike other institutions that can deny undocumented immigrants access to services, the Supreme Court has repeatedly ruled that public schools cannot (Fass, 2007; Rothstein, 1994). Historically, public schools in the United States have served as the primary institution responsible for integrating and assimilating waves of immigrant children (Fass, 1989; Olsen, 2000). Once again, they have been

---

[1] For an example of such a prediction, see Clark (1998).

[2] Marcelo and Carola Suarez-Orozco (2001) are some of the leading scholars on the education of immigrant children. For a discussion of how immigrant children are faring in the nation's public schools, see Kao and Tienda (1998) and Olsen (2000).

called upon to carry out this important task, particularly with respect to ensuring that immigrant children learn the English language. During the current period, schools must figure out how best to serve the needs of immigrant children within an increasingly hostile political climate. In such a context, educating a new generation of immigrant children has become a highly politicized project in many communities, and not surprisingly, many schools find themselves at a loss for how best to meet the educational needs of the immigrant children they serve.

Economic forces are largely responsible for driving the current influx of immigrants, and these forces work in two different directions. South of the border there is the ongoing reality of widespread poverty, gross inequity, unemployment, and underdevelopment in the Caribbean and Latin America, most especially Mexico, that serves as the primary *push* factor prompting migration. Liberalized trade policies such as NAFTA have in some cases contributed to economic hardships in the region and prompted large numbers of displaced farmers to migrate north.[3] Others have been prompted to leave their home countries by war, natural disasters, and political unrest. Even in nations like Mexico, Columbia, Peru, and Trinidad where economic growth has occurred, the inequitable distribution of resources and wealth has driven the poor to find ways to migrate to the United States in pursuit of economic opportunity. Undoubtedly, for as long as imbalances in wealth and living standards between rich and poor regions of the world remain unaddressed, it appears unlikely that current trends will reverse.[4]

On the other side of the immigration equation lie the *pull* factors that draw immigrants to the United States, and for that matter other wealthy nations. First and foremost are the insatiable demands of the US economy for cheap labor. Several sectors of the US economy including agriculture, construction, food processing, hotels and restaurants, and healthcare are highly dependent upon legal and undocumented immigrant labor. The unwillingness of the US Congress to adopt laws that would legalize the movement of labor across borders has not prevented foreign workers from finding ways to secure jobs in industries desperate for their services. It is for this reason that some of the strongest proponents of a more liberal immigration policy have come from business organizations in the private sector. In addition to the search for jobs, once immigrants settle in an area their presence creates its own dynamic. Family unification is another major factor prompting immigration, as is news of opportunity in a new land in communities of origin (Valdez, 1999). The settlement of immigrants is never a random process. When immigrants move into a community, it is almost always because they have followed a path, a network, or

---

[3]For a discussion of how liberal trade policies such as NAFTA have contributed to migration from Latin America to the United States, see "Immigrants Come Here Because Globalization Took Their Jobs Back There" by Jim Hightower in Lowdown, February 7, 2008.

[4]Imbalance in wealth and the lack of economic opportunity in other parts of the Third World are also responsible for migration to Europe as well as internal migration in nations such as China and Russia. See *Many Globalizations* by Peter Berger and Samuel Huntington (London: Oxford University Press, 2002).

a channel created by those who arrive first or the employers who have drawn them there.

The current backlash against immigrants ignores the push–pull factors that drive demographic change. Instead, it appears that much of the opposition to immigration is due to two other significant considerations: (1) the greatest number of immigrants coming to the United States today are non-white and do not speak English as their first language. Their presence is transforming the racial and ethnic makeup of several communities (Suarez-Orozco & Suarez-Orozco, 2008); and (2) in some sectors, immigrant labor is being used to displace US-born workers because they can be paid substantially less (Valenzuela, 1999). Television commentator Lou Dobbs has emerged as one of the leading spokespersons of the backlash against immigration, and though he and other opponents of immigration often claim that their hostility is directed at illegal immigration and not immigrants generally, they typically refuse to acknowledge that the hostility is increasingly directed at foreigners generally. In fact, many of the punitive laws adopted by local governments and much of the harassment and even overt violence carried out by vigilantes have been directed at Latinos.[5] In an act of remarkable hypocrisy, several prominent figures in both major political parties have attempted to curry favor among anti-immigration groups and have used rhetoric that has contributed to the attacks upon immigrants, even as they have also courted Latino voters. Similarly, no one within the federal government has publicly acknowledged the duplicity of the preoccupation with border security as it proceeds with the construction of a fence on the Mexican border while the longer Canadian border remains largely open and unobstructed.

Lurking in the background of the political debate over immigration is the growing awareness that by the year 2050 individuals regarded as "white" will no longer constitute the majority of US population.[6] While a small number of racist organizations openly express alarm over this impending transformation, most mainstream politicians and civic groups generally do not. Instead, leaders like US Congressman Tom Tancredo, former Massachusetts Governor Mitt Romney, and Lou Dobbs frame their opposition to illegal immigration as a matter of national security, as a concern that immigrants are taking jobs from American citizens, and as an alarm that American identity and the English language are threatened by immigrants who refuse to assimilate.

While some of those expressing such concerns may legitimately fear the changes brought about by immigration, it is also true that the new immigration has evoked a backlash because it differs from previous patterns in two important respects. First, prior to the Immigration Act of 1965, the majority of immigrants settling in the United States came from Europe, and while many European immigrants experienced

---

[5] For a discussion of some of the attacks against new immigrants, legal and undocumented, by local governments and vigilante groups such as the Minute Men, see Chavez (2008)

[6] For a discussion of demographic trends and the emerging non-white majority, see the *California Cauldron* by Clark (1998). I use the term "regarded as white" because these racial classifications are not universally accepted and are subject to change over time. For a discussion of race as a social and political category, see *Racial Formation in the United States* by Omi and Winant (1986).

hostility and discrimination, today, few question their claims to citizenship in the United States. Since 1965, the overwhelming majority of new immigrants have been from Latin America and Asia, and though many Asians and Latinos have resided in the United States for generations, it is not uncommon for their citizenship to be questioned. As historian Ron Takaki has said with reference to Asian Americans, many are treated as though they are "forever foreign" (Takaki, 1989) because of a pervasive assumption that a person of Asian origin cannot be an "American". A similar argument could be made regarding dark-skinned Latinos, who often experience a greater degree of discrimination and racial bias in schools and the workplace due to their phenotype (Fergus, 2004).

Additionally, whereas the settlement of new immigrants was once largely confined to the major cities on the east and west coasts, today immigrants are settling throughout the nation, in small towns, suburbs, and rural areas, wherever the demand for their labor is greatest. As they arrive in large numbers, immigrants invariably change the character of the communities, schools, churches, and workplaces where they reside. Even when they settle in communities where their labor is needed, in many cases their presence still generates conflict and tension with those who feel threatened or displaced by their presence. In many communities, older residents resent the changes that occur as immigrants who speak different languages and practice different customs transform the environment and local institutions. Even though there is considerable evidence that immigrants generally contribute more to local economies than they take and have been responsible for revitalizing a number of depressed cities and towns, many Americans still express opposition to allowing them to settle in this country.[7]

Though it is rarely discussed publicly, much of this backlash appears to be related to race, or more precisely to racism. Though there is ample evidence that a number of undocumented immigrants from Ireland and Canada reside in the United States, there have been no reports of immigration raids targeting these groups. Instead, in communities throughout the United States, Latinos have been the primary targets of political attacks against illegal immigration (Lovato, 2008). Documenting recent attacks against Mexican immigrants in Georgia and the complicity in these attacks by elected public officials, journalist Roberto Lovato writes,

> . . . the surge in Latino migration (the Southeast is home to the fastest-growing Latino population in the United States) is moving many of the institutions and actors responsible for enforcing Jim Crow to resurrect and reconfigure themselves in line with new demographics. Along with the almost daily arrests, raids and home invasions by federal, state and other authorities, newly resurgent civilian groups like the Ku Klux Klan, in addition to more than 144 new "nativist extremist" groups and 300 anti-immigrant organizations born in the past three years, mostly based in the south, are harassing immigrants as a way to grow their ranks. (2008, p. 33)

While much of the hostility toward immigrants has been manifest in white communities, there have also been sporadic acts of violence directed at immigrants in

---

[7]For a discussion of how immigrants contribute to local economies, see Portes and Rumbaut (2002) and Riech (1992).

several historically African American communities. Particularly in Los Angeles and other communities throughout southern California, there has been a significant increase in violence and tension between recent Latino immigrants and older Black residents.[8] Though both groups share a history of experiencing discrimination and racial injustice, in many communities they find themselves competing for jobs, services, political office, and control over the public schools.

Today, US immigration policy, or more precisely the question of how to control the borders and what to do about the estimated 12 million undocumented immigrants who now reside in the United States, has emerged as one of the most potent political issues of the 2008 electoral season. Against this backdrop, how public schools will be affected and respond to the changes brought about by immigration and the backlash to it will increasingly be a subject that educational leaders will not be able to avoid.

What Schools Can Do

Just as they have in the past with other immigrant groups, public schools will continue to serve as the primary institutions of socialization and support for immigrant children today (Katznelson & Weir, 1994). Given the growing hostility toward immigrants and their families (particularly the undocumented) and given the vast array of needs the poor immigrant children bring with them (i.e., they are more likely than other children to lack health insurance),[9] providing immigrant students with a quality education that prepares them adequately for life in this country will require an expansive vision and commitment to enacting policies and programs that support the education and well-being of immigrant youth. The following is a brief listing of some of the strategies schools can adopt to meet the needs of the immigrant students they serve:

(1) Provide Support as Students Acculturate
    Unlike their parents who arrived in the United States with their identities intact, immigrant youth often find themselves caught between two worlds, neither fully American nor fully part of the country of their parents (Jiobu, 1988). Many also arrive without having received formal education in their countries of origin. Such children are often not literate in their native language and, consequently, experience greater difficulty learning academic English (August & Shanahan, 2006; García, Wilksinson, & Ortiz, 1995). As they go through this

---

[8]For a discussion of the factors influencing racial conflict between African Americans and Latino immigrants in southern California, see "Beyond the Racial Divide: Perceptions of Minority Residents on Coalition Building in South Los Angeles" in TRPI Policy Brief, June 2007.

[9]For a discussion of the health challenges confronting immigrant children and their families, see Guendelman, Schauffler and Pearl (2001) and Capps, Fix, Ost, Reardon-Anderson and Passel (2004).

difficult acculturation process, immigrant youth are often susceptible to a variety of hardships and pressures that many adults, including their parents, do not fully understand. Some of these pressures include the following: a tendency to become alienated from adults and to be drawn toward gangs or groups involved with criminal activity, teen pregnancy, or dropping out of school altogether (Garcia, 2001; Zentella, 2002). Certainly, there are many immigrant youth that manage to avoid these pressures. In fact, in some schools, immigrant students are among the highest achievers, especially if they come to the United States as literates, with several years of education in the previous country, or from highly educated parents (August & Hakuta, 1997; Cummins, 1981; Kao & Tienda, 1998). However, for those whose parents are struggling financially and particularly for children of undocumented parents, the challenges they encounter both within and outside of school can be quite formidable.

Educators can respond to these challenges and mitigate the effects of hostility in the external environment in a variety of ways. For example, research has shown that one of the most effective means to counter the influence of gangs is to provide young people who may be susceptible to recruitment with a variety of extracurricular activities (that appeal to their interests to join) (Coltin, 1999). Additionally, scholars such as Ricardo Stanton Salazar (2001) and Angela Valenzuela (1999) have shown that when schools hire caring adults as teachers, counselors, and administrators – at least some of whom are from backgrounds that are similar to those of their students – they can have a positive effect on achievement, graduation, and college attendance. Such individuals can help in generating the kinds of social capital that middle-class students typically have access to by opening doors to internships, jobs, and various social services and by writing recommendations for admission to college (Bryk & Schneider, 2003).

(2) Address the Needs of Transnational Families

Immigration often compels families to make tough choices about who will leave and who will remain, and these choices often take a toll on families. When the decision to leave is made, some families are forced to separate and leave children or even a parent behind, often with the hope that with time, reunification will be possible. The development of transnational families, separated by borders and thousands of miles, often results in children experiencing disruptions in school attendance (Ada, 1988). To ensure that relationships are maintained, usually immigrant parents send a child to their country of origin for 6 weeks during the middle of the school year. For educators who are concerned with academic progress, such a choice might seem nonsensical and even negligent, but to a family that is coping with the hardships caused by separation, such choices may be the only way to maintain the bonds of family.

Migrant workers often return to Mexico for several weeks during the winter because there is no work available during the non-growing season. Although they generally return to their jobs, it is often the case that their children lose instruction and may even lose their seats in classrooms because of adjustments that are made during their absence. Those interested in supporting immigrant youth and their families must at the minimum demonstrate a capacity to understand the difficult choices transnational families face (Olsen, 2000). Finding ways to help reduce the strains caused by separation, while minimizing the losses in learning associated with extended absences, is an important pedagogical consideration for schools that serve large populations of Latino immigrant youth.

A growing number of schools have adopted strategies to support Latino youth who miss extended amounts of time because they are part of transnational families. For example, one elementary school in Los Angeles modified the academic year so that students could take off for 4 weeks at the end of December and beginning of January. An additional 2 weeks of school was added to the end of the year to make sure that students do not miss out on instruction (Gullatt & Lofton, 1996). A school in Texas located near the Mexican border established a cooperative relationship with a Mexican school across the border to ensure that its students received similar instruction in school while they are in Mexico. Finally, several schools in Miami and New York that serve immigrant youth, whose parents reside in the Caribbean, have hired social workers who are familiar with students' living arrangements and who can provide additional social and emotional support to youth in need (Ada, 1988). Such measures do not eliminate the difficulties experienced by immigrant youth who are separated from their families, but they do help to lessen the hardships they endure and demonstrate that the school is not interested in punishing students for a situation they cannot control. Employing staff with language and cultural skills to work effectively with immigrant youth and their families is also of vital importance, if trust and respect between home and school are to be established (Fix & Zimmermann, 2001; Valdez, 1999).

(3) Develop Full-Service Community Schools

Several schools that serve low-income immigrant students have adopted a community school approach to meeting student needs. The community school approach is an idea that can be traced back to the early writings of John Dewey. It is premised on the notion that the conditions for academic learning must include attention to the cognitive, emotional, social, physical, and moral development of children (Bronfenbrenner, 1979, 1988). The current movement of community schools began in the late 1980s when various organizations (e.g., Children's Aid Society, Communities In Schools, Beacon Schools) embarked on a reform strategy aimed at forming concrete relationships between schools and non-profit service organizations in school districts throughout the country. The initial rationale for these community school partnerships was based upon the recognition that the nutritional, mental health, and physical needs of low-income children are primary developmental issues that impact learning. In most cases, schools cannot respond to this broad array of needs without additional support (Dryfoos, Quinn, & Barkin, 2005). During the late 1980s and throughout the 1990s, the unmet social needs of poor children were exacerbated by changes in state and federal policies (e.g., Welfare to Work) that had the effect of compounding many of the difficulties facing poor children and their families and overwhelmed community and school-based resources (Hayes-Bautista, 2002). The combination of these trends has made it increasingly clear that high-poverty schools are in need of assistance.

A number of schools serving low-income immigrant children have adopted the community school approach, sometimes called the full-service school. Schools such as Edison Elementary in Portchester, New York, and Henshaw Middle School in Modesto, California, have shown that when immigrant children are provided with access social services schools can do a better job at meeting their academic needs (Hall, Yohalem, Tolman, & Wilson, 2003). Many community schools maintain a full-time licensed social worker, and for some community schools like the ones operated by the Children's Aid Society, mental health services or wellness centers are staffed by two to four social workers and a part-time psychologist. Community schools also enlist health professionals, such as dentists, optometrists, and nurse practitioners, which allows students to receive their annual physicals and prescriptions on the school site. Additionally, community schools provide an extensive after-school programs that include academic enrichment and recreation. Many community schools also attempt to extend their services to parents and families by providing adult education classes in the evening and weekends. All of these services occur in schools that typically operate 10–12 h per day and 6 or 7 days a week. While the overall number of community schools remains quite low, recognition of the need to address the developmental domains of children (i.e., cognitive, social, emotional, moral, and physical) in the social institution in which they are most influenced and spend majority of their developing years continues (Epstein et al., 2002). There is also evidence that addressing the social, emotional, and health needs of children can also have a positive impact on their academic performance (Coltin, 1999).

Creating a community school generally requires resourcefulness and creativity on the part of the staff and administration. Principals who are entrepreneurial generally take the lead in establishing partnerships with non-profits, local government agencies and community groups to meet the needs of the students and families they serve. Additionally, community schools focus on building a sense of community by engaging parents as partners and providing workshops to them on topics that meet their needs.

(4) Make Sure that English-Language Learners Are Not Prevented from Enrolling in College Preparatory Courses

In many schools that serve recent immigrant students, a student's inability to speak fluent English, or more precisely to display a command over academic literacy, is used as a justification for locating the student in courses designated for ELLs. While such placements are generally warranted to ensure that recent immigrant students learn English, in too many schools, ESL (English as a Second Language) and other language support courses serve as a means of tracking ELLs into courses that fail to prepare them for college. To make matters worse, in many cases such courses also fail to provide students with the ability to acquire proficiency in English even after several years of placement.

Tracking on the basis of language difference is one of the factors that has been cited by researchers as contributing to the high drop-out rates that are common among recent immigrant students (Orfield et al., 2005).

Educational leaders can ensure that students learning English are not denied the opportunity to enroll in rigorous college prep courses by providing the teachers in such courses with training on how to work with ELLs. Professional development in sheltered English is one strategy that schools have used to effectively address the needs of ELLs in mainstream courses (Ruiz de Valasco, Fix, & Clewell, 2001). More importantly, the schools that have demonstrated the greatest success in meeting the needs of ELLs make a deliberate effort to hire staff who can speak the language spoken by their students. Obviously, many schools are unable to make major changes in personnel in the short term and even those that are able to hire new faculty may have trouble recruiting bi-lingual teachers. Still, to the degree that educational leaders recognize the importance of providing all of their students with an education that prepares them for life beyond high school, they will find ways to ensure that their staff develops the capacity to meet the educational needs of the students they serve and will not allow their inability to speak English to be a permanent obstacle.

Immigration and America's Future

Like many immigrants today, earlier generations of European immigrants encountered hardships and discrimination. Despite the hostility they encountered, these groups gradually improved their social conditions and experienced the social mobility promised by the American Dream.

Schools played a major role in facilitating their social mobility by imparting the academic skills and the cultural competence needed to climb the economic ladder. Of course, social mobility often came with a price and some sacrifice. Many European immigrants found it necessary to abandon their native languages, to give up their cultures, and in many cases to "Anglocize" their names (Fass, 1989; Jiobu, 1988). For these groups, assimilation made social mobility possible, and over time, the early stigmas and hardships were gradually overcome (Glazer & Moynihan, 1963). Unlike many European countries where immigrants have never been fully accepted, in the United States groups that were once perceived as ethnically inferior were gradually accepted as full-fledged white Americans (Brodkin, 1999; Roediger, 1991).

The situation is very different for Latino immigrants and their children. Although Latinos represent the fastest growing segment of the US population and are now the largest minority group, it is not clear that the future will be as bright and promising for them as it was for European immigrants of the past. Globalization and de-industrialization have contributed to a worsening of circumstances for low-skilled Latino immigrants. Ironically, Latinos now constitute the ethnic group least likely to be unemployed, but most likely to be impoverished (Smith, 2002). This is occurring because Latinos are generally concentrated in the lowest paying jobs and many lack the skills and education needed to seek better paying alternatives (Smith, 2002). Unlike European immigrants whose offspring reaped the rewards from the sacrifices of earlier generations, Latino immigrants are not experiencing a similar degree of success (Portes & Rumbaut, 2002).

Despite having been present in the United States for centuries, Latinos are over-represented among the ranks of the poor and low-income groups, and at least part of the reason for this is the pervasiveness of racialized inequalities, particularly within education. Today, Latino youth are more likely than any other ethnic group to be enrolled in schools that are not only segregated by race, but by class as well (Orfield & Eaton, 1996). In cities such as New York, Los Angeles, and Chicago, where Latino youth comprise the majority of the school-age population, they are disproportionately assigned to schools that are over-crowded, under-funded, and woefully inadequate on matters related to educational quality (Garcia, 2001; Noguera, 2003, 2004; Oakes, 2002). Latino youth also have the highest high school dropout rates and lowest rates for college attendance (Garcia, 2001). In general, they are over-represented in most categories of crisis and failure (i.e., suspensions and expulsions, special education placements), while underrepresented in those of success (i.e., honors and gifted and talented classes) (Meier & Stewart, 1991).

Yet, in my work with schools, I often hear from administrators who speak favorably of the conduct of Latino immigrant students.[10] Though not all are described as studious, most are characterized as well behaved, courteous and deferential toward adults. Beyond focusing on their behavior, educators must make sure that Latino immigrant students are not over-represented in remedial classes and Special Education, nor trapped in ESL classes that bar them from courses that prepare students for college.

Like their parents, many immigrant youth have the drive, the work ethic and the persistence to take advantage of opportunities that come their way (Kao & Tienda, 1998). Of course, it is risky to generalize or to overstate the importance of will and work ethic. For immigrant youth who live in communities where economic and social opportunities are limited and who have no ability to control basic circumstances that shape the opportunities available to them – namely, the schools they attend, the neighborhoods where they live, or the hostility of others to their presence – will and determination may not suffice. In fact, research on the socialization of immigrant youth shows that in a reversal of past patterns, assimilation no longer serves as the pathway into mainstream American culture and middle-class status as it once did for European immigrants (Portes & Rumbaut, 2002). Instead, the evidence suggests that the socialization associated with acculturation and assimilation

---

[10] As a researcher and the Director of the Metro Center at NYU, I work with many schools throughout the United States. For a description of my research, see *City Schools and the American Dream* (NY: Teachers College Press, 2003).

often results in a lowering of the academic achievement and performance of Latino students (Suarez-Orozco & Suarez-Orozco, 2001).[11]

Theoretically at least, education should serve as means for immigrant children to escape poverty. For this to happen, education must serve as a source of opportunity and a pathway to a better life just as it has for other groups in the past. For this to happen, schools must not treat immigrant children as though their inability to speak fluent English is a sign of cognitive or cultural deficit. They must reach out to their parents and work with them, and they must find partners who can provide the resources and support their children need.

As was true in the past, the children of the new immigrants will eventually end up in America's public schools. How educators, parents and policy makers respond to their growing presence and the controversies that result will ultimately determine whether or not immigration will be a source of strength or lead to greater polarization and conflict in the years ahead.

References

Ada, A. F. (1988).The Pajaro Valley experience: Working with Spanish speaking parents to develop children's reading and writing skills through the use of children's literature. In T. Skutnabb-Kangas & J. Cummins (Eds.), *Minority education*. London: Multilingual Matters, Ltd.

August, D., & Hakuta, K. (1997). *Improving schooling for language-minority children: A research agenda*. Washington, DC: US Department of Education.

August, D., & Shanahan, T. (2006). *Developing literacy in second-language learners: Report of the national literacy panel on language-minority children and youth*. Mahaw, NJ: Lawrence Erlbaum Associates.

Brodkin, K. (1999) *How Jews became white folk*. New Brunswick, NJ: Rutgers University Press.

Bronfenbrenner, U. (1979). *The ecology of human development*. Cambridge, MA: Harvard University Press.

Bronfenbrenner, U. (1988). Forward. In R. Pence (Ed.), *Ecological research with children and families: Concepts to methodology* (pp. ix–xix). New York, NY: Teachers College Press.

Bryk, A., & Schneider, B. (2003). Trust in schools: A core resource for school reform. *Educational Leadership, 60*(6), 40–44.

Capps, R., Fix, M., Ost, J., Reardon-Anderson, J., & Passel, J. S. (2004). *The health and well-being of young children of immigrants*. Washington, DC: Urban Institute.

Chavez, L. (2008). *The Latino threat: Constructing immigrants, citizens and the nation*. Stanford: Stanford University Press.

Clark, W. (1998). *The California cauldron*. New York: The Guilford Press.

Coltin, L. (1999). Enriching children's out-of-school time. *Eric Clearinghouse on elementary and early childhood education,* Champaign, IL.

Cummins, J. (1981). Age on arrival and immigrant second language acquisition in Canada: A reassessment. *Applied Linguistics, 2,* 132–149.

Dryfoos, J., Quinn, J., & Barkin, C. (2005). *Community schools in action: Lessons from a decade of practice*. New York: Oxford University Press.

---

[11] In much of the sociological literature on immigration, it has been held that assimilation would lead to social mobility for immigrants. Second- and third-generation immigrants have generally fared better than new arrivals. For Latinos, available research suggests the opposite may be true.

Epstein, J. L., Sanders, M. G., Simon, B. S., Salinas, K. C., Joanshorn, N. R., & Van Voorhis, F. L. (2002). *School, family and community partnerships: Your handbook for action*(2nd ed.). Thousand Oaks: Corwin Press, Inc.

Fabienke, D. (2007) "Beyond the Racial Divide: Perceptions of Minority Residents on Coalition Building in South Los Angeles" in TRPI Policy Brief, June 2007.

Fass, P. (1989). *Outside in*. New York: Oxford University Press.

Fass, P. S. (2007). *Children of a new world: Society, culture, and globalization*. New York: New York University Press.

Fergus, E. (2004).*Skin color and identity formation: Perceptions of opportunity and academic orientation among Mexican and Puerto Rican Youth*. New York: Routledge.

Fix, M., & Zimmermann, W. (2001). All under one roof: Mixed-status families in an era of reform. *International Migration Review, 35*(2), 397–341.

Garcia, E. (2001). *Hispanic education in the United States*. New York: Roman and Littlefield.

García, S. B., Wilksinson, C. Y., & Ortiz, A. A. (1995). Enhancing achievement for language minority students: Classroom, school and family contexts. *Education and Urban Society, 27*(4), 441–462.

Glazer, N., & Moynihan, D. (1963). *Beyond the melting pot*. Cambridge, MA: MIT Press.

Guendelman, S., Schauffler, H. H., & Pearl, M. (2001). Unfriendly shores: How immigrant children fare in the US health system. *Health Affairs, 20*(1), 257–266.

Gullatt, D., & Lofton, B. (1996). The principal's role in promoting academic gain, *RIC Document Reproduction Service*.

Hall, G., Yohalem, N., Tolman, J., & Wilson, A. (2003). *How after school programs can most effectively promote positive youth development as a support to academic achievement: A report commissioned by the Boston after-school for all partnership*. Wellesley, MA: National Institute on Out-of-School Time.

Hayes-Bautista, D. (2002). The Latino health Research Agenda for the twenty-FIRST Century. In M. Suarez-Orozco & M. M. Paez (Eds.), *Latinos: Remaking America*. Berkeley, CA: University of California Press.

Jiobu, R. (1988). *Ethnicity and assimilation*. Albany, NY: State University Press.

Kao, G., & Tienda, M. (1998). Educational aspirations among minority youth. *American Journal of Education, 106*(3), 349–384.

Katznelson, I., & Weir, M. (1994). *Schooling for all*. Berkeley, CA: University of California Press.

Lipman, P. (1998). *Race, class and power in school restructuring*. Albany, NY:SUNY Press.

Lovato, R. (2008). Juan Crow in Georgia. *The Nation*, May 8.

Meier, K., & Stewart, J. (1991). *The politics of Hispanic education*. Albany, NY: State University Press.

Noguera, P. A. (2003). *City schools and the American dream*. New York: Teachers College Press.

Noguera, P. A. (2004). Social capital and the education of immigrant students: Categories and generalizations. *Sociology of Education, 77*(2), April.

Oakes, J. (2002). Adequate and equitable access to education's basic tools in a standards based educational system. *Teachers College Record*, special issue.

Olsen, L. (2000) *Made in America*. New York: New Press.

Omi, M., & Winant, H. (1986). *Racial formation in the United States*. New York: Routledge.

Orfield, G., & Boger, C. J. (2005). *Must the south turn back?* Chapel Hill: University of North Carolina Press.

Orfield, G., & Eaton, S. (1996). *Dismantling desegregation*. New York: New Press.

Portes, A., & Rumbaut, R. (2002).*Legacies: The story of the immigrant second generation*. Berkeley: University of California Press.

Riech, R. B. (1992). *The work of nations: Preparing ourselves for 21st century capitalism*. New York: First Vintage Books.

Roediger, D. (1991). *The wages of whiteness*. New York: Verso Press.

Rothstein, R. (1994). Immigration dilemmas. In N. Mills (Ed.), *Arguing immigration*. New York: Simon and Schuster.

Ruiz-de-Valasco, J., Fix, M., & Clewell, B. C. (2001). *Overlooked and underserved: Immigrant students in US secondary schools*. Washington, DC: The Urban Institute.

Smith, R. (2002). Gender, ethnicity, and race in school and work outcomes of second generation Mexican Americans. In M. Suarez-Orozco & M. M. Paez (Eds.), *Latinos: Remaking America*. Berkeley, CA: University of California Press.

Stanton Salazar, R. (2001). *Manufactruing hope and despair*. New york: Teachers College Press.

Suarez-Orozco, M., & Suarez-Orozco, C. (2001). *Children of immigration*. Cambridge, MA: Harvard University Press.

Suarez-Orozco, M., & Suarez-Orozco, C. (2008). *Learning a new land*. Cambridge, MA: Harvard University Press.

Takaki, R. (1989). *Strangers from a different shore*. New York: Penguin.

Valdez, G. (1999). *Con Respeto*. Stanford, CA: Stanford University Press.

Valenzuela, A. (1999). *Subtractive schooling*. Albany: SUNY Press.

Zentella, A. C. (2002). Latinos @ languages and identities. In M. Suarez-Orozco & M. M. Paez (Eds.), *Latinos: Remaking America*. Berkeley, CA: University of California Press.

Probing the Limits of Systemic Reform: The English Case

John Gray

In his remarkably prescient study, *The New Meaning of Educational Change*, Fullan and Stiegelbauer (1991) challenged policy-makers to pay more attention to the accumulated wisdom of research. "Armed with knowledge of the change process and a commitment to action," they argued, "we should accept nothing less than positive results on a massive scale – at both the individual and organisational levels" (p. 354). It was a call to arms which the New Labour government, under Prime Minister Tony Blair, was to take very seriously.

In this chapter I review some of the major developments which happened over the 10 years of the Blair administration from 1997 to 2007 and attempt to draw some broad conclusions. What were the key levers of educational change and what did they produce? Crucially, was the fabric and infrastructure of contemporary English schooling transformed in ways that have subsequently proved self-sustaining?

In calling for change, however, Fullan also counselled realism. There is a "huge negative legacy of failed reforms" littering the educational change literature. To rise above this legacy policy-makers would need more than "good intentions" and "powerful rhetoric." They would need not only to initiate reforms but to develop the capacity to learn from them.

The Commitment to a Third Way

Blair had made his election mantra "education, education, education." Consequently, many in the education professions assumed that when New Labour took office there would be a return to the values that had informed "old" Labour; although after some 17 years out of office, what precisely these values were beyond platitudes about equal opportunities and meeting the needs of the educationally disadvantaged had largely faded from memory.

J. Gray (✉)
University of Cambridge, Cambridge, UK
e-mail: jmg1004@cam.ac.uk

A. Hargreaves et al. (eds.), *Second International Handbook of Educational Change*, Springer International Handbooks of Education 23, DOI 10.1007/978-90-481-2660-6_17, © Springer Science+Business Media B.V. 2010

New Labour's strategic thinking has been described as the "Third Way". Anthony Giddens, widely credited as its intellectual architect, has argued that "investing in human capital" is a central "tenet" of Third Way thinking and that the "key force in human capital development obviously has to be education. It is the main public investment that can foster both economic efficiency and civil cohesion" (2000, p. 73). In short, he suggested, there were sound economic and social reasons for prioritising expenditure on education.

Giddens was dismissive of suggestions that Third Way thinking was less preoccupied with inequality than earlier Labour ideologies. It is concerned, he argued, "both with equality and pluralism, placing an emphasis on a dynamic model of egalitarianism . . . focusing primarily upon equality of opportunity but stressing that this also presumes economic redistribution" (2000, pp. 120–121). Inequality can be particularly addressed through strategies for tackling the needs of the long-term poor. "Enduring poverty," he concludes, "is usually coupled to exclusionary mechanisms and hence affects most aspects of life." Children from poor backgrounds get a raw deal in the womb and suffer "abuse and neglect" at home. These "disadvantages," he suggests, "carry on through their education or lack of it." "Schools in poor neighbourhoods are often under-funded (and) staffed by demoralised teachers, who have to concern themselves with keeping control in the classroom rather than with instruction" (op cit., p. 114).

The policies can almost be read off from the diagnosis – more funding for disadvantaged schools, greater attention to the sources of teacher morale, more focus on the sources of pupil disengagement which underpin unruly behaviour and, perhaps, more support for good teaching; in short, more investment in education. Interestingly, Giddens didn't have much to say about mechanisms for holding schools to account.

Whether there is anything distinctive here in Third Way thinking as regards the education of the socially and educationally disadvantaged is a moot point. There are strong echoes of the Plowden Committee's recommendations some 30 years earlier which lamented the fate of poor children caught up in "a seamless web of circumstances" in which one disadvantage was compounded by another (Plowden, 1967, para. 131). Although our understanding of what school improvement involves has moved on over the ensuing period, the underlying diagnosis is strikingly similar.

Where the Third Way has differed substantially from its predecessors has been in its thinking about *how* school improvement might best be pursued. In seeking to mobilise the forces for change New Labour has shown itself to be very flexible in interpreting the inheritance. More autonomy has been given to schools (where they have been prepared to take it) and public–private and public–voluntary partnerships have been fostered as a means of hastening reform. At the same time there has been some recasting of the lines of communication. In the process, central government has assumed more of the roles that, under earlier divisions of labour, had been reserved for local authorities.

Five Strategic Challenges

When New Labour assumed power it faced at least five strategic challenges in developing its reform programme.

First, *what organisational structures of schooling to maintain and promote.* The Conservatives had never completed the comprehensive reforms Labour had initiated. With a view to offering parents greater "choice and diversity", they had encouraged a range of different types of school to develop with a particularly prominent role for the grant-maintained sector. Should New Labour revisit its earlier agenda, accept the Conservative inheritance or take off in new directions? In the event, the commitments to "parental choice" and a diversity of school types were retained with the establishment of new Academies, eventually, extending the range.

Second, *how to improve individual schools, especially those serving socially and educationally disadvantaged populations.* There were considerable differences between schools in performance and some were getting left behind. How could stronger and more robust processes of school improvement be developed that were capable of creating "continuous improvement"? And what might they cost? Through an extensive system of target-setting individual schools were put under pressure to improve their performance. At the same time they received enhanced resources and other forms of support with a view to encouraging innovation and further development.

Third, *how far to intervene in the ways in which schools taught the National Curriculum through national initiatives.* The Conservatives had already started to pilot a National Literacy Strategy in primary schools. Should this kind of approach be extended to other core skills such as numeracy as well as to the secondary school? The decision to proceed was taken quickly; the Literacy Strategy went national, the National Numeracy Strategy started in 1999 and was followed by the Key Stage 3 (11–14) strategy in 2001. A major programme of additional funding for schools serving areas of social disadvantage was also launched under the Excellence in Cities initiative.

Fourth, *how to secure teachers' commitment to the reform agenda.* Teachers' pay had fallen behind that of other professions, some schools were experiencing severe recruitment and retention problems, and relationships between at least one of the unions (the largest – the National Union of Teachers) and the government had been fraught. In response a series of workforce reforms began to be implemented with the intention of raising teachers' pay and status and generally "modernising" the teaching profession.

And fifth, *how to use strategies for accountability to support the improvement process.* The Conservatives had claimed that league tables of schools' results and Ofsted inspections informed parental choice, held schools to account and encouraged them to improve their standards. Should these be maintained or modified? Again the decision was quickly reached to retain all of them, albeit with some modifications. Meanwhile a heavy programme of traditional school inspections was implemented until, in 2005, a so-called "self-evaluation" component was incorporated into a potentially lighter but conversely more frequent inspection regime.

Building on the Inheritance

In the event, New Labour's strategy for policy development was to build on much of the Conservative legacy that had emerged during the first half of the 1990s whilst selectively introducing new thinking. There was no radical break with the past. To the charge that such an approach simply represented a "middle way", Giddens has argued forcibly that "a concern for the centre should not be naively interpreted . . . as a forgoing of radicalism or the values of the left." "Many policies," he writes, "that can quite rightly be called radical transcend the left/right divide. They demand, and can be expected to get, cross-class support – policies in areas, for example, such as education, welfare reform, the economy, ecology and the control of crime" (2000, p. 44).

There were several respects however in which New Labour *sounded* distinctly different from its predecessors. First, and perhaps most importantly, it initially "talked tough". Borrowing from the language of crime reduction there was to be "zero tolerance for failure" and the pursuit of higher standards was to be "relentless". In an early move, shortly after assuming office, the secretary of state for education "named and shamed" ten of the worst-performing schools in the country, seemingly oblivious to the fact that a substantial part of the explanation for their apparent "failure" might lie in the socially blighted circumstances of the communities they served. Second, there was to be a much greater emphasis on results; the way to value and develop the outputs of education was to measure them. Third, there were arguments for more "joined up" thinking. And fourth, it began to talk up the case for the so-called "evidence-based" practice. In future educational policies would be researched and evaluated. In the course of these developments the rudiments of systemic thinking began to emerge.

The Court of Measurable Results

Evaluating educational reforms is a potentially complex business but, under New Labour, policy-makers have usually been quick to draw attention to improvements in measurable results. Over the course of the decade the percentages of primary school pupils achieving Level 4 in English (the "expected" national level of performance for an 11-year-old) climbed from 63% in 1997 to some 80% in 2007, an overall increase of 17% (see Table 1). Similarly with respect to maths the percentage rose from 62% to 77% over a decade.

These figures look impressive. However, when one tries to discern patterns and trends and offer explanations, the picture becomes more problematic. First, some

Table 1 Percentages of primary school pupils age 11 in England securing "expected level of performance" (Level 4) on headline measures at key stage 2 (1997–2007)

Description of the cohort of pupils passing through the system related government in office and to introduction of major policies	Key stage 1	Key stage 2	Level 4 English (%)	Level 4 Maths (%)	Level 4 Science (%)
Cohort affected mid-way by publication of primary schools' results	1993	1997	63	62	69
Cohort still experiences predominantly Conservative policies	1994	1998	65	59	69
Cohort affected mid-stream by New Labour's policies	1995	1999	71	69	78
Predominantly New Labour policies	1996	2000	75	72	85
First full New Labour cohort (the national literacy strategy cohort)	1997	2001	75	71	87
Second New Labour cohort (the first national numeracy strategy cohort)	1998	2002	75	73	86
Third New Labour cohort	1999	2003	75	73	87
Fourth New Labour cohort	2000	2004	77	74	86
Fifth New Labour cohort	2001	2005	79	75	86
Sixth New Labour cohort	2002	2006	79	76	87
Seventh New Labour cohort	2003	2007	80	77	88

comment about the timing of the changes is necessary. It takes a while for new policies to be rolled out and take effect. A new government's inheritance in its early years is inevitably dependent on the activities of its predecessors. New Labour was powerless to do anything about the 1997 results and it was not until 2001 that the national test results were picking up the full effects of any new policy developments.

Looked at from a statistical point of view, the trends in results seem to fall into three distinct phases. In the first phase, there was a 12% point increase in English over the period 1997–2000. In the second phase (2000–2003) the results plateaued with zero growth followed by a more modest phase in which over the next 4 years (2003–2007) results increased by a further 5%.

Looked at another way, however, more than half the growth over the decade occurred amongst just two cohorts (1994–1998 and 1995–1999). The fact that these improvements were sustained over subsequent years suggests that they were neither illusory nor ephemeral – if they had been one might have anticipated some backward steps or a rougher ride. But drawing conclusions about the effects of policy development is more problematic. What is most notable about this period is that it was one of transition – politically from Conservative to New Labour but, perhaps more importantly, from a situation in which the nature and rules of the game were rapidly changing as schools became more and more caught up in the newly emerging "performance culture" New Labour was developing.

Further support for this emphasis on the impact of the "transitional stages" of the reforms comes from the evidence on pupil performance in maths. Here no less than half the growth over the course of the decade came from a single cohort; the performance of the 1994–1998 cohort had dipped to 59% but the 1995–1999 cohort bounced back with an impressive increase to 69%. Over subsequent years, however, progress slowed down considerably; whilst the results continued to creep up, year on year, the overall gains were less impressive.

Rising Achievement in Secondary Schools

Much of the international attention has been focused on reforms at the primary level. Table 2 reports the results of pupil performance in the national GCSE examinations taken at age 16. These are nationally examined and taken in a wide range of different subjects; pupils are entered for them according to their aptitudes and interests. The results are subsequently captured in a headline figure which reports the proportions of pupils who secured grades A* to C in five or more subjects.

There has been a fairly inexorable trend in the percentages climbing over the 5+ A*–C hurdle since the previously separate examinations for more and less able

Table 2 Percentages of secondary school pupils achieving the traditional headline measure of "5 or more A*–C grades" in GCSE examinations at age 16

Description of the cohort of pupils passing through system related to government in office and to introduction of major policy initiatives	Year entered secondary school	Year took GCSE exams	Percentage of pupils achieving 5+A*–C grades	Percentage achieving 5+A*–C grades including English and Maths
Last cohort fully educated in secondary school under Conservative policies	1993	1997	45.1	35.6
Cohort experiences predominantly Conservative policies	1994	1998	46.3	37.0
Cohort affected mid-stream by New Labour's policies	1995	1999	47.9	38.6
Predominantly New Labour policies	1996	2000	49.2	40.0
First (full) New Labour cohort	1997	2001	50.0	40.7
Second New Labour cohort	1998	2002	51.6	42.1
Third New Labour cohort	1999	2003	52.9	41.9
Fourth New Labour cohort	2000	2004	53.7	42.6
Fifth New Labour cohort (experienced both secondary *and* primary strategies)	2001	2005	57.1	44.9
Sixth New Labour cohort	2002	2006	59.2	45.8
Seventh New Labour cohort	2003	2007	62.0	46.7

pupils were amalgamated into the national GCSE exam in 1988. The reasons for this increase are annually disputed when the results are published being variously attributed to declining standards on the part of the examiners, improved teaching methods, greater student commitment and so on. There has also been extensive use of what Gray et al. (1999) have described as "tactical" approaches.

The results for the decade under review are reported in Table 2. In 1997 some 45% got over the hurdle, by 2007 62% did so – in all a considerable increase. Nonetheless, the table again reinforces the view that educational policies are typically slow to unfold and take effect.

For most of New Labour's first term in office the table simply records the results of its predecessor's efforts. It is not until the turn of the millennium that the effects of the new regime can begin to be discerned. Over the period 1997–2000 the head-line statistic improved at a rate of about 1% a year; this continued the seemingly inexorable trend launched in 1988. From 2000 onwards it improved a little faster; the figures unfortunately do not satisfactorily take account of numerous minor (but in combination important) changes in the arrangements for counting up what could contribute to the indicator these gave a particular boost to the results in 2005. The changes included such things as counting in some vocational subjects which had previously been excluded and allowing some qualifications to count as more than one grade.

Concerns that schools were focusing on "easier" subjects in order to boost per-ceptions of their pupils' performance led to debates in the early 2000s about the need to include passes in maths and English in the basket of subjects to be counted in the headline measure (see last column of Table 2 above). Progress with respect to this indicator seems to have been steadier over the period. In 1997 performance lagged behind by some 10% points. Unfortunately, over the course of the decade, whilst the numbers reaching this hurdle rose by some 11% points, performance on this indicator fell still further behind. By 2007 the gap between the two had widened to some 15% points. Furthermore, the rate of improvement during the second half of the decade was only a little more rapid than that pertaining in the first half. On neither indicator did the step change in performance trends that had been anticipated actually emerge.

The Arena of International Comparisons

For most of the late twentieth century England was a sporadic and reluctant par-ticipant in studies based on international comparisons. It was largely content to evaluate itself in terms of its own national assessments. At the turn of the century, however, these predominantly isolationist attitudes began to change. They were rein-forced, no doubt, by the impressive performance of its 9-year-olds in the Progress in International Reading Literacy Study (PIRLS, 2001) which seemed to offer wel-come confirmation of the success of New Labour's reforms. England came third out of 35 countries, just behind the Netherlands and Sweden. But trumpeting success was possibly premature; in the 2006 survey the country slumped to 19th position

(Baer, Baldi, Ayotte, Green, & McGrath, 2007: Table 2). And whereas in 2001 the performance of English pupils stood out, by 2006, regardless of which measure was employed, they appeared merely average. It was possibly some consolation that performance in the Netherlands and Sweden also appeared to have declined, although not to the same extent.

There was some limited support for more optimistic interpretations of the performance of English pupils from the Trends in International Mathematics and Science Study (TIMMS) which studied 10-year-olds. The period 1995–1999 had seen little or no change in performance levels in primary schools but between 1999 and 2003 they leapt up (Ruddock et al., 2005).

The vagaries of such comparisons, however, are underlined by some of the results from the OECD's Programme for International Student Assessment (PISA). In science the United Kingdom's students (not just England) performed significantly above the OECD average (OECD, 2007: Table 2). In reading the United Kingdom appeared in the upper half of the table but its performance was not significantly different from the OECD average (OECD, 2007: Table 4). Performance, meanwhile, in maths in 2006 was also not significantly different from the OECD average (Table 5). Comparisons over time were restricted to just 3 years (the changes between 2003 and 2006) but the position was broadly unchanged. This could be seen as disappointing since the 2006 cohort will have been more exposed to both the primary and secondary strategies for raising performance.

The court of international comparisons provides fertile territory for those who are prepared to pick selectively over the evidence in support of their cases. The safest conclusion to be drawn, however, is that the international surveys do not as yet provide convincing evidence that England is performing at anything other than the sorts of levels one would expect a relatively well-developed and resourced educational system to produce – a good performance but not yet, perhaps, an outstanding one.

Systemic Thinking and the Search for Powerful Levers

In their study of systemic reform Goertz, Floden, and O'Day (1996) refer to the growth of so-called systemic approaches in the USA during the 1990s. Systemic reforms, they suggested, "embodied three integral components":

– "the promotion of ambitious student outcomes for all students;
– the alignment of policy approaches and the actions of various policy institutions to promote such outcomes; and
– the restructuring of the public education governance system to support improved achievement."

The terminology was a little slower to emerge in England than the USA but New Labour's intentions were clearly similar. At least two distinct phases of systemic thinking can be identified. During the first there was a determined edge to New Labour's policy-making. The vision came from outside schools themselves.

Accountability in the form of inspection loomed large as did national testing, targets and league tables. Neither was school "failure" to be tolerated. The drive for higher standards in literacy and numeracy, exemplified in the National Strategies, was to the fore.

Michael Fullan has always been clear that both "pressure" and "support" are needed if change programmes are to deliver. But he has also stressed that they are needed in *equal* measure. Broadly speaking, if the driving characteristic of the first phase had been pressure, by the early 2000s some of the rhetoric had mutated into what, retrospectively at least, can be characterised as a greater commitment to support. There was to be a New Relationship With Schools; accountability was to be more "intelligent"; there was to be a greater emphasis on supporting teaching and learning through more "personalised" approaches; and the quest for excellence was to be combined with the pursuit of enjoyment, if only at the primary stages. Importantly, some of the vision for change was to come from schools themselves. The role of school leadership was increasingly cast as one of building capacity. An arguably highly prescriptive and hard-edged vision had given way to a somewhat softer one.

To deliver systemic reform government needs access to a variety of levers on the processes of change. It is beyond the scope of a short review to enumerate the wide range of reforms New Labour initiated, let alone to evaluate them all. I have therefore deliberately confined myself to considering just four developments: the use of external inspection of schools, the National Strategies, the Specialist Schools programme and the Excellence in Cities (EiC) initiative.

These areas have been chosen for three main reasons: First, because they exemplify different facets of New Labour's reform agenda to improve standards – the development of accountability, the restructuring of the teaching of basic skills, the moulding of new forms of school organisation and the creation of enhanced support for disadvantaged schools; second, because their supporters have consistently maintained that they "worked"; and third, because each, in its different way, when scaled up to the national level, represents a very substantial investment whether it is judged in terms of the consumption of educational energy or of educational finance.

The Effects of Inspection

When New Labour came to power in 1997 Ofsted was still completing its first cycle of inspections. Its motto of "improvement through inspection" fitted the reform agenda and, to the dismay of many teachers and schools, its remit was expanded. In inspection government had discovered a powerful instrument for achieving compliance to its wishes. It could use inspection to shape institutions in its desired image and it was fairly ruthless in doing so. The key question for this analysis, however, is whether inspection pushes up *measured* results and, somewhat surprisingly, this has turned out to be a matter for debate. Most of the evidence on the effects of inspection was essentially anecdotal; it certainly seemed to confirm inspection "worked" but systematic research was in short supply.

Three independent studies have studied the effects of inspection. They differed in their samples, time scales and the sophistication of methods. The first study, by Cullingford and Daniels (1999), claimed that "Ofsted inspections have the opposite effect to that intended." They reported that inspected schools fell behind others. However, there were some doubts about the representativeness of their sample. A second, more sophisticated study by Shaw, Newton, Aitkin, and Darnell (2003) had similar difficulty in isolating an "inspection effect". They found that in comprehensive schools, which made up 90% of the schools in the study, "inspection did not improve exam achievement" although, in the small minority of schools where there was formal selection, there was "a slight improvement". A third study by Rosenthal (2004) reached similar conclusions. She found "adverse effects on the standards of exam performance achieved by schools in the year of inspection" and noted that "no offsetting later effects for inspection were discernible."

Eventually, some 12 years after its foundation, Ofsted replied to its critics (Matthews & Sammons, 2004). The results were finely balanced. The analysis spanned the period from 1993 to 2002. It found that in some years (5 out of the 9 years covered) "a higher proportion of inspected schools improved over a 2-year span than all schools" whilst in other years (4 out of the 9) the proportion was lower. A second analysis compared the results of schools that were inspected and not inspected 4 years later. Matthews and Sammons report that "the results indicated that, in general, there was little difference between those schools that were inspected and all schools." They concluded that their analyses "failed to show any consistent evidence that results spanning the inspection event over the last 8 years are either enhanced or depressed relative to other schools" (2004, p. 37).

These findings did not receive much publicity neither, for that matter, do they appear to have had much influence on Ofsted's hegemony. But the fact that the agency felt obliged to justify its contribution to schools' performance in such terms and that it reached such an ambivalent conclusion is of considerable relevance. Given the wide variety of states and circumstances of schools being inspected, it is probably unrealistic to expect some all-embracing "inspection effect". In many schools an inspection is unlikely to add much to what is already known although it may help to catalyse matters or even, in some instances, galvanise action. But whether it will actually do so depends on many factors beyond the inspectors' control.

The Impact of the National Strategies

The decision to go nationwide with the National Literacy Strategy (NLS) was made soon after New Labour took over and whilst the pilot was still underway. They had committed themselves to ambitious targets – in due course 80% of primary pupils would be expected to reach Level 4 compared with the 63% that were achieving this when they took over.

In the event the gamble paid off. The pilot showed significant improvements in children's test scores (Sainsbury, 1998). Nonetheless going to scale was expensive and brought problems. Many primary teachers felt they already understood how to teach reading and that they did not require further assistance; consequently there was some resistance. The National Numeracy Strategy (NNS), on the other hand, did not encounter the same problems. Teachers were generally less confident about their ability to handle maths and some of the "mistakes" made during the implementation of the NLS were avoided.

The team commissioned to evaluate the programmes were enthusiastic about what had been achieved in the early stages. "The Strategies," they reported, "have had an impressive degree of success, especially given the magnitude of the change envisaged; in many ways they have succeeded in transforming the nature of the country's primary schools" (Earl et al., 2003, pp. 127–128). Their observations, however, were mainly based on the ways in which classroom practice had been influenced. "It was more difficult," they felt, "to draw conclusions about the effects of the Strategies on pupil learning than on teaching practice."

Understanding the contribution of the National Strategies to enhancing pupil performance is problematic. Research on the implementation of educational reforms might lead one to expect that the reform dividends would emerge slowly over time – the major rewards would begin to flow when the changes were fully bedded down. The English experience, however, belies this expectation. The most remarkable thing about the NLS is, perhaps, that most of the changes took place during the *early* stages of its development; between 1997 and 2000 performance rose from 63 to 75% (see Table 1). Somewhat surprisingly, the first cohort to experience the strategy in its entirety did not improve on this position neither did the second. In fact, across four successive cohorts standards of performance stood still.

The NNS produced equally conflicting results. After initially promising developments, the pace of improvement slowed dramatically; again standards essentially plateaued across four cohorts (2000–2003) before resuming a slower upward trend. In science, meanwhile, results rose from 69% in 1997 to 88% in 2007. Yet this was an area in which there had been no National Strategy at all; teachers had been largely left to their own devices.

As with the GCSE results discussed earlier, possible changes in the performance metrics have made interpretations of trends over time more difficult. A detailed but little-publicised report for the Qualifications and Curriculum Authority, for example, concluded that, "around half of the apparent improvement in national results (between 1996 and 2000) may have arisen from more lenient test standards" (Massey, Green, Dexter, & Hamnett, 2002, p. 224).

Other researchers have also questioned the extent of improvement. Tymms (2004) sought support from the independent Statistics Commission (2005) for validation of his claims that the gains had been overstated. Their conclusion provided some support for both sides. "It has been established," they concluded, "that the improvement in Key Stage 2 test scores between 1995 and 2000 substantially over-states the improvement in standards in English primary schools over that period" but added that "there was nevertheless some rise in standards."

Renewing the Comprehensive School

The idea that there should be "diversity and choice" in the educational market place was already firmly established by the mid-1990s. New Labour launched the Specialist Schools programme as an important strategy for revamping the some-what jaded ideals of the comprehensive school. By 2005 some two-thirds had been given this status. Applicants were expected to raise some external sponsorship and to present a convincing case for being given specialist status in one (or possibly two) areas of the school curriculum. In exchange they were offered additional funding (up to 5% per pupil).

In their *5 Year Strategy* the DfES maintained that "specialist schools have improved faster than the average and add(ed) more value for pupils, regardless of their prior attainment" (DfES, 2005, 4: 15). A report by the Specialist School Trust claimed, furthermore, that "the longer that schools are specialist, the greater the specialist school dividend" (Jesson, Crossley, Taylor, & Ware, 2005).

Other researchers have been more skeptical about the extent of this premium. An early analysis by Schagen, Davies, Rudd, and Schagen (2002), for example, found very little edge in favour of specialist schools once differences in intakes were tightly controlled for. This general picture was confirmed in a later analysis by Levacic and Jenkins (2006). They reported, at best, a very small edge for the specialist sector.

Did this performance edge for the sector result from the schools' new status as *specialist* institutions, as the government claimed, or from other related factors? Schagen and colleagues have pointed out that early recruits to the programme had to demonstrate that they were already performing at "acceptable levels" in value-added terms. The Select Committee on Education and Skills (2005, para. 11) also drew attention to fact that the schools needed "school management and leadership compe-tencies" in place before they sought specialist status and that they got extra funding as a result. Might not better funding and superior management be responsible for the differences?

The suggestion that the specialist dividend flowed from schools' established characteristics rather than added to them was underlined, albeit indirectly, by Ofsted (2004, p. 3). They identified a range of pre-existing factors contributing to these schools' success including "working to declared targets, dynamic leadership by key players, a renewed sense of purpose, the willingness to be a pathfinder, targeted use of funding and being part of an optimistic network of like-minded schools." Doubts were also expressed about whether the requirement for private sponsorship biased take-up in the direction of schools which had historically commanded parental sup-port. And, related to this was the finding that schools with such strong 'parental support' tended to be located in more middle-class areas.

Spending More on the Educationally Disadvantaged

The EiC initiative, in various ways, embodied five key tenets of New Labour's policy discourse (Power, Whitty, Dickson, Gerwitz, & Halpin, 2003): First, that improved educational provision could combat social disadvantage; second, that good leaders could improve schools in any kind of context; third, that "joined-up problems require joined up solutions" through the development of multi-agency partnerships; fourth, that improvement is best secured by tying resources to outcomes; and fifth, that private sector involvement can help in securing change.

In seeking to tackle the causes of educational disadvantage New Labour faced one of its stiffest challenges. Furthermore, some of its early forays into this field had proved problematic. When Ofsted had looked at Education Action Zones it had provided a fairly cautious endorsement. "Some zones," they reported, "have made more consistent progress and had a greater impact than others" (Ofsted, 2001, para. 10). And, they added, "they have not often been test-beds for genuinely innovative action. More often, they have offered programmes which enhance or intensify existing action."

When the EiC programme was launched it represented the largest single investment ever made in tackling educational disadvantage. There were seven major strands. These included programmes to support "gifted and talented" children, the provision of learning mentors; the establishment of Learning Support Units for children with special needs and City Learning Centres to provide ICT resources for groups of schools and their communities; Action Zones which sought to link primary and secondary schools to address local priorities; and an expansion of the existing Specialist and Beacon school programmes.

Opinions varied about whether this menu of activities amounted to a coherent, "joined-up" strategy. When the programme came to be evaluated there were lots of outcomes, mostly worthwhile and predictable but none in themselves very dramatic. The evaluators commented that "most of the teachers and senior managers taking part . . . were very positive about the policy." They added tellingly that "although only a minority directly linked EiC with raiscd attainment, many noted the ways in which EiC was creating a better environment for learning, improving pupils' motivation and raising their aspirations and contributing to improved teaching and learning, all of which would lead in the longer term to improved levels of attainment" (Kendall et al., 2005, p. 16).

Regrettably, the desired improvements in measured results proved more elusive. Pupil attendance had improved amongst EiC schools, but only by "slightly more than 1 day per pupil." Some modest gains in pupil performance amongst 14-year-olds in maths received some publicity as did improvements in the proportions of pupils achieving the GCSE hurdles in some of the lowest-achieving schools. But the more the evaluators were able to compare like with like, the more modest the outcomes appeared to be. "Taken together," they concluded, "these findings do not support the hypothesis that pupils in EiC areas were, overall, making greater progress than those in non-EiC areas" (op. cit., 2005, p. 16). Given the social and educational importance of the EiC agenda, this conclusion was disappointing.

Changing Tack

In the early years of the Blair administration every problem seemed to generate a new solution. Policies of one kind or another flowed from the centre with impressive regularity. Some schools rose to the new challenges and exploited the opportunities but others, lacking a clear sense of their own identities, became embattled. On the surface there was a great deal of change but not all of it took root. The majority of schools committed themselves fairly wholeheartedly to the central agenda of raising measured attainment but even here the more successful found it difficult to keep going for long. Improvement was often rapid but soon tailed off. It was unusual for a school to boost pupils' attainment for more than 3 years at a time; only a minority managed it a second time over the course of a decade (Mangan, Gray, & Pugh, 2005). Not surprisingly, "sustainability" became the watchword and, to its credit, New Labour learnt from some of the bruises it had received in the battle for educational change.

As it entered its third term of office there were perceptible signs that some of the tougher messages had been absorbed. Crucially, there was a shift away from some of the grander schemes, driven from the centre, towards more localised and contextualised approaches in which, ostensibly, schools were to be given a greater say in how they would direct their energies. As Hopkins (2007, p. 171) has put it, schools need incentives rather than legislation and a greater sense of their own agency if they are to see themselves as test-beds for their own improvement. Central to this revised vision was the realisation that the strongest educational reform is built, both in practice and in theory, institution by institution. How this change of strategy will play out remains, at the time of writing, to be seen.

Fostering educational change is, by its nature, a highly risky enterprise. Governments that commit themselves to ambitious targets must expect, at times, to stumble. Some of New Labour's policies were successful, others less so; nearly all of them were ambitious but regrettably the returns were rarely as high as the expectations. The readers of this volume will not need much reminding that where changing schools is concerned there are few "easy wins".

References

Baer, J., Baldi, S., Ayotte, K., Green, P., & McGrath, D. (2007). *The reading literacy of US fourth-grade students in an international context: Results from the 2001 and 2006 progress in international reading literacy study (PIRLS)*. Washington DC: National Centre for Education Statistics, US Department of Education.

Cullingford, C., & Daniels, S. (1999). The effects of Ofsted inspections on school performance. In C. Cullingford (Ed.), *An inspector calls*. London: Kogan Page.

DfES (2005). *Five year strategy*. London: Department for Education and Skills.

Earl, L., Watson, N., Levin, B., Leithwood, K. et al. (2003). *Watching and learning 3: Final report of the external evaluation of England's national literacy and numeracy strategies*. Toronto: Ontario Institute for Studies in Education/DfES.

Fullan, M. & Stiegelbauer, S. (1991). *The new meaning of educational change*. London: Cassell Educational.

Giddens, A. (2000). *The third way and its critics*. Cambridge: Polity Press.

Goertz, M., Floden, R., & O'Day, J. (1996). *Systemic reform*. www.ed.gov/pubs/SER/SysReform/index.html.

Gray, J., Hopkins, D., Reynolds, D., Wilcox, B., Farrell, S., & Jesson, D. (1999). *Improving schools: Performance and potential*. Buckingham: Open University Press.

Hopkins, D. (2007). *Every school a great school: Realising the potential of system leadership*. Maidenhead: Open University Press.

Jesson, D., Crossley, D., Taylor, C., & Ware, C. (2005). *Educational outcomes and value added by specialist schools: 2004*. London: Specialist Schools Trust.

Kendall, L, O'Donnell, L., Golden, S., Ridley, K., Machin, S., Rutt, S., et al. (2005). *Excellence in cities: The national evaluation of a policy to raise standards in urban schools 2000–2003: Report summary*. London Department for Education and Skills, Research Report 675B.

Levacic, R., & Jenkins, A. (2006). Evaluating the effectiveness of specialist schools in England. *School Effectiveness and School Improvement, 17*(3), 229–254.

Mangan, J., Gray, J., & Pugh, G. (2005). Changes in examination performance in English secondary schools over the course of a decade: searching for patterns and trends over time. *School Effectiveness and School Improvement, 16*(1), 29–50.

Massey, A., Green, S., Dexter, T., & Hamnett, L. (2002). *Comparability of national tests over time: KS1, KS2 and KS3 standards between 1996 and 2001*, Report to the QCA. Cambridge: University of Cambridge Local Examinations Syndicate.

Matthews, P., & Sammons, P. (2004). *Improvement through inspection: An evaluation of the impact of Ofsted's work*. London: Office for Standards in Education.

OECD. (2007). *The programme for international student assessment (PISA) 2006: Science competencies for tomorrow's world (executive summary)*. Paris: Organisation for Economic Co-operation and Development.

Ofsted. (2001). *Education action zones: Commentary on first zone inspections – February 2001*. London: Ofsted.

Ofsted. (2004). *Specialist schools: A second evaluation*. London: Ofsted.

Plowden Committee. (1967). *Children and their primary schools*. London: HMSO (Advisory Council for Education).

Power, S., Whitty, G., Dickson, M., Gerwitz, S., & Halpin, D. (2003). *Paving a 'Third Way'? A policy trajectory analysis of education action zones*. Final Report to the ESRC. London: Institute of Education.

Rosenthal, L. (2004). Do school inspections improve school quality? Ofsted inspections and school examination results in the UK. *Economics of Education Review, 23*(1), 143–151.

Ruddock, G., Sturman, L., Schagen, I., Styles, B., Gnaldi, M., & Vappula, H. (2005). *Where England stands in the trends in international mathematics and science study (TIMMS) 2003: National Report for England,* Slough: NFER.

Sainsbury, M. (1998). *Evaluation of the national literacy project: Summary report*. Slough: NFER.

Schagen, S., Davies, D., Rudd, P., & Schagen, I. (2002). *The impact of specialist and faith schools on performance*. Slough: NFER.

Select Committee on Education and Skills. (2005). *Fifth report*, United Kingdom Parliament, (www.publications.parliament.uk./pa/cm200405/cmselect/cmeduski/86/8605.htm)

Shaw, I., Newton, D., Aitkin, M., & Darnell, R. (2003). Do Ofsted inspections of secondary schools make a difference to GCSE results? *British Educational Research Journal, 29*(1), 62–75.

Statistics Commission. (2005). *Measuring standards in English primary schools: Report by the statistics commission on an article by Peter Tymms*. London: Statistics Commission.

Tymms, P. (2004). Are standards rising in English primary schools? *British Educational Research Journal, 30*(4), 477–494.

How to Change 5,000 Schools

Ben Levin

This chapter describes the large-scale education improvement strategy implemented in the province of Ontario, Canada, from 2004 until the present, as a case of capacity building in education. While many education reforms around the world have focused on issues of structure and governance, the Ontario strategy aimed to make a difference for students by changing school and classroom practices across the province while also generating public support and engaging teachers and other education staff in a positive way. Capacity building does not happen in a vacuum, so the chapter places the case in the larger framework of vision, political leadership, and respectful dialogue that have also been central to Ontario's ability to improve student outcomes substantially while maintaining public confidence and stability in the education sector.

The Ontario strategy has focused on changing the experience of students. As Levin and Fullan (2008) put it:

> The central lesson of large scale educational change that is now evident is the following: Large-scale, sustained improvement in student outcomes requires a sustained effort to change school and classroom practices, not just structures such as governance and accountability. The heart of improvement lies in changing teaching and learning practices in thousands and thousands of classrooms, and this requires focused and sustained effort by all parts of the education system and its partners.

As Elmore (2004), Fullan (2007), and others have pointed out, there is no way to change classroom practices across an entire system without significant investment and work to improve the skills of teachers and principals as well as the support they receive from the wider system. This is what is meant by capacity building, and it takes a sustained effort well beyond what occurs in most education reforms.

Ontario's change process focused on a small number of key goals while still paying attention to a broad range of student outcomes. The overall approach has been respectful of professional knowledge and practice. Change strategies are

B. Levin (✉)
OISE/University of Toronto, Toronto, ON, Canada
e-mail: ben.levin@utoronto.ca

A. Hargreaves et al. (eds.), *Second International Handbook of Educational Change*,
Springer International Handbooks of Education 23, DOI 10.1007/978-90-481-2660-6_18,
© Springer Science+Business Media B.V. 2010

comprehensive with an emphasis not only on professional capacity building and strong leadership, but also on targeted resources and effective engagement of parents and the broader community. A substantial effort has been made to make main elements of change coherent and aligned at the provincial, district, and school level. Key partners – the provincial Ministry of Education; school boards; schools; and provincial and local organizations of teachers, principals, and other partners – work together even though they do not agree on every aspect of the changes. Of course the process has had its struggles and imperfections, described later. Readers should be aware that the author was a principal actor in these events, as deputy minister (chief civil servant) responsible for education and therefore for these policies from late in 2004 until early in 2007.

Context: The Ontario Education System

Ontario has about 2 million children in its publicly funded education system, which is organized into four sets of locally elected school boards with overlapping boundaries, reflecting Canada's constitutional requirement for public support of minority language and Catholic schools. Thirty-one English public school boards serve about 1.3 million students; 29 English Catholic boards serve about 560,000 students; 8 French Catholic boards have some 60,000 students; and 4 French public boards have 13,000 students. School boards range in size from a few hundred students to about 250,000 students in the Toronto District School Board – one of the largest in North America. In total there are nearly 5,000 schools extending across a huge geographic area – Ontario is 415,000 square miles, or about the size of the combined states of North and South Carolina, Tennessee, Mississippi, Alabama, Florida, Georgia, and Louisiana, or somewhat larger than France, Germany, Denmark, Belgium, and the Netherlands put together.

The population is about 80% urban with most people living in the very south of the province. The six largest school districts have about a third of all the students in the province. However many Ontario schools are small, with the average elementary school enrolling about 350 students and the average secondary school having fewer than 1,000. Ontario also has a very diverse enrolment, with 27% of the population born outside of Canada (1/3 of whom have arrived in the last 10 years), and 20% visible minorities. The Greater Toronto Area, which has nearly 40% of the province's population, is one of the most diverse urban areas in the world and receives more than 125,000 new immigrants each year.

The provincial government provides 100% of the funding to school boards using a formula that is always controversial but attempts to allocate money on a combination of per pupil or school amounts and elements that recognize differing needs across the province (Levin & Naylor, in press).

Ontario's 120,000 teachers are organized in four unions that roughly correspond to the four school systems. Most of the 70,000 support staff – caretakers, secretaries, maintenance staff, education assistants, and professional support workers such as social workers – are also unionized. School principals and superintendents must have specific Ontario qualifications. These, as well as teacher qualifications, are controlled under law by the Ontario College of Teachers, which is governed by its own council elected primarily by teachers.

Education in Ontario has all the challenges one might anticipate – large urban areas and very remote rural areas; significant urban and rural poverty levels; high levels of population diversity and many English as a Second Language (ESL) students; areas with sharply dropping enrolment and others with rapid growth.

Prior to 2004, Ontario education had experienced a decade of problems (Gidney, 1999). Two successive governments introduced measures that deeply offended teachers, including reductions in staffing levels and increased workloads. These led to substantial labor disruption including many strikes and sustained "work to rule" campaigns as well as lower morale and higher teacher turnover. In 1997 the governance system was changed dramatically, including a reduction in the number of local school districts from about 140 to 70, removal of all taxation powers from local districts coupled with 100% provincial financing, and removal of school principals from the teacher unions. Funding was cut significantly in the mid-1990s, leading to the reduction or elimination of many programs and services, often with the worst consequences for the most vulnerable students, such as recent immigrants. An entirely new and supposedly more rigorous curriculum was introduced in every grade and subject. A provincial testing agency was created and provincial testing of all students began.

Many other changes were also introduced including compulsory pencil-and-paper tests for new teachers, compulsory professional development requirements for all teachers, and a more intensive program of teacher evaluation. Perhaps most importantly, the government was vigorously critical of schools and teachers in public, including at one point broadcasting television ads that portrayed teachers as overpaid and underworked. Years of this environment led to significant public dissatisfaction, increasing private school enrolment, and poor morale among teachers. In short, nobody was happy with the state of public education (Hargreaves, 2003; Leithwood, Fullan, & Watson, 2003).

In October 2003, the Liberal opposition won the provincial election with the renewal of public education as one of its highest priorities and an ambitious set of policy commitments around improving education. Their platform was developed through intensive discussion with many stakeholder groups and through analysis of efforts in other jurisdictions. Michael Fullan also played an important role in advising the Liberals as they developed their plans.

A premier and ministers (Ontario follows the British parliamentary system in which ministers responsible for a portfolio are appointed by the premier from among those elected to the Legislature) with a deep commitment to public education brought strong political leadership. The importance of strong and effective political leadership is underestimated in the literature on education reform.

The Strategy

The new Ontario government understood clearly that public education can only thrive if citizens have confidence in the public school system so that they are willing to send their children and provide their tax support. The crafting of the platform reflected the political reality that to generate public attention, policy goals have to be few in number and relatively simple in expression (Levin, 2005).

One major commitment was to reduce class sizes in primary grades to a maximum of 20 students. Two other key promises were made around student achievement: to improve elementary school literacy and numeracy outcomes and to reduce high school dropout rates. These priorities reflected public concern about student performance in the province (Livingstone & Hart, 2005). Elementary literacy and numeracy skills as measured by curriculum-linked provincial tests had been roughly static over the previous several years (EQAO, 2006), while high school graduation rates had actually decreased following major changes to the high school program and curriculum in the late 1990s (King, Warren, Boyer, & Chin, 2005).

The three core priorities were complemented by a range of other commitments. Some of these, such as strengthening school leadership or changing curricula, were necessary to achieve the two key goals. Other initiatives, including unprecedented provincial involvement in 2005 in the negotiation of 4-year collective agreements with all Ontario's teachers, were essential so that all parties could focus on improving student outcomes instead of being consumed by labor issues. Still other initiatives, such as strategies to support safe and healthy schools, were necessary to sustain public support for improved outcomes by letting people know that the basic needs of students were also being attended to. Even where there is a strong focus on a small number of key goals, ancillary and potentially distracting issues still require attention. Indeed, the literature on school change gives insufficient attention to the challenge of focusing on teaching and learning while still managing a complex and diverse set of other issues in a volatile and highly political environment (Levin, 2005; Levin & Fullan, 2008).

Elementary School Literacy and Numeracy

Ontario's Literacy and Numeracy Strategy is aimed at improving literacy and numeracy skills for elementary school students. The government set a goal, as part of their election platform, of having at least 75% of grade 6 students able to read, write, and do mathematics at the expected level for grade 6 by the spring of 2008 – a 4-year time frame.

The Strategy assumes that improving student learning requires significant and sustainable change in teaching and learning practices in all of Ontario's 4,000 elementary schools (Literacy and Numeracy Secretariat, 2007). To achieve this, a multielement strategy was put in place. Main elements of the strategy include:

- creating the position of chief student achievement officer, filled by an outstanding Ontario educator, to bring constant attention to student achievement issues;
- creating a dedicated Literacy and Numeracy Secretariat to implement active and extensive capacity building around literacy and numeracy through a variety of means described below;
- adding some 5,000 new teaching positions over 4 years to reduce class sizes from junior kindergarten (age 4) to grade 3 to a maximum of 20 students in at least 90% of classrooms while also providing support to teachers to adopt instructional practices to take advantage of these smaller classes;
- adding about 2,000 specialist teachers to enrich teaching in areas such as art, music, and physical education while also providing more preparation and professional learning time for classroom teachers;
- implementing a voluntary "turnaround" program that provides additional support and expert advice for schools facing the most significant challenges in improving achievement; and
- supporting ancillary practices such as an expansion of tutoring (often by students in faculties of education) and a fuller engagement of parents and communities.

As a further measure, the provincial tests in grades 3 and 6 language and mathematics, which are closely linked to the Ontario curriculum, were changed in 2005 to take less time and give quicker results to schools. Although many teachers continue to have concerns about provincial testing, this is now a rather minor issue in Ontario education because of the increased support for improved teaching and learning including for using a range of student achievement data to support school improvement.

The test results are the main indicator of the success of the government's plan, but they have not been treated as the only significant measure of progress. Ontario has adopted a broader strategy for public accountability, in which the province and school districts report publicly on a variety of indicators of student progress. For example, the Ministry issues an annual report that provides information about all 72 school districts on 8 key indicators (http://www.edu.gov.on.ca/eng/bpr/). All of this is intended to foster and support public confidence in the quality of public education.

Increasing High School Graduation Rates

As of 2003–2004 only about 60% of Ontario students were graduating from high school in the normal 4 years, and only about 70% were graduating even after taking an extra year (King et al., 2005). These are clearly unacceptable levels in a knowledge society and are well below those of other Canadian provinces and many other comparable countries (OECD, 2005, p. 39). Within a year of being elected, the government set a target of having at least 85% of entering grade 9 students graduate from high school in a timely way by 2010. Although originally framed as a commitment to reduce dropout rates, Ontario's strategy was reframed to have a positive emphasis on improving high school graduation rates.

Many of the elements of this strategy are the same as those in the Literacy and Numeracy Strategy and are discussed below under the heading of "capacity building". However the high school strategy also had elements that take account of the specific challenges facing high school education, which has historically been harder to change than have elementary schools (World Bank, 2005).

Specific components of the high school graduation strategy beyond those just noted (Zegarac, 2007) include:

- building stronger transition models between elementary and secondary schools and paying attention to good transitions into high school for grade 9 students;
- developing a focus on and resources for literacy and numeracy in all areas of the high school curriculum;
- revising curricula in some key areas such as mathematics and career education;
- expanding program options through more cooperative education, credits for appropriate external learning, and dual credit programs with colleges and universities;
- creating a "high skills major" that allows school boards to work with employers and community groups to create packages of courses leading to real employment and further learning; and
- passing legislation to require students to be in a learning situation (school, college, apprenticeship, work with training, and so forth) until high school graduation or age 18.

Another noteworthy feature of the high school success strategy is the creation of a Student Success Commission, which brought together teacher unions, principals, and superintendents to support effective implementation of the strategy in schools so as to prevent disputes at the local level.

Capacity Building as a Central Focus

The most important element of each strategy involved measures to build the capacity of schools and educators to support improved student outcomes. The strategies assumed that outcomes would only improve if people in the schools were helped and supported in changing their practices to create and sustain student success. In both strategies, the focus was on raising the bar and closing the gap – on improving overall levels of achievement and on reducing gaps in achievement for key target groups who were underperforming.

In each case the Ministry of Education created structures to lead the capacity building. A new Literacy and Numeracy Secretariat was created headed by the chief student achievement officer (a new position for Ontario) and staffed by outstanding educators seconded from around the province to lead and guide the overall initiative. For high schools, the Ministry had begun funding, in 2003, a student success leader in each school district. An expanded secondary schools branch of the Ministry provided leadership and coordination at a provincial level.

The capacity-building strategy in Ontario was extensive. It focused on six interrelated elements:

- supporting effective planning for improvement in every school and board;
- supporting effective leadership for improvement in every school and board;
- developing specific approaches to reduce achievement gaps for target groups including boys in elementary schools, recent immigrants, visible minorities, Aboriginals, and students in special education;
- extensive, carefully designed professional development for educators, focused on key areas related to improvement;
- providing high quality, relevant materials to teachers and schools; and
- supporting use of data and research to inform school, district, and provincial policy and practice.

While the descriptions below may give the sense of a long list of separate initiatives, in fact all aspects of capacity building were connected through district leadership teams, through the provincial management structures, and through ongoing communication that kept front and center the overall goal around improving student learning.

These efforts were led and coordinated by the Ministry, but at all times had high levels of input and participation from all parts of the education system. The programs were designed to recognize and build on existing good practice in Ontario schools. Schools and districts were also invited to find their own ways to move forward on the agenda; while every school and district had to pay attention to issues of improvement, the Ministry did not impose mandatory strategies as to how this should be done. The provincial plan assumed that lasting results could only be obtained by building the commitment of local educators, and this cannot happen through mandating professional practices.

Planning for improvement. Every school district and school in Ontario was asked to develop a plan for improvement. However, the point of this work was not to produce a document but to create a real framework for the ongoing work of improvement. Planning was not mandated through a template or form but was led collaboratively by school district and Ministry staff. Plans could look different in each school, as long as they addressed real ways of improving teaching and learning and student outcomes. The staff of the Literacy and Numeracy Secretariat and the student success leaders worked closely with boards, reviewed many plans, and gave feedback around how these could be sharper and better grounded in evidence. People also came together across districts to share their ideas and learn from each other.

Closing gaps. The Ontario strategies were based on improvement occurring in every school, but they also recognized that some groups required additional particular attention. Special strategies were put into place to improve supports for Aboriginal students, English-language learners, French-language students, and students in special education by recognizing their particular needs and situations, including specific training, materials, policies, and stakeholder engagement.

Leadership for improvement. There can be no sustained improvement without effective leadership. The capacity-building work around leadership included extended training and learning opportunities for school principals (done in conjunction with the three provincial associations of principals), building of leadership networks within and across districts, the development of a provincial infrastructure for shared and coordinated leadership development, inclusion of principals in much of the training for teachers around literacy and numeracy, and, as noted below, efforts to address some of the workload pressures on principals in Ontario to allow them to focus on instructional leadership.

Professional development. The Ontario strategies recognized that one-shot workshop approaches to professional development would be insufficient. Instead, a whole range of approaches to learning and development have been implemented in various boards and schools across the province. These include use of literacy and numeracy coaches or lead teachers, a whole range of different forms of "learning communities" focused on literacy and numeracy, staff meetings keyed to provincial Webcasts, inter-school visits to study alternative practices, and many others. At all times the intent has been to embed professional learning in the ongoing work of teachers and schools. Professional development emphasized key areas such as differentiated instruction, use of data, and use of shared and guided reading. As well, the Ministry provided funds to the provincial teacher organizations to allow them to increase their professional development work.

Materials. The Ministry commissioned and produced a variety of documents and materials to support effective teaching and learning in priority areas, as well as making some revisions to key curriculum documents. Expert panels on literacy and numeracy produced detailed guidance for teachers, principals, and school boards around research implications for effective practice. All schools received copies of or online access to a whole range of materials for teachers, including teaching guides, videos, Webcasts for download, and others, all of which were tied to professional development priority areas.

Use of data and research. The Ontario plan emphasized policies and practices that are supported by research evidence while encouraging schools and districts to use their own data and action research as well as the broader research literature to inform their work. A provincial education research strategy was developed, universities were contracted to write short "what works" papers for schools, external evaluations of the main provincial strategies were commissioned, and schools and districts were supported in improving their use of data to guide their own improvement plans. Data use has actually had its own capacity-building strategy within the larger effort.

Sustaining Elements

Capacity building can only be successful in a stable education system, which means one that is respectful of all participants, comprehensive, coherent, and aligned.

Respect for Staff and for Professional Knowledge

The Ontario change strategy has consistently recognized and supported professional knowledge and skill. In addition to those elements already mentioned:

- The public statements of the government and ministry are supportive of public education and the work of educators and support staff.
- The government abolished some policy elements (such as paper-and-pencil testing of new teachers) which were seen by teachers as punitive and replaced them with policies (such as induction for new teachers and changes to teacher performance appraisal) that are seen as supportive of professionalism. Staffing levels have increased despite declining enrolment, while teacher workload has been reduced and preparation time increased.
- As noted already, the strategies build on successful practices in Ontario schools and involve extensive sharing of good practice. Almost everything that is happening at the provincial level draws on good practices that were already underway in schools somewhere in the province. Every effort is made to acknowledge publicly the good work of schools and districts.

Comprehensiveness

The Ontario strategy, while centered on these key student outcomes, is not limited to those. The focus on literacy and numeracy in elementary schools is complemented by strong support for other curricular areas such as physical activity and the arts, both of which have been expanded in the last 3 years. The strategy explicitly rejects narrow views of teaching and curriculum.

The Ontario theory of improvement recognizes schools as ecologies (Fullan, 2006, 2007), so gives attention to building capacity among teachers, to improving leadership, to involving parents, to changing policies, and to adding resources – all at the same time. It is also important to pay attention to the issues that could turn into huge distractions – such as having collective agreements in place with teachers and support staff, dealing with safety issues such as bullying, and ensuring that school buildings are in good repair. There has been action in each of these areas. The effort to be comprehensive, however, creates the challenge of overload, discussed a little later.

Coherence and Alignment Through Partnership

The nature of politics is that government directions can change quickly. Sustainable improvement in schools therefore requires real commitment and participation by all the partners – teachers, administrators, boards, and the broader community. Changing the negative and combative public discourse around education in order to build public confidence was itself an important policy goal of the government. However the efforts to build and sustain strong partnerships all take place within the common emphasis on improving student outcomes.

The Ontario approach built on Fullan's (2006) "trilevel solution," in which governments, school districts, and schools work together on common approaches and strategies. An explicit part of the strategy involves building strong relationships and close connections with boards, schools, and other organizations. Careful and explicit attention was given to building strong positive connections with every part of the education system.

The Ministry of Education implemented new mechanisms for consultation with partners on virtually all programs and policies. A Partnership Table brings the Minister of Education together with all the major stakeholders on a regular basis. The Minister and senior ministry staff meet regularly with the main provincial organizations, including teachers, principals, and superintendents. There is extensive consultation and ongoing communication with school boards.

The government took particular steps to involve teachers and their organizations in the development of policies and programs. In 2005, then-Minister Gerard Kennedy played a vital role personally in ensuring that 4-year collective agreements were put in place for all teachers across the province, giving teachers, students, and the public a multiyear assurance of stability. Steps have also been taken to work more closely with support staff groups and to recognize their need for involvement and for professional development.

Principals are widely recognized as playing key roles in school improvement. In 2005, the Ministry issued a paper on "role of the principal" that outlined a number of steps to support principals in focusing on leading improvement in student outcomes. Professional development for principals has been expanded, and efforts are being made to improve some of their key working conditions, though the job of principal remains a challenging one.

Targeted Additional Resources

The government has recognized that significant education renewal does require resources. From 2003 to 2007 funding for public education increased by 24%, or 28% on a per pupil basis. These funds have been allocated carefully to support the student achievement agenda. The largest single portion has gone to salary increases so that schools can attract and retain good staff. Another very significant amount has been used to expand staffing in key areas, such as smaller classes, student success teachers, specialist teachers in elementary schools, more support staff in key areas, repairs to aging buildings, antibullying programs, and the various other elements of the strategies. Additional funding has also gone to small and isolated schools to expand the services they can offer. The point has never been simply to provide more funds, but always to support better outcomes for students.

Political Leadership

It is important to mention again the vital role of strong political leadership across the education system. Change in Ontario has been driven by the premier and three successive ministers of education, each of whom has helped advance the same agenda. Many of the elements of this agenda are not particularly politically attractive but have still been supported. Schools and districts have been able to focus on the same priorities for 4 years. Sustainable change has also been supported by many other political actors, including elected school boards and the leadership of provincial organizations including trustees, parents, teachers, students, and administrators. This consensus has not been forced by the provincial government but has been carefully built through the kinds of measures just discussed. This political work of building consensus and trust must be an essential element in any program of education reform (Hubbard, Stein, & Mehan, 2006).

The success of these efforts can be seen in the much more positive public positions being taken by stakeholder groups in Ontario, including school boards and teacher unions. Differences and issues remain, and can be heated, but the overall tone of discussion has changed dramatically for the better, which also helps sustain public support for education.

In an atmosphere of increasing trust it is more common for all parties to attempt to work out differences through discussion and compromise rather than through public battles.

Results So Far

The two main strategies are relatively new. The Literacy and Numeracy Secretariat only began operation early in 2005, and the most important elements of the Student Success Strategy only came into place later in 2005, although both built on work already underway in a number of school boards and have been able in less than 2 school years to have a substantial impact on teaching practices and on students' results.

Results on Ontario's grade 3 and 6 provincial assessment have improved substantially and broadly over the last 3 years. Overall about 10% more students, or 15,000 per grade, are now achieving the provincial standard (Literacy and Numeracy Secretariat, 2007; full results are available at www.eqao.com). The number of schools with very low performance has fallen by three-fourths (Literacy and Numeracy Secretariat, 2007). The system as a whole is half way toward the target of 75%, though that target itself is not an end point. Nor are these results just a matter of test-taking. Gains on tests only matter if they represent real improvements in students' skills, and teachers across the province confirm that they are seeing real skill improvements for students, not just increases in test results.[1]

The indicators for high school improvement are also positive. Graduation rates have begun to rise – from 68 to 73% in 2007–2008. Results on the provincial

---

[1]This claim is based on the author's visits to more than 100 schools across Ontario as well as conversations with leaders in all districts and all major stakeholder organizations. All Ontario education leaders will acknowledge the very significant improvement in teacher morale since 2003.

grade 10 literacy test – itself not a particular focus of the changes – improved substantially in 2005 and 2006 (full results at www.eqao.com). Credit accumulation in grades 9 and 10, which so strongly predicts graduation, is also improving, so there should be further significant improvements in graduation rates in the next few years.

Just as importantly, there is a level of energy and enthusiasm in Ontario schools that has not been seen for quite some time. Fewer young teachers are leaving the profession and fewer teachers are choosing early retirement – tangible indicators of improved teacher morale.[2] Thousands of teachers are participating voluntarily in professional development programs. More teachers are giving positive responses to surveys of their level of satisfaction with their work (Ontario College of Teachers, 2006).

Challenges

No change of this magnitude occurs without challenges. Four are particularly important to note. First, 2 or 3 years of improvement are only a start. Much remains to be done. For example, although achievement levels are increasing, some groups, such as students in special education or recent immigrants or Aboriginal students, remain far behind (Literacy and Numeracy Secretariat, 2007). In other areas such as improving the physical condition of buildings and improving services to high-need students there has been progress but nobody would claim that these challenges have yet been fully met.

Despite improved morale, Ontario educators are feeling that they are being asked to address many initiatives all at the same time (Ontario College of Teachers, 2006). Even though most people are positive about the elements of change, putting them all together has brought stress – though of a more positive variety than was experienced a few years ago during all the labor disruption. Many teachers, and especially principals, feel overloaded, yet sustainability depends on people seeing the long-term task as feasible as well as challenging. Although this situation is slowly improving, at all levels of the system there is still a need for more alignment and coherence, and fewer distracting issues.

The next challenge has to do with resources. As noted, the government has increased funding for public education significantly, but schools and boards still face financial pressures in matching resources to demands. All partners will need to continue to work hard to ensure that resources are used as productively as possible. In addition to new resources, this means re-examining current allocations of

---

[2]The Ministry of Education spent an additional $30 million on salaries for teachers in each of 2005–2006 and 2006–2007 because the number of teachers actually retiring fell significantly below the projections based on teacher age profiles and previous years' retirement patterns. That is, many fewer teachers retired in each year than had been anticipated.

staff and funds to assess whether these actually are the most effective ways to use resources in support of students. The allocation of resources is an important area for more research and more effective application of existing research knowledge. For example, practices such as retaining students in grade or keeping students for a 5th year of high school effectively reduce the resources available for more effective strategies such as early intervention for success (Levin & Naylor, in press).

Finally, the Ontario approach poses challenges around the balance between support for and criticism of change. Even the strongest supporters of the Ontario strategy would admit that not everything is perfect; there have been bumps on the road and there remain areas of tension and insufficient progress. Governments do tend to try to focus on success and play down problems. Criticism based on evidence plays an important role in helping to identify areas for further improvement. That is why the Ministry of Education has funded credible third parties to undertake public evaluations of its major strategies, with initial results very positive (Audet et al., 2007; Ungerleider, 2007).

In his postwar novel, *Billiards at Half Past Nine*, Heinrich Boll (1959) makes the point that it is much quicker and easier to destroy something than it is to build it. This is certainly true of large-scale change in education, which is always fragile. If government policy were to change significantly, or if other issues were to occur that refocused attention on areas of conflict, the gains could be threatened. There are always groups, including political opposition groups and elements within each of the stakeholder organizations, that are looking for increased conflict; that is simply a reality of politics. In that sense, sustainable improvement, like many other human goods, requires constant and relentless attention and reinforcement. It can never be taken for granted but has to be recreated continually.

Conclusion

The strategy in Ontario is intended to create an atmosphere of "positive pressure" (Fullan, 2007) that creates the conditions for people at all levels to invest the energy and commitment necessary for the hard and rewarding work of continuous reform. Positive pressure provides resources, increases expectations, furnishes data on an ongoing basis connected to further reform, avoids unfair comparisons among schools, and interprets results based on multiyear trends. Success is celebrated, blame avoided, and lack of improvement is addressed in a transparent and supportive manner.

As this chapter testifies, there is a body of knowledge that can support effective and satisfying improvement in public education. The Ontario case is an example of large-scale change in education that is respectful of educators, fair to students and communities, and based on the best available knowledge. It is not perfect, and remains vulnerable, but it does show that when the right elements are brought together, both better results for students and higher satisfaction for educators can ensue.

References

Audet, W., Barnes, M., Clegg, M., Jaimeson, D., Klinger, D., Levine, M., et al. (2007). The impact of the literacy and numeracy secretariat: Changes in Ontario's education system. Unpublished report, Canadian Language and Literacy Research Network.

Boll, H. (1959). *Billiards at half-past nine*. London: Penguin.

Education Quality and Accountability Office. (2006). *The grades 3, 6, and 9, provincial report, 2005–2006: English-language schools*. Retrieved May 9, 2007, from http://www.eqao.com/pdf_E/06/06P031E.pdf

Elmore, R. (2004). *School reform from the inside-out*. Cambridge, MA: Harvard University Press.

Fullan, M. (2006). *Turnaround leadership*. Thousand Oaks, CA: Corwin; Toronto, ON: Ontario Principals Council.

Fullan, M. (2007). *The new meaning of educational change* (4th ed.). New York: Teachers College Press.

Gidney, R. (1999). *From hope to Harris: The reshaping of Ontario's schools*. Toronto, ON: University of Toronto Press.

Hargreaves, A. (2003). *Teaching in the knowledge society*. New York: Teachers College Press.

Hubbard, L., Stein, M., & Mehan, H. (2006). *Reform as learning*. New York: Routledge.

King, A. J. C., Warren, W. K., Boyer, J. C., & Chin, P. (2005). *Double cohort study. Phase 4: Report submitted to the Ontario ministry of education*. Retrieved March 9, 2007, from http://www.edu.gov.on.ca/eng/policyfunding/reports.html

Leithwood, K., Fullan, M., & Watson, N. (2003). *The schools we need*. Toronto, ON: OISE/UT.

Levin, B. (2005). *Governing education*. Toronto, ON: University of Toronto Press.

Levin, B., & Fullan, M. (2008). Learning about system renewal. *Educational Management, Administration and Leadership, 36*(2), 289–303.

Levin, B., & Naylor, N. (2007). Using resources effectively in education. In J. Burger, P. Klinck, & C. Webber (Eds.), Intelligent leadership (pp. 143–158). Dordrecht, NL: Springer.

Literacy and Numeracy Secretariat. (2007). *Making it happen*. Toronto, ON: Ontario Ministry of Education. Retrieved June 19, 2007, from http://www.edu.gov.on.ca/eng/literacynumeracy/makeithappen.pdf

Livingstone, D. & Hart, E. (2005). *Public attitudes towards education in Ontario, 2004*. Toronto, ON: OISE.

OECD. (2005). *Education at a glance*. Paris: OECD.

Ontario College of Teachers. (2006). State of the teaching profession 2006: Annual Survey. *A COMPAS report to the Ontario College of Teachers*. Retrieved May 7, 2007, from http://www.oct.ca/publications/PDF/survey06_e.pdf

Ungerleider, C. (2007). Evaluation of the Ontario ministry of education's student success/Learning to 18 strategy, Stage 1 report. Ottawa: Canadian Council on Learning. Unpublished report.

World Bank. (2005). Expanding opportunities and building competencies: A new agenda for secondary education. Washington, DC: World Bank.

Zegarac, G. (2007, April). *Secondary school reform in Ontario and the role of research, evaluation and indicator data*. Paper presented to the American Educational Research Association, Chicago.

Educational Change in Finland

Pasi Sahlberg

> *God mend us! The fact is that we don't even know the first letter of the alphabet, and that knowing how to read is the first duty of every Christian citizen. The power of law, of church law, may force us to it. And you know what kind of contraption the State has watching, eager to snap us up in its jaws if we don't obediently learn to read. The stocks are waiting for us, my brothers, the black stocks; their cruel jaws gaping wide like those of a black bear. The provost has threatened us with those hell his pincers, and he is bound to carry out his threat unless he sees us eagerly studying every day.*
>
> – Aleksis Kivi: Seven brothers (1870)

In the early 1970s – a century after the first Finnish novel *Seven Brothers* was published – Finland was known for its long-distance runners, introverted people, saunas on lakes, and successful political coexistence with the Soviet Union. In those days, the Finnish economy was characterized by traditional agriculture and it relied on forestry and heavy-metal industries. Being a rather poor member within a much wealthier family of industrial market economies, Finland was ranked in the lower half of the OECD nations. The Finnish education system had only a few features that attracted any praise among international observers and many education policy ideas were adopted from its wealthier Western neighbor, Sweden. Indeed, Finland's education system was recognized internationally exceptional only on one account: Finnish 10-year-olds were among the best readers in the world (Allerup & Mejding, 2003; Elley, 1992). Other than that, international education indicators – as they then existed – left Finland in the shadows of traditional education superpowers, such as Sweden, England, USA, and Germany. This chapter shows how Finland has been able to upgrade its human capital by transforming its education system from less-than-average to one of the best international performers since the 1970s. It then argues that although Finland has been claimed to be a "model pupil" in listening to advice from supranational organizations, success has been achieved

P. Sahlberg (✉)
Centre for International Mobility and Cooperation CIMO, Helsinki, Finland
e-mail: pasi.sahlberg@cimo.fi

A. Hargreaves et al. (eds.), *Second International Handbook of Educational Change*, Springer International Handbooks of Education 23, DOI 10.1007/978-90-481-2660-6_19, © Springer Science+Business Media B.V. 2010

by implementing education reforms that differ from those in many other nations. Finally, it suggests that much of the Finland's journey from the educational periphery to international limelight is explained by the contextual factors – especially sociocultural aspects and other public-sector policies. This article offers essential ideas for nations that aspire sustainable knowledge societies through educational and economic development. The main conclusion is that education and educational reform need to be incorporated into a common social mission that foster interdependency between education, other social sectors, and national economic development. Finnish experience suggests that education systems will continue to find it difficult to achieve good student learning if children live in a world outside school that does not provide enough of the caring in terms of health, safety, and moral support that are needed to be able to learn well in classrooms. This experience also raises some concerns for Finns themselves. As the family and state social capital decrease, conditions for universal good learning will also get more difficult. Reaching the top of the educational world has made politicians and policy-makers modest in their educational reform demands. As a consequence, the systemic evolution of education system has slowed down in Finland. However, changing social values, increasing immigration, aging population, emphasizing productivity, and demand for more creativity and innovation require continuous and sustainable improvement of education system.

Educational Progress in Finland since 1970

As Finland attracts global attention due to its high-performing education system, it is worth asking whether there was any progress in this performance since the 1970s. If progress can be reliably identified, then, consequently, the question becomes: What factors might be behind successful education reform? In my recent analysis of educational reform policies in Finland (Sahlberg, 2007), I describe how Finland changed its traditional education system, with little to celebrate in terms of international comparisons, into a model of a modern, publicly financed education system with widespread equity, good quality, and large participation – all of this at reasonable cost (OECD, 2007c; Sahlberg, 2007; Schleicher, 2006). What is significant from this analysis is the steady progress during the past three decades within four main domains: (1) increased level of educational attainment of the adult population, (2) widespread equity, (3) a good level of student learning, and (4) moderate overall spending, almost solely from public sources. Before describing the educational change since the 1970s, I will briefly summarize the main elements determining the level of Finnish educational system performance.

First, there has been a steady growth in participation in all levels of education in Finland since 1970. The growth has been especially rapid in the upper secondary education sector in the 1980s and, then, within the tertiary and adult education sectors in the 1990s, up to the present. Education policies that have driven Finnish reform since 1970 have prioritized creating equal opportunities, raising quality, and increasing participation within all educational levels across Finnish society. More than 99% of the age cohort successfully complete compulsory basic education, about 95% continue their education in upper secondary schools or in the 10th grade of basic school (some 3%) immediately after graduation, and 90% of those starting upper secondary school eventually receive their school leaving certification, providing access to tertiary education (Statistics Finland, 2007). Two-thirds of those enroll in either academic universities or professionally oriented polytechnics. Finally, over 50% of the Finnish adult population participates in adult education programs. What is significant in this expansion of participation in education is that it has taken place without shifting the burden of costs to students or their parents. According to recent global education indicators, only 2% of Finnish expenditure on educational institutions is from private sources compared to an OECD average of 13% (OECD, 2007a). Overall progress since 1970 in educational attainment by the Finnish adult population (15 years and older) is shown in Fig. 1. The current situation is congruent with a typical profile of the human capital pyramid in advanced knowledge economies (OECD, 2007a).

Second, education opportunities and, therefore, good learning outcomes have spread rather evenly across Finland. There was a visible achievement gap among young adults at the start of upper secondary school in the early 1970s due to very different educational orientations associated with the old parallel system (Aho, Pitkänen, & Sahlberg, 2006; Lampinen, 1998). This knowledge gap strongly corresponded with the socioeconomic divide within Finnish society at that time. Although students' learning outcomes began to even out by the mid-1980s, streaming through ability grouping in mathematics and foreign languages kept the achievement gap relatively wide. After abolishing streaming in comprehensive school in the mid-1980s and, therefore, making learning expectations similar

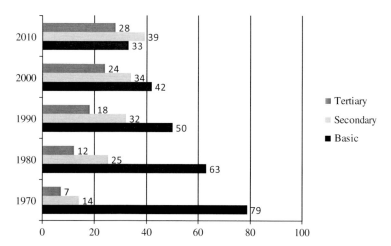

Fig. 1 Level of educational attainment among the Finnish adult population (15 years and older) since 1970 (Sahlberg, 2006b)
Note: Levels in 2010 are estimates.

for all students, the achievement gap between low and high achievers began to decrease. First evidence of this came from the OECD's Programme for International Student Achievement (PISA) survey in 2000. Finland had one of the smallest performance variations between schools, less than one-tenth of that variation for example in Japan, in reading literacy between schools of all OECD nations. A similar trend continued in the 2003 PISA cycle in mathematics and was strengthened in the PISA survey in 2006 (OECD, 2001, 2004, 2007b). Figure 2 illustrates performance variance within and between schools in different OECD nations as assessed by science scale in 2006 PISA survey.

According to Fig. 2, Finland has less than 5% between-school variance on the PISA science scale, whereas the average between-school variance in other OECD nations is about 33%. The fact that almost all Finnish inequality is within schools, as shown in Fig. 2, means that the remaining differences are probably mostly due to variation in students' natural talent. Accordingly, variation between schools mostly relates to social inequality. Since this is a small source of variation in Finland, it suggests that schools successfully deal with social inequality. This also suggests, as Grubb (2007) observed, that Finnish educational reform has succeeded in building an equitable education system in a relatively short time, a main objective of Finland's education reform agenda set in the early 1970s.

Third, Finnish students' learning is at a high international level as determined by recent comparative student achievement studies. Although it is difficult to compare students' learning outcomes today with those in 1980, some evidence can be offered using International Educational Assessment (IEA) and OECD PISA surveys since the 1980s (Kupari & Välijärvi, 2005; Martin et al., 2000; OECD, 2001;

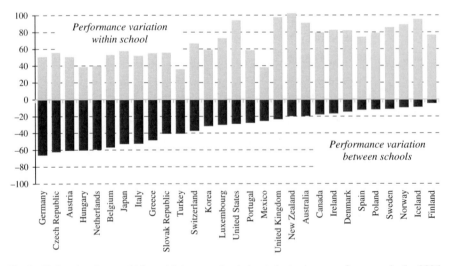

Fig. 2 National variance within and between schools in student science performance in the 2006 PISA cycle (OECD, 2007b)

Robitaille & Garden, 1989). Based on these data, I reported elsewhere a summary of Finnish students' mathematics performance since 1981 compared to their peers in other countries (Sahlberg, 2007). The studies used include the Second International Mathematics Study (SIMS) in 1981 (8th grade, 20 nations), Trends in Mathematics and Science Study (TIMSS-R) in 1999 (8th grade, 38 nations), and the OECD PISA survey in 2000 (15-year-olds, all 30 OECD member countries). These are the international student assessment surveys in which Finland participated since 1980. Since the nations participating in each international survey are not the same and the methodology of IEA and OECD surveys is different, the international average as a benchmarking value does not always provide a fully comparable or coherent picture.

Figure 3 shows another divergence of Finnish students' learning performance trend, as measured in the OECD PISA mathematics scale in comparison to some OECD countries over time. It is remarkable that student achievement in mathematics shows progress in Finland also according to the PISA data contrary to many other education superpowers. This indicates a continuing progress of student achievement in mathematics. There is an increasing debate of what these international tests really measure and it is beyond the scope of this chapter to discuss those issues or the validity of these studies. Criticism and proponents' arguments are available, for example, in Adams (2003), Bautier and Rayon (2007), Goldstein (2004), Nagy (1996), Prais (2003, 2004), Riley and Torrance (2003), Sahlberg (2007), and Schleicher (2007).

OECD PISA is increasingly being adopted as a global measure to benchmark nations' student achievement at the end of compulsory education. In 2006, the third cycle of this global survey was conducted within all 30 OECD member nations and in 27 other countries. It focused on "young people's ability to use their knowledge and skills to meet real-life challenges. This orientation reflects a change in the goals and objectives of curricula themselves, which are increasingly concerned with what students can do with what they learn at school and not merely with whether they have mastered specific curricular content" (OECD, 2007b, p. 16). In the 2006 PISA survey, Finland maintained its high performance in all assessed areas of student achievement. In science, the main focus of the 2006 PISA survey, Finnish students outperformed their peers in all 56 countries, as shown in Fig. 4.

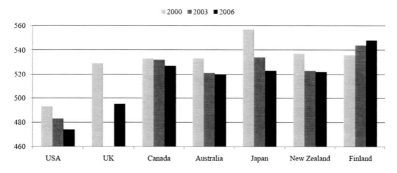

Fig. 3 Finnish 15-year-old students' performance in mathematics in three OECD PISA surveys between 2000 and 2006 in selected OECD countries

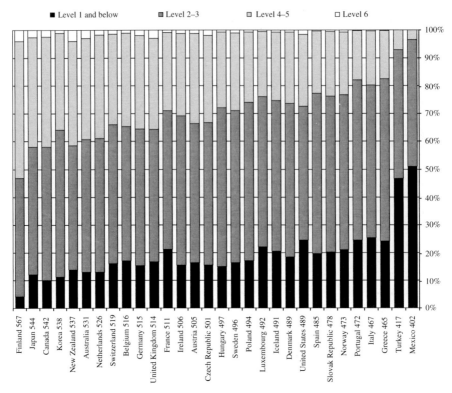

Fig. 4 Percent of students at each proficiency level on the science scale (OECD, 2007b, Table 2.1a), where level 2 refers to minimum and level 6 to excellent proficiency

Figure 4 suggests that Finnish students' learning achievement in science has advanced from the earlier international comparisons over the last 25 years. All three PISA survey cycles since 2000 also indicate that Finnish educational performance is consistent over all assessed educational domains and that Finnish students, on average, score high in every survey across all subjects – in mathematics, science, and reading literacy.

It seems that Finland has been able to reform its education system by increasing participation at all levels, making good education achievable to a large proportion of its population, and attaining comparatively high learning outcomes in most schools throughout the nation. All of this has been accomplished by financing education, including tertiary and adult education, almost exclusively from public sources. One more question regarding good educational performance remains to be addressed: How much does it cost the Finnish taxpayers? In OECD nations for which data on comparable trends are available for all educational levels combined, public and private investment in Finnish education increased 34% from 1995 to 2004 in real terms, while the OECD average for the same period was 42%. Expenditure on educational institutions as a percentage of GDP in Finland is at the OECD average,

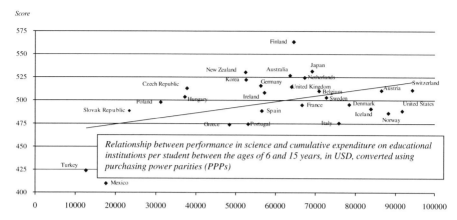

Fig. 5 Student performance on the PISA science scale and spending per student in USD converted to purchasing power parities (OECD, 2007b, Tables 2.1c and 2.6)

6.1% in 2004 (OECD, 2007a). Less than 2% of total Finnish expenditure on education institutions comes from private sources. At present, tertiary education remains fully financed from public funds, and therefore free, for everyone living in Finland. Figure 5 summarizes students' mean performance on the PISA science scale in relation to educational spending per student in 2006. These data indicate that good educational performance in Finland has been attained at reasonable cost.

Finnish educational success has encouraged people to search for causes of such favourable international performance. Most visitors to Finland discover elegant school buildings filled with calm children and highly educated teachers. They also recognize the large autonomy that schools enjoy; little interference by the central education administration in schools' everyday lives; systematic methods to address problems in the lives of students and targeted professional help for those in need. Much of this may be helpful to visitors in benchmarking their own country's practice in relation to a leading education nation such as Finland. However, much of the secret of Finland's educational success remains undiscovered: What has the educational change process been like? What was done behind the scenes when key decisions were made to make that success possible? How much did Finnish educators take note of global education reform movements in creating their own approaches? What is the role of other public-sector policies in making education system work so well?

Global Educational-Change Controversies

In our recent analysis of Finnish education policies and reform principles since 1968, my colleagues and I concluded that rather than introducing sequential educational revolutions, Finnish education policy has been built upon periodic change and systemic leadership led by commonly accepted values and common, compelling social vision that resonate closely with contemporary ideas of sustainable educational change (Aho et al., 2006; Fullan, 2005; Hargreaves, 2008; Hargreaves & Fink, 2006; Hargreaves & Goodson, 2006). Importantly, the main features for developing a competitive, well-performing education system are similar to those underlying the social and economic transformation of Finland into a welfare state and a knowledge society (Castells & Himanen, 2002; Saari, 2006; Sahlberg, 2006a). It is, therefore, difficult to identify particular reforms or innovations per se that served as driving forces in raising the level and quality of Finnish education. Thus, it becomes necessary to identify broader policies – and especially how different public-sector policies were interconnected with the education system. It is, furthermore, essential to emphasize that although Finland has been called "a model pupil" in listening to the policy advice from the supranational organizations, especially OECD and the European Union (Niukko, 2006; Rinne, 2006), the Finnish education system has remained quite unreceptive to influences from what is often called the *global education reform movement* or GERM (Sahlberg, 2004, 2007). GERM has emerged since the 1980s and has become increasingly adopted as an official agenda or accepted as educational orthodoxy within many education reforms throughout the world, including the USA, the UK, Germany, and some transition countries. Tellingly, GERM is often promoted through education strategies and interests of international development agencies, as well as by some bilateral donors through their interventions in national education and political settings.

Since the 1980s, at least five globally common features of education policies and reform principles have been employed to try to improve the quality of education, especially in terms of raising student achievement. First is *standardization* in education. Outcomes-based education reform became popular in the 1980s, followed by standards-based education policies in the 1990s, initially within Anglo-Saxon countries. These reforms, quite correctly, shifted the focus of attention to educational outcomes, that is, student learning and school performance. Consequently, a widely accepted – and generally unquestioned – belief among policy-makers and education reformers is that setting clear and sufficiently high performance standards for schools, teachers, and students will necessarily improve the quality of desired outcomes. Enforcement of external testing and evaluation systems to assess how well these standards have been attained emerged originally from standards-oriented education policies. Since the late 1980s, as Hargreaves (2003) also observed, centrally prescribed curricula, with detailed and often ambitious performance targets, frequent testing of students and teachers, and high-stakes accountability have characterized a homogenization of education policies worldwide, promising standardized solutions at increasingly lower cost for those desiring to improve school quality and effectiveness.

A second common feature of global education reform strategies is *increased focus on core subjects* in curriculum, in other words, on literacy and numeracy. Basic student knowledge and skills in reading, writing, mathematics, and natural sciences are elevated as prime targets and indices of education reforms. As a consequence of accepting international student assessment surveys, such as PISA and

IEA, as criteria of good educational performance, reading, mathematical, and scientific literacy have now become the main determinants of perceived success or failure of pupils, teachers, schools, and entire education systems.

The third characteristic that is easily identifiable in global education reforms is *the search for safe and low-risk ways to reach learning goals*. This minimizes experimentation, reduces use of alternative pedagogical approaches, and limits school risk-taking. Research on education systems that have adopted policies emphasizing achievement of predetermined standards and prioritized core subjects suggests that teaching and learning are narrower and teachers focus on "guaranteed content" to best prepare their students for tests (Au, 2007; Valli & Buese, 2007). The higher the test-result stakes, the lower the degree of freedom in experimentation and risk-taking in classroom learning.

The fourth globally observable trend in educational reform is *transfer of educational innovation from one context to another* as a main source of change (Levin, 1998; Phillips, 2005). This process where educational policies and ideas are lent and borrowed is often facilitated by international development organizations and motivated by national hegemony and economic profit, rather than by moral goals of human development. Faith in educational change through innovations brought and sold from outside the system undermines two important elements of successful change: First, it often limits the role of national policy development and enhancement of an education system's own capabilities to maintain renewal, and perhaps more important, it paralyzes teachers' and schools' attempts to learn from the past and also to learn from each other, or it prevents lateral capacity building in the system (Fullan, 2005).

The fifth global trend is adoption of *high-stakes accountability policies* for schools. School performance – especially raising student achievement – is closely tied to the processes of accrediting, promoting, inspecting, and, ultimately, rewarding or punishing schools and teachers. Success or failure of schools and teachers is often determined by standardized tests and external evaluations that devote attention to limited aspects of schooling, such as student achievement in mathematical and reading literacy, exit examination results, or intended teacher classroom behavior.

None of these elements of GERM have been adopted in Finland in the ways that they have within education policies of many other nations, for instance, in the United States, England, Japan, or some Canadian provinces. This, of course, does not imply that education standards focus on basic knowledge and skills or emphasis on accountability should be avoided in seeking better learning or educational performance. Nor does it suggest that these ideas were completely absent in education development in Finland. But, perhaps, it does imply that a good education system can be created using alternative approaches and policies orthogonal to those commonly found and promoted in global education policy markets.

By contrast, typical features of teaching and learning in Finland are, first, high confidence in teachers and principals as professionals. Second feature is to encourage teachers and students to try new ideas and approaches, in other words, to learn about and through innovations. Finally, teaching and learning aims to cultivate creativity in schools while respecting schools' pedagogic legacies. This does not mean that traditional instruction and school organization are nonexistent in Finland—quite the opposite. What is important is that today's Finnish education policies are a result of four decades of systematic, mostly intentional, development that has created a culture of diversity, trust, and respect within Finnish society, in general, and within its education system, in particular. This may be a reason for the commonly noted Finnish pedagogical conservatism that, for example, Simola (2005) has identified as a paradoxical feature of the Finnish teaching profession.

What education policy principles and related strategies were implemented in Finland to bring its education system to a high international level of overall performance? Schleicher (2006) suggests that one element of Finland's success has been "the capacity of policy makers to pursue reform in ways that went beyond optimizing existing structures, policies and practices, and moved towards fundamentally transforming the paradigms and beliefs that underlay educational policy and practice until the 1960s" (p. 9). Although Finnish education-policy discourse changed during the 1990s as a consequence of new public sector management and other neoliberal policies, Finland has been slow to implement dominant market-oriented education reforms. Instead, education sector development has been grounded on equal opportunities for all, equitable distribution of resources rather than competition, intensive early interventions for prevention, and building gradual trust among education practitioners, especially teachers. Moreover, Finland has been characterized as a consensus society, where major political decisions have been agreed upon by all key players in society (Aho et al., 2006; Routti & Ylä-Anttila, 2006; Saari, 2006). Importantly, the Finnish Teachers' Trade Union, a main negotiating partner in education, has consistently resisted adopting market-oriented management models. Table 1 highlights alternative approaches that were adopted by Finnish education policies since the early 1980, intending to enhance student school learning.

There is a lot of speculation regarding the reasons that could explain Finnish educational success in earlier mentioned international comparisons (Aho et al., 2006; Grubb, 2007; Hargreaves, Halasz, & Pont, 2007; Laukkanen, 2008; Linnakylä, 2004; Sahlberg, 2007; Schleicher, 2006; Simola, 2005; Välijärvi, Linnakylä, Kupari, Reinikainen, & Arffman, 2002; Valijarvi et al., 2007). These efforts to explain good educational performance often focus on factors within the education system, such as well-educated teachers or intelligent accountability policies (as shown in Table 1). Some argue, quite correctly, that cultural aspects of Finland such as the high social status of literacy or ethnic uniformity within Finnish society affect school performance. At the same time, educational, or technical, peculiarities of the Finnish model of educational change provide necessary, but insufficient conditions for understanding how an education system can be transformed to suit a modern knowledge society. What has been much less analyzed and researched among educators or social scientists, in general, is how since the 1970s the education system has operated as a part of larger, complex political and social system within Finnish welfare society (Saari, 2006) that covers economy, employment, social issues, and education.

Table 1 Some features of education policy development and reform principles globally and in Finland since the early 1980s

Education policies and reform principles	
Global education reform movement	Education development in Finland
Standardization	*Loose standards*
Setting clear, high, centrally prescribed performance standards for schools, teachers, and students to improve the quality of outcomes.	Setting clear but flexible national framework for school-based curriculum planning. Encouraging local solutions to national goals in order to find best ways to create optimal learning opportunities for all.
Focus on literacy and numeracy	*Focus on broad and creative learning*
Basic knowledge and skills in reading, writing, mathematics, and natural sciences serve as prime targets of education reform.	Teaching and learning focus on deep, broad learning, giving equal value to all aspects of the growth of an individual's personality, moral character, creativity, knowledge, and skills.
Teaching for predetermined results	*Encouraging risk-taking and uncertainty*
Reaching higher standards as criteria for success and good performance; minimizes educational risk-taking and narrowing teaching to content and methods beneficial to attaining preset results.	School-based and teacher-owned curriculum facilitates finding novel approaches to teaching and learning; hence, encourages risk-taking and uncertainty in leadership, teaching, and learning.
Transferring external innovations for educational revolutions	*Learning from the past and respecting pedagogical conservatism*
Sources of educational change are external innovations brought to schools and teachers through legislation or national programs. These often replace existing improvement strategies.	Teaching honors traditional pedagogical values, such as teachers' role and relationship with students. Main sources of school improvement are proven good practices from the past.
High-stakes accountability and control of schools	*Professional responsibility and trust*
School performance and raising student achievement are closely tied to the processes of promotion, inspection, and ultimately rewarding schools and teachers. Winners normally gain fiscal rewards, whereas struggling schools and individuals are punished.	Gradual building of a culture of responsibility and trust within the education system that values teachers' and principals' professionalism in judging what is best for students and in reporting their learning progress. Targeting resources and support to schools and students who are at risk to fail or to be left behind.

Three Perspectives on Educational Change

Finland offers an interesting case study to policy experts and researchers in explaining what might affect positive and rather rapid educational progress. In most cases, factors influencing good performance have been sought from within the education sector (Aho et al., 2006; Niukko, 2006; Rinne, 2006; Simola, Rinne, &

Kivirauma, 2002). Critical observers have particularly tried to identify technical, sociocultural, or political peculiarities that question the adequacy of international comparison efforts or would place Finland in a special position to succeed well in international comparisons (Bracey, 2005; Dohn, 2007; Messner, 2003). Quite rare, however, are attempts to analyze systemic characteristics that include the role of other key public-sector policies on Finnish education sector progress. Educational change in Finland can be viewed from three different perspectives that together form a complex framework for understanding the evolution and current state of the Finnish education system – technical (educational), sociocultural, and political (Fig. 6).

Much research on educational change over previous decades includes these three perspectives highlighted in Fig. 6. In the first edition of the *International Handbook of Educational Change*, House and McQuillan (1998) wrote that "an adequate understanding of school reform necessarily involves all three perspectives, though many reformers emphasize only one, a partial knowledge which often results in reform failure because of neglect of the other powerful factors" (p. 198). The *technical perspective* includes those educational aspects of reform that have been identified as factors in good performance. In the case of Finland, these include the same comprehensive school for all, a respected teaching profession, research-based teacher preparation, early prevention of failure and a system for special education, school autonomy, and professional leadership (Itkonen & Jahnukainen, 2007;

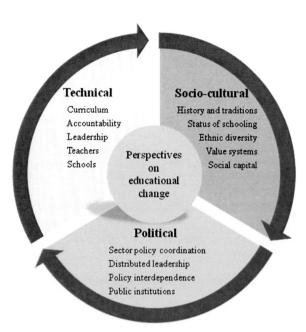

Fig. 6 Three perspectives enabling an understanding of educational change in Finland since 1970

Laukkanen, 2008; Linnakylä, 2004; Sahlberg, 2007; Salo & Johnson, 2008; Simola, 2005; Valijarvi et al., 2007).

The *sociocultural perspective* explains, in part, performance, or in some cases lack of proficiency, in terms of social, cultural, and historical features of the nation or its education system (Sahlberg, 2010; Simola, 2005). It includes both family and national social capital, ethnic and religious uniformity, mutual trust among people, traditional appreciation of literacy and reading, and also valuing integrity and the low level of corruption that this brings.

The *political perspective* explains how a small, rather poor nation that has been able to create, in a relatively short time, one of the world's most competitive and advanced modern economies with many characteristics of a welfare state (Alasuutari, 2004; Castells & Himanen, 2002; Routti & Ylä-Anttila, 2006; Saari, 2006). Studies of the Finnish model explain how strategies in other public-policy sectors are linked to educational change and to key processes that concern the entire society, such as globalization of the Finnish economy since the 1980s and integration into the European Union in the early 1990s. For example, rekindling Finnish competitiveness after the economic recession in the early 1990s required strategic investments in human capital in order to convert the education and training system to offer flexible learning paths to all including those who had already left education system. Accession to the European Union, in turn, challenged Finns to align their national identity and public institutions with those elsewhere in Europe. History and the personal mind-set of Finns suggest that they are at their best when faced with these kinds of global challenges – experiences such as the twentieth-century Olympics, war against the Soviet Union, and the deep economic recession of the early 1990s provide good evidence of the competitive and resilient Finnish spirit (called *sisu*). These educational and cultural attitudes were complemented by key economic, employment, and social policies since the 1970s and the establishing of welfare state, its institutions and policies were completed by the end of the 1980s.

Analysis of educational change often includes speculation about the basic nature of change, that is, whether it is *evolutionary* or *revolutionary*. These terms refer to change as smooth and continuous change or as radical transition points where new institutions and rules are introduced. Educational change in Finland has displayed periodic evolution, meaning that the nature of educational change has been different during these periods of change. What is important to realize is that the year 1990 marks an important watershed in Finnish history that also distinguishes two evolutionary periods in educational change (see Table 2). The time prior to 1990 was characterized by creating institutions and frameworks for a welfare-based education system. The post-1990 is more concerned with interests, ideas, and innovations that have formed the education system as an integral part of the complex social, economic, and political system. Part of the success of the Finnish model, in general, is claimed to emerge from an ability to create punctuated equilibrium between periods of changes (Gersick, 1991; Saari, 2006).

Two simultaneous processes have played an important role in developing the education sector in Finland since 1970. On the one hand, increased interaction among various public-sector policies has strengthened the coherence of economic

Table 2 Increased interdependency among public-sector policies in Finland since 1970

	Economic policies	Employment policies	Social policies	Education reform principles
1970s: Institutionalization Consolidation of the pillars of welfare state and strengthened state-driven social capital. Fostering conventional industrial production structures	Small, open economy that depended on exports and was state-regulated. Investments mainly in physical capital.	Establishing active employment policies and unemployment benefit system. Strengthening direct training for labor markets.	New risk-management systems for adults. Systems for unemployment, work-life balance, access to further education and housing.	Emphasis on equity and equal access to good primary and secondary education for all. Securing public provision of education.
1980s: Restructuring Welfare state completed. Restructuring economic regulations, information technology infrastructure, and public administration.	Rapid public-sector growth. Industrial production concentrates on metal and wood sectors.	Restructuring unemployment benefit system. Using early retirement as part of new employment policies.	Student welfare services and medical-care system. Student loan and social benefit systems. Restructuring unemployment legislation.	Restructuring upper secondary education to increase access for all students. Transferring upper secondary schools to municipal authority.
1990s: Ideas and innovation Public-sector liberalization. Diversification of exports through innovation-driven markets and dissemination of ideas through a network society.	Public-sector growth halts and starts to decline. Private service sectors starts to grow and new ICT industries emerge. Investments in R&D increased. Restructuring of banking sector.	Recession cuts employment benefits. New labor market benefit system to encourage employment. Employment policy system reform.	Fixing social consequences of Big Recession, especially for in-debt and long-term unemployed. Re-training and further education of unemployed.	Empowering teachers and schools through school-based curricula, coordinated innovations and networking schools and municipalities for sharing ideas and change. Expansion of higher education sector.
2000s: Renewal Strengthening well-performing parts of economy and renewing social policies (further privatization) to match financial realities.	Focus on services increases. Central administration loses its role and productivity of public sector is emphasized.	Aging population casts a shadow on employment. Accent on rights and obligations of unemployed. Cross-sectoral approach emphasized.	Renew immigration legislation. Adapting social system for further diversification.	Renewing education legislation, strengthening evaluation policies and tightening state control over schools and productivity in education sector. Sizes of schools increases.

Establishing institutions ↓ Interests, ideas, and innovations

⇐ Interdependency between public sector- policies strengthen ⇒

and social reforms and, therefore, created conditions for what Hargreaves & Fink (2006) term *sustainable leadership* in education. This enables systematic commitment to longer-term vision and inter-sector cooperation among different policies and strategies. On the other hand, internationalization and especially Finland's integration into the European Community have harmonized and intensified consolidation and development of public institutions and their basic functions (Saari, 2006). In this light, three conclusions can be drawn regarding how Finnish educational success can be understood from a political perspective:

(1) The success of Finnish education reform from an international perspective is mainly based on institutions and institutional structures established in the 1970s and 1980s, rather than on changes and improvements implemented from the 1990s. This state-driven social capital that has been created through government regulations and the responsibility to provide basic conditions of well-being for all have provided a favorable social context for educational achievement.

(2) Changes in Finnish education after 1990 are more about interests, ideas, and innovations than about new institutional structures. Institutional changes in the 1990s have been smaller, except in tertiary education where a new polytechnic system was introduced in the 1990s. However, directions remain clear and are based on the earlier policies.

(3) The emphasis on national competitiveness that has been a key driving force in most public-sector policies in the European Union has not been converted to clear targets or operations in Finnish public-policy sectors during the 1990s and 2000s. At the same time, equity principles promulgated in the early 1970s have gradually lost influence in these policies.

Since 1970, there have been two interconnected change periods, but differing in terms of the logic of change and sources of ideas and innovations. On the one hand, education reform principles have increasingly been created in coherence and interdependently with other public-policy sectors following a *complementarity* principle. On the other hand, ideas for educational change   particularly improving teaching and learning in schools – have been transferred from past good practices and traditions in Finland. This has sometimes been labeled as *pedagogical conservatism* (Sahlberg, 2007; Simola, 2005) and has created a pedagogical equilibrium between progressivism and conservatism through learning from the past and teaching for the future. Further analysis of social and economic policies in Finland since the 1970s show how context makes a difference in educational achievement, in other words, how social capital can explain student learning in international comparisons.

Educational Change for a Welfare State

Finland has traveled a long way from being a rather poor agrarian state in the early twentieth century to a modern knowledge economy at the start of the third millennium. Postwar decades were marked by significant migration in Finland, as many left their homes to seek a better life abroad or in urban parts of Finland. In 1950, the structure of the Finnish economy corresponded closely to that of Sweden's in 1910 (Kokkinen, Jalava, Hjerppe, & Hannikainen, 2007; Routti & Ylä-Anttila, 2006). Social policy decisions in the 1950s and 1960s underscored the economic importance of family farms. However, the general perceived image of Finland remained agrarian despite rapid industrialization and agriculture's declining contribution to the GDP over the second half of the twentieth century. Regardless of drastic changes in the way of life and emerging cosmopolitanism among Finnish people, traditional values endured. According to Lewis (2005), these included such cultural hallmarks as a law-abiding citizenry, trust in authority including schools, commitment to one's social group, awareness of one's social status and position, and a patriotic spirit. Policies that guided education reforms since the 1970s relied on these cultural values and principles of consensus-building that have all been distinguishing characteristics of Finnish society.

The structure of the Finnish education system until the early 1970s was based on two parallel streams that had maintained social division and created unequal opportunities for good education (Aho et al., 2006). This parallel education system caused a wide gap in learning achievement among Finnish youth by the end of compulsory school, typically at age 16. Only a minority of that age cohort enrolled in upper secondary school programs that provided them with access to higher education.

The 1970s marked a turning point in Finnish education (Hirvi, 1996; Lampinen, 1998). A new publicly financed 9-year comprehensive school (*peruskoulu*) harmonized the curriculum and offered identical educational opportunities to all young Finns, regardless of their socioeconomic background, domicile, gender, or mother tongue. Key drivers of educational change at that time were the ideals of equal access to education and a steady increase in the level of educational attainment by all Finnish citizens. Together with more equal opportunities to learn, new *peruskoulu* also offered other social services, such as health and dental care, special education support, free meals, and transportation. Education reform in the 1970s sparked bitter political debate and divided opinions among politicians and the public-at-large regarding the future of knowledge and skills of the nation (Aho et al., 2006). Interestingly, teachers who entered this new *peruskoulu* from the two parallel streams had the fewest doubts about the value of this reform. Teacher education was upgraded in universities by the end of the 1970s; it was converted into research-based masters-level programs (Jakku-Sihvonen & Niemi, 2006; Jussila & Saari, 2000; Westbury, Hansen, Kansanen, & Björkvist, 2005). This also led to a slow but steady rise of quality of Finnish primary school teachers as college-trained teachers began to be replaced by university-trained teachers. This also guaranteed that the teaching profession in primary schools remained the favorite career choice for Finnish upper secondary school graduates (Laukkanen, 2008; Sahlberg, 2006b).

Finland followed the main postwar social policies of other Nordic countries. This led to the creation of a type of welfare state, where basic social services, including education, became public services for all citizens, particularly for those most in need of support and help. This increased the level of social capital, so did national government policies that affected children's broader social environment and improved their opportunities and willingness to learn. Carnoy (2007) calls this *state-generated social capital*. State-generated social capital is expressed as social context for educational achievement that is created by government social policies. The influence of social restructuring and education reform in Finland was profound and immediate. Eager to improve their children's economic and social opportunities, Finnish families turned to the education system. In 1955–1956, the nation's grammar schools enrolled approximately 34,000 pupils. Five years later, enrollment had swelled to 215,000 and it continued to soar, rising to 270,000 in 1965 and 324,000 in 1970 (Aho et al., 2006). Finland's old system could barely hold together as parents demanded an improved and more comprehensive basic education for their children in the hope of securing better lives for them. Such social pressure introduced a new theme in the education policy debate: the individual's potential for growth. Researchers then argued that an individual's abilities and intelligence always rose to the level required by society and that education systems merely reflected these limits or needs. An agricultural country has different educational needs than a high-tech industrial powerhouse. By the mid-1980s, the idea of comprehensive basic education was fully realized and enrollment in upper secondary schools began to increase.

Political and Economic Context of Educational Change

Educational progress in Finland should be viewed in the broader context of economic and social development and renewal, both nationally and globally. Interestingly, the growth of the Finnish education sector coincided with an impressive economic transformation from an agrarian, production-driven economy to a modern information society and knowledge-driven economy. Indeed, Finland has transformed itself into a knowledge economy in a relatively short time. The Finnish experience of the 1990s represents one of the few documented examples of how education and therefore knowledge can become driving forces of economic growth and transformation. During that decade, according to Routti and Ylä-Anttila (2006), Finland became the most specialized economy in the world in information and communication technologies and thus completed its transition from resource-driven to knowledge- and innovation-driven development. In the 2000s, Finland has consistently scored high in international comparisons in terms of economic competitiveness, levels of good governance, network readiness, and implementation of sustainable development policies (Castells & Himanen, 2002; Saari, 2006; Sahlberg, 2006a; Routti & Ylä-Anttila, 2006). Figure 7 highlights how rapidly economic transformation affected changes in employment in terms of the emergence of knowledge- and skills-intensive labour market needs and thereby declining needs of low know-how labour during the last two decades of the twentieth century. In a small economy that is almost fully dependent on its own labor, this had an immediate impact on educational policies.

The major economic transformation and need for sophisticated knowledge and skills in new high-tech industries provided the education system with unique

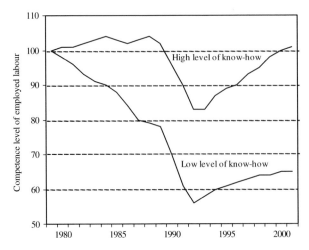

Fig. 7 Structural changes in Finnish industry in terms of changes in employment of high and low level know-how labor between 1980 and 2000 (Pajarinen & Ylä-Anttila, 2001)

opportunities for radical renewal in the 1990s. This happened at the same time as three significant economic and political processes unfolded: the collapse of the Soviet Union; a deep and severe economic recession triggered by a Finnish banking crisis, accelerated by vanishing Soviet trade; and integration with the European Union. Each of these changes influenced the Finnish education sector either directly or indirectly. By the middle of the 1990s, a clear Finnish consensus emerged that information and communication technologies would eventually foster the transformation to a knowledge economy and that this was perhaps the best way out of the economic crisis and into the heart of European power. It was also realized that the knowledge economy is not only about preparing human capital for higher know-how. It is also about having highly educated consumers able to benefit from technological products in markets requiring better technological literacy.

The information society and knowledge economy have been important contextual factors for educational change in Finland. The economic sector in Finland has expected that the education system should provide not only the needed quantities of skilled professionals but also those with appropriate knowledge and skills to deal with rapidly changing environments. In their call for raising standards of knowledge and skills, Finnish employers, for example, were reluctant to advocate narrow specialization and early selection to schools. Although Finnish industry has actively promoted better learning of mathematics, sciences, and technology, it simultaneously supported rather innovative forms of school-industry partnerships as part of the formal curriculum. Rapid emergence of innovation-driven businesses in the mid-1990s introduced creative problem-solving and innovative cross-curricular projects and teaching methods to schools. Some leading Finnish companies, such as Nokia, reminded education policy-makers of the importance of keeping teaching and learning creative and open to new ideas, rather than fixing them to predetermined standards and accountability through national testing.

Membership in the European Union in 1995 marked a mental change within Finland. The Soviet Union had disappeared only half-decade earlier—an event that boosted consolidation of Finland's identity as a full member of Western Europe. The accession process of becoming an EU member was equally important as attaining actual membership in 1995. As a new Finnish identity emerged during the years of EU accession, Finnish people were motivated to ensure that they and their institutions were at least up to the level of other European nations. In fact, the poor reputation of mathematics and sciences in Finnish schools, compared to European peers in the 1970s and 1980s, became a reason to try harder to move Finnish educational performance up to a good European level. Although education is not included in formal EU membership requirements, the accession process had a tangible positive impact on strengthening public institutions, including schools in Finland, especially in the midst of the worst economic recession since the years of World War II. Moreover, Finnish educators became increasingly aware of various European education systems. This gave a positive impetus to innovation and new ideas within Finland's education sector as more information became readily available about practices within other systems.

Transfer of Educational Know-How

International tests comparing how well young people in different countries perform in reading, mathematics, and science have provided a worldwide pretext for education reforms and has increased focus on educational "quality." When the first PISA results were published in late 2001, they induced a shock in many countries and also in Finland. They created an educational pilgrimage from all over the world to see the "miracle of PISA" that took all Finns by surprise: Finnish education experts were not sure what made them educationally so successful. Later on, other nations like Korea, and most recently Estonia and Canada have experienced similar international attention. Interestingly, Cuba has also joined the league of educational powerhouses due to its good performance in UNESCO's *Latin American Laboratory of Educational Evaluation* in the late 1990s. In their search for reasons why Cuban children outperform their peers from all other Latin American countries, Carnoy's research team concluded that "state-driven social capital is an important construct for understanding why children in some countries do better in school" (Carnoy, 2007 p. 155). There are certain contextual similarities between Nordic welfare states and Cuban society as far as sociocultural conditions for educational achievement are concerned. These contextual factors of high social capital and the role of education in generating national well-being provide valuable insights for those who are concerned with raising student achievement.

Due to recent educational success documented by all three PISA surveys, many want to learn from Finns how to build a good education system (Barber &

Mourshed, 2007; Grubb, 2007; Hargreaves et al., 2007; Schleicher, 2006). Yet understanding Finnish educational success needs to include the sociocultural, political, and economic perspectives discussed in this chapter. Indeed, there is more to the picture than meets the eye. An external OECD expert review team that visited Finland observed that "it is hard to imagine how Finland's educational success could be achieved or maintained without reference to the nation's broader and commonly accepted system of distinctive social values that more individualistic and inequitable societies may find it difficult to accept" (Hargreaves et al., 2007). Another visiting OECD team confirmed that the Finnish experience advice that approaches to equitable schooling should rely on multiple and reinforcing forms of intervention with support that teachers can get from others, including special education teachers and classroom assistants (Grubb, 2007). Furthermore, educational change should be systematic and coherent, in contrast to current haphazard intervention efforts in many other countries. The conclusion was that "developing the capacities of schools is much more important than testing the hell out of students, and that some non-school policies associated with the welfare state are also necessary" (Grubb, 2007, p. 112).

These observations about transferability of educational change ideas contradict with the thinking of those who claim that context, culture, politics, or governance are not the most important things to the school system and its leaders for achieving real improvement in educational outcomes. The McKinsey Report that analyzed education policies and practices in 25 countries concluded that the following three educational reform principles go before anything else: (1) the quality of teachers; (2) education outcomes will only improve by improving instruction; and (3) system-wide excellence is only possible by "putting in place mechanisms to ensure that schools deliver high-quality instruction to every child" (Barber & Mourshed, 2007, p. 40). Another example is the US education reform known as *No Child Left Behind*. This legislation, according to many teachers and scholars, has led to fragmentation in instruction, further interventions uncoordinated with the basic classroom teaching, and more poorly trained tutors working with students and teachers. As a consequence, schools have experienced too many instructional directions for any student with an increase of unethical behaviors and a loss of continuity in instruction and systematic school improvement (Grubb, 2007; Nichols & Berliner, 2007; Valli & Buese, 2007). Difference between this and the Finnish approach is notable: The Finns have worked systematically over 35 years to make sure that competent professionals who can craft the best learning conditions for all students are in all schools, rather than thinking that standardized instruction and related testing can be brought in at the last minute to improve student learning and turn around failing schools. Both of these examples resonate with the key ideas of GERM and can be found in education policies of numerous nations and jurisdictions.

Indeed, only importing specific ideas from Finland about curricula, teacher training, accountability, or educational leadership is of little value to those aiming to improve their own education systems within their own context. The Finnish welfare state has guaranteed all children with a sociopolitical context inside and outside of school that provide the safety, health, and moral support needed to function well in a classroom environment performing well in school. As the passage from the novel *Seven Brothers* in the beginning of this chapter illustrates, literacy and education in general have historically played a central role in becoming a full member of the Finnish society. In this respect, one of the transferable principles of educational change for other nations may be that successful educational reform comes with interdependent social and economic reforms.

What then can be transferred from good educational practice in Finland to other systems? One common mistake carried by GERM is underestimating the complex nature of education as a subsystem of the economic and political national system. As described by Kauffman (1995), for example, separate elements of a complex system rarely function adequately in isolation from their original system in a new environment. Therefore, rather than "borrowing" only specific ideas and innovations from a well-performing education system, more readily transferrable aspects may be the features and properties of a larger, complex system, in this case, the Finnish model. In the complex system, interactions among elements of the system determine the behavior of that system as much as its individual elements. Therefore, some concerns that should be included in contemplating the transfer of ideas from the Finnish education system are:

1. *Technical drivers of good educational performance.* These include common comprehensive basic schooling for all, research-based teacher education, intelligent accountability policies, relatively small schools, and good educational leadership especially within schools.
2. *Sociocultural factors.* These include long reliance on the social value of literacy and education, high work morality, trust in public institutions including schools, and state-driven social capital created by the welfare state.
3. *Links to other public-policy sectors.* Success of one sector depends on the success of all others. Therefore, good educational performance may only be explained through larger policy principles, including those of other public policies.

Conclusion: Waking Up for the Change

In the first decade of the third millennium, Finland has established a global reputation as a model educational nation. There is, indeed, evidence that Finland's education performance has progressed steadily in terms of international comparisons since the early 1980s. Mobile phone makers, symphony-orchestra conductors, and Formula 1 drivers are marks of what the Finnish culture and society that values ingenuity, creativity, and risk-taking over selfish competition for irrelevant standards is able to nurture. The question is, "Will the Finnish education system continue to be a model in the future?"

On the one hand, Finland's systemic educational leadership since the 1970s, its stable political structure, and its established *complementarity* among public-policy sectors would suggest that its educational performance will remain strong. On the other hand, PISA survey results, in particular, have created a feeling of complacency among education policy-makers, politicians, and the public-at-large regarding the status of Finnish education. This may lead to a condition favoring the *status quo*, where education policies and leadership of a high-performing system are motivated by a desire to maintain the current situation, rather than seeing what possible futures might require from a reformed Finnish education system.

Educational change in Finland since the 1970s has been driven by culture and emotion in the context of social, political, and economic survival. A lesson from Finland is that technical knowledge or political interests are not enough to renew society without emotional engagement. Indeed, global education reforms show that too rational approach on change does not work because renewal requires energy, and energy is driven by emotion. In the era of Big Changes, emotional passion often emerges from crisis – or a sense of survival – as it did in Finland. But it can also come from viewing new economical, technological, or cultural opportunities.

In the beginning of the twenty-first century, Finland has become a model nation for other reasons also: It has been able to build a competitive knowledge economy while maintaining much of social justice of Nordic welfare state model. A high-level think tank named the New Club of Paris that considered possible futures for Finland stated that survival is not the impetus for renewal anymore to keep all the good that Finland has been able to build (Ståhle, 2006). In their recommendations to the Finnish government, they suggested that

> other drivers with emotional effect need to be identified. The question is how to broaden the scale of emotional recognition and exploitation. Instead of survival the driver for change could be a powerful vision, or the Big Dream of Finland. If people do not love the idea, it is futile to publish new strategies. The new strategy with cultural and emotional dimensions should be simple; a couple of words that people can immediately and emotionally relate to. This is currently missing. (Ståhle, 2006, p. 2)

The spirit of that general recommendation should also be considered in education. The chief instrument that guides Finnish education policies and educational renewal is the Development Plan for Education and Research for 2007–2012 (Ministry of Education, 2007). This, as its former document for 2003–2008, continues earlier policies and principles. These documents emphasize equal opportunities, quality education, skilled workers, and developing tertiary education and teachers as main resources of education. Furthermore, these documents place strong emphasis on the *complementarity* principle and developing the education system as a whole. All this assumes that the Finnish education system will continue to perform well in the coming years also. However, there are some trends within the governance of education system that provide cause for concern.

First, national education authorities have tightened the grip of control over schools and signaled that there is not a high level of confidence in schools' ability to judge what is best for pupils and parents. For example, the new national curriculum of 2004 reduces schools' role in curriculum planning. Second, the governmental Education Sector Productivity Program for 2006–2010 (Ministry of Education, 2005) calls for schools to do more with less and proposes school mergers and increasing class sizes. In some cases, productivity gains are sought by reducing schools' special education and counseling services. This may turn out to be harmful for the high social capital of Finnish schools. Finally, there is no clear idea within the Finnish education system of what the direction of education should be in the future. For example, the Development Plan for Education and Research for 2007–2012 is silent about how education should react to needs expressed in the economic sector to intensify innovation and create new products.

Increasing productivity and improved efficiency lead to financial savings and perhaps temporarily better services but, as Finnish futurologists Ståhle and Wilenius (2006) point out, in the economic context, the plan's strategy of shrinking budgets will never create sustainable improvements unless there are simultaneous investments in something new. There are enough signals through forecasts of the Finnish economy and society in general to suggest that more investments are needed to create new ideas and innovations both in education and in economic development and to maintain the high level of social capital that has traditionally been the driver of strong educational performance (Castells & Himanen, 2002; Routti & Ylä-Anttila, 2006; Ståhle, 2006). Finland was able to benefit from one of the most competitive national economies when competition within its education system was minimized in the 1990s. A component of educational change that creates new ideas and innovation should be providing enough encouragement and support for risk-taking that will enable creativity to flourish in classrooms and schools. This is possible only with continuous renewal of Finnish education, guided by wise educational leadership in close relation to other public-sector policies. The political and strategic challenge that is both ironic and paradoxical remains: "Which measures need to be taken to wake up the Finns for the change."

Acknowledgments I wish to thank Henry Heikkinen and David Oldroyd for their constructive suggestions on this chapter. I also wish to acknowledge several colleagues in Finland who provided their comments and corrections to the data and the conclusions presented above. However, any lack of clarity, errors, and omissions are the author's responsibility alone.

References

Adams, R. J. (2003). Response to 'Cautions on OECD's recent educational survey (PISA)'. *Oxford Review of Education, 29*(3), 377–389.

Aho, E., Pitkänen, K., & Sahlberg, P. (2006). *Policy development and reform principles of basic and secondary education in Finland since 1968*. Washington, DC: World Bank.

Alasuutari, P. (2004). Sunnittelutaloudesta kilpailutalouteen. Miten muutos oli ideologisesti mahdollinen? [From planned economy to competition economy. How was the change ideologically possible?] *Yhteiskuntapolitiikka, 69*(1), 3–16.

Allerup, P., & Mejding, J. (2003). Reading achievement in 1991 and 2000. In S. Lie, P. Linnakylä, & A. Roe (Eds.), *Northern lights on PISA: Unity and diversity in Nordic countries in PISA 2000* (pp. 133–146). Oslo: University of Oslo, Department of Teacher Education and School Development.

Au, W. (2007). High-stakes testing and curricular control: A qualitative metasynthesis. *Educational Researcher, 36*(5), 258–267.

Barber, M., & Mourshed, M. (2007). *The McKinsey report: How the world's best performing school systems come out on top*. London: McKinsey & Company.

Bautier, E., & Rayon, P. (2007). What PISA really evaluates: Literacy or students' universes of reference? *Journal of Educational Change, 8*(4), 359–364.

Bracey, G. (2005). Research: Put out over PISA. *Phi Delta Kappan, 86*(10), 797.

Carnoy, M. (with A. Gove, & J. Marshall). (2007). *Cuba's academic advantage. Why students in Cuba do better in school*. Stanford: Stanford University Press.

Castells, M., & Himanen, P. (2002). *The information society and the welfare state. The Finnish model*. Oxford: Oxford University Press.

Dohn, N. (2007). Knowledge and skills for PISA – Assessing the assessment. *Journal of Philosophy of Education, 41*(1), 1–16.

Elley, W. B. (Ed.). (1992). *How in the world do students read?* Hamburg: Grindeldruck GMBH.

Fullan, M. (2005). *Leadership and sustainability. System thinkers in action*. Thousand Oaks: Corwin Press.

Gersick, C. (1991). Revolutionary change theories. A multilevel exploration of the punctuated equilibrium paradigm. *Academy of Management Review, 16*(1), 10–36.

Goldstein, H. (2004). International comparisons of student attainment: Some issues arising from the PISA study. *Assessment in Education: Principles, Policy and Practice, 11*(3), 319–330.

Grubb, N. (2007). Dynamic inequality and intervention: Lessons for a small country. *Phi Delta Kappan, 89*(2), 105–114.

Hargreaves, A. (2003). *Teaching in the knowledge society. Education in the age of insecurity*. New York: Teachers College Press.

Hargreaves, A. (2008). The fourth way of change: Towards an age of inspiration and sustainability. In A. Hargreaves & M. Fullan (Eds.), *Change wars*. Toronto: Solution Tree.

Hargreaves, A., & Fink, D. (2006). *Sustainable leadership*. San Francisco: Jossey-Bass.

Hargreaves, A., & Goodson, I. (2006). Educational change over time? The sustainability and nonsustainability of three decades of secondary school change and continuity. *Educational Administration Quarterly, 42*(1), 3–41.

Hargreaves, A., Halasz, G., & Pont, B. (2007). *School leadership for systemic improvement in Finland. A Case study report for the OECD activity "Improving School Leadership"*. Paris: OECD.

Hirvi, V. (1996). *Koulutuksen rytminvaihdos. 1990-luvun koulutuspolitiikka Suomessa* [The rhythm change in education. Finnish education policy in the 1990s]. Helsinki: Otava.

House, E., & McQuillan, P. (1998). Three perspectives on school reform. In A. Hargreaves, A. Lieberman, M. Fullan, & D. Hopkins (Eds.), *International handbook of educational change* (pp. 198–213). Dordrecht: Kluwer.

Itkonen, T., & Jahnukainen, M. (2007). An analysis of accountability policies in Finland and the United States. *International Journal of Disability, Development and Education, 54*(1), 5–23.

Jakku-Sihvonen, R., & Niemi, H. (Eds.). (2006). *Research-based teacher education in Finland: Reflections by Finnish teacher educators*. Research Report 25. Turku: Finnish Educational Research Association.

Jussila, J., & Saari, S. (Eds.). (2000). *Teacher education as a future-molding factor: International evaluation of teacher education in Finnish universities*. Helsinki: Higher Education Evaluation Council.

Kauffman, S. (1995). *At home in the universe. The search for the laws of self-organization and complexity*. Oxford: Oxford University Press.

Kivi, A. (2005). *Seven brothers*. [Seitsemän veljestä, first published in 1870, translated by R. Impola]. Beaverton: Aspasia Books, Inc.

Kokkinen, A., Jalava, J., Hjerppe, R., & Hannikainen, M. (2007). *Catching up in Europe: Finland's convergence to Sweden and EU15*. Working Papers 93. Helsinki: Pellervo Economic Research Institute.

Kupari, P., & Välijärvi, J. (Eds.). (2005). *Osaaminen kestävällä pohjalla. PISA 2003 Suomessa* [Competences on solid ground. PISA 2003 in Finland]. Jyväskylä: Institute for Educational Research, University of Jyväskylä.

Lampinen, O. (1998). *Suomen koulutusjärjestelmän kehitys* [Development of the Finnish education system]. Tampere: Tammer-paino.

Laukkanen, R. (2008). Finnish strategy for high-level education for all. In N. C. Sognel & P. Jaccard (Eds.), *Governance and performance of education systems* (pp. 305–324). Dordrecht: Springer.

Levin, B. (1998). An epidemic of education policy: (what) can we learn from each other? *Comparative Education, 34*(2), 131–141.

Lewis, R. (2005). *Finland, cultural lone wolf.* Yarmouth: Intercultural Press.

Linnakylä, P. (2004). Finland. In H. Döbert, E. Klieme, & W. Stroka (Eds.), *Conditions of school performance in seven countries. A quest for understanding the international variation of PISA results* (pp. 150–218). Munster: Waxmann.

Martin, M. O., Mullis, I. V. S., Gonzales, E. J., Gregory, K. D., Smith, T. A., Chrostowski, S. J., et al. (2000). *TIMSS 1999 international science report: Findings from IEA's repeat of the third international mathematics and science study at the eighth grade.* Chestnut Hill: Boston College.

Messner, R. (2003). PISA und Allgermeinbildung. *Zeitschrift fur Padagogik, 48*(3), 400–412.

Ministry of Education. (2005). Opetusministeriön hallinnonalan tuottavuusohjelma 2006–2010 [Education Sector Productivity Programme 2006–2010]. *Opetusministeriön julkaisuja 2005:32.* Helsinki: Ministry of Education.

Ministry of Education. (2007). *Development plan for education and research 2007–2012.* Helsinki: Ministry of Education.

Nagy, P. (1996). International comparisons of student achievement in mathematics and science: A Canadian perspective. *Canadian Journal of Education, 21*(4), 396–413.

Nichols, S., & Berliner, D. (2007). *Collateral damage: How high-stakes testing corrupts America's schools.* Cambridge: Harvard Education Press.

Niukko, S. (2006). OECD in the eyes of Finnish education policy makers. In J. Kallo & R. Rinne (Eds.), *Supranational regimes and national education policies – encountering challenge. Research in educational sciences 24* (pp. 299–333). Turku: Finnish Educational Research Association.

OECD. (2001). *Knowledge and skills for life: First results from PISA 2000.* Paris: OECD.

OECD. (2004). *Learning for tomorrow's world. First results from PISA 2003.* Paris: OECD.

OECD. (2007a). *Education at a glance. OECD indicators 2007.* Paris: OECD.

OECD. (2007b). *PISA 2006. Science competencies for tomorrow's world* (Vol. 1). Paris: OECD.

OECD. (2007c). *No more failures. Ten steps to equity in education.* Paris: OECD.

Pajarinen, M., & Ylä-Anttila, P. (2001). *Maat kilpailevat investoinneista: Teknologia vetää sijoituksia Suomeen.* [Nations competing for investments: Technology attracts foreign investments to Finland]. B 173. Helsinki: ETLA.

Phillips, D. (2005). Policy borrowing in education: Frameworks for analysis. In J. Zajda (Ed.), *International handbook on globalisation, education and policy research. Global pedagogies and policies* (pp. 23–34). Dordrecht: Springer.

Prais, S. J. (2003). Cautions on OECD's recent educational survey (PISA). *Oxford Review of Education, 29*(2), 139–163.

Prais, S. J. (2004). Cautions on OECD's recent educational survey (PISA): Rejoinder to OECD's response. *Oxford Review of Education, 30*(4), 569–573.

Riley, K., & Torrance, H. (2003). Big change question: As national policy-makers seek to find solutions to national education issues, do international comparisons such as TIMSS and PISA create a wider understanding, or do they serve to promote the orthodoxies of international agencies? *Journal of Educational Change, 4*(4), 419–425.

Rinne, R. (2006). Like a model pupil? Globalization, Finnish education policies and pressure from supranational organizations. In R. Rinne & J. Kallo (Eds.), *Supranational regimes and national education policies – encountering challenge. Research in Educational Sciences 24* (pp. 183–215). Turku: Finnish Educational Research Association.

Robitaille, D. F., & Garden, R. A. (Eds.). (1989). *The IEA study of mathematics II: Context and outcomes of school mathematics.* Oxford: Pergamon Press.

Routti, J., & Ylä-Anttila, P. (2006). *Finland as a knowledge economy. Elements of success and lessons learned.* Washington, DC: World Bank.

Saari, J. (2006). Suomen mallin institutionaalinen rakenne [The institutional structure of the Finnish model]. In J. Saari (Ed.), *Suomen malli – Murroksesta menestykseen?* [The Finnish model – From reformation to success] Helsinki: Yliopistopaino.

Sahlberg, P. (2004). Teaching and globalization. *International Research Journal of Managing Global Transitions, 2*(1), 65–83.

Sahlberg, P. (2006a). Education reform for raising economic competitiveness. *Journal of Educational Change, 7*(4), 259–287.

Sahlberg, P. (2006b). Raising the bar: How Finland responds to the twin challenge of secondary education? *Profesorado, 10*(1), 1–26.

Sahlberg, P. (2007). Education policies for raising student learning: The Finnish approach. *Journal of Education Policy, 22*, 147–171.

Sahlberg, P. (2010). Rethinking accountability in a knowledge society. *Journal of Educational Change, 11*(1).

Salo, P., & Johnson, P. (2008). Action research revealing paradoxes and tensions of education reforms. Lessons learned in Finland. In E. Furu, P. Salo, & K. Rönneman (Eds.), *Nurturing praxis. Action research in partnership between school and university in a Nordic light.* Rotterdam: Sense Publishers.

Schleicher, A. (2006). *The economics of knowledge: Why education is key for Europe's success.* Brussels: The Lisbon Council.

Schleicher, A. (2007). Can competencies assessed by PISA be considered the fundamental school knowledge 15-year-olds should possess? *Journal of Educational Change, 8*(4), 349–357.

Simola, H. (2005). The Finnish miracle of PISA: Historical and sociological remarks on teaching and teacher education. *Comparative Education, 41*(4), 455–470.

Simola, H., Rinne, R., & Kivirauma, J. (2002). Abdication of the education state or just shifting responsibilities? The appearance of a new system of reason in constructing educational governance and social exclusion/inclusion in Finland. *Scandinavian Journal of Education Research, 46*(3), 247–264.

Ståhle, P. (Ed.). (2006). *Five steps for Finland's future. Technology Review 202.* Helsinki: Tekes.

Ståhle, P., & Wilenius, M. (2006). *Luova tietopääoma: Tulevaisuuden kestävä kilpailuetu* [Creative intellectual capital: Sustainable competitive advantage of the future]. Helsinki: Edita Publishing.

Statistics Finland. (2007). Education. Retrieved from the Internet at http://www.stat.fi/til/kou_en.html, on 30 December, 2007.

Valijarvi, J., Kupari, P., Linnakyla, P., Reinikainen, P., Sulkunen, S., Törnroos, J., et al. (2007). *Finnish success in PISA and some reasons behind it II.* Jyväskylä: University of Jyväskylä.

Välijärvi, J., Linnakylä, P., Kupari, P., Reinikainen, P., & Arffman, I. (2002). *Finnish success in PISA and some reasons behind it.* Jyväskylä: Institute for Educational Research, University of Jyväskylä.

Valli, L., & Buese, D. (2007). The changing roles of teachers in an era of high-stakes accountability. *American Educational Research Journal, 44*(3), 519–558.

Westbury, I., Hansen, S.-E., Kansanen, P., & Björkvist, O. (2005). Teacher education for research-based practice in expanded roles: Finland's experience. *Scandinavian Journal of Educational Research, 49*(5), 475–485.

China as a Case Study of Systemic Educational Reform

Yong Zhao and Wei Qiu

Introduction

Over the last 30 years or so, China has engaged in a series of systemic educational reforms. These reforms aimed to "improve the quality of the citizenry, produce more talents, and produce high quality talents" (MOE, 1985) through actions in all domains of education: governance and management, financing, teacher preparation, curriculum, and assessment. As a highly centralized political society, these reforms were always initiated by the central government and naturally their intended impacts were system-wide. However, not all reforms met with the same level of success. Some of them were much more fruitful than others.

In this chapter, we review the major systemic educational reforms that China has undertaken over the past three decades and analyze the reasons behind their different degrees of success. Among the ups and downs of the reform, we focus on two major themes in China's system-wide education reform: decentralization and marketization. Both themes appear to be prominent in the worldwide education reform discourse. Meanwhile, both themes have strong "Chinese flavor," reflecting the specific contexts facing the Chinese reformers and the driving forces underlying the reform. While each theme may have different driving forces, both witness the achievements and setbacks in China's system-wide reforms. In our discussion, we first introduce the key laws and policies related to the two themes and then analyze the Chinese way of decentralization and marketization. Then we identify the driving forces of the reforms and assess the reforms. Finally, we highlight the lessons to take away from China's journey of systemic reform in the past three decades.

Y. Zhao (✉)
Michigan State University, East Lansing, MI, USA
e-mail: zhaoyo@msu.edu

A. Hargreaves et al. (eds.), *Second International Handbook of Educational Change*,
Springer International Handbooks of Education 23, DOI 10.1007/978-90-481-2660-6_20,
© Springer Science+Business Media B.V. 2010

Major Themes of the Reforms

China's systemic reforms over the last 30 years have been intended to achieve two interconnected goals: expand access to and improve the quality of education. In terms of access, China has set the ambitious goal of universalizing 9 years of compulsory education, increasing high school enrollments, and expanding college enrollments. Regarding the quality of education, China wants its education system to prepare a citizenry that can participate and compete in the increasingly global economy and thus aims to transform its curriculum and pedagogy that support the education of the whole child; lead to the well-rounded development of the body, the mind, and the heart; and foster creativity, problem-solving skills, and practical knowledge.

While the overall goals remained the same in the last 30 years, the specific reform actions and strategies changed in accordance with the perceived obstacles at the time. For example, in 1977, when China emerged from a chaotic period of communist radicalism and the whole formal education system was in ruins, it quickly resurrected the college entrance exams with a milestone initiative entitled *1977 Suggestions for the Admissions to Higher Education Institutions*[1] issued by the State Council (referred to hereafter as "1977 Suggestion"). But today, as the country gradually emerges as a world economic power and wishes to transform itself from a manufacture economy into a knowledge economy, the college entrance exams are viewed as the largest obstacle that must be reformed.

The specific systemic reform initiatives come in different formats and may be approved by different agencies. However, system-wide reform initiatives in China always take a top-down approach, coming from the central government represented by different branches and agencies. The initiatives are launched in a limited number of forms: speeches of top political leaders; documents of the Central Committee of the Chinese Communist Party (CCCCP); documents and regulations of the State Council; laws passed by the People's Congress; and announcements, regulations, and documents of the Ministry of Education. Because of the nature of government in China, although the agencies announcing the initiatives may differ, it can be assumed that all bear the same power and have been sanctioned by the highest body of decision making.

Looking across the 30 years, the reform initiatives may vary in their titles launching agencies, formats, foci of reform, and other details, in one way or another. However, two persistent themes run through the reforms: decentralization and marketization.

---

[1] The 1977 Suggestion was launched in August 1977, immediately after Deng Xiaoping was reinstated after being purged twice during the Cultural Revolution (1966–1977). The College Entrance Exam (CEE) was cancelled for more than ten years during the Cultural Revolution, and its restoration was attributed to Deng. After Deng came to power, one of the first things he worked on was to reform China's higher education system, starting with the way to select students. In August, the State Council approved the proposal to restore college entrance exams as the way to select students by the Ministry of Education, based on Deng's suggestion.

Decentralization

Initiatives of Decentralization

Decentralization features as a prominent strategy in China's systemic education reforms. Since 1985, three key initiatives constitute a movement of decentralization in China's system-wide educational reform. The movement started with the *Decision to Reform the Education System* (MOE, 1985) released by CCCCP in 1985 (referred to hereafter as "1985 Decision"). It was advanced by the *Framework for China's Education Reform and Development* (MOE, 1993) launched jointly by CCCCP and the State Council in 1993 (referred to hereafter as "1993 Framework"). The journey was furthered by the *Decision to Further Educational Systemic Reform and Promote Quality-oriented Education* (MOE, 1999) another policy jointly released by CCCCP and the State Council in 1999 (referred to hereafter as "1999 Decision").

The 1985 Decision was the first comprehensive systemic reform policy document after China started the reform and opening policy. The foci of reform included decentralization, implementation of the 9-year compulsory education, development of vocational and technical education, and reform of teacher education. *The 1985 Decision* pointed out that "the government control of schools was too rigid and inefficient," and it suggested that "authority be 'devolved' to lower level" and "multiple methods of financing be sought" (MOE, 1985). *The Decision* specified that the administration of elementary schools and secondary schools belong to provincial- and county-level authorities, instead of the central government (MOE, 1985, p. 9). According to *the 1985 Decision*, the State Education Commission (SEC), the education branch of the central government, would continue to monitor the process and provide basic guidelines, but local governments would have more power and bear financial costs (MOE, 1985, p. 20). Meanwhile, the *1985 Decision* cautioned that the decentralization be implemented gradually from relatively developed coastal cities to less developed interior regions.

The 1993 Framework furthered the decentralization movement. There were four points worth highlighting. First, it decentralized the fiscal duties from central government to local government and schools. While state-run institutions should remain the majority, the new education system welcomed the establishment of private institutions. Moreover, the *Framework* encouraged a variety of sources to invest in both state-run and private schools. Second, it stressed that principals should be given the authority to manage their schools including employment and fiscal planning. Third, the decentralization expanded from elementary and secondary schools to higher education. Specifically, it stated that the central government and provincial government should both be responsible for higher education. While the central government would continue to manage a number of higher education institutions in addition to providing guidelines, provincial governments were responsible for the operation of the majority of them. Fourth, college graduates should no longer be assigned positions upon graduation, meaning that the employment of college graduates were no longer planned by the state but to be managed by individual students.

The 1999 Decision advanced the decentralization movement. It focused on two areas: college entrance examination (CEE) and curriculum. It endeavored to break up the governmental monopoly of exam, curriculum, and textbooks. Specifically, it abolished entrance examination to middle school, and encouraged secondary schools to implement their own graduation examinations. It claimed to reform college entrance exams and admission procedures. Qualified provincial governments were encouraged to carry out a variety of experiments with the college admissions and exam system. Colleges would enjoy more autonomy in admission. Furthermore, it determined to reform school curriculum and diversify textbooks.

Chinese Way of Decentralization

The decentralization has taken place in all aspects of the system, including administration, finance, curriculum, examination, and enrollment. The first was to decentralize the fiscal responsibility and management of basic education to local governments. The 1985 *Decision* and a number of subsequent policies made it clear that the local governments at county level and *village* level were responsible for raising the funds for the 9-year compulsory education and high school education. As far as post-secondary education was concerned, except for 72 universities that were directly managed by the central government, the rest of China's 1,500-plus post-secondary institutions were funded and managed by provincial governments or private groups.

The 1999 *Decision* marked the beginning of a movement to break state monopoly of curriculum and textbooks. Prior to 1999, the central government had control over what was taught in schools through one national syllabus, one set of national textbooks, and one national college entrance exam. Since 1999, the curriculum for basic education has moved from a centralized system toward a three-layered system in which curriculum is codeveloped by the state, the provinces, and the schools. Textbook development and selection have adopted a similar system: The central government approves textbooks published by any Chinese publisher, provincial governments select textbooks to be allowed in each province, and county-level governments decide what to use in local schools.

Correspondingly, the college entrance examination has undergone substantial changes in terms of the scheme and content. By 2004, 11 provinces have been granted the autonomy to implement their own college entrance exams instead of using the national one (XinhuaNews, 2004). Fifty nine of China's nearly 1,700 colleges have been granted the right to select 5% of freshmen using their own criteria in addition to their test scores in the national entrance exam (XinhuaNews, 2007). In addition, a new scheme of national college entrance exam has been implemented. In the new scheme, commonly known as 3 + X, the central government requires only three subjects (math, Chinese language, and English), provinces and colleges can decide what else to test, hence the X, which can be one comprehensive test encompassing many subjects or several separate tests (Luo, 2001).

But decentralization in China is not complete devolution of power and authority. Bray (1999) differentiates three types of decentralization: deconcentration, delegation, and devolution. Deconcentration is to transfer task and work, but not authority, to lower levels, while delegation is to transfer decision-making authority, but the authority can be withdrawn. Devolution is to transfer authority to an autonomous unit that can act independently without permission from the higher-level body (Bray, 1999). In China, decentralization takes more of the forms of deconcentration and delegation, but not devolution (Hawkins, 2000; Mok, 1997b).

Whether it is decentralization of fiscal responsibilities, management authority, curriculum content, or examination and admissions, the central government never gives up real authority, and the central government can withdraw what is delegated to lower-level units at anytime (Hawkins, 2000; Mok, 1997b). For example, in 2001, when *the State Council's Decision on Compulsory Education Reform and Development* (MOE, 2001) was issued, the government determines to reclaim the village level responsibility back to the county level. The reason was due to the damages occurred in school finances and teacher recruitment when power was devolved too low to the village government (Yang, 2006). The MOE's decision to provide free education to freshmen in teacher education major with government funding was another example of recentralization (Kwan, 2007).

Marketization

Initiatives of Marketization

Marketization is another major theme of China's educational systemic reform. It emphasizes personal choice, competition between schools, quasi-market educational services, and multichannel financing. Prior to 1980, all education institutions were state owned and education was free at all levels. Since 1980, a number of significant policies introduced, emphasized, and pushed forward the movement of marketizing education.

The first significant initiative was the *Decision to Universalize Primary Education* released by CCCCP in 1980 (referred to hereafter as "1980 Decision"). *The 1980 Decision* was significant in two ways. It was the first document after China reopened its door to the world in 1977 that aimed to universalize primary education. Meanwhile, it was the first document that singles out "marketization" as a crucial means to realize the goal of 9-year compulsory education. Not only did the law stress the importance of marketization rhetorically, it pointed out two specific policies of marketization. First, education reform should "walk on two legs." As stated in the *Decision*, "in a populous and economically underdeveloped country like ours, the task of universalizing primary education cannot be completed by just relying on the State. While the state remains the primary sponsor, we should at the same time mobilize communities, enterprises, and factories to sponsor schools. It is also important to encourage the people to operate schools with their own funding" (CCCCP, 1980, p. 1). This policy was emphasized and expanded in the above-mentioned

1993 Decision, which not only encouraged Chinese citizens to invest in education, but also welcomed international organization and individuals to donate. Second, the reform encouraged alternative schooling opportunities. "In addition to full-day school, half-day schools and programs became legitimate alternative schoolings that fulfill the needs of students and parents from different backgrounds. However, alternative schooling should carefully tailor the curriculum and pedagogy to their students" (CCCCP, 1980, p. 1).

Marketization of education received more intensive attention in 1998, when the State Council approved the policy entitled *Action Plan to Reinvigorate Education for the Twenty-First Century* (MOE, 1998) (referred to hereafter as "the 1998 Action Plan"). This document aimed at applying the strategy of marketization to post-secondary education and outlined a package of policies in order to realize this aim. The policies included several large-scale projects that linked universities and research institutes to market economy. For example, the *Action Plan* introduced "High Level Creative Workforce Project" to strengthen scientific research, and the "University-Based New and High-Tech Industrialization Project" to drive the development of high-tech industries in China.

The marketization movement became more refined when the State Council released *the Decision on the Reform and Development of Basic Education* in 2001 (referred to hereafter as "2001 Decision"). The 2001 Decision claimed to further reform school operation system and support alternative schoolings, especially in less developed regions. It called upon non-governmental organizations and individuals to support the basic education reform. The purpose of the *2001 Decision*'s call on marketization was not only to produce more talents but also to improve the quality of talents.

Chinese Way of Marketization

China's education has introduced the market mechanism, just like the country's economy, in a number of ways. First, private education institutions have been flourishing in China. Although China prefers to use the term *minban* (or people-operated) instead of "private" when referring to these schools, these institutions are in essence funded and operated by non-governmental organizations. Since the first *minban* higher education was founded in 1982 (Mok, 1997a), *minban* educational institutions have grown significantly. Table 1 is a summary of regular *minban* educational institutions in China in 2006. As the data show, both in terms of the number of institutions and the number of students they serve, *minban* education has become a significant part of China's education system. To further promote and regulate *minban* education, China enacted the *Law to Promote Minban Education* in 2002, which recognizes the legal status of *minban* education as an essential component of "socialist education system (MOE, 2002)."

However, it should be noted that there is a reason for these schools to be called *minban* instead of private. Unlike private schools in many western countries, Chinese *minban* education institutions are highly regulated. They must follow the same curriculum as state-owned schools. Higher education institutions must obtain

Table 1 Number and enrollment of non-state/private education institutions in 2006

	No.	Graduates	New entrants	Total enrollment
Regular HEIs	278	222,991	498,562	1,337,942
Independent colleges[a]	318	142,139	527,284	1,467,040
Other HEIs	994			
Senior secondary	5,805	1,102,202	1,852,010	4,503,451
Junior secondary education	4,561	1,102,088	1,323,872	3,943,973
Regular primary schools	6,161	643,121	712,489	4,120,907
Pre-school education	75,426	2,628,256	4,104,503	7,756,871

Data Source: Ministry of Education (MOE, 2002)
[a]Independent colleges are joint ventures of state universities and private companies. These are operated independent from the state universities as private higher education institutions.

permission and quota each year to enroll full-time degree-earning students. While they can charge higher tuitions, than state-schools the government reviews their prices and sets a cap on what they can charge. Consequently, these schools do not operate in a free market. A more accurate term for China's education marketization in this sector is quasi-marketization (Mok, 1997a).

Second, in addition to private education institutions, government education institutions also participated in marketization. Since the mid-1980s, government higher education institutions began to enroll "self-sponsored" students (Bray & Borevskaya, 2001), who were essentially students whose scores in the college entrance exams were not high enough to be admitted to universities. However, they could pay a fee to be admitted. But their scores must be good enough because the slots were still controlled by the government. These students in essence were buying education opportunities in higher education. Self-sponsored students would then find their own employment upon graduation, unlike the students who were enrolled as regular "within-plan" students, who were assigned a post upon graduation. Gradually, this dual-track system was abolished when all college students began to pay for their college education and the government stopped the practice of job assignment around 1989.

Education opportunities were marketed as commodities not only in higher education, but also in basic education. Well-known, high-quality state primary and secondary schools also marketed opportunities in a similar fashion. Although as state schools, they were supposed to provide education for free to eligible students, they collected "school choice fees" from those who did not perform well enough to be admitted or came from outside the communities they were supposed to serve. On top of the annual school choice fee, a large amount of one-time "donation" was collected upon entrance.

Third, public educational resources were put into the education market in a very interesting and controversial form in China. Since the mid-1990s, some government universities in China began to jointly establish private education entities with funds from non-government sources. These entities often took the form of colleges within a university, but they could be located on the existing campus or in a different location, some even in different cities. They were operated as *minban* institutions and charged much higher fees and tuitions than the parent university. The parent university provided the reputation, some faculty, and other educational resources as the investment, while the other partners invested in cash, hardware, and land. This form of private education started more as an experiment in the beginning. It was then legalized by the 2002 *Law to Promote Minban Education in China* (MOE, 2002), which encouraged public universities to work with private entities to establish "independent colleges" (Wang, 2006). As shown in Table 1, there were 318 independent colleges in China as of 2006. Similarly, well-known primary and secondary public schools began to establish *minban* schools in collaboration with private entities in the mid-1990s.

Fourth, "socialization" of support services and facilities of public education was another form of marketization of education in China. Beginning in 1999, public higher education institutions were asked to hand over their support services and facilities, such as student housing, food services, and medical services, to external agencies (Fu, 2002). Prior to this point, these services were all provided as part of the universities. This movement in effect began to commercialize a large part of functions of universities. Universities were no longer responsible for constructing and maintaining student housing and cafeteria and providing other support services.

Lastly, another prominent form of marketization was school-operated enterprises. Both K-12 and higher education institutions entered the business of operating factories, companies, and other types of enterprises since the 1980s (Bray & Borevskaya, 2001). These business operations directly commercialize resources of the schools, be it inventions of the faculty or school-owned facilities.

Driving Forces of the Reforms

Decentralization and marketization (not necessarily privatization) are apparently the two most prominent features of China's systemic education reform in the past 30 years. While they in many ways correspond to the overall pattern of changes in China a movement from a socialist planned economy toward a socialist market economy – they are motivated by two primary concerns: finance and quality.

China has ambitious goals in education, but as a developing country, the central government does not have the financial resources to realize them. Hence, the central government decentralized the fiscal responsibilities to local governments and introduced the market mechanism to bring in financial resources from the non-government sectors, including foreign donations and investments. Thus it can be said that China's systemic reform in education has been primarily motivated by financial concerns (Bray & Borevskaya, 2001; Kwong, 1997; Mok, 1997b; Wang & Zhou, 2002; Wang, 2006).

Another major driver of the movement has been the concern over education quality. The decentralization of curriculum and textbooks, college entrance exams, and authority over basic education is undoubtedly motivated by the concern that the central government's excessively tight control has been a barrier to improving the quality of education and that the more local autonomy would bring innovative ideas and strategies. The biggest concern that China has, after it has accomplished the goal of making education more accessible is the quality of education. The quality problem in China has been interpreted as the inability to produce creative talents needed to transform China from the world's factory into an innovation-driven society. Chinese students are generally considered not as creative as their western peers (Farrell & Grant, 2005) and not well prepared to compete in the global economy. According to a McKinsey study, only 10% of Chinese graduates are eligible for global job market competition. Although China produces 3.1 million college graduates and 600,000 engineers annually, there is a huge talent shortage for jobs such as that of designers, researchers, etc. (Farrell & Grant, 2005). China seems to have a limitless potential for high-rate economic growth, but it could falter badly if the workforce continued to be labor intensive and lacking of creativity.

Assessing the Reforms

After 30 years of continuous systemic reform, China's education has certainly become much more diversified, accessible, and decentralized. How successful are the reforms in accomplishing the two overarching goals: expanding access and improving quality? There is no definitive research-based answers, and the answers, as usual, vary depending on one's perspective. To some, China's basic education reform has been a clear success.

> ... the basic education system has experienced significant transformation in the two decades of reform. First and foremost, the reform goals of 9-year compulsory schooling and literacy have been largely realized. Second, resource mobilization has resulted in relatively adequate financial resources for 9-year compulsory schooling. Lastly, the educational landscape of diversity beyond the Ministry of Education (MOE) system has taken shape, particularly along with the significant expansion of private schools and NGO-sponsored Hope Schools and the indispensable contribution of Maoist *minban* ("people-managed," or community-supported) teachers in rural areas. Admittedly, governmental decisions were crucial in transforming the basic education system in a fundamental way. These decisions included moves to decentralize educational governance, universalize 9-year schooling and improve literacy, diversify educational financing, and enforce education taxation by garnering resources from communities and households. In the final analysis, China's basic education reform has been, in short, a success. (C. Wang & Zhou, 2002)

The same can be said of higher education. In 1978, 400,000 out of 11 million who participated in the first College Entrance Exam after the Cultural Revolution (winter of 1977 and summer of 1978) were admitted to colleges, with an admission rate of 29 to 1. In 2007, about 9.5 million students took the College Entrance Exam, and about 6 million of them were admitted to colleges with an admission rate of 1.9 to 1, which meant nearly 60% of those who took the exam were admitted to higher education institutions. Both in terms of enrollment rate and the number of students, higher education in China has successfully transformed from serving a few elites to serving the mass. The decentralization and marketization reforms have been undoubtedly successful to enlarge the capacity of higher education for increased number of students.

But to others, the reforms have not been so successful. "Whether it is the vaunted concept of quality education or the reform of the exam-oriented system, I would say education reform is the most unsuccessful of all reforms in China since the 1980s," according to Xu Haoyuan, a psychologist in China, as quoted by China Daily (Tao, 2003). This view is shared by many Chinese people. A 2005 survey found that over 77% of the public were either "very dissatisfied" or "somewhat dissatisfied" with the overall situation of education in China. Only 4.1% reported that they were "very satisfied" or "somewhat satisfied" (Yang, 2006).

The discontent mainly comes from two sources. First, the curriculum decentralization movement and other associated reforms have not achieved their objectives: more flexibility in curriculum, all-round education of the child, more independent thinking and creative talents, and less student burdens. Today, students and schools continue to be burdened by excessive amount of academic work and tests, which have been blamed for depriving students of time to engage in other activities and hurting students' health, independent thinking, and overall psychological and mental development (Zhao, 2007).

Second, the decentralization and marketization movement has resulted in more inequality in education. Because of the uneven economic development in different regions in China, different provinces and cities have different levels of investment in education. The disparity in terms of government education input is appalling. According to data released by the MOE in 2006, Shanghai invested an average of over 9,400 *yuan* RMB per student in its primary schools, while Henan's per pupil input was only 948 *yuan*, a difference of 10 times (MOE&NSB&MOF, 2006).

The inequality also comes from the financial capacity of families to pay education expenses. Despite the government's efforts to make loans available, many families in China still cannot afford higher education. In 2004, the average annual tuition was about 5,000 *yuan* and dormitory rent was about 1,200 *yuan*, while the average net income of city residents and rural residents was 9,400 *yuan* and 2,400 *yuan,* respectively. In other words, it would take a city worker 4 years and a farmer 13 years to pay for 1 year's higher education expenses, without them spending on anything else (XinhuaNews, 2007).

While the mixed reactions are expected of such large-scale reforms that span 30 years, it is apparent that the devolution of fiscal responsibilities and marketization of education have had positive effects on the education system. They have brought in more financial resources, diversified the system, and led to more educational opportunities. Of course, these reforms have created inequalities. And the government has begun to address these new inequalities through a new series of efforts – mostly recentralization. For example, the central government has devoted billions in recent years to building schools and boarding facilities, developing technology infrastructure and digital content, and covering the costs of textbooks and supplies for students in less-developed regions. The central government has also taken a more active role in controlling higher education costs and providing financial assistance to poor students.

The reforms around curriculum, pedagogy, assessment, and other reform practices that aimed to enhance the quality of education or to transform traditional modes of education have been much less successful. Despite these efforts, the essence of education remains the same as before the reforms:

> According to a recent national study by the Ministry of Education, although many educators seem to have accepted the concept of "quality education" and some teachers have changed their teaching practices, by and large the focus on the whole child remains lip service. "Quality education is loudly spoken, but test-oriented education gets the real attention," notes the report. As a result, competition among students remains fierce, schools and teachers continue to teach to the test at the expense of students' physical and mental health, test preparation overrides national curriculum requirements, and some schools resort to militaristic ways of managing their students. Under intense pressure, students spend all their time and energy on schoolwork. (Zhao, 2007)

Conclusions

China's reform, like any other systemic reforms, have been neither straightforward nor completely successful. There are a number of lessons we can learn from China's 30 years of systemic reforms.

First, reforms are always iterative and have unexpected consequences. In the case of China, while decentralization and marketization have been the consistent themes, they have resulted in some serious negative consequences that were not anticipated. Thus, reform agents should be prepared to be persistent and ready to introduce corrective actions. In China, when decentralization and marketization took place, the once tightly controlled system was suddenly liberated, which resulted in many unplanned actions at the local level. Some of these actions were positive and others not. The positive ones included bold experimentations with different financing models. As documented earlier in this chapter, public education institutions developed very creative ways to enhance their revenues. But such experiments also brought chaos, public discontent, and inequality. The government took action to recentralize some functions and passed laws to regulate the education market.

Second, structural changes are easier than cultural changes. In the case of China, decentralization and marketization of fiscal responsibilities, administrative structures, school governance, and even curriculum and textbooks took effect quickly. But the school culture, that is, how teaching and learning occur and what students, parents, and teachers value did not change much. Test-oriented education, which has been one of primary targets of the reforms, remains strong.

Third, governments must be actively involved in education reforms. Although decentralization and marketization seem to have been the trend in world education reforms, governments cannot remove itself from education, particularly in addressing the inequalities that inevitably result from decentralization and marketization. In China's case, for a period time, the central government significantly reduced its role in education financing, which resulted in increasing disparity in school funding. Growing disparities in turn resulted in serious social and educational problems. Fortunately, the central government has reassumed its responsibility and has taken actions to reduce the funding gap.

Lastly, it should be noted that what works in China may not work in other countries due to cultural differences. In this chapter, we have mostly discussed political actions but not much about the economic and historical context of education in China. But it should be emphasized that China's systemic reform strategies – decentralization and marketization – mimic its economic reforms over the past 30 years. In addition, shifting fiscal responsibilities to society and families works in China because it has a long tradition of valuing education. Education, in the eyes of most Chinese, is noble and practically the only means for upward mobility. These may not be the case in some other countries.

References

Bray, M. (1999). Control of education: Issues and tensions in centralization and decentralization. In R. F. Arnove & C. A. Torres (Eds.), *Comparative Education: The Dialectic of the Global and the Local*. Lanham, MD: Rowman & Littlefield.

Bray, M., & Borevskaya, N. (2001). Financing education in transitional societies: Lessons from Russia and China. *Comparative Education, 37*(3), 345–365.

CCCCP. (1980). Decision to universalize primary education. Retrieved January 20, 2008, from http://www.moe.edu.cn/edoas/website18/info4987.htm

Farrell, D., & Grant, A. J. (2005). China's looming talent shortage. *The McKinsey Quarterly: The Online Journal of McKinsey & Co.* Retrieved December 19, 2007, from http://www.mckinsey.com/mgi/publications/chinatalent.asp

Fu, Z. (2002, December 24). A summary of socialization of support services in China's higher education: Three years' achievement more than fifty years. *People's Daily (Overseas Edition)* (p. 2).

Hawkins, J. N. (2000). Centralization, decentralization, recentralization: Educational reform in China. *Journal of Educational Administration, 38*(5), 442–454.

Kwan, C. (2007). Free teacher education stirs hot discussions. *China Daily*. March 14, 2007. Retrieved December 28, 2008, from http://www.chinadaily.com.cn/china/2007-03/14/content_827801.htm

Kwong, J. (1997). The reemergence of private schools in socialist China. *Comparative Education Review, 41*(3), 244–259.

Luo, D. (2001, September 29). 31 Provinces implement 3+X exams. *Beijing Morning*.

MOE. (1985). Decision on systemic educational reform (Zhonggong Zhongyang Guanyu Jiaoyu Tizhi Gaige de Jueding). Retrieved December 19, 2007, from http://www.moe.edu.cn/edoas/website18/level3.jsp?tablename=208&infoid=3318

MOE. (1986). Compulsory education law of P.R.C. (Zhongguo Yiwu Jiaoyufa). Retrieved December 19, 2007, from http://www.moe.edu.cn/edoas/website18/info1431.htm

MOE. (1993). Framework for China's education reform and development (Zhongguo Jiaoyu Gaige he Fazhan Gangyao). Retrieved December 19, 2007, from http://www.moe.edu.cn/edoas/website18/level3.jsp?tablename=208&infoid=3334

MOE. (1998). Action plan to reinvigorate education for the 21st century (Mianxiang 21 Shiji Jiaoyu Zhenxin Xingzheng Jihua). Retrieved January 20, 2008, from http://www.moe.edu.cn/edoas/website18/info3337.htm

MOE. (1999). Decision to further educational systemic reform and promote quality-oriented education (Guanyu Shenhua Jiaoyu Tizhi Gaige Quanmian Tuijin Suzhi Jiaoyu de Jueding). Retrieved December 19, 2007, from http://www.chinapop.gov.cn/flfg/xgflfg/t20040326_30741.htm

MOE. (2001). Decision on compulsory education reform and development (Guanyu Jichu Jiaoyu Gaige yu Fazhan de Jueding). Retrieved December 19, 2007, from www.fjjyjy.net/UploadFiles/20057416581892.doc

MOE. (2002). Law to encourage minban education in the People's Republic of China (PRC Minban Jiaoyu Cujinfa). Retrieved January 20, 2008, from http://www.moe.edu.cn/edoas/website18/info1433.htm

MOE. (2006). Data on the number of non-state/private schools of all levels. Retrieved January 20, 2008, from http://www.moe.gov.cn/edoas/website18/info33446.htm

MOE&NSB&MOF. (2006). 2006 National statistical report on educational expenditure. Retrieved January 20, 2008, from http://www.moe.gov.cn/edoas/website18/info36955.htm

Mok, K. H. (1997a). Privatization or marketization: Educational development in Post-Mao China. *International Review of Education, 43*(5/6), 547–567.

Mok, K. H. (1997b). Retreat of the state: Marketization of education in the pearl river delta. *Comparative Education Review, 41*(3), 260–276.

State Council. (1977). Suggestions for the admissions to higher education institutions (Guanyu 1977 Gaodeng Xuexiao Zhaosheng Gongzuo de Yijian). Retrieved January 20, 2008, from http://www.moe.edu.cn/edoas/website18/info4986.htm

Tao, X. (2003). Lessons to learn on education reform [Electronic Version]. *China Daily, June, 13*. Retrieved January 20, 2008 from http://www.china.org.cn/english/culture/67092.htm

Wang, C., & Zhou, Q. (2002). Basic education reform in China: Untangling the story of success, *Education Policy Analysis Archives* (Vol. 10).

Wang, W. (2006). An analysis of "private schools operated by famous schools" in China. Retrieved January 20, 2008, from http://www.bpedu.org.cn/xxlr1.asp?ID=427

XinhuaNews. (2004). Chinese college entrance examination: Autonomy draw public attention. Retrieved January 20, 2008, from http://news.xinhuanet.com/focus/2004-06/14/content_1521059.htm

XinhuaNews. (2007). 59 Universities are free to enroll students, Special talents are valued. Retrieved January 20, 2008, from http://news.xinhuanet.com/edu/2007-12/11/content_7229930.htm

Yang, D. (2006). *Bluebook of education: The development report of China's education (2005)*. Beijing, China: Social Sciences Archives Press.

Yang, D. (2006). From the 1980s to the 1990s. In D. Yang (Ed.), *The ideal and reality of China's education equality (Zhongguo Jiaoyu Gongping de Lixiang yu Xianshi, in Chinese)*. Beijing: Beijing University Press.

Zhao, Y. (2007). China and the whole child. *Educational Leadership, 64*(8), 70–73.

Educational Leadership in Racially Divided Communities

Jonathan D. Jansen

Leading in deeply divided societies is at the same time an emotional, spiritual and political task. The volumes of instrumental writing on the subject of leadership, whether in the tentative language of academic writing or in the language of corporate certainty ("six steps or seven habits or twenty one laws ..."), hardly begin to capture this complexity. It is much more than *balancing* the interests of very different groups – like black and white, men and women, and majority and minority; leadership in divided communities is about engaging and transforming diverse constituencies even as the leader seeks to keep everyone in conversation. It is more than seeking out and applying the right technologies, for the challenges at hand extend way beyond manipulable techniques or validated instruments. Human behaviour where the rawness of racial division is still fresh is far more complex than such reductionist measures presume. And it is not simply about imposing change on others; leading in divided contexts is about being transformed even as one sets out, perhaps presumptuously, to transform others. This chapter offers an extended deliberation on the nature, purposes and consequences of leadership and educational change in post-conflict societies, invoking the South African experience as a case in point.

Over the Rainbow

Soaked in religious metaphor, South Africa attracted the admiration of people around the world for its peaceful transition to democracy after more than 350 years of colonialism and apartheid. Part of a deeply religious country, citizens of the new South Africa followed the cue of the great moral figure of Archbishop Tutu talking about the rainbow people of God; white political leaders spoke about Damascus Road experiences, referring to their political conversion; a few among black

J.D. Jansen (✉)
University of the Free State, Bloemfontein, South Africa
e-mail: rector.rd@ufs.ac.za

A. Hargreaves et al. (eds.), *Second International Handbook of Educational Change*, 363
Springer International Handbooks of Education 23, DOI 10.1007/978-90-481-2660-6_21,
© Springer Science+Business Media B.V. 2010

leaders saw nothing short of divine intervention that brought together sworn enemies to agree on a political settlement; and one remarkable white politician, the former minister of police, dropped to his knees in an act of contrition and washed the feet of the chief of staff of the Presidency, a black activist his forces once tried to kill.

Despite stubborn inequalities, a rampant AIDS pandemic, and waves of violent crime, South Africa managed to hold the centre with respect to racial tolerance, if not embrace. Schools integrated with relative ease; black and white mingled freely together in public spaces once rigidly segregated; corporate boardrooms gradually integrated as blacks, albeit a minority, gained economic muscle in an openly capitalist society; and black and white politicians populated the leadership of both the ruling party and the main opposition parties in a richly diverse parliament.

And, then, the wheels came off. In a short space of time, dramatic incidents of white racism suddenly threatened the common belief that South Africans had overcome the horrific racial prejudices of the past through a permanent settlement that would eventually lead to what the natives call *a non-racial society*. Four white high school students kick a homeless black man to death. An 18-year-old white youth takes a loaded gun into an impoverished black settlement and empties the weapon on the inhabitants, killing four people including a baby. And four white students capture on video their racist attack on black women workers at their university, including an act that coerced the staff to ingest food on which these students had allegedly urinated. In an instant, the public mood shifted, and South Africans started to question whether they were, in a manner of speaking, over the rainbow era of racial harmony and reconciliation.

What was striking about these three incidents was that the students were all senior high school and junior undergraduates, all male and all from the dominant group of white South Africans, the Afrikaners, who established and maintained the apartheid state with the generous support of English-speaking whites. This was the predominant ethnic group of the historically Afrikaans University of Pretoria where I served as the first black Dean of the largest of nine academic units, the Faculty of Education. In this essay, I will reflect on what I learned about pursuing educational change within this community, which, overnight, became both a demographic and a political minority within a democratic state in which black South Africans dominated postapartheid politics.

Into the Heart of Whiteness

It was always unreasonable to think that centuries of racial conflict and division would dissipate in the euphoria of liberation in the 1990s. What is striking about South Africa was that there were not more incidents of racial confrontation among black and white in a generally peaceful transition. Yet the seeds of antipathy and animosity still run deep. It was not, therefore, the coming together of black and white in previously segregated public spaces that caused the difficulties of racial tension; it was, I will argue, the unresolved problems of bitter knowledge about history, identity, culture and politics that lay at the root of an untransformed society. And this failure to interrupt received knowledge is, in the first and last instance, an educational change problem.

How is it possible that young white students, born around the time of Mandela's release from prison, could hold such firm views about the past, such rigid views about black people and, especially among the boys, such fatalistic views about the future? This was the question that dogged me during my early years as Dean of Education at the University of Pretoria. It made no sense. These white students had no direct experience of apartheid; they did not live as masters and madams through the worst years of racial oppression; they did not police the townships during states of emergency; and the boys did not have to face the trauma of compulsory military service on and often beyond the borders of South Africa. Despite the fact that these were, technically speaking, postapartheid children, their beliefs and behaviours mirrored those of their parents – the people who upheld, supported and benefited directly from white domination in the decades before they were born. The more I listened to my almost all-white undergraduate class of more than 2,000 students, the more this question besieged me. After 7 years as Dean, I resigned from the University of Pretoria to complete a book that seeks to answer that question. The book is titled *Knowledge in the Blood* (2009).

The answer to the opening question first emerged when I encountered the work of Eva Hoffman, and in particular her book, *After Such Knowledge* (2004). Hoffman poses the question personally: how is it, she asks, that as second-generation Jews, who did not live through the horrors of the Holocaust as did our parents, we nevertheless behave as if we were there? She names this phenomenon *the paradoxes of indirect knowledge*. Indirect knowledge results from the intergenerational transmission of spoken and unspoken knowledge from the parents who were there to the children who were not. The consequences are devastating for the second generation, for they bear and express the bitterness and the loss of their parents long after the initial terror was actually lived. This insight stretched way beyond the trauma of the Holocaust; it explained the beliefs and the behaviours of my white students.

For those 7 years, I tried to immerse myself inside the lives of my white students. I attended and spoke in their different Afrikaans churches. I visited their homes. I spent time with their parents, often talking about adjustment and change to the promised non-racial order. I observed teaching and learning in white Afrikaans primary and high schools. I gave speeches at Afrikaans cultural festivals and workshops at Afrikaans cultural associations. I trained with principals and teachers from the Afrikaans school community and gave endless talks about sameness and difference at school events such as prize-giving ceremonies. I took the students to the malls and the movies and attended their sporting events. In their university residences and in bush camps, we talked for countless hours about race, identity and the transition into a new country and a changing university. And this is what I found.

The single most important finding from this intense experience working with white (mainly) Afrikaans students is that like all South African youth, they are decent, idealistic and committed to their country and are capable of change. These young people are not wide-eyed racists going about the university seeking out black people for racial attack and humiliation. This is not my experience. There is however a serious problem. They carry within them the seeds of bitter knowledge that, left unchallenged, can easily germinate into the most vicious racial attacks on and outside the university campus.

In the case of white Afrikaner youth, how is this troubled knowledge transmitted? It is channelled through five influential agencies: the family, the church, the school, cultural associations and the peer group. In itself, such an observation about knowledge transmission is hardly novel within sociological observation. The problem is that these agencies transmit the same dangerous messages in all-white social circles over and over again; worse, these messages have not been interrupted over the period of transition despite the spectacular changes in the formal institutions of democracy. To be sure, some of the potency of these messages might have been diluted as a result of the collapse of some of the historical agencies of socialization – such as the state media under apartheid. But by and large, the three core messages of transmission have remained intact.

The first message is about *racial exclusivity* (we belong by ourselves), the second about *racial supremacy* (we are better than them) and the third about *racial victimization* (we are being targeted by them). What reinforces these messages in the hearts of young white people is the threat of social collapse around them through things like rampant crime, electricity failures, corruption in government and affirmative action. In the belief system of white youth, these social events are interpreted through a singular lens: black incompetence, black greed, black barbarism and black retaliation.

It is not difficult to understand, therefore, why white students stepping into their first integrated experiences in the undergraduate university years would revolt against learning and especially living together with black students. It is also not hard to grasp why right-wing political parties, without any chance of prominence within the broader society, would exploit the bitter knowledge of white students. This has been the primary strategy of the Freedom Front Plus, a conservative political party, as it infiltrated the white Afrikaans universities to wreak racial havoc on these campuses.

The strategy of the Freedom Front Plus was brilliant in its perversity. It would not appeal to *race* to purvey its inflammatory ideas; it would appeal to *rights*. Students should not be forced to live together; they have the rights of association. Students have the right to learn in their own languages, implying Afrikaans and therefore largely, if not exclusively, white classes. Students who pay for their education (erroneously implying only white students) should have the right to choose where they live on campus and in what language they are taught.

For institutions that for many years ran their student elections along party political lines, like the University of Pretoria, the Freedom Front Plus sailed into the perfect storm. It won every student election by substantial margins with election posters that contained the most grievous racial insults. And on campuses like the University of the Free State, where this bitter knowledge was fed through separate residences long after other institutions had deracialized their living arrangements, the advent of the Freedom Front Plus was like fire attracted to an oiled rag.

South Africa's education policies since 1994 have had as their presumptive audience black students in schools and universities – as the national curriculum so clearly demonstrates. Our national policies do not speak of engaging and disrupting the bitter knowledge of white students, from a policy standpoint. National education policy appears to assume that white knowledge either does not exist or that by some miraculous feat, white and black students (and teachers) thrown together in the same educational spaces would simply find each other despite the rival knowledges they bring into the learning commons.

Interrupting Bitter Knowledge

In our years of research and living among white students, we achieved some measure of success with educational change at this one institution, the University of Pretoria and, in particular, its Faculty of Education. What follows is some discussion of the limits of critical theory and the possibilities within a new approach to racial conflict and divided histories in post-conflict situations.

Critical theory remains a crucial body of scholarship in education that offers a lens for understanding the role of schools in perpetuating and subverting the race, class and gender interests of state and society. But critical theory, interpreted broadly,[1] is severely limited in post-conflict situations for making sense of troubled knowledge and for transforming those who carry the burden of such knowledge on both sides of divided communities. Critical theory both receives and constructs the world as divided between black and white, the working classes and the privileged classes, legal citizen and illegal immigrant, men and women, straight and queer, and oppressors and oppressed; its dialogical pretenses notwithstanding, the world is taken as torn among rival groups.

Critical theory then takes sides once this divided world is constructed in terms of these polarities. The goal of a critical education is liberation, to free the oppressed (those on the underside of history) from the shackles of their oppression and to take on evil systems and resist the agents of exploitation. As one review put it, "The primary goal of critical pedagogy is to empower students to understand the links between knowledge, history, and power and to use this knowledge to resist hegemonic structures and dominant ideologies (Hesford, 1999)." The evangel of critical theory therefore enables us to see the world from the perspective of those denied human rights or economic access or racial justice. And while critical theory has moved beyond the incisive class analyses of the 1960s into a more richly textured account of the *intersectionalist* character of oppression, it remains a *pedagogy of the oppressed* (Freire, 2000; Knudsen, 2007; Weis, McCarthy, & Dimitriadis, 2006).

---

[1]For a useful discussion of the narrow and broad meanings of critical theory see the Stanford Encyclopedia of Philosophy's entry on Critical Theory (first published on Tuesday 8 March 2005), accessible on http://plato.stanford.edu/entries/critical-theory accessed on 26 January 2008.

Of course, much of the intellectual labor that spawned critical theories of education comes from within advanced capitalist societies, principally the United States, and this location in part explains the rather fixed terms of the debate – the oppressed classes struggling against the overwhelming power of an oppressive system (Choules, 2007). Still, the focus of this critical literature is less on what to do with the racist or tribalist in the classroom and more to do with how to *empower* or give *voice* or lend *recognition* to those marginalized within school and society.[2] The often facile deployment of these categories of course tend to gloss over the complexities of power and inequality represented in the classroom, a point made elegantly in Ellsworth's (1989) famed critique of the limits of critical pedagogy.

Yet it is not only that critical theory divides the world; in its more radical version, the enemy is not a human Other but a capitalist system, oppressive processes, imposing ideologies, the neoliberal state, and so forth. The task is to *face capital down*"[3] to challenge oppressive structures and to destabilize regnant pedagogies and beliefs. Such a conception of the other side, without real human beings to encounter, engage, confront and change, has little value for a post-conflict pedagogy. This is not to deny the systemic and institutionalized character of oppression; it is simply to lament the denial of what confronts teachers in schools and universities in the aftermath of genocide and conflict – real human beings. There is a different and more compelling question that confronts teachers within post-conflict societies, one posed so poignantly by Freema Elbaz-Luwisch (2004): "How is education possible when there is a body in the middle of the room?" Elbaz-Luwisch talks about the kind of pedagogy appropriate to contexts where Arab/Palestinian and Jewish students face each other in the same classroom. By extension, this is a question that applies equally to black and white children in the postapartheid classroom; to Catholic and Protestant children in Northern Island; to Hutu and Tutsi children in Rwanda, and so on (Davies, 2004).

These are of course extreme examples, but inequality and prejudice exist everywhere, and what critical theory does is to assume that a critical pedagogy can lead what is sometimes presented as a socially homogenous group of teachers and students towards a common understanding of the nature of oppression and how to confront its systemic elements.[4] But classrooms are themselves deeply divided places where contending histories and rival lived experiences come embodied with indirect (and sometimes *direct*) knowledge into the same pedagogical space to create deeply complex challenges for teachers. And of course even within this space the divisions are not restricted to the student body.

---

[2]Two important criticisms of the conceptual and philosophical claims and assumptions of critical theory can be found in Maddock (1999) and Tubbs (1996).

[3]See the review of two books, one by and one on Peter McLaren, by Kahn (2005) and also McLaren (2006).

[4]It is a point made by Gur-Ze'ev (1998) as well, noting the tendency of critical theory to assume a "weak, controlled, and marginalized collectives" sharing a "common optimistic view of change"; see next footnote for full source details.

It follows therefore that it is not simply the master narratives of the official curriculum or the controlling ideologies of state examinations or the capitalist interests of the textbook industry that is at stake in the critical classroom; it is also the people there, the bodies in the classroom, who carry knowledge within themselves that must be engaged, interrupted and transformed. Moreover, these bearers of received knowledge do not come with one story about the past, a common understanding of the present and a shared vision of the future. It is divided knowledges *within* the classroom that constitute the starting point for a post-conflict pedagogy.

Taking sides, as in critical theory, is not therefore a very productive stance in settings where *the clash of martyrological memories* (Hoffman, 2004, pp. 140–141) confronts the teacher of the memory holders. The goal of a post-conflict pedagogy under these circumstances is first to understand the emotional, psychological and spiritual burden of indirect knowledge carried by all sides in the aftermath of conflict. The teacher takes position, for sure, but in a way that creates safe spaces within which the afflicted on all sides can speak openly and without fear of dismissal. Furthermore, even from positions in which the teacher is herself implicated – like the black teacher hearing white grievances about black people – there is at least an attempt to understand how such knowledge came about, what it does to white students and, then, how that knowledge can be productively engaged.

The important point here is that in the rush to judgment and openly taking one side, critical theory dislodges the teacher from a compassionate involvement with the knowledge of the other side. Such positioning estranges the teacher from those who are arguably most in need of critical engagement with their troubled knowledge and makes it impossible for constructive confrontation and transformation of this knowledge.

Critical Theory as Post-Conflict Pedagogy

What I have tried to convey is an argument that undoing oppression in dangerous and divided communities requires the bringing together of black and white into the same dialogic space. This means that there is diminished opportunity for such a social and educational encounter in segregated classrooms, for the presence and passion of the other enables the clash and engagement with conflicting and conflicted knowledges. The longer schools remain segregated and in cases where schools become re-segregated, the chances of creating opportunities for a post-conflict pedagogy to take root are dramatically reduced.[5] This does not mean that inventive teachers cannot and do not create such extracurricular moments of encounter with others or that white teachers in black schools, for example, cannot provide such opportunities for cross-racial engagement through skilful teaching and exemplary leadership. But it does mean that intense and sustained opportunities for prolonged

---

[5]There is empirical substantiation for this point in the excellent study of integrated and non-integrated Catholic and Protestant schools in Northern Ireland; see Byrne (1997).

engagement among white and black students, in this case, are absent, and the chances of separate knowledges being retained, with all the consequences of stereotype and racism, will remain. With this in mind, what constitutes the *critical* in such a critical theory of education? More specifically, what are the critical elements of a post-conflict pedagogy?

The Power of Indirect Knowledge

A post-conflict theory of education recognizes the power of indirect knowledge. Students come into the school or university classroom with powerful ideas and constructs about the past, the present and the future. They carry knowledge of a past in which they did not live or which they did not experience, and yet it is a knowledge that has profound individual and social consequences for how they live, how they learn and how they see. This knowledge is not only cognitive knowledge but also emotional knowledge, for what the second generation of children carries with them is strongly attached to their ethnic, cultural, religious, language and even political identities.

It is not that these second-generation children carry knowledge of specific historical events, for they probably do not *know* the detail of dates and commanders in the war between Boer and Briton, or information about specific atrocities in specific encounters between the English imperialists and Zulu warriors. What they carry with them is thematic knowledge, meaning knowledge of broad themes about conquest and humiliation, struggle and survival, suffering and resilience, poverty and recovery, and black and white.[6] While the more outrageous racial themes of apartheid are no longer trumpeted in public spaces, the underlying ideological and emotional attachments that come with such knowledge claims remain more or less undisturbed (da Cruz, 2005).

Because indirect knowledge is also emotional knowledge, it can be explosive in classroom situations in which teachers are unprepared to mediate such engagement. When such pedagogical explosions happen, from the side of white students, they do not simply round on the teacher but also on the black students in the same space. To say therefore that indirect knowledge is consequential is to imply that teacher preparation programs need to take account of this thinking in the development of educators and that in-service programs must prepare teachers in practice for something they did not have to encounter before.

Indirect knowledge is also partial knowledge. Of course, it needs to be remembered that all knowledge is partial and that the choices that every school and teacher makes about what to teach are not simply intellectual decisions about appealing

---

[6] As she digs into the personal history of apartheid's most notorious killer, the man called "Prime Evil" in the South African press, Pumla Gobodo-Madikizela (2003) uncovers the operation of what she calls "constant themes" and "refrains" in Afrikaner family and adult discourses that shaped Eugene de Kock's knowledge of past and future enemies, and that motivated his deadly ambitions (p. 21).

knowledge or a planning decision about appropriate knowledge (say for a particular grade level) but also a political decision about valued knowledge.

Any teacher who fails to recognize the existence and influence of indirect knowledge in, say, a history classroom or a language seminar, walks in the direction of a field littered with hidden landmines. It is true that teachers have found nimble ways of navigating these minefields in ways that circumvent any controversy or conflict by relaying official knowledge in very technical ways or doing so in all-white (or all-black) classrooms or avoiding it all together. Such curricular or pedagogic aversion postpones deep-rooted problems, continues to extend the supremacist ideas of white children, leaves unresolved the burden of knowledge they carry and denies the possibility of building community towards what Paul Gilroy (2000a, b) calls a planetary humanism.

The Importance of Listening

The natural compulsion of any teacher is to tell, to demonstrate authority and to inculcate (what a brutal word) knowledge. This is especially the case in authoritarian societies and explains the spectacular failure of Western pedagogies in third world states because of its insistence on open, critical, and student-centred classrooms (Jansen, 2005). When students initiate a question, the familiar impulse of the educator is to anticipate and correct, to respond and to direct an answer towards the goals of the lesson. This representation of the teacher as the authority who knows all and who controls the classroom is routinely presumed in texts and manuals on classroom management and student discipline. It is especially the case that when controversial questions or difficult subjects emerge, the teacher is even more attentive to *managing* the classroom situation lest things get out of control.

Unfortunately, this is the direct opposite of what is required for a critical dialogue in divided societies, schools and classrooms on subjects of history, identity and power. What a post-conflict pedagogy demands is a very different approach where the teacher has to consciously position himself/herself to listen; this will not come naturally, but without it, there is no chance of any speaking and certainly no opportunity for listening. This kind of proposition implies a highly skilled teacher who is not only confident in the subject matter and comfortable with different students but competent to manage difficult thematic knowledge. In other words, the success of a post-conflict pedagogy depends almost entirely on the qualities of those who teach.[7]

The problem with listening is that even well-intentioned teachers are emotionally drawn into student stories in ways that could render them off-balance in critical dialogues of the kind required for cross-border engagements. A white teacher under

---

[7]Few post-conflict interventions have achieved such resonance among black and white teachers than the listening that comes through hearing stories of the Other, as in *Facing the Past*, a nongovernmental organization in South Africa. See Tibbits (2006).

attack for an action perceived by black students to be racist or taking sides could become defensive and find it difficult to listen to what students have to say. This is emotionally taxing work, and yet the steady position of the teacher is crucial for critical dialogue.

Listening is obviously more than the physical act of receiving auditory stimuli that flow from student to teacher. It is, more correctly, a process of hearing. This means listening for the pain that lies behind a claim, the distress that is concealed in an angry outburst and the sense of loss that is protested in a strident posture. Listening in a post-conflict pedagogy does not mean that anything goes and that the recklessness of accusation is simply tolerated – not at all. The teacher has a crucial role in setting an atmosphere that enables talking and listening to take place in the first place (more about this later) and, at crucial points, to reprimand where talking randomly insults other students or the teacher herself. But hearing in this sense means delaying interruption, enabling expression and understanding the claims and the silences, the body language and the spoken word, and the pain inside the voice.

Listening in a post-conflict pedagogy is therefore an active rather than a passive event, but it is also attentive to being even-handed in allowing all to speak in equal measure. This is difficult, for on the one hand the teacher has to listen to and follow what is being said, and on the other hand, the teacher has to be conscious of who spoke, what they said, how they said it and what they failed to say. The identity of the speaker matters; giving voice to students in a tense and intense critical dialogue is all about allowing for expression, yet being conscious of one's own identity all the time. Listening is also important in terms of who does not speak at all; an observant teacher is listening for silences, sulkiness, anger, and disappointment. This requires emotional attunement to the classroom as a whole, and is another level of listening crucial for enabling and sustaining critical dialogues between white and black students. It is also critical knowledge for disrupting received knowledge.

The Disruption of Received Knowledge

Listening signals respect not agreement; it is an empathetic attempt to understand, not an amoral attempt to condone. The indirect knowledge that students receive and carry should be directly challenged and critically engaged as a matter of social justice – for white students. The indirect knowledge that the second generation brings into learning and living spaces comes from closed circles of socialization that reinforce single messages about white superiority and black subordination. It essentializes and triumphalizes a white ethnic identity in opposition to rival identities – black, English and other – and in the process, assigns differential and hierarchical value to these subordinate identities. For these reasons alone, indirect knowledge should be made explicit and its potential and real harm discussed openly.

The harm that white knowledge imposed on black children is well documented before and since apartheid (Barbarin & Richter, 2001; Burman & Reynolds, 1986; Straker, 1992) and is readily visible in the social, economic, psychological and educational consequences of racism and inequality deep into the years of democracy in South Africa. What is less obvious in the critical literatures on schooling is what indirect knowledge does to white children, the second generation of apartheid's rulers. Their received knowledge renders white students incapable of competent cross-cultural communication; it limits their ability to gain freely from the richness of the intercultural experience; it has done an as yet unmeasured harm to their racial psyches – one moment the masters , equal citizens the next and minority subjects forever in the new social order; it leaves them isolated and fearful within the new national arrangement where, no matter what they do, whites are framed by the majority as racial suspects all the time; it deprives them of the skills, knowledge and values to meaningfully access the changing and more cosmopolitan knowledge of the new regime; and it leaves them stunted in their social, moral and emotional development in the same way that apartheid distorted their parents' sense of themselves within the human community, a distortion transmitted to the children.[8]

It does not help that the postapartheid state constructs official victims, those who deserve empathy, support and resources, and those who do not. Official victims do not include poor whites even though socio-economic status is a more equitable and sensible way of accounting for difference in a capitalist society that professes a commitment to what is called *non-racialism*. In the new narrative, official victims alone carry a burden from the past; white parents and their children do not. This is crucial, for the pain of white second-generation students show that even though they were not directly involved in the atrocities, not being born at the time, they nevertheless inherit relative economic privilege as well as the pounding burden of guilty knowledge.

The disruption of received knowledge requires attention to a relational pedagogy. The disruptive knowledge advocated requires that white students be set in critical dialogue with black students, observe examples of leadership and living that counters and confronts their own logics of race and identity, and engage critical knowledge presented through the re-examination of the old knowledge received.

The Significance of Pedagogic Dissonance

The value of pedagogic dissonance cannot be overstated. It is *pedagogic* because it is designed and lived to teach, without the necessity of speaking, the contradictions inherent in a racially organized and a racist world view. Dissonance happens when, for example, a white student observes a black student outperforming him in

---

[8]Throughout the research for this book I would only encounter brief, often very emotional, reflections by white children on incidents in the course of growing up that had a lasting impact on their racial formation; there is, to my knowledge, no systematic inquiry on this subject in educational contexts.

mathematics, and when the evidence is irrefutable in this subject that white patriarchs singled out as *not for him*, then white doubt sets in and the process of disruption unfolds.

This was the case with Surgeon Xolo, a brilliant young black high school graduate who scored reasonable marks in his rural, black high school in mathematics. Sought out to come into the Faculty of Education and given the unfamiliar resources, he started to score the highest marks in mathematics in all his education classes from the 1st to 4th year of study, and he did this in the midst of almost all-white classes composed of students from well-endowed white schools with qualified teachers in mainly middle-class suburbs. At one of the many prize-giving ceremonies, this one for a team task, a white woman student in her acceptance speech tells the mainly white crowd: "I was only able to do this because of Surgeon." A massive pedagogic dissonance is on display here, one that does not need a moralizing *see-what-happens-when* lesson by teachers. It is simply there in a public and disruptive way and it is all the more powerful because it is not *taught* directly.

One incident of pedagogic dissonance does not of course lead to personal change, but it can *begin* to erode sure knowledge. It is, moreover, the collection of dissonant events, spread over multiple school years, that eventually collapses the foundations of indirect knowledge. Dissonance happens when black school or university leaders step forward with acts of kindness and generosity towards their white staff. Seen from the other side of the bridge, dissonance is unavoidable when a white woman undergraduate student comes into the office of a black male Dean to hold his hand and to bless him. Dissonance is imposed on a school or university campus when the institutional culture and the public curriculum includes and integrates multiple knowledges within a social justice framework.

The case for dissonance in a post-conflict pedagogy is not, however, a simplistic concern for *overcoming resistance*[9] or *motivating the disinterested* among privileged students. It is, rather, a pedagogical commitment to locate, interrogate and engage troubled knowledge within (in this case) white students in ways that allow for disruption of received authority. Only in this way, through human engagement, can a broader inquiry into the ideological and structural foundations of racism proceed.

Even so, direct and unmediated confrontation with disruptive knowledge seldom works; it is more likely to fuel egotistical aggression. Taking the commonsense with which white students live, and asking them to reflect on that which they embrace, is much more likely to begin to alter secure and intimate knowledge. For the interruption of received knowledge to work, the white student must first be drawn into a trusting relationship (more later), but again, knowledge disruption is a complex endeavour not attained by the simple (simplistic?) ambition of the new nationalists to merely inscribe victor knowledge onto a new curriculum.

---

[9] I am arguing here with McFalls and Cobb-Roberts (2001).

The Acknowledgement of Brokenness

The construct of brokenness carries the idea that in our human state we are prone to failure and incompletion and that as imperfect humans we constantly seek a higher order of living. Brokenness is the realization of imperfection, the spiritual state of recognizing one's humanness and the need for forgiveness and love. Yet brokenness is even more than this; it is the profound outward acknowledgement of inward struggle done in such a way as to invite communion with other people and with the divine.

In a post-conflict pedagogy, therefore, the teacher and the leader are part of the classroom story. They are not distant and *objective* pedagogues floating above the emotional and political divides that separate those in the classroom. Teachers in this pedagogy not only bring in their own identities, they also carry their own knowledge of the past. Such knowledge is out in the open and shared as part of the process of making sense of how to live together in the shadow of a shared history and with the prospects of a common future.

Brokenness compels dialogue. I have worked with white high school girls that want to share their own stories about how they wrestle with parents and other significant adults in their lives and are caught between an old knowledge that is faltering and a new knowledge that is compelling. They have questions about what happened and how it could have happened, and as they move forward to talk, they risk confiding in a (black) stranger but also breaking primordial bonds of loyalty with the (white) family. This is a highly significant moment in a post-conflict pedagogical situation and the beginning of the end for the certainty conveyed thus far through indirect knowledge. And it is only possible when, and because, white students witness the humanity of the other side through the concession of brokenness.

Contrary to the logic of masculine thought, brokenness is not weakness. By contrast, brokenness reveals inner strength, the capacity to acknowledge not only human frailty but also human sameness. It is the paradox conveyed in Christian verse: "when I am weak, then I am strong." This sounds like a near-impossible task for a teacher trained to and, indeed, eager to establish her authority in the classroom. And yet it is crucial to draw the students in and, more importantly, to demonstrate what it means to live openly and honestly with one's own knowledge about and in relation to those in the classroom.

The Importance of Hope

A post-conflict pedagogy is founded on hope. It does not get lost within a circularity of oppression talk where whites retell stories of *them* as being less and blacks retell stories of *us* as being harmed. It is strongly against any sense of victimhood, which traps white and black in an endlessly downward spiral of defeat. This kind of critical pedagogy recognizes the power and the pain at play in school and society and its effects on young people and then asks *how* things could be better. It shifts *martyrological memories* (Hoffman, 2004) towards seeing the possibility in others, and in ourselves. But this kind of sight (vision) is not possible when the characters in the divided setting are seen as essentially evil, as white racists, or as terminally disempowered, as black victims. Hope imagines, in a very real sense, a way out of the two quagmires, one black and one white. Hope starts by asking that same question within the pedagogical situation: "how do I move towards ..." in order to relocate to a safer and more secure place, with others.

Hope in a post-conflict pedagogy is not some empty, airheaded and aspirational quest of pedagogical Pollyannas detached from the hard ideological and material conditions that constrain and shape interracial relations. In this argument, hope recognizes and works through those conditions of oppression by recognizing the common bonds and bondage of white and black students and teachers in school and community. Hope requires the recognition of racism and the privilege it bestows, and hope demands that these consequences of white history and power be redressed. However, it cannot be taken on without the bonds of solidarity being first established between white and black, and this in turn cannot happen until the participants in the classroom and indeed in the community come to understand and confront themselves, and their disparate knowledges, in the historical and contemporary story.

Hope in this kind of pedagogy therefore begins with the quest for individual and collective understanding within the classroom. Under post-conflict conditions, there can be no discourse of, or even desire for, hope unless and until human beings within the same lived and learning space achieve some amount of self-understanding, some measure of common humanity, and some degree of disrupted knowledge. And, in this context, the teachers and the students are drawn into the same ambition.

A post-conflict pedagogy founded on hope once again requires that intergenerational stories of victimhood be disrupted. It is my firm belief that in addition to the very real structural fault lines that sustain divided communities, there are also the repeated and well-worn stories of defeat transmitted from one generation of children to the next. In this regard, I distinguish stories that remind black children about their shared heritage of a colonial past or a slave history (that is crucial) from stories that conclude with terminal endings of despair and distress. What destroys hope is that the story of the bondage of slavery is not always accompanied by a story of the bravery of the enslaved. One pedagogical story told by a black parent to the next generation might be to see Nelson Mandela as imprisoned for his beliefs by evil white captors; a complementary way of telling the story is to show how he imprisoned his white guards by the sheer force of his moral authority and political cause. The first story alone leads to despair; the story added signals hope.

Hope in a post-conflict pedagogy inside divided communities insists that the stories about oppressing and overcoming are mutually conceived and resolved. In other words, it is absolutely crucial that students understand that from the very beginning there were white resisters to slavery and colonialism fighting alongside the black cause. It is crucial in Rwanda that stories be told of Hutu resisters who lost their lives as one of the most efficient genocides in history was visited on the Tutsi minority by their Hutu neighbors. That there were Germans who stood by Jews, that there were Afrikaners who stood with blacks, that there were whites in the civil rights marches of the United States – all of whom faced the same ferocity of attack as those originally targeted because of their race or ethnicity or religion. Embedded in such stories of solidarity are stories of hope. And what students learn is that there is no genetic or social *essence* that predisposes any group of people towards hatred or, for that matter, towards love.

The Necessity for Establishing Risk-Accommodating Environments

White students do not rush into pedagogic spaces confessing guilt or acknowledging racism, nor do white parents suddenly own up to years of privilege at the expense of black citizens. Even when such compulsion is felt, it is extremely difficult for human beings to unburden themselves in private or public spaces. This was the most important mistake of the Truth and Reconciliation Commission (TRC) in South Africa, the assumption that whites, given the platform, would stream forward to tell the truth about their complicity in, and benefiting from, apartheid. The chair of the TRC, Archbishop Tutu was adamant: whites should use this invitation to not only speak the truth but, in the process, advance reconciliation. This of course did not happen, for a very good reason: human beings do not willingly release painful memories, especially not on a public platform, that could draw the ire of black victims and impose the shame of association with and support of apartheid.

When I did such workshops on risk accommodation within the classroom, invariably a teacher or professor would become adamant: there can be no reconciliation without truth. People need to acknowledge their racism and privilege as a very first step, or there's nothing to talk about. This is a particularly Western way of thinking: "fess up," as if this is an involuntary reflex to some central command. The explosion of talk shows in American public culture in which the most personal and the most bizarre behaviours are displayed without restraint to live audiences on national television strikes many in the third world as disgusting. This is not the real world. Guilt and shame are more common responses to burdensome knowledge than the apparent reveling in extreme and obnoxious behaviour.

Nevertheless, when I sense the adamant position that whites must simply step forward and acknowledge their racism, I ask a simple question: "Do any of you here have a memory of something so painful that you have not shared that memory with anyone, even those closest to you?" As the thud of this unexpected question takes hold in the room, I scan the faces of the participants as they struggle for a few seconds to process what was just asked. Slowly, most of the hands in the room would go up, acknowledging that there is a knowledge of something known only to them that cannot be spoken. Nothing demonstrates this point more powerfully that the acknowledgement of Gunter Grass, after so many years, that the Nobel Laureate for literature was actually a youthful member of Hitler's notorious Waffen-SS during the Second World War. For half a century, the author of *The Tin Drum* was the moral conscience of postwar Germany, urging his fellow citizens to own up to their terrible knowledge about the Holocaust and their role in that horrendous conflict. But he harboured secret knowledge such that "What I had accepted with the stupid pride of youth I wanted to conceal after the war out of a recurrent sense of shame" (Isaacson, 2007).

It is crucial in a post-conflict pedagogy that the teacher creates the atmosphere and structures the teaching–learning episodes in ways that reduce the risk of speaking openly about direct and indirect knowledge. Students must be able to speak without feeling that they will be judged or despised for what they believe. They must know that in a divided classroom there will be an attempt to *hear them out* even if their ideas are, on the face of it, outrageous, even offensive. The students must be reassured through the example of the teacher–leader that she/he can be trusted with such personal and ethnic knowledge. What is true, in this example, for white students is of course true also for black students, especially when the latter group is a minority within the classroom. To repeat, this creation of risk-accommodating environments does not mean that *anything goes* and that a student can spout offensive words about another group without consequences. Long before the pedagogic encounter, the atmosphere should have been set, the terms of engagement explained, the rules of the dialogue shared. Such difficult dialogues can only take place if trust in the teacher–leader is already ensured through the demonstration of a profound example of conciliation within and outside the classroom. The notion that *the lesson* starts in the classroom is clearly misguided.

Nonetheless, such encounters remain risky. I used to speak about risk-removing classroom climates; that is clearly impossible. At best the teacher will work towards a risk-accommodating environment in which students, in taking risks, are assured that they will be treated fairly and their positions given serious consideration irrespective of what they hold. It is only when students trust the teacher–leader, however, that the ability to speak is made possible. It is also when such trust is established that the teacher can take what is said and steer the students in the divided classroom towards a dialogue that counters racism, sexism and classism (among other things that divide) and demonstrate the harmfulness and the offensiveness of bigotry in school and society.

The Value of Demonstrative Leadership

For a post-conflict pedagogy to gain any traction in divided and suspicious learning contexts, the critical key is the quality and depth of leadership. I take leadership to be not as much a formal position but a set of dispositions and not an allocated posting but the ability to influence the behaviour of followers.[10] This kind of conception of leadership therefore accepts as given the notion of distributed leadership, and it

---

[10]I am grateful to Gene Carter, Executive Director of the Association for Supervision and Curriculum Development, for sharing this conception of leadership with me.

also understands that such leadership can be student, teacher or principal leadership within any educational setting.

The one thing that became repeatedly clear to me over the years of leadership among white students, staff and parents is that they had absolutely no reason to accept my authority outside of the formal designation of *Dean of the Faculty*. Indeed, in the first months of my appointment, there was very little contact with white students. They walked right past me, heads dropping or staring straight ahead to avoid eye contact. They always seemed to be in a hurry when I was around and engaged in tight conversation with friends when I passed by. When I did initially introduce myself there were cold stares, and, out of sheer demands of Afrikaner decency, they would mumble a greeting. I could not, at that time, sustain any conversation without making a fool out of myself. For many this was, after all, their first contact with a black person in authority of any kind, and I had more than a fair suspicion that the subject of my deanship must have come up at home and among peers.

Words, with teenagers, have very little meaning in a cynical world. Civic, political, religious, sporting, artistic and family leaders dominate the front pages of a globalised media testifying to a profound breakdown in leadership at all levels and across national borders. Young people know this and see this. In post-conflict situations where divides run deep, the credibility of leadership is more important than ever. Conventional leadership training focuses on and measures performance in terms of technical competency; this is not enough to bridge deep divides. The credibility of the leader is crucial to convince black and white students or black and white staff to even consider the possibility of crossing over.

Teachers and leaders (here, the same thing) are being watched more than they are being heard, for we know that what students remember and value is not the subject matter content taught as much as the life led, the example set and the actions demonstrating value. In a racially divided community, it makes no sense whatsoever for those who teach about multicultural education or who espouse values of interracial community when their daily lives do not demonstrate the living out of such commitments in practice. This is crucial. Do students see within the teacher a choice of close friends that goes against the grain of her own ethnic or religious origins? If not, no amount of professing in the classroom will have much meaning with youth. Do leaders speak out against injustice of any kind but especially when it is committed by those regarded as part of his/her ethnic or religious or national group? If not, such leaders should not expect strong responsiveness to taught ideals within the student body. Do leaders demonstrate the same distress when their nation's children are killed as when the children of a self-designated *evil empire* are horrifically wounded or killed in battle? The superficiality of common school plans that isolate compassion and consciousness within a global week or ethnic holiday or AIDS day or even a black history month is clearly wasting valuable curricular and pedagogical resources. Students do not respond, I found, to empty symbolism or occasional bouts of liberal conscience; they are drawn towards personal involvement in their lives and daily, demonstrable commitments of what is worthwhile in the pursuit of social justice.

Students are surprised by lives and leaders who act against the grain of their own biographies. Touching leadership in a post-conflict pedagogy does the unexpected. It is the story of the white principals whom I have studied as they integrate their former all-white Afrikaner schools by transforming the student body, the teaching staff, the curriculum as well as the culture and ethos of the school in ways that embrace black citizens as part of the school community. It is the story of Sipho Ngobeni, the residence student head, as he welcomes white parents onto their historical campus in ways that embrace and include the surprised parents. It is the story of a white student who comes to pray for her black Dean. And when this happens, those who observe leadership come to respect it and wish to emulate it. But this is not always the case.

Such leadership against the grain can be a costly exercise. It risks losing friends and alienating family. It often draws criticism from those still comfortable within the racialized zones defined by their received knowledge. It means that invitations to homes and special events like weddings dry up. This is a painful isolation that must not be underestimated in the life of the courageous leader. But leadership on principle draws in new friends and eventually enlarges circles of friendship; crucially, it eventually demands the respect, also, of those watching from a distance. Like any critical position, a post-conflict pedagogy takes a stand on what is important and demonstrates in practice what is possible by leading upstream in divided schools and society.

Conclusion

Pursuing change in deeply divided communities is exacting work on the human emotions of educational leaders. In such contexts, politics and emotions collide in the classroom as new knowledge confronts received knowledge among white students. The argument in this essay is that the conventions of critical theory do not allow for a compassionate and transformative engagement between perpetrator and victim, and that a different methodology, a different idiom, for talking about educational change is required. I have called this a post-conflict pedagogy, one that fundamentally alters the terms and the terrain on which racial division is bridged. Ignoring the fact that bitter knowledge exists in *the bodies in the classroom* is to risk further alienation, hatred and division among black and white students. More than anything else, the power of demonstrative leadership, guided by the principles of a post-conflict pedagogy, can begin to confront, to heal and to reconcile the second generation in the aftermath of conflict.

References

Barbarin, O. A., & Richter, L. (2001). *Mandela's children: Growing up in post-Apartheid South Africa*. New York: Routledge.

Burman, S., & Reynolds, P. (1986). *Growing up in a divided society: The contexts of childhood in South Africa*. Johannesburg: Ravan Press.

Byrne, S. (1997). *Growing Up in a divided society: The influence of conflict on Belfast schoolchildren*. New Jersey: Associated University Presses.

Choules, K. (2007). Social change education: Context matters. *Adult Education Quarterly, 57*(2), 159–176.

da Cruz, P. (2005). *From narrative to severed heads: The form and location of white supremacist history in textbooks of the Apartheid and post-Apartheid eras*. A case study. Master of Philosophy (History of Education), School of Humanities, University of Capetown.

Davies, L. (2004). *Education and conflict: Complexity and chaos*. New York: Routledge Farmer.

Elbaz-Luwisch, F. (2004). How is education possible when there is a body in the middle of the room? *Curriculum Inquiry, 34*(1), 9–27.

Ellsworth, E. (1989). Why doesn't this feel empowering? Working through the repressive myths of critical pedagogy. *Harvard Educational Review, 59*(3), 297–324.

Freire, P. (2000). *Pedagogy of the oppressed*. New York: Continuum.

Gilroy, P. (2000a). *Against race: Imagining political culture beyond the color line*. Cambridge, MA: Harvard University Press.

Gilroy, P. (2000b). *Between camps: Nations, cultures and the allure of race*. London: Allen Lane.

Gobodo-Madikizela, P. (2003). *A human being died that night: A South African story of forgiveness*. Boston: Houghton Mifflin.

Gur-Ze'ev, I. (1998). Toward a non-repressive critical pedagogy. *Educational Theory, 48*(4), 463–486.

Hesford, W. S. (1999). *Framing identities: Autobiography and the politics of pedagogy* (p. xxxvi). Minneapolis, MN: University of Minnesota Press.

Hoffman, E. (2004). *After such knowledge: Memory, history, and the legacy of the Holocaust*. Cambridge, MA: PublicAffairs.

Isaacson, M. (2007, July 15). A brave and riveting confession. *Sunday Independent* (p. 13).

Jansen, J. (2005). Why recitation persists: The relationship between authority and pedagogy in third world classrooms. In M. Beveridge, K. King, R. Palmer, & R. Wedgewood (Eds.), *Reintegrating education, skills and work in Africa: Towards informal economies? Towards autonomy or dependency in development?* (pp. 105–136). Edinburgh: University of Edinburgh, Centre for African Studies.

Jansen, J. (2009). *Knowledge in the blood: Confronting race and the apartheid past*. Stanford, CA: Stanford University Press.

Kahn, R. (2005). Reviews. *Learning for Democracy, 1*(3), 85–88.

Knudsen, S. V. (2007). *Intersectionality—a theoretical inspiration in the analysis of minority cultures and identities in textbooks*. www.caen.jufm.fr/colloque_jartem/pdf/knudsen.pdf, accessed January 26, 2008.

Maddock, T. (1999). The nature and limits of critical theory in education. *Educational Philosophy and Theory, 31*(1), 43–61.

McFalls, E. L., & Cobb-Roberts, D. (2001). Reducing resistance to diversity through cognitive dissonance instruction: Implications for teacher education. *Journal of Teacher Education, 52*(2), 164–172.

McLaren, P. (2006). *Life in schools: An introduction to critical pedagogy in the foundations of education* (5th ed.). New York: Allyn & Bacon.

Straker, G. (1992). *Faces in the revolution: The psychological effects of violence on township youth in South Africa*. Athens, Ohio: Ohio University Press.

Tibbits, F. (2006). Learning from the past: Supporting teaching through the Facing the past history project in South Africa. *Prospects: Quarterly Review of Comparative Education, XXXVI*(3), 295–318.

Tubbs, N. (1996). Becoming critical of critical theory of education. *Educational Philosophy and Theory, 28*(2), 42–54.

Weis, L., McCarthy, C., & Dimitriadis, G. (2006). *Ideology, curriculum, and the new sociology of education: Revisiting the work of Michael Apple*. New York: Taylor and Francis.

Educational Change in Chile: Reform or Improvements? (1990–2007)

Beatrice Avalos

Very soon after Michelle Bachelet, the new president of Chile, took office in 2006, secondary public school students went out onto the streets to protest. Initially, their complaints had to do with specific issues such as free bus tickets on weekends, but gradually the movement became a more serious call to improve education in the public school system including private subsidised schools. They had many complaints, but underlying them all was the notion that large numbers of young people in public schools lacked the opportunities open to the affluent groups who attend the private school system. The student movement gained support from the public, and from many organisations such as the Teachers Union, political groups and university students, as well as private school students who perhaps recognised their own privileged situation.

As the protests became more centred on macro issues, there were three that stood out:

- the need to enact a new Education Law to replace the existing Organic Law;
- the need to change the municipal system of administration of public schools and
- the need for greater funding for the improvement of teaching and learning in the public school system.

Recognising that these demands were serious and hit at the heart of the education system, the government agreed to form an Advisory Presidential Commission on the Quality of Education with representatives from a wide array of civil society institutions: political parties, teachers' union, churches, students (secondary and university) and academics. The Commission produced its report towards the end of 2006, and as this chapter is being written two laws have been passed in Parliament that address the issues of concern.

To those who know of the Chilean government's involvement in improving the quality and equity of education since the early 1990s, the impact of this massive

B. Avalos (✉)
Centre for Advanced Research in Education, Universidad de Chile, Santiago, Chile
e-mail: bavalos@terra.cl

A. Hargreaves et al. (eds.), *Second International Handbook of Educational Change*, 383
Springer International Handbooks of Education 23, DOI 10.1007/978-90-481-2660-6_22,
© Springer Science+Business Media B.V. 2010

protest may have come as a surprise. The purpose of this chapter, then, is to discuss these changes, their focus and their achievements; to highlight the tensions involved in the process of improving the education system including the conflicting ideologies underlying the efforts and finally to assess the importance of what effectively can be considered an improvement as well as the reforms that are still needed to better the education results of students.

From Improvement Programmes to Reform (1990–1996)

The 1990s began with the key political overhaul from a military dictatorship to a democratically elected government, in the context of transition and not revolution. This meant that whatever was to change had to be done with caution, so as not to arouse suspicions on the part of the relatively large group that still supported the military government and feared "reforms" that might appear as veiled intentions to reinstate the principles of the socialist government that had been overthrown by the military government in 1973. The educational situation in 1990 was adequate in quantitative terms compared to other Latin American and developing countries (Matear, 2007). There was almost full primary level coverage, that is, 97% Basic Education (8 years), around 75% secondary enrolment (4-year secondary school) and 5.2% illiteracy compared to 16.4% in 1960. However, the fundamental issue then and now is not so much the expansion of enrolments in schools but the quality of education provided to students. In order to explore the quality of education in Chile in this chapter, we will

- examine how the education system was handed over to the new democratic government;
- identify the urgent needs of change detected at the time and
- discuss how these were converted into what were called "improvement" programmes.

The Education System and the Legal Structure Inherited from the Military Government

The last major structural education reform before 1990 took place in 1965, when, in line with UNESCO recommendations at the time to extend compulsory education from 6 to 8 or 9 years, the 6-year primary education system was converted into an 8-year Basic School and made compulsory for all. The secondary system at the time was in turn shortened to a 4-year Middle School with two streams: an academic and a technical-vocational, both of which in turn would make it possible to apply for higher education programmes. In line with this structure, the system of teacher education was also modified so as to prepare generalist teachers for the Basic school and specialised university trained teachers for the Middle school. Despite curricular changes, the structure of the system has remained the same until today and, as we shall see later, stands in need of reform.

Until the early 1980s, the education system was primarily a public one with a limited number of private schools geared to the more affluent social groups. In 1981 the military government transferred the administration of public schools to the municipalities, arguing that this would allow for a better and more participatory form of school management, although such participation was limited given the non-elected condition of municipal authorities until the system was changed in the 1990s. In reality, the municipalisation of schools responded to the market economy principles upheld by the military authorities involving the belief that educational quality could be assured through competition among schools in line with their degree of effectiveness in achieving learning results. Accordingly, the military government modified the funding of schools introducing a system of vouchers. The system was a variation of Milton Friedman's (Friedman & Friedman, 1980) voucher scheme, as subsidies would go to school managements (municipal and private) on the basis of actual student attendance rather than directly to parents. It was expected that through this system private subsidised schools would attract more students than the less effective municipal ones and gradually produce a shift from a public to a private school system. This shift did not happen in the 1980s, but since the end of the 1990s it has begun to occur. At present around 49% of students are enrolled in municipal schools compared to 43% in private subsidised schools, while the rest attend the paid private schools (Ministerio de Educación de Chile, 2007).

In terms of overall funding levels, the last decade of the military government showed a major decrease in funding levels for the publicly subsidised system (27% between 1982 and 1990) that affected teacher salaries and their working conditions and the money available for teaching resources in schools (Cox, 2003). This decrease in funding also lowered Basic School education enrolment between 1985 and 1990 from 98 to 93% (Cox, 2003).

The most contentious inheritance of the Military Regime was the Organic Law of Education, which was passed 1 day before the change of government (10 March 1990). This Law was designed to ensure the maintenance of the changes put in place by the military government such as the municipal administration of schools and the voucher system of funding (Cox, 2003), because it required a very high quorum of agreement in Parliament to be changed, a condition which has been impossible to fulfil until very recently.

Change Needs Faced by the Newly Elected Government in the Early 1990s

Bound by the restrictions of the Organic Law, the political coalition (known as the *Concertación*) that took office in 1990, and is now in its fourth period of government, needed to address two urgent situations: improve the working conditions of teachers and the educational opportunities of students in the light of equity and quality principles.

Teachers had undergone grave injustices during the military government. Not only had many been arbitrarily dismissed, but they had also lost their former rights as public servants (Avalos, 2004a) and suffered a substantial reduction of their salaries compared to what they earned in the early 1970s. Improving the situation of teachers meant altering their status as employees of the municipal school system and improving their salaries and working conditions. This was achieved through the passing of the Teacher Statute (Law 19.070, 1991), which recognised teaching as a profession and the right to continuing professional development as well as to adequate working conditions. While municipal authorities retained the power to appoint teachers, they no longer could dismiss tenured ones.[1] There would be a minimal national salary with added benefits on the basis of experience, professional development courses, work in difficult areas and managerial responsibilities. Salary increases for municipal teachers would be negotiated periodically by the Teachers Union and the government, while teachers in private subsidised schools would be bound by the general labour laws. From 1991 onwards, teachers' salaries have increased to the point that they are now, around 150% higher than what they were in 1990. While this salary improvement is not entirely satisfactory in the eyes of the Union, the problems are more clearly focussed on the high number of pupils per class (officially 45) and of teaching hours (around 30 per week for a full-time teacher), as well as low differentials between beginning teachers, teachers with 15 years experience and teachers at the end of their career (see OECD, 2005).

The forecast that municipal administration of schools would show poorer learning results as compared to the private subsidised ones appeared true at the beginning of the 1990s and has remained so for several reasons. Municipal schools enrol students from the lowest socio-economic groups who in turn, despite the efforts of better municipal schools, tend to show lower results on national assessments than their counterparts in private subsidised schools. Municipal schools also are not allowed to select their students on the basis of ability (nor for other reasons), which in fact puts them in an unequal situation with private schools that practice selection. Another reason is that private subsidised schools, within limits, are allowed to charge fees, thus increasing the amount of money per student that these schools have. This has brought to the fore the negative effects of providing an equal subsidy per student regardless of their condition and needs, a situation that affects the municipal schools more drastically as they are faced with having to compensate for the advantages of students in private schools without sufficient resources for this purpose.

---

[1] This is a controversial issue as municipalities find themselves very limited in their possibilities of selecting good teachers while others considered less competent remain in post. Thus there has been a longstanding demand from municipalities and the political opposition to change or eliminate the Teachers Statute.

At the start of the 1990s the issues of equity in education were a key concern (García-Huidobro, 1999). It was obvious that students in more disadvantaged conditions who attended municipal schools were not learning as expected, but also that across the subsidised system teaching and learning processes were inadequate. The situation required urgent attention.

Nine hundred schools were first identified as in need of special educational assistance, and the programme put in place for this purpose, appropriately known as P-900, gained worldwide recognition (Filp, 1994). The P-900's target was to improve learning results through several actions: teacher development workshops, special help for students standing behind in their achievement and resources such as textbooks and teaching/learning materials. The key intervention of the programme was the organisation of "learning workshops" with 15–20 children (first to fourth grade) with learning difficulties. They worked, after school hours, with monitors or facilitators (generally secondary school graduates in the communities where the children belonged) who were prepared for the task by programme staff. While the programme continued all through the 1990s (gradually covering all of the eight grades of the Basic School), it did not target the same schools, as once a school attained reasonable learning levels as measured by the national assessment test, it left the programme and another school took its place. An external evaluation showed that over the decade of the 1990s there was a continued lowering of the achievement gap in relation to the mainstream Basic School results and also there were better results compared to schools with similar characteristics not in the programme (García-Huidobro, Jara, & Sotomayor, 2002).

About 16% of students attend rural schools, many of which are small and managed by one or two teachers. An innovative programme known as Programme for the Improvement of Quality and Equity in Education (MECE) Rural targeted these schools from the early 1990s on. Rural schools had been operating in impoverished conditions and with little support for their teachers. While the MECE Rural programme provided funds for the improvement of buildings and teaching/learning resources, its most important intervention was the establishment of the "Rural Microcentres". These were monthly professional development meetings of teachers from nearby schools at a host school. Assisted by a school supervisor and often with invited guests, teachers exchanged experiences, discussed their problems and examined the demands of the curriculum and how to manage multigrade teaching as most lacked any prior preparation in this respect. The external evaluation of the programme carried out at the end of the 1990s (Avalos, 2004b) showed that the Microcentre meetings together with other professional development opportunities contributed around 40% to learning results in the schools, and that these in turn improved over time in national learning assessments.

Beyond these actions focused on the poorest and more vulnerable school population, the government initiated in 1992 a programme that was to continue throughout the 1990s directed to the overall qualitative improvement of schooling. Known as the MECE and partially funded through a World Bank loan, it gradually covered the entire school system from pre-school to secondary level. School building infrastructure was improved; free textbooks were provided first for all Basic School students and after 1995 for secondary students in the subsidised system (municipal and private). A new curriculum framework was approved for Basic schools (1995) and for secondary schools (1998) together with syllabuses for each one of the main curriculum subjects that schools could use if they so wished (in practice most schools use them). Resources were provided for classroom libraries in Basic schools, improvement of school libraries and the setting up of educational material resource centres. Opportunities for school-based teacher professional development were especially structured and supported for secondary schools (Avalos, 1998) besides those already in place in P-900 and rural schools.

Perhaps the most innovative of the improvement initiatives of the 1990s was the introduction of computing into schools. Beginning in 1990 the ENLACES programme, as it came to be known, gradually extended the provision of computers to schools (beginning with primary level), established a platform for communication later superseded by widespread Internet connection and an education portal, set up training opportunities for teachers in schools and provided software for educational purposes. Today, practically all the schools have a computer laboratory, and teachers and students have access to a rich education portal to assist in the teaching and learning activities of the school (Hinostroza & Guzmán, 2002).

Change or Reform?

Throughout the effervescence produced by the development of these improvement programmes in the early 1990s, the word *reform* was never used. Essentially, this was related to the nature of the transition period from a military dictatorship to democracy and the fact that the former dictator remained as head of the Armed Forces. There was a certain degree of concern that anything that might appear as a radical change (i.e. reform) might unleash unnecessary suspicion and resistance. However, when Eduardo Frei, the second democratic president, took office in 1995, the time seemed ripe to use the word *reform*. On the basis of proposals embodied in the report of a national commission on education convened in 1994, President Frei used the concept of "education reform" in the announcement of three major policy targets in his Address to the Nation (1996): education as a government priority, doubling of expenditure within a 6-year period and lengthening of the school day. The speech also informed of the provision of special funds to strengthen the teaching profession (initial preparation and continuing professional development) and a programme to support the development of a number of high-quality municipal secondary schools throughout the country.

The next two governments in fact continued the trend to expand public expenditure in education (2.4 of GDP in 1990 to 3.2 of GDP in 1996) with big increases in infrastructure to support the longer school day and assist the development of teacher education and other related teacher programmes. The existing MECE and ENLACES programmes continued their expansion throughout the decade as stated above.

Progress and Setbacks in Education Quality (1996–2006)

Perhaps the most important policy that became a law in 1997 was the lengthening of the school day from six 45-min periods to eight, meaning that double-shift schools would gradually give way to single-shift ones, involving a substantial increase in investments in building and infrastructure. The lengthening of the school day was considered an important equity factor under the assumption that students with poorer cultural background need more time to engage in the kind of learning that the new curriculum and more constructivist teaching strategies require (Cox, 2003). The process of transforming the system in this direction is now almost completed. Most students today remain in schools longer, and many teachers are concentrating their teaching in one school rather than in two or three as occurred before.

The effects of lengthening the school day on learning are not yet visible (as far as national assessment results show), and there still is not an adequate use of the extra time for learning. As shown in independent evaluations, there are a number of schools that use the time to repeat curricular content already taught, thus increasing the boredom of students (DESUC, 2005). Nevertheless, there is a new context for furthering better teaching practices and more interesting educational opportunities for students.

Teacher Policies: Education, Incentives and Evaluation

Other than dealing in 1991 with the vexing issue of teacher salaries and contractual conditions through the Teacher Statute, insufficient attention was given to engaging teacher participation in the reform initiatives. From a sociological perspective, Bellei (2001) concluded that while privately and with greater or lesser willingness teachers accepted the reforms of the 1990s, in their public expressions they complained about their lack of participation in the framing of reform initiatives and continued to complain about their working conditions. From the perspective of teacher education, although each improvement programme had considered some form of professional development action, no comprehensive and long-term policy directed to teacher development (including initial preparation) had been embedded in the reform policies (Avalos, 2003).

Teachers began to get increased attention after the presidential address of 1996 in several ways: improvement of initial teacher education and better opportunities for professional development, incentives based on student results and the establishment of a system of formative teacher evaluation.

Teacher Initial Education and Professional Development

Around 1996 it was publicly acknowledged that initial teacher education was in poor condition, due to insufficient funding, inadequate curriculum and low institutional prestige resulting from contradictory policies during the military government.[2] To deal with the situation, the government provided a fund to be allocated on a competitive basis to teacher education programmes that presented reasonable improvement projects. Thus, 17 university teacher education programmes that covered about 80% of the future teacher population were able to engage in 5-year projects (1997–2002). These projects addressed practically all the key areas in need of change: curriculum improvement, capacity building of teacher educators and greater practical experience covering the entire period of teacher preparation. The teacher education institutions were able to improve their libraries, their computing facilities and their buildings (for example, office space for lecturers and meeting space for students). International links were established with teacher education institutions in a number of countries as a result of study visits, and participation of well-known researchers and teacher education practitioners in workshops and seminars organised in Chile. By the end of the programme, there was a noticeable increase in the qualifications of applicants for teacher education, in the qualifications of teacher educators and in the overall structure and quality of the teacher education curriculum.[3] During the period of implementation of the projects the Ministry of Education held an important support role, which unfortunately was not continued to the same degree after the completion of the projects.

Teacher professional development was also encouraged in several ways. A programme was established to send teachers on study visits abroad with the purpose of visiting innovative schools and classrooms that provided examples of different ways of facing subject-teaching, dealing with diversity, multicultural learning as well as school organisation and leadership. Around 6,000 teachers benefited from this programme between 1996 and 2003. Currently, the programme has focused on a smaller number of teachers being awarded grants to complete post-degree diplomas in their field of teaching.

Changes in the curriculum made it imperative to provide teachers with short informative courses to acquaint them with the nature of these changes. Thus, year after year, as the changes were implemented teachers were offered curriculum upgrading through short summer courses. However, this form of curriculum upgrading was shown not to be appropriate for the change of teachers' prior view of the curriculum and much less for adequate implementation of changes in their classrooms. Thus, more recently and with the assistance of university lecturers, the courses are being designed with a stronger opportunity to understand changes and with continued support in the classroom during the year. Also, more recently the Curriculum and Evaluation Unit has been working on curriculum support materials that contain performance standards for each of five subjects along the continuum

---

[2]For example, the secondary (and much of primary) teacher initial education that had traditionally been offered at university level was demoted to tertiary non-university level and then again restored to its former position towards the end of the military government. This, as well as low status, salary and working conditions of teachers deterred qualified school graduates from pursuing teaching as a profession.

[3]For an account of this programme see Avalos (2005).

from 1st to 12th grade. These materials, known as Progress Maps, are the result of joint collaboration between Chilean and Australian professionals, based on similar materials developed by the Australian Council of Education Research. To ensure that teachers understand and feel motivated to use the materials, one of the universities piloted a strategy for the purpose with a group of around 200 teachers. At the end of the 4-month activity participant teachers had recognised the potential of these materials to improve their teaching strategies and student learning (UMCE, 2007). But it will take some time to broaden the experience to other teachers within the system.

More in line with the concept of school-based teacher development over time, the Ministry of Education has undertaken a number of activities that engage teachers in workshops, professional discussions and interactions across schools with and without assistance from facilitators. However, as these activities cease to be experimental and are engulfed within the Ministry of Education's structure, they tend to lose prominence in relation to other priorities and new initiatives. Thus, for example, the Teacher Professional Groups, which was a very successful programme for secondary teachers (Avalos, 1998), no longer receives specific support, so that only schools that are strongly motivated and able to continue with the Groups have done so.

More recently and linked to policies involving teacher evaluation, a network structure of teachers who act as professional developers for other teachers has begun to operate. These teachers are selected from those who are judged to be highly competent by the teacher evaluation system.

Improving Teacher Performance Through Incentives and Teacher Performance Evaluation

The 1991 Teacher Statute included a clause requiring municipal teacher performance to be evaluated, but more as a means of control than as a stimulus for improvement. This interpretation resisted by the Teachers Union stopped for some years the development of a system of teacher evaluation. However, political pressures to establish such a system and the recognition on the part of the Union that evaluation in itself could be a useful tool for teacher improvement prepared the way for all parties to undertake a lengthy series of discussions and negotiations that finally led to the establishment in 2002 of a formative evaluation system (Avalos & Assael, 2006). The system, which is being gradually implemented, is based on a framework or set of criteria describing competent teaching against which teachers are judged, and which was approved through wide teacher consultation. Teachers are evaluated on the basis of a portfolio, peer interviews and head-teacher reports, as well as the video of one of their lessons. As a result they may be considered "excellent", "competent", "basic" or "unsatisfactory". Teachers judged as "basic" and "unsatisfactory" are entitled to extra professional development opportunities in their area of weakness, and unsatisfactory teachers are evaluated in two further opportunities before they are asked to leave the municipal education system. Teachers who are willing to pass a content-knowledge test are eligible for a salary bonus. Additionally, a voluntary system to reward excellent performance similar to the USA National Board examination has been implemented since 2002. Teachers who apply must pass a content-test as well as provide a portfolio and video as evidence of their performance. Those who are successful receive a salary bonus for 10 years.

As can be seen, Chile has followed the tendencies towards greater teacher accountability in systems such as the USA and British ones that link controls and incentives. However, the measures in place have critics on both sides of the ideological spectrum: for conservatives the evaluation system is too soft (formative), while for some left-wing teacher groups the system expresses neo-liberal market policies that confront teachers with each other in pursuit of a reward.

Learning Results: How Equitable Have the Changes Turned Out to Be?

Chile has a system of student assessment in place since the 1980s known as the System for Measurement of Educational Achievement (SIMCE). Since its inception, the system has undergone a serious of changes, of which the most recent one is a modification of the way in which results are communicated.[4] SIMCE covers language, mathematics, science and social studies in fourth, eighth and tenth grades. Students in fourth grade are assessed every year, while students in eighth and tenth grades are assessed every 2 years. Besides this national assessment, Chile has participated in Trends in International Mathematics and Science Study (TIMSS), the UNESCO Latin American assessment (LLECE) and PISA evaluations.

As can easily be noted, the country has a fair amount of information on the learning progress of students. Furthermore, each time SIMCE or other assessment results are published, there is no lack of public comment and judgement about how the education system is performing and how effective are its reform programmes.

Until SIMCE changed the frequency of measurement of fourth grade students (2006), it was not possible to follow cohorts from fourth to eighth and tenth grades, and therefore to get value-added measures. Each administration of the tests offered a snapshot of the learning levels of the school population. Because results have not been as expected in the light of investments and efforts to improve educational provisions and because they generally show lower results for the municipal schools, there is a recent effort to examine (even without value-added measures) how the different types of schools perform in relation to the socio-economic level of their students. Although the presentation of results in relation to the school population attended allows for a more nuanced assessment of effects, with municipal schools sometimes outperforming the private subsidised schools in relation to the same socio-economic

---

[4]Thus instead of each school getting a score for each subject measured which compares with scores of other schools and the mean score, results will be reported against two standards or learning levels each with a description of what the level means.

group, there is a continuous critique of the municipal management system vis-à-vis the private subsidised ones. Those favouring the concept of "private is good" help to create a public feeling that municipal education is failing, and this explains the constant exodus of students from municipal to private subsidised schools. On the other hand others, including the government, recognise that municipal schools operate in unfavourable conditions in terms of funding, decision-making power of school heads and type of school population attended. In other words, students who are poorer have less chance of reaching satisfactory achievement levels. The laws under discussion at present are attempting to deal with the situation.

Beyond the discussion of what type of school is better, it is still a fact that learning results have not improved much since reforms began in the early 1990s. The report prepared by the Chilean government on occasion of the OECD external review of Chilean policies (OECD, 2004) notes fluctuations in results over the period 1992–2002 in terms of decreasing the achievement gap between municipal and private schools. Those programmes that got special attention in the 1990s (P-900 and Rural Schools) progressed consistently upwards, thus decreasing the achievement gap with the rest of the system. But on the whole as the Report suggests, "national achievement averages remain below the objectives defined by the curriculum and far from the international standards to which they aspire" (OECD, 2004, p. 44).

The People's View: Report of the President's Advisory Commission on Education

The "penguin revolution" referred to at the start of this chapter bore its fruits. The discussions among the 80-plus members of the President's Advisory Committee reflected not only the concerns but also the tensions that have accompanied the implementation of reforms since these begun in the 1990s. The discussions served as well to highlight avenues for change that had not been considered earlier. We look at the tensions and situations that emerged as critical for the improvement of education, and in the last section of the chapter we hypothesise about what the future of education of Chile may look like.

Tensions

Throughout the entire period under description, a persistent ideological dichotomy has marked discussions, proposals and critiques. The following word dyads aptly describe these dichotomies: private–public, outcomes–processes, programmes–policies, centralisation–decentralisation and improvement–reform. To some extent we dealt earlier in this chapter with the conceptual shift in the mid-1990s from "improvement programmes" to "educational reform", illustrating the tension between the need to move ahead and the need to contain the opposition of former military government supporters. The "public–private" relationship however exemplifies one of the acute tensions that remain a part of policy discussions and reform efforts. The tension is illustrated in many ways but mainly in the extent to which the power to administer the education system is vested in the State (either the central government or decentralised municipalities) or devolved to subsidised private institutional management. One of the key issues brought out for discussion in the President's Advisory Committee (Consejo Asesor, 2006) precisely refers to where the power to regulate education and secure education quality should reside. The education law and a subsidiary law under parliamentary discussion at present grant greater regulatory power to the State and to its ministry of education. However, the law proposal has been challenged in an alternative proposal by the political opposition that calls for an independent regulatory institution and for more managerial autonomy for public municipal schools.

Within the same logic of a public–private tension, the political opposition considers that the unsatisfactory learning results of students in municipal schools are the effect of their management system (mostly vested on municipal authorities rather than the school principal). It also blames the situation on the difficulty of dismissing teachers who are deemed ineffective due to protective clauses in the Teachers' Statute. Without disagreeing with this view, the government and especially the Teachers' Union consider that the main reason for poor results in municipal schools is the school population they attend and the lack of selection practices. However, neither side sufficiently considers the effect also of high student–teacher ratios (up to 45 students per class) and high teaching loads (up to 36 periods per week) that affect many of the schools that serve poorer social groups.

The policies set in place by the governments of the past 15 years to improve teacher performance (besides more opportunities for professional development), such as teacher performance evaluation and monetary incentives, are not considered entirely appropriate by the political opposition. Their criticism is directed to the "formative" character of the evaluation (not linked to student results) that makes it very difficult to dismiss a teacher with unsatisfactory performance. Their preferred method is to have a stringent form of evaluation and very good incentives for effective teaching as measured by student results.

Perhaps the most vexing issue also resulting in different explanations of why this occurs is the growing inequality in educational results between the lower and the affluent social groups with greater cultural capital. The most obvious explanation provided by all groups is that there has been insufficient investment per student in education giving the same to rich and poor. The voucher system in place has been criticised on this account, and as a result a new law will grant bigger subsidies per student to schools that cater for the poorer social groups. These schools will also get extra funding to improve their resources and/or contract better qualified teachers able to deal with the different educational needs of their students. The schools getting these additional funds will need, however, to prove that they are using them well for improvement and will be closely monitored in this regard.

Finally, and only recently acknowledged in the new education law, is the problem of the education structure and the system of teacher preparation which follows this structure. As indicated earlier in the chapter, there is an 8-year basic school set in place by the 1965 Education Reform Law. Although the curriculum of Basic Education is divided into two cycles (1–4 and 5–8), both cycles tend to be taught by generalist Basic Education teachers. This has had a detrimental effect on the learning opportunities of those students attending municipal schools (mostly the poorer ones), as private schools tend to contract subject specialists for the second cycle of the Basic School. Teacher education institutions are beginning to reform their programmes so as to provide Basic Teachers with subject specialisation for grades 5–8. But this will probably not happen in all institutions, unless the curricular structure of the system is altered, and specialised teacher education becomes a necessity. In the meantime, this situation exacerbates the already unequal opportunities of students who attend municipal schools in relation to their peers in private schools.

Conclusion

The educational system has moved well beyond the situation it was in at the beginning of the 1990s. In sheer numbers, there is practically universal coverage in Basic Education and over 90% enrolment in secondary school. The curriculum has been updated and new curricular materials are being offered to teachers to assist them in dealing with the diversity of student learning needs. In almost all schools there is a longer day and better infrastructure and learning resources. Teachers are getting more opportunities for professional development and have an evaluation system that helps them detect their needs and deal with them accordingly. But there is still a way to go in terms of deciding what kind of an education system needs to be put in place to provide equal learning opportunities, especially for the poor, and to improve learning results, especially among the more vulnerable social groups.

The current discussion involving new education laws deals with issues related to governance, funding and monitoring of quality. The role of the Ministry of Education and of semi- or non-governmental regulating institutions has recently been agreed upon. Systemic policies have been wanting and must be considered when the new conditions are implemented. The current preparation of teachers, especially for primary and lower secondary level, needs reform. The questions raised by the "penguin movement" and the solutions proposed by the President's Advisory Committee may get blurred in the ensuing discussions that are taking place among all stakeholders, but especially among the politicians who have to approve the new laws. The policies needed to provide opportunities in the public education system need to be put in place, even if this requires a radical change in the municipal system of management. Selection policies and fee charges in subsidised schools need to be stopped. The role of civil society in maintaining the key issues and their most adequate (as well as feasible) solutions alive in public discussions is essential, so that the changes of the 1990s do result in better educational conditions for all when Chile celebrates the bicentennial of its independence (2010).

References

Avalos, B. (1998). School-based teacher development. The experience of teacher professional development groups in Chile. *Teaching and Teacher Education, 14*(3), 257–271.

Avalos, B. (2003). La formación de profesores y su desarrollo professional. Prácticas innovadoras en busca de políticas. In C. Cox (Ed.), *Políticas Educacionales en el Cambio de Siglo. La Reforma del Sistema Escolar de Chile* (pp. 559–594). Santiago de Chile: Editorial Universitaria.

Avalos, B. (2004a). Teacher regulatory forces and accountability policies in Chile: From public servants to accountable professionals. *Research Papers in Education, 14*(1), 67–86.

Avalos, B. (2004b). Desarrollo docente en el contexto de la institución escolar. Los microcentros rurales y los grupos profesionales de trabajo. In *Maestros en América Latina: Nuevas Perspectivas sobre su Formación y Desempeño* (pp. 213–248). Santiago de Chile: PREAL and Banco Interamericano de Desarrollo.

Avalos, B. (2005). How to affect the quality of teacher education: A four-year policy driven project implemented at university level. In P. M. Denicolo & M. Kompf (Eds.), *Connecting policy and practice: Challenges for Teaching and Learning in Schools and Universities* (pp. 39–43). London: Routledge.

Avalos, B., & Assael, J. (2006). Moving from resistance to agreement. The case of Chilean teacher performance evaluation. *International Journal of Educational Research, 45*(4–5), 254–266.

Bellei, C. (2001). El talon de Aquiles de la Reforma: Análisis sociológico de la política de los 90 hacia los docentes en Chile. In S. Martinic & M. Pardo (Eds.), *Economía Política de las Reformas Educativas en América Latina*(pp. 227–258). Santiago: CIDE & PREAL.

Consejo Asesor. (2006). Informe final. Consejo asesor presidencial para la Calidad de la Educación. Santiago.

Cox, C. (2003). Las políticas educacionales de Chile en las últimas dos décadas del siglo XX. In C. Cox (Ed.), *Políticas Educacionales en el Cambio de Siglo. La Reforma del Sistema Escolar de Chile* (pp. 19–113). Santiago de Chile: Editorial Universitaria.

DESUC. (2005). Informe uso del tiempo Enseñanza Básica. Evaluación Jornada Escolar Completa. Santiago: Dirección de Estudios Sociológicos, P. Universidad Católica de Chile.

Filp, J. (1994). Todos los niños aprenden. Evaluaciones del P-900. In M. Gajardo (Ed.), *Cooperación Internacional y Desarrollo de la Educación* (pp. 179–250). Santiago de Chile: Agencia de Cooperación Internacional.

Friedman, M., & Friedman, R. (1980). *Freedom to choose*. New York: Harcourt Brace Yovanovich.

García-Huidobro, J. E. (1999). *La Reforma Educacional Chilena*. Madrid: Editorial Popular.

García-Huidobro, J. E., Jara, C., & Sotomayor, C. (2002). *El Programa de las 900 Escuelas: Trayectoria de una Década*. Santiago de Chile: Ministerio de Educación.

Hinostroza, J. E., & Guzmán A. (2002). Innovative uses of ICT in Chilean Schools. *Journal of Computer Assisted Learning, 18*(4), 459–469.

Matear, A. (2007). Equity in education in Chile: The tensions between policy and practice. *International Journal of Educational Development, 27*(1), 101–113.

Ministerio de Educación de Chile. (2007). Indicadores de la Educación en Chile http://w3app.mineduc.cl/mineduc/ded/documentos/Indicadores_de_la_Educacion_2007.pdf

OECD. (2004). *Reviews of national policies for education: Chile*. Paris: OECD.

OECD. (2005). *Teachers matter. Attracting, developing and retaining effective teachers*. Paris: OECD.

UMCE. (2007). *Evaluación del Programa Piloto de Mapas de Progreso del Aprendizaje*. Santiago: Universidad Metropolitana de Ciencias de la Educación.

A Market for Knowledge?

Frederick M. Hess

For more than a decade, market-oriented education reformers have touted the ability of competition to improve American education. While arguing that competition will nonetheless promote quality, efficiency, and innovation, these advocates have avoided the blunt, self-interested language of markets.

The result has been a strange politics of half-hearted debate. Proponents of deregulation have hesitated to use the instrumental language of markets. Even the champions of reform have opted for the gentler language of "choice" – while paying homage to the societal mission of schooling and its value as a public good. This has made for some astonishing, or astonishingly inept, efforts at market making. In K-12, for instance, champions of competition have chosen to ignore questions about existing incentives for schools or managers, or the manner in which collective bargaining agreements restrict the ability of schools to respond to competition.

In the context of deregulatory politics, it is vital to understand that American education is not a regulated system in any conventional sense. K-12 schooling is, quite simply, a government-operated system with a small private sector. As for "deregulation," most such policy is not concerned with reducing government restrictions on private entities but with encouraging publicly managed entities to act "as if" they were private entities. These realities of the education sector have seldom been recognized by proponents and opponents of market-based reform, whose debates rest on the unstated assumption that publicly governed schools and colleges will behave like traditional profit-seeking firms when confronted with students empowered to attend the school of their choice.

In K-12 education, there is substantially less competition and much more ambivalence about whether schools and educators should be subject to competition. Nonetheless, teachers compete to win positions in advantaged districts, superintendents and principals vie for the career-making accolades showered upon innovators, school districts compete with private firms to provide tutoring under the federal

F.M. Hess (✉)
American Enterprise Institute for Public Policy Research, Washington, DC, USA
e-mail: rhess@aei.org

A. Hargreaves et al. (eds.), *Second International Handbook of Educational Change*,
Springer International Handbooks of Education 23, DOI 10.1007/978-90-481-2660-6_23,
© Springer Science+Business Media B.V. 2010

No Child Left Behind Act (NCLB), and principals eagerly explain how they contend for students who could attend other schools. More obviously, for-profit firms have always competed to supply schools with academic products and services such as testing, textbooks, curricula, professional development, and instructional supplies.

In short, rather than suggesting that competition does not exist in education, it is more accurate for proponents of market reform to argue that education is currently subjected to *inadequate* or *unhealthy* competitive pressures, and that market-based reform will yield more constructive dynamics. This, however, places a particular burden upon reformers. If the problem is that existing competition is unproductive or toothless, then simply promoting increased choice is an insufficient solution. It becomes paramount for reformers to embrace changes that will trump existing pressures, alter the rules of the game, and rationalize behavior in the intended manner.

Education has two purposes: a "private" purpose and a "public" purpose. Education is a private good to the extent that individuals benefit from the skills and training produced by schooling and is a public good insofar as one is learning skills, dispositions, or values that make for a better citizen and neighbor. It is generally agreed that the public content of schooling is highest in the elementary grades and declines through secondary school and higher education, though there is no objective way to determine the size of the public component at any particular grade level. To the extent that education is a private matter, proponents of choice-based reform contend that public officials should regulate with a light hand and should not privilege state-run institutions. Those who see education as primarily a public good, meanwhile, argue that the state should oversee its provision and ensure its quality.

In both K-12 and postsecondary education, a persistent difficulty for market proponents has been the disparity between the rhetoric and reality of competition. Confusingly, there has been a tendency to conflate two very different dynamics and call them both "competition": one is the unleashing of self-interested incentives to compel public providers to improve, and the other is a loosening of restraints that hobble nontraditional and private providers.

It is vital to distinguish between competition intended to force public school systems to change in desirable ways and competition intended to permit new providers to emerge and thrive. This distinction yields two theories of change. The most straightforward way to unleash competition is to make it relatively simple for private providers to receive public funding for their educational services. If the accompanying regulation does not erect immense barriers to entry, this kind of *displacement* can yield immense change whether or not existing institutions respond productively. The alternative course is to use the threat from private providers and changes in public agency funding to compel a productive *public sector response*, trusting that self-interest will drive public schools to improve in response to competitive pressure. In contemporary policy debates, the rhetoric of public sector response is more common than that of displacement.

The Landscape of Education Competition

Competitive forces are most evident in four areas of K-12 education, each a product of relatively recent changes to state or federal policy. First, somewhere between 1 and $1\frac{1}{2}$% of children are currently homeschooled. State laws rendered homeschooling illegal in nearly all states until the 1970s, when Christian groups spearheaded an effort to relax school attendance laws and ensure the right of parents to educate their children at home. Today, homeschooling is legal in all fifty states, operating under a variety of statutory restrictions. Estimates vary, but most place the homeschooling population at about 1 million. This has fostered a variety of opportunities for entrepreneurial providers, as families seek curricular materials and web-based instructional support.

Second, as of fall 2006, 1,150,000 students were enrolled in 3,977 "charter schools" nationwide. These schools held charters from state-designated entities that permitted them to operate independently from the local school district. Charter school legislation, first enacted in Minnesota in 1991, funds schools with formulas based on enrollment, thus linking competitive performance to revenue. States fund charters to varying degrees, some at the same level as other public schools but many at a considerably reduced level. Only a few states offer charter schools substantial support when it comes to facilities and construction. As a result, entrepreneurs have encountered significant difficulty in getting charter schools started, often relying on philanthropic support and using third-rate facilities.

Third, publicly funded school voucher programs, first enacted in Milwaukee in 1990, now operate in some cities (e.g., Cleveland and Washington, D.C.) and on a limited statewide basis in Florida. Under voucher arrangements, the government provides individuals with a specified amount of money to be used toward tuition at any eligible provider. In each case, students are able to use the vouchers to attend private schools, including religious schools. Vouchers make the financial state of a school directly dependent on whether students enroll there, though most programs set per-pupil funding at a substantially lower level than for local public schools.

Fourth, the landmark No Child Left Behind Act of 2002 requires low-performing districts to use federal funds to create a competitive market for after-school tutoring services. More than 2,500 state-approved supplemental service providers are now competing for federal funds that average $800–900 per eligible student. While many of the approved providers are school districts themselves or other nonprofits, a number are small for-profits and larger national for-profits. Harvard University business professor Clay Christensen has argued that most disruptive innovation tends to be pioneered by low-cost "down-market" providers who find ways to undercut established, pricey producers by delivering functional substitute products at dramatic savings (Christensen, 1997; Christensen & Raynor, 2003). Historically, the absence of for-profits, coupled with K-12 funding formulas and higher education subsidies, has stifled the emergence of cost-effective providers.

Existing arrangements insulate educational leaders, administrators, and teachers from the consequences of their performance. Because individual teachers are not promoted or rewarded for exemplary performance, and because they do not face termination or demotion for poor performance, it is difficult for even determined leadership to spur employees to efforts beyond those they are disposed to put forth. And because neither school principals nor district superintendents are rewarded for attracting enrollment, they have little incentive to engage in controversial or unpopular measures to do so. Lacking the ability to readily assess, reward, or select subordinates, and in an environment where only the rarest school systems resort to layoffs, most principals and superintendents lack the means to answer market forces.

Competitive Response of Public Schools

Markets work precisely because they are neither gentle nor forgiving. They are impersonal mechanisms that gain their power by harnessing self-interest and drawing on desire and fear. The power of the market lurks in the knowledge that even dominant firms may be only one innovation away from being overthrown, that hungry garage inventors may be only one breakthrough away from success. It is the handful of entrepreneurs who take the chances and embrace the risk that drive innovation and growth, as with the entrepreneurs who have exploited new opportunities in vocational colleges or in services to homeschooling families.

In the private sector, when competition is threatening enough – such as when American electronic manufacturers were met with an onslaught of Japanese competitors in the 1980s – it can bring these protective edifices crashing down. Firms either cast off inefficient rules and procedures or are overtaken by new providers. This is not a pleasant process or a painless one, and it raises concerns about capriciousness and equity. Nonetheless, this is how competition actually works.

It is immediately clear that the very nature of public organizations such as schools, colleges, and universities makes it possible to limit the effects of markets in two key ways. First, the market threat can be neutralized by political fiat. Public agencies are not threatened by bankruptcy in the same way that private firms are. Legislatures may require a public agency to begin competing against other entities, but they are free to buffer schools and colleges from the revenue losses that might attend a shrinking clientele. Second, the incentives for officials in public school districts are fundamentally different from those for executives of private firms. Private firms are driven by investors anxiously watching profitability or by owner-managers who have their own wealth riding on the future of the firm. When confronted by competitors, the pressure to improve profitability propels executives to find new market opportunities, root out organizational inefficiencies, and pursue increased profitability. If executives do not take these steps, they risk being displaced by leaders who will.

Public schools, in particular, are not well suited to act boldly. Public employees face extensive procedural requirements. Given substantial penalties for violating a statute and few rewards for effective performance, public servants have incentives to hew to procedural requirements – even when the requirements seem inefficient.

Employees who respect these prosper, while entrepreneurs who violate norms or offend constituencies encounter difficulties. Consequently, when compelled to launch a public response to the threat of market competition, leaders are constricted in their course of action. One response is to enhance advertising and public outreach. A second, more interesting, response is the tendency of officials to relax procedures so as to permit the development of new programs and initiatives.

Even for managers in the private sector, it is arduous and unpleasant to undertake significant organizational changes. They do so only when they have to, relying upon their capacity to recruit and promote supportive managers, reward cooperative employees, monitor performance, and sanction or fire the uncooperative. Managers in public schools generally lack such tools. So, rather than forcing change upon their subordinates, they prefer reforms that allow entrepreneurial employees to step forward. The result is enhanced opportunities for principals to launch new specialty schools. This solution avoids the conflicts provoked by coercion, while producing visible evidence of organizational change.

Unorthodox opportunities to provide new services appeal to entrepreneurial personalities, the same individuals marginalized in process-oriented public sector agencies. In fields such as education, these entrepreneurs are rarely motivated by self-interest as traditionally understood in economic discourse. Having forgone more lucrative opportunities of the private sector, they are frequently motivated by a sense of calling, intrinsic desire, or a desire for new challenges.

Competition-induced pressure can encourage influential constituencies to accept some relaxation of procedures, enabling entrepreneurs to punch small holes through regulatory barriers. Though inefficient practices are not rooted out, new initiatives – such as new schools, departments, or hiring programs – may spring up beside existing practices. Pressured to provide a visible response, officials may chip holes in the regulations and procedures that run like kudzu through public sector organizations. These holes permit entrepreneurs to bypass traditional gatekeepers, creating new pockets of reform and possibly starting to topple the existing edifice.

Policy and Educational Competition

Most proposals to reform education through enhanced competition fail to wrestle seriously with what that course of action entails. In areas where competition is driving change, providers have exploited new opportunities to offer narrowly defined services and displace existing public agencies. Efforts to compel public schools to respond through market-based measures have enjoyed less success.

There is a stark difference between reforms that create new room for nonpublic operators and those that harness competition to force public providers to change. Ambivalence toward this distinction is at the heart of market-based reform. On one hand, reformers highlight the need for competition to challenge insulated institutions, unleash entrepreneurial energies, focus attention on productivity, and create incentives to find efficiencies. On the other hand, they hesitate to violate established notions of educational decorum, worry that vulnerable students may be harmed by marketplace dislocations, feel uncertain about for-profit educators, and prefer a "kinder, gentler" competitive regime.

Proponents of educational competition have proceeded with studied inattention to the central truth of market-based reform. Competition requires that producers have incentives to address consumer demands in ways that promote performance and productivity. However, this is precisely where public agencies, especially those with high levels of public support, can pursue rules and regulations that stifle potential competitors and buffer themselves from the consequences of competition. When asked to compete with private providers, public providers have significant incentive to choke off entry, lobby for protections, and satisfy constituents with symbolic gestures, while using the resulting slack to avoid structural changes that competition intends to force. Incentives of this nature suppress the pressures driving the technology of change.

Although the public might be expected to support efficiency-minded proposals intended to control costs, there is no evidence of a coherent or influential constituency for cost-effectiveness at the K-12 level. Rather than express any concerns about productivity, public opinion has consistently supported increased spending, and a plurality of the public routinely says that a lack of money is the greatest single challenge facing schools. While some observers trace undisciplined spending to the influence that teachers' unions exert on school boards, the reality is that President George W. Bush increased federal spending on K-12 education more rapidly than any previous president – and was criticized primarily for not spending enough. Ultimately, the centrality of education to American notions of opportunity and meritocracy, sensitivity to questions of educational access and equity, and the public's abiding affection for educators and local institutions make it inordinately difficult to promote radical policy change in this area or to rally support on behalf of productivity or cost containment.

Americans have great faith in the ideal of public schooling, express a high rate of satisfaction with their local school, and are averse to proposals for radical change (Moe, 2002). Hence, it ought not be a surprise that they are uncomfortable with importing into education the "creative destruction" that is the signature of market-driven improvement. There is also much ambivalence about embracing a new breed of educators who are expansionist, profit seeking, or focused on cost-efficiencies, especially when it cannot be proven that they will be more effective than traditional educators. Given the hesitance of both the public and reformers toward market-based school reform, political efforts to promote specific deregulatory measures – such as relaxing the licensure of teachers and administrators, allowing money to follow students more readily from school to school, or instituting more flexible compensation – might ultimately prove to have a more dramatic effect on educational provision than proposals for choice-based reform.

Exactly how deregulation will proceed in such an environment is unclear. How will it impel a public that regards educational expenditure as a rough proxy for quality to endorse cost-effectiveness? And how will it spur publicly managed schools to compete as if they were private sector organizations or encourage nonprofits to behave more like profit-maximizing firms? If the success of market-based reform ultimately hinges upon the entry and expansion of for-profits, precious little consideration has been devoted to either desirable regulatory measures or the political implications. Given that markets do not implement themselves but are ultimately dependent on the rules within which they operate and the fidelity with which their rules are monitored and maintained, this inattention leaves unclear what meaningful educational deregulation would even look like.

"Deregulating" a marketplace can mean very different things, depending on the sector, the politics, and the context. Thatcherite reform in Great Britain consisted of dismantling state monopolies and creating competitive markets. Deregulation of the airline and trucking industries was a matter of the government making it easier for firms to pursue profit-driven agendas. In education, not even the most ardent champions of markets wish to see the government dismantle its system of schools. Meanwhile, the vast majority of non-state providers are nonprofit institutions, in which concerns about culture, comfort, and prestige, for example, often take precedence over the imperatives of maximizing revenues or minimizing costs. Exactly how deregulation will proceed in such an environment is unclear. In the end, the abiding American faith in markets and in public institutions comes to a head in the case of schooling, where strong and passionate defenders of existing public institutions exist.

References

Christensen, C. M. (1997). *The innovator's dilemma*. Cambridge, MA: Harvard Business School Press.

Christensen, C. M., & Raynor, M. E. (2003). *The innovator's solution*. Cambridge, MA: Harvard Business School Press.

Moe, T. M. (2002). *Schools, vouchers, and the American public*. Washington, DC: Brookings Institute.

Marketization and Post-Marketization in Education

Geoff Whitty

Education has become increasingly "marketized" in recent years. Although the detail in this chapter relates to the situation in England, where neo-liberal policies have been in place for more than three decades now, these developments are now part of a much broader trend. The emergence of comparable reforms across continents has led some to suggest that the current restructuring of education needs to be understood as part of the economic, political and cultural processes of globalization in which national differences erode, state bureaucracies fragment and mass systems of public welfare disintegrate.

Although we always need to bear in mind both the commonality and specificity of contemporary education reform, the English case is of particular interest, partly because of its longevity and also because it has been looked to as a source of evidence by advocates and critics of neo-liberal reforms alike. It is also of interest because it is sometimes suggested that the neo-liberalism of Thatcherism was superseded by something significantly different under Tony Blair's New Labour government of 1997–2007 and this shift too has been echoed in other countries (see, for example, FPCJ, 2007).

I will begin by outlining the emergence of neo-liberal policies in England under the Conservatives from the 1980s and show how these relate to notions of the "free economy and the strong state" (Gamble, 1988) and "steering at a distance" (Neave, 1988). I then turn to the record of New Labour and the tensions that have resulted from New Labour's commitment to tackling disadvantage within the broader policy context established by the preceding Conservative administrations.

G. Whitty (✉)
Institute of Education, University of London, London, UK
e-mail: g.whitty@ioe.ac.uk

A. Hargreaves et al. (eds.), *Second International Handbook of Educational Change*,
Springer International Handbooks of Education 23, DOI 10.1007/978-90-481-2660-6_24,
© Springer Science+Business Media B.V. 2010

Education Policy under the Conservatives, 1979–1997

Marketization

Neo-liberal reforms were spearheaded in England by the Conservative government that came to power in 1979 under Margaret Thatcher. In the case of education, the government's public sector reforms focused primarily on the local government – or local education authority (LEA) – allocation of school places by catchment area. If governments allow schools a captive market in this way, it was argued, schools have no need to innovate or to respond efficiently, if at all, to consumer (parental) preferences (Shleifer, 1998). At the same time, the Conservatives regarded the LEAs as having been "captured" by the so-called "educational establishment" of teachers and the universities that trained them, whom they saw as left-leaning and favouring what in their view were highly questionable "progressive" or "child-centred" approaches to teaching. Together, they argued, state allocation of places and "progressive" teaching methods had brought a dull uniformity to the system and a levelling down of standards.

Accordingly, throughout its time in office the Conservative government acted to reduce the power of the "producers" and increase that of the "consumer." The key piece of legislation in this respect was the 1988 Education Reform Act. This gave state schools the opportunity to "opt out" of their LEAs and run themselves as grant-maintained schools with direct funding from central government. Even those schools that chose to remain with their LEAs had to take greater control over their own budgets and day-to-day management. Equally significantly, 80% of that devolved budget would be determined directly by the number and ages of its pupils.

This per capita funding was coupled with open enrolment and the right for all families to express a preference for any school, even one outside their local authority. Some radical Conservatives characterized this as moving towards a "virtual voucher" system (Sexton, 1987). Open enrollment allowed popular schools to attract as many students as possible, at least up to their physical capacity. Consequently, schools could no longer rely on a given intake and had to attract sufficient numbers themselves to remain viable. The market choice argument was that schools which failed to attract pupils should not be "buttressed" but closed. In practice, existing rules on admission, such as prioritizing sibling enrolment and those living closest to the school, were retained once schools were oversubscribed. This obviously weakened the market in education that the government wanted to achieve, but its overall policies were still successful in embedding a change of ideology in education policy.

Subsequent to the 1988 Act, the Conservatives continued to divert even more money away from LEAs into schools, and extended the right for schools to opt out of LEA control. The government also encouraged diversity and choice by introducing a new type of school within the state sector. Known as specialist schools, these schools had a curriculum specialism, received additional funding to support their area of specialization and were permitted to select up to 10% of their pupils by aptitude.

Accountability

However, while the Conservatives were enthusiastic about making schools more receptive to parents' wishes, they were unwilling to relinquish control over the outcomes that schools should achieve. In this, Conservative education policy provides a clear illustration of the tendency for liberal democracies to develop along the lines of the "strong state" and the "free economy" (Gamble, 1988) and the associated shift in the way the public sector is coordinated and controlled by government – to what can be characterized as "steering at a distance". While processes of devolution appear to offer organizations greater autonomy, the state retains overall strategic control by setting the outputs that providers need to achieve and publishing tables of performance against them (Neave, 1988, p. 11; Whitty, Power, & Halpin, 1998). These indicators arguably influence the priorities of service users, who in turn reinforce the pressure on providers to work to them (Adnett & Davies, 2003).

The main mechanism for such central steering under the Conservatives was the establishment of a standard "National Curriculum" and related system of student assessment for all schools. While seen largely as a centralizing measure, standardizing the curriculum generated important data on school performance, thereby facilitating school choice. The more intensive approach to school inspections introduced under the Conservatives through the 1992 Education (Schools) Act generated similar data on school performance (see Wilcox & Gray, 1996).

New Labour and the attempt to balance Choice and Equity

The approach to public sector management that emerged during the 1980s has since become a major policy thrust across countries and political parties. As indicated earlier, choice and competition, devolution and performativity and centralization and prescription now represent global trends in education policy (Ball, 2001; Whitty et al., 1998). Nevertheless, their acceptance by the New Labour government represented a significant move away from the party's traditional ideology. It therefore sought to differentiate its policies from those of the Conservatives, but perhaps more importantly to "spin" them differently in an effort to bridge the ideological divide.

Rhetorically, New Labour's education policy has been rooted in the government's commitment to the "Third Way," which has been presented as a creative partnership between neo-liberal capitalism and social democracy (Lawton, 2005) and a means of linking market approaches with social justice (Barber, 1997; Blair, 1998; Giddens, 1998). In practice, however, many commentators have concluded that New Labour has not delivered a substantially new education policy (see Power & Whitty, 1999). Indeed, in some respects it has gone further down the marketization route, and much further down the privatization route, than the Conservatives ever achieved, as well increasing the central steerage of the system. The effect of this has been to limit the impact of the more progressive aspects of New Labour rhetoric that were initially intended to differentiate the "new" policies from those of the previous government.

Targeted attempts to tackle Disadvantage

Yet that rhetoric was partly a response to claims that marketization under the Conservatives had led to inequalities in educational provision and outcomes (Mortimore & Whitty, 1997; Whitty et al., 1998). "High quality education for the many rather than excellence for the few" was the Labour Party's slogan immediately following the 1997 election. Early initiatives focused on raising educational attainment in areas of particularly intense social exclusion through the allocation of additional resources. These initiatives included the "Education Action Zones" (EAZs), "Excellence in Cities", "London Challenge" and the "extended schools" programme, whereby schools offer access to a range of after-school, health and welfare services.

Evaluation findings for EAZs have generally been disappointing (Power, Whitty, Gewirtz, Halpin, & Dickson, 2004), showing a failure to raise attainment and improve skills and attitudes across *all* students, especially the most disadvantaged (see also Machin, McNally, & Meghir, 2007). In contrast, the recent evaluation of the extended schools pilot found that, despite the challenges, such provision has had some positive outcomes for poorer families by providing stability and improving their children's engagement in learning. Encouragingly, its final report indicated that the achievement gap between advantaged and disadvantaged pupils, based on eligibility for Free School Meals, was narrower in these schools than in others (Cummings et al., 2007). London Challenge too appears to have had some success, both in reducing the number of "failing" schools and increasing the relative achievement of disadvantaged children within them (see Ofsted, 2006).

What is significant is that these gains, though small, have been identified from initiatives that, to some extent at least, run counter to the marketization of recent policies in that they recognize the importance of structural and cultural influences on educational performance. Oddly, New Labour has long seemed to recognize the importance of such factors in its broader policies, but it has seemed reluctant to apply these insights to its understanding of differential performance in schools. Instead, too many of New Labour's school policies have been founded ". . . on the belief that quality differences between schools are primarily the responsibility of schools themselves and can therefore be tackled by initiatives at the school level" (Thrupp & Lupton, 2006, p. 315). This is reflected in the government's focus on "standards, not structures."

"Standards, not Structures"

In 1997 New Labour committed itself to an "unrelenting" focus on raising educational standards through a system of "high challenge and high support" (DfEE, 1997). This school improvement approach – based around the "exemplary school discourse" and the idea that all schools can replicate the example of the best (Thrupp & Lupton, 2006) – has included the setting of ambitious standards for pupil attainment and clear targets for schools to reach. A particularly important component has been the principle of government intervention in inverse proportion to a school's success.

"Successful" schools – those that perform well against government targets and in school inspections – are rewarded with new freedoms. From 2003, and reminiscent of earlier neo-liberal thinking on education markets, this included the opportunity for the best schools to expand their pupil numbers. In contrast, "failing" schools are subjected to tough measures and targeted support. Not surprisingly, there is a high correlation between the results of Ofsted inspections and schools' indicators of pupil disadvantage (Gorard, 2005), with the majority of schools in "special measures" or facing closure located in areas of socio-economic disadvantage. This provides a stark illustration of the systematic effects of social class on children's attainment, which New Labour has consistently understated (Plewis & Goldstein, 1998).

Important here is the research showing that, with the same input, children from advantaged homes tend to progress at a faster rate than those from disadvantaged backgrounds. Thus, if all schools performed as well as the best schools, the stratification of achievement by social class would be even starker than it is now (Mortimore & Whitty, 1997). Indeed, data released by the government itself in 2005 seemed to show the deficiencies of its approach in this respect. They showed that while all primary school pupils achieved higher standards in English and mathematics in 2004 than in 1998, those from higher income families had made more progress than disadvantaged pupils – resulting in a persistent attainment gap between these two groups of pupils (Kelly, 2005).

These findings have now prompted action on the part of the government. Importantly, this has led to a greater focus on disadvantaged pupils themselves, rather than just on schools in disadvantaged areas – as was the case with some of the interventions I noted earlier. The 2005 schools White Paper (DfES, 2005) emphasizes the tailoring of education around the needs of each child, including catch-up provision for those who need it. This shift includes the expansion of the "Reading Recovery" programme, which offers one-to-one support for children who have fallen behind with their reading in the early years.

Such provision may or may not have a significant impact on the social class achievement gap in the future. In 2006, then Education Minister Ruth Kelly announced that new research would show that "... if anything, there has been a slight closing of the [attainment] gap at age 14 and 16" (Kelly, 2006). To have achieved only a very modest closing of the gap after three terms in office still reflects poorly on the record of a government committed to social justice and might have been expected to stimulate a fundamental reassessment of the benefits of diversity and choice.

"Diversity and Choice"

Alongside its "high challenge, high support" approach to school improvement, New Labour has favoured the "modernization" of the comprehensive system through the differentiation of schools. It has increasingly placed an emphasis on the supposed link between school diversity and higher standards for all (Blair, 2006. See also Evans, Castle, Cooper, Glatter, & Woods, 2005). Accordingly, the amount of differentiation among schools has increased under New Labour with academies and trust schools being added to the existing mix of community, foundation and faith schools. Increasing numbers of secondary schools have curricular specialisms. But the key ingredient for linking differentiation to standards and excellence has remained choice.

Even so, the evidence to support the case that diversity and choice are the key to higher standards for all remains weak and highly contested. That the superior performance of some schools may be partly due to the nature of their pupil intakes does not seem to have been fully acknowledged by the government. Yet the data on the proportions of children on Free School Meals in different types of school is telling in this respect (Braswell, 2005; Sutton Trust, 2006). The school types that are generally most academically successful typically have higher proportions of middle class pupils and correspondingly lower proportions of disadvantaged pupils, thus generating a "virtuous circle" of strong performance against government attainment targets and popularity among more affluent families. The danger of the diversity and choice agenda, then, is the creation of a "multi-tier" system of secondary schools based on the sorts of children who attend them (Riddell, 2003).

This outcome is made more likely by a peculiar feature of the English system. Some schools, including many faith-based schools, have control over admission of their pupils, while the allocation of pupils to some other schools is undertaken by local authorities. There has long been a suspicion that schools use their control over their own admissions to operate systems of academic and social selection. For example, Tough and Brooks (2007) found that schools that are their own admissions authorities are six to ten times more likely to be highly unrepresentative of their surrounding area than schools where the local authority is the admissions authority.

In this context, the evidence on the positive impact of diversity and choice is therefore not sufficiently robust to justify New Labour's strong commitment to this approach. Furthermore, a well-balanced assessment of the evidence concluded that ". . . whatever performance advantages it offers [and they did show some], further expansion of market mechanisms . . . may come at the cost of increased social polarisation" (Gibbons, Machin, & Silva, 2006).

The extent to which recent policies have or have not increased social segregation is, however, contested in the literature (Gorard, Taylor, & Fitz, 2003; Jenkins, Micklewright, & Schnepf, 2006). Whether or not the position has become worse as a result of these policies, there is no doubt that advantaged schools and advantaged parents have been able to seek each other out.

A new admissions code introduced in 2007 requires all schools to act in accordance with common national guidelines. It prohibits schools from giving priority to children on the basis of their interests or knowledge, and this is to be combined with existing plans for free school transport to open up choice to less advantaged families and "choice advisers" to assist these families in negotiating their child's transition to secondary school (DfES, 2005). This is a belated recognition of the impact of structural and cultural factors on the capacity of different groups to exercise choice meaningfully in a diverse system of schooling. But it will take these provisions many years to begin to address more covert forms of selection and the way in which middle class parents learn to decipher the "real" admissions criteria, as revealed in research by Gewirtz, Ball, and Bowe (1995) and by Reay and Ball (1998).

Beyond Marketization?

Meanwhile, there have been other attempts to counter the negative effects of marketization and its associated hierarchies of schools. "Collegiates" in Birmingham and federations of schools elsewhere seek to foster collaboration rather than competition and enable schools to work together in the interests of optimum provision for all pupils. However, early evaluation evidence suggests that, although there is widespread professional support for this move, its impact on outcomes has been limited (Lindsay et al., 2007). It is questionable whether genuine, long-term and productive collegiality among schools can be easily established where schools are on different legal and budgetary footings, have very different pupil intakes and have their results reported separately (Adnett & Davies, 2003).

Many opponents of marketization have united around the call for good schools in all areas – for all children (Education Alliance, 2006). Unfortunately, the evidence suggests that a good school in every locality is very much harder to achieve in some areas than others (Lupton, 2005; Thrupp & Lupton, 2006). So, while diversity and choice may not be the way of ensuring high standards for all, neighbourhood schools may not be the answer either. As I have indicated, wider structural influences mean that the performance of schools is significantly affected by the sorts of children who attend them and a critical mass of children from more aspirational backgrounds does make a difference in raising a school's overall attainment (Maden, 2003; Thrupp, 1999).

Unfortunately, it is not easy to find ways of balancing intakes academically and socially in a politically acceptable way. As Giddens (1998) recognizes, social exclusion is a dual process that operates at the "top" as well as the "bottom" of society. Unless they feel their needs are being met, there is always a danger that more middle class parents will withdraw their children from the state sector and move them into private schools (Whitty, 2002). For electoral reasons, New Labour has felt that its policies have to speak particularly to the middle class and aspiring middle class voters who constitute the "swing" vote that decides modern elections – especially in the first-past-the-post electoral system that exists in England. New Labour was initially so concerned about this electoral logic that it was very wary of limiting the opportunities for middle class advantage and this included putting limits on school choice.

However, the new admissions code noted earlier permits local authorities to seek to balance intakes by ensuring that schools have to take pupils from all ability bands. It also permits oversubscribed schools to allocate places by ballot. Nevertheless, neither of these measures is mandatory and the evidence so far is that they are unlikely to prove popular with either schools or parents.

If a climate of public opinion that supports policies to balance school intakes is now to be created, the implications of school mix need to be better understood. This need not centre exclusively on the social costs of a highly segregated schooling system, but also on the way in which interventions to balance admissions could reduce what is at stake for individual middle class families when selecting their secondary schools. Clearly, such a re-adjustment of public opinion will take time. But only by using its powers more robustly to counter the negative effects of marketization can New Labour properly claim to be fostering social justice rather than sustaining the manifestly unjust system it inherited from the Conservatives.

It remains to be seen whether the replacement of Tony Blair by Gordon Brown as prime minister in 2007 will lead to a clearer break with neo-liberal policies and a decisive move into a post-marketized era of education policy in England. As Peter Wilby puts it, "a Brown government will need courage and ingenuity to reconcile egalitarian ambitions with political realities" (Wilby, 2007).

References

Adnett, N., & Davies, P. (2003). Schooling reforms in England: From quasi-markets to co-opetition? *Journal of Education Policy, 18*(4), 393–406.

Ball, S. J. (2001). Labour learning and the economy: A policy sociology perspective. In M. Fielding (Ed.), *Taking education really seriously: Four year's hard labour*. London: RoutledgeFalmer.

Barber, M. (1997). *The learning game: Arguments for an education revolution*. London: Gollancz.

Blair, T. (1998). *The third way: New politics for the new century*. Fabian Pamphlet 588 London: Fabian Society.

Blair, T. (2006). Education is the most precious gift. Speech at Specialist Schools and Academies Trust Conference, November. http://www.number-10.gov.uk/output/Page10514.asp

Braswell, S. (2005). *Choice and social segregation in education: The impact of open enrolment on the social compositions of English secondary schools*. Unpublished DPhil thesis.

Cummings, C., Dyson, A., Muijs, D., Papps, I., Pearson, D., Raffo, C., et al. (2007). *Evaluation of the full service extended schools initiative: Final report*. Research Report RR852. http://www.dfes.gov.uk/research/data/uploadfiles/RR852.pdf

DfEE [Department for Education and Employment]. (1997). *Excellence in schools*. London: TSO.

DfES [Department for Education and Skills]. (2005). Schools white paper. *Higher standards, better schools for all*. Norwich: HMSO.

Education Alliance. (2006). A good local school for every child: Will the education bill deliver? Conference report. 25 March 2006, Institute of Education, University of London.

Evans, J., Castle, F., Cooper, D., Glatter, R., & Woods, P. (2005). Collaboration: The big new idea for school improvement? *Journal of Education Policy, 20*(2), 223–235.

FPCJ [Foreign Press Centre Japan]. (2007). http://www.fpcj.jp/e/mres/japanbrief/jb_740.html

Gamble, A. (1988). *The free economy and the strong state*. London: Macmillan.

Gewirtz, S., Ball, S., & Bowe, R. (1995). *Markets, choice and equity*. Buckingham: Open University Press.

Gibbons, S., Machin, S., & Silva, O. (2006). *Competition, choice and pupil achievement*. London: LSE/CEE.

Giddens, A. (1998). *The third way: The renewal of social democracy*. Cambridge: Polity Press.

Gorard, S. (2005). Academies as the 'future of schooling': Is this an evidence-based policy? *Journal of Education Policy, 20*(3), 369–377.

Gorard, S., Taylor, C., & Fitz, J. (2003). *Schools, markets and choice policies*. London: Routledge Falmer.

Jenkins, S., Micklewright, J., & Schnepf, S. (2006). *Social segregation in secondary schools: How does England compare with other countries?* Southampton Statistical Sciences Research Institute. (S3RI Applications and Policy Working Papers, A06/01).

Kelly, R. (2005).*Education and social progress.* Speech to the Institute of Public Policy Research, July.

Kelly, R. (2006). *Education and social mobility: Progress for all.* Speech to the Institute of Public Policy Research, April.

Lawton, D. (2005). *Education and labour party ideologies – 1900–2001 and beyond.* Abingdon: RoutledgeFalmer.

Lindsay, G., Muijs, D., Harris, A., Chapman, C., Arweck, E., & Goodall, J. (2007) *School federations pilot study 2003–2007,* DCSF Research Report DCSF-RR015. London: DCSF.

Lupton, R. (2005) Social justice and school improvement: Improving the quality of schooling in the poorest neighbourhoods. *British Educational Research Journal, 31*(5), 589–604.

Machin, S., McNally, S., & Meghir, C. (2007). *Resources and standards in urban schools.* London: Centre for the Economics of Education.

Maden, M. (2003). Has choice, diversity and marketisation improved the quality and efficiency of education? Means to which ends?. *Journal of Educational Change, 4,* 64–72.

Mortimore, P., & Whitty, G. (1997).*Can school improvement overcome the effects of disadvantage?* London: Institute of Education.

Neave, G. (1988). On the cultivation of quality, efficiency and enterprise: An overview of recent trends in higher education in Western Europe, 1968–1988. *European Journal of Education, 23*(1/2), 7–23.

Ofsted. (2006). *Improvements in London schools 2000–2006.* http://www.ofsted.gov. uk/publications/2509 (December).

Plewis, I., & Goldstein, H. (1998). Excellence in schools – a failure of standards. *British Journal of Curriculum and Assessment, 8*(1), 17–20.

Power, S., & Whitty, G. (1999). New labour's education policy: First, second or third way? *Research Papers in Education, 14*(5), 535–546.

Power, S., Whitty, G., Gewirtz, S., Halpin, D., & Dickson, M. (2004). Paving a 'third way'? A policy trajectory analysis of education action zones. *Research Papers in Education, 19*(4), 453–475.

Reay, D., & Ball, S. (1998). Making their minds up: Family dynamics and school choice. *British Educational Research Journal, 24,* 431–448.

Riddell, R. (2003). *Schools for our cities: Urban learning in the 21st Century.* Stoke on Trent: Trentham Books.

Sexton, S. (1987). *Our schools – a radical policy.* Wartingham: Institute of Economic Affairs, Education Unit.

Shleifer, A. (1998). State versus private ownership. *Journal of Economic Perspectives, 12*(4), 133–150.

Sutton Trust. (2006). *The social composition of top comprehensive schools: Rates of eligibility for free school meals at the 200 highest performing comprehensive schools.* London: Sutton Trust.

Thrupp, M. (1999). *Schools making a difference: Let's be realistic! School mix, school effectiveness and the social limits of reform.* Buckingham: Open University Press.

Thrupp, M., & Lupton, R. (2006). Taking school contexts more seriously: The social justice challenge. *British Journal of Educational Studies, 54*(3), 308–328.

Tough, S., & Brooks, R. (2007). *Fair choice – choosing a better admissions system.* London: IPPR.

Whitty, G. (2002). *Making sense of education policy.* London: Sage.

Whitty, G., Power, S., & Halpin, D. (1998). *Devolution and choice in education: The school, the state and the market.* Buckingham: Open University Press.

Wilby, P. (2007). Why education remains the priority. *New statesman,* 14 May, p. 14.

Wilcox, B., & Gray, J. (1996). *Inspecting schools: Holding schools to account and helping schools to improve.* Buckingham: Open University Press.

Large-Scale Assessment for Accountability Purposes

Peter W. Hill

The past two decades have witnessed a dramatic increase in the importance and prevalence of large-scale assessment for accountability purposes. Programs have been introduced with the expectation of realizing significant collective and individual benefits, including raised educational standards, particularly for traditionally low-achieving groups of students; greater attention to important curriculum content; better information about student progress for the purposes of informing parents and guiding and improving teaching and learning; and greater transparency regarding the performance of schools and systems.

These are worthy and legitimate reasons for pursuing large-scale assessment. Unfortunately, the anticipated benefits are not always fully realized and sometimes costs outweigh benefits. It would be contended that the majority of systems are now committed to large-scale assessment programs that are less than optimal in delivering what they were supposed to achieve.

This is not news to most educators. Much has been written and said about the real and potential negative consequences of pursuing accountability for student learning through large-scale assessment (e.g., Black, 1998; Hursh, 2007; Linn, 2000; Mehrens, 1998). This is not to suggest that policy-makers should abandon current systems, but rather that most need significant adjustments. Unfortunately, misunderstandings and indeed misinformation persist about what exactly large-scale testing can and cannot do, negative washback effects have been underestimated, and design and/or implementation problems need fixing.

This chapter is in three parts. The first part is a brief overview of the emergence of large-scale assessment for accountability purposes. The second part identifies some of the key dimensions of change along which "assessment for accountability" systems vary and what can be done to improve them. The third and final part speculates on the likely future evolution of assessment for accountability purposes.

P.W. Hill (✉)
Hong Kong Examinations and Assessment Authority, Wan Chai, Hong Kong
e-mail: pwhill@hkeaa.edu.hk

A. Hargreaves et al. (eds.), *Second International Handbook of Educational Change*,
Springer International Handbooks of Education 23, DOI 10.1007/978-90-481-2660-6_25,
© Springer Science+Business Media B.V. 2010

The Emergence of Large-Scale Assessment for Accountability Purposes

Large-scale educational assessment is not a new phenomenon, nor is it of Western origin. It was invented by the Chinese centuries, if not millennia, ago. The practice of basing selection for the bureaucracy on results achieved in national examinations or tests can be traced back to the Han Dynasty (206BC–AD220) (Ingulsrud, 1994). These were very tough assessments and required years of preparation and study of classical texts. Competition was fierce and some candidates spent a lifetime trying to pass them and to secure access to what remains to this day in the Orient a coveted goal – a position in the senior ranks of the civil service. In modern-day Nanjing one can visit the remains of the Jiangnan Gongyuan Imperial Examination Center. First built in 1169, it became the largest imperial civil examination center in the Ming-Qing period with 20,644 rooms for examinees. This was assessment on a scale that is impressive even by today's standards.

China's examination system was copied by the Japanese as early as the eighth century, but the concept was unknown in the West for another 900 years when the Chinese system was described in letters written by missionary members of that most academic of Catholic orders, the Jesuits. Examinations were subsequently advocated by eighteenth century thinkers including Adam Smith and Voltaire, but the idea did not catch on in the West until the nineteenth century. Western nations have since made up for lost time.

Traditionally, large-scale assessment in education has existed for placement, progression, end-of-school certification, graduation, and above all, for selection purposes. In other words, it has been carried out to facilitate decision-making that has potentially serious or "high stakes" consequences for the examinee or test-taker. It has determined which school one went to, whether one would progress to the next grade, graduate from high school, get into the university program of one's choice, or get a job. It has been the instrument by which societies have moved from an aristocratic to a meritocratic basis for regulating access to the professions and to opening up opportunities for people in all strata of society.

In Europe, subject-based examinations, typically including a significant proportion of open-ended, subjective questions requiring extended written responses (especially essays), have prevailed, as exemplified by the British "General Certificate of Secondary Education" (GCSE) and "A-Level" examinations, the French "Baccalaureate," and the German and Finnish "Arbitur."

In the USA, large-scale educational assessment had its origins not in the context of recruitment to the civil service, but rather to the military. In World War I, some 1.9 million men were tested on the Army Alpha test of intelligence for "literates," and the Army Beta test of intelligence for illiterates and non-English speakers, especially new immigrants (Wigdor & Green, 1991). The numbers are staggering. These were "mental" tests associated with the new science of intelligence testing, new theories of psychometrics, and the invention of the multiple-choice question, allowing fast and efficient testing of large numbers of people. This history goes a long way to explaining the predominance in North America of objectively scored academic aptitude tests. The Standard Attainment Tests (SAT) evolved in the 1920s out of the Army intelligence quotient (IQ) tests and modern-day school graduation tests build on the same assessment technology.

Modern large-scale assessment got underway in the mid-60s as the result of the convergence of two factors. The first was a concern about the educational roots of inequalities in society that in the USA had become manifested through the civil rights movement. The second was advances in computer technology that made it possible for the first time to conduct and analyze the results from large-scale surveys of educational outcomes. The report into educational opportunities of Coleman et al. (1966) initiated a new era of educational research inspired by the twin notions that education is the key to maintaining social stability and progress, and that the key to improving educational outcomes is through scientific study of the factors that lead to improvement.

Much of the assessment technology underpinning current uses of large-scale assessment for accountability purposes was developed through programs that got underway in the wake of the Coleman Report, notably the National Assessment of Educational Progress (NAEP) in the USA and successive international surveys of educational achievement conducted by the International Association for the Evaluation of Educational Achievement (IEA). These surveys set new standards of excellence in test construction, sampling design, psychometrics to equate performances and enable the monitoring of standards over time, and research methods to understand influences on achievement for different groups of students within and across countries. These programs have typically been "low stakes" programs.

Since the 1980s, however, large-scale assessment has been used for more "high-stakes" purposes to hold providers (systems, schools, and teachers) directly accountable for the performance of their students. Justification for much of the current emphasis on assessment for the purposes of accountability was provided by research conducted from the mid-70s onwards into school effectiveness. School effectiveness research revealed modest but nonetheless significant differences among schools in the value that they add to learning by students having adjusted for resource inputs and student backgrounds and starting points. Evaluations of various school-reform initiatives reinforced the notion that the route to improvement lay in adopting evidence-based approaches to determining what works. This was in general agreement with the practices first introduced decades earlier by pioneers such as William Edwards Deming to improve quality and reduce costs in business and industry, and into later reforms that have transformed other areas of government service provision.

The shift in logic from the notion that it is possible to create schools that systematically adopt mechanisms for bringing about ongoing improvements in student learning to the notion of holding schools and school systems directly accountable for the progress of their students as measured by scores on tests was a small one, and one that resonated well with increasingly frustrated and anxious voters who were losing confidence in the capacity of public school systems to deliver a quality education.

And so the accountability movement arrived. Its declared aim has been to define standards, measure progress toward those standards, and hold schools publicly accountable for the progress their students make. While previous assessment programs involved "high stakes" consequences for the examinee or test-taker, assessment programs for the purpose of provider accountability are "high stakes" for teachers and school administrators, though with spillover consequences for parents and students. In a context in which market forces have increasingly been allowed to operate in determining school enrolments, these programs have influenced which schools flourish and which will be subject to remedial measures of even closure. They have been used to decide whose careers will be advanced and whose careers will be questioned.

Policy-makers have moved with boldness to ensure that pressure is applied to schools and school systems to improve student performance. For example, in the UK, national testing of all students at the end of each Key Stage of schooling, including the dissemination of individual reports to parents and the publication of individual schools' results, was first introduced in 1995 as part of the Conservative Government's education policies, but consolidated and extended under the Blair Labour Government. Students were required to take SATs at the ages of 7, 11, and 14 and national examinations (typically GCSEs) at the age of 16. The term "league tables" (after the tables used to rank soccer clubs) was coined to refer to the rankings of schools published annually in the media. Apart from the impact of being "named and shamed," some "failing" schools have been restructured or even in a very small number of cases closed down as a result of consistently poor performance on the SATs.

In the USA, the *No Child Left Behind* (NCLB) legislation enacted in January 2002, required states to:

- establish standards for academic proficiency in reading, mathematics and science;
- establish measures for assessing all students in public schools each year in English and math in grades 3–8 and in one of grades 10–12, and later on in science;
- develop a definition of what would constitute "adequate yearly progress" (AYP) toward the standard that has been set for academic proficiency; and
- set targets for schools to enable them to achieve 100% academic proficiency over 12 years.

In addition, the NCLB legislation incorporated the requirement that states will implement "high-stakes" consequences for schools and districts that fail to demonstrate AYP.

What is significant in the two countries cited is the way in which large-scale assessment for accountability purposes has been supported by opposing political parties. It came as a surprise to many when the Blair Labour Government continued the Conservative Party policies with respect to national key stage testing in the UK. In the USA, the NCLB legislation was passed with overwhelming support from both sides of politics. While this may have been due in no small measure to the fact that the legislation reinforced what was already a central theme of many state policies (Linn, Baker, & Betebenner, 2002), it was nonetheless a rare example of bipartisan cooperation.

Why have opposing parties in these two countries supported large-scale testing for accountability purposes? In part the answer is that it is regarded as a powerful means of promoting very different political goals. For example, from the perspective of social democratic liberalism, it is seen as a means whereby society can promote greater equality of opportunity by focusing on the performance of those students traditionally achieving low educational outcomes and seeking to have these students achieve at a level of proficiency that will enable them to cope effectively in the modern world. At the same time, from a neoliberal perspective it is seen as the necessary response to the challenges of globalization; free market capitalism; deregulation and privatization, requiring the creating of an informed public that can exercise choice in where they send their children to school (Hursh, 2007), and leading to ongoing improvements in the quality of educational provision as schools compete with one another for students.

In part the answer may come down to pragmatic considerations. After all, as Bismark famously said a century and a half ago: "Politics is the art of the possible" and large-scale testing has some compelling features given the real world in which politicians need to operate. Linn (2000) cites four: (1) it is inexpensive relative to most policy initiatives; (2) it is easy to mandate relative to other interventions; (3) it can be rapidly implemented within the term of office of elected officials; and (4) it generates visible results which typically show an increase in scores in the first few years of any new program. One can think of other reasons, including the public perception that test scores can be trusted, which in turn lends credibility to policy-makers who promote assessment-based policies.

And over and above political considerations, there are those mega trends in the consciousness of people everywhere (Caldwell & Spinks, 1992), of which one is the belief that justice and progress can occur only under conditions of transparency, full knowledge of the facts, (Fullan, 2008) and accountability for any failures to meet expectations. One manifestation of this mega trend is the growing conviction among parents that they are entitled to know how their child is progressing and how the child's school and school system is performing. It comes with a corresponding belief in the right to remediation or withdrawal of support when their child is not making adequate progress, and when the child's school or school system is not performing to expectation.

As a consequence, and for varied reasons, the accountability movement has prompted major initiatives in many countries to centrally prescribe content and performance standards in core areas of the curriculum, especially literacy and numeracy; to undertake annual population testing of cohorts of students; to implement policies governing the publication or otherwise of results; to implicitly or explicitly provide incentives for high performance or improvement; and to mandate support and sanctions for low performance. This is now true in most countries, although with some notable exceptions, including some that get excellent results in the Organization of Economic Development and Cooperation's (OECD) Programme for International Student Assessment (PISA) and that have thus far eschewed accountability testing programs (notably Finland and Japan).

Optimizing Large-Scale Assessment for Accountability Purposes

While large-scale assessment for accountability purposes is now widespread, much remains to be done to ensure that it is effective. This is particularly so because most programs were designed without taking into account their likely "washback" or test impact effects (Bachman & Palmer, 1996, pp. 29–35). This section considers some of the ways in which large-scale assessment systems differ and identifies some lessons regarding what can be done to optimize their fitness for purpose; to avoid negative washback effects; and to promote positive washback on the curriculum, learning, professional practice, motivation, decision-making, and trust.

Fitness for Purpose

In any area of endeavor, getting the right match between the intended purpose and a technical solution is critical. Assessment programs can only be effective if there is a good fit between their design and how the results are used. Assessment programs designed for one purpose are often unsuited for other purposes. For example, a test that measures generic outcomes and the ability to apply knowledge involving a wide span of curricula content will be of little assistance to schools in improving instruction. Such a test will indicate whether students are achieving broad educational goals, but it will not indicate what needs to be attended to in order to improve outcomes for these students.

In order to maximize the benefits of large-scale assessment, transparency and clarity of purpose is critical. In many programs there are significant differences between declared purposes, undeclared purposes, and perceived purposes. When such differences exist, problems almost always arise.

For example, the *declared* purposes of a state or national assessment program may be to monitor the overall standards of instruction in different areas of the curriculum, to provide information to assist schools to improve learning, and to ensure that students at risk of falling behind are given the necessary support to catch up. However, *undeclared* purposes may include ensuring compliance with the curriculum and greater effort by teachers to improve student performance. School principals and teachers may *perceive* the purpose of the program as being to expose poorly performing schools; to shift responsibility for poor system-wide performance and lack of support to them; and to accumulate the evidence to justify school closures, restructuring of schools, and dismissal of poorly performing staff. Students may have no clear idea about the purpose of the tests, but nevertheless make some effort to do well on them if for no other reason than to please their anxious teachers. Parents may perceive the purpose of the program as to give them access to the information they have always wanted, namely definitive rankings of schools to enable them to decide which is best for their child. When purposes are this confused, the interests of stakeholders cannot be satisfied.

Newton (2007) identifies three kinds of purposes that are particularly important to clarify, namely:

- the technical or measurement purpose;
- the decision purpose, or what use will be made of the assessment; and
- the consequential purpose, or the intended impact of the assessment program.

If the primary decision purpose is to monitor the performance of systems and schools over time with reference to an overall standard representing proficiency or basic competence, then it is important that the technical or measurement purpose is aligned to that purpose. For example, the measurement purpose might be to provide a series of unique tests that remain valid over time, provide maximum discrimination around the designated cut score representing achievement of the standard, and allow equating with tests administered in previous years. Such an assessment program is unlikely, however, to be useful in making decisions about the performance of the school as a whole because it will do a poor job in assessing those who are operating well above the cut score. The school may be doing a good job in targeting those students at risk of not meeting the minimum standard, but a poor job with its more able students. While the intended impact of the program may have been to improve outcomes of "at risk" students, neglecting other students would clearly be an unintended consequence.

Lesson 1
Ensure that what you seek to measure, the use you make of the results and what you intend to achieve by using results in this manner, are in alignment; that you declare your purposes, and don't undermine trust by retaining undeclared purposes, or allowing others to believe you have a hidden agenda.

The Curriculum

A recurring criticism of many large-scale accountability assessment programs is that they have the effect of narrowing the curriculum to a subset of the basic knowledge and of focusing on minimum competencies at the expense of promoting excellence across a wide range of outcomes. There is research evidence that this does occur in most cases, but with significant exceptions, depending on the nature and structure of the tests used (Au, 2007).

Many systems opt to measure a fairly narrow albeit critical subset of curriculum outcomes, namely those concerned with core competences within the domains of literacy and numeracy. At the same time, modern curricula typically require students to not only master a defined body of content but also to be able to apply this knowledge in order to solve problems or address issues. They emphasize higher-order thinking skills including creativity, the ability to be a strategic learner, the ability to learn independently, and the ability to make sensible and rationale choices.

Objectively scored multiple-choice test items struggle to assess many of these competencies. Examination questions that make use of open-ended response formats and that require students to refer to a range of information in answering the question fare much better, but they bring with them accompanying considerations of development and marking costs and costs in maintaining acceptable levels of interrater reliability. Assessment tasks conducted at the school level and involving the extended projects, laboratory work, fieldwork, and so on can go even further, but generate other problems, including the amount of time involved, ensuring that the work is genuinely that of the student, and the need to moderate assessments made by different schools.

In short, there are challenges in designing and implementing assessment programs that fully reflect the intentions of modern curricula. These challenges are primarily a matter of ensuring the validity of assessments. Baker (2007) is of the view that this is an unexamined aspect of most assessment programs:

> "How well do any of our external tests work?" The answer is that we don't know enough to know. We have little evidence that tests are in sync with their stated or de facto purposes or that their results lead to appropriate decisions. Nevertheless, we act as if tests were valid in the face of weak or limited evidence. We make heavy and far-reaching decisions about schools and students, talk about gaps, and applaud progress . . .. Yet test validity languishes as a largely unexamined, prior question because of inexorable schedules and budget constraints. With tests of uncertain validity, adequate yearly progress (AYP), value-added, or other growth modeling analyses will have limited meaning in accountability interpretations. (p. 310)

In other words, if the tests themselves are invalid, then all else that may be done with them is also invalid.

Lesson 2
Build into the accountability system tests that can assess all key curriculum outcomes and work with the best teachers in the system and with the test developers to ensure that tests are well designed, comprehensive, and contain high-quality questions that probe students' ability to apply the knowledge and understandings they have learnt in school to solving real and challenging problems. Consider developing different forms of each test, so that a wider range of outcomes can be assessed, but administer each student only one form to minimize the amount of testing. Remember, you get what you pay for and that quality is generally more important than quantity.

Impact on Learning

Most large-scale assessment for accountability programs make the claim that through the information provided and the associated incentives, support, or consequences, learning will improve. This is particularly so for those systems in which there are high-stakes consequences for failure to meet targets. In most programs, the necessary and sufficient evidence that improvement has occurred is taken to be the scores on the accountability tests themselves. If the test scores go up, then it is concluded that learning has improved.

There are many factors that get in the way of such an interpretation. If the same test is used on more than one occasion, or even if successive tests closely follow the same "blueprint," there is a real risk that any improvements in scores are due to familiarity with the test or tests. If new tests are used each year (the preferred arrangement), one must be sure that they have been properly and rigorously equated. Assuming rigorous equating of successive tests, one must exclude the possibility that any gains are not due to changes regarding which students have been excluded from the testing program. Even then, one must ask whether any improvements are due to excessive drilling of students on ways of maximizing their test scores and a host of other actions that may be taken by teachers, school administrators, and system officials to "game the system."

For these reasons, it is important to establish whether gains on high-stakes accountability tests are reflected in gains on other measures of learning. In the UK, following accusations that official statistics of National Curriculum Key Stage test scores for monitoring standards in primary schools over time exaggerated improvements in performance (Tymms, 2004), the Statistics Commission initiated an investigation which concluded that the improvement in Key Stage 2 (KS2) test scores between 1995 and 2000 substantially overstated the improvement in standards in English primary schools over that period, but that there was nevertheless some rise in standards (Statistics Commission, 2005).

In the USA, a number of studies have compared performance on high-stakes state-wide testing programs with scores on low-stakes NAEP tests (Carnoy & Loeb, 2002). While the evidence is mixed, some of the most widely publicized success stories almost certainly overstate gains. For example, there is evidence that the dramatic improvements reported for Texas were largely accounted for by various strategies to "game the system" especially through exclusions and retention practices (Heilig & Darling Hammond, 2008).

In other words, test scores can improve but learning may not improve. It is important for the credibility of any scheme that alternative explanations are explored before rash claims are made on the basis of an improvement in test scores, especially when the improvements are dramatic. This applies to individual schools as well as to school systems.

Lesson 3
Make sure you have a way of confirming whether gains on accountability tests reflect real improvements in learning and of investigating any alternative explanations, or you risk being misled and/or discredited.

Impact on Motivation

"Gaming the system" can be a polite term for what others might describe as "cheating" or "professional misconduct." Self-preservation will cause people to defend themselves and even to justify as ethical behavior action others would question if it conflicts with what they see as the best interests of those whom they are duty-bound to protect. For example, inflating students' scores may be regarded by some school administrators as ethical if it avoids closure of the local school.

It is therefore critical that systems consider carefully the role of motivation and incentives in determining the actual consequences of their policies. In any large-scale assessment program for accountability purposes, one must assume that those for whom the stakes are high will exploit *all* avenues to improve measured performance (Meyer, 1996). In so doing, they can subvert the outcomes that the accountability system was intended to promote, generate loss of confidence in the system and diminish the validity and reliability of the assessments.

Punitive measures may act as a deterrent, but are not good for morale. Openness, transparency, and frank discussion of the purposes of any accountability program are essential, so that there is alignment between declared and perceived purposes. But positive steps to build motivation are even more important.

Lesson 4
Avoid policies and perceptions of high-stakes negative consequences for those charged with bringing about improved performance. These may indeed be appropriate in extreme cases, but perceptions of threat should be removed from the majority for whom the emphasis should be on persuasion regarding the moral purpose of the program and on rewards for improvement.

Professional Practice

One of the claims often made by many accountability assessment programs is that they provide schools and teachers with valuable information for guiding and improving teaching and learning. In other words, an important reason for administering the tests is that the feedback they provide can enhance teachers' professional practice. Often schools and teachers are given access to detailed breakdowns of the performance of different group of students on individual test items or on subsets of items assessing specific aspects of the curriculum.

Certainly, it is important that teachers have access to objective information on both the absolute and relative levels of performance of their students. But the potential of the test results to improve teaching and learning is often overstated. Results typically reach schools many weeks or even months after students take the tests, by which time they may be in another grade, in another class and with another teacher, so the information is too late to inform practice. Even when there is timely feedback to schools, the information is rarely specific or precise enough to inform practice or improve learning in any but a very general way.

Tests can be thought of as being located along two dimensions, one relating to breadth of curriculum coverage and the other to depth of ability assessed, as indicated diagrammatically in Fig. 1.

Fig. 1 Test dimensions

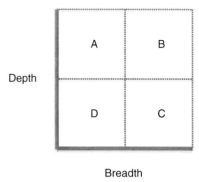

Depth

Breadth

A test located in quadrant A assesses a wide range of abilities on a narrow range of curriculum outcomes. A test in quadrant B assesses a wide range of abilities on a wide range of curriculum outcomes, and so on.

Most accountability tests are designed to provide both depth and breadth. In other words, they are quadrant B tests. But in order to keep them to a manageable length, light sampling of items is necessary so that there is a wide spread of item difficulties and few items per content area. This leads to imprecision in the measurement of abilities around any given cut score and less information about student performance on any given curriculum outcome. While the tests can provide global information with respect to the goals achieved by diverse students – information that is particularly relevant at a system level – they are unable to provide accurate or specific information of the kind necessary to improve instruction for particular students. There is then the danger that teachers will read too much into any detailed analysis of performance on individual test items. Instruction is about the steps required to reach longer-term outcomes and the most useful assessments will be quadrant D assessments. So-called formative assessments belong in this quadrant. Their purpose is to facilitate "instructional adjustment decisions" by teachers or "learning tactic adjustment decisions" by students (Popham, 2008), and so they need to be aligned to the ability of the learner and narrow in what they assess in order to reflect the current instructional focus.

As we will discuss later on, if there is a desire to provide schools and teachers with valuable information for guiding and improving teaching and learning as part of a system of accountability – and this is a perfectly legitimate desire – then consideration needs to be given to how formative assessment can become a pervasive, systemic endeavor and not just something left to teachers to figure out and implement at a classroom level.

Lesson 5
Be cautious in assuming that providing schools with detailed information on the performance of their students on accountability tests is going to be useful to teachers in improving instruction. Most accountability tests provide little more than a general indication of strengths and weaknesses of students within a given school. If you want

to assist teachers to improve their instruction you need to invest in good formative assessment.

Decision-Making

In most accountability assessment programs, results are used to inform high-stakes policy decisions that affect individual schools. These include decisions about the level and kind of support a school will receive or about consequences for the staff of failure to demonstrate satisfactory outcomes.

Good decisions require the right information and a proper understanding of this information. In making decisions about the performance of individual schools, it is important to have, in addition to test scores, data on the school context and on other aspects of school performance. In particular, it is important that in addition to measures of *status* (e.g., the percent meeting a defined standard), there are measures of growth or trends over time. Status measures typically say more about the nature of the school's student intake than they do about the value that the school is adding to the students' learning. Status is important, but equally important, and arguably even more important, is knowing whether individual schools are improving over time. A school serving a disadvantaged intake that has low absolute standards but is showing steady improvement may be less cause for concern than a school that has higher absolute standards but is in decline.

Few accountability systems make good use of value-added measures or time-series analyses to plot trends over several years, with adjustments for the nature of the student intake. Partly this is because of the technical complexity in undertaking the relevant analyses and in presenting the information in a readily understandable way. Partly it may reflect a lack of longitudinal data or simply a conscious but misguided decision by policy-makers to keep the focus on absolute standards.

In making high-stakes policy decisions about schools it is also important that decision-makers understand the limitations of the data. In particular, they need to be aware that in any assessment of student achievement, measurement error is unavoidable. This is something that does not resonate well with the general public who typically adopt the view that any "error" is inexcusable and that all assessments should be completely accurate. The notion that a school ranked at the 80th percentile may be, from a statistical point of view, indistinguishable from a school ranked at the 70th percentile is something that is rarely made clear to users of school-performance data. Unfortunately no assessment system can deliver completely accurate information on student performance and it is important to be upfront about this and to let users know how accurate the data are in order to minimize incorrect decisions.

Confidence intervals around scores of individual students are readily calculated, although not all systems take the trouble to report them. "Truth in testing" requires that they should. Typically, results for schools are reported in terms of the percentages of students at or above a given level (e.g., "proficient" or "competent") as represented by one or more cut scores on the test or examination. Such statistics are commonly adopted because they are intuitive and readily understood in the community at large. But they are much more unstable than say a mean score on a test. This is a serious issue in view of the high-stakes consequences of many testing programs. For many small schools, the degree of uncertainty around the school's percentage of students meeting a given standard turns out to be greater than the percentage change which the system has declared to be necessary in order to demonstrate adequate progress. As a consequence of the failure to understand confidence intervals, many schools erroneously conclude that they did very well one year but poorly the next, when in fact the differences were not statistically different. This can have serious implications for decision-making.

As an aside, there is no direct way of calculating confidence intervals around the percentages within schools meeting a given standard, although they can be estimated using various statistical inference procedures such as bootstrapping. It should be standard practice to report them if such statistics (i.e., percent meeting a given standard within the school) are to be used, but it would be even better if greater attention was paid to more stable statistics such as averages scores. Averages summarize the performance of all students: percent meeting the standard statistics can conceal critical details. For example, they can hide cases of mediocre performance of students performing above the cut score.

One further issue relating to the use of test-score data in making accountability decisions relates to problems arising from the creation and use of pseudoscientific indices of a school's performance, as for example when scores on examinations are converted into a limited set of grades or levels of performance which in turn are assigned points, which are then combined together across subjects to give an overall index. At the first stage, fine-grained score-point information is reduced to broad ordinal categories, while at the second stage, "apples and oranges" are added together as if they were equivalent, when often the difficulty of obtaining say a grade of B in one subject is not the same as the difficulty in gaining a B in another. The final indicator may hide more than it reveals and create perverse incentives to game the system (say focus on improving scores of those likely to be just below the threshold grade or level of performance, or encouraging students to opt for "easier" subjects).

Lesson 6
Make use of multiple indicators in judging the performance of a school, including measures that give an indication of trends over time having adjusted for student intake characteristics. Be aware of the limitations of the data and the degree of uncertainty around measures of status or growth and do not project a false impression of accuracy. Be wary of creating bogus indices from test results that hide the true performance of those tested and create perverse incentives to "game the system."

Trust

The standard explanation for the emergence of the accountability movement, not just in education, but also in other aspects of public life, is that it is the successor to trust

(Fukuyama, 1995; Putnam, 2000). Trust according to this explanation was once the social "glue" that held civil society together. When trust in the institutions of civil society was lost, it was replaced by accountability for performance. According to this explanation, once trust is lost, it cannot readily be restored. (Many would argue that modern media, particularly the high-circulation dailies, have played a key role in undermining trust in social institutions through their relentless focus on negative reporting. Interestingly enough, while trust in education systems is invariably lacking, trust in local schools and individual teachers is often quite high.)

O'Neil (2005) takes issue with this interpretation and argues that accountability can never replace trust because it is not possible to have any system of accountability unless there is trust in the system itself. She says:

> Trust-free accountability is a mirage. We should not be surprised that replacing trust with accountability, life world with system world, only pushes the question of where to place and where to refuse trust further back. We need to ask of any system of accountability why it should—or should not—command our trust. The various systems of accountability that use the outcomes of educational assessment are no exception. We need to ask whether and when we have reason to trust them. (p. 6)

In other words, she argues for a form of intelligent accountability in which stakeholders trust the accountability system because they are sufficiently informed and persuaded of its value and are provided with the evidence they need as a basis for placing or refusing trust in schools, teachers, and assessments.

The reality is, however, that in many systems there is widespread misunderstanding and mistrust of assessment for accountability, and this is most evident within the teaching profession itself, which then undermines the trust that the public at large should have in the system. Unless the profession supports the system, the likelihood of it working properly and not generating perverse incentives and negative backwash effects are minimal. The answer is not to abandon such accountability systems or to impose them in spite of opposition from the profession, but to fully engage the profession in the design and implementation of systems that *do* have their support. This is perhaps a tall order and in the past may have seemed unthinkable, but there has been a sea change in attitudes to assessment and the use of data in schools and while challenging, is something with which the teaching profession must eventually come to grips in the same way other professions have embraced enhanced accountability.

An important avenue for building trust by the profession in accountability systems is through embracing the concept of *reciprocal accountability*, which Elmore (2004) states as implying that "For each unit of performance I demand of you, I have equal and reciprocal responsibility to provide you with a unit of capacity to produce that performance, if you do not already have that capacity" (pp. 244–245). Tucker and Codding (2002) have observed that the theory of change underpinning so many accountability systems often appears to involve the somewhat disingenuous notion "... that educators have always known how to greatly improve student performance, but were just waiting for someone to put more pressure on them to do it" (p. 2). However, the reality is typically that teachers and principals don't know how to significantly improve learning outcomes for their students and need help from someone who does. The implications of reciprocal accountability for how systems operate and are staffed are enormous. But reciprocal accountability is not just about system–school responsibilities, it also applies to parent–school responsibilities and internal school administration – teacher responsibilities.

Lesson 7
Involve the profession in the design and implementation of the accountability system, seek their support for it, and give them an active role in assisting other stakeholders, particularly parents, to understand and support it. Accept the notion of reciprocal accountability and ensure that you can provide schools and teachers with the capacity to meet your expectations.

The Future Evolution of Assessment for Accountability Purposes

What of the future of large-scale assessment for accountability purposes? One thing that can be said with some confidence is that it is here to stay. The issue is what form it will take and at what pace change will occur. In this final section, some thoughts are offered on the possible future evolution of assessment for accountability purposes.

In the short term, changes can be expected as a result of pressures to modify existing accountability systems in order to minimize negative washback effects, to better meet public expectations, and to improve the quality of information available for decision-making purposes. Systems will realize that they need to conduct systematic, expert audits of their assessment programs and accountability frameworks, and to use the findings as a basis for negotiating with stakeholders' progressive modifications to existing arrangements to ensure a greater chance of delivering intended outcomes. Significant improvements are possible through greater transparency, increased awareness of the impact of various kinds of programs, and a commitment to ongoing use of data to drive improvement.

In the middle to longer term, it can be expected that systems will adopt a multi-level approach to assessment for accountability purposes. At a macrolevel, they will want to benchmark their performance internationally. For example, they will wish to know the answers to questions such as, "How does, say, the province of Alberta or the states of Texas or of Western Australia compare with say Finland or Hong Kong in terms of student performance, and what lessons can be learnt from international comparisons with high-performing nations?" For this purpose, systems will continue to seek to participate in international surveys, especially the OECD's triannual PISA surveys.

At an intermediate level, they will want to continue to monitor performance against local curricula and standards using national or statewide tests. Indeed, for many systems there is a legislative requirement to do so. However, at a more microlevel, it is to be expected that they will also increasingly wish to lever the power of feedback and of formative assessment to improve teaching and learning. The reviews of the relevant research by Black and Wiliam (1998) and of Hattie and Timperley (2007) bear ample testimony to the positive effects of using assessment to provide the kind of feedback that can, as Popham (2008) has expressed it, facilitate "instructional adjustment decisions" by teachers or "learning tactic adjustment decisions" by students. But so far, systems have tended to leave it to teachers to work out how to embed formative assessment in their daily instructional practice and very few have considered how it could and why it should be incorporated into an overall accountability framework.

The trouble is that formative assessment is too difficult for most teachers to implement on a daily basis unaided. As we argue in *Breakthrough* (Fullan, Hill, & Crévola, 2006), there are a number of missing ingredients that systems need to provide, namely:

(1) A set of powerful and aligned assessment tools . . . that give the teacher access to accurate and comprehensive information on the progress of each student on a daily basis, and that can be administered without unduly interrupting normal classroom routines.
(2) A method to allow the formative assessment data to be captured in a way that is not time-consuming; of analyzing the data automatically, and; a means of converting it into information that is powerful enough to drive instructional decisions not sometime in the future, but tomorrow.
(3) A means of using the assessment information on each student to design and implement personalized instruction.
(4) A built-in means of monitoring and managing learning, of testing what works, and of systematically improving the effectiveness of classroom instruction so that it more precisely responds to the learning needs of each student in the class (pp. 36–37).

Having provided the missing ingredients, namely the tools, there is also the substantial professional learning and instructional leadership needed for change to occur, much of which assumes principals who understand instructional leadership and have the time and mandate to exercise it, and site-based learning and the appointment of school-based coaches that can work alongside teachers in their classrooms to effect changes in professional practice. Once these are in place, new possibilities exist for implementing powerful and localized forms of accountability based on access to information that can let teachers, school administrators, parents, and the system know precisely and at any point in time the current status of the learner, what has been provided by way of instruction, and what have been the outcomes of that instruction. What is more, because the information would be updated daily, it could allow for immediate adjustments when progress is unsatisfactory, rather than having to wait many months, by which time remedial action is all too late. Above all, such microlevel accountability could be expected to rebuild trust from the bottom up, through direct and daily feedback to the major stakeholders, especially to parents.

Some commercial providers have begun to develop assessment systems that begin to provide tools for a more systemic approach to formative assessment. Examples include Wireless Generation's mCLASS:DIBELS and Pearson's DRA

Online Management System. But school systems are only just beginning to take ownership of the task of building the kind of solutions called for in *Breakthrough* that would ultimately transform approaches to assessment for accountability purposes. Building such systems is a major task that can only be done through a rigorously planned and adequately resourced research and development effort and require high levels of investment and a partnership between publicly funded university research centers, school systems, and private companies.

Building such systems is just the technical challenge. The more difficult challenge is bringing about the necessary changes in thinking and practice at the level of classrooms, schools, and systems that are entailed in implementing a systemic approach to formative assessment as part of an overall accountability and instructional framework. However, all the indications are that a quantum breakthrough of this kind is tantalizingly close and that a tipping point has been reached that will propel systems in this direction over the next decade.

References

Au, W. (2007). High-stakes testing and curricular control: A qualitative metasynthesis. *Educational Researcher, 36*(5), 258–267.

Bachman, L. F., & Palmer, A. S. (1996). *Language testing in practice*. Oxford, UK: Oxford University Press.

Baker, E. L. (2007). The end(s) of testing. *Educational Researcher, 36*(6), 309–317.

Black, P. J. (1998). *Testing: Friend or foe? The theory and practice of assessment and testing*. London: Falmer Press.

Black, P., & Wiliam, D (1998). Assessment and classroom learning. *Assessment in Education, 5*(1), 7–71.

Caldwell, B. J., & Spinks, J. M. (1992). *Leading the self-managing school*. London: The Palmer Press.

Carnoy, M., & Loeb, S. (2002). Does external accountability affect student outcomes? A cross-state analysis. *Educational Evaluation and Policy Analysis, 24*(4), 305–331.

Coleman, J., Campbell, E., Hobson, C., McPartland, J., Mood, A., Weinfield, F., et al. (1966). *Equality of educational opportunity*. Washington, DC: US Government Printing Office.

Elmore, R. F. (2004). *School reform from the inside out: Policy, practice and performance*. Cambridge, MA: Harvard Education Press.

Fullan, M. (2008). *The six secrets of change: What the best leaders do to help their organizations survive and thrive*. San Francisco, CA: Jossey-Bass.

Fullan, M., Hill, P., & Crévola, C. (2006). *Breakthrough*. Thousand Oaks, CA: Corwin Press.

Fukuyama, F. (1995). *Trust: The social virtues and the creation of prosperity*. New York: Free Press.

Hattie, J., & Timperley, H. (2007). The power of feedback. *Review of Educational Research, 77*(1), 81–112.

Heilig, J. V., & Darling Hammond, L. (2008). Accountability Texas-style: The progress and learning of urban minority students in a high-stakes testing context. *Educational Evaluation and Policy Analysis, 30*(2), 75–110.

Hursh, D. (2007). Assessing no child left behind and the rise of neoliberal education. *American Educational Research Journal, 44*(3), 493–518.

Ingulsrud, J. E. (1994). An entrance test to Japanese universities: Social and historical context. In C. Hill & K. Parry (Eds.), *From testing to assessment: English as an international language* (pp. 61–81). New York: Longman.

Linn, R. L. (2000). Assessments and accountability. *Educational Researcher, 29*(2), 4–16.

Linn, R. L., Baker, E. L., & Betebenner, D. W. (2002). Accountability systems: Implications of requirements of the No Child Left Behind Act of 2001. *Educational Researcher, 31*(6), 3–16.

Mehrens, W. A. (1998). Consequences of assessment: What is the evidence? *Education Policy Analysis Archives, 6*(8).

Meyer, R. H. (1996). Comments on chapters two, three, and four. In H. F. Ladd (Ed.), *Holding schools accountable: Performance-based reform in education* (pp. 137–145). Washington, DC: The Brookings Institution.

Newton, P. (2007). Clarifying the purposes of educational assessment. *Assessment in Education, 14*(2), 149–170.

O'Neil, O. (2005). *Assessment, public accountability and trust.* Paper presented to Cambridge Conference: A quality of confidence: Maintaining trust in national assessment systems. Cambridge Assessment Network, 17 October, 2005.

Popham, W. J. (2008). *Transformative assessment.* Alexandria, VA: Association for Supervision and Curriculum Development.

Putnam, R. (2000). *Bowling alone: The collapse and revival of American community.* New York, NY: Simon & Schuster.

Statistics Commission. (2005). *Measuring standards in English primary schools.* Statistics Commission Report No 23. London: Statistics Commission.

Tucker, M. S., & Codding, J. B. (Eds.). (2002). *The principal challenge: Leading and managing in an era of accountability.* San Francisco, CA: Jossey-Bass.

Tymms, P. (2004). Are standards rising in English primary schools? *British Educational Research Journal, 30*(4), 477–494.

Wigdor, A. K., & Green, B. F., Jr. (Eds.). (1991). *Performance assessment for the workplace.* Volume I. Committee on the Performance of Military Personnel, Commission on Behavioral and Social Sciences and Education, National Research Council. Washington, DC: National Academy Press.

Digital Technologies and Educational Change

Juana M. Sancho

> *The essence of technology is by no means anything technological. Thus we shall never experience our relationship to the essence of technology so long as we merely conceive and push forward the technological, put up with it, or evade it. Everywhere, we remain unfree and chained to technology whether we passionately affirm or deny it. But we are delivered over to it in the worst possible way when we regarded it as something neutral*
>
> (Heidegger, 1977, p. 4).

Among all the forces that can bring about positive and deliberate educational change, one of the most strongly and persistently advocated is new technology. Technology has been hailed as the savior of educational change many times in the past. Television, video, language laboratories, audio-recorded reading programs, and pocket calculators have all been proposed as ways to move learning from the teacher to the learner – and all have fallen short of initial expectations.

But today's digital technologies are different. They are faster, more ubiquitous, and more integrated into the everyday lives of the children, youth, and young adults who were "born" more digital than at any other time before. But the benefits of technological transformation are hotly debated. Are the digital generations more connected or more distracted? Is the knowledge that instant technology makes available also always reliable? These are just some of the questions that are being posed about the relationship between education and technology and they are as much questions about technology and society as they are about technology and schools.

Mapping out the interconnections between digital technologies and educational change therefore requires taking into account the wider societal and political context in which these technologies and educational systems are located. Digital technologies are not merely teaching and learning aids that have a given impact on

J.M. Sancho (✉)
University of Barcelona, Barcelona, Spain
e-mail: jmsancho@ub.edu

A. Hargreaves et al. (eds.), *Second International Handbook of Educational Change*, 433
Springer International Handbooks of Education 23, DOI 10.1007/978-90-481-2660-6_26,
© Springer Science+Business Media B.V. 2010

learning achievement. They are embedded in and part of technology-driven change in practically all social realms.

In the educational field, new situations that schools have to tackle (often brought about by unpredictable, unwanted, and unwelcome change) can be explained not only by the impressive growth of digital technologies, but also by the political and economic forces that shape the development and uses of these technologies as well as the nature of educational reform. Nevertheless, the massive influence of digital technologies on new generations is transforming not only children's and young people's ways of learning along with their attitudes and predispositions to learn, but also how knowledge is conceived, used, and valued.

In practically all countries, but especially in those that are technologically and economically developed, children's and young people's culture has changed dramatically. Young people's expectations, views on life, values, ways of learning, and modes of accessing information have undergone deep and fundamental changes. However, schools, as institutions in charge of providing education to these groups, are finding it extremely hard to introduce the changes needed to soften their structures and offer more meaningful learning experiences to students. Digital technologies are being regarded more and more as powerful levers of educational change and as clear means for updating education and making it more meaningful to students.

However, schools and school systems have adapted slowly and sporadically to the opportunities of technologically driven change and have often become disconnected from the learning patterns and lives of the children and young people whose development is profoundly influenced by it. Though there are Smart Boards, interactive whiteboards, computer labs, laptops, and PowerPoint presentations, most lesson structures and school structures remain fundamentally the same.

In 1998, in the first *International Handbook of Educational Change*, Bigum and Kenway (1998) identified and described four different perspectives that had been adopted by experts and others in relation to the possibilities and pitfalls of new technology in relation to teaching and learning and in relation to the ways in which they could be interpreted into learning in schools.

- *Boosters* were optimistic advocates of new technology and its potential and even predictable future impact on the transformation of teaching and learning.
- *Anti-schoolers* went even further and argued that these technologies would make the 150-year-old models of subjects, classes, and schools as separate institutions obsolete as learning through technology occurred in other ways.
- *Doomsters* dwelled on the problems of new technology narrowing or trivializing learning, making it less deep and critical and dividing the privileged who had easy access from the underprivileged who did not.
- *Critics* were more evenhanded – enthusiastic about the opportunities while also articulate and aware of the obstacles and threats.

In the last 10 years, the number of boosters has considerably increased, doomsters' voices seem to be fading, anti-schoolers are gaining their greatest footholds in higher education and homeschooling, and critics continue to argue for a more rigorous and evidence-based approach to the benefits and drawbacks of digital technologies and their adaptation in educational policy and practice. I am among the critics – searching to look for the best ways to use and integrate the digital technologies that have transformed young people's lives into the ongoing processes of teaching and learning within and outside schools. How do we bring together the transformative world of digital technology in the life, learning, and culture of young people, with the largely untransformed traditional structures of schooling?

The Social Context of Digital Technologies

The last decade has witnessed deep and fundamental change not only in the field of digital technology but also in almost all realms underpinning social organization and values. Digital technology applications have become second nature, especially to people from the most developed countries, who would find it difficult to live without having access to computers, mobile phones, MP3 players, play stations, digital TV, or the multiple forms of digital equipment developed and used in homes, labs, hospitals, companies, farming, agriculture, and so on. If, as Roberts, Foehr, and Rideout (2005, p. 36) stress, "a typical 8-to-18-year old is exposed to 81/2 hours of recreational media content daily," it is not hard to see the impact of the world outside and its digital aspects on students' developmental processes. In these 10 years through the ubiquitous and intangible Internet, a dense and multimodal fabric has been woven. The developmental trends and impacts of digital technology have also been influenced by new systems of thought, values, and positions. These include the globalization of change, of finance and capital, and now of debt and economic collapse; the growth of immigration and mobility and the increasing acceptance and interaction of diverse points of view; the idea that ordinary people are producers and circulators rather than merely consumers of new knowledge; and the conviction that we are living in an unstable and uncertain "liquid" life where interactions are fast and fleeting, identities are unstable, and are transient and temporary.

New information and communication technologies alter the structure of our interests (the things we think about), change the nature of symbols (the things about which we think), and modify the nature of the community (the area in which we develop our thought) (Sancho, 2005).

In this context of global change and constant movement, where almost everything is transforming beyond recognition, one institution – the school – remains practically unchanged after almost 150 years of becoming practically universal.

- Educational systems are still highly dependent on political party-related interests and political decision-making. Only a few countries, among them the highly-praised Finland due to its excellent results in PISA, consider education a national question not to be *used* for the benefit or interest of confronting political parties (Hargreaves, Halász, & Pont, 2007).
- Compared with other social institutions, schools are subject to huge expectations to eliminate achievement gaps and advance all children's development that

exceed their real power and available resources (Bransford, Brown, & Cocking, 1999; Hargreaves, 2003).

- Schools are continually urged to introduce, adopt, adapt, and integrate new products and organizational models such as Taylorism, Total Quality Management, or Toyotism – developed in other contexts and for other aims (Darling-Hammond, 1997; Noble, 1991) or are required to *buy* services producing significant profits for selling companies. This pressure can paradoxically reinforce stagnation, keeping schools and teachers busy with superficial matters (Rowan, 2002).

- Models of teaching have remained basically the same. While students in some countries have been given a little more space to make their voice heard, and while several countries have sought to overcome transmission models of teaching by fostering constructivist approaches, the prevailing "school grammar" (Tyack & Tobin, 1994) and cultural beliefs about education still support the idea that teaching is telling, learning is listening, and knowledge is what is in books (Cuban, 1993), or now in educational software. Indeed, countries like the United States and England have introduced and increased standardized testing that reinforces the most traditional aspects of drill and practice teaching, along with other *collateral effects* (Nichols & Berliner, 2007).

This juxtaposition of a fast-moving world, where children and young people's lives are undergoing rapid changes and are surrounded by myriad stimuli, competing with a rather *immobile* institution that fails to understand the educational needs of a population of whom everyone seems afraid, helps explain why a considerable percentage of young people do not feel engaged with school. According to the OECD (2003), there is a low sense of belonging at school among an average of one in four 15-year-old students, with one in five admitting to being regularly absent. As more and more young people feel completely at home in the digital world, there is a widening gap between schools that were founded in the nineteenth century and the current population they serve in the technological and cultural age of the twenty-first century.

Evidence of Impact

Over recent decades, digital technology-driven proposals have been heralded as the quintessence of educational innovation. Parallels with the fundamental contributions of digital technologies to business, commerce, agriculture, and medicine have been repeatedly drawn. It is commonly claimed that these technologies could considerably improve learning results and economic modernization if used in the *right* way and if educators were able to use their *full potential* (Ogilvy, 2006).

At the moment, it would be difficult to find a country not caught up in the rhetoric of digital technologies, not only as educational improvement levers, but also as forces of economic modernization. For example, according to Järvelä (2006, p. 40),

Based on research and practical experience, the following principles are the best arguments for implementing ICT in learning:

- ICT can increase authenticity and interest.
- ICT can build virtual communities among different schools, collaborating teams, and teachers.
- ICT can help to share perspectives among students with different expertise, proving peer support and "benchmarking practices" in different fields.
- ICT facilitates the use of technology-supported inquiry approaches and problem-based models for increasing learning-to-learn skills.
- ICT provides innovative ways (e.g., mobile tools) of integrating "just-in-time" support and interaction in different learning contexts.

In contrast to these promises, evaluations of the educational use of digital technologies give an uncertain picture of their contribution to improvement in learning results. Findings are often inconsistent or difficult to generalize. Even studies conducted by boosters such as Järvelä, discussed earlier, could not find significantly better results for digital technology versus nondigital technology mediated learning. Yet digital technology did seem to have an indirect impact on the overall learning environment in terms of the creation of more innovative pedagogical models; increased collaboration among teachers, students, and administrators; and enhanced lifelong learning among the students (Järvelä, 2006).

Balanskat, Blamire, and Kefala (2006) accomplished a review of 17 impact studies and surveys carried out at national, European, and international levels. All the studies acknowledge a set of important benefits of digital technologies in learning, ranging from students' motivation and skills to independent learning and teamwork. Some of these studies show statistical evidence that digital technologies can enhance achievement in subjects such as English, science and design, and technology. Interactive whiteboards in the UK had a positive effect on pupil performances in literacy, mathematics, and science tests compared to students in other schools.[1] They especially improved the performance of low-achieving pupils in English and impact was greatest on writing. Nevertheless, only a few studies – mainly in the UK – actually establish a direct link between the use of computer technology and achievement.

On the other hand, international studies such as SITES-M2 have focused on the innovative pedagogical uses of digital technologies in 174 schools in North and South America, Africa, Europe, Asia, and Australia. Overall, the schools in the study report, through opinion-based questionnaires, a substantially positive effect of their innovative use on students: 62% reported increased subject matter acquisition; 68% of schools reported increased positive attitudes by students toward learning; and 63% improved collaborative skills (Kozman, 2003).

These studies, and others carried out in the last 30 years, largely concentrate on how technology affects conventional kinds of learning, achievement, and results (as

---

[1]It has to be noted that devices such as whiteboards tend to reinforce traditional transmissive models that seem to suit test achievement levels, but generate serious doubts about its power to foster lifelong learning skills.

measured by standardized tests). These evaluations are less likely to show impacts on how to transfer knowledge and experience to other contexts, how to confront new situations, or how to collaborate with others. Moreover, it is not always clear that improvement in learning is due to the use of computers and digital technologies and not to other factors such as teaching methods, students' predispositions, or previous learning experiences. As McFarlane, Harrison, Somekh, Scrimshaw, Harrison & Lewin (2000, p. 9) state, "The problem is analogous to that of asking whether books are having an impact on learning: books are a medium for transmitting information, they cover a vast range of content, structure and genres, and they can be used in infinitive ways." Thus, rather than speaking about the impact of computer and digital technologies, we should start looking at concrete applications, paying special attention to the educational value of end users' learning experience. The key question is how technology can help transform schools into cutting-edge educational institutions ready to cater for students' individual and social needs.

Several studies reveal that even if computers are available in a good number of schools, not all teachers use them (Becker, 2001; Conlon & Simpson, 2003; Pelgrumn, 2001; Plomp, Anderson, Law, & Quale, 2003; Wilson, Notar, & Yunker, 2003). When computers *are* used, teachers find it difficult to modify their classroom routines and their expectations about students' predispositions to learn. Technology by itself does not produce "mega-changes" in teaching and learning practices (Cuban, 2001; Cuban, Kirkpatrick & Peck, 2001; Kozman, 2003; Ringstaff & Kelley, 2002; OECD, 2004; Sancho, Hernández, Bosco, Müller, Larraín, Giró, Nuri & Cernochova, 2004; Schofield & Davidson, 2002). In fact, the majority of teachers seem to explore digital technologies as tools to enhance existing traditional practice, then progressively build it into the curriculum and only eventually transform their teaching practice (Comber, Watling, Lawson, Cavendish, McEune & Paterson, 2002).

Although we lack an integrated framework to guide effective educational change by making an effective use of digital technologies, knowledge of what affects school and classroom use (or nonuse) of computers is steadily growing (Becker & Ravitz, 2001; Cuban, Kirkpatrick, & Peck, 2001; Rosen & Weil, 1995; Sandholtz, Ringstaff, & Dwyer, 1997; Specht, Wood, & Willoughby, 2002; Wood, Willoughby, Specht, Sterne-Cavalcante, & Childs, 2002). In a European project, we found *re-engineering* the school environment in order to convert it into a cutting-edge educational institution through making the most of digital technology proved to be difficult. The main constraints for implementing innovative approaches by taking advantages of digital technology were set by:

- lack of governmental policy to support changes in education
- specifications and standards of national curricula
- centralized systems of supervision of schools
- conventional structures of teaching (standard lessons lasting 45–50 min)
- space allocation – access to computers; number of students in classrooms; school building architecture; arrangement of desks inside of classrooms.

- professional development of teachers in technology that does not encourage profound educational change
- subject-oriented curricula that avoid transdisciplinary and problem-driven teaching
- lack of teachers' motivation in applying new methods and lack of understanding of why to apply digital technology
- reduced student and teacher autonomy in curriculum and pedagogical decisions (Sancho et al., 2004).

In summary, digital technology-driven change in education is practically impossible while the rest of the educational system remains virtually the same. And yet, as the problem continues to remain unaddressed and unresolved, the new generations that are making up the rest of the world are changing beyond recognition.

The Digital Generations

Children and young people are living in settings where they are bombarded by aural, visual, and sensorial stimuli providing them with very distinctive life and learning experiences that are often neglected or rejected by the unchanging structures and orientations of schools. According to Twenge (2006), those who were between the ages of 7 and 36 in 2006 belong to Generation Me. GenMe moves through the world beholden to few social rules and with the unshakable belief that *I am important*. It is the first generation plainly speaking the language of self as its native tongue. "Just be yourself." "Believe in yourself." "Express yourself." "Respect yourself." "Be honest with yourself." "You have to love yourself before you can love someone else." "Yes, stand up for yourself" (Twenge, 2006). Many members of this generation find it difficult to fit into an institution aimed more at homogenizing rather than individualizing people, where it is hard to discover their own sense of being and have their voice heard. As a result, one of OECD's objectives in meeting current educational challenges is that of "personalizing education" (OECD-CERI, 2006).

The philosophy of the so-called Web2.0 seems perfect for expressing the "self" as a second generation of Web-based communities and hosted services – such as social networking sites (e.g., MySpace and Facebook mostly used in the Anglosphere and Friendster in Asia), wikis, folksonomies (e.g., Flickr or del.icio.us), Weblogs (blogs), social bookmarking, podcasts, RSS feeds, and so on. These facilitate authorship, creativity, collaboration and sharing between users, and effective information handling. Howe and Strauss (2000) call those people born from the 1980s onward, and who have been raised in a context where digital technologies are a consubstantial part of daily life, *Millennials.*[2] These are the first generations to grow

---

[2]In 2006, the Centre for Educational Research and Innovation (CERI) of the OECD launched a research and development project called New Millennium Learners. http://www.oecd.org/document/10/0,3343,en_2649_35845581_38358154_1_1_1_1,00.html

up surrounded by digital media. Most of their activities dealing with peer-to-peer communication and knowledge management are mediated by these technologies. Millennials are thought to be skillful with computers, creative with technology and, above all, highly proficient at multitasking in a world where ubiquitous connections are taken for granted. These generations are also often referred to as the *Instant-Message Generation* (Lenhart, Rainie, & Lewis, 2001), *homo zappiens* (Veen & Vrakking, 2006), the *Net Generation* (Oblinger & Oblinger, 2005), or the *Gamer Generation* (Carstens & Beck, 2005).

Millenials usually take multitasking for granted as the normal approach to using digital media: being online while watching TV, speaking on the phone, and doing homework, for example. Their recurrent activity with these technologies fundamentally shapes their notions of communication, knowledge management, learning, and even personal and social values.

In a world with apparently unlimited technology and information, everyone is seeking to attract the attention of individuals. Human relations, publicity, media, schools, and churches are all trying to obtain this limited human attribute. Without paying attention (which implies time), friendship, love, family, followers, business, work, and learning, are impossible. In the new economy, the scarcest product is attention (Lanham, 2006; Lankshear & Knobel, 2001). As people's capacities for producing consumer goods, information, and so forth surpass their capacity for consuming them, the need to attract attention and the changes of increased distractibility are becoming a key focus.

In this *war for attention*, schools are the losers. In the media-saturated environment no sense is left free; there is no more attention span remaining. Saturation produces lack of concentration and attention and hyperactivity disorders multiply in school, where children increasingly lack the required amount of concentration and attention to accomplish school work. A key issue today is how to educate people who are overstimulated and feel bored. The crux of the matter is not the *pedagogy of the oppressed*,[3] but the *pedagogy of the bored* (Corea & Lewkowicz, 2004). This task is massive and its solution is not to be found in more technology and more information, but in our ability to meet the emergent challenges that they raise.

Challenges

To respond to the disparity of children's and young people's experiences in and out of school, educational systems will need to address a set of essential challenges.

Bridging the past with future knowledge. Today's generations admire the present, are attracted by the future, and look down on the past. They increasingly find curriculum content irrelevant to their lives and take it as a pill to be swallowed to pass to the next educational stage, forgetting what they have been taught as soon they have passed the exams. For Bauman (2005), in the current precariousness and

---

[3] Referring to Paulo Freire's seminal work.

uncertainty of life, people no longer think it is advisable to learn from experience and trust in strategies and tactics successfully used in the past, because past endeavours are regarded as useless for the dizzy, unforeseen, and unpredictable changes of circumstance. Within this frenetic setting, educational systems must decide the basic foundation needed for the next generation in order to take advantage of what is already known and avoid making the same mistakes, and also to *pass this foundation on* to students in a meaningful way.

Engaging students in passionate personal and social projects. In a media-saturated world, schools cannot be just another source of fragmented information. In schools, students are grateful when new media breaks down routine or gives them more active roles to play. Schools cannot compete with the huge amount of dynamic information to which children and young people have access. But they can help make sense of it. People need frameworks to make information meaningful, and schools should consider how to connect with students' interests, curiosity, and desire to learn in order to enable them to move on from superficial information to depth of personal and social knowledge.

Maintaining social cohesion. Historically, public educational systems have played a fundamental role in promoting social cohesion. Nowadays, movements toward privatization, high stakes testing, competition among schools, and intensified accountability systems are enemies of social cohesion. So too is the asymmetrical use of digital technologies outside school. While PISA 2003 data reveal a generally positive relationship between ICT use and educational attainment (OECD, 2003), greater achievement is related to better access to technology, previous experience, frequency of use (where moderate use gives the best results), and a level of confidence with computers. These data provide further evidence for the digital divide as all these factors are more likely to converge in middle-class students. If educational systems are not to contribute to this new form of exclusion, they should try to bridge the digital divide by extending use of the collaborative mode and mood of more and more computer-literate students.

Updating educators' knowledge of contemporary world issues. In the OECD countries, more than 50% of teachers – and sometimes up to 75% of teachers – are more than 40 years old (OECD, 2005). The same is true for teacher educators and educational policy-makers. Most people working in the field of education could have finished their initial professional development as teachers between 1968 and 1988. Most of them were baby boomers socialized in a discrete world made up of the family and the neighborhood, the church and the school, that was gradually enlarged by books and magazines, cinema and television. This large group of people started their careers in an analogue world and today they have to teach, train teachers, or develop educational policies in a digital one. School systems must therefore seek ways of bringing aging educators and administrators closer to the complexities of the current world and to the changing values and learning processes of young people. As the Millennial generation moves more into teaching positions and then more importantly into leadership roles, it will become increasingly probable that digital modes of being will be incorporated into the teaching and learning processes, as well as the systems and structures of schools.

References

Balanskat, A., Blamire, R., & Kefala, S. (2006). *The ICT Impact Report. A review of studies of ICT impact on schools in Europe.* Accessible at: http://insight.eun.org/shared/data/pdf/impact_study.pdf. [Download: May 21, 2007].

Bauman, Z. (2005). *Liquid life.* Cambridge: Polity.

Becker, H. (2001). *How are teachers using computers in instruction?* Paper presented at the 2001 meetings of the American Educational Research Association

Becker, H. J., & Ravitz, J. L. (2001). *Computer use by teachers: Are Cuban's predictions correct?* Paper presented at the 2001 annual meeting of the American Educational Research Association, Seattle. Available at: http://www.crito.uci.edu/tlc/findings/conferences-pdf/aera_2001.pdf. [Downloaded, April 4, 2005].

Bigum, C., & Kenway, J. (1998). New information technologies and the ambiguous future of schooling – some possible scenarios. In A. Hargreaves, A. Liebernan, M. Fullan, & D. Hopkins (Eds.), *International Handbook of Educational Change* (pp. 95–115). Dordrecht: Kluwer Academic Publishers.

Bransford, J. D., Brown, A. L., & Cocking, R. R. (Eds.). (1999). *How people learn: Brain, mind, experience, and school.* Washington, DC: National Academy Press.

Carstens, A., & Beck, J. (2005). Get ready for the gamer generation. *TechTrends, 49*(3), 22–25.

Comber, C., Watling, R., Lawson, T., Cavendish, S., McEune, R., & Paterson, F. (2002). *'ImpaCT2: Learning at Home and School – Case Studies' UK:* Becta. Accessed at: http://www.becta.org.uk/page_documents/research/ImpaCT2_strand_3_report.pdf. [Downloaded, October 24, 2004].

Conlon, T., & Simpson, M. (2003). Silicon Valley verses Silicon Glen: The impact of computers upon teaching and learning: A comparative study. *British Journal of Educational Technology, 34*(2), 137–150.

Corea, C., & Lewkowicz, I. (2004). *Pedagogía del aburrido. Escuelas destituidas, familias perplejas.* Buenos Aires: Paidós.

Cuban, L. (1993). *How teachers taught: Constancy and change in American classrooms, 1890–1990.* New York: Teachers College Press.

Cuban, L. (2001). *Oversold and underused: Computers in the classroom.* Cambridge, MA: Harvard University Press.

Cuban, L., Kirkpatrick, H., & Peck, C. (2001). High access and low use of technologies in high school classrooms: Explaining an apparent paradox. *American Educational Research Journal, 38*(4), 813–834.

Darling-Hammond, L. (1997). *The right to learn.* San Francisco: Jossey-Bass Pu.

Hargreaves, A. (2003). *Teaching in the knowledge society: Education in the age of insecurity.* Buckingham [England], Philadelphia: Open University.

Hargreaves, A., Halász, G., & Pont, B. (2007). *School leadership for systemic improvement in Finland. A case study report for the OECD activity improving school leadership.* Paris: OECD. http://www.oecd.org/dataoecd/43/17/39928629.pdf

Heidegger, M. (1977). *The question concerning technology.* New York: Harper Books.

Howe, N., & Strauss, W. (2000). *Millennials rising: The next great generation.* New York: Vintage Original.

Järvelä, S. (2006). Personalised learning? New insights into fostering learning capacity. In OECD-CERI (Eds.), *Personalising education* (pp. 31–46). Paris: OECD/CERI.

Kozman, R. B. (2003). *Technology, innovation, and educational change – A global perspective.* Washington, DC: ISTE.

Lanham, R. A. (2006). *The economics of attention: Style and substance in the age of information.* Chicago: The University of Chicago Press.

Lankshear, C., & Knobel, M. (2001). Do we have your attention? New literacies, digital technologies and the education of adolescents. In D. Alvermann (Ed.), *New literacies and digital technologies: A focus on adolescent learners.* New York: Peter Lang.

Lenhart, A., Rainie, L., & Lewis, O. (2001). *Teenage life online: The rise of instant-message generation and the internet's impact on friendship and family relationships*. Washington, DC: Pew Internet & American Life Project.

McFarlane, A., Harrison, C., Somekh, B., Scrimshaw, P., Harrison, A., & Lewin, C. (2000). *Establishing the relationship between networked technology and attainment: Preliminary study 1*. Coventry: Becta.

Nichols, S. L., & Berliner, D. (2007). *Collateral damage: How high-stakes testing corrupts America's schools*. Cambridge, MA: Harvard Education Press.

Noble, D. D. (1991). *The classroom arsenal: Military research, information technology, and public education*. Bristol, PA: Taylor & Francis/Hemisphere.

Oblinger, D., & Oblinger, J. L. (Eds.). (2005). *Educating the net generation*. Washington, DC: Educause.

OECD. (2003). *Student engagement at school. A sense of belonging and participation: Results from PISA 2000 (PISA)*. Paris: OECD.

OECD. (2004). *Education at a glance 2004*. París: OECD.

OECD. (2005). *Teachers matter education and training policy. Attracting, developing and retaining effective teachers* (p. 17). París: OECD.

OECD/CERI. (2006). *Personalising education*. Paris: OECD/CERI.

Ogilvy, J. (2006). Education in the information age: Scenarios, equity and equality. In OECD-CERI *Think Scenarios, Rethink Education* (pp. 21–38). Paris: OECD-CERI.

Pelgrumn, W. J. (2001). Obstacles to the integration of ICT in education: Results from a worldwide educational assessment. *Computers & Education, 37*, 163–187.

Plomp, T., Anderson, R. E., Law, N., & Quale, A. (Eds.). (2003). *Cross-national policies and practices on information and communication technology in education*. Greenwich, CT: Information Age Publishing Inc.

Ringstaff, C., & Kelley, L. (2002). *The learning return on our educational technology investment. A review of findings from research*. WestEd. Accessed at: http://www.wested.org/cs/we/view/rs/619. [Downloaded, November 2, 2003].

Roberts, D. F., Foehr, U. G., & Rideout, V. (2005). *Generation M: Media in the lives of 8–18 year-olds*. A Kaiser family foundation study. http://www.kff.org/entmedia/entmedia030905pkg.cfm

Rosen, L. D., & Weil, M. M. (1995). Computer anxiety: A cross-cultural comparison of university students in ten countries. *Computers in Human Behavior, 11*(1), 45–64.

Rowan, B. (2002). The ecology of school improvement: Notes on the school improvement industry in the United States. *Journal of Educational Change, 3*(3), 283–314.

Sancho, J. M. (2005). Virtual geographies of educational change: The more complex the problems the simpler the answers. In F. Hernández & I. Goodson (Eds.), *Social geographies of educational change* (pp. 143–167). Dordrecht: Kluwer.

Sancho, J. M., Hernández, F., Bosco, A., Müller, J., Larraín, V., Giró, X., Nuri, A., & Cernochova, M. (2004). *Final report. School + More than a platform to build the school of tomorrow*. Luxembourg: European Commission.

Sandholtz, J. H., Ringstaff, C., & Dwyer, D. C. (1997). *Teaching with technology: Creating student-centered classrooms*. New York: Teachers College Press.

Schofield, J. W., & Davidson, A. L. (2002). *Bringing the internet to school: Lessons from an urban district*. San Francisco, CA: Jossey-Bass.

Specht, J. A., Wood, E., & Willoughby, T. (2002). What early childhood educators want to know about computers to enhance the learning environment. *Canadian Journal of Journal of Learning and Technology, 28*(1), 31–40.

Twenge, J. (2006). *Generation me*. New York: Free Press.

Tyack, D., & Tobin, W. (1994). The "Grammar" of schooling: Why has it been so hard to change? *American Educational Research Journal, 31*(3), 453–480.

Veen, W., & Vrakking, B. (2006). *Homo zappiens: Growing up in a digital age*. London: Continuum International Publishing Group.

Wilson, J. D., Notar, Ch. C., & Yunker, B. (2003). Elementary in-service teacher's use of computers in the elementary classroom. *Journal of Instructional Psychology*. December 01. http://www.findarticles.com/p/articles/mi_m0FCG/is_4_30/ai_112686159

Wood, E., Willoughby, T., Specht, J. A., Sterne-Cavalcante, W., & Childs, C. (2002). Developing a computer workshop to facilitate computer skills and minimize anxiety for early childhood educators. *Journal of Educational Psychology, 94*, 164–170.

Toward a Theory of Teacher Education for Social Justice

Marilyn Cochran-Smith

During the last decade, dramatic changes have occurred in education policy and practice and in the larger economic and political contexts in the USA and elsewhere. Based on the widely shared view that education and the economy are inextricably linked, it is now assumed that teachers can – and should – teach all students as per world-class standards, serve as the linchpins in educational reforms of all kinds, and produce a well-qualified labor force to preserve the nation's position in the global economy. In the face of these daunting – and arguable – expectations, the question of how teachers are recruited and prepared has become a hot topic in the educational discourse of many nations. In the USA, despite many critiques (e.g., Earley, 2005; Michelli, 2005; Sleeter, 2009), a "new teacher education" (Cochran-Smith, 2005) has emerged, which is regarded as a problem that can be solved by the "right" public policies, based on evidence rather than values or ideals, and judged by outcomes rather than processes, resources, or curricula.

What has also emerged over the last decade is increasing emphasis on "social justice" as a theme in teacher education. There is great variation in the use of this language, however. Some programs emphasize teachers' beliefs and identity, others focus on democratic education, and many others concentrate on multicultural issues. Although a few programs feature community partnerships or other structural innovations (e.g., Murrell, 2001; Quartz, 2003; Seidl & Friend, 2002), most concentrate on changing course requirements or other aspects of curriculum within traditional programs (Zeichner, 2006). Both internal and external critics assert that "teacher education for social justice" is conceptually ambiguous with multiple instantiations and inadequate theoretical grounding (Cochran-Smith, Barnatt, Lahann, Shakman, & Terrell, 2009; Crowe, 2008; Damon, 2005; Zeichner, 2006). Further, only a few of those who write about teacher education and social justice are explicit about the philosophical and political roots of social justice education (McDonald & Zeichner, 2009; North, 2006), which increases the likelihood that it exists in name only (Grant & Agosto, 2008) or that it is diluted, trivialized or co-opted.

M. Cochran-Smith (✉)
Boston College, Chestnut Hill, MA, USA
e-mail: cochrans@bc.edu

A. Hargreaves et al. (eds.), *Second International Handbook of Educational Change*, 445
Springer International Handbooks of Education 23, DOI 10.1007/978-90-481-2660-6_27,
© Springer Science+Business Media B.V. 2010

This chapter[1] offers ideas toward a contemporary theory of teacher education for social justice, which is especially significant within the context of sharp critiques of social justice agendas (e.g., Hess, 2005; Lukianoff, 2007; Mac Donald, 1998); the political climate which, until very recently, has been acutely conservative; and policy makers' preoccupation with testing regimes that may reinforce existing inequities and systems of power and privilege. The chapter begins by laying the groundwork for a theory in terms of major premises and critiques. Next the chapter outlines a theory with three aspects: (1) a theory of justice that makes explicit its ultimate goals and considers the relationships of competing conceptions of justice; (2) a theory of practice that characterizes the relationship of teaching and learning, the nature of teachers' work, and the knowledge, strategies, and values that inform teachers' efforts for social justice; and (3) a theory of teacher preparation that focuses on how teachers learn to teach for justice, the structures that support their learning over time, and the outcomes that are appropriate for preparation programs with social justice goals. It is important to point out that the three parts of this theory are integrated and overlapping with one another rather than discrete. Likewise, the questions they engender are interdependent: What do we mean by justice? How do we think about teaching and learning in a way that enhances justice? How do we conceptualize and assess teacher education that prepares teachers to foster justice and supports them as they try to live out this commitment by working in educational settings? Figure 1 introduces this theory, which is then elaborated in Figs. 2, 3, and 4. The chapter devotes proportionately more space to the first aspect of the theory because it has received less attention in teacher education previously.

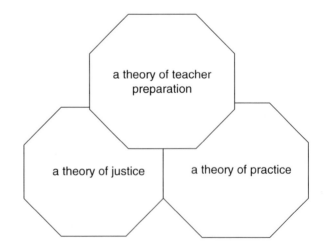

Fig. 1 Toward a theory of teacher education for social justice

---

[1] The author wishes to acknowledge the very helpful comments of Kenneth Howe and Susan Lytle on earlier drafts of this chapter as well as feedback from Boston College Evidence Team members, Sarah Enterline, Ann Marie Gleeson, Larry Ludlow, Karen Shakman, and Dianna Terrell.

Laying the Groundwork for a Theory

Four major premises form the groundwork for a theory of teacher education for social justice. First, although the term "social justice" has been used to mean almost any aspect or method of teacher education even loosely related to equity or multi-cultural education, the premise here is that teacher education for social justice is *not* about methods. That is, teacher education for social justice is not about requiring a fieldwork experience in a diverse setting nor is it about having teacher candidates read something like Peggy McIntosh's (1989) widely used article on "white privilege." Although either of these might be valuable for teacher candidates, the point of offering a theory is that teacher education for social justice is *not* merely activities, but a coherent and intellectual approach to the preparation of teachers that acknowledges the social and political contexts in which teaching, learning, schooling, and ideas about justice have been located historically as well as acknowledging the tensions among competing goals.

Second, this chapter takes as a premise that teaching and teacher education are inescapably political and ideological activities in that they inherently involve ideas, ideals, power, and access to learning and life opportunities. On the other hand, many of the critiques of teacher education for social justice, which I have analyzed in detail elsewhere (Cochran-Smith et al., 2009),[2] are based on the twin assumptions that academic knowledge, professional education, and educational policy can be – and ought to be – neutral and that current structures of teacher preparation (and schooling more broadly) neither create nor reinforce systems of power and privilege. These assumptions lead critics to the conclusion that preparation for social justice is blatantly political, biased, and even proselytizing as opposed to some other imagined kind of teacher preparation that is apolitical and objective. This chapter assumes that neutrality is impossible and that democracy depends on some core skills, such as civic deliberation, and some core values, such as respect for differences.

The third premise is that teacher preparation is a key interval in the process of learning to teach with the potential to be a site for educational change. Although teacher preparation has long been considered a weak intervention (Kennedy, 2005), we now know that what teachers learn from preparation depends in part on the beliefs and perspectives they bring with them (Wideen, Mayer-Smith, & Moon, 1998). Whether, how, how much, and when new teachers use what they have learned once they get into classrooms also depends on the cultures of schools, including resources, supports and constraints, and mentoring and induction programs (Achinstein & Ogawa, 2006; Cohen, Raudenbush, & Ball, 2002; Grossman et al., 2000). What this adds up to, then, may not be that the impact of preparation is cancelled out in the press of school life, but that it interacts in complex

---

[2]We argue that four major critiques of teacher education for social justice can be identified in the current educational discourse: the ambiguity critique, the knowledge critique, the ideology critique, and the free speech critique. These are connected to differing professional and political agendas and play out in policy and practice in highly politicized ways.

ways with the conditions and cultures of schools and the larger accountability contexts in which these are embedded. In addition, given the high rate of new teacher attrition (Ingersoll, 2003), which truncates the impact of school-based professional development, what new teachers learn during initial preparation may have greater importance than previously thought.

The final premise of this chapter is that teacher education for social justice is for all teacher candidates – not only for monolingual, middle-class white teachers who are preparing to teach those who are not like them and not only for teachers (whatever their own racial, cultural, or linguistic backgrounds) preparing to teach in urban or other schools where the pupils are poor or minority and where disparities in resources and achievement are large. This premise about teacher education for social justice depends on its corollary about teaching for social justice: teaching for social justice is for all pupils, not only those who are poor, minority, or historically disadvantaged by the system but also those whom the system advantages. The point here, as I elaborate in the pages that follow, is that teaching and teacher education for social justice are fundamental to the learning and life chances of all teachers and pupils who are current and future participants in a diverse democratic nation and who are able to both imagine and work toward a more just society. Without the perspectives inherent in social justice goals, the understandings and opportunities of all teachers and students are attenuated.

The theory I propose in this chapter is informed by research in many areas of education, pedagogy, schools, and communities as well as teacher education, professional development, and teacher quality. This also draws on my experience as a teacher education practitioner and researcher over 30-some years, my previous conceptual and empirical research on this topic, and collaborative work with my Boston College colleagues who are members of the *Teachers for a New Era* cross-disciplinary Evidence Team,[3] which has attempted to conceptualize learning to teach for social justice as a legitimate and measurable outcome of teacher education.

A Theory of Justice

Although social justice has become a watchword for teacher education, the concept is undertheorized, as indicated by reviews of the literature (Grant & Agosto, 2008; North, 2006; Wiedeman, 2002) and related discussions (Gewirtz, 1998; Westheimer & Suurtamm, 2009; Zeichner, 2006). Despite the lack of conceptual

---

[3]The Evidence Team includes Boston College faculty members and administrators, Marilyn Cochran-Smith (chair), Alan Kafka, Fran Loftus, Larry Ludlow, Patrick McQuillan, Joseph Pedulla, and Gerald Pine; TNE administrators, Jane Carter and Jeff Gilligan; and doctoral students Joan Barnatt, Robert Baroz, Lisa D'Souza, Sarah Enterline, Ann Marie Gleeson, Cindy Jong, Kara Mitchell, Emilie Mitescu, Aubrey Scheopner, Karen Shakman, Yves Fernandez Solomon, and Diana Terrell.

clarity about social justice in teacher education generally, a number of educators, myself included, have forwarded social justice as a major theme of preservice teacher education over the last two decades. (See, for example: Cochran-Smith, 1991, 1995, 1999, 2005; Gay, 1993, 2000; Gay & Howard, 2000; King, 2006, 2008; King & Castenell, 2001; King, Hollins, & Hayman, 1997; Ladson-Billings, 1994, 1999, 2000, 2001; Michelli, 2004; Michelli & Keiser, 2005; Oakes, Blasi, & Rogers, 2004; Oakes & Lipton, 1999; Oakes, Rogers, & Lipton, 2006; Sleeter, 1989, 1995, 1996; Villegas, 1991; Villegas & Lucas, 2002, 2004; Zeichner, 1993, 2003, 2006; Zeicher & Hoeft, 1996.) Much of this work is cited in the next two sections of this chapter.

In general, however, and with very few exceptions (e.g., McDonald, 2005), references to or discussions of teacher education for social justice have not been grounded in an articulated theory of justice, outside of occasional references to Rawls' (1971) concept of distributive justice (e.g., Grant & Agosto, 2008; Keiser, 2005). In this chapter, then, I turn to the first question in a theory of teacher education for social justice: How should we conceptualize justice in relation to teacher education? This question draws on conceptualizations of justice from other disciplines, primarily political philosophy, the field that has taken up this issue most extensively. Figure 2 portrays a concept of justice for teacher education, which I develop below. The figure is intended to emphasize two pairs of justice goals – distribution and recognition, and autonomy and identity – which are in tension with one another. The graphic also suggests that a theory of justice for teacher education is necessarily multiperspectival, combining critical and democratic perspectives with commitments to anti-oppressive policies and practices.

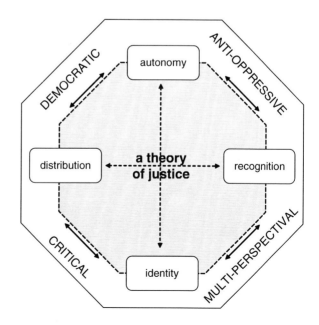

Fig. 2   A theory of justice

Distribution and Recognition

The distributive paradigm dominated theories of justice for the latter half of the last century (Fraser, 2003; Howe, 1997), especially after the publication of Rawls' now classic text on justice in 1971. However, in contemporary debates about justice, the "politics of difference," which emerged from group-based social movements of the 1960s and 1970s and emphasized recognition rather than redistribution (Young, 1990), has now taken center stage. The heading of this section, "Distribution and Recognition," reflects Fraser and Honneth's (2003) political-philosophical exchange about these seemingly opposing paradigms of justice and also draws from analyses by Gewirtz (1998), Gewirtz and Cribb (2002), and North (2006).

In short, the distributive paradigm of justice, which grows out of liberal democratic theory, focuses on equality of individuals, civic engagement, and a common political commitment to all citizens' autonomy to pursue their own ideas of the good life (Rawls, 1971). Here *in*justice is defined as inequalities rooted in the socioeconomic structure of society, including exploitation, economic marginalization or deprivation of classes or class-like groups (Fraser, 2003). From this perspective, the remedy for injustice is redistribution of material and other goods, including opportunity, power, and access with the goal of establishing a society based on fairness and equality. Canadian philosopher Will Kymlycka (1995), who argues for the rights and status of minority cultures, particularly immigrants, puts it this way: "According to this principle, injustice is a matter of arbitrary exclusion from the dominant institutions of society, and equality is a matter of non-discrimination and equal opportunity to participate" (p. 59). In education, the distributive paradigm has often taken the form of compensatory programs, such as Head Start or transitional bilingual education programs, or add-on curricula, such as adding a unit of study on Native Americans to an otherwise Eurocentric American history curriculum.

Despite the deepening socioeconomic inequalities in contemporary society, most political philosophers now agree that focusing solely on equality and distribution of goods is theoretically inadequate to the task of conceptualizing justice in today's diverse society. As Young (1990) points out, the social movements of the 1960s and 1970s, such as feminism, black liberation, American Indian movements, and gay and lesbian liberation, made it clear that failure to recognize and respect social groups was a central dimension of injustice, and thus the goal of recognition had to be central to justice theories. These social movements tried to "politicize vast areas of institutional, social and cultural life in the face of welfare state liberalism which operates to depoliticize public life" (Young, 1990, p. 10). In doing so, they challenged liberalism's notions of neutrality, the common good, and equality, as did postmodernists' endeavors to "decenter" these and other previously assumed impartial concepts (e.g., Lather, 1991; Popkewitz & Brennan, 1997). From a recognition perspective, efforts to achieve equality are presumptuous in that they presume to know what is good for everybody. In this sense, efforts for equality can work to deny difference and foster the oppression of social groups. From the perspective of recognition, the argument is that justice is not reducible to distribution, since as Honneth (2003) argues, even distributional injustices reflect "the institutional expression of social disrespect – or unjustified relations of recognition" (p. 114).

In contemporary political philosophy, then, the question really is not whether to theorize justice as a matter of distribution or as one of recognition. Rather the question is how to conceptualize the relationship between the notion of distributive justice that is central to modern liberal democracies, on one hand, and, on the other hand, contemporary struggles for the recognition of social groups based on culture, race, gender, religion, nationality, language, sexual orientation, and ability/disability – in short, in relation to the politics of identity and difference.

To address this question, American critical feminist, Nancy Fraser (2003) posits the notion of "perspectival dualism" wherein distribution and recognition are regarded as "co-fundamental" and "mutually irreducible" (p. 3) aspects of justice. In contrast, feminist political theorist Iris Marion Young (1990) rejects the idea of a unitary theory of justice, emphasizing that although distributive aspects are important, they should be limited to material goods, not things like self-respect or opportunity. She argues that justice is "co-extensive" with the political (p. 9), and that oppression and domination should be the primary terms for conceptualizing justice. Also in contrast to Fraser, German social theorist and philosopher Axel Honneth (2003) sees recognition as the overarching moral category with redistribution a subcategory of the struggle for recognition. British sociologists Sharon Gewirtz and Alan Cribb (2002) make the point that even though most current conceptions of social justice now acknowledge its plural dimensions, few adequately engage with the tensions between multiple facets.

Theories of Justice and Teacher Education

At a general level, these perspectives from political philosophy are instructive for theorizing teacher education for social justice, even though none of them addresses teaching or teacher education directly. There are many people in education and teacher education who have pushed the social justice agenda, such as those whom I list at the beginning of this section on justice. In the interest of space constraints, however, I mention just three additional concepts here, which are directly relevant to teacher education in the USA and are particularly helpful in developing a theory of teacher education for social justice: educational philosopher Kenneth Howe's (1997) "radical liberal theory of democracy, justice and schooling" (p. *x*), which offers a political understanding of what equality of educational opportunity requires; political scientist and ethicist Rob Reich's (2002) articulation of "liberal multiculturalism," a theory that integrates "the insights of both liberalism and multiculturalism, and takes seriously the history of schooling" (p. 5); and Black Studies scholar and sociologist Joyce King's (2008) argument for a "blues epistemology" in teacher education that challenges the hegemony of ideologically based knowledge in school and teacher education by drawing on the knowledge traditions and lived experiences of marginalized and oppressed groups.

In his "radical liberal theory of democracy, justice and schooling," Howe (1997) argues that only liberal-egalitarian theories offer an adequate foundation for the principle of educational opportunity "consistent with the demands of justice in a liberal democracy" (p. 23). Building on both Gutmann's (1987) "democratic threshold" for equal participation and Young's (1990) call for recognition of a differentiated humanity, Howe argues for a "participatory paradigm" (p. 130) wherein justice, democracy, and equality are so intertwined, it is impossible to have any of them without all. With a participatory approach, Howe suggests that in many cases, true equality of educational opportunity can be achieved only when historically marginalized groups have a genuine voice in "negotiating what educational opportunities have worth" (p. 27). It is important to note here that Howe does not mean mere recognition of previously unrecognized groups. Rather, following Young (1990), he argues that schooling is obligated to actively eliminate the oppression of social groups, especially cultural imperialism, as manifested in curriculum, educational policies and practices, school structures, and norms.

Reich (2002) posits a "liberal theory of multicultural education" (p. 5) that is respectful of both cultural differences and a democratic society's need to cultivate "autonomy and common political values" (p. 115). He concedes to multiculturalism that a liberal democratic state cannot be truly neutral (as Rawls' theory of justice originally suggested) about the ways of life pursued by its citizens, since autonomy itself is a culture-based and privileged way of life. Nevertheless his theory depends on the non-neutral (but necessary) aim of "minimal autonomy" (p. 116) for all persons, which includes the capacity to reflect critically on a variety of ideas and beliefs and thus to benefit from a range of genuine life options. Reich argues that this is not simply about identity politics, which benefit minority groups, but civic society, which benefits everybody. Reich rejects "mainstream multicultural pedagogy," which he claims essentializes groups and is based on stereotyping. Instead he calls for "hermeneutical pedagogy," which supports cross-cultural discussion and efforts to understand others' points of view from their own perspectives, thus building "interpretive capacity" for all participants in society (p. 185).

King (2006) argues that "if justice is our objective" (p. 337) in education, then we must recognize and account for the ways "ideologically distorted knowledge sustains societal *in*justice, particularly academic and school knowledge about black history and culture" (p. 337). King (2008) asserts that there is a "crisis of knowledge" (p. 1095) in teacher education research and in practice caused by the absence of the epistemologies of African Americans and other marginalized groups as a foundation for teacher learning and teaching. Noting that there is no consensus in teacher education about what teachers should know and be able to do with regard to "promot[ing] and safeguard[ing] the cultural well-being, sense of belonging, and agency" of historically marginalized students, King advocates for the epistemological and social perspectives conveyed by "the blues." She points out that these contrast sharply with the deficit theories of minority life and culture that continue to dominate the schools and much of teacher education. Acknowledging that many white teacher candidates resist ideas related to what she calls "racial-social justice teaching" (p. 1101) by claiming color blindness or innocence, King calls for research, pedagogy, and practice explicitly intended to challenge these views.

What should teacher education take from these ideas about justice? My argument here is that a theory of justice for teacher education must connect the key ideas of distributive justice, which locates equality and autonomy at the center of democratic societies (Howe, 1997, 1998), with current political struggles for recognition, which challenge the school and knowledge structures that reinforce disrespect and oppression of social groups (King, 2006; Young, 1990). This connection cannot simply be declared or glossed over, however. Both Howe and Reich suggest bridging concepts related to autonomy and civic participation for all members of diverse societies, which require revised curriculum and different instructional goals related to students' capacity for deliberation, disagreement, and interpretation. However, these concepts must also be connected to strategies for broader participation by all social groups in the discourse about what is fundamental in education in the first place, including those historically marginalized. Otherwise, as King (2006) points out, we are left with the untenable situation in which "equal access to a faulty curriculum" (p. 337) is assumed by some to constitute justice.

Applying these concepts to the day-to-day work of teaching and teacher education is difficult. In this work, there are ongoing and on-the-ground tensions between, for example, the idea of a knowledge and skills base that all new teachers should know, on one hand, and acknowledgment that school knowledge and curricula historically have been constructed in ways that privilege some cultural and racial groups and dismiss the knowledge traditions of other groups, on the other hand; between a curriculum that promotes what some presume to be core civic democratic values, on one hand, and a curriculum that explores a range of cultural positions about participation itself, on the other; and between efforts to provide educational services and modes of instruction that support the learning of individuals and social/cultural/racial groups, on one hand, and efforts to avoid stereotyping and essentializing particular groups, on the other. As Gewirtz and Cribb (2002) argue, most contemporary theorizing about social justice in education has glossed over the inherent tensions at an "a priori level or at a high level of abstraction" (p. 506) rather than understanding and managing them concretely. My intention here is to offer a theory of teacher education for social justice that addresses this problem by weaving together a theory of justice, a theory of teaching and learning practice, and a theory of teacher preparation, and by acknowledging all along the way that there are inherent tensions involved in doing so.

What I want to argue, then, is that a theory of justice for teacher education has three key ideas that are overlapping and integrated with one another:

(1) *Equity of learning opportunity:* promoting equity in learning opportunities and outcomes for all students, who are regarded as future autonomous participants in a democratic society, and simultaneously challenging classroom (and societal) practices, policies, labels, and assumptions that reinforce inequities;

(2) *Respect for social groups:* recognizing and respecting all social/racial/cultural groups by actively working *against* the assumptions and arrangements of schooling (and society) that reinforce inequities, disrespect, and oppression of these groups and actively working *for* effective use in classrooms and schools of the knowledge traditions and ways of knowing of marginalized groups;

(3) *Acknowledging and dealing with tensions:* directly acknowledging the tensions and contradictions that emerge from competing ideas about the nature of justice and managing these in knowingly imperfect, but concrete ways.

As noted, Fig. 2 is intended to suggest the multiple aims and aspects of justice, positing these as co-fundamental but also in tension with one another, rather than reducible to a single overarching focus.

A Theory of Practice

The second question in a theory of teacher education for social justice is this: How can we conceptualize teaching and learning practice in a way that enhances justice? The answer to this question is essential because it is the intermediate link that connects teacher preparation and justice. In other words, a theory of teacher education for social justice must have a well-theorized idea about the kind of teaching practice that enhances justice since preparing teachers for practice is the goal of all preparation programs and pathways. My argument here is that in order to support justice, teaching practice must be theorized as an amalgam of the following: knowledge; interpretive frameworks; teaching strategies, methods, and skills; and, advocacy with and for students, parents, colleagues, and communities, all with the larger goal of improving students' learning and enhancing their life chances. The idea of practice as defined by teachers' knowledge, interpretations, methods and advocacy is highlighted in Fig. 3, which also emphasizes that practice is theoretical as well as practical, critical and relational. These ideas are elaborated in the following section.

According to the federal education policy, No Child Left Behind, which was firmly in place in the USA when this chapter was written, teachers need just two things to practice successfully: subject matter knowledge and teaching skills based on scientific research (Cochran-Smith & Lytle, 2006). From this perspective, practice is what teachers *do* in classrooms, which can be prescribed and assessed independent of local communities and cultures. A theory of practice consistent with justice, however, rejects the narrow view that teaching practice is "simply" what, when, or how teachers do things. Rather, from the perspective of justice, teaching practice also involves how teachers think about their work and interpret what is going on in schools and classrooms; how they understand competing agendas, pose questions, and make decisions; how they form relationships with students; and how they work with colleagues, families, communities and social groups. The idea that practice is not a bundle of "proven" techniques is consistent in some ways with the professionalization agenda in teacher education, which stresses that new

Fig. 3 A theory of practice

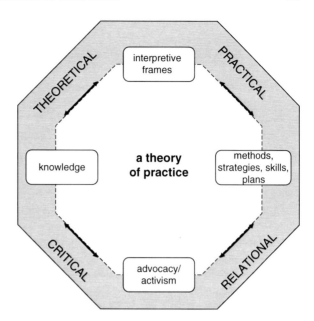

teachers need certain knowledge and dispositions as well as a repertoire of skills in order to teach well (e.g., Darling-Hammond & Bransford, 2005; NCATE, 2002). But a theory of practice consistent with justice also critiques aspects of the professionalization agenda, especially its tendency toward a universalist perspective on knowledge, which does not adequately account for the knowledge traditions and experiences of marginalized groups (King, 2008), and its lack of attention to preparing new teachers to challenge the "cultural imperialism" of curriculum, educational policies and practices, and school norms (Howe, 1997).

Knowledge

The mainstream professional view in teacher education is that there is a body of knowledge every new teacher should know. *Preparing Teachers for a Changing World* (Darling-Hammond & Bransford, 2005), for example, identifies eight knowledge domains. All of these are important in the theory of practice posited here. However, if practice is to foster justice, teachers also need to critique the very idea of a knowledge base and understand its limitations. They need to deal with the tensions created by traditional school knowledge that privileges the western canon and omits other cultural and linguistic "funds of knowledge" (Moll, 1992), which limits what can be known and who is considered a knower (Cochran-Smith & Lytle, 1990; King & Hollins, 1997; Sleeter, 2001). Along these lines, Michelli (2005) suggests that those committed to teaching for justice and democracy agree with the prevailing belief that the fundamental purpose of schooling is providing access to knowledge, but at the same time, they question what kinds of knowledge and for whom. Similar questions include who decides what knowledge counts in school, whose interests are served, and whose perspectives are/are not included (Castenell & Pinar, 1993). From the perspective of social justice, then, the knowledge teachers need includes much of the traditional canon of school knowledge, but also includes critiquing the universality of traditional knowledge in the first place (Gore, 1993; King, 2008; Lather, 2004) and teaching students to do the same.

Interpretive Frames

From the perspective of justice, interpretive frames, which emerge from a co-mingling of knowledge, experience, beliefs, and values, are an essential aspect of practice. As the filters through which teachers make decisions, form relationships, and support learning, they are powerful mediators of practice and thus of students' opportunities and experiences. When the goal of practice is social justice, several interpretive frames are key. An understanding of educators as potential agents of social change (Freire, 1970) means acting on the idea that teachers can influence students' learning and life chances, which depends on the belief that all students can learn academically challenging material (Oakes & Lipton, 1999). This is related to an asset-based (as opposed to deficit-based) view of the cultural, linguistic, and experiential backgrounds of students (Ladson-Billings, 1995; Moll, 1992). "Cultural consciousness" (Gay & Howard, 2000; Villegas & Lucas, 2002) is the understanding that all persons have multiple identities and have life histories structured by race, class, culture, and other aspects of existing societal systems of privilege and oppression. In addition, when teaching practice is aimed at justice, teachers interpret their work through an inquiry stance (Cochran-Smith & Lytle, 1999) by questioning their own and others' assumptions, posing and researching problems, and using curricula, tests, and research as generative rather than prescriptive. Finally, when practice is consistent with the aims of social justice, it is framed by the understanding that teaching practice, whether by design or default, always takes a stand on society's current distribution of resources and current respect/disrespect for social groups (Ginsberg & Lindsay, 1995).

Methods, Skills, Strategies, Techniques

A theory of teaching practice that supports justice is not about specific techniques or best practices, but about guiding principles that play out in a variety of methods and strategies, depending on the particular circumstances, students, content, and communities. Many teacher education scholars have discussed in depth the nature of pedagogy and practice that foster justice (e.g., Cochran-Smith, 1999; Gore, 1993; Ladson-Billings, 1995; Sleeter & McLaren, 1999; Villegas & Lucas, 2001; Zeichner, 1993). Across these, a common theme is developing caring relationships with students (Irvine, 1990; Witherell & Noddings, 1991) and providing rich and relevant learning opportunities for all students (Oakes & Lipton, 1999;

Oakes et al., 2006), including English language learners, students with special needs, students labeled "at risk" by the system, and students unlikely to increase a school's yearly progress on test scores. Another theme is using the resources and interests students bring to school to generate curriculum and instruction that are culturally, linguistically, and experientially relevant (Ballenger, 1998; Gay, 2000; Ladson-Billings, 1995), but at the same time, challenging the hegemony of the canon (King & Castenell, 2001). This includes providing social supports and scaffolding for students' learning of new skills and materials, such as explicitly teaching those without knowledge of mainstream language and interactional patterns how to negotiate the system, but also teaching how to critique the system and consider alternatives (Delpit, 1995). A final theme is that teaching practice that fosters justice makes equity/inequity and respect/disrespect for individuals and social groups explicit parts of the curriculum and allowable topics in the classroom. This supports cross-cultural discussion and the development of "interpretive capacity" (Reich, 2002, p. 185) in all students, which are essential skills in a diverse democratic society and an increasingly interdependent global community.

Advocacy and Activism

Central to the discussion of justice in the first section of this chapter is the idea of teachers deliberately claiming the role of advocate and activist based on political consciousness, deep respect for differences, and commitments to diminishing the inequities of American schooling and society. The idea of teachers as activists and advocates is related to Westheimer and Kahne's (2004) three versions of citizenship education. Their first version is implicit in civic education programs that seek to promote personally responsible, hard-working, and law-abiding citizens. Their second version of citizenship, on the other hand, is related to participatory citizen programs, which promote active participation in civic organizations and social life at all levels. However, Westheimer and Kahne's third version of citizenship education, or what they call "justice-oriented" citizen programs, "call explicit attention to matters of injustice and to the importance of pursuing social justice goals" (p. 243). My point here is that a notion of teaching practice that fosters justice is consistent with Westheimer and Kahne's third justice-oriented view of citizenship in that teachers who are advocates and activists call explicit attention to school and classroom injustices and work actively with their students, other teachers, parents, and community groups to pursue justice goals. This means realizing that competing approaches to teaching and schooling are often forwarded in the same name of equity, accountability, and serving the citizenry. This also means critiquing the processes of schooling and asking questions about whose interests are served, whose needs are met, whose knowledge is included, and whose goals are forwarded by different teaching practices. There is no assumption here that teachers alone, whether through individual or group efforts, can substantially fix the schools or alter the life chances of students. But a major assumption is that they can join with others as part of larger social movements for change.

A Theory of Teacher Preparation

The third question that must be answered by a theory of teacher education for social justice is this: How can we conceptualize teacher preparation intended to prepare teachers to engage in practice that enhances justice? Again, the answer to this question is central because it reflects the direct link between teacher preparation and teaching practice. My argument here is that in order to support teaching and learning practices that foster justice, teacher preparation must be theorized in terms of four key issues: who should teach, which is instantiated in practices and policies related to the selection and recruitment of teacher candidates; what teachers and students should learn, which plays out in the curriculum and pedagogy to which teacher candidates are exposed; how and from/with whom teachers learn, which has to do with the intellectual, social, and organizational contexts and structures designed to support candidates' learning; and how all of this is assessed, or how the outcomes of preparation are constructed and measured and what consequences these have for whom. Figure 4 provides a graphic representation of teacher preparation for justice in terms of the interrelationships of decisions regarding selection, curriculum, structures, and outcomes. The figure emphasizes that teacher preparation for social justice is transformative and collaborative, but also involves working within and against the accountability system.

The overarching idea in theorizing teacher preparation for social justice is that it is intended to challenge the educational status quo and be transformative. In sharp contrast to preparation intended to be ever more closely aligned with the accountability system (e.g., Janofksy, 2005), teacher preparation for social justice

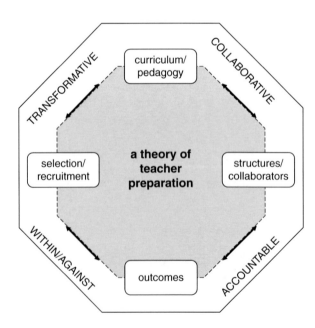

Fig. 4 A theory of teacher preparation

challenges the testing regime and the inequities it reinforces: limited rather than enriched learning opportunities for poor and minority students, increased drop-out rates, narrowed curriculum, and schools less connected and accountable to their local communities than before (Center on Education Policy, 2006; Darling-Hammond, 2004; Meier & Wood, 2004; Orfield, Losen, Wald, 2004). This does not mean that teacher education for justice simply sits outside the accountability system, however. Rather the point is to construct a different kind of accountability by working simultaneously within and against the system, an idea I return to below.

Recruitment/Selection/Retention of Teacher Candidates

In the first section of this chapter, I concluded that challenging inequities and respecting differences were at the heart of a theory of justice for teacher education. Consistent with these goals, the question of which teachers are recruited and selected is critical to a theory of teacher preparation. Two guidelines are important: diversifying the teaching force in terms of cultural, racial, and linguistic backgrounds and recruiting teachers whose beliefs, experiences, and values are consistent with social justice goals. Based on their analysis of demographic trends in the workforce and evidence regarding diversification, Villegas and Lucas (2004) conclude that increasing the diversity of the teaching force provides needed role models for all students and also infuses essential cultural knowledge into the workforce. Other research suggests that the experiences and maturity of minority and non-traditional candidates often make them more likely to succeed in high-need areas than traditional candidates (Clewell & Villegas, 2001; Haberman, 1991, 1996; Villegas et al., 1995), although minority candidates often experience alienation in primarily white institutions (Hollins & Guzman, 2005; Villegas & Davis, 2008). In addition, given that young white women currently make up the vast majority of teacher candidates in collegiate programs, selecting and retaining those whose attitudes, beliefs, and values are consistent with social justice goals must be an essential goal in teacher preparation for social justice.

Curriculum and Pedagogy

In keeping with the perspective on knowledge outlined in the previous section of this chapter, teacher education curriculum that fosters justice must include opportunities for candidates to learn about subject matter, pedagogy, culture, language, the social and cultural contexts of schooling, and the purposes of education. However, teacher education curriculum and pedagogy also need to be theorized and interrogated as "political text" (Castenell & Pinar, 1993), which I have suggested (Cochran-Smith, 2000; Cochran-Smith & Demers, 2007) means attending to more than the sequence of courses or experiences required for credentialing purposes. Rather this means calling attention to what is left out, implied, or veiled in the curriculum (Ginsburg & Clift, 1990) as well as uncovering what is subtly signaled as the norm or default perspective in discussions about pedagogy, growth, learning, experience, expectations, or family. This also means analyzing the messages about race, class, culture, and language background that are sometimes explicit, but often implicit in inconsistencies between the formal documents describing curriculum and what is actually conveyed to teacher candidates through a program's readings, written assignments, fieldwork placements, student body, and leadership. Along these lines, King (2008) has argued that in teacher education there has been an "absent presence" in teacher education theory and practice generated from the work and lives of people of color, resulting in a curriculum that primarily "meets the needs and dispositions of white teachers." Teacher preparation that fosters justice must deal with the tensions involved in meeting the needs of both white teachers and teachers of color and also focusing in the curriculum on the worldviews of social groups that have been marginalized or oppressed.

Contexts, Structures and Collaborators

At the heart of any theory of teacher preparation is a set of assumptions about how and from/with whom teacher candidates learn as well as the contexts and structures that support that learning. Today most programs assume that teachers need to learn in the context of university partnerships with the schools. With the justice goals of challenging inequities and respecting cultural knowledge and differences, however, the idea behind partnerships is not that candidates are evaluated on how well they imitate the "best practices" of expert teachers. Rather the point is that candidates learn in the company of their more experienced mentors who are also engaged in the life-long processes of teaching "against the grain" (Cochran-Smith, 1991) by working with others in inquiry communities to construct "local knowledge of practice" that enhances equity, access, and participation (Cochran-Smith & Lytle, 1999). From the perspective of social justice, teacher preparation also includes parents, families, and community groups as collaborators, especially those from historically marginalized groups (McDonald & Zeichner, 2009). Murrell (2001) and Murrell and Diez (1997) also argues that urban teaching and teacher education need to emphasize the role of parents and the community in educational reform. What these approaches have in common are organizational structures that make both experienced teachers who are working within and against the system and parents and community activists who are challenging the dominant ideology into collaborators in the enterprise of teacher preparation.

Outcomes

Teacher preparation that generates practice that fosters justice is squarely committed to promoting students' learning and takes accountability for both teachers' and students' learning very seriously. From this perspective, however, the point is to redefine learning so that it includes a wide range of academic, social, emotional, civic, and life skills, thus rejecting scores on standardized tests as the sole measure of either students' academic success or teacher education programs' effectiveness. Rather, from the perspective of justice, with its goal of challenging inequities, the focus is on ensuring that all students have rich opportunities to learn, not just opportunities to be held accountable to the same high stakes (which Howe, 1997, would call a "bare" rather than a genuine opportunity) and not just an equal slice of a curriculum pie that is, in the first place, faulty (King, 2006). On the other hand, however, if they are working from the perspective of justice, preparation programs must acknowledge that under the current accountability regime, poor performance on tests is often an insurmountable barrier to an array of life options (Michelli, 2005). These goals are contradictory and thus create enormous tensions, of the sort I referred to in the section on justice – preparing teachers whose students pass standardized tests, on one hand, but, on the other hand, simultaneously working to radically recast the whole notion of accountability by challenging both test and curriculum content that omit the knowledge traditions of marginalized groups and the social structures that reinforce educational disparities along the lines of race, class, culture, and language. To address these and other tensions, teacher educators in some places are working within the system by focusing on outcomes and owning accountability, but also working against the system by recasting accountability in terms of rich learning opportunities for all students, preparation for participation in a democratic society, teacher candidates' commitments to social justice goals, and their retention in careers as social justice educators as legitimate and measurable outcomes (e.g., Chou, 2006; Cochran-Smith, Mitescu, Shakman, & the Boston College Evidence Team, in press; Ludlow et al., 2008; Quartz & TEP Research Group, 2003; Villegas, 2007; Villegas & Lucas, 2006).

Conclusion

This chapter has offered ideas toward a contemporary theory of teacher education based on three questions: What is justice? What is teaching and learning practice that fosters justice? What is teacher preparation that generates teaching practice that fosters justice? Clearly these three complex questions – and their equally complex and necessarily partial answers – are not discrete pieces of a larger theory of teacher education for social justice that can simply be layered or piled up on top of each other. Rather these three are overlapping, interdependent, and intertwined with one another. The point of a theory of this kind is to be useful to practitioners, researchers, and policy makers by providing guidelines for curricula and programs, suggesting a framework for understanding outcomes and dilemmas, generating research questions and interpretive frameworks, and guiding recruitment and credentialing policies.

My argument here is that the bottom line of a theory of teacher education for social justice – and the goal that subsumes all other goals and objectives – is promoting students' learning and enhancing their life chances in the world. This goal does not imply that teacher education should be "un-accountable" for outcomes related to the learning of students and teachers. But it does assume a radically different kind of accountability, infused with the ideas discussed throughout this chapter – challenges to the hegemony of the knowledge base and the curricular canon, rich and real learning opportunities for all students (not just opportunities to be held to the same high stakes tests), outcomes for students that include true preparation for participation in a diverse democratic society, and roles for teachers as activists as well as educators.

References

Achinstein, B., & Ogawa, R. (2006). (In)fidelity: What the resistance of new teachers reveals about professional principles and prescriptive educational policies. *Harvard Educational Review, 76*(1), 30–63.

Ballenger, C. (1998). *Teaching other people's children: Literacy and learning in a bilingual classroom.* New York, NY: Teachers College Press.

Castenell, L., & Pinar, W. (Eds.). (1993). *Understanding curriculum as racial text: Representations of identity and difference in education.* Albany, NY: SUNY Press.

Chou, V. (2006). *Going where the greatest needs are: Gauging progress in urban teacher education by our impact on the hardest-to-staff* schools, Paper presented at Annual Meeting of the American Educational Research Association, April 2006, San Francisco.

Cochran-Smith, M. (1991). Learning to teach against the grain. *Harvard Educational Review, 51*(3), 279–310.

Cochran-Smith, M. (1995). Uncertain allies: Understanding the boundaries of race and teaching. *Harvard Education Review, 65*(4), 541–570.

Cochran-Smith, M. (1999). Learning to teach for social justice. In G. Griffin (Ed.), *The education of teachers: Ninety-eighth yearbook of the national society for the study of education* (pp. 114–144). Chicago, IL: University of Chicago Press.

Cochran-Smith, M. (2000). Blind vision: Unlearning racism in teacher education. *Harvard Educational Review, 70*(2), 157–190.

Cochran-Smith, M. (2005). The new teacher education: For better or for worse? *Educational Researcher, 34*(6), 181–206.

Cochran-Smith, M., Barnatt, J., Lahann, R., Shakman, K., & Terrell, D. (2009). Teacher education for social justice: Critiquing the critiques. In W. Ayers, T. Quinn, & D. Stovall (Eds.), *The handbook of social justice in education* (pp. 625–639). Philadelphia: Taylor and Francis.

Cochran-Smith, M., & Demers, K. (2007). Teacher educaton as bridge? Unpacking curriculum controversies in teacher education. In M. Connelly (Ed.), *Handbook of curriculum research* (2nd ed.). Mahwah, NJ: Lawrence Erlbaum.

Cochran-Smith, M., & Lytle, S. (1990). Research on teaching and teacher research: The issues that divide. *Educational Researcher, 19*(2), 2–11.

Cochran-Smith, M., & Lytle, S. L. (1999). Relationship of knowledge and practice: Teacher learning in communities. In A. Iran-Nejad & C. Pearson (Eds.), *Review of research in education* (Vol. 24, pp. 249–306). Washington, DC: American Educational Research Association.

Cochran-Smith, M., & S. Lytle (2006). Troubling images of teaching in no child left behind. *Harvard Education Review, 76*(4), 668–697.

Cochran-Smith, M., Mitescu, E., Shakman, K., & the Boston College Evidence Team. (in press). Just measures: Social justice as a teacher education outcome. *Teacher Education and Practice.*

Clewell, B.-C., & Villegas, A. M. (2001). *Ahead of the class: A handbook for preparing new teachers from new sources.* Washington, DC: Urban Institute.

Cohen, D., Raudenbush, S., & Ball, D. (2002). Evidence matters: Randomized trials in education research. In F. Mosteller & R. Boruch (Eds.), *Evidence matters: Randomized trials in education research*. Washington: Brookings Institute Press.

Crowe, E. (2008). Teaching as a profession: A bridge too far? In M. Cochran-Smith, S. Feiman Nemser, J. McIntyre, & K. Demers (Eds.), *Handbook of research on teacher education: Enduring questions in changing contexts*. Mahwah, NJ: Lawrence Erlbaum Publishers.

Darling-Hammond, L. (2004). From 'separate but equal' to 'no child left behind': The collision of new standards and old inequalities. In D. Meier & G. Wood (Eds.), *Many children left behind, how the no child left behind act is damaging our children and our schools* (pp. 3–32). Boston, MA: Beacon Press.

Darling-Hammond, L., & Bransford, J. (Eds.). (2005). *Preparing teachers for a changing world. Report of the committee on teacher education of the national academy of education*. San Francisco: Jossey Bass.

Damon, W. (2005). Personality test: The dispositional dispute in teacher preparation today, and what to do about it. *The Education Gadfly*.

Delpit, L. (1995). *Other people's children: Cultural conflict in the classroom*. New York, NY: The New Press.

Earley, P. (2005). Standards alignment and government policy: Unresolved policy dilemmas. In *After standards alignment* (pp. 29–68). Amhurst, MA: National Evaluation Systems.

Fraser, N. (2003). Social justice in an age of identity politics: Redistribution, recognition and participation. In N. Fraser & A. Honneth (Eds.), *Redistribution or recognition: A political-philosophical debate* (pp. 7–109). London: Verso.

Fraser, N., & Honneth, A. (2003). *Redistribution or recognition: A political-philosophical debate*. London: Verso.

Freire, P. (1970). *Pedagogy of the oppressed* (M. B. Ramos, Trans.). New York, NY: Seabury Press.

Gay, G. (1993). Building cultural bridges: A bold proposal for teacher education. *Education and Urban Society, 25*(3), 285–289.

Gay, G. (2000). *Culturally responsive teaching: Theory, research and practice*. New York, NY: Teachers College Press.

Gay, G., & Howard, T. C. (2000). Multicultural teacher education for the 21st century. *The Teacher Educator, 36*(1), 1–16.

Gewirtz, S. (1998). Conceptualizing social justice: Mapping the territory. *Journal of Education Policy, 13*(4), 469–484.

Gewirtz, S., & Cribb, A. (2002). Plural conceptions of social justice: Implications for policy sociology. *Journal of Education Policy, 17*(5), 499–509.

Ginsberg, M., & Clift, R. (1990). The hidden curriculum of preservice teacher education. In R. Houston. *Handbook of research on teacher education*. New York, NY, MacWilliams Publishing Company: 450–465.

Ginsberg, M., & Lindsay, B. (1995). *Comparative perspectives on policy formation, socialization, and society*. Philadelphia, PA: Falmer.

Gore, J. (1993). *The struggle for pedagogies: Critical and feminist discourses as regimes of truth*. New York, NY: Routledge.

Grant, C., & Agosto, V. (2008). Teacher capacity and social justice in teacher education. In M. Cochran-Smith, S. Feiman Nemser, J. McIntyre, & K. Demers (Eds.), *Handbook of research on teacher education: Enduring questions in changing contexts* (3rd ed.). Philadelphia: Taylor and Francis.

Grossman, O., Valencia, S., Evans, K., Thompson, C., Martin, S., & Place, N. (2000). Transitions into teaching; learning to teach writing in teacher education and beyond. *Journal of Literacy Research, 32*(4), 631–662.

Gutmann, A. (1987). *Democratic education*. Princeton: Princeton University Press.

Haberman, M. (1991). Rationale for training adults as teachers. In C. Sleeter (Ed.), *Empowerment through multicultural education* (pp. 275–286). Albany: SUNY Press.

Haberman, M. (1996). Selecting and preparing culturally competent teachers for urban schools. In
    J. Sikula, T. Buttery, & E. Guyton (Eds.), *Handbook of research on teacher education* (2nd ed.,
    pp. 747–760). New York, NY: Macmillan.
Hess, F. (2005). The predictable, but unpredictably personal, politics of teacher licensure. *Journal
    of Teacher Education, 56*, 192–198.
Hollins, E., & Guzman, M. (2005). Research on preparing teachers for diverse populations. In
    M. Cochran-Smith & K. Zeichner (Eds.), *Studying teaching: The report of the aera panel on
    research and teacher education* (pp. 477–548). Mahwah, NJ: Lawrence Erlbaum.
Honneth, A. (2003). Redistribution as recognition: A response to nancy fraser. In N. Fraser &
    A. Honneth (Eds.), *Redistribution or recognition: A political-philosophical debate* (pp. 110–
    197). London: Verso.
Howe, K. (1997). *Understanding equal educational opportunity: Social justice, democracy, and
    schooling*. New York: Teachers College Press.
Howe, K. (1998). The interpretive turn and the new debate in education. *Educational Researcher,
    27*(8), 13–20.
Ingersoll, R. (2003). *Is there really a teacher shortage? A report co-sponsored by the center for
    the study of teaching and policy and the center for policy research in education*. Seattle, WA:
    Center for the Study of Teaching and Policy, University of Washington.
Irvine, J. (1990). *Black students and school failure: Policies, practice and prescriptions*. New York,
    NY: Greenwood Press.
Janofksy, M. (2005). A Bush-style education school in texas. *New York Times*.
Keiser, D. (2005). Learners not widgets: Teacher education for social justice during transforma-
    tional times. In N. Michelli & D. Keiser (Eds.), *Teacher education for democracy and social
    justice*. New York: Routledge.
Kennedy, M. (2005). *Inside teaching: How classroom life undermines reform*. Cambridge: Harvard
    University Press.
King, J. (2006). If our objective is justice: Diaspora literacy, heritage knowledge, and the praxis of
    critical studyin' for human freedom. In A. Ball (Ed.), *With more deliberate speed: Achieving
    equity and excellence in education – realizing the full potential of brown v. Board of education,
    105th yearbook of the national society for the study of education* (pp. 337–357). Chicago:
    University of Chicago Press.
King, J. (2008). Critical and qualitative researchin teacher education: A blues epistemology, a
    reason for knowing for cultural well-being. In M. Cochran-Smith, S. Feiman Nemser, &
    J. McIntyre (Eds.), *Handbook of research on teacher education: Enduring issues in changing
    contexts* (pp. 1094–1135). Mahweh, NJ: Lawrence Erlbaum, Publishers.
King, J., Hollins, E. et al., (Eds.). (1997). *Preparing teachers for cultural diversity*, New York, NY:
    Teachers College Press.
King, J. E., Hollins, E. R., & Hayman, W. (Eds.). (1997). *Preparing teachers for cultural diversity*.
    New York: Teachers College Press.
King, S., & Castenell, L. (Eds.). (2001). *Racism and racial inequality: Implications for teacher
    education*. Washington, DC: AACTE.
Kymlycka, W. (1995). *Multicultural citizenship*. Oxford: Clarendon Press.
Ladson-Billings, G. (1994). Who will teach our children: Preparing teachers to successfully teach
    African American students. In E. Hollins, J. King & W. Hayman (Eds.), *Teaching diverse
    populations: Formulating a knowledge base* (pp. 129–162). Albany, NY: State University of
    New York Press.
Ladson-Billings, G. (1995). Toward a theory of culturally relevant pedagogy. *American
    Educational Research Journal, 32*(3), 465–491.
Ladson-Billings, G. (1999). Preparing teachers for diverse student populations: A critical race
    theory perspective. In A. Iran-Nejad & D. Pearson (Eds.), *Review of research in education*
    (Vol. 24, pp. 211–248). Washington, DC: American Educational Research Association.
Ladson-Billings, G. (2000). Fighting for our lives: Preparing teaches to teach African American
    students. *Journal of Teacher Education, 51*(3), 206–214.

Ladson-Billings, G. (2001). *Crossing over to Canaan.* San Francisco, CA: Jossey-Bass.

Lather, P. (1991). *Getting smart: Feminist research and pedagogy within the postmodern.* London: Routledge, Chapman, and Hall.

Lather, P. (2004). This is your father's paradigm: Government intrusion and the case of qualitative research in education. *Qualitative Inquiry, 10*(1), 15–34.

Ludlow, L., Pedulla, P., Enterline, S., Cochran-Smith, M, Loftus, F., Salomon-Fernandez, Y., et al. (2008). From students to teachers: Using surveys to build a culture of evidence and inquiry. *European Journal of Teacher Education, 31*(4), 319–337.

Lukianoff, G. (2007). Social justice and political orthodoxy. *The Chronicle of Higher Education, 53*(30), B8. Retrieved May 17, 2007, from Academic OneFile database.

Mac Donald, H. (1998). Why Johnny's teacher can't teach. *City Journal, 8*(2), 14–26.

McDonald, M. (2005). The integraton of social justice in teacher education. *Journal of Teacher Education, 56*(5), 418–435.

McDonald, M., & Zeichner, K. (2009). Social justice teacher education. In W. Ayers, T. Quinn, & D. Stovall (Eds.), *The handbook of social justice in education* (pp. 595–610). Philadelphia: Taylor and Francis.

McIntosh, P. (1989). White privilege: Unpacking the invisible knapsack. *Peace and Freedom, 1*(1), 10–12.

Meier, M., & Wood, G. (Eds.). (2004). *Many children left behind: How the no child left behind act is damaging our children and our schools.* Boston: Beacon Press.

Michelli, N. (2004). Preparing highly qualified teachers: A contested concept. In N. E. Systems (Ed.), *Highly qualified teachers.* Amherst, MA: National Evaluation Systems.

Michelli, N. (2005). Education for democracy: What can it be? In N. Michelli & D. Keiser (Eds.), *Teacher education for social justice and democracy.* New York: Routledge.

Michelli, N., & Keiser, D. (Eds.). (2005). *Teacher education for democracy and social justice.* New York: Routledge/Taylor & Francis.

Moll, L. (1992). Funds of knowledge for teaching: Using a qualitative approach to connect homes and classrooms. *Theory into Practice, 31*(1), 32–41.

Murrell, P. (2001). *The community teacher.* New York: Teachers College Press.

Murrell, P., & Diez, M. (1997). A model program for educating teachers for diversity. In J. King, E. Hollins, & W. Hayman (Eds.), *Preparing teachers for cultural diversity* (pp. 113–128). New York, NY: Teachers College Press.

National Council for the Accreditation of Teacher Education. (2002). *NCATE standards for accrediation.* Washington: National Council for the Accreditation of Teacher Education.

North, C. (2006). More than words? Delving into the substantive meaning(s) of 'social justice' in education. *Review of Educational Research, 76*(4), 507–535.

Oakes, J., Blasi, G., & Rogers, J. (2004). Accounting for adequate and equitable opportunities to learn. In K. Sirotnik (Ed.), *Holding accountability accountable* (pp. 82–99). New York: Teachers College Press.

Oakes, J., & Lipton, M. (1999). *Teaching to change the world.* Boston: McGraw Hill Publishers.

Oakes, J., Rogers, J., & Lipton, M. (2006). *Learning power: Organizing for education and justice.* New York: Teachers College Press.

Orfield, G., Losen, D., & Wald, J. (2004). *Losing our future: How minority youth are being left behind by the graduation rate crisi*s. Cambridge, MA: The Civil Rights Project at Harvard University, Contributors: Advocates for Children of New York, The Civil Society Institute.

Popkewitz, T., & Brennan, M. (1997). Restructuring of social and political theory in education: Foucault and a social epistemology of school practices. *Educational Theory, 47*(3), 287–313.

Quartz, K., & TEP Research Group. (2003). Too angry to leave: Supporting new teachers' commitment to transform urban schools. *Journal of teacher education, 54*(2), 99–111.

Rawls, J. (1971). *A theory of justice.* Cambridge, MA: Belknap Press of Harvard University Press.

Reich, R. (2002). *Bridging liberalism and multiculturalism in American education.* Chicago: Chicago University Press.

Seidl, B., & Friend, G. (2002). The unification of church and state: Working together to prepare teachers for diverse classrooms. *Journal of Teacher Education, 53*(2), 142–152.

Sleeter, C. (1989). Multicultural education as a form of resistance to oppression. *Journal of Education, 171*(3), 51–71.

Sleeter, C. (1995). Reflections on my use of multicultural and critical pedagogy when students are white. In C. Sleeter & P. McLaren (Eds.), *Multicultural education, critical pedagogy: The politics of difference*. Albany, NY: State University of New York Press.

Sleeter, C. (1996). *Multicultural education as social activism*. Albany: State University of New York Press.

Sleeter, C. (2001). Preparing teachers for culturally diverse schools: The overwhelming presence of whiteness. *Journal of teacher education, 52*(2), 94–106.

Sleeter, C. (2009). Teacher education, neoliberalism, and social justice. In W. Ayers, T. Quinn & D. Stovall (Eds.), *The handbook of social justice in education*. (pp. 611–624). Philadelphia: Taylor and Francis.

Sleeter, C. E., & McLaren, P. L. (1999). *Multicultural education, critical pedagogy, and the politics of difference*. Albany, NY: State University of New York Press.

Villegas, A. M. (1991). *Culturally responsive pedagogy for the 1990's and beyond*. Princeton, NJ: Educational Testing Service.

Villegas, A. (2007). Dispositions in teacher education: A look at social justice. *Journal of Teacher Education, 58*(5), 370–380.

Villegas, A. M., Clewell, B.-C., Anderson, M., Goertz, M. E., Joy, F., Bruschi, B. A., et al. (1995). *Teaching for diversity: Models for expanding the supply of minority teachers*. Princeton, NJ: ETS.

Villegas, A., & Davis, D. (2008). Preparing teachers of color to confront racial/ethnic disparities in educational outcomes. In M. Cochran-Smith, S. Feiman Nemser, J. McIntyre, & K. Demers (Eds.), *Handbook of research on teacher education: Enduring questions in changing contexts* (3rd ed.). Philadelphia: Taylor and Francis.

Villegas, A. M., & Lucas, T. (2002). *Educating culturally responsive teachers: A coherent approach*. Albany, NY: SUNY Press.

Villegas, A., & Lucas, T. (2004). Diversifying the teacher workforce: A retrospective and prospective account. In M. Smilie & D. Miretzky (Eds.), *Developing the teacher workforce: The 103rd yearbook of the national society for the study of education* (pp. 70–104). Chicago: University of Chicago Press.

Villegas, A., & Lucas, T. (2006). *Holding ourselves accountable: Assessing preservice teachers' development as culturally and linguistically responsive educators*. Paper for the Annual Meeting of the American Educational Research Association, April 2006, San Francisco.

Westheimer, J., & Kahne, J. (2004). Educating the 'good citizen': Political choices and pedagogical goals. *Political Science and Politics, XXXVII*(2), 241–247.

Westheimer, J., & Suurtamm, E. (2009). The politics of social justice meets practice: Teacher education and social change. In W. Ayers, T. Quinn, & D. Stovall (Eds.), *The handbook of social justice in education* (pp. 589–594). Philadelphia: Taylor and Francis.

Wideen, M., Mayer-Smith, J., & Moon, B. (1998). A critical analysis of the research on learning to teach: Making the case for an ecological perspective on inquiry. *Review of Educational Research, 68*(2), 130–178.

Wiedeman, C. (2002). Teacher preparation, social justice, equity: A review of the literature. *Equity and Excellence in Education, 35*(3), 200–211.

Witherell, C., & Noddings, N. (Eds.). (1991). *Stories lives tell*. New York, NY: Teachers College Press.

Young, I. M. (1990). *Justice and the politics of difference*. Princeton: Princeton University Press.

Zeichner, K. (1993). Connecting genuine teacher development to the struggle for social justice. *Journal of Education for Teaching, 19*(1), 5–20.

Zeichner, K. (2003). The adequacies and inadequacies of three current strategies to recruit, prepare, and retain the best teachers for all students. *Teachers College Record, 105*(3), 490–515.

Zeichner, K. (2006). Reflections of a university-based teacher educator on the future of college- and university-based teacher education. *Journal of Teacher Education, 57*(3), 326–340.

Zeichner, K., & Hoeft, K. (1996). Teacher socialization for cultural divetsity. In J. Sikula, T. J. Buttery & E. Guyton (Eds.), *Handbook of research on teacher education*. New York, NY, Macmillan: 525–547.

Connecting Learning Communities: Capacity Building for Systemic Change

Louise Stoll

Piecemeal educational reform is yesterday's news. The environment is characterised by increasingly rapid change and complexity. Meanwhile, intractable challenges of quality and equity persist in numbers of jurisdictions, and standards have plateaued in several systems promoting centralised strategies.

Using the same change strategies doesn't make sense, but many systems' models are still based on seventeenth-century scientific theories of simple cause and effect relationships and on trying to improve individual parts of the system. Many of these strategies have reached the limit of their effectiveness. Against a fast-moving backdrop, reformers in some countries have turned to messages from the new sciences that propose a world conception underpinned by webs of relationships with implications for focusing on interconnected systems (e.g., Capra, 1983; Wheatley, 2006). Because each individual part of the system is affected by others and individual actions have rippling effects on their environment, a holistic view is needed of what it will mean to improve any part of the system. In short, we're talking about systemic change.

Bringing about systemic change is a change in itself, and a major one at that. Sustainable change depends on an ongoing process of learning by individuals, singly and collectively. This means both better learning and learning in new ways. But it's not just learning. As parts of the system previously unreached are now as significant as those traditionally receiving all of the attention, people at all levels of the system need to learn. Different parts of the system must also be aligned to provide a coherent and consistent picture and strategy for change, and this means that people with diverse roles in the system have to connect and learn together. What we're talking about is connecting learning communities. Learning communities are inclusive, reflective, mutually supportive and collaborative groups of people who find ways inside and outside their immediate community to investigate and learn more about their practice in order to improve all students' learning. To have a system where the idea and practices of learning communities are the norm and where

L. Stoll (✉)
Institute of Education, University of London, London, UK
e-mail: l.stoll@ioe.ac.uk

A. Hargreaves et al. (eds.), *Second International Handbook of Educational Change*, 469
Springer International Handbooks of Education 23, DOI 10.1007/978-90-481-2660-6_28,
© Springer Science+Business Media B.V. 2010

learning communities connect with other learning communities doesn't just happen, capacity building is necessary.

In this chapter, I first define what I mean by capacity and capacity building, before exploring connected learning communities. I examine who needs to be involved and describe an example illustrating a connected learning community. Finally, I propose sets of learning processes and connecting conditions that appear to underlie capacity building for systemic change that is generated through connected learning communities.

Building Capacity

What makes schools, school systems and the people within them ongoing, capable learners? It requires going beyond identifying a number of different improvement-related capacities. Separating out capacities insufficiently captures the complexity, interconnectedness and potential of different facets of the change process, especially right now. Capacity has to be viewed as a more generic and holistic concept (Stoll, 1999). In relation to systemic educational change, it can be seen as *the power to engage in and sustain learning of people at all levels of the educational system for the collective purpose of enhancing student learning.* Capacity is a quality that allows people, individually and collectively, to routinely learn from the world around them and to apply this learning to new situations so that they can continue on a path towards their goals in an ever-changing context (Stoll & Earl, 2003). It also helps them to continuously improve learning and progress at all levels, but particularly and ultimately that of students such that their collective efficacy is enabling them to "raise the bar and close the gap of student learning for all students" (Fullan, 2006, p. 28). Capacity, therefore, is oriented towards making a difference for all students and in all aspects of learning (Delors et al., 1996). A system with capacity is also able to take charge of change because it is adaptive. In short, capacity lies at the root of success (Fullan, 2006).

Capacity exists at different levels: in individuals – personal capacity; in groups within organisations; and in whole organisations, whether schools, districts or departments/ministries of education. We've known for some time that successful educational reform depends on teachers' individual and collective capacity (e.g., Lieberman, 1995), school capacity (King & Newmann, 2001) and system capacity (Elmore, 2002). But the significance of the *mutually influencing and interdependent* nature of different levels (Mitchell & Sackney, 2000) has only more recently become clearer, and this is what matters most for systemic change. Essentially, capacity building has to attend to all levels simultaneously.

To bring about systemic change, capacity building has to be *multifaceted* (Fullan, 2006, p. 85) which comprises the following:

- creating and maintaining the necessary conditions, culture and structures;
- facilitating learning and skill-oriented experiences and opportunities; and

- ensuring interrelationships and synergy between all the component parts (Stoll & Bolam, 2005).

Connecting learning communities demonstrates the multifaceted nature of capacity building at work. Who do we mean when we refer to connecting learning communities?

Membership of Connecting Learning Communities

We all belong to different communities. They're generally held together by shared beliefs and understandings, interaction and participation, interdependence, concern for individual and minority views, and meaningful relationships through personal connections (Westheimer, 1999). Increasingly, communities aren't just face to face but also virtual, with soaring numbers of people connecting through social networking sites. Those involved tend to view the group as a collective enterprise and, as shared memory develops, it's passed on to newcomers. Collaboration is a norm for most communities. But communities don't have to be concerned with learning, so in considering capacity building for systemic change in education, those of particular interest are ones with learning at their core, as defined above. These communities focus on the learning of all of their members and, most especially, on enhancing learning for and of all children and young people.

Learning communities can be found at all levels of the educational system. Within schools there are classroom learning communities (Watkins, 2005), including those between students networked by technology (Brown & Campione, 1998; Scardamalia & Bereiter, 1994) that also provide opportunities for international online student learning conferences; communities among groups of teachers sharing and analysing their work (Little, 2002; McLaughlin & Talbert, 2006; Thompson & Wiliam, 2007), sometimes referred to as communities of practice (cf. Lave & Wenger, 1991); and communities operating at whole school level (e.g., Bolam, Stoll, & Greenwood, 2007; Louis, Kruse, & Associates, 1995), frequently known as professional learning communities, and sometimes including support staff (e.g., Bolam et al., 2007). Personnel in school districts also collaborate as enquiry and learning communities (e.g., Stoll & Temperley, 2009).

At the policy level, while knowledge is viewed as social, growing from previous ideas and relationships (Levin, 2007), the concept of policy learning communities is little articulated (Stoll, 2008). Scanning government websites, however, highlights cases of such activity. For example, the Ontario Ministry of Education's research coordination team, a Ministry-wide committee, has a specific remit to identify and respond to Ministry staff's own capacity-building needs by creating new opportunities for sharing knowledge and effective practices across the ministry as well as offering learning sessions for colleagues. Other communities exist within the educational system, for example, research communities, although the emphasis in university education departments has historically often been focused on individual achievement, tending to inhibit the kind of collaborative learning of interest here.

If each of these groups or organisations is viewed as a system, developing a thriving and challenging learning community offers the potential for positive change within any of these systems. However, it is when learning communities cross the boundaries of particular organisations or interest groups that systemic change on a broad scale is most likely. Any one group of stakeholders is likely to be insufficient to serve the needs of *all* students in diverse contexts, as well as bring about the changes required in a complex and fast-changing world. This suggests that a more divergent approach to the concept of professional learning communities is needed, one that includes systemic extensions with broader membership and involving divergent knowledge bases (Stoll & Louis, 2007). The term *professional learning communities* itself may come across as exclusive, even though it is intended to be inclusive.

From a social capital perspective, this means that *bonding* social capital – building trust and networks with people of similar demographic characteristics – is insufficient. *Bridging* social capital, while still horizontal in nature, extends links to others who don't share many of the same characteristics, whereas *linking* social capital (e.g., Grootaert, Narayan, Jones, & Woolcock, 2004) sees connections that are vertical in nature, operating across power differentials.

There are increasing numbers of examples of *bridging social capital*: through learning networks of teachers in different schools (Lieberman & Wood, 2001); between leaders of schools, both nationally and internationally (Stoll, Robertson, Butler-Kisber, Sklar & Whittingham, 2007); and between whole schools (Earl & Katz, 2006; Veugelers & O'Hair, 2005;), as well as many other collaborative arrangements established for a range of educational and financial reasons. Networking connections also exist between superintendents of different school districts, extending opportunities for members to co-construct new knowledge as they learn from experience and practice of peers elsewhere.

In many ways, learning networks, or networked learning communities, as they are sometimes known (e.g., Jackson & Temperley, 2007), are professional learning communities operating across a broader landscape. They share many commonalities with school-based professional learning communities and some similar goals. But their additional purposes include enlarging individual schools' repertoire of choices and moving ideas and good practice around the system in order to help transform the whole system, not just individual schools, thus improving education for *all* students. This lateral capacity building (Fullan, 2006) is a collective responsibility and moral purpose is writ large. Teacher learning benefits are well documented (e.g., Lieberman & Wood, 2001), but evidence is also emerging of links with student outcomes (e.g., Earl & Katz, 2006; Kaser & Halbert, 2005). The potential of learning networks' positive influence on the development of leadership capacity is also appealing at a time when succession planning is an issue in many countries due to impending retirements of large numbers of school principals (Pont, Nusche, & Moorman, 2008). While networked learning is seen to support sustainability (Hargreaves & Fink, 2006a), a strong internal professional learning community is still necessary because most new knowledge and learning gained through network experience is channelled back into schools where changed practice has its main impact (Earl & Katz, 2006).

Where *linking social capital* is concerned, a long research tradition has generally concentrated on what parents and the wider community can do for schools, although recent research presents a multidirectional perspective (Mulford, 2007). As greater numbers of multiagency communities are formed to address the social, health and well-being challenges that teachers clearly can't address alone (e.g., Cummings et al., 2007; Mitchell & Sackney, 2007), power issues need to be tackled head on, as people ask, "Whose community is this?" This suggests that a more fruitful approach might be to see this as bridging diverse partners of equal status. The relationship between learning and community becomes multifaceted (Stoll, Earl, & Fink, 2003) as well as multidirectional. Taking parents as an example, it's possible to see *learning of* community, where the school helps the parents support their children's learning and may help promote community development; *learning from* community, as they share their knowledge with the school; *learning with* community, as exemplified in schools that involve students, their parents and teachers in intergenerational dialogue; *learning for* community, to enhance relationships; and *learning as* community, that is, *deeply inclusive and broadly connected* and based on deep respect, collective responsibility, appreciation of diversity, a problem-solving orientation and positive role modelling (Mitchell & Sackney, 2007).

How can this multidirectional learning community relationship be applied to relationships between different stakeholder communities? The following example of the Austrian Leadership Academy (LEA, 2007) illustrates an attempt to build a connected learning community to build systemic capacity. It was selected as a case study during the OECD's Improving School Leadership activity (Pont et al., 2008) to illustrate innovative practice in leadership development. In 2004, the Austrian Minister of Education, Science, and Culture founded the academy, in association with the Universities of Innsbruck and Zurich. Its initial intent was to prepare school head teachers – who possessed newly acquired autonomy but had little experience in operating outside a hierarchical, bureaucratic structure – with the capacity to act more independently, take greater initiative and manage their schools through changes entailed by a stream of government reforms. Quickly, the benefits of involving a wider group of participants became apparent, and the Leadership Academy (LEA) began including district inspectors, staff of teacher training institutes and executives from the Ministry of Education and provincial education authorities. These participants learn together in four forums, where they are introduced through a range of creative pedagogical techniques to research on leadership for learning, school development and personal capacity, which they are invited to reflect on and explore. They also select and work with a learning partner and a collegial coaching team (3 pairs of learning partners) in and between the forums, focusing on a development problem that each person brings to the group. The change in relationships, attitudes and orientation to leadership for the vast majority of LEA participants has produced a groundswell at the various levels of the system where people have been involved – schools, districts, regions, teacher training institutes and parts of the Ministry. Ministry leaders who have participated for the most part find the programme and experience as powerful as their peers, some particularly valuing the connections they make with school and inspector colleagues (Stoll, Moorman, & Rahm, 2007). Involvement of the head of one Ministry Directorate had a particularly powerful effect on the system when he followed up his participation by replicating LEA learning processes with all of his Directorate staff.

This example represents an effort to build systemic capacity by developing learning and leadership connections across community boundaries. These communities – school leaders, district and regional leaders, Ministry leaders and leaders from teacher training institutes – are learning together and making the connections. So what kinds of learning processes and activities are developed in such connecting communities?

Learning Processes and Activities in Connecting Learning Communities

Learning communities engage in many joint activities. The focus here is on processes and activities oriented towards community learning. Individuals and groups need access to multiple sources of learning, but in connecting learning communities the social component of learning processes takes centre stage. Learning communities deconstruct knowledge through joint reflection and analysis, reconstructing it through collaborative action, and co-constructing it through collective learning from their experiences. Processes and activities involved are interconnected and can be construed in different ways. In this chapter, I have chosen to describe them as supported practice, collaborative inquiry, knowledge animation, joint planning and review, and meta-learning. At the heart of all of this activity are dialogue and learning conversations (see Fig. 1).

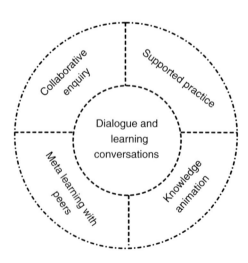

Fig. 1 Learning processes and activities

Dialogue and Learning Conversations

Dialogue is the key mechanism by which members of communities connect, not discussion or debate. Debate depends on the dominance of one position over another, while discussion avoids *undiscussables*, blocking true and honest communication (Bohm, 1985). Dialogue is a critical community process, although difficult to achieve, because all participants play equal roles, suspending their individual assumptions as they enter into a genuine *thinking together* (Senge, 1990). In connecting learning communities, dialogic processes are oriented towards articulating and exploring members' tacit knowledge (Nonaka & Takeuchi, 1995). Through dialogue, presuppositions, ideas and beliefs are brought to the surface, examined and challenged. Collective intelligence is harnessed, and new ideas and practices are created as initial knowledge is enhanced or transformed.

Learning conversations involve dialogue, but the learning goal is more overt. A learning conversation in connecting learning communities can be seen as a planned and systematic approach to professional dialogue that supports community members to reflect on their practice. As a result, they gain new knowledge, which they use to improve their practice (definition adapted from GTC, 2004). Reflection on process is intentionally built in. Learning conversations typically feature questioning and active listening.

Both dialogue and learning conversations are fundamental to the process of connecting learning communities. When operating at their optimum level, the following learning processes and activities all feature genuine dialogue and actively promote learning conversations.

Supported Practice

New ways of learning don't come easily: learning means coming to terms with different ideas and ways of doing things. This usually necessitates trying something out again and again, tinkering (Huberman, 1983), working at it, feeling uncomfortable for a while, and experiencing new responses. A systematic review of evidence on the effect of sustained, collaborative continuing professional development on teaching and learning highlights benefits of peer support to teachers' practice (Cordingley, Bell, Rundell, & Evans, 2003). Learning and teaching are strengthened when teachers support each other in examining new methods, questioning ineffective practices and supporting each other's growth (Little, 2005), for example, through focused peer observation and feedback across communities, coaching and mentoring. In connecting learning communities, particularly those involving stakeholders with diverse knowledge bases and skills, supported practice is likely to be enhanced by different partners bringing an open mind to the process, acting as critical friends (Costa & Kallick, 1993) and asking challenging but supportive questions that lead their partner to reflect deeply on their practice.

Collaborative Inquiry

Collaborative inquiry is a key learning process, where learning and inquiry are facilitated, encouraged, challenged and co-constructed (Jackson & Street, 2005). Inquiry can be the means by which teachers identify important issues related to learning, become self-regulated drivers for acquiring the necessary knowledge to solve the issues, monitor the impact and adjust practice as necessary (Timperley, Wilson, Barrar, & Fung, 2008). As a basis for professional learning, inquiry builds teachers' knowledge of their own practice (Cochran-Smith & Lytle, 2001). Here, colleagues from different schools, agencies or other stakeholder groups throughout the system decide on a common issue as an inquiry focus and commit to exploring this together using common methodology. Sometimes, they gather data in their own site, while, at other times, they collect data from each other's sites before analysing the data jointly. Collaborative review activities, such as moderating samples of students' work across sites, or reviewing support for students and their families across a whole community partnership, also provide data for such analysis.

Evidence-based dialogue carried out in a spirit of inquiry has the potential to promote powerful professional learning, because as people engage in conversations about what evidence means new knowledge can emerge as they come across new ideas or discover that ideas that they believe to be true don't hold up when under scrutiny; this recognition is used as an opportunity to rethink what they know and do (Earl & Timperley, 2008). Such collaborative inquiry skills are new for many educators, which means investing time and expert support in their development (Earl & Katz, 2006).

Knowledge Animation

Sharing knowledge between different communities – including learning experiences, the findings of collaborative inquiry and other research – can be challenging. What makes sense to and works well for one community may not easily translate, and yet a core activity of connecting learning communities is sharing knowledge that might help enhance others' practice. Ways are needed to bring knowledge to life such that others can engage with the ideas, locate them within their context and in relation to prior experiences and learning, make meaning and construct new knowledge from them that can be used to develop their practice. This learning is social as learners test the veracity of their beliefs and knowledge by comparing them to the beliefs and knowledge of others, and together they relate this to other external knowledge, processing it jointly and thereby creating new knowledge. A model of three fields of knowledge from England's National College for School Leadership's networked learning communities (NCSL, 2006) programme captures this relationship (see Fig. 2).

I describe this process of connections as *knowledge animation*. The word *animate* comes from the Latin word *anima*, which means breath, life or soul. Animate

Fig. 2 Three fields of
knowledge

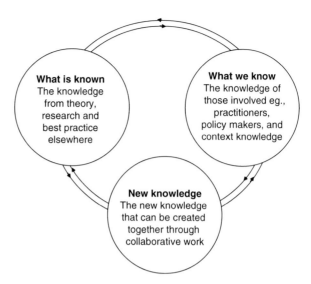

means to bring to life, put in motion. It suggests action and movement, dynamism and vibrancy, and invigoration and innovation. The focus of knowledge animation is helping people learn and use knowledge generated elsewhere and, through it, create valuable new knowledge (Stoll, 2008). It is more than just dissemination. Knowledge animation can be seen as ways of making knowledge accessible and mobile to help people make the necessary learning connections that enable them to put knowledge to use in their contexts. As learning communities generate knowledge, they want to share; they need to be thinking of knowledge animation strategies that will help others make the necessary *learning connections*, also ensuring that they engage in quality assurance processes so they do not share mediocre practice. Knowledge animation is also a way that the research community can connect with practitioner and policy communities.

Meta-Learning with Peers

Members of learning communities need to understand their own learning and internalise learning as a *habit of mind*. Meta-learning (Watkins, Carnell, Lodge, Wagner, & Whalley, 1998) not only means each member of a community demonstrating that they are a learner, but also engaging in in-depth learning about their own learning: their goals, strategies, feelings, effects and contexts of learning. In particular, in connecting learning communities, it means taking time to focus together on what all of the diverse members understand about their collective learning and knowledge creation, the conditions that support these and what these mean for the way they collaborate.

Conditions Supporting Learning Community Connections

Processes and activities that connecting learning communities engage in depend
on the right supporting conditions to motivate and sustain them. Here, I focus on
three key conditions – a common culture, trusting and respectful relationships and
supportive structures – and a fourth overarching one, leadership (see Fig. 3).

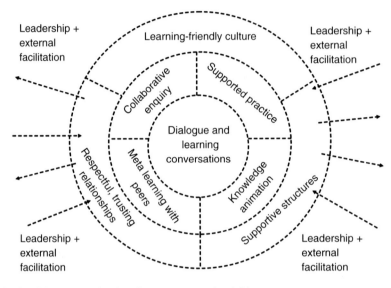

Fig. 3 Conditions supporting learning processes and activities

A Common Culture

Communities' values and beliefs play a major role in how they see themselves and
operate, the norms of acceptable behaviour and practice and even the language they
use to express themselves. Lave and Wenger (1991) propose that when learning in
communities of practice, participants gradually absorb and are absorbed in a *culture of practice*, giving them exemplars that lead to shared meanings, a sense of
belonging and increased understanding. The kind of deep learning processes on
which learning communities depend are best supported and nurtured in a culture
that values such processes and creates opportunities for them to occur. This requires
two shifts in mindset and expectation at all levels of the system: first, that engaging
in collaborative learning is not just other people's business – everyone must keep
learning, and second, that whenever people are learning, they are not only learning
for themselves but also on behalf of others (NCSL, 2006) – this is the commitment
to a wider moral purpose that characterises a systemic approach.

A challenging issue when different learning communities connect is coming to
common understandings because the communities often use different language. So,
while educators tend to see a child as a *learner*, for parents he or she is *my child*,

whilst social workers may see an *abused child* and health workers tend to see a *patient*. This creates opportunities for misunderstanding and conflict as learning communities consider the purposes for and focus of their collaboration and when they are implementing plans. Openness to learning about other communities is therefore essential; unless people make the effort to understand where others are coming from, the potential of connecting learning communities is unlikely to be realised.

Trusting, Respectful and Equal Relationships

Connecting learning communities is a human and emotional enterprise with the associated complexity of bringing about change. Developing social capital depends on positive relationships (Field, 2003), and working together productively requires collegiality and interdependence between people that allows serious challenge and adjustment of practice. Earl and Katz (2006) have described learning networks as "rigorous and challenging joint work". While personal friendships aren't necessary, dysfunctional relationships clearly have a negative effect. Each person needs to feel that they are a valued participant with something to offer (Mitchell & Sackney, 2007). Without a climate of trust and respect, people don't feel safe to take the risks associated with collaboration, open dialogue and opening up their practice to potential scrutiny by others. Equality is also important in the orientation to learning processes; for example, how coaching group members involved in the Austrian Leadership Academy rotated roles such that no one person became the sole expert. Coaching therefore becomes an equal partnership where both parties learn (Robertson, 2008).

Social trust among members of staff has been found to be the strongest facilitator of professional community within schools (Bryk, Camburn, & Louis, 1999). A base level of such trust seems necessary for learning communities to emerge. In networks and online communities, collaborative relationships appear to build trust and respect, essential for willingness to collaborate, risk taking and the exchange and development of ideas (Kahne, O'Brien, Brown, & Quinn, 2001). This becomes particularly important in contexts where schools have been used to a climate of competition and also seems to be predicated on networks involving voluntary participation and collaboration. Building trust across diverse communities can be even more challenging where hostile perceptions of other groups may have previously prevailed. Trusting relationships are insufficient on their own, but the evidence appears overwhelming that they are essential to connect learning communities if there is to be any chance of success.

Supportive Structures

Structures shape organisations' capacity to develop learning communities. At their best, structures enable better and deeper communication between members of learning communities. While coordination, communication mechanisms, joint governance structures and collaborative plans are all important, I have chosen here to focus on two particular structures, time and space.

Time is a critical resource for any meaningful learning (Stoll et al., 2003). Talk, exchange about and joint reflection on professional issues are key elements of the collaborative activity necessary to develop and connect learning communities. These require time, which doesn't only mean being able to cover staff who engage in network activities, including visiting other schools or attending meetings in the local community, but how any of the organisations involved plan and organise their time such that learning with and from communities beyond them can be fed back into their internal learning community and reconstructed to create new knowledge appropriate to their context and needs. The challenge is to find creative ways to deal with the perennial challenges of time, or else learning community activities just become an *add on* to an already overloaded agenda. In the Austrian example, time was allocated for the learning and networking sessions, although some participants talked of challenges of finding time and efforts to structure in time to follow up outside these sessions.

Space can also be a facilitating condition, and one with interesting shifts in meaning. In schools, professional exchange is facilitated by physical proximity (e.g., Louis et al., 1995), for example, teachers in a department having neighbouring classrooms and interdependent teaching roles, such as team teaching and joint planning. In learning networks, the need for equality and equal access between partners suggests that meetings and school and classroom visits should be rotated around schools, whilst similar concerns in extended learning communities implies that meetings should either be rotated around the different community partner locations, for example, schools, health centres or police stations, or held within neutral community locations such as community centres or coffee shops. Coffee houses were known in the eighteenth century as locations for stimulating and sociable conversations, offering a combination of both intimate and private spaces as well as ones that were public and open to speakers of all status, wealth or power (Ellis, 2004). In the coffee house, everyone's contributions were treated as equal.

Community space now includes the virtual space through which networks of users of the internet connect and communicate. In this world of mass collaboration through *wikinomics*, democratic networks of individuals are sharing, adapting and updating knowledge (Tapscott & Williams, 2008). The internet also provides a connecting communication mechanism when time to meet is hard to find. Essentially, connecting learning communities means rethinking the meaning of *location* and *space*.

Leadership and External Facilitation

Leadership provides the energy source; it is the umbrella within which all other conditions and processes of connecting learning communities fit. Communities depend on key individuals' involvement to keep processes going and facilitate enabling conditions. In learning communities within, between and beyond schools, leadership isn't just the realm of senior leaders in organisations, although their commitment is important (e.g., Bolam et al., 2005; Earl & Katz, 2006). Rather, the evidence points to the importance of distributed leadership, reciprocal leadership actions of people at different levels and from various stakeholders. Distributed leadership and empowerment, important for professional learning communities within schools (Hargreaves & Fink, 2006b), also contribute to success of learning networks (Hopkins, 2003; Wohlstetter, Malloy, Chau, & Polhemus, 2003), with decisions being taken at the place of greatest action. Taking distributed leadership seriously means being committed to collective responsibility.

Leadership is a facilitator, but external facilitation and support for connecting learning communities can also make a difference, as the example highlights. External agents may bring specialist expertise as mediators of community dialogue, or supporting networks' inquiry efforts, for example, by helping members interpret and use data (Lee, 2008). Facilitation takes on a particularly significant role in networks and networked learning communities and can be key to success (Wohlstetter et al., 2003).

Conclusion

Systemic capacity building depends on harnessing and channelling collective energy. It means paying attention to developing deep and positive learning relationships within and across different levels of the system and connecting educators with communities and agencies whose interests or remits go beyond education but who, fundamentally, share a common interest in the present and future well-being and success of children and young people. Such collaborative, connected learning can be extremely powerful, as common understandings and shared knowledge are co-constructed, but this depends on serious and equal participation of members of diverse communities. Such collective commitment and openness takes time and effort to develop, but is essential if learning communities are to connect meaningfully and achieve systemic change.

Acknowledgements With grateful thanks to Lorna Earl and Julie Temperley who commented on an earlier draft.

References

Bohm, D. (1985). *Unfolding meaning*. New York: Doubleday.

Bolam, R., McMahon, A., Stoll, L., Thomas, S., & Wallace, M. with Greenwood, A., Hawkey, K., Ingram, M., Atkinson, A., & Smith, M. (2005). *Creating and sustaining effective professional learning communities*. Research Report 637. London DfES and University of Bristol.

Bolam, R., Stoll, L., & Greenwood, A. (2007). The involvement of support staff in professional learning communities. In L. Stoll & K. S. Louis (Eds.), *Professional learning communities: Divergence, depth and dilemmas*. Maidenhead and New York: Open University Press/McGraw-Hill Education.

Brown, A. L., & Campione, J. C. (1998). Designing a community of young learners: Theoretical and practical lessons. In N. M. Lambert & B. L. McCombs (Eds.), *How students learn: Reforming schools through learner-centered education*. Washington, DC: American Psychological Association.

Bryk, A., Camburn, E., & Louis, K. S. (1999). Professional community in Chicago elementary schools: Facilitating factors and organizational consequences. *Educational Administration Quarterly, 35*(Supplement), 751–781.

Capra, F. (1983). *The turning point: Science, society and the rising culture*. London: Flamingo.

Cochran-Smith, M., & Lytle, S. L. (2001). Beyond certainty: Taking an inquiry stance on practice. In A. Lieberman & L. Miller (Eds.), *Teacher caught in the action: Professional development that matters*. New York: Teachers College Press.

Cordingley, P., Bell, M., Rundell, B., & Evans, D. (2003). The impact of collaborative cpd on classroom teaching and learning. In: *Research evidence in education library*. Version 1.1. London: EPPI-Centre, Social Science Research Unit, Institute of Education

Costa, A. L., & Kallick, B. (1993). Through the lens of a critical friend. *Educational Leadership, 51*(2), 49–51.

Cummings, C., Dyson, A., Muijs, D., Papps, I., Persona, D., Raffa, C., et al. (2007). *Evaluation of the full service extended schools initiative: Final report*. RR 852. Nottingham: DfES.

Delors, J., Al Mufti, I., Amagi, A., Carneiro, R., Chung, F., Geremek, B., et al. (1996). *Learning: The treasure within – Report to UNESCO of the international commission on education for the twenty-first century*. Paris: UNESCO.

Earl, L., & Katz, S. (2006). *How networked learning communities work*. Centre for strategic education seminar Series Paper No. 155. Jolimont, Victoria: CSE.

Earl, L., & Timperley, H. (Eds.). (2008). *Professional learning conversations: Challenges in using evidence for improvement*. Dordrecht: Springer.

Ellis, M. (2004). *The coffee house: A cultural history*. London: Weidenfeld & Nicholson.

Elmore, R. (2002). *Bridging the gap between standards and achievement*. Washington, DC: Albert Shanker Institute.

Field, J. (2003). *Social capital*. London: Routledge.

Fullan, M. (2006). *Turnaround leadership*. San Francisco: Jossey-Bass.

Grootaert, C., Narayan, D., Jones, V., & Woolcock, M. (2004). *Measuring social capital*, Working paper no. 18. Washington, DC: The World Bank.

GTC. (2004). *The learning conversation: Talking together for professional development*. Birmingham: General Teaching Council for England.

Hargreaves, A., & Fink, D. (2006a). *Sustainable leadership*. San Francisco: Jossey-Bass.

Hargreaves, A., & Fink, D. (2006b). Redistributed leadership for sustainable professional learning communities. *Journal of School Leadership, 16*(5), 550–565.

Hopkins, D. (2003). Understanding networks for innovation in policy and practice. In OECD (Ed.), *Networks of innovation: Towards new models for managing schools and systems*. Paris: OECD.

Huberman, M. (1983). Recipes for busy kitchens: A situational analysis of routine knowledge use in schools. *Knowledge: Creation, Diffusion, Utilization, 4*(4), 475–510.

Jackson, D., & Street, H. (2005). Introduction. In H. Street & J. Temperley (Eds.), *Improving schools through collaborative enquiry*. London: Continuum.

Jackson, D., & Temperley, J. (2007). From professional learning community to networked learning community. In L. Stoll & K. S Louis (Eds.), *Professional learning communities: Divergence, depth and dilemmas*. Maidenhead and New York: Open University Press/McGraw-Hill Education.

Kahne, J., O'Brien, J., Brown, A., & Quinn, T. (2001). Leverage, social capital and school improvement: The case of a school network and a comprehensive community initiative. *Educational Administration Quarterly, 37*(4), 429–461.

Kaser, L., & Halbert, J. (2005). *What is the inquiry network in BC learning from rural schools?* Paper presented at the annual conference of the International Congress for School Effectiveness and Improvement (ICSEI), Barcelona, January.

King, M. B., & Newmann, F. M. (2001). Building school capacity through professional development: Conceptual and empirical considerations. *The International Journal of Educational Management, 15*(2), 86–93.

Lave, J., & Wenger, E. (1991). *Situated learning: Legitimate peripheral participation.* Cambridge: Cambridge University Press.

LEA. (2007). *Leadership academy: Generation I executive summary.* bm: ukk. www.leadershipacademy.at/index.en.php

Lee, L. E. (2008). Honey, wooden spoons and clay pots: The evolution of a Lithuanian learning conversation. In L. Earl & H. Timperley (Eds.), *Professional learning conversations: Challenges in using evidence for improvement.* Dordrecht: Springer.

Levin, B. (2007). *Knowledge for action in education research and policy: What we know, what we don't know and what we need to do.* Paper presented at the German Ministry EU Conference on Knowledge for Action in Education Research and Policy, March.

Lieberman, A. (1995, April). Practices that support teacher development: Transforming conceptions of professional learning. *Phi Delta Kappan, 76*(8), 591–596.

Lieberman, A., & Wood, D. (2001). When teachers write: Of networks and learning. In A. Lieberman, & L. Miller (Eds.), *Teacher caught in the action: Professional development that matters.* New York: Teachers College Press.

Little, J. W. (2002). Locating learning in teachers' communities of practice: Opening up problems of analysis in records of everyday work. *Teaching and Teacher Education, 18*(8), 918–946.

Little, J. W. (2005). *Nodes and nets: Investigating resources for professional learning in schools and networks.* Unpublished paper. Nottingham: NCSL.

Louis, K. S., Kruse, S. D., & Associates. (1995). *Professionalism and community: Perspectives on reforming urban schools.* Thousand Oaks, CA: Corwin Press Inc.

McLaughlin, M. W., & Talbert, J. E. (2006). *Building school-based teacher learning communities: Professional strategies to improve student achievement.* New York: Teachers College Press.

Mitchell, C., & Sackney, L. (2000). *Profound improvement: Building capacity for a learning community.* Lisse, The Netherlands: Swets & Zeitlinger.

Mitchell, C., & Sackney, L. (2007). Extending the learning community: A broader perspective embedded in policy. In L. Stoll & K. S Louis (Eds.), *Professional learning communities: Divergence, depth and dilemmas.* Maidenhead and New York: Open University Press/McGraw-Hill Education.

Mulford, B. (2007). Building social capital in professional learning communities: Importance, challenges and a way forward. In L. Stoll & K. S Louis (Eds.), *Professional learning communities: Divergence, depth and dilemmas.* Maidenhead and New York: Open University Press/McGraw-Hill Education.

NLC. (2006). *Learning about learning networks.* Nottingham: NCSL.

Nonaka, I., & Takeuchi, H. (1995). *The knowledge creating company: How japanese, companies create the dynamics of innovation.* New York: Oxford University Press.

Pont, B., Nusche, D., & Moorman, H. (2008). *Improving school leadership: Volume 1 – Policy and practice.* Paris: OECD.

Robertson, J. (2008). *Coaching educational leadership building leadership capacity through partnership.* London: SAGE Publications Ltd.

Scardamalia, M., & Bereiter, C. (1994). Computer support for knowledge-building communities. *Journal of the Learning Sciences, 3*(3): 265–283.

Senge, P. M. (1990). *The fifth discipline: The art and practice of the learning organization.* London: Century Business.

Stoll, L. (1999). Realising our potential: Understanding and developing capacity for lasting improvement. *School effectiveness and school improvement, 10*(4), 503–532.

Stoll, L. (2008). Leadership and policy learning communities: Promoting knowledge animation. In B. Chakroun & P. Sahlberg (Eds.), *Policy learning in action: ETF yearbook 2008.* Torino, Italy: European Training Foundation.

Stoll, L., & Bolam, R. (2005). Developing leadership for learning communities. In M. Coles & G. Southworth (Eds.), *Developing leadership: Creating the schools of tomorrow.* Maidenhead: Open University Press.

Stoll, L., & Earl, L. (2003). Making it last: Building capacity for sustainability. In B. Davies & J. West-Burnham (Eds.), *The handbook of educational leadership and management*. London: Pearson Education.

Stoll, L., Fink, D., & Earl, L. (2003). *It's about learning (and it's about time)*. London: RoutledgeFalmer.

Stoll, L., & Louis, K. S. (2007). *Professional learning communities: Divergence, depth and dilemmas*. Maidenhead and New York: Open University Press/McGraw-Hill Education.

Stoll, L., Moorman, H., & Rahm, S. (2007). School leadership development strategies: The Austrian leadership academy, a case study report for the OECD improving school leadership activity. In D. Pont, D. Nusche, & D. Hopkins (Eds.), *Improving school leadership volume 2: Case studies on system leadership*. Paris: OECD.

Stoll, L., Robertson, J., Butler-Kisber, L., Sklar, S, & Whittingham, T. (2007). Beyond borders: Can international networks deepen professional learning community? In L. Stoll & K. S. Louis (Eds.), *Professional learning communities: Divergence, depth and dilemmas*. Maidenhead/New York: Open University Press/McGraw-Hill Education.

Stoll, L., & Temperley, J. (2009). Creative leadership: A challenge of our times? *School Leadership and Management, 29*(1), 65–78.

Tapscott, D., & Williams, A. D. (2008). *Wikinomics: How mass collaboration changes everything* (revised ed.). London: Atlantic Books.

Timperley, H., Wilson, A., Barrar, H., & Fung, I. (2008). *Teacher professional learning and development: Best evidence synthesis iteration (BES)*. New Zealand: Ministry of Education and the University of Auckland.

Thompson, M., & Wiliam, D. (2007). *Tight but loose: A conceptual framework for scaling up school reforms*. Paper presented at the annual meeting of the American Educational Research Association, Chicago, April.

Veugelers, W., & O'Hair, M. J. (Eds.). (2005). *Network learning for educational change*. Maidenhead: Open University Press/McGraw-Hill Education.

Watkins, C. (2005). *Classrooms as learning communities: What's in it for schools?* Abingdon: Routledge.

Watkins, C., Carnell, E, Lodge, C., Wagner, P., & Whalley, C. (1998). *Learning about learning*. Coventry: National Association for Pastoral Care in Education.

Westheimer, J. (1999). Communities and consequences: An inquiry into ideology and practice in teachers' professional work. *Educational Administration Quarterly, 35*(1), 71–105.

Wheatley, M. (2006). *Leadership and the new science: Discovering order in a chaotic world*. San Francisco, CA: Berrett-Koehler.

Wohlstetter, P., Malloy, C. L., Chau, D., & Polhemus, J. (2003). Improving schools through networks: A new approach to urban school reform. *Educational Policy, 17*(4), 399–430.

International Comparisons of Student Learning Outcomes

Andreas Schleicher

Parents, students and those who teach and run education systems seek good information on how well their education systems prepare students for life. Most countries monitor students' learning in order to provide answers to this question. Comparative international assessments can extend and enrich the national picture by providing a larger context within which to interpret national performance. They have gained prominence, over recent years, since the benchmarks for public policy in education are no longer solely national goals or standards, but increasingly the performance of the most successful education systems internationally. International assessments can provide countries with information that allows them to identify areas of relative strengths and weaknesses and monitor the pace of progress of their education system. They can also stimulate countries to raise aspirations by showing what is possible in education, in terms of the quality, equity and efficiency of educational services provided elsewhere, and they can foster better understanding of how different education systems address similar problems.

Following a brief introduction to the history of international assessments, the chapter sets out the potential that international assessments offer for educational policy and practice as well as some of the challenges they face in providing valid, comparable and reliable evidence.

International Assessments

History

While efforts to compare education systems internationally can be traced back to the early-nineteenth century (e.g. Jullien, 1817), the discourse on international comparisons of learning outcomes started to emerge during the 1950s and 1960s. In 1958, an expert group led by William Douglas Wall and including prominent

A. Schleicher (✉)
Organisation for Economic Co-operation and Development, Paris, France
e-mail: andreas.schleicher@oecd.org

researchers such as Benjamin Bloom, Robert Thorndike, Arthur Wellesley Foshay, Arnold Anderson, Gaston Mialaret and Torsten Husen met under the auspices of UNESCO's International Institute of Education in Hamburg to launch a feasibility study to compare student performance internationally. The feasibility study involved 12,000 13-year-olds in 12 countries and its results were published in 1962 (Foshay, Thorndike, Hotyat, Pidgeon, & Walker, 1962). The International Association for the Evaluation of Educational Achievement (IEA) emerged out of this collaboration which then conducted a series of international assessments (see Table 3). The most prominent regular surveys conducted by the IEA are now the 4-yearly Trends in Mathematics and Science Study (TIMSS) and the 5-yearly Progress in Reading Literacy Study (PIRLS).

In 1988 the Education Testing Service in the United States conducted the International Assessment of Educational Progress (IAEP) (Lapointe, Mead, & Phillips, 1989) and a follow-up study in 1991 (Lapointe, Mead, & Askew, 1992).

The latest generation of international assessments has been developed by the Organisation for Economic Co-operation and Development (OECD) as part of the Programme for International Student Assessment (PISA). PISA surveys have been conducted every 3 years since 2000 in key content areas such as reading, mathematics and science, but they also cover cross-curricular domains such as problem-solving as well as a range of non-cognitive outcomes. PISA is one of the most rigorous and comprehensive assessments, not least in terms of its geographic coverage, with the latest survey in 2006 testing over 400,000 students who represented more than 20 million 15-year-olds in 60 countries that made up close to 90% of the world economy.

Research Frameworks of International Assessments

OECD and IEA assessments seek to contextualise measures of student learning outcomes with background information collected from students, school principals and sometimes teachers and parents in order to interpret the observed variation in learning outcomes between students, classrooms, schools and education systems. To facilitate this, they operate with research frameworks that provide data at up to four levels of the education system, namely

(i) the education system as a whole;
(ii) the educational institutions and providers of educational services;
(iii) the classrooms or instructional setting and
(iv) the learners themselves (see Table 1).

The research frameworks address different classes of research areas:

(1) A first class relates to comparing learning outcomes at each of the four levels.
(2) The second class provides information on the policy levers or circumstances which shape the outputs and outcomes at each level of the education system.

Table 1 Research frameworks for international assessments

	(1) Education and learning outputs and outcomes	(2) Policy levers and contexts shaping educational outcomes	(3) Antecedents or constraints that contextualise policy
(I) Individual participants in education and learning	(1.I) The quality and distribution of individual educational outcomes	(2.I) Individual attitudes, engagement and behaviour	(3.I) Background characteristics of the individual learners
(II) Instructional settings	(1.II) The quality of instructional delivery	(2.II) Curriculum, pedagogy and learning practices and classroom climate	(3.II) Student learning conditions and teacher working conditions
(III) Providers of educational services	(1.III) The output of educational institutions and institutional performance	(2.III) School environment and organisation	(3.III) Characteristics of the service providers and their communities
(IV) The education system as a whole	(1.IV) The overall performance of the education system	(2.IV) System-wide institutional settings, resource allocations and policies	(3.IV) The national educational, social, economic and demographic contexts

This includes, for example, measures of attitudes and behaviours at the level of students, measures of student learning and teacher working conditions and human and material resources at the level of instructional settings and institutions and measures of structures and resource allocation policies and practices at the level of the education system. These policy levers and contexts typically have antecedents – factors that define or constrain policy, and which are represented in a third class of research areas.

(3) This third class which, for example, provides information on the socio-economic context of students, schools or systems is particularly important in an international comparative context, as it allows to ensure "like with like" comparisons, that is comparisons of schools that have a similar socio-economic intake or countries that operate under similar socio-economic conditions.

Each of the cells resulting from cross-classifying the above two dimensions can then be used to address a variety of research issues from different perspectives relating, for example, to the quality of educational outcomes and educational provision; to issues of equality of educational outcomes and equity in educational opportunities; or to the adequacy, effectiveness and efficiency of resource management. Subsequent sections of this chapter will illustrate the application of this framework.

The Potential of International Assessments for Policy and Practice

The design and conduct of international assessments was originally motivated by research objectives. More recently, governments too have begun to attribute growing importance to international assessments and have invested considerable resources into their development and implementation. This interest derives from several considerations:

- By revealing what is possible in education in terms of the performance levels demonstrated in the best performing countries, international assessments can enhance the quality of existing policies but also create a debate about the paradigms and beliefs underlying policies.
- While international assessments alone cannot identify cause-and-effect relationships between inputs, processes and educational outcomes, they can shed light on key features in which education systems show similarities and differences, and make those key features visible for educators, policy makers and the general public.
- International assessments can also help to set policy targets in terms of measurable goals achieved by other systems and help to identify policy levers and establish trajectories as well as delivery chains for reform.
- International assessments can assist with gauging the pace of educational progress and help reviewing the reality of educational delivery at the frontline.
- Last but not least, international assessments can support the political economy of educational reform, which is a major issue in education where any pay-off to reform almost inevitably accrues to successive governments if not generations.

Some of these issues are examined more closely in the remainder of this section.

Revealing What Is Possible in Education and Identifying Factors that Contribute to Educational Success

International assessments seem to impact more on countries whose performance is comparatively low (Hopkins, Pennock, & Ritzen, 2008). Although it is sometimes argued that weighing the pig does not make it fatter, diagnosing underweight can be an important first step towards therapy. Also, the level of public awareness rose by international comparisons, has in some countries created an important political momentum and engaged educational stakeholders, including teacher or/and employer organisations, in support of policy reform.

Equally important, international assessments have had a significant impact in some countries that did not do poorly in absolute terms, but that found themselves confronted with results that differed from how educational performance was generally perceived. In Germany, for example, equity in learning opportunities across schools had often been taken for granted, as significant efforts were devoted to ensuring that schools are adequately and equitably resourced. The PISA 2000 results, however, revealed large socio-economic disparities in educational outcomes between schools. Further analyses that separated equity-related issues between those that relate to the socio-economic heterogeneity within schools and those that relate to socio-economic segregation through the school system suggested that German students from more privileged social backgrounds are directed into the more prestigious academic schools which yield superior educational outcomes while students from less privileged social backgrounds are directed into less prestigious vocational schools which yield poorer educational outcomes, even where their performance on the PISA assessment was similar. This raised the spectre that the German education system was reinforcing rather than moderating socio-economic background factors. Such results, and the ensuing public debate, inspired a wide range of equity-related reform efforts in Germany, some of which have been transformational in nature. These include giving early-childhood education, which had hitherto been considered largely an aspect of social welfare, an educational orientation and better institutionalising early-childhood provision; establishing national educational standards for schools in a country where regional and local autonomy had long been the overriding paradigm; or enhancing the support for disadvantaged students, such as students with a migration background.

For many educators and experts in Germany, the socio-economic disparities that PISA revealed were unsurprising. However, it was often taken for granted and outside the scope of public policy that disadvantaged children would fare less well in school. The fact that PISA revealed that the impact which socio-economic background has on students and school performance varied considerably across countries, and that other countries appeared to moderate socio-economic disparities much more effectively, showed that improvement was possible and provided the momentum for policy change.

Showing that strong educational performance and improvement are possible seems to be two of the most important aspects of international assessments. Whether in Asia (like in Japan, Korea or Singapore), in Europe (like in Finland or in the Netherlands) or in North America (like in Canada), many countries display strong overall performance in international assessments and, equally important, some of these countries also show that poor performance in school does not automatically follow from a disadvantaged socio-economic background. Last but not least, some countries show that success can become a consistent and predictable educational outcome: In Finland for example, the country with the strongest overall results in PISA, the performance variation between schools amounted in 2006 to only 5% of students' overall performance variation. So parents could rely on high and consistent performance standards in whatever school they choose to enrol their children. Considerable research has been invested into the features of these education systems. In some countries, governments have used knowledge provided by PISA as a starting point for a peer review to study policies and practices in countries operating under similar context that achieve better results (Döbert, Klieme, & Sroka, 2004). Such peer reviews, each resulting in a set of specific policy recommendations for educational improvement, are also being carried out by the OECD, the results of which have been published so far for Denmark and Scotland (OECD, 2004, 2007).

As a result, the benchmarks for public policy in education are no longer national goals or standards alone, but increasingly the performance of the most successful education systems internationally. International assessments have at times raised awareness which led to a public debate about education, with citizens recognising that their countries' educational performance will not simply need to match average performance, but that they will need to do better if their children want to justify above-average wages.

Putting National Targets into a Broader Perspective

International assessments can also play an important role in putting national performance targets into perspective. Educators are often faced with the following dilemma: If, at the national level, the percentage of students achieving good exam scores in school increases, some will claim that the school system has improved. Others will claim that standards must have been lowered, and behind the suspicion that better results reflect lowered standards is often a belief that overall performance in education cannot be raised. International assessments allow those perceptions to be related to a wider reference framework, by allowing schools and education systems to compare themselves with schools and education systems in other countries. Some countries have actively embraced this perspective and systematically related national performance to international assessments, for example, by embedding components of the PISA or TIMSS assessments into their national assessments.

Assessing the Pace of Change in Educational Improvement

A third important aspect is that international comparisons provide a frame of reference to assess the pace of change in educational development. While a national framework allows progress to be assessed in absolute terms, an internationally comparative perspective allows an assessment of whether that progress matches the pace of change observed elsewhere. Indeed, while all education systems in the OECD area have seen quantitative growth over past decades, international comparisons reveal that the pace of change in educational output has varied markedly. For example, among 55–64-year-olds, the United States is well ahead of all other OECD countries in terms of the proportion of individuals with both school and university qualifications. However, international comparisons show that this advantage is largely a result of the "first-mover advantage" which the United States had gained after Word War II by massively increasing enrolments. It has eroded over last decades as more and more countries have reached and surpassed qualification levels in the United States in more recent cohorts. While many countries are now close to ensuring that virtually all young adults leave schools with at least a high school qualification, which the OECD benchmarks highlight as the baseline qualification for reasonable earnings and employment prospects, the United States stood still on this measure and among OECD countries only New Zealand, Spain, Turkey and Mexico now have lower secondary school completion rates than the United States (OECD, 2008). By contrast, two generations ago, South Korea had the economic output equivalent to that of Afghanistan today and was at rank 24 in terms of schooling performance among today's OECD countries. Today it is the top performer in terms of the proportion of successful school leavers, with 96% of an age cohort obtaining a high school degree. In college education, the pace of change has been even more dramatic, and so has been its impact on the relative standing of countries: Within less than a decade, the United States has slipped from first to 15th rank in terms of the proportion of the relevant age cohort graduating from college. While progress in a national perspective matters, in a global framework, an internationally comparative perspective is having a growing impact not just on public policy but on institutional behaviour too. International assessments of learning outcomes are beginning to show similar trends.

A Tool for the Political Economy of Reform

International assessments can also support the political economy of reform. For example, in the 2007 Mexican national survey of parents 77% of parents interviewed reported that the quality of educational services provided by their children's school was good or very good. However, in OECD's PISA 2006 assessment, roughly half of the Mexican 15-year-olds who are enrolled in school performed at or below the lowest level of proficiency established by PISA (IFIE-ALDUCIN, 2007; OECD, 2007). There may be many reasons for such a discrepancy between perceived educational quality and performance on international assessments. For example, in part this may be due to the fact that the educational services which Mexican children receive are significantly enhanced over the quality of schooling that their parents experienced. However, the point here is that justifying the investment of public resources into areas for which there seems no public demand poses difficult challenges for the political economy of reform. One recent response by the Mexican presidential office has been to include a "PISA performance target" into the new Mexican reform plan. This performance target that is based on the outcome of an international assessments and that is to be achieved by 2012 will serve to highlight the gap between national performance and international standards and monitor how educational improvement feeds into closing this gap. It is associated with a reform trajectory and delivery chain of support systems, incentive structures as well as with improved access to professional development to assist school leaders and teachers in meeting the target. Such reforms draw on the experience of other countries. Brazil has taken a similar route, providing each secondary school with information on the level of progress that is needed to perform at the OECD average performance level on PISA in 2021.

Japan is one of the best performing education systems on the various international assessments. However, PISA revealed that while students tended to do very well on tasks that require reproducing subject matter content, they did much less well on open-ended constructed tasks requiring them to demonstrate their capacity to extrapolate from what they know and apply their knowledge in novel settings. Conveying that to parents and a general public who are used to certain types of tests poses a challenge for the political economy of reform too. The policy response in Japan has been to incorporate "PISA-type" open-constructed tasks into the national assessment, with the aim that skills that are considered important become valued in the education system. Similarly, Korea has recently incorporated advanced PISA-type literacy tasks in its university entrance examinations, in order to enhance excellence in the capacity of its students to access, manage, integrate and evaluate written material. In both countries, these changes represent transformational change that would have been much harder to imagine without the challenges revealed by PISA.

Design Issues and Challenges for International Assessments

The design of international assessments of learning outcomes needs to fulfil different, and sometimes competing, demands:

- First, international assessments need to ensure that their outcomes are valid across cultural, national and linguistic boundaries and that the target populations from which the samples in the participating countries are drawn are comparable.
- Second, they need to offer added value to what can be accomplished through national analysis.
- Third, while international assessments need to be as comparable as possible, they also need to be country-specific so as to adequately capture historical, systemic and cultural variation among countries.
- Fourth, the resultant measures need to be as simple as possible to be widely understood, while remaining as complex as necessary to reflect multi-faceted educational realities.
- Fifth, while there is a general desire to keep any set performance measures as small as possible, it needs to be large enough to be useful for research and policy across countries that face different educational challenges. Some of the design issues involved in meeting and balancing these various demands are laid out in the remainder of this section.

Cross-Country Validity and Comparability in the Assessment Instruments

International assessments necessarily are limited in their scope. This is because

- there is no overarching agreement on what fundamental competencies students in a particular grade or at a particular age should possess,

- an international assessment can only capture a selection of competencies and
- various methodological constraints limit the nature of competencies that are currently amenable to large-scale assessment (international assessments necessarily are limited in their scope).

International assessments have made considerable progress towards assessing knowledge and skills in content areas such as mathematics, reading, science and problem-solving. However, they have not yet been able to evaluate, for example, interpersonal dimensions of competencies which are of increasing importance, such as the capacity of students to relate well to others, to manage and resolve conflicts or to respect and appreciate different values, beliefs or cultures. Similarly, they provide only very crude self-reported measures of intrapersonal dimensions of competencies, which are of increasing importance as individuals need to be able to constantly adjust to their right place in an increasingly complex world.

Even in established content areas, internationally comparative measurement poses major challenges. Countries vary widely in their intended, implemented and achieved curricula. Inevitably, international assessments need to strike a balance between narrowing the focus to what is common across the different curricula of school systems, on the one hand, and capturing a wide-enough range of competencies to reflect the content domains to be assessed adequately, on the other. Leaning towards the former, as has been the tendency for the assessments of the IEA, ensures that what is being tested internationally reflects what being taught nationally. This is an important aspect of fairness, but it risks that the assessment reflects just the lowest common denominator of national curricula and lacks important aspects of curricula that are not taught in all countries as well as the content validity that is required to faithfully represent the relevant subject area. Leaning towards the latter, as is the case for the assessments of the OECD with their focus on the capacity of students not merely to reproduce what they have learned but to extrapolate from what they have learned and apply their knowledge and skills in novel settings, enhances content validity but risks that students are being confronted with assessment material they may not have been taught.

In whatever way the various international assessments have struck these balances, they have tried to build them through a carefully designed interactive process between the agencies developing the assessment instruments, various international expert groups working under the auspices of the respective organisations and national experts charged with the development and implementation of the surveys in their countries. Often, a panel of international experts led, in close consultation with participating countries, the identification of the range of knowledge and skills in the respective assessment domains that were considered to be crucial for student's capacity to fully participate in and contribute to a successful modern society. A description of the assessment domains – the assessment framework – was then used by participating countries, and other test development professionals, as they contributed assessment materials, which typically involved

- the development of a working definition for the assessment area and description of the assumptions that underlay that definition;

- an evaluation of how to organise the set of tasks constructed in order to report to policy makers and researchers on performance in each assessment area among 15-year-old students in participating countries;
- the identification of a set of key characteristics to be taken into account when assessment tasks were constructed for international use;
- the operationalisation of the set of key characteristics to be used in test construction, with definitions based on existing literature and the experience of other large-scale assessments;
- the validation of the variables, and assessment of the contribution which each made to the understanding of task difficulty in participating countries and
- the preparation of an interpretative scheme for the results.

In the case of PISA, for example, the assessment is defined through three interrelated dimensions, namely the knowledge or structure of knowledge that students need to acquire (e.g. familiarity with scientific concepts); competencies that students need to apply (e.g. carrying out a particular scientific process); and the contexts in which students encounter scientific problems and relevant knowledge and skills are applied (e.g. making decisions in relation to personal life, understanding world affairs) (see Table 2).

Once the assessment framework is established and agreed, which tends to be the most challenging aspect of an international assessment, assessment items are developed to reflect the intentions of the frameworks and they need to be carefully piloted before final assessment instruments can be established. To some extent, the question to what extent the tasks in international assessments are comparable across countries can be answered empirically. Analyses to this end were first undertaken for the IEA TIMSS (Beaton et al., 1996). The authors compared the percentage of correct answers in each country according to the international assessment as a whole with the percentage correct in each country on the items said by the country to address its curriculum in mathematics. Singapore, for example, had 144 out of 162 items that were said to be covered by the Singaporean curriculum. The percentage of items correct on the whole test and on the items covered in the curriculum was 79 in both cases. Singapore also scored between 79 and 81% correct on the items that other countries considered as covered in their own curricula. These ranged from 76 items in Greece to 162 items in the United States. For most countries, the results were similarly consistent, suggesting that the composition of the tests had no major impact on the relative standing of countries in the international comparisons. Such analyses have also been conducted for PISA, which yielded similar results.

International assessments pay close attention to reflecting the national, cultural and linguistic variety among participating countries. OECD's PISA assessments employ the most sophisticated and rigorous process to this end. The agency charged with the development of the instruments uses professional test item development teams in several different countries. In addition to the items developed by these teams, assessment material is contributed by participating countries that is carefully evaluated and matched against the framework. Furthermore, each item included in the assessment pool is rated by each country:

Table 2 Defining an assessment domain – an example from PISA

	Science	Reading	Mathematics
Definition and its distinctive features	The extent to which an individual: – Possesses scientific knowledge and uses that knowledge to identify questions, acquire new knowledge, explain scientific phenomena and draw evidence-based conclusions about science-related issues – Understands the characteristic features of science as a form of human knowledge and enquiry – Shows awareness of how science and technology shape our material, intellectual and cultural environments – Engages in science-related issues and with the ideas of science, as a reflective citizen *Scientific literacy* requires an understanding of scientific concepts, as well as the ability to apply a scientific perspective and to think scientifically about evidence	The capacity of an individual to understand, use and reflect on written texts in order to achieve one's goals, to develop one's knowledge and potential and to participate in society In addition to decoding and literal comprehension, *reading literacy* also involves interpretation and reflection and the ability to use reading to fulfil one's goals in life The focus of PISA is on reading to learn rather than learning to read, and hence students are not assessed on the most basic reading skills	The capacity of an individual to identify and understand the role that mathematics plays in the world, to make well-founded judgements and to use and engage with mathematics in ways that meet the needs of that individual's life as a constructive, concerned and reflective citizen *Mathematical literacy* is related to wider, functional use of mathematics; engagement includes the ability to recognise and formulate mathematical problems in various situations

Table 2 (continued)

	Science	Reading	Mathematics
Knowledge domain	*Knowledge of science*, such as • "Physical systems" • "Living systems" • "Earth and space systems" • "Technology systems" *Knowledge about science*, such as • "Scientific enquiry" • "Scientific explanations"	The form of reading materials: • *Continuous texts*: including different kinds of prose such as narration, exposition, argumentation • *Non-continuous texts*: including graphs, forms and lists	Clusters of relevant mathematical areas and concepts: • *Quantity* • *Space and shape* • *Change and relationships* • *Uncertainty*
Competencies involved	Type of scientific task or process: • *Identifying scientific issues* • *Explaining scientific phenomena* • *Using scientific evidence*	Type of reading task or process: • Retrieving information • Interpreting texts • Reflecting and evaluating of texts	Competency clusters define skills needed for mathematics: • *Reproduction* (simple mathematical operations) • *Connections* (bringing together ideas to solve straightforward problems) • *Reflection* (wider mathematical thinking)
Context and situation	The area of application of science, focusing on uses in relation to personal, social and global settings such as • "Health" • "Natural resources" • "Environment" • "Hazard" • "Frontiers of science and technology"	The use for which the text is constructed: • *Private* (e.g. a personal letter) • *Public* (e.g. an official document) • *Occupational* (e.g. a report) • *Educational* (e.g. school-related reading)	The area of application of mathematics, focusing on uses in relation to personal, social and global settings such as: • *Personal* • *Educational and occupational* • *Public* • *Scientific*

  (i) for potential cultural, gender or other bias;
 (ii) for relevance to the students to be assessed in school and non-school contexts and
(iii) for familiarity and level of interest.

Another important aspect concerns the nature and form of the assessment, as reflected in the task and item types. While multiple-choice tasks are the most cost-effective way to assess knowledge and skills, and have therefore dominated earlier international assessments, they have important limitations in assessing more complex skills, particularly ones that require students not just to recall but to produce knowledge. Moreover, since the nature of assessment tasks, and in particular student familiarity with multiple-choice tasks, varies considerably across countries, heavy reliance on any single item type such as multiple-choice tasks can be an important source of response bias. The PISA assessments have tried to address this through employing a broad range of assessment tasks, with about 40% of the questions requiring students to construct their own responses. Another way to improve the nature of the assessments task is by either providing a brief answer (short-response questions) or by constructing a longer response (open-constructed response questions), allowing for the possibility of divergent individual responses and an assessment of students' justification of their viewpoints. Partial credit is given for partly correct or less complex answers, with questions assessed by trained specialists using detailed scoring guides which gave direction on the codes to assign to various responses. Open-ended assessment tasks, however, raise other challenges, in particular the need to ensure inter-rater reliability in the results. For PISA, sub-samples of the assessment booklets are coded independently by four coders and examined by the international contractor. In order to examine the consistency of this coding process in more detail within each country and to estimate the magnitude of the variance components associated with the use of coders, an inter-coder reliability study on the sub-sample of assessment booklets is being applied and homogeneity analysis is applied to the national sets of multiple coding. Similarly, at the between-country level, an international coding review is implemented to check on the consistency of application of response-coding standards across all participating countries, with the objective to estimate potential bias (either leniency or harshness) in the coding standards applied in participating countries.

In order to cover the intended broad range of content while meeting the limits of individual assessment time, most modern international assessments are now using multiple forms which are spiralled among students.

Ensuring that international assessments are comparable across countries is one thing, but the more important challenges actually relate to their external validity, which involves verifying that the assessments measure what they set out to measure. An important question is whether the knowledge and skills that are being assessed are predictive for the future success of students. In the case of PISA, the Canadian Youth in Transition Survey (YITS), a longitudinal survey which investigates patterns of and influences on major educational, training and work transitions in young people's lives, provided a way to examine this empirically. In 2000, 29,330

15-year-old students in Canada participated both in YITS and PISA. Four years later, the educational outcomes of the same students, then aged 19, were assessed and the association of these outcomes with PISA reading performance at age 15 was investigated (Knighton & Bussiere, 2006). The results showed that students who had mastered PISA performance Level 2 on the PISA reading test at age 15 were twice as likely to participate in post-secondary education at age 19 than those who performed at Level 1 or below, even after accounting for school engagement, gender, mother tongue, place of residence, parental, education and family income. The odds increased to eight-fold for those students who had mastered PISA Level 4 and to sixteen-fold for those who had mastered PISA Level 5. A similar study undertaken in Denmark led to similar results, in that the percentage of youth who had completed post-compulsory, general or vocational upper-secondary education by 19 increased significantly with their reading ability assessed at age 15 (see http://www.sfi.dk/sw19649.asp). Last but not least, the International Adult Literacy Study allowed reading and numeracy skills (defined in similar ways to those measured by PISA) to be related to earnings and employment outcomes in the adult population. The analyses showed that such competencies were generally a better predictor for individual earnings and employment status than the level of formal qualification individuals had attained (OECD and Statistics Canada, 2000).

Comparability of the Target Populations

Even if the assessment instruments are valid and reliable, meaningful comparisons can only be made if the target populations being assessed are also comparable. International assessments therefore need to use great care when

  (i) defining comparable target populations;
 (ii) ensuring that they are exhaustively covered with minimal and well-defined population exclusions and
(iii) ensuring that the sampled students do participate in the assessment.

As regards defining target populations, important trade-offs need to be made between international comparability, on the one hand, and relating the target populations to national institutional structures, on the other. Differences between countries in the nature and extent of pre-primary education and care, the age of entry to formal schooling and the institutional structure of educational systems do not allow the establishment of internationally comparable grade levels of schooling. Consequently, international comparisons of educational performance typically define their populations with reference to a target age group. International assessments of the IEA have defined these target groups on the basis of the grade level that provides maximum coverage of a particular age cohort (such as the grade in which most 13-year-olds are enrolled). The advantage of this is that a grade level can be easily interpreted within the national institutional structure and provides a cost-effective way towards assessment, with minimal disruption of the school day. However, a disadvantage is that slight variations in the age distribution of students across grade levels often lead to the selection of different target grades in different countries, or between education systems within countries, raising serious questions about the comparability of results across, and at times within, countries. In addition, because not all students of the desired age are usually represented in grade-based samples, there may be a more serious potential bias in the results if the unrepresented students are typically enrolled in the next higher grade in some countries and the next lower grade in others. This excludes students with potentially higher levels of performance in the former countries and students with potentially lower levels of performance in the latter. To address these problems, the assessments of the OECD use an age-based definition for their target populations, i.e. a definition that is not tied to the institutional structures of national education systems. For example, PISA assesses students who were aged between 15 years and 3 (complete) months and 16 years and 2 (complete) months at the beginning of the assessment period and who were enrolled in an educational institution, regardless of the grade levels or type of institution in which they were enrolled, and regardless of whether they were in full-time or part-time education. The disadvantage of this age-based approach is that this is costly and that the assessment process becomes more disruptive and it is more difficult to relate the results of individual students to teachers and classrooms.

The accuracy of any survey results also depends on the quality of the information on which national samples are based as well as on the sampling procedures. For the latest international assessments, advanced quality standards, procedures, instruments and verification mechanisms have been developed that ensure that national samples yielded comparable data and that the results could be compared with confidence.

Comparability in Survey Implementation

Last but not least, well-designed international assessment needs to be well implemented to yield reliable results. The process begins with ensuring consistent quality and linguistic equivalence of the assessment instruments across countries. PISA, which provides the most advanced procedures to this end, seeks to achieve this through providing countries with equivalent source versions of the assessment instruments in English and French and requiring countries (other than those assessing students in English and French) to prepare and consolidate two independent translations using both source versions. Precise translation and adaptation guidelines are supplied, also including instructions for the selection and training of the translators. For each country, the translation and format of the assessment instruments (including test materials, marking guides, questionnaires and manuals) are verified by expert translators appointed by agency charged with the development of the assessment instruments (whose mother tongue was the language of instruction in the country concerned and who were knowledgeable about education systems) before they are used.

The assessments are then implemented through standardised procedures. Comprehensive manuals typically explain the implementation of the survey, including precise instructions for the work of school co-ordinators and scripts for test administrators for use during the assessment sessions. Proposed adaptations to survey procedures, or proposed modifications to the assessment session script, are reviewed internationally before they are employed at a national level. In the case of PISA, specially designated quality monitors visited all national centres to review data-collection procedures and school quality. Monitors from the international agency visited a sample of 15 schools during the assessment. Marking procedures are designed to ensure consistent and accurate application of the internationally agreed marking guides.

Conclusions

In a globalised world, the benchmarks for public policy in education are no longer national goals or standards alone, but increasingly the performance of the most successful education systems internationally. International assessments can be powerful instruments for educational research, policy and practice by allowing education systems to look at themselves in the light of intended, implemented and achieved policies elsewhere. They can show what is possible in education, in terms of quality, equity and efficiency in educational services, and they can foster better understanding of how different education systems address similar problems. Most importantly, by providing an opportunity for policy makers and practitioners to look beyond the experiences evident in their own systems and thus to reflect on some of the paradigms and beliefs underlying these, they hold out the promise to facilitate educational improvement. As the chapter has shown, designing and implementing valid and reliable international assessments poses major challenges, including defining the criteria for success in ways that are comparable across countries while remaining meaningful at national levels, establishing comparable target populations and carrying the surveys out under strictly standardised conditions. However, more recently, international assessments such as PISA have made significant strides towards this end.

Some contend that international benchmarking encourages an undesirable process of degrading cultural and educational diversity among institutions and education systems, but the opposite can be argued as well: In the dark, all institutions and education systems look the same and it is comparative benchmarking that can shed light on differences on which reform efforts can then capitalise. Who took notice of how Finland, Canada or Japan run their education systems before PISA revealed the success of these education systems, in terms of the quality, equity and coherence of learning outcomes?

Of course, international assessments have their pitfalls too: Policy makers tend to use them selectively, often rather in support of existing policies than as an instrument to challenge them and to explore alternatives. Moreover, highlighting specific features of educational performance may detract attention from other features that are equally important, thus potentially influencing individual, institutional or systemic behaviour in ineffective or even undesirable ways. This can be like the drunken driver who looks for his car key under a street lantern and, when questioned whether he lost it there, responds no, but that it was the only place where he could see. This risk of undesirable consequences of inadequately defined performance benchmarks is very real, as teachers and policy makers are led to focus their work on those issues which performance benchmarks value and put into the spotlight of the public debate.

While the development of international assessments is fraught with difficulties and their comparability remains open to challenges, cultural differences among individuals, institutions and systems should not suffice as a justification to reject their use, given that the success of individuals and nations increasingly depends on their global competitiveness. The world is indifferent to tradition and past reputations, unforgiving of frailty and ignorant of custom or practice. Success will go to those individuals, institutions and countries which are swift to adapt, slow to complain and open to change. The task for governments will be to ensure that their citizens, institutions and education systems rise to this challenge and international benchmarks can provide useful instruments to this end.

Annex

Table 3 International assessments conducted by the IEA

	Study	Data collection	Target population	Coverage
1960	Pilot study	1960	13 years	Mathematics, science, reading, geography, non-verbal abilities
	First International Mathematics Study – FIMS	1964	13 years and last year of upper secondary education	Mathematics
1970	The six subject survey	1970–1971	10, 14 years and last year of upper secondary education	Reading comprehension
				Literature
				First international science study
				English as a foreign language
				French as a foreign language
				Civic education
1980	Second International Mathematics Study – SIMS	1980–1982	13 years and last year of upper secondary education	
	Classroom environment study	1982–1983	9 and 15 years	Instructional methods in mathematics, science and history
	Second International Science Study – SISS	1983–1984	10, 14 years and last year of upper secondary education	Science
	Written composition	1985	10, 14–16 years and last year of upper secondary education	Writing
	Computers in education – COMPED	1989 e 1992	10 and 13 years	Availability and use of computers and technology
	Pre-primary project	1986–1994 1989–2003 1993–2003	Longitudinal study following children from 4 to 7 years	Quality of early-childhood provision

Table 3 (continued)

	Study	Data collection	Target population	Coverage
1990	Reading Literacy Study – RLS	1990–1991	9 and 14 years	Reading comprehension
	Third International Mathematics and Science Study – TIMSS 1995	1994–1995	9 and 13 years and last year of upper secondary education	Mathematics and science
	Civic education study – CIVED	1996–1997 1999–2000	14 years and 16–18 years	Civic education
	Second Information Technology in Education Study Module 1 – SITES-M1	1998–1999		Availability and use of technology
	Third International Mathematics and Science Study Repeat – TIMSS-R 1999	1998–1999	9 and 13 years and last year of upper secondary education	Mathematics and science
	Study	Data collection	Target population	Coverage
2000	Progress in International Reading Literacy Study 2001 – PIRLS	2001	9 years	Reading comprehension
	Trends in Mathematics and Science Study 2003 – TIMSS 2003	2002–2003	9 and 14 years	Mathematics and science
	(In progress) Progress in International Reading Literacy Study 2006 – PIRLS 2006	2005–2006	9 years	Reading comprehension
	(In progress) Second Information on Technology in Education Study 2006 – SITES 2006	2006		Availability and use of technology
	(In progress) Teacher Education and Development Study-Mathematics – TEDS-M 2008	2007–2008		Teacher training
	(In progress) Trends in International Mathematics and Science Study 2007 – TIMSS 2007	2006–2007	9 and 13 years	Mathematics and science
	(In progress) TIMSS advanced 2008	2007–2008	Last year of upper secondary education	Mathematics and physics
	(In progress) International Civic and Citizenship Education Study – ICCS 2009	2008–2009	13 years	Civic education

Source: Siniscalco (2007).

References

Beaton, A. E., Mullis, I. V. S., Martin, M. O., Gonzales, E. J., Kelly, D. L., & Smith, T. A. (1996). *Mathematics achievement in the middle school years*. Chestnut Hill: Center for the Study of Testing, Evaluation, and Educational Policy, Boston College.

Döbert, H., Klieme, E., & Sroka, W. (2004). Vertiefender Vergleich der Schulsysteme ausgewählter PISA-Teilnehmerstaaten, Frankfurt a. M., Deutsches Institut für pädagogische Forschung.

Foshay, A. W., Thorndike, R. L., Hotyat, F., Pidgeon, D. A., & Walker, D. A. (1962). *Educational achievement of thirteen-year-olds in twelve countries*. Hamburg: UNESCO Institute for Education.

Hopkins, D., Pennock, D., & Ritzen, J. (2008). *Evaluation of the policy impact of PISA,* Paris: OECD.

IFIE-ALDUCIN. (2007). *Mexican national survey to parents regarding the quality of basic education.* Mexico City: IFIE

Jullien, M. A. (1817). Esquisse et vues préliminaires d'un ouvrage sur l'éducation comparée, Paris, L. Colas.

Knighton, T., & Bussiere, P. (2006). *Educational outcomes at age 19 associated with reading ability at age 15 (research paper)*. Statistics Canada, Ottawa.

LaPointe, A. E., Mead, N. A., & Askew, J. M. (1992). *The international assessment of educational progress report*. Princeton, NJ: Educational Testing Service.

LaPointe, A. E., Mead, N. A., & Phillips, G. W. (1989). *A world of differences: An international assessment of mathematics and science*. Princeton, NJ: Educational Testing Service.

OECD. (2004). *Reviews of national policies for education – Denmark: Lessons from PISA 2000.* Paris: OECD.

OECD. (2007). *Reviews of national policies for education: Quality and equity of schooling in Scotland*. Paris: OECD.

OECD. (2008). *Education at a glance – OECD indicators 2007*. Paris: OECD.

OECD and Statistics Canada. (2000). Literacy skills for the information age, Ottawa and Paris, OECD and Statistics Canada.

Siniscalco, M. T. (2007). PISA e le valutazioni internazionali dei risultati della scuola. In M. T. Siniscalco, R. Bolletta, M. Mayer, & S. Pozio (Eds.), *Le valutazioni internazionali e la scuola italiana*. Bologna: Zanichelli.

Teaching and Educational Transformation

Linda Darling-Hammond

As they entered the twenty-first century, most nations around the world undertook major transformations of their governmental and education systems to respond to changing economic, demographic, political, and social imperatives. Nearly all countries are engaged in serious discussion of school reform to address demands for much higher levels of education for much greater numbers of citizens – demands created by a new information age, major economic shifts, and a resurgence and redefinition of democracy around the world. These demands are being imposed upon educational institutions designed a century ago for a different time. In the United States as elsewhere, the need to prepare future citizens and workers who can cope with complexity, use new technologies, and work cooperatively to frame and solve novel problems – and the need to do this for a much more diverse and inclusive group of learners – has stimulated efforts to rethink school goals and curriculum, to better prepare teachers, and to redesign school organizations.

This rapidly changing economic base has stimulated political concerns as well as rapid job changes, industrial restructuring, and the need for many workers to learn new occupations and new roles. Manufacturing industries can no longer pay high wages for low-skilled work. High wages and corporate growth characterize industries that rely on high levels of skill, complex technologies, and new knowledge and information. "An economy in which knowledge is becoming the true capital and the premier wealth-producing resource" means that "once again we will have to think through what an educated person is" (Drucker, 1989, p. 232). The changes demanded of workers and of educational institutions are striking:

> The great majority of the new jobs require qualifications the industrial worker does not possess and is poorly equipped to acquire. They require a good deal of formal education and the ability to acquire and to apply theoretical and analytical knowledge. They require a different approach to work and a different mind-set. Above all, they require a habit of continuous learning. Displaced industrial workers thus cannot simply move into knowledge

---

L. Darling-Hammond (✉)
Stanford University, Stanford, CA, USA
e-mail: ldh@stanford.edu

This chapter draws in part on Darling-Hammond (2000a)

A. Hargreaves et al. (eds.), *Second International Handbook of Educational Change*,   505
Springer International Handbooks of Education 23, DOI 10.1007/978-90-481-2660-6_30,
© Springer Science+Business Media B.V. 2010

work or services the way displaced farmers and domestic workers moved into industrial work (at the turn of the last century). At the very least, they have to change their basic attitudes, values, and beliefs (Drucker, 1994, p. 62).

Furthermore, the nature of work will continue to change ever more rapidly. Whereas during much of the twentieth century, most workers held 2 or 3 jobs during their lifetimes, the US Department of Labor (2006) estimates that today's workers hold more than 10 jobs before they reach the age of 40. The top ten in-demand jobs projected for 2010 did not exist in 2004 (Gunderson, Jones, & Scanland, 2004). Thus, we are currently preparing many students for jobs that do not yet exist using technologies that have not yet been invented to solve problems that we don't even know are problems yet.

Meanwhile, knowledge is expanding at a breathtaking pace. It is estimated that 5 exabytes of new information (about 500,000 times the volume of the Library of Congress print collection) was generated in 2002, more than three times as much as in 1999. Indeed in the 4 years from 1999 to 2003, the amount of new information produced approximately equaled the amount produced in the entire history of the world previously (Varian & Lyman, 2003). The amount of new technical information is doubling every 2 years, and it is predicted to double every 72 h by 2010 (Jukes & McCain, 2002). As a consequence, effective education can no longer be focused on the transmission of pieces of information that, once memorized, comprise a stable storehouse of knowledge. Education must help students learn how to learn in powerful ways, so that they can manage the demands of changing information, technologies, jobs, and social conditions.

Factory Model Schools Confront New Demands

In the United States and many other countries, reaching these new goals will require fundamental transformation of existing school organizations and ways of managing teaching. At the turn of the twentieth century during the last major era of system reform, the prevailing model of school organization that took hold in the United States mimicked the then-popular factory line managed by centralized bureaucracy. Automated means for mass producing goods created specialized divisions of labor and a proliferation of routinized, semiskilled jobs requiring limited knowledge. The "Taylor system," widely adopted in the decade after 1910, provided techniques for using rules and routines to manage the work of people assigned to simplified, discrete tasks. "Scientific management" brought with it a distinct division of responsibility between a new class of managers, who did all the thinking, and the workers, who followed procedures developed by the managers (Callahan, 1962, pp. 37–38).

This approach was carried over from manufacturing industries to schools, which sought to develop standardized procedures engineered to yield standard products. Teachers, like factory workers, were viewed as unskilled laborers who would implement the schemes developed by others, rather than developing lessons tailored to the needs of their students. For both teachers and students, schools stressed compliance and the capacity for repetitive, rote tasks in response to the demands from industry (Tyack, 1974). Based on faith in the power of rules to direct human behavior, and in the ability of administrators to discover and implement the common procedures that would produce desired outcomes, twentieth-century education policy assumed that continually improving the design specifications for schoolwork – required courses, textbooks, testing instruments, and management systems – would lead to student learning.

The twentieth-century search for a bureaucratic route to the "one best system" of education (Tyack, 1974) was based on the assumptions that students are standardized and that educational treatments can be prescribed. Because most major teaching decisions were to be handed down through administrative channels and encapsulated in packaged teaching materials, teachers were viewed as needing little knowledge or expertise (Darling-Hammond, 1990). In the factory model conception, if it is possible to fix teaching by developing better regulations, there is no incentive to develop better teachers. Because decisions are made at the top of the educational hierarchy, there is no rationale in this kind of organization for substantial teacher preparation or professional development, aside from "in-servicing" designed to ensure more exact implementation of prescribed teaching procedures. The presumption of regularity means that schools are designed to function without major investments in teachers' professional knowledge and without time for collegial consultation and planning. It is this logic that has allowed policymakers to avoid investing substantial resources in teacher preparation or teacher salaries.

This kind of schooling system may have worked reasonably well many decades ago for helping most students acquire minimal basic skills and prepare for routine work, and for enabling a few to develop higher-order thinking and performance skills. However, it has proved increasingly inadequate to the new mission of schools: teaching large numbers of very diverse learners to think critically, solve complex problems, and master ambitious subject matter content – a task that requires a different, more sophisticated kind of teaching than merely covering the curriculum or "getting through the book" (Darling-Hammond et al., 2008).

In contrast to the assumptions underlying the factory model, a growing body of research suggests that highly skilled teachers are essential to this task, and that perhaps the greatest school influence on student learning is the quality of the teacher. Students lucky enough to have teachers who know their content and how to teach it well achieve substantially more (for reviews, see Darling-Hammond, 2000b; Wilson, Floden, & Ferrini-Mundy, 2002). And the effects of a very good (or very poor) teacher last beyond a single year, influencing their students' learning for years to come (Sanders & Rivers, 1996). Indeed, expert teachers are the most fundamental resource for improving education.

However, in the United States, teachers are the most inequitably distributed resource. On any measure of qualifications – extent of preparation, level of experience, certification, content background in the field taught, advanced degrees, or scores on college admissions and teacher licensure tests – studies show that students of color, and low-income and low-performing students, particularly in urban and poor rural areas, are disproportionately taught by less qualified teachers (Darling-Hammond, 2004a; Lankford, Loeb, & Wyckoff, 2002). In many high-minority schools, the most vulnerable students are taught by a revolving door of inexperienced and untrained teachers (NCTAF, 1996).

These disparities are largely a function of the nation's inequitable funding of education, which translates into lower salaries and poorer working conditions for teachers in districts serving the neediest students. The tradition in the United States has been to lower standards rather than to increase incentives when there are too few teachers willing to work under suboptimal conditions. Unfortunately, in these places, especially, the factory model is held in place while other parts of the system strive to create a more productive approach to change.

Cross-Currents in Policy

Over the last 20 years, an alternative vision for education – based on a professional conception of teaching and a more intellectually ambitious conception of learning – has begun to emerge. The profession has engaged in serious standard setting that reflects a growing knowledge base about what teachers should know and be able to do to help all students learn in ways that develop higher-order thinking and performance skills. Some states have successfully launched efforts to restructure schools and to invest in greater teacher knowledge (Lieberman, 1995). New, more effective models of teacher preparation have been created in partnership with schools (Darling-Hammond, 2007; Fullan, 2007). Grassroots networks like the National Writing Project and the Coalition of Essential Schools have helped to support teacher development, reorient curriculum and teaching toward more thoughtful educational goals, and rethink schools. These efforts to build the capacity of teachers differ from past educational change strategies in their concern for building capacity rather than tightening controls over education. In some places, new initiatives are seeking to invest more in the front lines of education – well-prepared and well-supported teachers – rather than in regulations to direct what they do.

Several professionalizing reforms have provided critical linchpins for transforming teaching. The National Board for Professional Teaching Standards (NBPTS) was established in 1987 to certify accomplished veteran teachers through standards and assessments that respect the complex demands of teaching and place student learning at the heart of the enterprise. The board's efforts paved the way for major changes in teacher education, professional development, evaluation, recognition and reward systems, and retention. The prospects for extending these breakthroughs to all teachers are enhanced by the work of more than 30 states and major professional organizations involved in the Interstate New Teacher Assessment and Support Consortium (INTASC). This consortium has established a set of model standards for beginning teacher licensing that are based on the National Board's standards, and is beginning to develop prototype assessments for teacher licensing modeled after those of the board. At least 40 states have adopted these standards and have begun to invest in stronger teacher education, induction, and professional development systems that could assure learning opportunities for teachers throughout their careers.

Reforms of teacher education have included the creation of hundreds of professional development school (PDS) partnerships between schools and universities, designed to focus on professional preparation for novices and veteran teachers, school-based research linking theory and practice, the improvement of teaching, and the redesign of schooling. The importance of the PDS idea is that it can institutionalize the process of ensuring that entering teachers are supported in learning how to apply complex knowledge in practice in settings that allow for the development of high levels of competence rather than encouraging counterproductive teaching and coping strategies. Such partnership schools also address the age-old problem of educational change: If teacher educators prepare teachers for schools as they are, they will be unable to teach more effectively or help schools become more effective than the status quo permits. PDSs create a means to prepare teachers for schools that do not currently exist in large numbers by combining the work of preservice education, staff development, and school restructuring (Fullan, 1993).

In many of these and other forward-looking schools, pedagogy has become more student centered, and curriculum is aimed at deeper understanding, buttressed by performance assessments of learning that require students to show what they know through applications to authentic problems. Evidence suggests that this kind of teaching – which demands higher-order thinking, consideration of alternatives, and development of intellectual products – develops stronger and more equitable learning on both conventional measures and more complex performance tasks (Darling-Hammond et al., 2008; Lee, Smith, & Croninger, 1995; Newmann et al., 1996). Such teaching is, of course, grounded in a deep understanding of both the demands of disciplined thinking and the learning processes of students.

These promising new initiatives, however, must contend with deeply entrenched barriers. While some states and districts have redefined teaching, learning, and schooling, with strong results for students (see, e.g., Darling-Hammond, 2000b, 2004b; Lieberman, 1995), these efforts have been piecemeal and nonsystematic. Despite recent improvements in some places, teaching as an occupation is still characterized by extremely uneven preparation – some excellent and some very poor; vague and haphazardly enforced standards; submarket wages; chronic shortages in key fields like mathematics and science; high levels of turnover for beginners; and vast differences in resources and performance across classrooms, schools, and communities.

While extraordinary teachers grace many classrooms, others struggle without assistance to learn to teach in ways they themselves have never encountered. The systems responsible for recruiting, preparing, and supporting teachers are generally disconnected from one another and frequently unaware of advances in knowledge that should inform what they do. Teachers in many communities still work in isolation from one another in settings that provide them with little time for collaboration and learning.

Meanwhile, the factory model view of teaching is alive and well, especially in states and districts that have invested the least in high-quality teaching. The view that students are raw materials to be "processed" by schools according to standard specifications has led to a resurgence of policies in many states that seek to drive teaching through standardized tests that are externally developed and scored and tied to tightly scripted teaching materials. In some states and in some of the nation's largest city school districts, like Chicago, Los Angeles, and Philadelphia, particularly in schools serving the least advantaged students where large numbers of untrained teachers are hired, teacher-proof curriculum attempts have recurred with regularity, despite their lack of success in previous iterations. In the most extreme cases, teachers are supplied with a standardized curriculum outlining the scope and sequence for instruction in each subject in each grade, complete with a pacing schedule showing how much time teachers should spend on each topic and lesson plans for each day of the school year. Grading standards are also prescribed, showing how much weight teachers should give to each type of assignment (also prescribed), and how they should calculate grades. Promotion standards are determined by standardized tests developed to match the curriculum. The assumption is that marching the students through these procedures is all that is necessary to ensure learning. Unfortunately, this kind of teaching cannot address the higher-order thinking and problem-solving skills needed for success in the twenty-first century.

Contrasting Approaches

This lesson has been well learned by societies that top the international rankings in education on such measures as the Program in International Student Assessment (PISA). A study of twenty-five of the world's school systems, including ten of the top performers, found that investments in teachers and teaching are central to improving student outcomes. These focus on purposeful recruitment; preparation and development; and systemic supports for instruction (Barber & Mourshed, 2007). The highest-achieving countries around the world routinely prepare their teachers extensively, pay them well in relation to competing occupations, and provide them with lots of time for professional learning. They also distribute well-trained teachers to all students – rather than allowing some to be taught by untrained novices – by offering equitable salaries, sometimes adding incentives for harder-to-staff locations.

Supports for High-Quality Teaching

In Scandinavian countries like Finland, Sweden, Norway, and the Netherlands, all teachers now receive 2–3 years of graduate-level preparation for teaching, completely at government expense, including a living stipend. Typically, programs include at least a full year of training in a school connected to the university, like the professional development school partnerships created by some US programs, along with extensive coursework in pedagogy and a thesis researching an educational problem in the schools. Unlike the United States, where teachers either go into debt to prepare for a profession that will pay them poorly or enter with little or no training, these countries made the decision to invest in a uniformly well-prepared teaching force by recruiting top candidates and paying them to go to school. Slots in teacher training programs are highly coveted and shortages are rare.

Finland has been a poster child for school improvement since it rapidly climbed to the top of the international rankings after it emerged from the Soviet Union's shadow. Leaders in Finland attribute these gains to their intensive investments in teacher education. Over 10 years the country overhauled preparation to focus more on teaching for higher-order skills like problem solving and critical thinking. Teachers learn how to create challenging curriculum and how to develop and evaluate local performance assessments that engage students in research and inquiry on a regular basis. Teacher training emphasizes learning how to teach students who learn in different ways – including those with special needs. The egalitarian Finns reasoned that if teachers learn to help students who struggle, they will be able to teach all students more effectively (Buchberger & Buchberger, 2004).

Policymakers also decided that if they invested in very skillful teachers, they could allow local schools more autonomy to make decisions about what and how to teach – a reaction against the oppressive, centralized system they sought to overhaul. This bet seems to have paid off. Teachers are sophisticated diagnosticians, and they work together collegially to design instruction that meets the demands of the subject matter as well as the needs of their students. Finnish schools are not governed by standardized tests, but by teachers' strong knowledge about how students learn (Laukkanen, 2008).

Top-ranked Singapore, by contrast, is highly centralized, but it treats teaching similarly. Singapore's Institute of Education – the tiny nation's only teacher training institution – is investing in teachers' abilities to teach a curriculum focused on critical thinking and inquiry – the twenty-first-century skills needed in a technologically oriented economy. To get the best teachers, students from the top one-third of each graduating high school class are recruited into a fully paid 4-year teacher education program (or, if they enter after they have already completed college, a 1- to 2-year graduate program) and immediately put on the Ministry's payroll. When they enter the profession, teachers' salaries are higher than those of beginning doctors.

As in other high-ranked countries, novices are not left to sink or swim. Expert teachers are given release time to serve as mentors to help beginners learn their craft. The government pays for 100 h of professional development each year for all teachers in addition to the 20 h a week they have to work with other teachers and visit each others' classrooms to study teaching. Currently teachers are being trained to undertake action research projects in the classroom so that they can examine teaching and learning problems, and find solutions that can be disseminated to others.

And teachers continue to advance throughout the career. With help from the government, Singapore teachers can pursue three separate career ladders that help them become curriculum specialists, mentors for other teachers, or school principals.

These opportunities bring recognition, extra compensation, and new challenges that keep teaching exciting.

In these and other high-achieving countries, schools are organized to support teacher success. Typically, teachers have 15–20 h a week to work with colleagues on developing lessons, participating in research and study groups, and engaging in seminars and visits to other classrooms and schools. Meanwhile, most US teachers have no time to work with colleagues during the school day: They plan by themselves and get a few "hit-and-run" workshops after school, with little opportunity to share knowledge or improve their practice. In their study of mathematics teaching and learning in Japan, Taiwan, and the United States, Jim Stigler and Harold Stevenson (1991) noted that "Asian class lessons are so well crafted [because] there is a very systematic effort to pass on the accumulated wisdom of teaching practice to each new generation of teachers and to keep perfecting that practice by providing teachers the opportunities to continually learn from each other."

A Focus on Higher-Order Learning

Having well-prepared teachers who focus on continually improving instruction is only part of building an educational system that can respond to twenty-first-century needs. Teachers need to work with students on critical skills that will allow them to transfer and apply their knowledge to new situations, and enable them to learn how to learn. The transmission curriculum that dominated schools for the last 100 years – which assumed a stable body of knowledge could be codified in textbooks and passed onto students who could "learn" it by remembering all the facts – is counterproductive today. Rigid approaches to defining knowledge cannot accomplish what is currently needed. Today's students need an education that will help them learn how to learn in powerful ways, so that they can manage the demands of changing information, knowledge bases, technologies, and social conditions.

Unfortunately, in the United States, curriculum is still too often defined by standards and textbooks that are, in many states, a mile wide and an inch deep, and by tests that focus on recall and recognition, rather than production and application of knowledge. By contrast, most high-achieving countries teach (and test) fewer topics each year and teach them more thoroughly so students build a stronger foundation for their learning. Their assessments focus on critical thinking and problem solving, whether they are developed nationally (as in the small countries of Japan and Singapore), at the state or provincial level (as in larger countries like Australia, Canada, and China, where Hong Kong and Macao score well on assessments like PISA) or locally (as in top-ranking Finland).

In most cases, these assessment systems combine centralized (state or national) assessments that use mostly open-ended and essay questions with local assessments given by teachers, which are factored into the final examination scores. These local assessments – which include research projects, science investigations, mathematical and computer models, and other products – are mapped to the syllabus and the standards for the subject and are selected because they represent critical skills, topics, and concepts. They are generally designed, administered, and scored locally. In the United States, by comparison, multiple-choice tests – which focus the curriculum on low-level skills – direct attention to modes of learning that are increasingly out of date. Whereas students in most parts of the United States are typically asked simply to recognize a single fact they have memorized from a list of answers, students in high-achieving countries are asked to apply their knowledge in the ways that writers, mathematicians, historians, and scientists do.

The Road Ahead

These distinctive realities describe a crossroads for American education. There are two futures at hand. One maintains the current features of teaching in the face of major demographic and economic changes and expanding expectations of schools. In the year 2013, 30 years after the issuance of the *Nation at Risk* report, it looks something like this:

Following a brief and familiar flurry of education reform activity in the early 1990s, schools settled back down to business as usual. The education governors had come and gone; educational leaders were relieved to have the proliferation of commission reports shelved and out of the way. A period of teacher shortages was addressed by modest salary increases and increased use of emergency and alternative certification, which brought teachers into classrooms with little initial preparation. Although teacher salaries climbed by 2005 to match the peak levels they had reached in the early 1970s (following the previous teacher shortage), they remained significantly below the salaries of other occupations requiring similar education and training. Many schools of education had substantially improved their programs, producing teachers who were more expert than ever before, but lack of attention to recruitment in high-need fields and locations coupled with continued inequalities in salaries and teaching conditions across states and districts made it difficult to recruit and retain staff in underfunded urban and rural communities.

In rapidly growing, high-immigration states like California that had disinvested in education over many years, tens of thousands of individuals entered teaching on emergency permits, working almost exclusively with low-income and minority students in central city and poor rural school districts. Another 20 states joined the 25 who by then had initiated quick routes into teaching through alternative certification. Many of these programs offered minimal training focused on classroom management and teaching formulas and then assigned recruits as teachers of record, hoping for mentoring that only sometimes materialized. Thus, classrooms, especially in the cities, were staffed. Students' access to highly capable teachers became increasingly inequitable, expanding the already large achievement gap.

Throughout the decade, students in the public education system changed, but schools did not. Great waves of immigration boosted the numbers of poor, minority, and non–English speaking children to more than 40% of public school enrollments.

The vast majority of children in large urban districts were low-income students of color. This made it easier for the broader public to write off these school districts, allowing a steady downward slide in their funding levels while resources were directed to affluent suburbs and private schools.

Because a majority of the teaching staff in city districts had retired, and the large numbers of vacancies were hard to fill at the low salaries offered, shortages led to larger classes and emergency hiring. The many teachers whose formal pedagogical preparation consisted of only a 5-week summer course desperately wanted to address the learning needs of their students, but their knowledge of child development, language acquisition, learning styles, and teaching methods was too skimpy to provide them with adequate ammunition for the job. As schools were increasingly filled with teachers who had never had the opportunity to practice under the guidance of an expert veteran or to study how children learn or how to teach effectively, the quality of practice deteriorated. Because these teachers had so little knowledge about teaching and barely knew how to plan from one day to the next, teacher-proof curriculum packages that had been rejected for their ineffectiveness in the 1980s returned once again to city school systems.

This exacerbated the flight of bright, well-prepared teachers from these systems as they refused to teach according to scripts that they found undermined their ability to teach creatively or to meet individual students' needs. Coupled with the high attrition rates of underprepared teachers, this produced chaotic conditions in many schools, with continuous turnover resulting in the most vulnerable students being taught by a parade of short-term substitutes and untrained, inexperienced teachers for their entire school careers.

The public's periodic concern for low student performance was answered by the enactment of "stiffer" requirements: more frequently administered tests for students to determine promotion, placement, and graduation; more carefully specified grade level objectives and curricular requirements matched to the standardized tests; more rigid procedures for tightening school management; more record keeping requirements for keeping tabs on administration, instruction, and student progress; and more frequent testing of teachers. Accountability systems offered greater sanctions for the growing share of public schools that failed to raise test scores.

Teaching in public schools was increasingly determined by these regulatory requirements rather than by knowledge about teaching and the needs of learners. Teachers taught for the required multiple-choice tests from mandated texts and curriculum packages aligned with the tests. Except in specially segregated programs for the "gifted and talented," affluent public schools, or private schools exempted from state testing requirements, students no longer read books, wrote papers, conducted experiments, or completed projects in class; their learning was structured by worksheets, practice tests, packaged instructional modules, and more practice tests. Businesses looking for high-skilled labor for the growing number of technology jobs increasingly turned to workers educated overseas to fill these positions.

Test-based accountability systems resulted in more students being held back and dropping out. Schools responded to the pressure to raise their test scores by pushing out, holding back, or refusing to admit students who did poorly on the standardized tests. For many, this increased the appearance of their scores without actually improving the quality of education they provided. Schools that served highly transient students, those with severe learning disabilities, or new immigrants lacking English language skills were increasingly labeled failures in systems that looked at average test scores, rather than the quality of teaching or longitudinal measures of student learning over time. This caused them to lose funding in states that tied dollars to test scores and further undermined their ability to recruit or retain capable teachers. Their students, increasingly treated as society's throwaways, were also unwanted by public schools of choice or the few private schools willing to accept vouchers.

Graduation rates, which had reached nearly 80% by the mid-1990s, began to reverse in the late 1990s and fell to 69% by 2005 and only 60% by 2013. The students who left school were disproportionately African American, Latino, and recent immigrant students who found themselves with few employment opportunities. With less than a high school education, their odds of finding work were less than 1 out of 4 while their odds of being imprisoned were greater than 50%. States with diverse populations and unequal school spending like California, Florida, Georgia, New York, and Texas, where test-based accountability policies were not accompanied by increased school investments, found that their prison populations more than tripled over the decade, further reducing available resources for education. A growing number of states found themselves spending as much on prisons as they spent on higher education. Scores on basic skills tests climbed slowly while scores on tests of higher-order thinking continued to decline. US students continued to perform ever more poorly relative to students in other countries on international assessments; colleges continued to decline in the production of math, science, engineering, and technology graduates; and corporations imported more workers for high-tech jobs, while moving other jobs overseas.

Earlier enthusiasm for reforms gave way to disillusionment and lower school budgets, as middle class parents fled to private schools and the general population, comprised largely of older citizens without children in schools, voted down tax levies for education. Just as the progressive education initiatives of the 1960s had been replaced in the 1970s by a movement to cap taxes for school support and go "back to the basics," so the restructuring rhetoric of the early 1990s gave way to a movement to fund private school vouchers and standardize education in public schools. By the year 2013, public frustration with the schools resurfaced with cries from the business community for employees who could function in an information-based and technological economy. New commissions were born to declare the nation, once again, at risk.

Another future – one that envisions different resolutions of these dilemmas – is possible. In this future, teaching continues its progress toward becoming a profession focused on the needs of students and informed by a growing knowledge base about effective teaching. Efforts to redesign schools to make them more supportive of in-depth learning and strong teacher–student relationships are advanced through public charter initiatives, a small schools movement in big cities, and district-initiated redesign of faltering schools. And strategies to equalize educational opportunity through litigation and legislation are successful in allocating a fair share of resources to all schools. In the year 2013, a different public education system has emerged. It looks something like this:

Much had changed since the last "crisis" in education during the 1980s. A second wave of reform impelled new coalitions between teachers, school administrators, and teacher educators, all of whom began thinking of themselves as members of the same profession with common goals. They articulated the first professional definition of teaching knowledge through the National Board for Professional Teaching Standards. As more and more teachers undertook the challenge of passing the board's rigorous assessments and the standards were infused into beginning licensing standards, new assessments for beginning teachers, and teacher education, the board's vision began to create a consensus about the features of accomplished teaching.

A growing number of teacher education programs, professional development programs, and teacher evaluation strategies began to focus on helping teachers understand and support student learning, rather than marching lockstep through textbooks or implementing routines that were ultimately often ineffective. Over time, teacher educators, teaching mentors, and principals were chosen from among the ranks of board-certified teachers, creating a stronger base of shared knowledge and expertise across the profession as a whole. By returning the role of school leadership to that of the "principal teacher," it became possible to base decisions in many schools on professional knowledge rather than idiosyncratic beliefs.

The National Board also helped to support the creation of analogous state boards which built upon its standards and assessments to establish more effective systems of teacher preparation and licensure in the states. Universities established 5-year teacher education programs that supported more intense and integrated study of both subject matter content and pedagogy, along with year-long student teaching experiences in professional development schools. Most also created high-quality post-baccalaureate programs of preparation for mid-career entrants into teaching to assure more streamlined coursework and well-mentored entry into teaching for talented individuals who wanted to learn how to make their expertise accessible to young people. Districts created well-supported internships for new teachers, with expert mentors who could continue to guide their on-the-job learning after they had completed their master's degree in teaching. Many states followed the lead of Connecticut, Vermont, Wisconsin, and California to establish beginning teacher programs that coupled mentoring with portfolio assessments that both boosted teachers' effectiveness and reduced the early attrition that had long plagued teaching. The new cohort of teachers – over a million of them – was better prepared than any that had preceded them.

Teacher shortages were met with higher salaries and differentiated staffing arrangements. These responses also began to change the shape of school organizations and the allocations of school resources. As bureaucratization had taken hold in American schools after 1950, classroom teachers comprised an ever smaller share of school employees (just over 40% by the mid-1990s, as compared to 60–80% in other industrialized countries), and teachers' salaries had dipped to only 36% of the total education budget. This trend was reversed as salaries climbed to a level comparable with other occupations for college-educated workers, and schools began to invest in quality teaching rather than futile efforts at teacher-proofing.

As the supply of prospective teachers willing and able to undergo rigorous preparation programs grew and the qualifications of teachers increased, the perceived need to spend large portions of education budgets on massive control and inspection systems diminished. Long hierarchies that had grown to design, regulate, and monitor teaching flattened out. The plethora of special categorical programs and pullout approaches which had pulled resources to the periphery of the classroom and fragmented the lives of students and schools were replaced by investments in the front lines of the classroom: more and better-trained teachers supported by new technologies and more time with the students they sought to teach. Teachers took on more professional responsibilities for mentoring, curriculum development, school improvement, and assessment design and scoring, and schools took on new shapes conducive to professional teaching.

As in other professions, differentiated roles and responsibilities emerged as a means for balancing the requirements of supply and qualifications. Most practitioners worked in teams which jointly assumed responsibility for groups of students. This supported both collaborative planning, which improved the quality and coherence of instruction across classrooms, and greater accountability for the overall welfare and progress of students. Those less extensively trained practiced under the direct supervision of career professionals, performing more routine tasks for which they had been prepared. Many of these were in teachers-in-training working in the classrooms of expert teachers. In settings where, for example, three professional teachers and two instructors were responsible for 100 students over 2–3 years, many possibilities emerged for developing collegial learning, for assuring effective supervision, for organizing large- and small-group instruction, for consulting about teaching plans and decisions, and for developing strategies to meet individual children's needs. Not incidentally, such structures promoted the kinds of consultation and peer review of practice that are central to a professional role.

Teachers began to insist on selecting and inducting their peers, and on collective decision making in schools over the best uses of knowledge and resources to meet students' needs. Professional knowledge and effectiveness grew as serious induction, sustained professional development, and collaboration in problem-solving replaced the sink-or-swim, closed door ethos of an earlier era.

Instructional practices changed, too. As schools became more learning centered and teachers more skilled, the conveyor belt approach to processing students gave way to more varied and appropriate methods of teaching and learning. All adults in schools served as advisors to small numbers of students for whom they became family liaisons and in-school advocates to assure personalized attention to students' progress and needs. Lectures, text questions, and worksheets were no longer the preponderant school activities: though still used when appropriate, these strategies were augmented by cooperative and experiential learning opportunities, projects, research activities, debates, essays, and exhibitions that encouraged students to construct and solve intellectual problems, engaged students of varied learning styles, and created more meaningful and useful ways by which to assess students' progress.

With the help of their teachers and advisors, students worked intensely on exhibitions of their learning, including graduation portfolios that demonstrated their abilities to conduct scientific inquiries, evaluate and produce works of literature and art, research and understand social science concerns, frame and solve mathematical problems, and contribute responsibly to their communities. Some of these pieces of work were evaluated as part of district and state assessment systems, which also included common tasks that asked students to demonstrate their reading, writing, and mathematical skills in the more authentic ways pioneered by Vermont, Maryland, Kentucky, and Connecticut during the 1990s.

A wide variety of more productive approaches to organizing the school day and the school year and to grouping students gave individual teachers and students more time together, reducing the pull-outs, pass-throughs, start-ups, and wind-downs that had stolen teaching time and decreased teachers' capacity to come to know students well. Like schools in other high-achieving countries, American schools enabled teachers to stay with the same students for longer blocks of time over more than 1 year, structured collaborative planning within and across disciplines, and reduced the total number of teachers students were expected to encounter. Schools became smaller and more personalized. Fewer students fell through the cracks.

Incentives to attract the most expert teachers to the profession's greatest needs and challenges also emerged. Following the lead of the successful new schools movements in New York, Chicago, Cincinnati, San Antonio, and Oakland, master teachers redesigned inner-city schools as smaller, more communal places where partnerships with parents and communities were joined with expert professional practice. In a set of these schools that served as professional development schools, school- and university-based faculties coached new teachers, put research into practice – and practice into research – and put state-of-the-art knowledge to work for children. Equity and excellence became joined with professionalism.

By the year 2013, a renaissance had occurred in American education. The best American students performed as well as students anywhere in the world. The vast majority of students graduated with not only minimal basic skills, but with the capacity to write, reason, and think analytically. Complaints from the business community about the quality of graduates subsided for the first time since World War II. And for the first time since the beginning of the twentieth century, a decade was launched without a chorus of commission reports crying crisis in the American public schools. The road taken, as it turned out, was the one that finally made a difference.

References

Barber, M., & Mourshed, M. (2007). *How the world's best-performing school systems come out on top*. London: McKinsey and Company.

Buchberger, F., & Buchberger, I. (2004). Problem solving capacity of a teacher education system as condition of success? An analysis of the "Finnish case." In F. Buchberger & S. Berghammer (Eds.), *Education policy analysis in a comparative perspective*. Linz, Austria: Trauner.

Callahan, R. E. (1962). *Education and the cult of efficiency*. Chicago: University of Chicago Press.

Darling-Hammond, L. (1990). Teacher professionalism: Why and how? In A. Lieberman (Ed.), *Schools as collaborative cultures: Creating the future now*. New York: The Falmer Press.

Darling-Hammond, L. (2000a). Futures of teaching in American education. *Journal of Educational Change, 1*(4), 353–373.

Darling-Hammond, L. (2000b). Teacher quality and student achievement. *Educational Policy analysis archives, 8*(1), http://epaa.asu.edu/epaa/v8n1

Darling-Hammond, L. (2004a). The color line in American education: Race, resources, and student achievement. *W.E.B. DuBois Review: Social Science Research on Race, 1*(2), 213–246.

Darling-Hammond, L. (2004b). Standards, accountability, and school reform. *Teachers College Record, 106*(6), 1047–1085.

Darling-Hammond, L. (2007). *Powerful teacher education: Lessons from exemplary programs*. San Francisco: Jossey-Bass Publishers.

Darling-Hammond, L., Barron, B., Pearson, D., Schoenfeld, A., Stage, E., Zimmerson, T., et al. (2008). *What we know about teaching for understanding*. London, UK: Wiley and Sons, Ltd.

Drucker, P. F. (1989). *The new realities*. New York: Harper & Row.

Drucker, P. F. (1994). The age of social transformation. *Atlantic Monthly, 62*, 53–80.

Fullan, M. (1993). Why teachers must become change agents. *Educational Leadership, 50*(6), 12–17.

Fullan, M. (2007). *The new meaning of educational change* (4th ed.). New York: Teachers College Press.

Gunderson, S., Jones, R., & Scanland, K. (2004). *The jobs revolution: Changing how America Works*. Washington, DC: Copywriters, Inc.

Jukes, I., & McCain, T. (2002, June 18). *Living on the future edge*. The InfoSavvy Group and Cyster.

Lankford, H., Loeb, S., & Wyckoff, J. (2002). Teacher sorting and the plight of urban schools: A descriptive analysis. *Educational Evaluation and Policy Analysis, 24*(1), 37–62.

Laukkanen, R. (2008). Finnish strategy for high-level education for all. In N. C. Soguel & P. Jaccard (Eds.), *Governance and performance of education systems* (pp. 305–324, Springer, at p. 319). Dordrecht: Springer.

Lee, V. E., Smith, J., & Croninger, R. (1995). Another look at high school restructuring. *Issues in Restructuring Schools, No. 9*. Madison, WI: University of Wisconsin, Center on Organization and Restructuring of Schools.

Lieberman, A. (1995). *The work of restructuring schools: Building from the ground up* (pp. 87–110). New York: Teachers College Press.

National Commission on Teaching and America's Future [NCTAF]. (1996). *Doing what matters most: Teaching for America's future*. NY: NCTAF.

Newmann, F., & Associates. (1996). *Authentic achievement: Restructuring schools for intellectual quality*. San Francisco: Jossey-Bass Publishers. http://www.amazon.com/Authentic-Achievement-Restructuring-Intellectual-Education/dp/0787903205/ref=sr_1_1?ie=UTF8&s=books&qid=1263672628&sr=1-1

Sanders, W. L., & Rivers, J. C. (1996). *Cumulative and residual effects of teachers on future student academic achievement*. University of Tennessee Value-Added Research and Assessment Center. http://www.mdk12.org/practices/ensure/tva/tva_2.html

Stigler, J. W., & Stevenson, H. W. (1991). How Asian teachers polish each lesson to perfection. *American Educator, 15*, 12–47.

Tyack, D. B. (1974). *The one best system: A history of American urban education*. Cambridge, MA: Harvard University Press.

U.S. Department of Labor. (2006). *Number of jobs held, labor market activity, and earnings growth among the youngest baby boomers: Results from a longitudinal survey*. Washington, DC: Bureau of Labor Statistics. Retrieved on 9/22/07 from http://www.bls.gov/news.release/pdf/nlsoy.pdf

Varian, H., & Lyman, P. (2003). *"How much information? 2003"* *UC Berkeley School of Information Management & Systems (SIMS)*. Retrieved on 9/22/07 from www2.sims.berkeley.edu/research/projects/how-much-info-2003/printable_report.pdf

Wilson, S., Floden, R., & Ferrini-Mundy, J. (2002). *Teacher preparation research: Current knowledge, gaps, and recommendations*. Working Paper, February 2002, Center for the Study of Teaching and Policy, University of Washington.